Celebrating Life Customs around the World

Celebrating Life Customs around the World

From Baby Showers to Funerals

Volume 3

Aging and Death

VICTORIA WILLIAMS

An Imprint of ABC-CLIO, LLC
Santa Barbara, California • Denver, Colorado

Copyright © 2017 by ABC-CLIO, LLC

All rights reserved. No part of this publication may be reproduced, stored in a retrieval system, or transmitted, in any form or by any means, electronic, mechanical, photocopying, recording, or otherwise, except for the inclusion of brief quotations in a review, without prior permission in writing from the publisher.

Library of Congress Cataloging-in-Publication Data

Names: Williams, Victoria, author.
Title: Celebrating life customs around the world : from baby showers to funerals / Victoria Williams
Description: Santa Barbara, California : ABC-CLIO, 2017. | Includes bibliographical references and index.
Identifiers: LCCN 2016036558 (print) | LCCN 2016037544 (ebook) | ISBN 9781440836589 (hardback) | ISBN 9781440846519 (volume 1) | ISBN 9781440846526 (volume 2) | ISBN 9781440846533 (volume 3) | ISBN 9781440836596 (ebook)
Subjects: LCSH: Manners and customs. | Rites and ceremonies.
Classification: LCC GT76 .W54 2017 (print) | LCC GT76 (ebook) | DDC 390—dc23
LC record available at https://lccn.loc.gov/2016036558

ISBN: 978-1-4408-3658-9 (set)
ISBN: 978-1-4408-4651-9 (vol. 1)
ISBN: 978-1-4408-4652-6 (vol. 2)
ISBN: 978-1-4408-4653-3 (vol. 3)
EISBN: 978-1-4408-3659-6 (set)

21 20 19 18 17   1 2 3 4 5

This book is also available as an eBook.

ABC-CLIO
An Imprint of ABC-CLIO, LLC

ABC-CLIO, LLC
130 Cremona Drive, P.O. Box 1911
Santa Barbara, California 93116-1911
www.abc-clio.com

This book is printed on acid-free paper ∞

Manufactured in the United States of America

Contents

Preface	xxi
Introduction	xxiii
Geographical List of Entries	xxxiii

Volume 1: Birth and Childhood

Akan Baby-Naming Ceremonies, Ghana	1
Akka Goddess Customs, Saami	4
Apache Baby Ceremonies, Apache	7
Atiq Ceremony, Inuit	9
Baba Marta, Bulgaria	13
Babinden: Day of the Midwife, Bulgaria	17
Baby Gender Prediction Chart, China	20
Baby Racing, International	21
Baby Showers, International	22
Baby Welcoming, Paganism	24
Baptism and Christening, Christianity	25
Bedwetting Remedies, Traditional, International	29
Beschuit met Muisjes, Suikerboon, and *Dragées*, Europe	31
Birth Trees, International	33
Birthday Cakes, International	34
Birthday Candles, International	37
Birthday Cards, International	38
Birthday Torments, International	40
Birthdays, International	42
Birthstones, International	44
Bismillah Ceremony, Islam	47

CONTENTS

Blessingway Ceremony, Navajo	48
Blidworth Cradle Rocking Ceremony, England	51
Blooding, United Kingdom	53
Blue Peter Badge, United Kingdom	54
Breastfeeding, International	55
Brit Milah, Judaism	59
Bulgarian Birth Customs, Bulgaria	63
Burying the Placenta, International	67
Calabash Chalk, Nigeria, United Kingdom, United States, and Canada	71
Cardboard Box Beds, Finland	72
Cerne Abbas Giant, England	75
Changeling Beliefs, International	77
Child Beauty Pageants, International	80
Childermas, Christianity	83
Childhood Vaccinations, International	85
Children's Laureate, United Kingdom	87
Chinese Pregnancy and Birth Rituals, China (including Taiwan)	89
Christening Gown, Christianity	93
Christingle, United Kingdom	95
Related Primary Document: Christingle Service Script	97
Churching of Women, Christianity	98
Related Primary Document: Churching of Mothers Ceremony Script, Greek Orthodox	100
Couvade, International	104
Covering the Belly Button Traditions, Latin America	108
Cradleboard, Native American	109
Crying-Baby Sumo Competition, Japan	111
Cutting the Umbilical Cord Traditions, International	112
Dala Horse, Sweden	115
Devadasi System, India	116
Dream Catcher, Native American	119
Eating Human Placenta, International	123

CONTENTS

El Bolo, Mexico	125
El Salto del Colacho Baby Jumping Festival, Spain	126
Entering the *Bashali*, Pakistan	128
Fady, Madagascar	133
Fairytales, International	134
Father's Day, International	138
Fire-Hair Shaving and *Khwan* Ceremonies, Thailand	140
First Communion, Christianity	142
Food Taboos in Pregnancy, International	144
Ghanaian Birthday Traditions, Ghana	149
Girl Guides, International	151
Government-Approved Baby Names, International	153
Related Primary Document: Government-Approved Names, Iceland	157
Grasmere Rushbearing, England	164
Groaning Cheese and Groaning Cake, United Kingdom and North America	166
"Happy Birthday" Song, International	171
Hesono-o: Wrapping Umbilical Cord as Keepsake, Japan	173
Hindu Baby Rituals, Hinduism	175
Hopi Naming Rites, Hopi	177
Jamu Medicine and Massage, Indonesia	181
Kangaroo Care, International	183
Kodomo No Hi: Children's Day, Japan	184
Korean Childbirth Customs, Korea	186
Kumari and *Deuki*, Nepal	189
Kyrgyzstani Childhood Traditions, Kyrgyzstan	193
La Cuarentena, Latin America	197
Ladybird Books, England	198
Lamaze Technique and Bradley Method, International	201
Latvian Birth Traditions, Latvia	203
Legong, Indonesia	204
Little Edith's Treat, England	207
Lohusa Şerbeti, Turkey	208

CONTENTS

Lotus Birthing, International	210
Lullabies, International	213
May Crowning Ritual, Catholicism	217
Mistletoe, International	218
"Monday's Child," England	220
Monstrous Punishments for Naughty Children, International	221
Moon-Yuet, China	226
Mother Roasting, Southeast Asia	228
Mothering Sunday, Christianity	230
Mundan Ceremony, India	232
Muslim Birth Rites, Islam	234
Muslim Male Circumcision, Islam	235
Mutterpass, Germany, and *Carnet de Santé Maternité*, France	237
Name Days, Catholic and Orthodox, and *Slava*, Serbian Orthodox	241
Nativity Play, International	244
Navjote Ceremony: Zoroastrian Initiation, Zoroastrianism	246
Nordic Napping, Europe	249
Nursery Rhymes, International	250
Nyabutan Ceremony, Indonesia	253
Obando Fertility Dance, Philippines	255
One-Child Policy, China	256
Oshichiya Meimeishiki, *Hyakunichimairi*, and *Okuizome*, Japan	259
Pantomime, United Kingdom	261
Parental Leave, International	265
Related Primary Document: Maternity Leave Guide, United Kingdom	267
Related Primary Document: Parental Leave Guide, Australia	269
Related Primary Document: Paternity Leave Guide, United Kingdom	270
Party Games, International	273
Pasni Weaning Ceremony, Nepal	275
Phallus Festivals, International	277
Pidyon Haben: Redemption of the First Born, Judaism	280
Piñata, Mexico	283

Potty Training, International	286
Pregnancy Yoga, International	289
Quccija, Malta	291
Saining, Scotland	293
Saint Nicholas, Christianity	294
Sambatra Mass Circumcision Festival, Madagascar	298
Sarung Buaian, Malaysia	300
Scouts, International	302
Scroggling the Holly, England	304
Sebou, Egypt	305
Setsubun: Children's Bean-throwing Festival, Japan	307
Shengxiao, China	310
Sikh Baby Rites and *Naam Karan* Naming Ceremony, Sikhism	311
Silver Spoon, United Kingdom	313
Slow Parenting Movement, International	314
Spitting on Babies, International	316
Sprinkling Cake, Ireland	317
Steiner Schools, International	318
Swaddling, International	320
Tibetan Pregnancy and Birth Customs, Tibet	323
Tooth Fairy and Tooth Mouse, International	324
Traditional Teething Remedies, International	327
Trokosi: Female Ritual Servitude, Ghana, Benin, and Togo	330
Tuj, Guatemala	333
Upanayana: Sacred Thread Ritual, Hinduism	337
Waldkindergärten, International	341
Warding Off the Evil Eye, International	342
Water Birth, International	346
Wedding Ring Test, United Kingdom	348
Weihnachtsmärchen and Advent Calendars, Germany	349
Wetting the Baby's Head, International	350
Whuppity Scoorie and Lanimer Day, Scotland	351

CONTENTS

Wiccaning, Wicca	353
Wik-Mungkan Naming Ceremony, Aborigine, Australia	355
Witch Ball, International	356
Worry Dolls and *Katsina* Dolls, Guatemala and Hopi	357
Zuo Yuezi, China	361
Zur-zur and *Yankan Gishiri*, Sub-Saharan Africa	362
Selected Bibliography for Volume 1	365
Comprehensive Index	369

Volume 2: Adolescence and Early Adulthood

Afghani Betrothal, Afghanistan	1
Andrzejki: St. Andrew's Eve, Poland	3
Arranged Marriage and Forced Marriage, International	5
Assyrian Betrothal and Weddings, International	9
Baccalauréat and *Matura*, Europe	15
Bachelor and Spinster Balls, Australia	16
Bar Mitzvah and *Bat Mitzvah*, Judaism	19
Beards, International	21
Bed-Courtship, Amish	23
Birthday Humiliations for Singletons, Denmark and Germany	26
Blackening the Bride, Scotland	28
Breast Ironing, Africa and Elsewhere	30
British Wedding Traditions, United Kingdom	32
Bulgarian Weddings, Bulgaria	37
Bullet Ant Initiation, Brazil	41
Burning the Ashen Faggot, England, and The Burning of the Clavie, Scotland	43
Cajun Weddings, United States	47
Chinese Coming-of-Age Ceremonies, China	49
Chisungu, Zambia	52
Chokha Thavani Viddhi: Devipujak Purification Trial, India	55
Choosing Options, England, Wales, and Northern Ireland	56
Christian Wedding Ceremony, Christianity	58

Coming of Age Day, Japan	61
Courtship Whistling, Mexico	64
Cow Jumping, Ethiopia	66
Dastaar Bandi and *Amrit Sanchar*, Sikhism	69
Dipo Womanhood Ceremony, Ghana	71
Diwali and *Kali Pooja*, India	73
Related Primary Document: Sandip Roy, "The Great Diwali Fight and Obama," 2009	76
Dunmow Flitch Trials, England	78
Dyngus Day, Eastern Europe and United States	79
Ear-Piercing Ceremonies, Myanmar and Malaysia	83
Face in Birthday Cake, Mexico	85
Fattening Room Seclusion, Nigeria	86
Female Genital Cutting, Africa, Middle East, Asia, and Elsewhere	89
Fidanzamenti, Italy	94
Filipino Debut, Philippines	95
Forehead-Cutting Initiation, Africa	98
Gap Year, International	103
Gretna Green, Scotland	104
Gwallye, South Korea	105
Hadaka Matsuri, Japan	109
Hair Removal, International	111
Hajj, Islam	113
Handfasting, Scotland, also Neo-Paganism	117
Related Primary Document: Handfasting Ceremony (Sample)	118
Handparting, Wicca	127
Hijab, Islam	128
Hijra, Indian Sub-Continent	131
Hindu Wedding Ceremony, Hinduism	133
Hmong Names, Laos, Myanmar, Vietnam, Cambodia, and Thailand	136
Hora, Eastern Europe, and *Horah*, Judaism	139
Horseshoes, International	141

CONTENTS

Human Tooth Sharpening, Indonesia and Africa	142
Inter-Railing, Europe	147
Initiation by Semen Transferal, Papua New Guinea and Vanuatu	148
Iria Ceremony, Nigeria	153
Isanaklesh Gotal, Mescalero Apache	155
Jewish Wedding Customs, Judaism	159
Jumping Over the Broom, United Kingdom and United States, also Neo-Paganism	163
Jury Duty, International	165
Related Primary Document: Jury Duty Guide, United States	169
Related Primary Document: Jury Summons Guide, United Kingdom	170
Kumbh Mela, Hinduism	173
La Quinceañera, Latin America, the Caribbean, and the United States	177
La Soupe, France	180
Ladouvane and St. Sylvester's Day, Bulgaria	182
Land Diving, Vanuatu	183
Lazarovden, Bulgaria	186
Leap Year Proposal, International	189
Lindo, Croatia	190
Lip Plugs, Africa and South America	191
Lobola, Southern Africa	195
Log Riding, Japan	197
Looking for Fern Blossoms, Eastern Europe	199
Lovespoons, Wales	201
Maasai Warrior Initiation, Kenya and Tanzania	205
Majáles, Czech Republic	208
Marriage Banns, Christianity	210
Related Primary Document: Marriage Banns Legislation, United Kingdom	211
Matis Hunting Trials, Brazil	215
Maypoles, Europe	219
Mehndi, International	222

Menstrual Customs, International	224
Menstrual Taboos, International	228
Money Dance, International	233
Moonie Weddings, International	235
Moroccan Weddings, Morocco	237
Muslim Wedding Ceremony, Islam	241
Neck Elongation, Thailand, Myanmar, and South Africa	243
Nkumbi, Democratic Republic of Congo	245
Nyumba Ntobhu: Traditional Same-Sex Marriage, Tanzania	247
Omiai: Japanese Matchmaking, Japan	251
Pika and *Nyora*, Zimbabwe and Mozambique	253
Polterabend, Germany	254
Polyandry, International	258
Polygyny, International	261
Povitica, Eastern Europe	263
Purity Ball, United States	264
RAG Week, United Kingdom and Ireland	267
Reed Dancing Chastity Ceremony, Kingdom of Swaziland	269
Ritual Tattooing, International	272
Rumspringa, United States and Canada	277
Russefeiring, Norway, and Schoolies Week, Australia	281
Same-Sex Marriage, International	285
Related Primary Document: Same-Sex Civil Partnership Ceremony Text, United Kingdom	288
San-San-Kudo, Japan	291
Scarification, Africa and Papua New Guinea	293
Schuhplattler and *Ländler*, Germany and Austria	297
Secular Confirmation, Europe	300
Shabka, Islam and Coptic Christianity	302
Shanghai Marriage Market, China	305
Sharo: Public Flogging, Nigeria and Benin	307

CONTENTS

Shinbyu, Buddhism	310
Sikh Wedding Ceremony, Sikhism	312
Singles' Day, China, and Black Day, South Korea	315
Sisters' Meal Festival, China	317
Sock Garland, Germany, and Sock Dance, Canada	318
St. Catherine's Day, France	320
St. Dwynwen's Day, Wales	322
Sünnet, Turkey	323
Sunrise Ceremony, Apache, United States	326
Thaipusam: Extreme Ritual Flesh Modification, Hinduism	333
Tooth-Filing Ceremony, Indonesia	335
Training Bras, United States, Europe, and Australasia	338
Trobriand Ritualized Sex and Commitment, Papua New Guinea	341
Twenty-First Birthday Traditions, International	344
Urethral Subincision, Australia, Africa, and South America	347
Vinok, Ukraine	353
Virginity Testing, International	355
Vision Quest, Native American	358
Visiting-Girls Courtship Tradition, China	361
Walkabout, Australia	365
Wedding Anniversaries, International	367
Wedding Cakes, International	369
Wedding Dress and Wedding Ring, International	373
Related Primary Document: Yumi Sakugawa, "An Asian American Wedding," 2009	377
Wedding March and Bridal Chorus, International	379
White Coat Ceremony and Pinning Ceremony, International	381
Wodaabe Courtship Dance and Festival, Africa	383
Xhosa Circumcision, South Africa	387
Zou Hun: Mosuo Walking Marriages, China	391
Selected Bibliography for Volume 2	395
Comprehensive Index	399

Volume 3: Aging and Death

"Abide With Me," United Kingdom, North America, and Australasia	1
Albanian Funeral Customs, Albania	3
Alkaline Hydrolysis, United Kingdom, Australia, and United States	5
All Souls' Day, Europe and South America	6
Ankou, France and England	10
Assisted Suicide, International	11
Bees, United Kingdom	17
Buddhist Attitudes Toward Death, Buddhism	18
Cairn, International	23
Changing of the Guard Ceremony, United States	24
Chelsea Pensioners, England	26
Chinese Death Customs, China	29
Christian Death Rituals, Christianity	35
Condemned Prisoner's Last Meal, United States	37
Condolences, International	40
Cremation, International	41
Croning, Saging, and Elderling Ceremonies, Paganism	44
Crucifixion Rituals, Philippines	47
Death Dance, International	51
Delaware Indian Death Rituals, North America	53
Related Primary Document: Ray Fadden, Letter to President Harry S. Truman Regarding Burial of an Indian at Arlington National Cemetery, September 3, 1951	55
Denville Hall & Brinsworth House, England	56
Dia de los Muertos: Day of the Dead, Latin America and United States	58
Doom Metal and Funeral Doom, International	62
Easter Eggs, Christianity	65
Eating the Ashes of the Dead, Brazil and Venezuela	67
Edir, Ethiopia, and *Engozi*, Uganda	70
Eleanor Crosses, England	72
Embalming, United States	73

Endocannibalism, Papua New Guinea and Brazil	76
Eulogies, International	80
Related Primary Document: President Reagan's Address to the Nation Following the Challenger *Shuttle Disaster, 1986*	81
Eyam Plague Sunday Service, England	83
Famadihana, Madagascar	85
Fantasy Coffins, Ghana	87
Finger Amputation, Papua New Guinea	90
Funeral Cakes and Funeral Candy, International	92
Funeral Plants, Europe	94
Funeral Songs, International	97
Goth Subculture, International	99
Grave Rental and Exhumation, Europe and Asia	102
The Great Passing, Romania	105
Hallowe'en and *Martinstag,* International	109
Halva, International	113
High-Platform Exposure of the Corpse, Australia	115
Hindu Death Customs, Hinduism	118
Isola di San Michele: Venice's Cemetery Island, Italy	121
Japanese Death Customs, Japan	123
Jazz Funeral, United States	127
Jewish Death Customs, Judaism	129
Koliva, International	135
Lakota Death Rituals, Lakota, North America	139
Related Primary Document: Native American Grave Protection and Repatriation Act, 1990	142
"The Last Post" and "Taps," International	152
Living with the Dead, Indonesia	155
"Lyke-Wake Dirge," England	158
Maidens' Garlands, England	161
Malagan, Papua New Guinea	162
Maundy Money, United Kingdom	164
Memento Mori and *Vanitas,* International	167

Message from the Queen, United Kingdom	171
Minute's Silence, International	173
Mirila, Croatia	175
Missing Man Formation, International	177
Mizuko Kuyo: Japanese Fetus Memorial Service, Japan	180
Mortuary Totem Poles, Haida and Tlingit	183
Mummification, International	185
Muslim Death Rituals, Islam	188
National Mourning, International	191
Ngaben, Indonesia	193
Nine-Nights, Caribbean	196
Obituary, International	199
Ossuaries, Europe	200
Passing Bells, England and Scotland	205
Passion Play, Christianity	206
Pauper's Funeral, United Kingdom	209
Personalized Hearses, United Kingdom	211
Plastination, Germany	213
Pregnancy and Infant Loss Remembrance Day, International	216
Qingming Festival, China	219
Remembrance Day and Remembrance Sunday, International	223
Related Primary Document: Remembrance Sunday Early Day Motion, United Kingdom	226
Retirement and Pensions, International	228
Related Primary Document: Social Pension/Superannuation Guide, New Zealand	232
Related Primary Document: State Pension Government Guide, United Kingdom	234
Riderless Horse, International	236
Romanian Funeral Customs, Romania	237
Royal Wootton Bassett, England	239
Sakalava Royal Death Traditions and *Fitampoha*, Madagascar	243
Sallekhanā, Jainism	245

San La Muerte, South America	246
Santa Muerte, Mexico and United States	249
Saturday of Souls, Orthodox Christianity, Bulgaria, and Serbia, and *Radonitsa*, Russia	251
Senior Sporting Events, International	254
Shrunken Heads, Peru and Ecuador	255
Sikh Death Customs, Sikhism	257
Sky Burials, Autonomous Tibet and China	259
Soul Cakes and Soul Breads, Europe	263
Space Burial, Outer Space	267
Spontaneous Shrines, International	269
State Funeral, International	271
Stations of the Cross, Christianity	275
Suicide Landmarks, International	278
Tangihanga: Māori Mourning Ritual, New Zealand	281
Taxidermy, International	283
Tear Catchers and Mourning Jewelry, International	286
Tết Nguyên đan, Vietnam	288
Tomb of the Unknown Soldier, International	292
Tombstone Tourism, International	297
Tongan Funerals, Tonga	300
Traditional Mourning Colors, International	302
University of the Third Age, International	307
Vrindavan: The City of Widows, India	309
Wake, International	313
Wearing Flowers to Honor War Dead, International	314
Wiccan Funerals, Wicca	318
Related Primary Document: Wiccan Funeral for an Elderly Woman	321
Windmills, The Netherlands	323
Yew Trees, Europe	327
Yu Lan Jie: The Hungry Ghost Festival, China	329

Zaduszki, Poland	333
Zombies and Voodoo Death Traditions, Haiti	335
Zoroastrian Funerals, India	338
Selected Bibliography for Volume 3	343
Comprehensive Index	347

Preface

It is not often that an author can claim (truthfully) that all readers should find something in her book to which they can relate. That is, however, certainly true of this book, a three-volume encyclopedia of life customs around the world. While not everyone that reads this book will marry or have children, all readers are born and all will die, so there is, I hope, something in this book to interest everyone.

This multivolume encyclopedia concentrates on rites of passage, traditions, rituals, and life customs that take place around the world. While I deliberately focused on activities that may be less familiar to American readers, many of the activities detailed are American or at least occur in the United States. Some of these customs involve millions of participants, such as breastfeeding, while others are known of by only a handful of people, such as the "Blidworth Cradle Rocking Ceremony." Many of the customs included in this book are rooted in the real world—such as potty training and jury duty—while others are deeply indebted to folklore such as "Monstrous Punishments for Naughty Children" and "Akka Goddess Customs." Meanwhile, some customs, such as those surrounding fairytales and lullabies, were not customs I had really considered as being associated with childhood until I wrote them. Having written my PhD thesis on fairytales, I had rather forgotten that fairytales are, primarily, intended for children rather than as texts to study.

The scope of this book takes in North America, South America, Europe, Africa, Asia, the Middle East, Oceania, and even outer space, and covers customs experienced by men, women, children, and animals (e.g., "Taxidermy"), in groups or as individuals. Volume 1 examines customs pertaining to birth and early childhood. Volume 2 looks at the coming-of-age customs of adolescents and those in early adulthood. Volume 3 covers entries relating to aging and death. A number of the entries in the books deal with subject matter that some readers may find distressing or distasteful, particularly entries such as "Female Genital Cutting," "Breast Ironing," "Initiation by Semen Transferal," and various entries on circumcision, but I have endeavored to write these entries as sensitively as possible. The same is true with the many entries on death customs and tombs.

This book is primarily aimed at researchers though I have purposely kept the writing as jargon-free as possible so that the general reader can also read the book from cover to cover for entertainment. Keeping the researcher in mind, however, every entry can be looked at as a stand-alone item or as part of an overarching theme. Each entry details the known history and evolution of the particular custom or rite but I have also detailed the myths and legends that lie at the heart of several of the entries. Where space allows, I have also attempted to note artworks, literature, films, and television programs that depict the various activities detailed in the entries. In addition, each entry is followed by a "See also" section that enables cross-referencing plus a brief Further Reading list. A number of selected primary document excerpts are also included that support specific entries. Finally, each volume has a selected bibliography.

The writing of this book would not have been possible without the generosity and enthusiasm of Kaitlin Ciarmiello, acquisitions editor at ABC-CLIO. I would also like to thank my family and friends for listening when I mentioned random information about obscure customs or asked them if they knew anyone that had taken part in certain activities. Most especially, I would like to thank my Mum, Rosemary Williams, who has a knack for alerting me to newspaper articles on unusual traditions and the like. An interview with my Mum is included in the entry entitled "Christingle." Thank you also to Dr. Nida Suri for her input on Indian customs and for guidance when I was writing about Islamic rituals. Thank you as well to Andrew Levicki who, as a fluent Japanese speaker and former long-time resident of Japan, provided a valuable insight into Japanese culture.

Introduction

The various points in an individual's or group's life cycle are marked by a variety of rituals, traditions, customs, and rites of passage, all of which can be placed under the umbrella term "life customs." Today the most commonly experienced life customs are associated with pregnancy, childbirth, initiation or attainment of adult physical maturity, mating or betrothal, marriage, and death, with thousands of different life customs occurring each year around the world involving living (and dead) men, women, children, and animals. The term life customs can be applied to myriad events and occasions though distinctions exist between those events dubbed rites of passage, customs, and traditions. From the beginning of an individual's life to its end, life's milestones are denoted through a huge number of time-honored traditions and unique customs. These ceremonial events have occurred in all societies throughout time. The classification of these different events varies, however, with differences existing between rituals, traditions, and rites of customs.

Many life customs are religious in nature while even more are secular. Moreover, some life customs may not even be considered to be life customs by the people undergoing them. For example, pensioners in the United Kingdom receiving their so-called bus pass is an everyday occurrence that happens without fanfare, yet when individual senior citizens are sent their pass by the government it is indeed a rite of passage as it is an official confirmation that someone has reached a certain age and, therefore, is officially classified as a senior citizen. For the most part, however, communities tend to denote these life events by holding ceremonial occasions. These ceremonial occasions tend to include at least one ritual that demonstrates that the individual experiencing the rite of passage has symbolically separated from his or her former state. This is exemplified by the Korean *Gwallye* coming-of-age ceremony for males and females turning 19 years old. The ceremony sees the 19-year-olds don special ceremonial clothing that denotes that they have attained adulthood.

Special celebrations may also be held to announce to a community as a whole that an individual has entered a new state of being (or in terms of death, beyond a state of being). In the most highly evolved societies, these types of ceremonial occasions are woven into the life of society with literal interpretations of separation, death, and rebirth tending to be portrayed through symbolism. This can be seen in the example of Christian baptisms during which the person being baptized may undergo a ritual drowning and re-emergence from sacred water as a form of initiation into the Christian faith. In addition, many communities in Western society practice customs that can be traced back to earlier times, with certain practices having their basis in ancient sacred activities. For example, the Japanese Onbashira festival sees men ride logs downhill in honor of Suwa-no-Kami, the primary goddess in the pantheon of Shinto, the main religion of Japan, while the custom of dancing around the maypole that is a summer activity in many European countries is often considered to have ancient fertility rites as its basis. Another Western custom that has its roots in earlier, sacred practices is the frequently occurring custom of the baby shower. Though a seemingly recently invented secular custom, the custom of holding baby showers can be traced back to an ancient Greek ritual that saw a baby five or seven days old undergo a rite called the *Amphidromia*, or Running Round. Then, on the 10th day, the baby's mother would invite her friends and family to a ritual called *Dekate* for a celebratory meal during which the baby's mother would dedicate gifts to Eileithyia, a goddess of childbirth.

RITUALS, TRADITIONS, AND CUSTOMS

The various life customs experienced by an individual or group can be divided into different classifications. Though the terms ritual, tradition, and custom are often used interchangeably in everyday conversation, there are, technically, different parameters for each term. Rituals are religious rites or earnest secular ceremonies consisting of a number of actions performed according to a prescribed order. Rituals usually occur at important times of life such as birth, marriage, and death and often confer protection on an individual. Examples of this kind of protective occasion linked to a life event include spitting on babies to ward off the evil eye, placing a veil over a bride's face to protect her from malignant supernatural entities, or performing a vigil for a corpse, perhaps to prevent a cat from jumping over it, and thereby precluding the reanimation of the corpse after burial as a vampire-like supernatural being, as occurs in Albania. Rituals often involve special amulets or charms that ensure the individual transitions safely to another state of being. An example of this is the skin decoration known as *mehndi* that is intended to confer blessings, grace, and good luck to Indian brides and grooms as a kind of amulet worn upon the skin.

In the popular imagination, rituals are often confused with customs and traditions, yet differences exist between the types of occasion. As opposed to a ritual, a custom is a widely accepted, conventional mode of behavior that is specific to a particular society or place. Similarly, a tradition is a practice passed down within a community that holds some symbolic meaning or special significance that connects to its origins in the past. An example of a seemingly recently invented tradition occurs at British weddings for it is now traditional when newlyweds go on honeymoon for a collection of tin cans, boots, and assorted junk to be attached to the vehicle that they use as transport, often together with a sign declaring the couple to be "Just Married." Typically, the cans are attached to a car's back fender resulting in them clanging against each other and the road surface as the car drives away. This is a fairly recently instituted custom since cars were not invented until the end of the 19th century, but the tradition most likely harks back to the French custom of the *chivari* or the German *Polterabend*. Both of these noise-making traditions are associated with weddings and are intended to drive away from newlyweds evil spirits that might harm the newlyweds out of spite or jealousy. Tradition is, therefore, essentially retrospective, nostalgic, and governed by invariance, even in the case of newly invented traditions. For this reason it is common for people to refuse to change their manner of performing an action arguing that they cannot because it is traditional to perform the action in a certain way. Hence many people's Christmas celebrations are the same year after year because they feel that they must mark their celebrations in the way that they always have on account of it being traditional to do so. Therefore, whether old or new, traditions are governed by the imposition of fixed practices that are performed repetitively and do not waver. Customs on the other hand are not as backward looking as traditions for they do modify over time, though at the same time the customs must still conform in essence to what has gone before thereby allowing for continuity. In short, therefore, custom permits flexibility while tradition prefers to adhere to precedent especially through the use of symbolic actions and paraphernalia. Though there are, therefore, differences between traditions and customs the two terms do overlap, and, moreover, intertwine. Tradition may also become bound up with ritual for although a tradition may not have had any symbolic function when it originated it may acquire a sense of ritual where none was intended while, simultaneously, establishing a set of conventions and rules that are passed on to new participants. For this reason, some traditions that began as secular traditions seem increasingly like ritual.

RITES OF PASSAGE

Another type of life event marked by certain types of actions are so-called rites of passage. Rites of passage occur the world over with the universal distribution of rites of passage a matter of fascination for scholars for centuries. Perhaps the most famous and influential work on the phenomena of rites of passage is *Les Rites de Passage* (*The Rites of Passage*, 1909), written by European anthropologist, ethnographer, and folklorist Arnold van Gennep. In this work, van Gennep coined the phrase rite of passage to describe a celebration of the transition that occurs when a person leaves one group to enter another, thereby experiencing a significant change of social status. The term rite of passage is used today in cultural anthropology to describe ceremonial events in which an individual progresses through the stages of life within their society. Van Gennep suggested that rites of passage are the means by which people shift, without causing social disturbance, from one social role to another. Van Gennep also proposed that rites of passage consist of three discernible yet consecutive elements: separation, transition, and reincorporation, or, correspondingly, pre-liminal, liminal, and post-liminal stages (from the Latin word *limen* meaning threshold). According to van Gennep, the individual that is the focus of a rite of passage is severed symbolically from his or her previous status before undergoing an adjustment to a new status. This occurs during a period of transition that culminates in the initiate's reincorporation into society under the cloak of his or her new social status. Despite the fact that the most frequently observed rites of passage correspond to crises in the life cycle of an individual, van Gennep observed that the ceremonies attendant upon rites of passage are significant for the whole of a society or culture not just the individual. This is most likely due to the fact that the most oft-celebrated rites of passage are sociocultural events.

Rites of passage occur worldwide and, if archeological findings are to be believed, have most likely taken place since time immemorial. Most societies consider the key rites of passage to be childbirth, initiation or the attainment of adulthood, marriage, and death. Indeed many of the rites of passage considered most important by society, and therefore most frequently enacted, are associated with these biological milestones of life: birth, maturity, reproduction, and death. This is because these biological crises bring about changes in an individual's social status and, therefore, in the individual's relationship with society. Rites of passage that are unconnected to biology mark transformations that are cultural. This is exemplified by initiations into societies consisting of people with specific interests or concerns such as the white coat ceremony that is a rite of passage for first-year medical students that welcomes the students into the medical profession.

There is no generally accepted classification of rites of passage, though many names have been suggested to distinguish the various types and elements of such rites. For example the term "purification ceremony" can be applied to a ritual that occurs frequently as an element of rites of passage, particularly rites associated with birth and death, but also refers to other religious events. In most cases, the aim of a purification ceremony is to prepare an individual for some kind of communication with a supernatural being. However a purification ceremony can also occur as a rite of passage that signifies the symbolic erasing of an individual's old status in readiness for his or her taking on a new social rank. For example, the post-birth Christian purification ceremony called the churching of women is held for women that have recently given birth thereby assuming the social status of a mother while the Hindu *Upanayana*, or sacred thread, ritual marks the stage of a young boy's life when he enters into Vedic education. The Upanayana ceremony also signifies the end of a boy's childhood for once a boy has undergone the ritual he is expected to immerse himself in the task of acquiring knowledge and responsibility. These examples demonstrate the way in which rituals focused on social transformation and religious transformational ceremonies overlap. This is also the case with religious transformational rites such as baptism, which also involves a degree of social transformation and celebration. Certain coming-of-age rites may also cause a change of religious status, as is the case with *Shinbyu*, the obligatory period of initiation in the life of Theravada Buddhist males that boys living in some Asian countries experience between the ages of 9 and 12 years. Not only is this a religious rite but Buddhist parents also consider their son's Shinbyu as his rite of passage to manhood.

LIFE-CYCLE CEREMONIES

Life-cycle ceremonies—the ritual counterparts of the biological crises of the life cycle—exist in all societies. All societies observe some forms of ritual surrounding the major life-cycle occasions of childbirth, marriage, and death, though the degree of elaboration of the rites and the significance accorded to them varies greatly between societies even when societies are comparable. These life-cycle ceremonies include the numerous rites attendant upon childbirth, ranging from pre-birth and pregnancy rites (such as baby showers and the wedding ring test) to practices observed during the actual moment of childbirth and post-birth rituals such as the churching of women. Rites associated with pregnancy and birth tend to stipulate different roles to the mother, father, and other family members as well as the non-family members of a community with respect to the baby. Pregnancy rites may begin when a pregnancy is confirmed and may continue until the time the baby is delivered, and, possibly, for a variable period of time after birth. This ritual process is exemplified by Korean birth customs, for a Korean woman will normally believe she has fallen pregnant after she has experienced a dream of conception called a *tae-mong*. Then, when a pregnancy is confirmed, she will inform her mother-in-law first, followed by her husband, and then, finally, her own mother. While a Korean woman is pregnant she will follow a strict diet of prescribed foods and act in a certain way. Then during the birthing process the woman will be attended to by certain female relatives and perform particular actions that are intended to hasten delivery while enhancing the *qi* life force. Then, after birth the placenta is treated in a ritual manner and the new mother must abide by certain ritual rules for a period of time.

Just as there are numerous birth rites around the world, so there are also very many coming-of-age and death rituals. The holding of coming-of-age rites varies much more than the holding of other types of rites of passage. While births and deaths are marked by most communities, some societies hold coming-of-age rites for only one sex, while some hold elaborate coming-of-age rites for one sex and contrastingly simple rites for the other. Then again other countries do not hold any coming-of-age rites at all for either sex. In the West initiation and coming-of-age rites have become increasingly secular. Though all major world religions include some sort of coming-of-age rites—such as the Jewish bar mitzvah and bat mitzvah and the Sikh *Dastaar Bandi* ceremony—coming of age rites in Western societies either are not observed or are viewed as vestiges of ancient religious rituals. An example of this is the noisy, German pre-wedding custom known as the

Polterabend. This custom is most commonly thought to have evolved from ancient pagan tribal beliefs. These ancient Germanic tribes believed that evil spirits and malign forces could be banished from weddings if guests made a great deal of noise by breaking crockery, cracking whips, and banging pans together. The ancient Germans believed that once such malign supernatural entities had been banished from the wedding they could not then go on to sabotage the newly wedded couple's married life.

A great many coming-of-age rites are socially transformational as they see individuals initiated into certain sections of society that have no direct connection with biological changes. Moreover in the West coming-of-age rites tend not to be religious occasions but rather to be secular ceremonies that are not lineage-based or the result of tribal societies. Secular Western coming-of-age rites mark the individual's induction into societies based on age, social hierarchy, or common interests. An example of a purely secular coming-of-age rite is the European rite of inter-railing. This secular rite of passage sees students travel independently across the continent, and possibly beyond, thereby symbolizing their ability to act as independent, responsible adults. Other coming-of-age rites of passage are attendant upon puberty and physical maturation with many coming-of-age rites of passage being rites of initiation that coincide with puberty. For this reason such rites are sometimes referred to as puberty rites. Puberty among females is often defined as the time when a female experiences the onset of her menstrual flow, however there is no such clearly defined criteria for the sexual maturation of males. Furthermore the age at which rites pertaining to the attainment of maturity are observed varies hugely between societies thereby suggesting that maturation is as much a social or cultural concern as it is a matter of biology. Coming-of-age rites of passage connected with puberty are often marked by ordeals or tests of manhood and womanhood the experience of which qualifies an individual to assume a new social status. Common examples of this type of trial include numerous types of circumcision (male and female), the Apache Sunrise Ceremony, and the Ghanaian Dipo Womanhood Ceremony. This latter ceremony occurs when a female is aged between 12 and 16 years and it is divided into many individual stages that involve ritual cleansing, virginity testing, and education, and it culminates in the initiate returning to society as a woman. The Dipo Womanhood Ceremony exemplifies the fact that coming of age-of-age rites, more than any other type of life custom, emphasize appropriate modes of dress, demeanor, and morality. Indeed in the run-up to certain coming-of-age rites an initiate may undergo a period of instruction to teach them the correct behavior.

Another rite of passage that involves some form of prior instruction or education is marriage. Traditionally, women that are about to be married have to undergo preliminary rites providing them with instruction in how to be a wife. Such educational rites may occur informally or as a part of a prescribed ritual and tend to include instruction on a wife's role in society while communicating her economic and social duties with regard to pleasing her husband, children, and family in general as well as her community on the whole. Women may also have to undergo tests of sexual maturity and rites that promote fertility or ensure sexual faithfulness. This pre-wedding education still occurs in Morocco where it is traditional for a bride-to-be to undergo a *beberiska* ceremony. This ceremony sees the married members of a bride's entourage give the bride a sex education lesson, for, traditionally, the bride is a young virgin who is generally ignorant of such matters. Sometimes during the beberiska ceremony the bride sits behind a curtain that symbolizes the imminent change in her life.

As well as being important events in the lives of individuals, marriage ceremonies may be considered especially significant in the stressing of social bonds between the kinship groups of the newlyweds. To this end, throughout history romantic love has not been the criterion by which individuals have found spouses. According to convention, marriage normally occurred only between people belonging to certain classes or groups with mutual love and sexual attraction being considered a matter of little or no importance. Instead what really mattered was that a marriage could provide a couple with children and maintain social norms. For this reason, some societies have long-standing traditions of matchmaking and arranged marriage. Such traditions are particularly prevalent in Bulgaria, China, Japan, and India and in expatriate communities around the world.

Many factors, such as changing religious views, a lessening in the belief in the supernatural, and social change, all seem to be contributing to a decline in the frequency with which rites of passage occur, at least in the West. As a rite of passage, marriage continues to be popular in the West, and indeed around the word. However like so many other rites of passage the popularity of marriage in the West is frequently reported as being in decline. In recent years the conventions on which marriage is based have changed significantly in some locations with the legalization of same-sex marriage. The advent of same-sex marriages demonstrates that even the most long-standing and celebrated traditions are open to change and modification. Anthropologists suggest that marriage is one of the earliest socially constructed institutions, for rites of marriage have been observed in every known society since time immemorial. The form that marriage rites take varies hugely, however, from extremely elaborate rituals to simple ceremonies that view marriage as a formal agreement of unity between families. Additionally, some marriages are religious ceremonies while others are secular events. Some societies also hold pre-marriage rites such as betrothal ceremonies that consist of complex formalities governing the exchange of material goods. Customs involving the mock capture of the bride by the groom and his relatives also occur. Like coming-of-age rites, marriage ceremonies often include obvious emblems of an individual's new social status, such as wedding rings and hair adornments. There are also a huge number of courtship traditions, rituals, ceremonies, and festivals around the world, though these vary greatly in terms of propriety and solemnity. For instance bawdy events such as Bachelor and Spinster Balls occur regularly in rural Australia. These events are one of Australia's best-loved traditions though they are also notorious for being the scene of casual sexual encounters and binge drinking. Similarly, the Eastern European custom of looking for fern blossoms during the summer solstice is more or less a euphemism for looking for a sexual encounter. Other courtship practices are more chaste, such as Kickapoo Courtship Whistling and Amish bed-courtship. Then again other rituals are intended to safeguard young adults' (especially young women's) sexual virginity. For example virginity testing takes place in various locations around the world while purity balls take place in the United States.

After the rite of passage that is marriage, the next life-cycle event that is marked by ritual and considered a rite of passage is death. All societies pay ceremonial attention to death with rituals associated with death tending toward the religious and nearly always viewed as extremely important. All societies consider the dead to be significant and so they are the focus of much ritual attention both at the time of death and over periods of time after death. Since death is universally considered a supremely significant occasion, death rites tend to be elaborate and include all of the stages of separation, transition, and reincorporation, as set out by van Gennep in his model of rites of passage. Death involves a great deal of social transformation not just for the person that dies but for their family too. For example when an individual dies they take on a new social role as a spirit or ancestor that may be considered important by the community of which they were a part when they were alive. Meanwhile the deceased's surviving spouse will experience a change in his or her social status because he or she will change from being a married partner to becoming a widow or widower. The couple's children, if any, will also see their status change from that of having two parents to being without a parent. Death rites need not be governed by religion however as the practice of erecting spontaneous shrines to the dead testifies. While writing this book this author's hometown was the center of international headlines when, in August 2014, 14-year-old Alice Gross went missing in Hanwell, west London, prompting residents to tie handmade yellow ribbons around trees, lampposts, cars, monuments, and railings to keep her disappearance in the collective memory. As police searched for Alice the so-called Alice Ribbons covered the local clock tower and spread across London and beyond. Also, as the search by the police for Alice entered its fifth week, 6,000 runners in the Ealing Half Marathon chose to wear the ribbons, some inscribed with the hashtag #FindAlice pointing to the Twitter campaign that had gathered international support including help from celebrities. When the schoolgirl's murdered body was found in a local river, the Alice Ribbons transformed from objects aiming to show hope for Alice to memorial emblems of grief with accumulations of Alice Ribbons collecting at the clock tower serving as spontaneous shrines as locals gravitated toward the landmark. The ribbons were ultimately removed in October 2014 at the request of Alice's family. Though not in any way religious, the phenomenon of the Alice Ribbon highlighted the ritual nature of so many death practices. Other newly established death customs see people take to social media to express their grief.

As well as the rites of passage that are birth, initiation, marriage, and death, the term rites of passage is also sometimes applied to institutionalized, cyclic ceremonies such as agricultural festivals that are intended to ensure bountiful harvests. Though this type of ceremony does not see participants attain a new social status these occasions are viewed as rites of passage because they contain similarities in their ritual procedures. Elements of ceremonies relating to changes in the seasons also involve acts of separation and incorporation as they symbolically bid farewell to the previous season while welcoming the new.

A wealth of symbolism is normally attendant upon all kinds of elaborate rites of passage. Often this is due to the fact that such symbols represent the discarding of one social status and the adoption of another status. Typically the symbols of new status connected to rites of passage include modifications made to visible parts of the body, distinctive clothing and jewelry, and the adoption of special emblems. Examples of ritual body modification denoting a change of status include the various types of circumcision found around the world including the type experienced by boys belonging to the South African Xhosa tribe, Indonesian tooth-filing, African pika-marking, and Papua New Guinean scarification rituals. Special ceremonial clothing worn for rites of passage include the Western wedding dress that is bought especially for the wedding service and various types of kimono that can be worn to mark the attainment of adulthood or on the occasion of a death. Symbolic ritual jewelry includes the wedding ring, whose circular shape denotes eternal fidelity and mourning jewelry that may be black to denote bereavement or contain body parts such as hair taken from the dead. Meanwhile emblems related to rites of passage include the symbols of office ranging from the badges adopted by Girl Guides and the pins presented to nurses during a nurses' pinning ceremony—a ceremony dedicated to enshrining newly qualified nurses within the fold of the nursing profession.

As well as special symbolism, many rites of passage are also associated with taboos and prohibited behavior or actions during the rites. For example, some Native Americans consider it taboo for an initiate to scratch the body with the fingers during rituals. Other taboos include the various menstrual taboos that exist around the world and that may be enacted every time a female experiences her monthly menstrual bleed.

The frequency with which rites of passage such as marriage and coming-of-age customs are conducted does seem to be decreasing, at least in the West, due in part to the seeming incompatibility of such rites with modern life and also escalating costs associated with holding certain ceremonies. However the social and psychological value of such rites in making the transition to adulthood are substantial, meaning that such ceremonies are unlikely to die out completely. Moreover, such ceremonies continue to be considered extremely important in other parts of the world. Rites associated with birth and death are universally upheld, however, and even seem to be increasing in number and importance. This may well be because birth and death are two rites of passage that everyone of all nations, religions, and sexes has no choice but to experience.

Further Reading

Berns, Roberta. *Child, Family, School, Community: Socialization and Support.* Tenth edition. Stamford, CT: CENGAGE Learning, 2016.

Hobsbawm, Eric, and Terence Ranger, eds. *The Invention of Tradition.* Cambridge, UK: Cambridge University Press, 2012.

Horrox, Camilla. "Alice Gross Yellow Ribbons of Hope to Be Removed." Get West London, October 10, 2014. Accessed September 9, 2015, at http://www.getwestlondon.co.uk/news/local-news/alice-gross-yellow-ribbons-hope-7914799.

Jones, Alison. *Larousse Dictionary of World Folklore.* Edinburgh, UK: Larousse, 1996.

Laing, Jennifer, and Warwick Frost, eds. *Rituals and Traditional Events in the Modern World.* Abingdon, UK: Routledge, 2015.

van Gennep, Arnold. *The Rites of Passage.* Abingdon, UK: Routledge, 2010.

Geographical List of Entries

VOLUME 1: BIRTH AND CHILDHOOD

Africa and Middle East
Akan Baby-Naming Ceremonies (Ghana)
Fady (Madagascar)
Ghanaian Birthday Traditions (Ghana)
Sambatra Mass Circumcision Festival (Madagascar)
Sebou (Egypt)
Trokosi: Female Ritual Servitude (Ghana, Benin, and Togo)
Zur-zur and *Yankan Gishiri* (Sub-Saharan Africa)

Asia (Central and North)
Entering the *Bashali* (Pakistan)
Kyrgyzstani Childhood Traditions (Kyrgyzstan)
Kumari and *Deuki* (Nepal)
Pasni Weaning Ceremony (Nepal)
Tibetan Pregnancy and Birth Customs (Tibet)

Asia (South and Southeast)
Baby Gender Prediction Chart (China)
Chinese Pregnancy and Birth Rituals (China including Taiwan)
Crying-Baby Sumo Competition (Japan)
Fire-Hair Shaving and *Khwan* Ceremonies (Thailand)
Hesono-o: Wrapping Umbilical Cord as Keepsake (Japan)
Jamu Medicine and Massage (Indonesia)
Kodomo No Hi: Children's Day (Japan)
Korean Childbirth Customs (Korea)
Legong (Indonesia)
Moon-Yuet (China)
Mother Roasting (Southeast Asia)
Nyabutan Ceremony (Indonesia)
Obando Fertility Dance (Philippines)
One-Child Policy (China)
Oshichiya Meimeishiki, *Hyakunichimairi*, and *Okuizome* (Japan)
Sarung Buaian (Malaysia)
Setsubun: Children's Bean-Throwing Festival (Japan)
Shengxiao (China)
Zuo Yuezi (China)

GEOGRAPHICAL LIST OF ENTRIES

Australia and Pacific
Wik-Mungkan Naming Ceremony (Australia)

Europe and Russia
Baba Marta (Bulgaria)
Babinden: Day of the Midwife (Bulgaria)
Beschuit met Muisjes, *Suikerboon*, and *Dragées* (Europe)
Bulgarian Birth Customs (Bulgaria)
El Salto del Colacho Baby Jumping Festival (Spain)
Latvian Birth Traditions (Latvia)
Lohusa Şerbeti (Turkey)
Mutterpass (Germany) and *Carnet de Santé Maternité* (France)
Name Days (Catholic and Orthodox) and *Slava* (Serbian Orthodox)
Nordic Napping (Europe)
Quccija (Malta)
Weihnachtsmärchen and Advent Calendars (Germany)

India
Devadasi System (India)
Hindu Baby Rituals (Hinduism)
Mundan Ceremony (India)
Sikh Baby Rites and *Naam Karan* Naming Ceremony (Sikhism)
Upanayana: Sacred Thread Ritual (Hinduism)

International
Baby Racing (International)
Baby Showers (International)
Baby Welcoming (Paganism)
Baptism and Christening (Christianity)
Birth Trees (International)
Birthday Cakes (International)
Birthday Candles (International)
Birthday Cards (International)
Birthday Torments (International)
Birthdays (International)
Birthstones (International)
Bismillah Ceremony (Islam)
Breastfeeding (International)
Brit Milah (Judaism)
Burying the Placenta (International)
Calabash Chalk (Nigeria, United Kingdom, United States, and Canada)
Changeling Beliefs (International)
Child Beauty Pageants (International)
Childermas (Christianity)
Childhood Vaccinations (International)
Christening Gown (Christianity)
Churching of Women (Christianity)
Couvade (International)
Cutting the Umbilical Cord Traditions (International)
Eating Human Placenta (International)
Fairytale (International)
Father's Day (International)
First Communion (Christianity)
Food Taboos in Pregnancy (International)
Girl Guides (International)
Government-Approved Baby Names (International)
Groaning Cheese and Groaning Cake (United Kingdom and North America)
"Happy Birthday" Song (International)

Kangaroo Care (International)
Lamaze Technique and Bradley Method (International)
Lotus Birthing (International)
Lullabies (International)
May Crowning Ritual (Catholicism)
Mistletoe (International)
Monstrous Punishments for Naughty Children (International)
Mothering Sunday (Christianity)
Muslim Birth Rites (Islam)
Muslim Male Circumcision (Islam)
Nativity Play (International)
Navjote Ceremony: Zoroastrian Initiation (Zoroastrianism)
Nursery Rhymes (International)
Parental Leave (International)
Party Games (International)
Phallus Festivals (International)
Pidyon Haben: Redemption of the First Born (Judaism)
Potty Training (International)
Pregnancy Yoga (International)
Saint Nicholas (Christianity)
Scouts (International)
Slow Parenting Movement (International)
Spitting on Babies (International)
Steiner Schools (International)
Swaddling (International)
Tooth Fairy and Tooth Mouse (International)
Traditional Bedwetting Remedies (International)
Traditional Teething Remedies (International)
Waldkindergarten (International)
Warding Off the Evil Eye (International)
Water Birth (International)
Wetting the Baby's Head (International)
Wiccaning (Wicca)
Witch Ball (International)

North America
Apache Baby Ceremonies (Apache)
Atiq Ceremony (Inuit)
Blessingway Ceremony (Navajo)
Cradleboard (Native American)
Dream Catcher (Native American)
Hopi Naming Rites (Hopi)
Worry Dolls and *Katsina* Dolls (Guatemala and Hopi)

Scandinavia
Akka Goddess Customs (Saami)
Cardboard Box Beds (Finland)
Dala Horse (Sweden)

South and Central America
Covering the Belly Button Traditions (Latin America)
El Bolo (Mexico)
La Cuarentena (Latin America)
Piñata (Mexico)
Tuj (Guatemala)
Worry Dolls and *Katsina* Dolls (Guatemala and Hopi)

United Kingdom and Ireland
Blidworth Cradle Rocking Ceremony (England)
Blooding (United Kingdom)
Blue Peter Badge (United Kingdom)

Cerne Abbas Giant (England)
Children's Laureate (United Kingdom)
Christingle (United Kingdom)
Grasmere Rushbearing (England)
Ladybird Books (England)
Little Edith's Treat (England)
"Monday's Child" (England)
Pantomime (United Kingdom)
Saining (Scotland)
Scroggling the Holly (England)
Silver Spoon (United Kingdom)
Sprinkling Cake (Ireland)
Wedding Ring Test (United Kingdom)
Whuppity Scoorie and Lanimer Day (Scotland)

VOLUME 2: ADOLESCENCE AND EARLY ADULTHOOD

Africa and Middle East

Breast Ironing (Africa and Elsewhere)
Chisungu (Zambia)
Cow Jumping (Ethiopia)
Dipo Womanhood Ceremony (Ghana)
Fattening Room Seclusion (Nigeria)
Forehead-Cutting Initiation (Africa)
Hajj (Islam)
Iria Ceremony (Nigeria)
Lobola (Southern Africa)
Maasai Warrior Initiation (Kenya and Tanzania)
Moroccan Weddings (Morocco)
Nkumbi (Democratic Republic of Congo)
Nyumba Ntobhu: Traditional Same-Sex Marriage (Tanzania)
Pika and *Nyora* (Zimbabwe and Mozambique)
Reed Dancing Chastity Ceremony (Kingdom of Swaziland)
Sharo: Public Flogging (Nigeria and Benin)
Wodaabe Courtship Dance and Festival (Africa)
Xhosa Circumcision (South Africa)

Asia (Central and North)

Afghani Betrothal (Afghanistan)

Asia (South and Southeast)

Chinese Coming-of-Age Ceremonies (China)
Coming of Age Day (Japan)
Ear-Piercing Ceremonies (Myanmar and Malaysia)
Filipino Debut (Philippines)
Gwallye (South Korea)
Hadaka Matsuri (Japan)
Hmong Names (Laos, Myanmar, Vietnam, Cambodia, and Thailand)
Log Riding (Japan)
Omiai: Japanese Matchmaking (Japan)
San-San-Kudo (Japan)
Shanghai Marriage Market (China)
Singles' Day (China) and Black Day (South Korea)
Sisters' Meal Festival (China)
Tooth-Filing Ceremony (Indonesia)
Visiting-Girls Courtship Tradition (China)
Zou Hun: Mosuo Walking Marriages (China)

Australia and Pacific

Bachelor and Spinster Balls (Australia)
Initiation by Semen Transferal (Papua New Guinea and Vanuatu)
Land Diving (Vanuatu)
Trobriand Ritualized Sex and Commitment (Papua New Guinea)
Walkabout (Australia)

Continental Europe and Russia

Andrzejki: St. Andrew's Eve (Poland)
Baccalauréat and *Matura* (Europe)
Birthday Humiliations for Singletons (Denmark and Germany)
Bulgarian Weddings (Bulgaria)
Fidanzamenti (Italy)
Hora (Eastern Europe)
Inter-Railing (Europe)
Ladouvane and St. Sylvester's Day (Bulgaria)
La Soupe (France)
Lazarovden (Bulgaria)
Lindo (Croatia)
Looking for Fern Blossoms (Eastern Europe)
Majáles (Czech Republic)
Maypoles (Europe)
Polterabend (Germany)
Povitica (Eastern Europe)
Schuhplattler (Germany) and *Ländler* (Austria)
Secular Confirmation (Europe)
Sock Garland (Germany)
St. Catherine's Day (France)
Sünnet (Turkey)
Vinok (Ukraine)

India

Chokha Thavani Viddhi: Devipujak Purification Trial (India)
Dastaar Bandi and *Amrit Sanchar* (Sikhism)
Diwali and *Kali Pooja* (India)
Hijra (Indian Sub-Continent)
Kumbh Mela (India)

International

Arranged Marriage and Forced Marriage (International)
Assyrian Betrothal and Weddings (International)
Bar Mitzvah and *Bat Mitzvah* (Judaism)
Beards (International)
Christian Wedding Ceremony (Christianity)
Dyngus Day (Eastern Europe and United States)
Female Genital Cutting (Africa, Middle East, Asia, and Elsewhere)
Gap Year (International)
Hair Removal (International)
Handfasting (Scotland, also Neo-Paganism)
Handparting (Wicca)
Hijab (Islam)
Hindu Wedding Ceremony (Hinduism)
Horah (Judaism)
Horseshoes (International)
Human Tooth Sharpening (Indonesia and Africa)
Jewish Wedding Customs (Judaism)
Jumping Over the Broom (United Kingdom and United States, also Neo-Paganism)

Jury Duty (International)
La Quinceañera (Latin America, the Caribbean, and the United States)
Leap Year Proposal (International)
Lip Plugs (Africa and South America)
Mehndi (International)
Menstrual Customs (International)
Menstrual Taboos (International)
Money Dance (International)
Moonie Weddings (International)
Muslim Wedding Ceremony (Islam)
Neck Elongation (Thailand, Myanmar, and South Africa)
Polyandry (International)
Polygyny (International)
Ritual Tattooing (International)
Russefeiring (Norway) and Schoolies Week (Australia)
Same-Sex Marriage (International)
Scarification (Africa and Papua New Guinea)
Shabka (Islam and Coptic Christianity)
Shinbyu (Buddhism)
Sikh Wedding Ceremony (Sikhism)
Thaipusam: Extreme Ritual Flesh Modification (Hinduism)
Training Bras (United States, Europe, and Australasia)
Twenty-First Birthday Traditions (International)
Urethral Subincision (Australia, Africa, and South America)
Virginity Testing (International)
Wedding Anniversaries (International)
Wedding Cakes (International)
Wedding Dress and Wedding Ring (International)
Wedding March and Bridal Chorus (International)
White Coat Ceremony and Pinning Ceremony (International)

North America
Bed-Courtship (Amish)
Cajun Weddings (United States)
Isanaklesh Gotal (Mescalero Apache)
Sock Dance (Canada)
Purity Ball (United States)
Rumspringa (United States and Canada)
Sunrise Ceremony (Apache, United States)
Vision Quest (Native American)

South and Central America
Bullet Ant Initiation (Brazil)
Courtship Whistling (Mexico)
Face in Birthday Cake (Mexico)
Matis Hunting Trials (Brazil)

United Kingdom and Ireland
Blackening the Bride (Scotland)
British Wedding Traditions (United Kingdom)
Burning the Ashen Faggot (England) and The Burning of the Clavie (Scotland)
Choosing Options (England, Wales, and Northern Ireland)
Dunmow Flitch Trials (England)
Gretna Green (Scotland)
Handfasting (Scotland, also Neo-Paganism)
Lovespoons (Wales)
Marriage Banns (Christianity)
RAG Week (United Kingdom and Ireland)
St. Dwynwen's Day (Wales)

VOLUME 3: AGING AND DEATH

Africa and Middle East
Edir (Ethiopia)
Engozi (Uganda)
Famadihana (Madagascar)
Fantasy Coffins (Ghana)
Sakalava Royal Death Traditions and *Fitampoha* (Madagascar)

Asia (Central and North)
Sky Burials (Autonomous Tibet and China)

Asia (South and Southeast)
Chinese Death Customs (China)
Crucifixion Rituals (Philippines)
Living with the Dead (Indonesia)
Ngaben (Indonesia)
Qingming Festival (China)
Tết Nguyên Đan (Vietnam)
Yu Lan Jie: The Hungry Ghost Festival (China)

Australia and Pacific
Finger Amputation (Papua New Guinea)
High-Platform Exposure of the Corpse (Australia)
Malagan (Papua New Guinea)
Tangihanga: Māori Mourning Ritual (New Zealand)
Tongan Funerals (Tonga)

Europe and Russia
Albanian Funeral Customs (Albania)
Funeral Plants (Europe)
The Great Passing (Romania)
Isola di San Michele: Venice's Cemetery Island (Italy)
Mirila (Croatia)
Ossuaries (Europe)
Plastination (Germany)
Romanian Funeral Customs (Romania)
Saturday of Souls (Orthodox Christianity, Bulgaria, and Serbia) and *Radonitsa* (Russia)
Soul Cakes and Soul Breads (Europe)
Windmills (The Netherlands)
Yew Trees (Europe)
Zaduszki (Poland)

Elsewhere
Space Burial (Outer Space)

India
Hindu Death Customs (Hinduism)
Sallekhanā (Jainism)
Sikh Death Customs (Sikhism)
Vrindavan: The City of Widows (India)
Zoroastrian Funerals (India)

International

"Abide With Me" (United Kingdom, North America, and Australasia)
All Souls' Day (Europe and South America)
Alkaline Hydrolysis (United Kingdom, Australia, and United States)
Ankou (France and England)
Assisted Suicide (International)
Buddhist Attitudes Toward Death (Buddhism)
Cairn (International)
Christian Death Rituals (Christianity)
Condolences (International)
Cremation (International)
Croning, Saging, and Elderling Ceremonies (Paganism)
Death Dance (International)
Dia de los Muertos: Day of the Dead (Latin America and United States)
Doom Metal (International)
Easter Eggs (Christianity)
Exhumation (Europe and Asia)
Endocannibalism (Papua New Guinea and Brazil)
Eulogies (International)
Funeral Cakes and Funeral Candy (International)
Funeral Doom (International)
Funeral Songs (International)
Goth Subculture (International)
Grave Rental (Europe and Asia)
Hallowe'en (International)
Halva (International)
Jewish Death Customs (Judaism)
Koliva (International)
"The Last Post" (International)
Martinstag (International)
Memento Mori (International)
Minute's Silence (International)
Missing Man Formation (International)
Mummification (International)
Muslim Death Rituals (Islam)
National Mourning (International)
Obituary (International)
Passion Play (Christianity)
Pregnancy and Infant Loss Remembrance Day (International)
Remembrance Day and Remembrance Sunday (International)
Retirement and Pensions (International)
Riderless Horse (International)
Santa Muerte (Mexico and United States)
Senior Sporting Events (International)
Spontaneous Shrines (International)
State Funeral (International)
Stations of the Cross (Christianity)
Suicide Landmarks (International)
"Taps" (International)
Taxidermy (International)
Tear Catchers and Mourning Jewelry (International)
Tomb of the Unknown Soldier (International)
Tombstone Tourism (International)
Traditional Mourning Colors (International)
University of the Third Age (International)
Vanitas (International)
Wake (International)
Wearing Flowers to Honor War Dead (International)

GEOGRAPHICAL LIST OF ENTRIES

North America
Changing of the Guard Ceremony (United States)
Condemned Prisoner's Last Meal (United States)
Delaware Indian Death Rituals (North America)
Embalming (United States)
Jazz Funeral (United States)
Lakota Death Rituals (Lakota)
Mortuary Totem Poles (Haida and Tlingit)

South and Central America and Caribbean
Eating the Ashes of the Dead (Brazil and Venezuela)
Japanese Death Customs (Japan)
Mizuko Kuyo: Japanese Fetus Memorial Service (Japan)
Nine-Nights (Caribbean)
San La Muerte (South America)
Shrunken Heads (Peru and Ecuador)
Zombies and Voodoo Death Traditions (Haiti)

United Kingdom and Ireland
Bees (United Kingdom)
Chelsea Pensioners (England)
Denville Hall & Brinsworth House (England)
Eleanor Crosses (England)
Eyam Plague Sunday Service (England)
"Lyke-Wake Dirge" (England)
Maidens' Garlands (England)
Maundy Money (United Kingdom)
Message From the Queen (United Kingdom)
Passing Bells (England and Scotland)
Pauper's Funeral (United Kingdom)
Personalized Hearses (United Kingdom)
Royal Wootton Bassett (England)

A

"ABIDE WITH ME," UNITED KINGDOM, NORTH AMERICA, AND AUSTRALASIA

"Abide With Me" is a Christian hymn often played at funerals in the United Kingdom, North America, Australia, and New Zealand. The hymn is almost always associated with mourning and sorrow. Scots-born Church of England pastor Henry Francis Lyte (1793–1847) wrote the hymn's haunting lyrics and also composed a melody for the hymn. However "Abide With Me" is usually sung to the tune "Eventide," composed by Englishman William Henry Monk (1823–1889).

The hymn's first of eight verse consists of the following lyrics:

> Abide with me; fast falls the eventide;
> The darkness deepens; Lord with me abide.
> When other helpers fail and comforts flee,
> Help of the helpless, O abide with me.

Lyte wrote the hymn's lyrics while he was dying of tuberculosis in 1847. Indeed it is said that Lyte only finished the text shortly before his last Sunday service at the Lower Brixham Church in Devon where he ministered to the poor. Parishioners recalled that on this occasion the ailing Lyte had to virtually crawl to the pulpit to deliver his sermon and it was clear that death would soon claim the clergyman.

Lyte's lyrics form a plea for God's companionship in the face of death. However the lyrics were inspired by Lyte's misremembering of a passage from the Gospel of Saint Luke (24:29) during which the disciples meet, but do not recognize, the newly resurrected Jesus, to whom they say "Abide with us, for it is toward evening, and the day is far spent." By changing the pronoun from "us" to "me" Lyte achieved a deeply melancholy quality to his lyrics. "Abide With Me" did not, however, become popular until it was published in 1850 in a book called *Lyte's Remains*. Five years later "Abide With Me" was published in Henry Ward Beecher's book *Plymouth Collection* together with an annotation indicating that the hymn was supposed to be read and not sung. Then in 1861 William Henry Monk, music editor of the Anglican Church book of hymns, *Hymns Ancient and Modern*, included "Abide With Me" in the first edition of the hymnal. It is said that Monk took less than half an hour to compose the tune, "Eventide," to which "Abide With Me" is usually sung.

The poignancy of Lyte's lyrics resulted in "Abide With Me" being sung frequently in the mud-filled trenches of World War I (1914–1918) where death and destruction were ever-present and, in one particularly noted instance of the hymn being sung during that war, British nurse Edith Cavell sang "Abide With Me" on the eve of her execution by the German authorities for helping British soldiers to escape from occupied Belgium in 1915. The hymn's association with death in wartime is reflected in the fact that it is sung at both the British Legion's Festival of Remembrance, an annual event commemorating all those who have lost their lives in times of conflict that is held on the Saturday before Remembrance Sunday, and on ANZAC Day, the national day of remembrance in Australia and New Zealand for those who have served and died during times of both conflict and peace-keeping. A particularly memorable unique occurance of the playing of "Abide With Me" occurred on September 21, 2001, at the site of ground zero in New York City when a Salvation Army band played the hymn during a commemoration service for those killed during the 9/11 attacks.

Aside from associations with death in conflict "Abide With Me" is also associated with civilian tragedy for eyewitnesses recall that the hymn was one of those played by the ship's orchestra during the sinking of the *Titanic* on April 15, 1912.

Despite the hymn's associations with death, "Abide With Me" is a favorite hymn of the British royal family and was played at the wedding of Elizabeth Bowes-Lyon to the future King George VI and at that of their daughter, Elizabeth (now Queen Elizabeth II) to Philip Mountbatten. The royal family's love of "Abide With Me" has given rise to a particular curiosity about "Abide With Me" for since 1927 it has been traditional for spectators to sing the hymn before the start of the annual FA Cup Final, a soccer game that decides the winners of the Football Association Challenge Cup. This custom arose because that year King George V and Queen Mary were attending the Cup Final between Arsenal and Cardiff City and it was well known that the hymn was a favorite of the royals. As 1927 was the year that community singing was reintroduced to the Cup Final, Football Association secretary Sir Frederick Wall arranged for the hymn to be sung by the crowd. Since then, "Abide With Me" has become part of the ritual of FA Cup Final Day. The hymn's stirring lyrics seem to unite opposing fans with their varying loyalties and backgrounds, and the communal singing of the hymn provides a moment of togetherness before battle commences on the soccer field.

"Abide With Me" has appeared in numerous films and television programs, almost always in scenes associated with death or distress. For example, the hymn is sung by wounded British soldiers at a field hospital in *A Bridge Too Far* (1977), and appears in funeral scenes in *Fist of Fury* (1972) and *The Full Monty* (1997).

See also: Funeral Songs; Jazz Funeral; "The Last Post" and "Taps"; "Lyke-Wake Dirge"; Remembrance Day and Remembrance Sunday; Tomb of the Unknown Soldier, Wearing Flowers to Honor War Dead

Further Reading

Christiansen, Rupert. "The Story Behind the Hymn," *The Telegraph*, September 22, 2007. Accessed October 28, 2014, at http://www.telegraph.co.uk/culture/music/3668058/The-story-behind-the-hymn.html.

The FA. "Abide With Me." *The FA Cup*, May 18, 2007. Accessed October 28, 2014, at http://www.thefa.com/TheFACup/News/2007/May/CupFinal_abide.
Mowbray, Jay Henry. *Sinking of the Titanic: Eyewitness Accounts*. Kirkland, WA: Tales End Press, 2012.
Norwich Cathedral. "Nurse Edith Cavell." Accessed October 28, 2014, at http://www.cathedral.org.uk/historyheritage/historical-characters-linked-in-people-s-minds-eg-dame-julian--sir-thomas-erpingham--edith-cavell-and-1.aspx.
Osbeck, Kenneth W. *101 Hymn Stories*. Grand Rapids, MI: Kregel Publications, 1982.

ALBANIAN FUNERAL CUSTOMS, ALBANIA

Like many other Eastern European countries Albania is a land steeped in folklore and traditions. Rituals and customs govern many aspects of Albanian culture and life events, perhaps none more so than funerals, which in Albania are surrounded by a great many customs and superstitions.

When someone dies in Albania it is traditional for the body's eyes to be shut, as an Albanian superstition tells that if the eyes of a corpse remain open then another death will occur in the family of the dead person. Then, as soon as news of the death is made public all the females belonging to the dead person's extended family begin to wail loudly, a tradition known as a "wailing funeral." This custom is particularly pronounced in rural areas of Albania. While the women wail the corpse is washed, dressed in his or her best clothes and placed in a coffin. Alternatively, in the Mirdita region of Albania it has also been known for the corpse to be sat upright holding a gun with a lit cigarette placed between its lips to give the impression that it is still alive. A vigil is performed over the corpse lying in the coffin. This is to ensure that a cat does not jump over the body for this would result in the reanimation of the corpse after burial with the dead individual becoming a vampire-like supernatural being of Slavic origin called a *lugat*.

Burials in Albania normally occur within 24 hours of death, so the day after someone dies the corpse travels in procession to the cemetery. In some areas of Albania (e.g., the Malësi e Madhe district), before the coffin is removed from the dead person's home it is lifted up and down three times in the doorway of the house before being taken outside feet first. A bowl of flour is then placed on the floor where the coffin stood with the flour later given to the poor.

There are many graveyard traditions in Albania. For instance, in the Maltsia e Vogel district the graves of women are traditionally dug just over one–and-a-half feet deeper than those for men. Meanwhile it is generally understood in Albania that people must never leap or walk over an empty grave, nor should a grave be left empty. For this reason a tool such as a spade or shovel should be left in the specially dug hole until it is occupied. Once a coffin is lowered into the grave a coin is placed alongside it. This is a widely followed custom that some folklorists think is upheld in case the new occupant of the grave needs to pay someone that inhabited the grave previously for use of the burial plot. Another possible explanation for the tradition is that the custom may hark back to ancient beliefs that it is necessary for the newly dead to pay for their safe conduct through the afterlife. Other objects also commonly placed into graves include smoking pipes, tobacco, and apples. Tradition also dictates that coffins in Albania are buried facing eastward so that the corpse's head reaches the dawn.

After the burial is complete, all the mourners go to the home of the bereaved family where they wash their hands. This ritual washing is intended to stop the soul of the departed from traveling home with the mourners thereby bringing death into their homes.

A particularly celebrated aspect of Albania funerals is the singing of dirges and lamentations for the dead by women, which is another element of the so-called wailing funerals. A wailing funeral consists of various actions designed to signal the pain of mourning including tearing out hair, scratching the face, and wearing clothes that have been turned inside out. However the most noted aspect of such funerals is the singing of dirges, known as wailing. To begin the singing one woman chants a few lines from a dirge or lamentation and then other women join in the singing. It is very unusual for men to sing any type of lamentation. Indeed only in the north of Albania are men known to sing lamentations, though men across Albania will grow their beards as a sign of mourning. The dirges laud the recently dead person and call on them to rise from the grave. If the dead person is a man then the songs suggest that his horse, sword, and herds of animals are all calling for him. Wealthy families may also hire professional mourners to perform the singing.

After a funeral it is usual for the friends and family of the deceased to gather on specific days in order to share a meal in the belief that the dead person may join in the feast. In Tirana, the capital city of Albania, as well as in the city of Gjirokastra, such ritual meals are held on the third-, seventh-, and 40th-day anniversaries of the person's death as well as six months and one year after the death. In the Korça region to the southeast of the country, which is mainly Orthodox in religion, such memorial meals take place nine days after death to reflect the nine ranks of angels as set out by Saint Dionysius the Areopagite and 40 days after death to mirror the 40 days between Jesus's Resurrection and the Ascension. People living in the Korça region also hold memorial meals on the first-, second-, and third-year anniversaries of a death. In the past, the three-year anniversary was marked by the exhumation of the deceased's skeletal remains that were then bathed in wine and milk before being placed in a crypt.

Foods eaten during the memorial feasts include lamb rissoles called *qofta*, *tzatziki* (a yoghurt and mint sauce), various salads, red peppers, olives, potatoes, a type of filo pastry pie filled with beans called *byrek me fasule*, boiled eggs, bread, and different types of soup. Memorial meals in honor of Christian Albanians are also marked by the eating of a type of *koliva* called *grurë*, which is sweetened wheat mixed with chopped nuts that is blessed by the local priest and shared among those present. Moreover, *grurë* is also distributed among the poor, some of whom are invited to partake of the feast as it is believed that showing such benevolence to the poor will benefit the soul of the departed. Memorial meals to honor Muslim Albanians serve a type of *halva* instead of *grurë*.

See also: *Halva*; *Koliva*; *Mirila*; Romanian Funeral Customs

Further Reading

Elsie, Robert. *A Dictionary of Albanian Religion, Mythology and Folk Culture*. London: C. Hurst & Co. Publishers Ltd., 2001.

Gëzuar. "Remembering Those Who Have Passed." Gëzuar: A Blog about Albania, Anthropology, and New Experiences, February 5, 2009. Accessed April 14, 2015, at http://chelsiabaniaadventure.blogspot.co.uk/2009/02/remembering-those-who-have-passed.html.

Gloyer, Gillian. *Albania*. Fifth edition. Chalfont St. Peter, UK: Bradt Travel Guides Ltd., 2015.

Vyshka, Gentian, and Bardhyl Çipi. "Death Rituals in Albania: An Anthropological Review," *Antrocom Online Journal of Anthropology*, 6(2), 2010, 235–246.

ALKALINE HYDROLYSIS, UNITED KINGDOM, AUSTRALIA, AND UNITED STATES

Alkaline hydrolysis, also known as liquid cremation, resomation, and aquamation amongst other names, is an environmentally friendly method of corpse disposal employed in the United Kingdom, Australia, and the United States, where the National Funeral Directors Association recognizes the process as fittingly dignified as far as it is approved by state law, properly regulated, and coherently explained to relatives of the deceased. In addition, such universities as the University of Florida use alkaline hydrolysis to dispose of cadavers used in medical research.

During alkaline hydrolysis of a body a corpse is submerged in a solution of water and potassium hydroxide that is heated and pressurized for up to three hours. Proponents of alkaline hydrolysis assert that the method merely accelerates the natural process of decomposition as heating and pressurizing the corpse breaks down body tissue. The resultant liquid can be poured into the sewer system or used as a fertilizer as tests have proven the emission is sterile, does not contain DNA, and is safe for the environment. Meanwhile, remaining bones are processed in a cremulator, the same machine that crushes bone into ash following cremation. Metals including mercury, which is often released into atmosphere during cremation, are safely recovered, as are any artificial joints or implants.

In the United Kingdom alkaline hydrolysis is championed by the Scottish company Resomation Limited, which has trademarked the name Resomator and has a patent pending on the resomation process. Resomation Limited is part owned by The Co-Operative Group, the largest funeral firm in the United Kingdom. The process is supported by several environmental pressure groups that aver that alkaline hydrolysis uses less energy, particularly fossil fuels, than cremation, and creates less carbon dioxide. Alkaline hydrolysis is offered at some U.K. crematoria and at present the process is legal in eight states in the United States: Colorado, Florida,

Illinois, Kansas, Maine, Maryland, Minnesota, and Oregon. In Queensland, Australia, the Aquamation Industries of Australia disposed of several corpses using a rival alkaline hydrolysis machine to the Resomator. The same design was also used to dispose of 19 corpses in Ohio in 2011 before the state court ruled that the machine used did not comply with state law.

While the ecological friendliness of alkaline hydrolysis is often stressed, such opponents as Republican New Hampshire State Representative John Cebrowski claim that alkaline hydrolysis is akin to flushing a loved one down a drain. Similarly, the Catholic Church opposes the process arguing that the chemical digestion of a human body does not treat a corpse with sufficient dignity.

See also: Cremation; Grave Rental and Exhumations; Wiccan Funerals; Zoroastrian Funerals

Further Reading

Bowdler, Neil. "New Body 'Liquefaction' Unit Unveiled at Florida Funeral Home." BBC News: Science & Environment, August 30, 2011. Accessed November 8, 2014, at http://www.bbc.co.uk/news/science-environment-14114555.

Catholic News Agency. "NY Catholic Conference Opposes 'Chemical Digestion' of Human Remains," *Catholic News Agency*, March 25, 2012. Accessed November 8, 2014, at http://www.catholicnewsagency.com/news/ny-catholic-conference-opposes-chemical-digestion-of-human-remains/.

Hansen, Kent. "Choosing to Be Flushed Away: A National Background on Alkaline Hydrolysis and What Texas Should Know about Regulating 'Liquid Cremation,'" *Estate Law Journal*, February 10, 2012. Accessed November 9, 2014, at http://www.estatelawjournal.org/site/wp-content/uploads/2012/02/10-Kent-Hansen-Choosing-to-be-Flushed-Away-.pdf.

Olson, Philip R. "Flush and Bone: Funeralizing Alkaline Hydrolysis in the United States." *Science, Technology, & Human Values*, 39(5), 2014, 666–693.

ALL SOULS' DAY, EUROPE AND SOUTH AMERICA

All Souls' Day, also known as Soulmas Day, Saumas, and The Commemoration of All the Faithful Departed amongst other names, is a Christian holy day generally celebrated annually on November 2, the day after All Saints' Day, a Christian day celebrating all martyrs and saints that is also known as All Hallows' Day. All Souls' Day is, therefore, closely linked to Hallowe'en, the name of which derives from All Hallows' Eve. Catholics in Europe and North America generally celebrate All Souls' Day and, though beliefs and customs connected to All Souls' Day vary widely between Christian denominations and from place to place, the day is regarded as an opportunity for people to unite in order to remember those who have died recently, particularly relatives and loved ones. All Souls' Day is also regarded as a time when the living can commune with the dead and when prayer can help cleanse those souls trapped in purgatory, that is, caught between heaven and hell thereby paying the price for their sins before entering Paradise, helping the souls to reach the Kingdom of Heaven. On All Souls' Day the dead are remembered, appeased, and called upon to look out for the living. Some churches hold special All Souls' Day services with music and prayers, during which the names of those who have died are read aloud, and commemorative candles are lit.

That Christians have a duty to pray for the souls of the departed is referred to in Chapter 12, verse 46 of 2 Maccabees, a book of the Christian Old Testament that is regarded as part of the Bible by Catholics and Orthodox Christians. This passage recommends praying for the dead so that they might be absolved of their sins. Praying for the departed was also performed in the ritual offering of the Eucharist for the repose of souls. This traditionally occurs on the day of a person's death, the day of their burial, the seventh and 30th day after death occurs and when the Month's Mind Mass is celebrated, as well as on the anniversary of a person's death. Of these masses only the funeral mass is obligatory. It is left to the discretion of the deceased's loved ones whether they celebrate the other masses. All Souls' Day is also an optional celebration in the Anglican Church and is celebrated several times per year in the Eastern Orthodox Church, which does not associate the day with November.

Traditions surrounding feasts for the dead date back to ancient Babylonia, Rome, and Greece and are well established in both world folklore and religions. For example, the Japanese Bon Festival and the Chinese Hungry Ghost Festival both fulfill a role similar to that of All Souls' Day. The history of All Souls' Day dates back to the 11th century when Saint Odilo of Cluny established All Souls' Day as a festival of prayer designed to release souls from purgatory. According to legend, Saint Odilo instituted the festival after a pilgrim returning from the Holy Land told him of an island on which the souls of those in purgatory could be heard crying out for prayers to be said as they knew these would lead to their release. Saint Odilo established All Souls' Day as a day when the monks at Cluny Abbey in central France, and its associated Benedictine monasteries, would hold requiem masses and pray for the souls of those they believed were trapped in purgatory. From Cluny Abbey the All Souls' Day custom spread to other monasteries and then across the Christian Church in the western hemisphere. However despite Saint Odilo's order that All Souls' Day be commemorated, the custom did not become truly accepted until the end of the 13th century and even then the Church had qualms about a day set aside purely for the commemoration of the dead. By the 14th century, the celebration of All Souls' Day had spread throughout France and to Germany, England, and Spain. By the end of the century, the Catholic Church had placed All Souls' Day (as the Day of the Commemoration of All the Faithful Departed) in the official books of the Western Church for November 2 (or November 3 if November 2 falls on a Sunday). Saint Odilo originally set All Souls' Day to fall in February but this was changed by the Church to the day after All Saints' Day so that the memory of all the departed, both saints in heaven and souls in purgatory, could be celebrated on two successive days, thereby expressing the Christian belief in *Communio Sanctorum* or Communion of Saints, the spiritual union of all members of the Christian Church whether living or dead and residing on earth, in heaven, or in purgatory. The Church decided that as All Saints' Day was celebrated on November 1, it was right that the memory of souls in purgatory should be commemorated the following day. It was also during medieval times that many of the traditions now associated with All Souls' Day were first instituted. For instance, bells were rung to comfort souls in purgatory and candles were lit to provide souls languishing in the dark of purgatory with a light.

In 1915, Pope Benedict XV gave permission for priests to say three masses on All Souls' Day as a way of increasing the aid through prayer available to souls suffering in purgatory. These masses belong to the group of requiem masses as they begin with the Latin words "*Requiem aeternam dona eis*" which translates as "Eternal rest grant unto them." During these masses it is common to sing the 13th-century poem "*Dies Irae*" ("Day of Wrath"). It also became customary for the Office of the Dead, a prayer cycle for the repose of the soul belonging to a departed descendent, to be recited by priests and congregations. It has also become traditional in many places for graves and cemeteries to be blessed either on the eve or morning of All Souls' Day. On the afternoon of All Souls' Day it is usual for practicing Christians to visit the graves of their loved ones. Sometimes a priest may lead a procession consisting of his congregation to the churchyard where prayers are said for the dead and graves sprinkled with holy water. After the procession relatives and friends say private prayers for the departed. In the week preceding All Souls' Day it is usual for Christians to decorate graves with fresh flowers, mow the grass in the churchyard and sprinkle white gravel around graves.

Individual countries also have their own particular All Souls' Day customs. For example, in Poland, and at Polish churches around the world, Catholics give their priests black-bordered paper sheets called *Wypominki* (Naming) on which are written the names of the dead. Then, during evening prayers throughout November, and on Sundays, these names are read aloud from the pulpit and prayers are offered for the souls of those named. Meanwhile, in rural Austria children pray aloud while walking through open spaces to churches and graveyards, as it is the Austrian belief that on All Souls' Day the dead wander in the forests praying and moaning, unable to reach out to the living. The children pray aloud in order to communicate to the dead that their moans have been heard and answered. Another All Souls' Day custom involving children occurs in Hungary where orphaned children are invited into family homes, fed a delicious meal, and given new clothes and toys. In Hungary it is also the custom to tend graves that are otherwise neglected. Hungarian families take turns tending these graves in addition to the graves of their own relatives, lighting candles, adorning tombs, and praying for the souls of those buried within.

In other parts of Europe All Souls' Day customs actually begin on All Saints' Day. For instance, in Germany little candles called *Seelenlichter* (lights of the holy souls) are placed around the graves of relatives and friends on All Saints' Day and then left to burn through the night for in Germany All Souls' Day, known as *Allersselen*, marks the start of an eight-day period of performing charity and penance known as *Seelënnacht*, meaning Soul Nights. Many German superstitions pertain to Allersselen, including the belief that hot cooking pans and knives should be hidden on All Souls' Day so that the dead cannot hurt themselves and bowls of butter should be visible to soothe the wounds of the dead. Another German superstition is that to walk three times round a church on All Souls' Day will make a wish come true and the belief that a girl can stop a man at random and ask his name in order to discern the name of her future husband.

In areas of central Europe where Catholicism is the prevailing religion it is traditional to ring church bells at the approach of dusk on All Saints' Day so that believers may be reminded of the need to pray for souls languishing in purgatory. On hearing the bells Catholic families congregate in one room of their home and put out all the lights except for a sanctified candle that they have kept since Candlemas Day, the Christian celebration held on February 2 that marks the Virgin Mary's ritual purification after the birth of Jesus and the presentation of Jesus at the Temple. The candle is placed on a table and the family kneels around it, reciting the rosary with prayers led by the males of the household. Meanwhile, in rural Brittany, France, four men alternate in tolling the church bell for an hour after sunset on All Saints' Day. Four other men then visit farms during the night, ringing hand-bells and chanting prayers for the souls of the dead to which those inside the farms reply saying "Amen."

In most countries of South America All Souls' Day is a public holiday. (*See* Plate 1.) In Brazil, thousands of people visit cemeteries in the morning, light candles, and pray at graves, while in Puerto Rico, people wear their best clothes to walk to the graves of their loved ones—women often carry water-filled vases of flowers as they know there will not be water available at the cemetery to keep the flowers fresh. At the cemeteries priests visit each grave in turn and recite prayers for the dead accompanied by mourners. This procession lasts for hours and usually ends around midnight.

In England, an All Souls' Day custom known as souling exists during which children visit houses, sing songs, and collect food, especially soul cakes, as well as

---

The Origins of the Name Candlemas

The festival of Candlemas is so-called because on this day all the church's candles to be used throughout the year would be blessed. Though a Christian occasion, as with many other Christian festivals, Candlemas draws on elements originating in pagan times. In pre-Christian days, the date of Candlemas, February 2, was considered the festival of light as it marked the mid-point of winter since it fell equidistant between the winter solstice (the shortest day of the year) and the spring equinox. Many ancient peoples felt the night brought forth evil spirits and so would light candles to frighten away dark forces.

money and drink. This customs may have been inspired by the medieval Christian (particularly Catholic) belief that the dead were allowed to leave purgatory for two or three days in order to call at the homes of relatives. Souling has a long history in England alluded to in William Shakespeare's play *The Two Gentlemen of Verona* (written between 1589 and 1592). However the custom really took off during the 19th century. The songs sung during souling vary but nearly always mentions lost souls, the desire for cake and religious references.

See also: Christian Death Rituals; *Dia de los Muertos*: Day of the Dead; Japanese Death Customs; *Koliva*; Passing Bells; *Qingming* Festival; Saturday of Souls and *Radonitsa*; Soul Cakes and Soul Breads; *Têt Nguyên đan*; *Yu Lan Jie*: Hungry Ghost Festival

Further Reading

Clements, Jane. "Christians Mark All Saints Day and All Souls Day." ITV News, November 1, 2009. Accessed November 2, 2014, at http://www.itv.com/news/london/2014-11-01/christians-mark-all-saints-day-and-all-souls-day/.

Jones, Alison. *Larousse Dictionary of World Folklore*. Edinburgh, UK: Larousse, 1996.

Morton, Lisa. *Trick or Treat: A History of Halloween*. London: Reaktion Books Ltd., 2012.

Norget, Kristin. *Days of Death, Days of Life: Ritual in the Popular Culture of Oaxaca*. New York: Columbia University Press, 2006.

Simpson, Jacqueline, and Steve Roud. *Oxford Dictionary of English Folklore*. Oxford, UK: Oxford University Press, 2000.

Trinity Communications. "Catholic Activity: Feasts of All Saints and All Souls." Accessed November 2, 2014, at http://www.catholicculture.org/culture/liturgicalyear/activities/view.cfm?id=1185 ().

ANKOU, FRANCE AND ENGLAND

Ankou, or *L'Ankou*, is the personification of Death in the Breton mythology prevalent in the Brittany region of northwestern France and the folklore of the English county of Cornwall. As the embodiment of Death, Ankou beckons the souls of those about to die and carries them away in a cart or carriage called the *karrigell an Ankou*, the wheels of which can be heard screeching during the night. Like the Grim Reaper, Ankou is a tall, thin figure usually resembling a skeleton dressed in a black robe, wearing a wide brimmed hat, sometimes with long flowing white hair and often carrying a scythe. In some parts of Brittany both Ankou and Ankou's servant *mervel an Ankou* are thought to be the last person to have died in the parish the previous calendar year or the last person to have been buried in the local graveyard. For this reason, Ankou is not an abstract figure but rather a particularly familiar or intimate figure as it is likely that those who believe in Ankou will know the person who is said to have become the personification of Death through being the last to die or be buried.

Some folklorists suggest that Ankou is a remnant of the prehistoric death-goddess once worshipped in Brittany while others opine that the figure of Ankou derives from the Celtic god of death who was said to transport the dead to his kingdom. In addition, a local legend tells that Ankou is the first-born son of Adam and Eve. Ankou has been present in Breton literature for a long time, appearing in many works of such 16th-century literature as *Le Mirouer de la Mort* (*The Mirror of Death*). The myth of Ankou continues in the many Breton funeral customs involving food. This is because Ankou and its minions are said to walk on earth on November's Eve and the living are expected to keep them well fed with a supply of milk, cider, and pancakes—foods for which Brittany is famous. As a result of this folk belief many Breton graveyards are built to accept offerings of food with gravestones embellished with small cup-like holes for receiving milk and cider. Meanwhile, it was a common belief that if a person died from cancer then a dish of butter should be placed near their corpse so that the butter could absorb the disease. The "infected" butter would then be removed and buried to prevent the disease from spreading. Another Breton death custom is that the corpse should eat, or be buried with, the amount of soil equivalent to the amount of bread that he or she wasted during their lifetime.

Since the 1940s, many of these customs have begun to die out gradually. However the presence of Ankou can still be seen in the numerous statuettes of Ankou that can be found in Breton churches. (*See* Plate 2.) Indeed in the church at Ploumilliau, a village in northwestern Brittany, a statue of Ankou appears amongst a collection of saints' effigies.

See also: *Memento Mori* and *Vanitas*; Ossuaries; *San La Muerte*; *Santa Muerte*

Further Reading

Gibson, Marion, Shelley Trower, and Garry Tregidga, eds. *Mysticism, Myth and Celtic Identity.* Abingdon, UK: Routledge, 2013.
History of Brittany. "Ankou a Legend from Brittany." April 18, 2009. Accessed November 23, 2014, at http://athomeinbrittany.typepad.co.uk/at_home_in_brittany/2009/04/ankou-a-legend-from-brittany.html.
Koch, John T., ed. *Celtic Culture: A Historical Encyclopedia Volumes 1–5.* Santa Barbara, CA: ABC-CLIO, 2006.
Nourishing Death. "Lower Brittany, The Land of the Dead." An Examination of the Relationship between Food and Death in Rituals, Culture, Religion and Society, June 28, 2013. Accessed November 23, 2014, at http://nourishingdeath.wordpress.com/2013/06/28/lower-brittany-the-land-of-the-dead/.
Spence, Lewis. *Legends and Romances of Brittany.* Mineola, NY: Dover Publications, 1997.

ASSISTED SUICIDE, INTERNATIONAL

Assisted suicide is the act of helping or encouraging another person to kill him- or herself. Assisted suicide is also often defined as a situation in which a terminally ill person requests the help of others to end his or her life. When this is requested of a doctor it may be referred to as physician-assisted suicide (PAS). Assisted suicide and physician-assisted suicide are not the same as euthanasia as this is the act of killing another living being in order to ease their suffering. Assisted suicide is a highly sensitive and emotive subject causing much argument on moral, ethical, and religious grounds. As such, assisted suicide is legal in only a few countries (usually only under certain circumstances or within the definition of euthanasia) in the world—Switzerland, the Netherlands, and Belgium—and in Oregon, Washington, Montana, New Mexico, and Vermont in the United States.

The Netherlands has long been legally tolerant of both euthanasia and assisted suicide with both practices legalized in 2001. Under Dutch law doctors can perform euthanasia and assist suicide if a patient has made repeated, well-thought-out arguments for ending his or her life or in cases where a person's physical suffering is deemed to be unacceptably immense—though the individual need not have been declared terminally ill. Any doctor that considers performing assisted suicide must discuss the case with a colleague and note all the actions he or she takes. In the Netherlands, assisted suicide is not limited to adults: with parental consent, doctors may help patients between 12 and 18 years old die. The year after assisted suicide and euthanasia were legalized in the Netherlands, Belgium made euthanasia lawful. Though the bill did not specifically deal with the topic of assisted suicide, it also did not spell out what was meant by euthanasia. Belgian law does not refer explicitly to assisted suicide because of a cultural taboo surrounding suicide in Belgium but assisted suicide is performed lawfully in Belgium under the cloak of euthanasia. As in the Netherlands, assisted suicide must only be performed after a patient has made frequent, well-considered requests to die and only in cases where the individual's suffering is judged to be intolerable. Unlike in the Netherlands, in Belgium assisted suicide may only be performed on people under 18 if they are suffering from an incurable medical issue. However in February 2014 Belgium became the first country in the world to legalize euthanasia for children. In Belgium there is no age limit for minors wishing to die by lethal injection, though the children must be terminally ill, near death, and suffering in a way that cannot be alleviated by medical intervention. The children must also be aware of the seriousness of their decision and have the agreement of their parents.

Meanwhile, Switzerland is unique in that the country's penal code allows assisted suicide by both doctors and lay-people as long as they are not motivated by personal gain when performing the killing. The Swiss penal code does, however, clearly forbid euthanasia. Such is Switzerland's attitude to assisted suicide that the country is famed for being a favored destination of individuals engaged in so-called suicide tourism, the act of traveling to a place with the sole intention of committing suicide there. Between 2008 and 2012, 611 suicide tourists travelled to Switzerland purely with the purpose of committing assisted suicide. The tourists came from 31 different countries though the majority came from Germany and the United Kingdom. Indeed "going to Switzerland" is a euphemism for assisted suicide in the United Kingdom where assisted suicide is illegal under section 2(1) of the Suicide Act 1961 and where voluntary euthanasia is considered to be murder. In September 2015 the subject of assisted suicide was debated in the U.K. parliament. Members of Parliament (MPs) representing English and Welsh constituencies were allowed to vote on whether to change the law so that people with less than six months to live could be prescribed a lethal dose of drugs that they would then take themselves. The proposal also stated that two doctors and a high court judge would have to approve each individual request. In a free vote 118 MPs favored a change in a law but were outnumbered by the 330 MPs that voted against the plans. The leader of the Church of England, the Archbishop of Canterbury Justin Welby, welcomed the decision as he felt that allowing assisted suicide to take place legally would mean that suicide was no longer regarded as a tragedy. Similarly, the union for British doctors, the British Medical Association, opposes all forms of assisted dying though the Royal College of Nursing adopts a neutral stance on the matter.

In Switzerland, six right-to-die organizations help in around 600 suicides per year of which between 150 and 200 of the deaths are cases of suicide tourism. The most well known right-to-die organization in Switzerland is Dignitas, a not-for-profit organization founded in the Swiss city of Zurich in 1998. Dignitas claims to provide people with the option of a dignified death via assisted dying. The people helped by Dignitas tend to be terminally ill or suffering from serious physical and mental illness. According to Swiss law, those that wish to end their life at a Dignitas clinic must be judged of sound judgment following an investigation by a Swiss psychiatrist. After a person has ended his or her life at a Dignitas clinic, a Dignitas doctor contacts the police and they, along with a medical examiner and another doctor, travel to the scene of the death. After a short enquiry the deceased is cremated in Zurich and their ashes transported back to their homeland. Leading reasons for people wishing to be assisted to die via suicide tourism in Switzerland include neurological diseases, cancer, rheumatic disease, or cardiovascular disease. The most common method of performing assisted suicide is the provision of the drug sodium pentobarbital, a fatal dose of which allows a patient to slip into a deep coma and paralyzes the patient's respiratory system, causing them to stop breathing.

In Germany, there is no formal legal term in the criminal code concerning assisted suicide though doctors are not allowed to assist someone to commit suicide for ethical reasons. Moreover, German doctors can be held responsible by law for not aiding a patient whom they have seen fall into an unconscious state. In German-speaking countries, the word euthanasia tends to be avoided because it is associated with the eugenics experiments of the Nazi era. For this reason, German law usually distinguishes between *beihilfe zum suizid* (assisted suicide) and *aktive sterbehilfe* (active assisted suicide). Active assisted suicide is illegal in Germany and is said to occur when a doctor prescribes and hands over a drug to a patient. In contrast, assisted suicide is legal and permitted under German law, as long as the person who wishes to die does so without the help of someone else, for example, without someone guiding their hand.

In the United States, Oregon became the first state to legalize assisted suicide after a public referendum in 1997. Under this law, known as the Death with Dignity

Act, a terminally ill adult considered to be competent may ask for a doctor's help to die under certain circumstances and as long as certain requirements are met. These safeguards are intended to prevent abuse. In Oregon, a person wishing to die must make two verbal and one written appeal for assisted suicide that are at least 15 days apart. Additionally, the person's terminal diagnosis must be confirmed and they must be judged to be in sound mind by a psychiatrist or psychologist. Lastly the person must be informed of alternatives to assisted suicide and the prescribing physician should suggest that the patient inform his or her family and friends of his or her intentions. Once these necessities have been completed the physician can prescribe a fatal dose of medicine before filing a report with the Department of Human Services.

In October 2015, a joint statement by the Canadian Conference of Catholic Bishops and the Evangelical Fellowship of Canada (an alliance of over 40 allied denominations) that was also supported by more than 30 other Christian denominations as well as Jewish and Muslim leaders set out opposition to assisted suicide in response to the Canada's decision to legalize assisted suicide from February 6, 2016. Canada's Supreme Court declared that the Criminal Code's prohibitions on assisted suicide would no longer apply in cases involving competent adults who had clearly consented to the termination of their life and who were suffering from serious and incurable medical conditions that caused intolerable suffering. The court also ruled that a doctor could not be forced to accelerate an individual's death. In response to this ruling the Canadian Conference of Catholic Bishops and the Evangelical Fellowship of Canada reaffirmed their belief in the sanctity of human life and argued in favor of compassion, improved pain relief, and better palliative care rather than assisted suicide.

See also: *Sallekhana*; Suicide Landmarks

Further Reading

Barone, Emily. "See Which States Allow Assisted Suicide," *Time*, November 3, 2014. Accessed November 3, 2015, at http://time.com/3551560/brittany-maynard-right-to-die-laws/.

Catholic News Agency. "Killing People Is Not Compassion—Religious Leaders Unite against Assisted Suicide," November 3, 2015. Accessed November 3, 2015, at http://www.catholicnewsagency.com/news/killing-people-is-not-compassion-religious-leaders-unite-against-assisted-suicide-44896/.

Gallagher, James, and Philippa Roxby. "Assisted Dying Bill: MPs Reject 'Right to Die' Law." BBC News: Health, September 11, 2015. Accessed November 3, 2015, at http://www.bbc.co.uk/news/health-34208624.

Guardian Staff. "Euthanasia and Assisted Suicide Laws around the World," *The Guardian*, July 17, 2014. Accessed November 3, 2015, at http://www.theguardian.com/society/2014/jul/17/euthanasia-assisted-suicide-laws-world.

Huxtable, Richard. *Euthanasia, Ethics and the Law: From Conflict to Compromise*. Abingdon, UK: Routledge, 2007.

McManus, Ruth. *Death in a Global Age*. Basingstoke, UK: Palgrave Macmillan, 2013.

Nitschke, Philip, and Fiona Stewart. *The Peaceful Pill Handbook*. International edition. Lake Tahoe, NV: Exit International US Ltd., 2006.
Picard, André. "Court Has Ruled on Assisted Death, But Canada Is Not Prepared," *The Globe and Mail*, August 31, 2015. Accessed November 3, 2015, at http://www.theglobeandmail.com/globe-debate/court-has-ruled-on-assisted-death-but-canada-is-not-prepared/article26167297/.
Werth Jr., James L., Elena Yakunina, and Jessica M. Richmond. "Assisted Suicide," in Bryant, Clifton D. and Dennis L. Peck, eds., *Encyclopedia of Death and the Human Experience 1*, 77–79. Thousand Oaks, CA: SAGE Publications Inc., 2009.
Wilson, Jacque. "'Suicide Tourism' to Switzerland Has Doubled Since 2009." CNN, October 7, 2014. Accessed November 3, 2015, at http://edition.cnn.com/2014/08/20/health/suicide-tourism-switzerland/.

B

BEES, UNITED KINGDOM

Bees are flying insects of the superfamily *Apoidea* of which there are nearly 20,000 known species of bee grouped into seven to nine recognized families. In the United Kingdom, particularly in England, bees have been regarded as wise, mysterious, and holy since medieval times probably because of their ability to produce beeswax, the substance used to make church candles, and honey, a God-given joy of heaven. However British folk tradition stresses that bees are liable to take offense easily thereby depriving humans of the beneficial substances they produce. Therefore it is important that bees be treated as part of a household and in particular must be informed of any births, marriages or, most importantly, deaths in the family. This is colloquially known as "the telling of the bees" and was a widespread tradition across England with many local variations that still exists today, though less frequently than in earlier times. It is considered especially important that bees be told of the death of their beekeeper, that their hives be adorned in such ways in keeping with the sad event as draping a black cloth across the entrance to the hives, and that they be given a share of any funereal food such as cakes and wine (or festive food if the occasion is a happy one). It is also believed that bees are extremely sensitive and that if they are not told of the change in family circumstance then they will either desert their hive or will themselves die.

The earliest association of bees being affected by the death of the keeper is found in *Historical Meditations* by P Camerarius, published in 1621, which notes that a beehive should be moved on the death of its master or mistress. Though it has been claimed that the oldest reference to telling the bees of a death, dressing their hive, and giving them funeral food comes as recently as the start of the 19th century, a reference to this practice occurs in *Modern Husbandmen* by William Ellis, published in 1750. This article relates that as soon as a woman beekeeper died a member of her family went outside at midnight to wake her hive of bees and tell them of their mistress's death.

Another association between bees and death comes in the form of an English superstition that if a swarm of bees settles on the dead branch of a tree then either there will be a death in the family to which the bees belong or the person who sees the bees settle will die. Similarly, it is believed that if a single bee flies into a home and then dies there then bad luck is sure to follow.

See also: Birthday Candles (Volume 1); Christian Death Rituals; Funeral Plants; Yew Trees

Further Reading
Jones, Alison. *Larousse Dictionary of World Folklore.* Edinburgh, UK: Larousse, 1996.
O'Malley, Michael. *The Wisdom of Bees: What the Hive Can Teach Business about Leadership, Efficiency and Growth.* London: Penguin Group, 2010.
Ransome, Hilda M. *The Sacred Bee in Ancient Times and Folklore.* London: George Allen & Unwin, 1937. Reprinted by Mineola: Dover Publications, 2004.
Roud, Steve. *The Penguin Guide to the Superstitions of Britain and Ireland.* London: Penguin Books, 2006.
Simpson, Jacqueline, and Steve Roud. *Oxford Dictionary of English Folklore.* Oxford, UK: Oxford University Press, 2000.

BUDDHIST ATTITUDES TOWARD DEATH, BUDDHISM

Buddhism originated in northwestern India around 2,500 years ago, with the enlightenment of Siddhārtha Gautama, later known as the Buddha (or the Awakened One). The Buddha's teaching, or *Dharma,* then spread from India to become widespread throughout Asia, and with Buddhist civilizations becoming established throughout East Asia especially China, Tibet, Thailand, Sri Lanka, and Japan. Buddhists also live in communities established outside these countries by families with ethnic links to these countries. Today, there are several forms of Buddhism including the Theravada, Tibetan, and Zen traditions. As a result of this diversity there is no one single funeral service or ritual common to all forms of Buddhists. It is, however, possible to say that the main Buddhist traditions—Theravada, Mahayana, and Vajrayana—seek to teach their followers about the three grades of existence that are suffering, impermanence, and lack of self, as well as the need to achieve liberation. It is also possible to generalize by saying that most Buddhists are cremated, as was the Buddha. Some Buddhist traditions allow at least four days to pass before a corpse is cremated though this depends on local customs and climatic conditions. Additionally many forms of Buddhism are not in favor of embalming though again this is by no means universal within Buddhism.

According to Buddhist belief, the worldview of Siddhārtha Gautama was transformed when he came upon a sick man, an old man, a dead man, and a man that renounced the world. Seeing these men shocked the Buddha into re-appraising the passage of life and the searching for freedom from the unceasing cycle of death and rebirth, *samsara.* Indeed ever since, Buddhism has considered old age, ill health, and death to be inherent aspects of life with death a mere separation of consciousness from the world of ignorance and desire. For this reason, Buddhists tend to appreciate forthrightness about the diagnosis of illnesses and the effects of treatment as well as likely prognosis. Moreover, since Buddhists consider it important for an individual to be aware of the state in which he or she exists, Buddhists are often concerned that pain relief and medication prevent them from feeling connected to what is happening to their body. Indeed Buddhists feel that dying and death should, if possible, take place in an atmosphere of tranquility and compassion that is not clouded by the side effects of medication.

Ultimately, the Buddha conquered death to achieve *nirvana*, or enlightenment. According to Buddhist tradition, nirvana is a deathless state free from the never-ending sequence of rebirth that is free from all suffering and experienced as a perfect state of rest. As part of their desire to achieve serenity in death, many Buddhists request that their bodies lay undisturbed for a period of time (often four hours) before being moved. Some Buddhist traditions stipulate that there should be a waiting period of at least three and a half days before any autopsy is performed on a body or a body is cremated.

Followers of Buddhism are bent on trying to achieve the ideal state of rest that is nirvana. To this end, various Buddhist meditations and customs have sprung up that are intended to teach Buddhists that death is an essential element of life—this is important as only by being aware of the constancy of death can Buddhists spend their lives in meaningful devotional practices and meditation that remove the practitioner from emotional attachments that might inhibit their chance of achieving nirvana. For this reason, every Buddhist denomination teaches that only spiritual development can benefit Buddhists when they die. The Theravada Buddhist tradition includes two meditations on death, an eightfold mindfulness of death and a contemplation on decaying bodies. The eightfold mindfulness leads the practitioner through consecutive steps that allow the practitioner to comprehend and face the reality of death as an essential ingredient of life. Only through coming to terms with this reality can the practitioner understand the true transience of life. Meanwhile, the contemplation on decaying bodies teaches followers about the physical realities of death and decomposition in order to subvert any physical desires the Buddhist holds that will impede his or her ability to renounce the world.

In Tibet, there are two literary traditions concerned with death and dying. The first of these traditions is called *lam-rim* (the gradual stages of the path tradition) that teaches that while death is a certainty the time of death cannot be predetermined and so life should be spent in preparation for death. In order to be sufficiently prepared for death, lam-rim suggests that people should adopt a practice known as the nine-round meditation on death that will allow the follower to find enlightenment. The nine-round meditation on death teaches three contemplations—firstly, that death is an inescapable certainty; secondly, that the actual time of death can be known in advance; and thirdly, that the only thing that can help during the moment of death is the dying person's state of mind. The second Tibetan Buddhist tradition is *bardo* (in between) that teaches that between death and rebirth exists a number of stages of existence that allow the deceased to undergo myriad experiences and visions.

In the earliest days of Buddhism funeral rituals were concerned with preventing the ghosts of the departed from harming the living as well as helping the dead achieve the optimum rebirth. The concept of helping a deceased individual achieve the best possible rebirth still lies at the heart of many Buddhist funeral rites, a concept known as merit transfer. This process sees the living perform rites that will reflect merit upon the dead thereby allowing the dead to achieve an auspicious rebirth. In the Sinhalese (north Indian), Burmese, and Thai Buddhist traditions merit transfer is an important part of funeral rituals and of commemorative ceremonies while in China, Japan, and Tibet merit transfer has melded with ideas of ancestor worship and soul transferal to create many customs that are concerned with the journey of the soul to the afterlife. When a person dies in Tibet, Tibetan Buddhists read the text known as the *Tibetan Book of the Dead, Liberation Through Hearing in the Bardo*, or similar that aims to unite the living and the dead thereby allowing the living to give up their attachment to the deceased and let the living get over their grief by connecting with the dead. This is important because grief and fear will have negative consequences for the karma of the dead that will in turn damage their chance of undergoing a favorable rebirth. Moreover, by instilling in the living the belief that grief will negatively effect their loved one's rebirth, Tibetan Buddhist leaders aim to help the living deal with death. Meanwhile, in Japan ideas of ancestor worship have fused with the Buddhist concept of merit transfer to create a way for people to remain emotionally connected to the dead while also dealing with their own personal grief. This attitude is evident in the Japanese custom of *mizuko kuyo* that allows Japanese parents to see their aborted fetuses as a *bodhisaattva*—a sentient being that has moved along the path of awakening in the direction of the Buddha. In this way, parents that have aborted fetuses feel that they have assisted their child and so fulfilled their parental obligation to give assistance to the unborn. In short, all forms of Buddhism sees grief recycled into acts of compassion intended to assist the dead. Moreover, death allows the living to perform spiritual acts that help the dead move onward either toward rebirth or toward the status of bodhisattva.

In Sri Lanka, if a person knows that he or she is dying, the person will invite a monk to his or her bedside so that the two can pray together and prepare for the impending death. When the person has died his or her body is removed and embalmed before being returned to its home—though embalming is not a typical Buddhist tradition it is necessary in the hot Sri Lankan climate. On the fourth day after the death the funeral of the deceased takes place. This involves the saying of prayers, chanting, and the presenting of a white cloth to the monks that are presiding over the ceremony. The offering of the white cloth is a form of merit transfer intended to help the deceased. Once the cloth has been given to the monks the burial (or cremation) is held in a cemetery and then everybody returns to the home of the deceased to enjoy a meal. On the sixth day after the death, a monk returns to the home and preaches for exactly one hour. This too is a form of giving merit to the deceased. The next day a number of monks return to the deceased's home, walking in single file and led by a layperson that carries a casket on his or her head. The monks say a short sermon and then are treated to a feast during which morsels of food are placed in the garden to feed hungry ghosts. After the meal, tools and cooking utensil are wrapped in brown paper and given to the monks—this too is intended to transfer merit to the deceased. This custom is repeated three months after the death of the deceased and again on the anniversary of the death and then every year afterward, all with the intention of effecting merit transfer.

In the West, the Buddhist concern with assisting the dead has given rise to a type of hospice movement based around Buddhists concepts with examples to be found in Australia and the United States. The aim of these hospices is to provide the dying with compassionate end-of-life care, to train volunteers in Buddhist principles, to aid the dying, and to offer the terminally ill medical and spiritual care as they approach their death.

See also: Cremation; Japanese Death Customs; *Mizuko Kuyo*: Japanese Fetus Memorial Service; Sky Burials; *Tết Nguyên đan*; *Yu Lan Jie*: The Hungry Ghost Festival

Further Reading

The Buddhist Society. "Buddhist Funerals." Accessed October 20, 2015, at http://www.thebuddhistsociety.org/page/resources/Buddhist-funerals.

Gleig, Ann. "Buddhism," in Brennan, Michael, ed., *The A–Z of Death and Dying: Social, Medical, and Cultural Aspects*. Santa Barbara, CA: ABC-CLIO, 2014.

Goss, Robert E., and Dennis Klass. "Buddhism and Death," in Garces-Foley, Kathleen, ed., *Death and Religion in a Changing World*. Abingdon, UK: Routledge, 2015.

Howarth, Glennys, and Oliver Leaman, eds. *Encyclopedia of Death and Dying*. Abingdon, UK: Routledge, 2013.

Langer, Rita. *Buddhist Rituals of Death and Rebirth: Contemporary Sri Lankan Practice and Its Origins*. Abingdon, UK: Routledge, 2007.

C

CAIRN, INTERNATIONAL

A cairn is a pile or stack of stones used as a grave marker or navigation tool, especially along upland or mountainous routes in Scotland and elsewhere in Europe, the Himalayas in Asia, in Texas, Alaska, and elsewhere in North America, and in desert and permafrost locations in both northern and southern Africa. Moreover, in the Scottish Highlands upland area and the Himalayas, cairns mark the summit of mountain peaks and the top of mountain passes with each visitor that survives to reach the cairn expected to add another stone to the pile or stack. (*See* Plate 3.) Cairns are especially associated with Scotland with the word cairn deriving from the Scottish Gaelic word *carn* and with an old Scottish blessing being "*Cuiridh mi clach air do charn*" ("I will put a stone on your cairn"). Although often associated with prehistoric mortuary customs, cairns are still constructed today in various places around the world, particularly in areas where the ground is too hard or stony for ground burials to take place. Cairns vary in size from small stone markers to large artificial hills. The construction of cairns also shows different levels of complexity from simple, loose rock piles to stone sculptures and feats of engineering. Additionally, some cairns are painted or decorated while others are left plain. Moreover, there are a number of different types of cairns including court cairns and chambered cairns.

Cairns are an extremely old manufactured landscape feature with Eurasian cairns dating back to prehistory. Indeed according to ancient Greek mythology, the god Hermes was buried under a pile of stones as punishment for slaying the servant of the goddess Hera. Near Inverness, Scotland, a cairn site known as the Prehistoric Burial Cairns of Balnuaran of Clava, or the Clava Cairns, are believed to date from around 2000 BCE. The Clava Cairns consist of three burial cairns making up a line of seven sites that lie along the River Nairn. This in turn helps to form a massive group of 45 separate cairns. The group of cairns is something of a tourist attraction as the cairns are situated inside a circular frame of large boulders known as a kerb.

When cairns are used as burial markers it is traditional for mourners or those that come across the burial mounds to deposit another stone on top of the pile of existing stones. As burial markers cairns perform a dual function. On a practical level cairns protect corpses from being eaten by scavenging animals while also guarding the living from the risen spirit of the departed. In recent times, cairns have been erected to commemorate large-scale death as well as the deaths of inidviduals. For example a series of many cairns can be found at the site of the 1879 Battle of Isandlwana in South Africa that mark the mass graves of British soldiers.

Occasionally people that reach a cairn will leave an offering of food. People that leave food at a cairn may do so partly as a presentation to a deity or as a general show of gratitude for reaching the cairn, and partly as a courtesy to others that manage to reach the stones. The act of using a cairn as depository for a food offering may well hark back to a possible previous use of cairns in sacrificial rituals, which, today, results in cairns being used as burial markers. That cairns have a spiritual function is suggested by that fact that in Mongolia a type of pre-Buddhist Mongolian cairn known as an *ovoo* can be found high on mountain plateaus. An ovoo is usually made of rocks or wood and used in folk religious ceremonies, especially in shamanistic worship of the skies and ground. Prior to leaving Mongolia it is traditional for travelers to circle an ovoo while depositing on the ovoo a *khadag*—a blue ceremonial scarf that symbolizes both Mongolia and the sky.

Coastal cairns, generically known as sea marks, occur frequently in the northern latitudes, particularly in Scandinavia, where the cairns are placed along seashores and on islands and off-shore land masses. The coastal cairns are typically painted white for improved offshore visibility, meaning that the carins can be used as navigation aids.

See also: *Mirila*; Ossuaries; Sky Burials; Spontaneous Shrines; Tombstone Tourism

Further Reading

Eternal Mongolia. "Mongolia's Sacred Ovoos." Blogging from the Wild in Mongolia, March 15, 2013. Accessed December 14, 2015, at http://eternal-landscapes.blogspot.co.uk/2013/03/stones-sticks-and-scarves-mongolias.html.

Jones, Alison. *Larousse Dictionary of World Folklore*. Edinburgh, UK: Larousse, 1996.

Scotland.com. "Cairns of Scotland." Accessed December 14, 2015, at http://www.scotland.com/blog/cairns-of-scotland.

Texas Beyond History. "Stone Cairns of West-Central Texas." August 2012. Accessed December 14, 2015, at http://www.texasbeyondhistory.net/cairn/.

CHANGING OF THE GUARD CEREMONY, UNITED STATES

The U.S. Changing of the Guard Ceremony occurs every hour on the hour at the Tomb of the Unknown Soldier (also known as the Tomb of the Unknowns) located at Arlington National Cemetery in Virginia. The ceremony is performed by impeccably uniformed, elite volunteer members of the U.S. Army's Third U.S. Infantry Regiment (The Old Guard) known as Tomb Guard Sentinels. The Sentinels watch over the Tomb of the Unknown Soldier every minute of every day all year round whatever the weather, though risk assessments are performed by the Chain of Command during changeable weather conditions to ensure that soldier welfare is never compromised by lightning or high winds while guarding the tomb.

The United State's Tomb of the Unknown Soldier was constructed in 1921 after Congress gave the go ahead for an unidentified U.S. soldier from World War I to be buried in the tomb. Other Unknown Soldiers have been buried there since. The non-stop guarding of the Tomb of the Unknown Soldier began in 1937 with the Sentinels watching over the tomb since 1948. To be chosen as a Tomb Guard a soldier must be extremely physically fit, be in possession of an untarnished military record, and stand between five-feet, ten-inches and six-feet, four-inches tall with their weight and height in proportion. Potential Tomb Guards are interviewed and undergo and a two-week trial to determine their capability for the role. During this two-week period would-be sentinels learn seven pages of information about Arlington National Cemetery's history that they must be able to recite word for word in order to earn a so-called walk-between-guard changes. A daylight walk lasts for one and a half hours in the summer and one hour in the winter. Night walks last for one hour. After these soldiers pass their first phase of training, they start their "new-soldier" training during which they learn more of the history of Arlington National Cemetery and the locations of 300 veteran graves. The new soldiers also learn how to enact the Changing of the Guard Ceremony. Sentinels are also instructed on how to keep their uniforms and weapons in pristine condition. The sentinels are then tested in order to earn the privilege of wearing a silver Tomb Guard Identification Badge. This test sees would-be sentinels tested on their manual of arms, preparation of uniforms, and their walks. Soldiers then face the Badge Test in which they are asked a hundred questions selected at random about the history of Arlington National Cemetery and the Tomb of the Unknown Soldier. In order to pass the test a would-be badge holder must achieve a score in excess of 95 percent. Once the soldiers have passed the test they are issued a temporary Tomb Guard Identification Badge that they hold until they have served honorably for nine months at the Tomb of the Unknown Soldier. After nine months, the temporary badge can be made permanent—an honor that the soldier may wear on the right pocket of his or her uniform jacket for the rest of the soldier's military career. The badge is silver and depicts an inverted laurel-leaf wreath surrounding an image of the front of the Tomb of the Unknown Soldier as well as portrayals of Peace, Victory, and Valor personified as Greek figures. More than 600 Tomb Guard Identification Badges have been awarded since the award's inception in the late 1950s, which is an average of 10 per year. A Tomb Guard Identification Badge can be revoked if an offense committed—as a soldier or civilian—is deemed to discredit the Tomb of the Unknown Soldier.

During the Changing of the Guard Ceremony sentinels take 21 steps north and south in front of the tomb, standing for periods of 21 seconds on either side. The pause lasts for 21 seconds as this represents the 21-gun salute that is the military's highest honor for any military personnel or foreign dignitary. While they are on duty the sentinels do not wear anything that would suggest their rank (.e.g, rank insignia) so as not to outrank the Unknown Soldier. The sentinels are relieved on the stroke of every hour, except during the cemetery's summer visiting hours, for during the summer (April 1 to September 30), the sentinels are relieved on the half hour. When the cemetery is closed the guard changes every two hours instead. The relieving of the sentinels instigates the Changing of the

Guard Ceremony for a relief commander emerges onto the plaza to announce the Changing of the Guard Ceremony. The new sentinel then leaves the quarters and unlocks the bolt on their fully functioning M-14 rifle. This signals to the relief commander to start the ceremony. Next, the relief commander strides out to the Tomb of the Unknown Soldier, salutes, and faces the people watching the ceremony. Visitors are then asked to stand silently during the ceremony. The relief commander inspects the rifle before the relief commander and the relieving sentinel meet the retiring sentinel in the middle of the path in front of the Tomb of the Unknown Soldier. All three military personnel salute the unknown soldiers that have been symbolically presented with the Medal of Honor. The relief commander then orders the relieved sentinel to "Pass on your orders," which the relieved sentinel does by commanding, "Post and orders, remain as directed." The newly positioned sentinel replies in turn, "Orders acknowledged" and retreats into place on the black matting. The newly positioned sentinel now walks at a cadence of 90 steps each minute as the relief commander passes by. The tomb guard then marches 21 steps down the black matting behind the tomb, turns to face east for 21 seconds, then turns and faces north for 21 seconds. The guard then takes 21 steps down the matting and duplicates the process. After the turn, the sentinel, whose gloves are wet so as to better grasp the rifle, performs a rapid "shoulder-arms" movement that positions the rifle on the shoulder that is closest to the onlookers. This signifies that the sentinel is positioned between the tomb and any potential threat from the crowd.

See also: "Abide With Me"; "The Last Post" and "Taps"; Remembrance Day and Remembrance Sunday; Royal Wootton Bassett; State Funeral; Tomb of the Unknown Soldier; Wearing Flowers to Honor War Dead

Further Reading

Kennedy, Royce. *Arlington National Cemetery Became My Classroom*. Baltimore, MD: PublishAmerica, 2011.

Sculetti, Justin. "Watch One of the U.S. Military's Most Sacred Rituals, The Changing of the Guard, in 4K." PBS Newshour, May 24, 2015. Accessed June 27, 2015, at http://www.pbs.org/newshour/rundown/changing-guard/.

Society of the Honor Guard, Tomb of the Unknown Soldier. "Frequently Asked Questions." Accessed June 27, 2015, at https://tombguard.org/society/faq/.

U.S. Army. "The Changing of the Guard." Arlington National Cemetery. Accessed June 27, 2015, at http://www.arlingtoncemetery.mil/Explore-the-Cemetery/Changing-of-the-Guard.

CHELSEA PENSIONERS, ENGLAND

Chelsea Pensioners are the scarlet-coated residents of the Royal Hospital Chelsea, situated near the banks of the River Thames in London, England's capital city. Royal Hospital Chelsea is a retirement and nursing home for former members of the British Army. Historically, however, the term Chelsea Pensioner refers to both in-pensioners and out-pensioners (i.e., the home's non-residents). Anybody of good character and aged over 65 years that has served as a regular soldier in the British Army, has no dependent spouse or family, and who finds him- or herself in need may apply to become one of the world famous Chelsea Pensioners.

The Royal Hospital Chelsea houses 300 veterans from the ranks of non-commissioned officers and below. All pensioners are looked after until they die, which in reality means that a new place becomes available each week. For several hundred years, Chelsea Pensioners were exclusively male but in 2009 Dorothy Hughes, 85 years of age, and Winifred Phillips, 82 years of age, became the first official female Chelsea Pensioners.

There is a long history of Chelsea Pensioners in London. Until the 17th century there was no state provision for wounded or aged soldiers. During the reign of Queen Elizabeth I (1533–1603) it was noted that some sort of provision should be made for soldiers who were ill, disabled, or had become penniless. Thus an Act of Parliament was passed in 1593 that levied a weekly tax on church parishes with funds raised going to sailors and soldiers. In 1681, King Charles II (1630–1685) issued a Royal Warrant permitting the building of the Royal Hospital Chelsea. Aware that the British Army was supporting an ever-increasing number of soldiers that were unfit for active duty, and inspired by Les Invalides in Paris (originally a retirement home for old or unwell French war veterans founded in 1676), Charles II committed to create a welcoming and safe home for army veterans who had fought for their country that would care for those who had been "broken by age or war." In 1692, work was completed on the building of the hospital, designed by Sir Christopher Wren, and the first Chelsea Pensioners were admitted in February that year. By the end of March 1692, 476 Chelsea Pensioners had taken up residency. The Hospital was initially paid for by deductions made from army pay plus occasional donations from other sources. Wage deductions and donations remained the hospital's chief sources of income until 1847. However since then the hospital has been supported by grant-in-aid from the Ministry of Defence as well as a small income from the Army Prize Money and Legacy Fund.

The Royal Hospital Chelsea provides pensioners with meals, accommodation, and activities and also features a purpose-built infirmary able to accommodate a hundred pensioners and that also has a specialist dementia ward. Those who live at the hospital enjoy a varied social life; for example, Chelsea Pensioners are regularly invited to attend such high-profile events as the Wimbledon tennis championships, Chelsea FC football matches, the Chelsea Flower Show, and horseracing meetings. Some Chelsea Pensioners reside in the infirmary permanently. However others stay in the infirmary for short periods when they feel unwell or are recovering from treatment or surgery. Pensioners' families are welcome to visit at any time and the hospital offers accommodation to close relatives of seriously ill pensioners.

> ### The First Female Chelsea Pensioner
>
> In the early 18th century, a woman, Mrs. Christian Davies, disguised herself as a man and enlisted in the British Army to track down her errant soldier husband. After many years of searching, Davies was reconciled with her husband but continued to be a soldier. Her subterfuge was only discovered when she was medically examined after incurring a fractured skull at the Battle of Ramilies in 1706. The Army allowed Davies to stay with them, though as a butler providing troops with food and drink, not as a soldier. Eventually Davies married again, and then later for a third time. Ultimately, however, Davies ended her days at the Royal Hospital Chelsea. When Davies died in 1739 she was buried alongside male Chelsea Pensioners with full military honors.

To become a Chelsea Pensioner a person must be over 65 years of age and in receipt of either an Army Service Pension or War Disability Pension that is surrendered upon entry to the hospital. Also eligible to become a Chelsea Pensioner are former British Army officers who meet the regular eligibility criteria and have served for at least 12 years in the ordinary ranks before obtaining a commission. If a Chelsea Pensioner does not receive an Army Pension then he or she is required to pay £175 per week as a contribution toward living costs. If a pensioner's Army Service Pension or War Disability Pension amounts to less than the £175 per week then he or she is required to pay the difference, though this is waived if doing so would place the pensioner in financial difficulty. Chelsea Pensioners must be able to care for themselves initially and live independently in the so-called Long Wards, that is, the Chelsea Pensioners' living quarters. The hospital does not accept direct entries to the infirmary.

Chelsea Pensioners take part in two particular customs of note. The first is Founder's Day that takes place at the hospital as close as possible to Charles II's birthday on May 29. Founder's Day is an annual celebration that commemorates the escape of the future King from parliamentary forces after the Battle of Worcester in 1651. After this battle Charles hid from his enemies inside an oak tree, known today as The Royal Oak or Boscobel Oak after the location of the oak tree. For this reason, on Founder's Day it is traditional for Chelsea Pensioners to shroud the statue of Charles II, located in the hospital's Figure Court, in oak leaves and all participating pensioners as well as spectators wear a sprig of oak. Also on this day, a member of the Royal Family, most recently by HRH The Duke of Kent, inspects the Chelsea Pensioners.

Another custom associated with the Chelsea Pensioners is The Ceremony of the Christmas Cheese during which cheese-makers from across the United Kingdom provide the Pensioners with a festive supply of cheese in gratitude for the pensioners serving their country in war. Cheese and other dairy products have been included in soldiers' rations for centuries, especially so in the two World Wars. In

2014, to mark the centenary of the start of World War I, cheese-makers from around the United Kingdom provided the Chelsea Pensioners with cheeses that have been made in Britain for more than 100 years plus a selection of modern varieties.

The Chelsea Pensioners are highly visible in their famous scarlet coats—to the point that they have been likened to a walking tourist attraction—and they often attend high-profile events. For instance, when Chelsea FC won the Premier League (English soccer's top division), Chelsea Pensioners formed a guard of honor as players and managers came out to receive their trophy. Chelsea FC have a long association with the Chelsea Pensioners who regularly sit in the main stand at the club's home ground, Stamford Bridge. From 1905 to 1952, Chelsea FC was nicknamed The Pensioners and the club occasionally includes scarlet, the color of the Chelsea Pensioners' uniform, in its strip. Another instance of the Chelsea Pensioners high profile came in November 2010 when seven pensioners released a debut album, *Men in Scarlet*, in order to help the Royal Hospital Chelsea raise £30 million to pay for refurbishments. The pensioners, between 68 and 81 years of age, accompanied by singers Dame Vera Lynne and Katherine Jenkins, recorded renditions of classic songs such as "White Christmas" and "I'll Being Seeing You," the latter receiving several thousand views on YouTube. The album entered the Top 20 and topped the easy-listening album chart.

See also: Denville Hall and Brinsworth House; Maundy Money; Retirement and Pensions; State Pension Government Guide, United Kingdom

Further Reading

Baker, Margaret. *Discovering London Statues and Monuments.* Princes Risborough, UK: Shire Publications Ltd., 2002.
Bates, Stephen. "Female Army Veterans Become First Women Chelsea Pensioners," *The Guardian*, March 12, 2009. Accessed January 11, 2015, at http://www.theguardian.com/uk/2009/mar/12/first-women-chelsea-pensioners.
Culture24. "Royal Hospital Chelsea." Accessed January 11, 2015, at http://www.culture24.org.uk/am16862.
Johnson, Simon. "Chelsea's Blues Will Be in the Red Next Season," *London Evening Standard*, April 14, 2010. Accessed January 11, 2015, at http://www.standard.co.uk/sport/football/chelseas-blues-will-be-in-the-red-next-season-6459077.html.
Ministry of Defence. "Meet Britain's Oldest Boy Band." Gov.uk. January 28, 2011. Accessed January 11, 2015, at https://www.gov.uk/government/news/meet-britains-oldest-boy-band.
Royal Hospital Chelsea. "Origins and History." Accessed January 11, 2015, at http://www.chelsea-pensioners.co.uk/origins-and-history-0.

CHINESE DEATH CUSTOMS, CHINA

Death customs vary throughout China. In general, the country's communist government has deemed traditional death practices as profligate and redolent of superstition. Cremations are common in urban areas while in rural locations burials are

> ### China Cracks Down on Funeral Strippers
>
> In April 2015, China instigated a crackdown on the increasingly popular practice of hiring exotic dancers to perform at funerals. Such performers are hired to attract mourners to funerals and show off the wealth of the deceased's family. However the Chinese Ministry of Culture has attacked the practice as illegal and morally corrupting. The ministry has compiled a blacklist of performers and venues that participate in such shows and singled out the burlesque dance act Red Rose Song and Dance Troupe because in February it had performed a striptease after a funeral held in the province of Hebei.

preferred as in these areas politics hold less sway allowing traditional customs to prevail. Indeed it has been known for corpses to be smuggled out of a city location to the countryside for burial. Moreover, in recent years there has been a discrete revival of traditional Chinese customs, including death customs. This revival has been achieved partly through a slight relaxation in the government's stance on such matters and also because private individuals now have their own wealth, meaning they can pay for more elaborate funeral rites. Furthermore, as people now have their own personal wealth they have become more conscious of social status and are concerned that death customs are appropriate for their social standing.

Traditionally, the burial of the dead is taken very seriously in China, as inappropriate funeral arrangements are believed to cause bad luck for the family of the deceased. Since the time of the Shang Dynasty (circa 1556 BCE–1046 BCE) the Chinese have believed that the souls of the dead reside in the netherworld and that graves are the dead's earthly residences. For this reason, the Chinese have traditionally held lavish funerals to send the dead to the next world. Today, in general, Chinese funerals are much simpler and economical, with only a few traditions needing to be observed.

To a certain extent Chinese funeral rites and burial traditions are determined by the age at which a person dies, their cause of death, and their marital status and position in society when alive. In general, however, Chinese death customs are eye-catching, attention-grabbing events intended to impress upon the living the importance of their relationship with the deceased. Familial and social obligations are key elements of Chinese death customs. Moreover, Chinese death customs do not try to memorialize the deceased or lessen the grief of the bereaved, as do Western death customs. Instead Chinese traditions aim to create a sense of ancestry and to allow the living to influence the existence of their loved one's soul in the afterlife. The basic themes of Chinese death customs include the need to lessen the polluting effect of death on the living, to protect the living from bad luck and evil spirits, and to maintain family order.

According to Chinese tradition, an elder must not show respect to someone younger than him- or herself. Therefore, for example, if the deceased individual is a young, unmarried man his body must remain at the funeral parlor and his parents must not offer prayers for him. Moreover, since he died unmarried, the man would not have had children who could perform these same rites hence the man's corpse must remain in the funeral parlor and must not enter the family home. Additionally, if the deceased is a baby or child then no funeral rites will be performed, as respect cannot be shown to the young person. For this reason, the youngster will be buried in silence. Conversely funeral rites for an elder person must follow a prescribed pattern of rites befitting his or her social standing, marital status, and age. These rites must be performed even if it means the deceased's family will need to owe money in order to pay for the arrangements.

In China, preparations for a funeral often begin before a person has died for when a person is near death his or her family will order a coffin from an undertaker who will also oversee the funeral rites. Chinese coffins are traditionally rectangular with three hump-like features, though in recent years Western-style coffins have been used in China too. Once a person has died, his or her family covers all the statues of gods kept within the family home using red paper. The red paper ensures that the deities are not exposed to the polluting influence of the corpse or coffin. Additionally, all the mirrors in the home are removed as it is commonly believed that anyone that sees the reflection of a coffin in a mirror will experience a death in his or her own family. Meanwhile, a white cloth is draped over the entrance to the house and a gong is placed in the doorway—the gong is positioned to the left of the entrance if the dead person was a male and to the right of the doorway if the deceased was a female. Before the corpse is placed in the coffin, it is cleaned with a moist towel that has been dusted with talcum powder and then dressed in his or her best clothes, though never red clothes, as these are believed to transform the deceased into a ghost. Instead white, black, brown, or blue clothes are used to dress the corpse. Footwear will also be placed on the corpse and if the deceased was female she will have make-up applied too. All other clothing belonging to the deceased is incinerated. Once the corpse is properly attired its face is covered with a yellow cloth while its body is draped in pale blue fabric before being placed in the coffin.

Once the body is placed in the coffin, the coffin is not sealed but is placed on a stand made from two stools so that the body rests about one foot from the ground. The coffin is left either in the deceased's house, if the person died at home, or in the courtyard of the house, if the person died somewhere else. The coffin is positioned in such as way that the head of the corpse faces inside the house. A wake then takes place during which wreaths, gifts, and an image of the deceased (either a portrait or photograph) are placed at the head of the coffin. Next, food is placed in front of the coffin as an offering to the dead whose comb is broken in two with one part placed inside the coffin and the other half kept by the deceased's family. For the duration of the wake, the family of the deceased does not wear any jewelry or clothes that are red in color—red is deemed unsuitable at times of mourning as it is the Chinese color of happiness. Traditionally, children and grandchildren of the deceased do not cut their hair for 49 days after their relative has died, but this custom is now usually only observed by older generations. It is also traditional for the blood relatives and daughters-in-law of the dead to moan and cry during the wake as a sign of respect and loyalty to the dead person, with the cries particularly loud if the person has left a sizeable fortune.

During the wake the family of the deceased congregate around the coffin in order of their rank within the family with the deceased's eldest son sitting at the left shoulder of his deceased parent and the deceased's spouse on the deceased's right. Other guests at the wake have to bow to the family as a sign of respect. The clothes worn by the various family members denote their relationship to the dead. For example, the children and daughters-in-law of the dead wear black to indicate that they feel the loss of the deceased more than anyone else and they also wear a hood of sackcloth over their heads. The grandchildren of the dead wear blue clothes and great-grandchildren wear light blue. Meanwhile sons-in-law wear bright colored clothing, usually made from white fabric, as they are considered to exist outside the family.

At the foot of the coffin an altar is set up on which burning incense and a lit white candle are placed. Joss paper and paper prayer money, intended to provide the deceased with an income in the afterlife, are burned throughout the wake. A donation box for money is also present during the wake as money is always offered to the family of the deceased as a sign of respect. On a more practical level the money also helps the deceased's family pay for the funeral.

Another custom during the wake is for a group of people to gamble in the front courtyard of the deceased's home. This custom is significant as according to Chinese tradition the corpse must be watched over, or guarded, at all time and the gambling helps those responsible for watching the corpse to remain awake during their vigil. Also, as the gaming is regarded as a fun pastime it helps ease the grief experienced by the participants.

The duration of the wake is dependent on the family's finances but it should last for at least one day, as this is the time necessary to allow for the offering of prayers. While the coffin is in place at the wake, a monk will chant verses from either Buddhist or Taoist scriptures while accompanied by musicians playing gongs, flutes, and trumpets. The chants, prayers, and music are thought to help the soul of the deceased to transition to the afterlife.

A Chinese funeral ceremony traditionally lasts over 49 days, though the first seven days of this period are the most significant. If the deceased's family, particularly the deceased's daughter who is responsible for paying, can afford it, prayers are said every seven days for 49 days. Otherwise, the funeral period will be shortened by several days. According to tradition, the head of the deceased's family should be present for at least the first and, optimally, the second prayer ceremony. However the actual number of prayer ceremonies performed also depends on the family's financial situation. The head of the deceased's family should also attend the deceased's interment or cremation. Prayer ceremonies should be held every 10 days within the 49-day funeral period with an initial ceremony followed by three succeeding periods of 10 days up until the final disposal of the corpse. An optional prayer ceremony may also be performed after 100 days. In the Mahayana tradition of Buddhism, which is the form of Buddhism to which most Chinese Buddhists belong, it is thought that an intermediate period known as *Antarabhava* (in Sanskrit) or *bardo* (in Tibetan) exists between death and rebirth. This in-between stage is considered an important period that will influence the form that the deceased's rebirth will take. If the deceased's family sees that the correct prayers and remembrances are performed, then it is thought that the deceased will achieve a favorable rebirth.

On the completion of the various prayer ceremonies, the wailing of the mourners reaches a climax. Also, the coffin is sealed shut in a process signifying the separation of the dead from the living. Once it is nailed closed, yellow and white paper known as holy paper is glued onto the coffin as it is thought to protect the corpse from evil spirits. As it is considered very inauspicious in China to witness the sealing of a coffin, everybody present must turn away as the coffin is shut. Once it is sealed the coffin is taken away from the home of the deceased using a piece of wood that is secured over the coffin. As the coffin is transported, the head of the corpse is kept facing forward. Since it is thought that the blessings of the deceased are conferred upon the pallbearers, it is usually the case that many people will volunteer to carry the coffin.

The coffin is not taken straight to the cemetery for it is first placed on the side of the road outside the home where it had rested prior to being moved. Here more prayers are said and holy paper is sprinkled. The coffin is then positioned on a slowly moving hearse with the deceased's eldest son and other family members trailing behind, their heads touching the hearse—if there are lots of relatives present then a length of white material is used to connect the hearse to the family members. The order in which the family members follow the hearse is determined by their status within the family with the eldest son normally sitting next to the coffin. Throughout the hearse's journey a lit joss stick symbolizing the soul of the deceased is held by a family member. If the joss stick is extinguished it is relit quickly. Sometimes other items such as paper models of cars or boats are carried by the procession as these represent the financial wealth of the deceased's family. Another interesting element of the funeral procession is that the corpse must be told when the procession crosses any body of water. This is because it is thought that an uninformed soul will be unable to pass across the water.

Chinese cemeteries are usually found on hillsides because this is thought to improve *feng shui*, the Chinese philosophical system that sees architecture in terms of the invisible lifeforce known as *qi* (or *chi*) that binds together the universe and humankind. According to the tenets of feng shui, the higher up the hillside a grave is located, the more auspicious it is. When the coffin arrives at its final location it is taken down from the hearse and lowered into the grave plot. As the coffin is lowered into the ground, everyone present turns away and only a few family members stay to throw handfuls of earth into the grave before it is filled in. Traditionally, before the mourners leave the cemetery the deceased's eldest son will retrieve soil from the grave. This is later placed into an incense holder and used by the family to worship the deceased at home. Once the coffin is buried, the keeper of the cemetery says prayers for the deceased and mourners are presented with a red packet. This package is a sign of appreciativeness on the part of the deceased's family though the money is not purely symbolic, as tradition dictates that the money must be spent. Mourners are also presented with a white towel. This too is a sign of the family's gratitude, as it should be used to wipe away sweat caused by strenuous mourning. After the funeral all the mourners burn the clothes that they wore to the graveside in order to stop the bad luck and pollution associated with death from finding them.

After the funeral the mourning period continues for 100 days unless the deceased is a wife or a child, in which case no mourning period is necessary. During this time all of the family members wears a piece of cloth on their sleeve to show that they are in mourning, though the most traditional families will wear the cloth for up to three years. The color of the cloth worn by mourners depends on their relation to the departed—the deceased's children wear black, grandchildren wear blue, and great-grandchildren wear green.

Chinese people believe that seven days after the death of a family member their soul returns home. For this reason a red inscribed plaque is sometimes left outside the home of the deceased on the seventh day after the death in order to guide the soul to their house. On the day that the soul is expected all family members within the house must stay in their rooms and flour or talcum powder is sprinkled on the floor of the house to show if the soul has visited.

See also: Buddhist Attitudes Toward Death; Japanese Death Customs; *Qingming* Festival; Sky Burials; Traditional Mourning Colors; Wake; *Yu Lan Jie*: The Hungry Ghost Festival

Further Reading

Bryant, Clifton D., ed. *Handbook of Death and Dying: Volume One The Presence of Death*. Thousand Oaks, CA: Sage Publications, 2003.

Ministry of Culture, People's Republic of China. "Chinese Funeral Customs." Accessed November 3, 2015, at http://www.chinaculture.org/gb/en_chinaway/2004-03/03/content_46092.htm.

Singapore Federation of Chinese Clan Associations. "Funeral Rituals." Accessed November 3, 2015, at http://www.sfcca.sg/en/node/62.

Victoria and Albert Museum. "Traditional Life in China: Burial Customs." Accessed November 3, 2015, at http://www.vam.ac.uk/content/articles/b/burial-customs-china/.

Wu, Anne. "A Grave Day—the Culture of Death!" China Highlights. Accessed November 3, 2015, at http://www.chinahighlights.com/travelguide/article/death-culture.htm.

CHRISTIAN DEATH RITUALS, CHRISTIANITY

Christians believe that death is the end of a person's time on earth. Moreover, Christians trust that when a person dies the individual will be judged by God with the good entering heaven and sinners going to hell, though Catholics also believe that people that have committed forgivable sins will travel to purgatory. For this reason, it is often the case that when a Christian is near death a minister will be asked to prepare the sick or injured person for death—in Roman Catholicism a priest will be called to anoint the dying person with holy oil, a process called the Last Rites, that also involves the dying person saying deathbed prayers of preparation and reconciliation with the minister. Meanwhile, the dying person's family and friends may say the Lord's Prayer and partake of Holy Communion. After the death of a Christian, a ceremony called a funeral is held for the individual to which their relatives and friends are usually invited. Funerals are often times of grief but also a way of giving thanks to God for the person's life. However there has never been a set pattern for a Christian funeral. Just as there are various kinds of Christian baptisms, weddings, and prayers, so there are different customs and traditions to mark the death of Christians depending on the denomination to which the person belonged and its location.

When a Christian dies, his or her corpse is typically placed in a coffin. Sometimes the coffin is left open so that the deceased's relatives and friends may say a final farewell to the dead person. The coffin may then be taken to a church where a minister may read from the Christian holy book, the Bible, and say a few prayers that aim to comfort the grieving and aid the deceased on his or her passage to heaven. A special church service called a Requiem Mass may also be held for deceased Roman Catholics during which prayers are said for the soul of the deceased. After this, the coffin is removed from the church to either be buried or cremated.

A Christian funeral takes place either at a church or a crematorium around a week after a person dies. It is sometimes the case that a Christian that has died will leave instructions for his or her funeral service such as which hymns to sing and prayers to be said as well as specifying whether they would like to be buried or cremated.

Though Christian funerals vary in their details, according to the Christian denomination to which the deceased belonged, a Christian funeral usually starts with the Gathering, a ritual that sees a minister open the service with a reading from scripture: "'I am the resurrection and the life,' saith the Lord; 'he that believeth in me, though he were dead, yet shall he live: and whosoever liveth and believeth in me shall never die,'" Next, more readings from the scriptures are read aloud, particularly readings from the Old Testament and New Testament together with a sermon. Often a psalm is read from the Bible too, usually this is Psalm 23, "The Lord Is My Shepherd."

After the psalm, the minister will often give a short oration about the deceased. Often this is a personal recollection that gives detail about the person's life and his or her connection to the church. A member of the deceased's family or a friend will then give a further talk about the dead person or they may read aloud a poem or passage from the Bible. The deceased may have specified the poem or section of the Bible that he or she would like read out. Next prayers will be said, including prayers of thanksgiving, penitence, and readiness for death. These prayers reflect that the main themes of a Christian funeral are the desire for salvation and the hope and expectation of resurrection from death. Once the prayers have been said there is often a short period of silent reflection during which the people gathered as the congregation remember the deceased. This period of reflection is followed by the commendation during which the minister says: "Let us commend [the deceased's name] to the mercy of God, our maker and redeemer" before reading another prayer. The commendation is followed by the most somber part of the funeral, the committal. At a burial the committal sees the coffin lowered into a grave while at a cremation the curtains will close around the coffin. During the committal the minister says the following words: "We therefore commit [his/her] body to the ground; earth to earth, ashes to ashes, dust to dust; in the sure and certain hope of the Resurrection to eternal life." These words may be accompanied by the singing of hymns that are also sung throughout the funeral service. When a Christian is buried, it is often considered traditional to throw soil on to the coffin.

A Catholic funeral is slightly different from other Christian funeral services and may or may not include a mass. Post-death Catholic rituals begin with a wake or the Vigil for the Deceased—a service of prayers, hymns, and talks that takes place either at the deceased's home or at a church. The Vigil for the Deceased occurs the day before the funeral. On the day of the funeral the funeral service begins with the priest greeting the congregation and saying, "The grace of our Lord Jesus Christ and the love of God and the fellowship of the Holy Spirit be with you all." The priest then leads the congregation and the coffin down the aisle of the church. When the coffin is in place it is draped with a white cloth called a pall that recalls the white garment worn by a Catholic at his or her baptism and a Paschal candle is placed close to the coffin or at the front of the church. A Paschal candle is a large white candle that is lit to symbolize that Catholics view Christ as the Light of the World. Moreover the pure beeswax from which a Paschal candle is made signifies that Christ was free from sin. The wick of the candle represents Christ's humanity while the flame signifies that Christ was divine in terms of both body and soul. Into the wax from which the candle is made five grains of incense are inserted in the shape of a crucifix. This incense evokes the aromatic spices that were used to prepare Christ's body before it was placed in the tomb following the Crucifixion while the number five recalls the five wounds that Christ received into his hands, feet, and torso during his execution.

Next, the priest sprinkles holy water and says an opening prayer and everyone present sings a hymn. After this the Liturgy of the Word occurs during which sermons from the Bible are read aloud, a psalm is read and the priest gives a homily. A homily is like a sermon but tends to be a practical talk rather than religious sermon. After the homily, the Liturgy of the Eucharist takes place. This involves the preparation of the Offertory Gifts (the bread and wine that will be consecrated during the mass), the saying of the Eucharist prayer, and the giving out of the Holy Communion. The final commendation then occurs and the mass ends. Prayers are then said and the coffin is removed from the church for the Rite of Committal. This rite sees prayers at the final resting place, which is either at the graveside where the deceased will be buried or before the curtains close prior to a cremation. In the past, the Catholic Church tended to disapprove of cremation on the grounds that burning a corpse meant that a person could not be resurrected on the Day of Judgment. Nowadays however it is a matter of personal choice as to whether a Catholic is cremated or interred.

See also: "Abide With Me"; Cremation; Eulogies; Funeral Songs; Jazz Funeral; "Lyke-Wake Dirge"; Maidens' Garlands; Passing Bells

Further Reading

BBC. "Christian Funerals." BBC News: Religion, June 23, 2009. Accessed October 17, 2015, at http://www.bbc.co.uk/religion/religions/christianity/ritesrituals/funerals.shtml.

Catholic News Agency. "The Paschal Candle." Accessed October 17, 2015, at http://www.catholicnewsagency.com/resources/holy-week/holy-saturday/the-paschal-candle/.

Long, Thomas G. *Accompany Them with Singing: The Christian Funeral*. Louisville, KY: Westminster John Knox Press, 2009.

Prince of Peace Parish. "A Guide to the Catholic Funeral." Accessed October 17, 2015, at http://www.princeofpeace.me/documents/A%20Guide%20to%20the%20Catholic%20Funeral_website.pdf.

Venbrux, Eric, Thomas Quartier, Claudia Venhorst, and Brenda Mathijssen, eds. *Changing European Death Ways*. Volume 1. Zurich, Switzerland: Lit Verlag, 2013.

CONDEMNED PRISONER'S LAST MEAL, UNITED STATES

The condemned prisoner's last meal is a custom observed in many countries across the world. The tradition typically sees a condemned prisoner allowed to select the dishes that will be served as his or her final meal before execution, within reason. The tradition of the condemned prisoner's last meal is most widely observed in the United States, where the practice of allowing the condemned to select his or her last meal is upheld by many states that support capital punishment. A notable exception is the state of Texas, which stopped providing last meals in 2011. The custom of the condemned prisoner's final meals is an enduring, if morbid, source of fascination. Request for last meals must, usually, fall within a set budget and it is usually the case that prisoners are not allowed to request alcohol. Requests for bubble gum and cigarettes have also been denied.

The exact history of the custom of providing the condemned with a last meal of his or her choosing is unknown. It has, however, been theorized that the custom goes back to pre-modern Europe, where it may have been the case that a superstition existed that suggested granting condemned prisoners their final meal was a symbolical way of allowing the soon-to-die to make peace with the host/executioner. Some people believe that the old European superstition held that if the prisoner accepted his or her last meal then the prisoner would not return in spirit form to haunt his or her executioner. In more recent folklore, the concept of the last meal request in the United States is thought to stem from the early 20th century when death row prisoners would ask for cakes to share amongst themselves as they waited to be exececuted.

Most of the final meals requested today tend to be calorific, high-fat meals, often featuring fast foods and comfort foods particularly, according to research by Cornell University, French fries, soda, ice cream (especially chocolate and vanilla), burgers, fried chicken, steaks, and pies. Indeed an average last meal is estimated to include 2,756 calories. Comfort foods are especially popular with condemned prisoners with very few choosing fruits or vegetables though around a quarter request salad. One prisoner, Robert Buell—executed for the murder and sexual assault of an 11-year-old girl in 1982—did, however, request a single pitted olive as his last meal.

Researchers have theorized that the frequency with which prisoners request meals containing comfort foods and such branded products as Coca-Cola could signify that the condemned try to process the extremely high levels of stress they are experiencing by surrounding themselves with familiar food and drinks. Researchers also suggest that the infrequency with which vegetarian meals are requested may reflect the poor socio-economic backgrounds of prisoners on death row. According to academics researching capital punishment, the foods chosen by these condemned prisoners remind the prisoners of good times from their pre-prison lives. Moreover, the foods requested tend to reflect how the prisoners spent their earlier lives and how they wish to face death. For outsiders not connected to the prisoner, finding out what a person chose to eat as his or her last ever meal offers a poignant human insight into the people that the law has judged should die for their crimes. To this end, the custom of the last meal functions partly as a way to assuage society's discomfort at the harsh reality that a fellow human being is shortly to be killed with the full sanction of the law. The custom of the last meal captivates public imagination because the activity of eating dinner is one that most people have experienced and also one to which people without any experience of prison life can relate. The ritualistic manner in which the last meal is served reminds people that the prisoner will never again eat dinner. The human drama of the last meal fascinates people that are not connected to the prisoners or their victims and the thought of someone having a last-ever meal may also recall the Last Supper as experienced by Jesus before his Crucifixion as detailed in Christian tradition.

Condemned prisoners' last meals were abolished in Texas after notorious killer Lawrence Russell Brewer requested two chicken fried steaks, a triple-meat bacon cheeseburger, fried okra, a pound of barbecue, three fajitas, a meat lover's pizza, a pint of ice cream, and a slab of peanut butter fudge with crushed peanuts before his execution for the hate killing of James Byrd Jr. Despite asking for the lavish spread, prison officials reported that Brewer did not eat any of the food provided. As a result of Brewer's spurning of his feast, authorities decided that from then on all prisoners facing execution would not be granted a last meal request but would, instead, be served the same food as all other inmates in their unit. State Senator John Whitmire denied claims that stopping the tradition of granting the condemned a last meal was mean-spirited and miserly. Instead Whitmire justified his drive to halt the custom by stressing that the denial of a last meal request was based on moral rather than financial concerns by pointing out the it was not the state's aim to comfort those inmates about to be executed and also that those inmates that are executed did not grant their victims any such comfort as a last last-meal request.

Other American states impose a limit on the cost of last meals. For example, in Florida the most a final meal may cost is $40 and food must be acquired locally. Meanwhile, Oklahoma is more parsimonious, providing prisoners with a budget of only $15 to spend on their last meal, which must be obtained from a restaurant within the town of McAlester where the death chamber is located. Furthermore, the request is subject to the approval of the prison warden.

A significant number of condemned prisoners waive their right to a last meal, either because they wish to defy convention or simply because they have lost their appetite. Other prisoners—for example, David Clark, who was executed in Texas in 1992 for a double murder—refused food on the grounds that he wished to fast for spiritual reasons. Similarly, before Danny Harris was executed in Texas in July 30, 1993, his last meal request was for God's saving grace, love, truth, peace, and freedom.

The 2004 book, *Meals to Die For*, written by Brian D. Price, a former prison cook responsible for making the final meals for prisoners at Texas's Huntsville unit, provides details of many condemned prisoners' last meals as well as their final statements before execution.

Odd last meal requests are often publicized online and there is even a blog devoted to detailing the last meal requests of American prisoners called *Dead Man Eating*. For instance, in 1990 James Smith is said to have requested a handful of earth to complete a Voodoo ritual before his execution in Texas for robbery-murder. Smith's request was denied as dirt was not included on the list of approved foods and he had to make do with a yoghurt instead. Another request that was refused by prison authorities was that made by Odell Barnes Jr, who asked for justice, equality, and world peace.

See also: Funeral Cakes and Funeral Candy; *Halva*; *Koliva*; Soul Cakes and Soul Bread

Further Reading

Associated Press. "Texas Execution Leads to Ban on Choice of Last Meal," *The Guardian*, September 23, 2011. Accessed November 6, 2015, at http://www.theguardian.com/world/2011/sep/23/texas-execution-ends-final-meal.

Duda, Doug. "Eat Like There's No Tomorrow and Other Lessons Learnt from Last Meals," in Friedland, Susan R., ed., *Food and Morality: Proceedings of the Oxford Symposium on Food and Cookery 2007*. Totnes, UK: Prospect Books, 2008, 103–108.
Hill, Michael. "Death Row Last Meals: Comfort Foods Most Popular Choice of Prisoners, Study Finds," *Huffington Post*, August 29, 2012. Accessed November 6, 2015, at http://www.huffingtonpost.com/2012/08/29/comfort-foods-last-meal_n_1839009.html.
Howe Verhovek, Sam. "Word for Word / Last Meals; For the Condemned in Texas, Cheeseburgers without Mercy," *New York Times*, January 4, 1998. Accessed November 6, 2015, at http://www.nytimes.com/1998/01/04/weekinreview/word-for-word-last-meals-for-the-condemned-in-texas-cheeseburgers-without-mercy.html.
Nasaw, Daniel. "Last Meal: What's the Point of This Death Row Ritual?" *BBC News Magazine*, September 26, 2011. Accessed November 6, 2015, at http://www.bbc.co.uk/news/magazine-15040658.
Untiedt, Kenneth L. *Death Lore: Texas Rituals, Superstitions, and Legends of the Hereafter*. Denton, TX: University of North Texas Press, 2008.

CONDOLENCES, INTERNATIONAL

Condolences are expressions of sympathy that ensue after a death and are directed at the family of the deceased. The word condolences derives from the Latin words *com*, which translates as together, and *dolere*, meaning to suffer pain or to grieve. Condolences can be verbal—for example, at a funeral or a wake—or written. Written condolences are often added to a special book called a book of condolence or in a letter to the bereaved. In Jewish communities, condolences are expressed in person to the family of the bereaved when people visit the home of the deceased during the period of mourning called *shiva*. Condolences are not, however, confined to Judaism as people of most faiths express them when a death occurs. In all cases condolences are intended to show solidarity with people mourning the death of a loved one and act as a form of emotional support.

The writing of condolences dates back to ancient Rome when in 45 BCE Servius Sulpicius Rufus conveyed his sympathy in writing to Marcus Tullius Cicero on the death of the latter's daughter during childbirth. It was, however, during the Victorian era that the writing of condolences peaked for this was an era during which, except for conversation, letter writing was the main method of communication. Indeed during the Victorian period of history special black edged stationery intended expressly for condolence writing became popular, as did the sending of condolence cards. In recent years a new tradition regarding the sending of condolences has evolved for it had become the norm to open a so-called book of condolence following any large-scale disaster or the death of a popular public figure. The most famous instance of a book of condolence was that following the death of the Diana, Princess of Wales in 1997. After Diana's death, books of condolence were opened in many locations and saw people from all over Britain and indeed the world wait in line for many hours to write in the books. Researchers have suggested that the books of condolence following the death of Diana are particularly significant as not only were they part of an array of public mourning proceedings but they also in some way removed taboos surrounding mourning in public. Academics have also highlighted the fact that the books of condolence that followed the death of Diana were highly unusual as the messages contained in the books were directed to the deceased herself, rather than to her family.

An even newer form of sending condolences sees social media websites such as Twitter and Facebook used to convey messages of admiration for someone that has died or to send sympathy to his or her family and friends. Indeed it now routine when a well-known person dies for people to convey their feelings of sympathy (or otherwise) via social media. The desire to express condolences via social media was evident in the hour following the announcement of the death of singer Whitney Houston in February 2012 for there was a surge of messages on Twitter pertaining to the subject with 2.4 million tweets sent—an average of 1,500 tweets per second. Moreover, when the name of a celebrity starts to trend on Twitter many users immediately assume it is because the celebrity has died and is trending because people are expressing their thoughts on the matter in 140 characters or fewer.

See also: Christian Death Rituals; Japanese Death Customs; Jewish Death Customs; Spontaneous Shrines; Wake; Windmills

Further Reading

Brennan, Michael, ed. *The A–Z of Death and Dying: Social, Medical, and Cultural Aspects.* Santa Barbara, CA: ABC-CLIO, 2014.

Brown, Alyson, ed. *Historical Perspectives on Social Identities.* Newcastle, UK: Cambridge Scholars Press, 2006.

Bryant, Clifton D., and Dennis L. Peck, eds. *Encyclopedia of Death and the Human Experience, Volume 1.* Thousand Oaks, CA: SAGE Publications Inc., 2009.

Mehta, Glenn. *Infinite Ripple—The Social Media Revolution.* Bloomington, IN: Xlibris Corporation e-book, 2013.

CREMATION, INTERNATIONAL

Cremation is a method of corpse disposal that involves the combustion, vaporization, and subsequent oxidation of corpses to their basic chemical compounds. Cremation is performed on both humans and animals. Cremated remains may be interred in memorial sites or cemeteries, or they may be kept in a receptacle by loved ones or dispersed in a variety of different ways. Cremation may occur in a specific building called a crematorium (pl. crematoria) though some countries such as India and Nepal allow cremations to occur in the open. The International Cremation Federation (ICF) was established in London in 1937 as an international non-profit organization devoted to providing information of cremation and promoting the processing of cremations to the best standard. In 1996 the ICF was allowed Consultative Status (Roster) with the Economic and Social Council of the

United Nations. The ICF has approved representatives at the United Nations headquarters in New York and at the United Nations offices in Vienna and Geneva for meetings of the United Nations' Economic and Social Council (ECOSOC).

Cremation is an ancient form of corpse disposal with cremated remains discovered in Australia in 1969 found to date back some 20,000 years. Cremation has a very long history in Asia where it is the preferred method of corpse disposal for Sikhs, Hindus, and Buddhists—in fact, the Buddha himself is said to have been cremated on a self-igniting funeral pyre. Cremation is also an ancient way of disposing of the dead in the West for references to cremation occur on prehistoric urns and burial mounds. There are also references to cremation in such classical texts as Homer's *The Iliad* and *The Odyssey*. After the Christianization of Europe, burial became the most popular method of corpse disposal as people wanted to identify with Christ who was buried and then rose from the dead during the Resurrection. Indeed the Emperor Charlemagne made cremation illegal in the Christian world in 789. The only exceptions to the illegality of cremation was in times of war, as cremation would prevent enemies for vandalizing the corpses of their foes and during outbreaks of communicable diseases. Moreover, except for the epidemic of bubonic plague in Europe during the 17th century, burial has been the pre-eminent form of corpse disposal in Christian Europe. It was not until the 19th century that interest in cremation was reignited through an interest in human biology and religious philosophical debates and a new interest in engineering and science brought about during the Industrial Revolution. During the late 19th century cremation association sprang up in the United Kingdom, the United States, and the Netherlands and there was a great deal of interest in cremation among high-profile physicians and influential thinkers in France, Italy, and Switzerland.

Despite the high level of interest in cremation in these countries, cremation as a method of corpse disposal did not take off until much later. For instance the first crematorium opened in the Netherlands in 1914 and the Roman Catholic Church did not accept cremation as acceptable for Christians until 1963. Similarly, it was not until the 1960s that cremation became the main method of corpse disposal in the United Kingdom, though the widespread slaughter of World War I (1914–1918) had previously softened attitudes to cremation in the United Kingdom. However the first crematorium was built in England in 1878 with the first person to be cremated officially in the United Kingdom being Jeanette Pickersgill who was cremated in 1885. By the end of the 20th century, rates of cremation were highest in northern Europe—countries where cultures tend toward Lutheranism and Anglicanism rather than Catholicism. In 1999, 71 percent of British and Danish people were cremated as were 68 percent of Swedes. Conversely, cremation does not occur in Greece because the Greek Orthodox Church strictly opposes cremation as a method of dealing with dead bodies.

Cremation is performed at temperatures ranging from 1400°F to 1800°F. Such intense heat is required to reduce the corpse to its basic elements and bone fragments. When cremation occurs at a crematorium, the procedure takes place in a cremation chamber, also called the retort. This chamber is preheated to a certain temperature and the corpse is placed in the chamber quickly via a mechanized door in order to avoid loss of temperature. The corpse is then incinerated having previously had any pacemakers or jewelry removed. During the incineration, the corpse is exposed to flames produced by a furnace that is fueled by natural gas, oil, or propane. Since the corpse is, typically, placed in a casket made from a combustible material before it enters the cremation chamber, the coffin will also burn. The heat of the cremation chamber dries out the corpse resulting in the hair and skin burning, the muscles contracting, and soft tissue evaporating. Meanwhile, the bones calcify and eventually crumble and the gasses released during the cremation process are removed from the chamber through an exhaust system, meaning that there is no unpleasant smell.

Occasionally a crematorium may offer a secondary afterburner that will burn the corpse until no trace of the body remains. Otherwise, a cremation technician may need to crush skeletal remains with a long implement. Skeletal remains (e.g., pieces of bone) are collected in a tray and allowed to cool. Other parts of the body that do not burn include metal screws and replacement joints, metal dental work, and implants that will be present together with any metal parts of the coffin such as hinges, screws, and nails. These items will have to be retrieved by crematorium staff using magnets or forceps and then disposed of in accordance with local laws. Meanwhile, tiny particles of the corpse may still remain in the cremation chamber where they will merge with residue left from subsequent cremations. Metal needs to be removed from the remains as metal fragments will damage the pulverization equipment called a cremulator that is used in the next step of the cremation process. This final stage of the cremation sees the fragments of dried bone ground down until they reach the consistency of fine sand. These finely ground remains are usually a pale, off-white color. Generally it takes between one and three hours to cremate an adult human, a process that yields three to seven pounds of remains. It is usual after a cremation for the remains to be placed in a cremation urn that is then presented to someone connected to the deceased, usually a spouse or relative.

Sati: The Ancient Indian Custom

Sati, also spelled *suttee*, was an ancient Indian funeral custom that saw an Indian widow place herself on her husband's funeral pyre or commit suicide in some other way soon after the death of her husband. The custom was most prevalent among India's Hindu and Sikh communities though it was also recorded elsewhere. When the British colonized India in the 19th century they outlawed the practice in British-held land. The Indian Sati Prevention Act of 1988 criminalized any type of aiding, abetting, or glorifying sati but incidents of sati have been reported as recently as 2006.

Today, religions such as Islam, Orthodox Judaism, and the Greek and Russian Orthodox Churches still oppose cremations. Cremation is also scorned by enviromentalists on the grounds that the process is wasteful and polluting. A cremator uses an average of around 285 kW-hours of gas and 15 kW-hours of electricity per cremation. This is about the same as a month's domestic energy demands for a single person. Nearly all cremators use gas and since gas is a finite resource, the cremation process could be argued to be highly energy inefficient. Moreover, cremation also produces large amounts of greenhouse gas emissions. As well as the greenhouse gas emissions created by cremation, the process also causes mercury pollution. Indeed in 2015 the United Kingdom's Environment Agency revealed that 16 percent of the country's mercury pollution arose from dental fillings being present during cremations. Such figures meant that the cremation industry was ordered to halve its mercury emissions by 2012, though, ironically, one way to ensure this decrease in mercury pollution was to cremate corpses at higher temperatures, which resulted in higher levels of greenhouse gas emissions. Environmentalists also point out that it is wasteful to use materials to make coffins, especially ones that will be burned. Wooden coffins are usually made from either solid oak or pine, or veneered chipboard that is bonded together using a formaldehyde resin. When the coffins are burned during cremation the residue from the wood, plus the residue of the formaldehyde resin, enters the atmosphere.

See also: Alkaline Hydrolysis; Eating the Ashes of the Dead; Finger Amputation; Hindu Death Customs; Japanese Death Customs; *Ngaben*; Sikh Death Customs; Space Burial; Zoroastrian Funerals

Further Reading

BBC. "How Cremation Became the Way to Go." *BBC News Magazine*, March 25, 2009. Accessed October 17, 2015, at http://news.bbc.co.uk/1/hi/magazine/7963119.stm.

Cremationresource.org. "How Is a Body Cremated?" Accessed October 17, 2015, at http://www.cremationresource.org/cremation/how-is-a-body-cremated.html.

Davies, Douglas J., and Lewis H. Mates, eds. *Encyclopedia of Cremation*. Aldershot, UK: Ashgate e-book, 2013.

Hickman, Leo. "Should I . . . Be Buried or Cremated?" *The Guardian*, October 18, 2005. Accessed October 17, 2015, at http://www.theguardian.com/environment/2005/oct/18/ethicalmoney.climatechange.

International Cremation Federation. "Home." Accessed October 17, 2015, at http://www.int-crem-fed.org/homepage.

CRONING, SAGING, AND ELDERLING CEREMONIES, PAGANISM

A croning ceremony is a New Age, neo-pagan (particularly Wiccan) or feminist ritual that celebrates the start of a woman's third stage of life and is viewed by those that undergo the ceremony as a rite of passage marking an age of freedom, wisdom, and personal empowerment. Women usually celebrate their croning ceremony when they start their menopause or when they reach 50 years of age. Traditionally, the word crone was used to denote the archetype of a physically unattractive, withered old woman. However in recent times the term has been embraced positively by Wiccans, proponents of New Age religions and feminists that envisage the crone as a wise woman figure that wishes to pass on her knowledge to the next generation of women. This view arises from the idea that the crone is one of the sacred trinity of aspects of the female—the Virgin, the Mother, and the Crone—that represent the different stages of a woman's life. As the Crone is the last stage of a woman's life she is, in all likelihood, the closest to death, which casts her as the wisest stage of all. Thus a croning ceremony is a major landmark in the lives of some women. While many women see the croning ceremony as a revolutionary way to celebrate ageing in Western society that usually idealizes youth, cynics suggest that the concept of the croning ceremony is merely a marketing strategy aimed at 50-something women with large disposable incomes as many forms of croning merchandise are available to buy in specialist Wiccan supply stores and online. This merchandise includes publications such as books, magazines, and cards; gifts such as mugs, jewelry, purses, and t-shirts; and ritual equipment such as candles, candleholders and cauldrons.

It is not known when croning ceremonies first began to be held though feminist writer Z Budapest is believed to have held such ceremonies in 1976, while in the early 1980s a women's group based in Maine self-published a book on the subject as a companion to their own croning ceremonies. Then, in 1987, a group called Crone was established in Seattle. By this time, a magazine titled *Crone Chronicle: A Journal of Conscious Aging* had been launched, gaining an international circulation of 15,000 readers. When *Crone Chronicle* ceased production in 2001 the magazine *Crone: Women Coming of Age* succeeded it. This publication explores and embraces women's role in the earth's cycle of life, death, and transformation and honors the wisdom of older women that style themselves as crones.

Croning rituals are usually designed as group rituals but they can also be modified for the solo practitioner. In the group version of a croning ceremony two women members of a coven portray the Goddess in both her Maiden form and as Mother. Thus a young woman represents the Maiden and a woman of childbearing age represents the Mother. Oftentimes these women are related to the woman whose croning ceremony it is, either because they are her coven sisters or because they are literally the woman's female family members—for example, her sisters, aunts, or nieces or with one of the women being the woman's biological mother. There is no set pattern for a croninng ceremony but during a croning ceremony a black candle representing the Crone may be placed on the altar along with herbs including mugwort, hellebore, tansy, elderberry, lilac, and lavender and spices such as anise and fresh ginger. These are all associated with the Goddess Crone and are placed on the altar either to disperse energy during the ceremony or to be burned as offerings. The altar may also feature a cauldron and a container to hold the black candle. Next, the Priestess stands in front of the altar facing outward to the gathering of women. The Priestess then invokes the energy of the Crone and asks that those present be imbued with her wisdom. The Priestess next lights white candles placed on the altar. A young woman carrying an unlit white candle approaches the Priestess who states that this young coven sister represents the Maiden. The Priestess lights the Maiden's candle using one of the white altar candles and the Maiden places the white candle on the altar. Next, the woman representing the Mother and carrying an unlit red candle approaches the Priestess who lights the Mother's candle using a white altar candle. The Mother then places the red candle on the altar. Next, the Priestess bids forth the woman whose Croning ceremony it is. The Crone then steps forward when called and asserts that she represents the wisdom, accomplishment, and knowledge of the Crone. The Crone then lights a black candle using an altar candle. This candle is placed between the candles placed on the altar by the women representing the Maiden and the Mother. All three women then turn to those looking on and family members and coven members then come forward to embrace the Crone. Some may also leave a flower on the altar as a gift for the Goddess. Next the women representing the Maiden, the Mother, and the Crone turn toward the altar and the Priestess who states that the Crone has entered a new phase of life. Next, the Priestess usually gives the Crone a piece of jewelry, often a ring or pendant, that commemorates the croning ceremony. The Priestess then says that the woman is now a Crone able to continue in life and charged with spreading her wisdom to the young. This concludes the ceremony and the spectators disperse. It is usual for a party or other celebration to be held after a croning ceremony.

There are no known precedents for pagan ceremonies to celebrate male ageing in the way that the croning ceremony rejoices in the older woman. However a saging ceremony can be held to mark the advancing years of a pagan man in much the same way as a croning ceremony is held for a woman. To adapt the ceremony for a man three aspects of the God may be represented: the Green Man, the Horned God, and, lastly, the Sage—or as the Page, Father, and Sage, just as the Maiden, Mother, and Crone are present during a croning ceremony. As it is generally agreed that men do not go through a physical menopause, their saging ceremony must take place at a time that corresponds to the female menopause, so a time when the man feels imbued with the wisdom of life is usually chosen, for a saging ceremony classes a sage as the older aspect of the God. Alternatively, a unisex elderling ceremony may be held to honor those who are regarded as mature, responsible, and knowledgeable within Paganism. However some pagans find the term elderling rather weak as it is a gender-neutral term that somewhat dilutes the importance of gender that is a feature of croning ceremonies. Unlike the word crone, which older women have reclaimed, the term sage does not tend to have negative connotations and has generally only been used to confer esteem on a man celebrated for his wisdom.

See also: Jewish Death Customs; *La Quinceañera* (Volume 2)

Further Reading

BBI Media. "Origins of Crone Chronicle." Crone: Women Coming of Age. Accessed February 16, 2015, at http://www.cronemagazine.com/cc_origins.html.

Bramshaw, Vikki. *Craft of the Wise: A Practical Guide to Paganism and Witchcraft*. Ropley, UK. O Books, 2009.

Grufferman, Barbara Hannah. "The Croning of America: How Post50 Women Are Learning to Love Their Inner Crone," *Huffington Post*: The Blog, September 10, 2012. Accessed February 15, 2015, at http://www.huffingtonpost.com/barbara-hannah-grufferman/what-every-post50-woman-s_b_1864921.html.

McCoy, Edain. *World Religion and Magic Series: Celtic Myth and Magick*. Woodbury, MN: Llewellyn Publications, 1995.

Raine, Amythyst. *The Gray Witch's Grimoire*. Alresford, UK: Moon Books, 2012.

CRUCIFIXION RITUALS, PHILIPPINES

The Philippines is the only Christian country in Asia with some 86 percent of the country's population claiming to be Roman Catholic, 6 percent belonging to a variety of Christian cults and another 2 percent belonging to numerous Protestant denominations. In addition, around 4 percent of Filipinos are Muslim. While the majority of Filipinos are Catholic, however, the country retains vestiges of local pre-Christian beliefs. This combination of Catholicism and folk religion results in a number of festivals and rituals. For example, every Good Friday during the Christian time of Eastertide a number of Filipino Christian males and females volunteer to be nailed to wooded crucifixes, often by other devotees dressed as Roman centurions, in order to reenact the execution of Christ. (*See* Plate 4.) The crucifixion reenactments are considered an Easter devotional practice by locals and are an essential element of the local observance of Holy Week, which is known in the Philippines as *Semana Santa* (Spanish) or as *Mahál na Araw* (Filipino).

The crucifixion reenactments, which can draw crowds of 30,000 spectators consisting of both locals and visitors, take place at various locations in the north of the Philippines. Although the crucifixion rituals clearly allude to the death of Christ, many observers have noted that the rituals are also informed by ancient, indigenous, pre-Christian attitudes. Some academics also suggest that the emphasis on the suffering and death of Christ is a particularly Filipino take on Christianity, something that has been dubbed Calvary Catholicism after Calvary, the site of Jesus's crucifixion. That there is a focus on devotional physical suffering in the Philippines is evinced by that fact that the spikes hammered through the hands and feet of crucifixion ritual participants are several inches long and made of metal. It can also take as long as 45 minutes for an individual to be fully nailed to their cross before allowing the participant to hang from his or her nailed body parts for many minutes. Therefore participants in Filipino crucifixion rituals feel real, extreme, physical pain and suffer bloody wounds that require medical attention. Since the crucifixion ritual participants wear microphones close to their mouths while they are nailed to their crosses their every agonized utterance is relayed to huge crowds of onlookers.

The history of Filipino crucifixion rituals is thought by historians to date from the Spanish colonization of the country (from around 1565) for it was then that Spanish Catholic monks settled in the country and brought with them the practice of self-flagellation as a disciplinary exercise. Though the monks performed this ritual discipline in private, the local male population came to know of it and began to perform self-flagellation too while also encouraging local women and children to do the same. Within 30 years of the Spanish settlement of the Philippines, self-flagellation had become a mass participation phenomenon throughout the country. Eventually the popularity of self-flagellation in the Philippines led the Catholic Church to forbid the practice throughout the nation but this ban proved ineffectual. Indeed self-flagellation in the Philippines has been continuing, uninterrupted, for many hundreds of years. In contrast, ritual crucifixion reenactments are a recent phenomenon in the Philippines. Indeed the rites were unknown until the latter half of the 20th century when in 1961 a self-flagellating faith healer called Arsenio Añosa, was crucified in San Fernando in an attempt to become closer to God than self-flagellation alone would permit and also in anticipation that by experiencing the suffering of Christ he would gain extra powers of healing. Such was Añosa's desire to gain healing powers that between 1961 and 1976 he was willingly crucified each year and in doing so garnered much media attention both in the Philippines and internationally.

The people that allow themselves to be nailed to a cross during Filipino crucifixion reenactment are usually devoutly religious penitents, referred to locally as *magdarame* (one who bleeds himself). The magdarame consider these actions to be a form of mortification of the flesh, and undertake their punishments for a variety of reasons. These reasons include seeking forgiveness for their sins, to fulfill a *panatà* (vow) that they have made to God, to ask for God's intercession, to appeal to God for miracles cure for an illness, and to express thankfulness for favors they believe that God has granted them. Just as the reasons behind participants' involvement in the rites differ so the details of each village's crucifixion rituals vary too. In the village of Kapampangan, the magdarame are crucified in commemoration of Christ's death having first performed self-flagellation using bamboo sticks attached to rope handles, crawled over rough stones, walked barefoot on cracked pavements, and carried the wooden crosses on which they will be hung. Meanwhile, The San Pedro Cutud Lenten Rites, held at Barangay San Pedro Cutud, San Fernando, Pampanga, reenact Christ's suffering and crucifixion through the performance of a Passion play that culminates in at least three penitents being nailed to wooden crosses on top of a hill that is decorated to resemble the Biblical Calvary. Sometimes at the San Pedro Cutud reenactments spectators also use pieces of broken glass to slice open the back of crucifixion participants. Also taking place in Pampanga is the *Siete Palabras* (*Seven Last Words*) Passion play that is performed in Angeles City, Pampanga. The play, which depicts the sufferings of Christ after he is sentenced to death by Pontius Pilate, is performed in the city's streets with dozens of men lugging wooden crosses weighing up to 110 pounds along city routes. Many locals also perform self-flagellating in Barangay Lourdes Northwest, Angeles City, as part of the local crucifixion rituals. Crucifixions also take place in Barangay Kapitangan, Paombong, Bulacan, an area considered by locals to be a place of pilgrimage and an area where faith healers congregate. Barangay Kapitangan is also home to a venerated wooden statue of Christ (known as *Sto Christo*) that is credited with facilitating miraculous acts of healing and mystical visions.

Although the crucifixion reenactments are intended to commemorate one of the most important events in Christianity, Catholic authorities have condemned the crucifixion rituals, suggesting that the gruesome rites are superstitious expressions of Folk Catholicism that are contrary to the church's view of how the human body should be treated. Meanwhile, the country's health authorities insist that crucifixion participants must have tetanus shots before being pierced by the stainless steel nails. Since there is, obviously, an inherent danger to experiencing crucifixion, medical professionals are on hand at the crucifixion reenactments to treat those people that have undergone the rite and to ensure that participants do not suffer complications from being crucified. Medical staff are also on hand at crucifixion reenactments because onlookers often become overcome while watching the gory rituals in the hot Filipino weather resulting in dizziness and fainting.

Despite the two-fold condemnation of the rites, the annual crucifixion rituals attract many participants some of whom experience the rites many times throughout their life, possibly even year after year. The rituals also draw huge crowds especially in the northern Pampanga province. In recent years, however, foreign tourists have been banned from the reenactments in some villages to prevent the imitation crucifixions becoming spectator attraction rather than a religious practice. For a similar reason, some villages forbid the involvement of foreign participants too. The ban on foreign participants is due, in part, to the fact that in recent years foreigners have taken part in the rites under dubious circumstances. For example, in 2009 an Australian comic took part while wearing an improvised crown of thorns under an assumed name for what he called personal reasons, while in 1996 a citizen of Japan tried to be crucified as part of a pornographic movie.

See also: Easter Eggs; Passion Play; *Thaipusam*: Extreme Ritual Flesh Modification (Volume 2)

Further Reading

Associated Press. "Crucifixion Rite: 24 Nailed to Crosses to Re-Enact Jesus Christ's Suffering," *The Guardian*, April 22, 2011. Accessed December 13, 2015, at http://www.theguardian.com/world/2011/apr/22/crucifixion-rite-jesus-christ-suffering.

Bräulein, Peter J. "Negotiating Charisma: The Social Dimension of Philippines Crucifixion Rituals," in Thomas Reuter and Alexander Horstmann, eds., *Faith in the Future: Understanding the Revitalization of Religions and Cultural Traditions of Asia*. Leiden, Netherlands: Brill, 2013, 63–89.

Favila, Aaron. "In the Philippines, Observers Perform Crucifixion Reenactment in Good Friday Ritual (PHOTOS)," *Huffington Post*, April 18, 2014. Accessed December 13, 2015, at http://www.huffingtonpost.com/2014/04/18/philippines-crucifixion-reenactment_n_5173257.html.

Hackney Blackwell, Amy. *Lent, Yom Kippur, and Other Atonement Days*. New York: Chelsea House, 2009.

Miller, Jack. "Religion in the Philippines." Asia Society. Accessed December 13, 2015, at http://asiasociety.org/religion-philippines.

News.com.au. "TV's John Safran Crucified in Philippines Easter Ritual." April 10, 2009. Accessed December 13, 2015, at http://www.news.com.au/world/safran-crucified-in-bizarre-easter-ritual/story-e6frfkyi-1225699241284.

D

DEATH DANCE, INTERNATIONAL

A death dance is a widespread ritual that can take many forms and is usually performed to mark a funeral. There are many reasons why mourners dance at or after a funeral. Sometimes people perform death dances to prevent the dead from envying the living—by performing a death dance the living pacify, mislead, or distract the dead so that they are too diverted to notice the living. It is for this reason that many death dances involve moves taken from other dances only performed backward as reversing the dance is supposed to confuse the dead and therefore distract the dead from being jealous of the living. Death dances may often feature sacrifices and the making of noise. Alternatively Native American peoples perform death dances to exorcise the spirits of the dead and to hasten the journey taken by the spirit of the deceased to the Great Spirit.

Meanwhile the Nyakyusa ethnic tribe living in Tanzania and Malawi perform a death dance upon the death of members of their tribe as a way to alleviate their sorrow and anger. The dance performed by the Nyakyusa is simultaneously both a dance of sadness and a war dance that allows those that perform the dance to express feelings that they would otherwise keep hidden. Moreover, the grief and anger that are channeled into the dance not only exhibits the qualities of a war dance but also honors the virility of dead men. Such is the desire to honor the dead that occasionally Nyakyusa men performing the dance will break into fights while Nyakyusa women will act passionately with each other. In the past, the Nyakyusa focused primarily on honoring the dead through a very warlike dance but today the emphasis is on sexuality. When danced as a war dance the Nyakyusa stress the virility and bravery of their dead males and when performed in a sexual manner, to mark the death of a female tribe member, the dance emphasizes that the woman was the mother of warriors. Since most Nyakyusa females are betrothed as soon as they reach puberty, social friction can be caused when females dancing the death dance act in a sexually suggestive manner. However this social scorn is countered by arguments that sexual displays stress the importance to continue life in the face of death. The Bara people of central Madagascar also perform a death dance as part of funeral activities. This dance sees girls dance in a slow circle in front of a house dubbed the house of many tears that is the location of the corpse that is being honored. The girls are then joined one-by-one by Bara boys so that two or three concentric rings of dancers are formed. Those dancers in the innermost ring dance slowly in double-time while those in the outermost circle move to a drumbeat. Sometimes outside of the outermost circle a few young boys will dance by themselves spinning in circles. The unending movement that is a characteristic of the Bara death dance is intended to epitomize *faha*, or vitality, in the face of death.

During the time of the Black Death in medieval Europe an allegorical figure called the *danse macabre* evolved to symbolize the omnipotence of death. The danse macabre features the figure of Death as a skeleton leading a hoard of living people taken from all walks of life, from the mightiest emperor to the lowliest peasant. Prior to the invention of the danse macabre there existed in the 13th century a literary genre known as *Vado Mori*, meaning, "I prepare myself to die." Vado Mori took the form of poems written in Latin in which representatives of the different social classes complain that they will die soon. The artistic genre referred to as danse macabre most likely developed in France with the painting *The Dance of Death of the Cimetière des Innocents in Paris* (1424), considered to be the first work that established the tradition. Later artworks to feature the danse macabre include frescoes created in London, England (in around 1430), in Basel, Switzerland (in 1440 and 1480), and at La Chaise-Dieu in Lübeck, Germany (circa 1463). The motif of the danse macabre gained in popularity in the second half of the 15th century leading to the painting of frescoes in France, Germany, Italy, Croatia, Denmark, Slovenia, Croatia, and elsewhere. Usually these frescoes were painted or sometimes carved on the outside of monastery cloisters, on family vaults, and on the exterior of ossuaries. Occasionally the danse macabre was also depicted inside churches. The frescoes always show either a skeleton or an emaciated corpse alongside members of various social classes. Often the skeleton or corpse is shown dancing a *farandole*, a lively French folk dance. The painting of the danse macabre is usually accompanied by verses that allow death to address its victims often in a threatening or accusatory tone or alternatively in a cynical manner while the victims of death cry out despairingly for mercy. However both the frescoes and verses reveal that death shows no regard for the social status, wealth, sex, or age of its victims and leads everyone in its dance of death.

The danse macbre was featured in the art, drama, and literature of Western Europe but was also included in carnivals in Germany, Spain, and parts of Latin America that had been colonized by the Spanish. Today the danse macabre is perhaps best known through musical works such as *Totentanz* (1849) by Franz Liszt and Camille Saint-Saëns's *Danse Macabre* (1874) while energetic skeletal figures are still central to *Dia de los Muertos* (Day of the Dead) processions in Spain and Mexico.

See also: *Ankou*; *Dia de los Muertos*: Day of the Dead; *Memento Mori* and *Vanitas*; Ossuaries; Tombstone Tourism

Further Reading

Jones, Alison. *Larousse Dictionary of World Folklore*. Edinburgh, UK: Larousse, 1996.

Metcalf, Peter, and Richard Huntington. *Celebrations of Death: The Anthropology of Mortuary Ritual*. Second Edition. Cambridge, UK: Cambridge University Press, 1991.

Pollefeys, Patrick. "Danse Macabre." La Mort Dans L'Art. Accessed October 21, 2015, at http://www.lamortdanslart.com/danse/dance.htm.

DELAWARE INDIAN DEATH RITUALS, NORTH AMERICA

The various Native American nations practice a wide variety of rituals and customs concerning death, funerals, and mourning. This variety of mourning practices, customs, and traditions reflects the rich variety of Native American beliefs and values. It is possible, however, to make a few generalizations about Native American mourning customs. For example, Native American funerals tend to be collective events that bring communities together and there is a general sense that the recently dead, like ancient ancestors, should be venerated. There is a universal feeling among Native American peoples that life is sacred and that since burial grounds contain the remains of people that were once alive the land should be treated as sacred areas. The way in which human remains are treated after death varies greatly between tribes. For instance some peoples wrap remains in a shroud-like cloth, blanket, or animal skin while others do not. Many tribes bury the deceased's property with the corpse but others give items away or burn the property. The vessel in which a Native American is placed after death also varies with some Native Americans buried in graves, ditches, mounds, cabins, canoes, scaffolds, trees, or pits. Then again, some Native Americans are cremated.

The Delaware Indians (or Lenape) traditionally reside along the Delaware River, in the west of Long Island and in the Lower Hudson Valley. Delaware Indians begin to prepare for their death when they reach their sixth decade of life or when they feel that they are near death. For women, this death preparation takes the form of sewing a special burial outfit consisting of a skirt, leggings, blouse, and moccasins, while a Delaware Indian man may ask for help in preparing his outfit. Delaware Indians sense that death is approaching because they notice their personality changes—they will become irritable and grumpy so as to make others dislike them and not grieve for them when they are dead. They will notice physical changes too. For example they will consider the white semi-circles at the base of their fingernails to have faded. This change is important as the Delaware Indians deem these half-moons to be spirit fingers or *lenapeokani sekelenja*. When Delaware Indians are close to death, they may expect that they will be enveloped in a white mist and their soul will separate from their physical being. Once the soul has disengaged itself it will rapidly travel around the universe visiting people and places. As soon as the person is dead a window is opened near his or her body as this is believed to let the person's soul fly freely, a handkerchief is placed over the person's face, and all mirrors and photographs are covered too. Next, the deceased's clothes are gathered together with one outfit selected to accompany the coffin and the others packaged together into two bundles alongside some tobacco.

In preparation for the funeral, women of the community will make corn bread, which is handled very carefully as it is intended for a sacred ceremony. Meanwhile, the family of the dead person will elect two men and two women that are not related to the deceased to perform the rest of the preparations. The women will prepare the rest of the refreshments while the men will fashion the wooden grave post, or *kikinhikan*. The form that the post takes differs depending on whether the dead person was a man or a woman—the post for a man is straight with its peak shaped like a diamond while a woman's post is shaped like a crucifix with three diamond shapes at each corner.

In addition to the four nonrelatives selected for funeral duties, the family also selects a tribal elder to conduct the ceremony. Once the family of the dead person has selected an elder they present him with a white cloth. The family also has to choose a close friend of the dead to sit with them so that the corpse is not left alone. The vigil over the dead coincides with a wake that lasts for one or more nights until the funeral takes place. At midnight, everyone at the wake except for the chief mourner goes outside and a rifle may be fired into the air. Then everyone present gathers around the corpse and says a prayer before the corpse's face is painted with red ochre. The painting rituals is performed so that the Creator, Kishelemukong, will recognize the deceased as a Delaware Indian—women have a red dot painted on each cheek and a line drawn on their hairline while men have three lines painted from each eye to their hairline.

The wake continues through the night followed by the burial, which occurs at noon. When making their way to the cemetery there is a strict order in which mourners proceed: the speaker, the family of the dead, and the deceased's friends head the procession and the corpse is the last in the procession. The coffin containing the corpse is painted red and has a notch cut in it to allow the soul to be free. All the while none of the mourners at the head of the procession are allowed to look back at the corpse as this is thought to make the deceased's spirit lag behind. Once the corpse arrives at the cemetery a grave is dug and then the deceased is laid to rest with its head pointing to the east. Mourners then encircle the grave in a clockwise direction starting from the east. Once the coffin is interred the deceased's clothes are laid on top of the coffin and then the grave is filled with soil. The grave post is then placed on top of the grave pointing eastward. This too is painted red so that the deceased is able to locate the spirit realm.

After the burial, a ritual feast is held at which the friend of the deceased selected as the chief mourner eats on behalf of the deceased. Once the feast is over a small fire is lit. This fire is relit each night for the next three nights just before sunset as the fires are thought to keep the spirit of the deceased warm as it journeys to the world of the spirits. Other post funeral customs see the relatives of the deceased not fix their hair for three days after the funeral as a sign of their bereavement. Additionally, mourners may tie a piece of deer skin around their wrists that they then allow to degrade naturally and fall from their arms and at night the mourners must keep their lights low. Meanwhile, mourners should also not mention the name of the deceased except in the morning.

An extended period of mourning is also observed for one year during which time members of the deceased's immediate family must not attend any community events. Moreover, the deceased's widow should not fix her hair during this period. Once the extended mourning period has concluded, a cedar tree is burned signaling that the widow may again take part in community events. As a secondary signal that the remaining spouse may again take part in society, and moreover, that they are free to remarry, the relatives of the deceased will often bring the widow a new set of clothes. If the family does not bring the widow a new outfit then this is a sign that they wish the widow to remain as a member of their own family. A special ceremony called a *Wihunge* may be held to mark the end of the extended mourning period, or if a relative is having recurrent visions of the deceased. The Wihunge takes the form of a special ceremonial feast and once a Wihunge is held the ceremony must continue to take place every year.

The Delaware Indians think that the souls of the deceased reside within the Milky Way, which they call *Ane*. According to Delaware Indian tradition, this is where the Creator lives. Spirit dogs guard the bridge to the realm of the spirits and for this reason any Delaware Indian then mistreats a dog will be forbidden from entering the realm of real souls. In contrast, the souls of people that have committed evil in life must reside in another place where they are tortured by insects. Moreover, if the realm of the evil spirits tires of the soul of an evildoer, the person may be transformed into an insect and placed among the living. Since the Delaware Indians believe in reincarnation, tribal elders will often inspect babies' earlobes to see pits on the skin where the babies have had their ears pieced in a previous existence.

See also: Mortuary Totem Poles; Native American Grave Protection and Repatriation Act, 1990; Ray Fadden, Letter to President Harry S. Truman Regarding Burial of an Indian at Arlington National Cemetery, September 3, 1951; Vrindavan: City of Widows; Wake

Further Reading

Cox, Gerry R. "The Native American Way of Death," in Clifton D. Bryant, ed., *Handbook of Death and Dying: Volume One The Presence of Death*. Thousand Oaks, CA: Sage Publications, 2003, 631–639.

Crawford, Suzanne J., and Dennis F. Kelley, eds., *American Indian Religious Traditions: An Encyclopedia*. Santa Barbara, CA: ABC-CLIO, 2005.

Lenape Lifeways. "Burial Customs." About the Lenapes, July 15, 2014. Accessed December 10, 2015, at http://www.lenapelifeways.org/lenape3.htm.

Popovic, Mislav. "Native American Death Rites." TraditionsCustoms.com. Accessed December 10, 2015, at http://traditionscustoms.com/death-rites/native-american-death-rites.

Related Primary Document: Ray Fadden, Letter to President Harry S. Truman Regarding Burial of an Indian at Arlington National Cemetery, September 3, 1951

Sergeant John R. Rice, a member of the Winnebago tribe (sometimes referred to as the Ho-Chunks) died on September 6, 1950, fighting in Korea. Almost one year after Sgt. Rice's death his remains were returned to his wife who organized his burial in a cemetery

located in Sioux City, Iowa. When the owners of the cemetery learned of Sgt. Rice's Native American heritage, however, they refused permission for Sgt. Rice to be interred in the cemetery. On hearing about this turn of events President Harry S. Truman became involved and approved a burial plot for Sgt. Rice at Arlington National Cemetery while also allowing Sgt. Rice to be buried with full military honors. The controversy surrounding the burial of Sgt. Rice led to both Sioux City and the owners of the cemetery becoming the focus of international attention. The issue of discrimination against Native Americans also became the subject of debate both in the United States and elsewhere. The following is a letter sent to President Truman by a member of a Mohawk counseling group. The letter was sent in order to express the appreciation felt by many Native Americans for the President's intervention in authorizing the burial of Sgt. Rice in Arlington Cemetery, something that highlighted the fact that Sgt. Rice died for his country.

President Harry Truman
Washington, D.C.
White House
Dear President Truman,

The members of our Indian organization read of your act as regards Sgt. John R. Rice who died in action in Korea. We are ashamed that officials of Sioux City did the cruel thing that they did, refusing to bury an Indian in their cemetery. We were proud of you, brother, when we read of you allowing our warrior to be buried in the Arlington Cemetery [sic]. We want you to know that we are grateful to you and appreciate it very much. May the Great Spirit bless your home for defending one of our people.

Cordially yours, Ray Fadden, Sec.

Source: *Textual Records from the President (1945-1953: Truman). Office of the President. (04/1945- 01/20/1953). Harry S. Truman Library and Museum, National Archives and Records Administration.*

DENVILLE HALL & BRINSWORTH HOUSE, ENGLAND

Denville Hall and Brinsworth House are English retirement/care homes for people connected with the entertainment industry. Denville Hall, which dates from the 18th century and is located in the northwest of London, England's capital city, is a charity founded and run by actors for members of their profession through funds donated by performers and theatre managers.

Denville Hall has been associated with the acting profession since 1925 when the impresario, actor-manager, and British member of Parliament Alfred Denville bought the hall. Denville dedicated the hall to the acting profession in memory of his son Jack, who died aged 26 years after an on-stage injury reactivated an injury sustained during World War I (1914–1918). Since then, the Hall has been enlarged and refurbished through contributions from show-business luminaries including Academy Award–winning director and actor Sir Richard Attenborough (who would also become president of Denville Hall) and media mogul Lew Grade, as well as legacies from Academy Award–winning actors Sir John Gielgud and Sir Alec Guinness, among others. Today, Denville Hall offers short stay and convalescence accommodation, residential care, nursing care, dementia care, and palliative care. On August 24, 2014, Sir Richard Attenborough died at Denville Hall five days short of his 91st birthday.

Brinsworth House, located in Twickenham in southwest London, is nicknamed "The Old Pro's Paradise" as it is a small retirement home for elderly artistes and members of the entertainment profession as well as their descendants. The house is appropriately decorated throughout to emphasize the house's theatrical connections. Brinsworth House is owned and maintained by the Entertainment Artistes' Benevolent Fund (EABF), which bought the property in 1911. In 1913, the EABF took over an existing music hall performers' retirement home relocating the music hall stars to Brinsworth House. In 1914, an enlargement to the house was proposed and King George V and Queen Mary consented to attend a Royal Command Performance at the Palace Theatre in London in order to raise funds for the expansion, while Frank Matcham, an architect famed for designing many of London's theatres and music halls, agreed to prepare plans for the expansion for free. The Royal Command Performance proved a great success and George V decreed that henceforth the reining monarch or the monarch's representative must attend an annual performance in aid of Brinsworth House and the EABF. The Royal Variety Performance, as the Royal Command Performance has been renamed, continues to be held annually in the form of a gala entertainment evening that has, over the years, attracted big name performers including the Beatles, Luciano Pavarotti, the Spice Girls, Bob Hope, the Jackson 5, Sir Elton John, and Kanye West. Brinsworth House also receives funds from a percentage of the proceeds from the reality television series *Britain's Got Talent* as well as voluntary donations.

See also: Chelsea Pensioners

Further Reading
Denville Hall. "History of Denville Hall." Accessed November 1, 2014, at http://www.denville hall.org.uk/history.html.
Donin, Janet. "Brinsworth House Retirement Home for Entertainers." Surrey Life, November 9, 2009. Accessed November 1, 2014, at http://www.surreylife.co.uk/people/brins worth_house_retirement_home_for_entertainers_1_1632734.
EABF. "History." Entertainment Artistes' Benevolent Fund. Accessed November 1, 2014, at http://www.eabf.org.uk/brinsworth-house/history.
EABF. "Royal Variety Archive." Entertainment Artistes' Benevolent Fund, May 24, 2009. Accessed November 1, 2014, at http://www.eabf.org.uk/news-feature-box;news/id/9.
Simkins, Michael. "Ageing Thespians Should Stick Together," *The Telegraph*, July 11, 2009. Access November 1, 2014, at http://www.telegraph.co.uk/comment/personal-view /5804497/Ageing-thespians-should-stick-together.html.

DIA DE LOS MUERTOS: DAY OF THE DEAD, LATIN AMERICA AND UNITED STATES

Dia de los Muertos, or Day of the Dead, is a lively annual Latin American holiday held to honor the dead. Despite being called the Day of the Dead, the holiday actually falls on both November 1 and 2 and, although the celebration occurs throughout Latin America and among Latin American communities in the United States, the holiday is synonymous with Mexico, particularly central and southern areas, where the holiday originated. Secure in the knowledge that the dead would be affronted by an atmosphere of sadness, Dia de los Muertos instead commemorates the lives of the deceased with food, drink, and general merrymaking. The celebrations also make people reflect on the fact that the dead are part of their community. In 2008, Dia de los Muertos was inscribed on UNESCO's Representative List of the Intangible Cultural Heritage of Humanity.

Dia de los Muertos honors the dead with fiestas and energetic celebrations that amalgamate native Aztec rituals with the Catholicism that was brought to Mexico by the Spanish *conquistadores*. The Spanish conquered the Aztecs in 1521, resulting in pre-Hispanic beliefs merging with Catholicism and producing a blending (*mestizaje*) of religions that is unique to the region. Prior to the arrival of the conquistadores, the Aztecs had prayed to a variety of gods including Miclantecuhtli, the god of death, who presides over the furthest reaches of the Aztec underworld, Mictlan, with his wife Mictlancihuatl, the goddess of death also referred to as Lady of Death. Nowadays, an integral part of modern Dia de los Muertos festivities is the making of offerings to Mictlancihuatl who was, traditionally, venerated in the ninth month of the solar calendar. Mictlancihuatl is brought to the world of the living each year when women paint their faces to resemble the goddess and offer her special foods and flowers during Dia de los Muertos. Impersonations of the goddess are referred to as *Catrinas* or *La Calavera Catrina* (The Elegant Skull). La Calavera Catrina is usually portrayed as having a crazed toothy grin and was first depicted in this way by artist José Guadalupe Posada in 1910. This image in turn was adopted by the muralist Diego Rivera who used the image to symbolize the Mexican ability to laugh at death. Rivera also suggested that death is a democratizing event as the skeleton woman may be dressed in fine clothing but is, nonetheless, just a set of bones.

According to Mexican beliefs, once per year these ancestors return to reunite with their living relatives. For this reason on November 1 each year Latino people celebrate Dia de los Muertos through various rituals and offerings (*ofrendas*) performed at home or at graveyards that are intended to honor their ancestors. In Mexico, the history of making offerings to the dead dates back some 3,000 years for ancient peoples living in Mexico believed that in order to make the transition to the afterlife more pleasant for the dead it was necessary to bury food with the recently deceased. It was also traditional to bury the dead's animal companions with them too. Ancient Aztecs believed that Mictlan could be a peaceful realm filled with butterflies or it could be extremely scary. Indigenous Mexicans treated death as a natural transition to another life that could not be avoided and was merely an element of the human experience that came after birth, childhood, adulthood, and old age. For this reason, images of skulls saturated all areas of life with carved skulls appearing on the side of buildings and made out of quartz and obsidian, a naturally occurring type of volcanic glass that forms from igneous rock, for offering to the gods. The Aztecs also wrote poetry celebrating the belief that life needs deaths and death needs life.

According to Catholic beliefs, November 1 is designated All Saints' Day and November 2 is All Souls' Day. In order to simplify ways of venerating the dead in pre-Columbian times, efforts were made to unite the two dates. This resulted in what is not known as Dia de los Muertos, although in actuality November 1 is intended to commemorate dead babies and children and November 2 is the day for remembering deceased adults. Today, Dia de los Muertos is celebrated with especial vigor in central and southern Mexico where people tend to observe indigenous traditions more closely than elsewhere in Mexico. Two Mexican states in particular, Michoacan and Oaxaca, are especially associated with Dia de los Muertos. That said, a particularly startling Dia de los Muertos custom occurs in the Mayan town of Pomuch in the southern state of Campeche. Here, relatives take the bones of their ancestors from their coffins and clean them as a celebratory act.

The principal belief behind Dia de los Muertos is that the spirits of dead ancestors will return to their families on the evening of November 1. On this evening the dead are said to leave Mictlan to visit their family and enjoy the special foods left for them. Days of preparation prior to Dia de los Muertos see families clean the tombs of their ancestors where they later leave gifts to the dead. Women and youngsters also decorate the tombs with *cempasuchits* or *zempoaxochitls* (marigolds), as these are the official Mexican flower of death. In particular, women may fashion a crucifix from the marigolds. These preparations conclude with the setting of an altar to celebrate Dia de los Muertos within family homes on October 30 and 31. These altars (*ofrendas*) are decorated with an embroidered or crocheted tablecloth that has been made by the women of the house. Sometimes the tablecloth is colored purple, as this is the color most associated with death in Mexico. Every altar is unique but there are certain items that should be displayed on it during Dia de los Muertos including flowers, photographs, or portraits of dead relatives and friends, incense, bread, skulls (usually made from sugar), foods, and candles. An item associated with the people being remembered should also be present—usually this takes the form of a cigarette for a deceased adult or a toy to remember a dead child. The photographs or portraits of the dead that are displayed on the altar should show the people that a family wishes to remember and whose graves might be visited on the night of Dia de los Muertos. It is also traditional to surround the altar with marigolds. Above the altar is strung a tissue paper garland called *papel picado*. This consists of colorful flags displaying images normally associated with death. Once the altar is prepared it is customary for a family to gather around it and stay up all night in expectation "for the dead to arrive." While they wait for the dead, the family will normally say prayers.

Food is the main offering during the celebrations as it is a core belief of the festivities that the dead return to partake of the feasts laid on in their honor. Consequently, it is usual for families to make the favorite foods of their ancestors. These foods must include *pan de mureto*, bread of the dead, which may be baked either fashioned into a round loaf or shaped to resemble bones before being colored red to symbolize blood. Pan de mureto is usually sweet tasting but some people prefer a salty version. Other foods that are typically made for ancestors on Dia de los Muertos include traditional Mexican dishes such as *moles* (chicken with chili sauce) and *tamales* (a type of steamed, filled corn dough cooked in a leaf). Hot chocolate, beer, and tequila are also prepared as these are thought to quench the thirst of the dead. These foods and drinks are also placed on top of the tombs that people visit during Dia de los Muertos. Indeed on the night of Dia de los Muertos families will sing and pray surrounded by the specially made foods because they believe that their deceased loved ones are close and wish to celebrate their special night with the living.

The Catholic element of Dia de los Muertos is seen in the offerings of crucifixes, rosaries and images of Jesus and patron saints that are put on display during the holiday. Usually the saints whose icons are displayed are the patron saints of the deceased people being venerated by their families. Another Christian element, candles, are kept burning all through the night of Dia de los Muertos too as these are thought to guide souls to their intended destinations. As a rule a family will light one candle for each departed person plus an extra candle for a soul. Meanwhile, the omnipresent smell of incense means that the atmosphere of death is pervasive on Dia de los Muertos. This air of death is complimented by the presence of sugar skulls. These have been made since the 17th century in order to initiate children into the Dia de los Muertos tradition and to encourage youngster to make and decorate the sugar skulls as a sign of esteem for their ancestors. It is not, however, only children that make sugar skulls for skilled artisans also create them with examples of their work displayed at the Museo de Arte Popular located in Mexico City.

As well as the altars, foods, and graveyard visits, Dia de los Muertos is marked by theatrical performances known as *comparsas* that represent the return of the dead to the living. Comparsas often feature masked men walk on stilts through the center of a town with the men willing to sing a witty epitaph to a deceased person in exchange for a few coins. Such activities are a boon to local tourist trades. Indeed each year the island of Janitzio sees many tourists arrive each year specifically to experience the island's Dia de los Muertos activities. Janitzio, located in Lake Patzcuaro in the Mexican state of Mchoacan, is one of the most traditional locations to witness Dia de los Muertos festivities. At night, tourists board small boats to take short trips to the island. The boats are guided by tar-covered wooden stakes that stick out of the water that are illuminated for a few hours, thereby emitting an eerie amber-colored half-light that creates an extremely unnerving atmosphere. Once on the island visitors enjoy a feast of Dia de los Muertos foods including pan de muerto and sugar skulls, while local musicians play mournful music and incense burns all around.

> ### *Isla de las Munecas*—The Island of the Dolls
>
> Located near Mexico City is a floating garden island, *Isla de las Munecas* (Island of the Dolls), which is dedicated to a girl who was found to have drowned nearby. When the man who discovered the girl found a doll floating in the same stretch of water where the girl died, the man assumed the doll belonged to the dead girl and hung it from a tree on the island. Ever since, visitors have brought dolls to the island and nowadays there are hundreds of dolls there, some with missing limbs or heads. According to local legend, the dolls are possessed by the dead girl's spirit and can move, speak, and open their eyes.

When night falls on November 2, the dead are thought to return to their repose and all festivities therefore end. To ensure that the dead disperse and revelers cease their activities, masked mummers walk the streets to frighten away both the dead and the living.

Dia de los Muertos has appeared frequently in popular culture. For example, the festival acts as the backdrop for the opening action scenes of the 2015 James Bond film, *Spectre*. Moreover, in recent years the holiday has become associated with everything from rock concerts by tribute act mimicking dead singers in Houston, Texas, to Dia de los Muertos cycle races and marathons. Furthermore, the image of La Calavera Catrina has been appropriated as a decoration for all manner of products, clothing, and jewelry as well as embroidery patterns, car mats, chopping boards, oven gloves, and hairbrushes.

See also: All Souls Day; Japanese Death Customs; *Qingming* Festival; *Santa Muerte*; Saturday of Souls and *Radonitsa*

Further Reading

Aguilar-Moreno, Manuel. *Handbook to Life in the Aztec World*. Oxford, UK: Oxford University Press, 2006.

Galvan, Javier A., ed. *They Do What? A Cultural Encyclopedia of Extraordinary and Exotic Customs from around the World*. Santa Barbara, CA: ABC-CLIO, 2014.

Gordon, Sarah. "The Dead Have Been Expecting You, Mr Bond," *The Daily Telegraph: Travel*. 2015, October 10, 8–9.

Herrera-Sobek, Maria. *Celebrating Latino Folklore: An Encyclopedia of Cultural Traditions*. Volume 1. Santa Barbara, CA: ABC-CLIO, 2012.

The Huffington Post. "'Day of the Dead' Traditions Cross Over into U.S. Mainstream Culture." Huffington Post: Latino Voices, 2011, January 11. Accessed October 15, 2015, at http://www.huffingtonpost.com/2011/10/31/spirit-of-day-of-the-dead-crosses-border_n_1067851.html.

National Geographic Society. "*Dia de los Muertos*." National Geographic: Education. Accessed October 15, 2015, at http://education.nationalgeographic.co.uk/media/dia-de-los-muertos/.

UNESCO. "Indigenous Festivity Dedicated to the Dead." Accessed October 15, 2015, at http://www.unesco.org/culture/ich/RL/00054.

DOOM METAL AND FUNERAL DOOM, INTERNATIONAL

Doom Metal is a form of extreme heavy metal music characterized by slow tempos, low-tuned guitars, and a distinctively heavier sound than other types of metal music. The name doom metal originates from the fact that both the music and lyrics of doom metal aim to induce a sense of imminent tragedy, despair, and dread.

The doom metal genre is a fairly recently invented genre of music, as the genre was greatly influenced by the early work of the English rock group Black Sabbath, which was formed in 1969. Black Sabbath was initially fronted by Ozzy Osbourne and the band formed a prototype for doom metal creating lyrical music with songs that included allusions to the occult and references to horror. The New Wave of British Heavy Metal music movement (often abbreviated to NWoBHM movement) of the late 1970s and early 1980s has also been cited as a major influence on the doom metal genre. The 1980s saw an increase in the number of bands producing doom metal across Europe as well as in the United States. For instance, at the vanguard of the genre in England were bands such as Witchfinder General and Pagan Altar while in Sweden Count Raven and Candlemass, which released the landmark album *Epicus Doomicus Metallicus* in 1986, were leading exponents of the genre. Meanwhile, in the United States doom metal was produced by bands including Pentagram, Trouble, and Saint Vitus while the Melvins helped shape the genre further and also led to the creation of other musical subgenres, particularly grunge.

Thus far, music scholars recognize four waves of doom metal. The first wave saw the creation of the genre followed by the second wave that began in the mid-1980s with the popularity of bands such as Candlemass and Saint Vitus. The third wave is said to have begun with the success of *Forest of Equilibrium*, the debut album by British doom metal band Cathedral in 1991, which is now considered a classic of the doom metal genre. Around the same time as *Forest of Equilibrium* was released, other British bands such as Anathema, My Dying Bride, and Paradise Lost fused doom metal with death metal, a particularly depressive form of extreme metal, to help form the European gothic metal music genre. European gothic metal takes the intense heaviness of doom metal and melds it with the sensibilities of gothic rock to produce music characterized by doom-laden, introspective lyrics inspired by both gothic literature and personal experience.

The fourth wave of doom metal began in the mid 1990s with the popularity of Finnish doom metal band Reverend Bizarre whose work was arguably influenced by Black Sabbath, Saint Vitus, and Pentagram. In recent years, doom metal bands such as Disembowelment and Celestial have been at the forefront of the doom metal genre.

Funeral doom is a sub-genre of doom metal that takes the slow intensity of doom metal to an extreme in a deliberate attempt to increase the atmosphere of despondency and desolation experienced by the listener. Funeral doom also often employs elements of ambient music to create a discordant, distorted, and melancholy sound that is, nonetheless, also dreamlike. Another common feature of funeral doom is that songs are growled rather than sung and that any vocals are secondary and included solely to give texture to the music. Bands, including the aptly named Funeral, as well as Skepticism and Thergothon, pioneered the funeral doom genre with Skepticism releasing the landmark albums *Lead and Aether* and *Farmakon* in 1998 and 2003 respectively. Noted funeral doom bands formed more recently include Shape of Despair (originally called Raven), Bloody Panda, Until Death Overtakes Me (often referred to as UDOM), and Stabat Mater, a one-man band, which, like Shape of Despair, hails from Finland.

See also: Funeral Songs; Goth Subculture; "The Last Post" and "Taps"

Further Reading

Azevedo, Pedro. "Doom Metal: The Gentle Art of Making Misery." Chronicles of Chaos, November 19, 2004. Accessed March 31, 2015, at http://www.chroniclesofchaos.com/articles.aspx?id=6-674.

Roccor, Bettina. "Heavy Metal: Forces of Unification and Fragmentation within a Musical Subculture," *The World of Music: Gothic, Metal, Rap, and Rave—Youth Culture and Its Educational Dimensions,* 42(1), (2000), 83–94.

Smith, Emily. *The Megadeth Handbook—Everything You Need to Know about Megadeth.* Queensland, Australia: Emereo Publishing, 2013.

"Symphony I—Deep Dark Red, Until Death Overtakes Me." Encyclopaedia Metallum: The Metal Archives. Accessed March 31, 2015, at http://www.metal-archives.com/reviews/Until_Death_Overtakes_Me/Symphony_I__Deep_Dark_Red/8866/.

E

EASTER EGGS, CHRISTIANITY

Easter eggs, also known as Paschal eggs, are an important part of the traditions associated with Eastertide, the annual Christian commemoration of the death and Resurrection of Christ, which is a central festival of the Christian calendar. Easter eggs are therefore a symbol of both death and new life. Easter eggs are made from a variety of materials including chocolate though they may also be ordinary eggs that have been decorated. Although a Christian tradition, the giving and receiving of Easter eggs is enjoyed by people without any particular religious beliefs, especially children, in Europe and North America. Often Easter eggs are hidden for children to find on Easter morning. The eggs are often placed in such a manner that they appear to have been left by the so-called Easter Bunny, possibly being placed in a basket filled with real or artificial straw that resembles a bird's nest.

There are many folk customs associated with Easter, many of which have their roots in pre-Christian times. For instance the traditional Easter bunny is most likely a modern re-working of the hare that was considered a symbol of fertility by the ancient Egyptians. Alternatively, the Easter bunny is thought by some folklorists to be connected to the ancient Germanic deity Ostora (known as *Ostern* in German and also called *Eostre*) who was the goddess of the spring and whose companion was a hare. Many people, including Jacob Grimm, theorise that the word Easter may have evolved from the goddess's name. Perhaps the most famous custom associated with Easter is, however, the giving of Easter eggs. The history of the Easter egg can be traced back to the time of the advent of Christianity in Mesopotamia (around the first to the third century), when people used to stain eggs red as a reminder of the blood spilled by Christ during the Crucifixion. In time, the Christian church in general adopted this custom with the eggs considered to be a symbol of both Christ's death and Resurrection. Moreover, in the earliest days of Christianity Easter eggs were considered symbolic of the tomb in which Jesus's corpse was laid after the Crucifixion for eggs, as a near universal symbol of fertility and life, were like Jesus's tomb, something from which new life came forth. The Roman Ritual—one of the official ritual works of the Roman Rite of the Catholic Church—which was first published in 1610 but which contains texts written before this date, contains the rite of the Easter Blessings of Food, including eggs.

In Europe, the Easter egg tradition may also derive from the celebrations held to mark the end of Lentern privations. The period just before the start of Lent was, traditionally, a time when households used up all of their eggs. It was necessary to use the eggs because, according to tradition, Christians were not allowed to eat eggs during Lent. This is true still among the Eastern Christian Churches. The need to use up eggs before Lent also gave rise to the British tradition of Pancake Day when great numbers of pancakes are traditionally made on Shrove Tuesday. This day is known as *Mardi Gras* (Fat Tuesday) elsewhere, thereby highlighting the fact that the day to marks the last consumption of eggs, and other ingredients, before Lent starts.

In the Orthodox and Eastern Catholic Churches, Easter eggs are colored red to symbolize the blood of Christ that was shed during the Crucifixion with the egg's shell representing the sealed tomb containing the body of the dead Christ. Moreover, the act of cracking open the eggs, is believed by Orthodox and Eastern Catholic worshippers to echo Christ's Resurrection. The red Easter eggs are blessed by a priest at the end of the Paschal Vigil, a church service traditionally held by Christian churches as the first celebration of the Resurrection of Jesus, before being distributed to the congregations. A similar custom, *święconka*, exists in the Roman Catholic Church in Poland and among Polish communities in the North America and the United Kingdom. Święconka, which takes place on Holy Saturday and is considered an extremely important ritual by Polish Catholics, sees the blessing of decorative baskets lined with white fabric and filled Easter eggs and a variety of symbolic foods. The foods contained in the Święconka baskets usually include *baranek* (pats of butter molded into the shape of a lamb), *kranszanki* (Easter eggs dyed different colors to symbolize life after death), *sauerkraut* (fermented cabbage to represent Christ's suffering during the Crucifixion), ham (denoting plenty), and bread (representing both the physical body of Christ and the symbolic body of Christ that is the Eucharist). In some Orthodox communities the tradition of giving Easter eggs is extended to the dead for on either the second Monday or Tuesday of Easter, a memorial service takes place during which worshippers take to cemeteries eggs that have been blessed. Once at the cemeteries the faithful exclaim, "Christ has risen" to their ancestors.

Another European Easter egg tradition is the folk custom of concealing brightly colored, batik-patterned eggs known as *pysanka* or *pisanka* (plural *pysanky*), in gardens where that can be found by children. This tradition occurs in Bulgaria, Poland, Romania, Russia, Ukraine, and other Central and Eastern European countries as well as other countries with sizeable Central and Eastern European communities. For instance, the world's largest pysanka is located not in Europe but in Vegreville, Canada, where a 27-foot sculpture of a pysanka can be found. The town also holds and annual Pysanka Festival celebrating Ukrainian culture.

The exact history of the pysanka is not known but one theory is that Ukrainian pagans invented the object to use in rituals to worship the sun. The pagans are thought to have considered the egg as a magical object because the yellow of the egg's yolk symbolized the sun while the albumen represented the moon. Following the Christianization of Ukraine in 988, the egg was embraced as a Christian religious symbol during Easter celebrations. Moreover, the designs of the pysanky began to be regarded as holding Christian significance with traditional pysanka decorations seen as symbolizing hope after the death of Christ and the promise of life eternal. To this end, the traditional sun symbol came to mean the Son of God, triangles symbolized the Holy Trinity, stars denoted God's love of humanity, dots stood for the tears of the Virgin Mary as her son was crucified, and the cross motif represented Christ's suffering during the Crucifixion. Newly instituted symbols are also applied to pysanky too. These designs include fish (representing the Christian faith), the number 40 to remind believers of both Christ's 40 days of fasting and the 40 days of Lent, butterflies to symbolize the Resurrection, and churches to remind the faithful to worship.

In Germany, meanwhile, Easter egg trees, *Osterbrunnen*, are erected. The word Osterbrunnen means Easter wells or Easter fountains and reflects the fact that in the Franconia region of Germany Osterbrunnen sees trees decorated with Easter eggs placed in locations served by public wells. (*See* Plate 5.) Osterbrunnen is a very old custom designed to celebrate the essential role of water as a giver of life at a time when the death of Christ is being recalled. In order for Osterbrunnen to take place every year women collect eggs, hollow them out, decorate them, and then string the eggs together to fashion colorful garlands that are used to decorate the village wells and fountains. The eggs are placed around the fountains one week before Easter Sunday and stay up until one week after Easter.

See also: Christian Death Rituals; Saturday of Souls and *Radonitsa*

Further Reading
Black, Vicki K. *Welcome to the Church Year: An Introduction to the Seasons of the Episcopal Church*. Harrisburg, PA: Morehouse Publishing, 2004.
Dues, Greg. *Catholic Customs & Traditions: A Popular Guide*. Revised and updated. New London, CT: Twenty-Third Publications, 2006.
Jones, Alison. *Larousse Dictionary of World Folklore*. Edinburgh, UK: Larousse, 1996.
Journey to Germany. "Easter in Germany." Accessed December 12, 2015, at http://www.journey-to-germany.com/easter-in-germany.html.
Nowak, Zachary. "Poland," in Lucy M. Long, ed., *Ethnic American Food Today: A Cultural Encyclopedia*. Lanham, MD: Rowman & Littlefield, 2015, 507–512.
Ukrainian American Society of Texas. "Pysanky." Accessed December 12, 2015, at http://www.uast.org/Pysanka.htm.

EATING THE ASHES OF THE DEAD, BRAZIL AND VENEZUELA

Eating the ashes of the dead is a form of endocannibalism and those who eat human ashes are technically known as endocannibalistic anthropophagers. Though eating ashes occurs in individual instances around the world, eating ashes is a funeral custom of the Yanomani people who live in the Amazon rainforest on the border of Brazil and Venezuela. Children's corpses produce less bone ash when burned than do the bodies of adults, and it is usual for the ashes of children to be eaten by their parents. Adults produce more bone ash and so the ash eating ceremony to mark the passing of an adult is suitably more extravagant. The Yanomani eat the ashes of their dead in order to cut all ties between the deceased and the physical realm, as they believe this means the dead's spiritual energy will leave the living unmolested. In this way, eating the ashes of the dead allows the Yanomani to free the dead from the energy that holds the dead in the physical world.

According to Yanomani folklore, the funeral custom of eating ashes originated when a tribesman called Poreími ate the ashes of his dead son as part of a soup of pareamu plantain, a very large variety of the fruit. A group of strangers visited Poreími and as they were leaving he instructed them to eat their dead too despite the fact that at this point in time it was usual for the Yanomani to bury their dead. As Poreími was known to be a particularly clever tribesman, the Yanomani have eaten the ashes of their dead ever since.

Today, the dead of the Yanomani are cremated in a ritual that is supposed to remove the deceased's living essence allowing the spirit of the dead to enter an eternal rest. To cremate the corpse, the Yanomani carry the body to a village clearing and place it on a pile of firewood with more firewood piled up around the corpse and on top of it too in order to ensure that it burns well. Children and ill members of the tribe are ordered out of the village in case they are contaminated by smoke billowing form the cremation. Similarly, after the burning the villagers will wash their weapons in case these too have become infected by smoke. A villager is charged with making sure the corpse is entirely incinerated and when the ashes have cooled sufficiently the villagers sift through them gathering together every piece of residual bone that are then placed in a hollowed-out log. The Yanomani believe that the vital power of the dead resides in the bones so a week after cremation residual bones are ground to a fine, soft powder by a close male kinsman or friend of the deceased who uses a five-foot-long pole as a pestle. This resultant powder is poured into a leaf and then from the leaf into gourds. The ashy dust that remains in the log is added to a plantain soup that is drunk by the tribe. As they drink the soup, the tribe members wail, claw at their hair with their hands, and cry. Once the soup is finished the log is burned. The ash contained in the gourds is reserved for use in a feast at a later date, possibly when a kinsman from a far off village visits. During such a visit an elaborate ceremony takes place in which the ashes are added to gourds filled with plantain soup that are passed among kinsfolk while spectators sob and mourn loudly.

The ashes of Yanomani men who die at the hands of enemy raiders receive special attention. Village women drink the ashes of warriors killed in this way on the eve of a revenge attack on the rival village. This means that the ashes of the dead warriors may be held in their home village for many years, or at least as long as it takes for their kinsfolk to feel that their deaths have been avenged. Indeed it has been known for a warrior's ashes to be kept in the roof of his brother's house for 10 years during which time his village had raided the opposing village and killed many opposing tribesmen in revenge for the warrior's death. Another circumstance demanding special measures is in cases of large-scale deaths such as after an epidemic of illness. In this case, corpses are taken into the rainforest and placed in trees having been enveloped in bark. Once the bodies have rotted any flesh clinging to the bones is scraped off and the bones incinerated, stored and then consumed in soup.

The Yanomani also cremate beloved pets, particularly prized hunting dogs. However the tribe does not eat the ashes of animals but rather buries them. Non-hunting dogs are treated less respectfully—ordinary dogs are abandoned in the forest, sometimes before they are dead.

The eating of human ashes is not, however, practiced exclusively by the peoples of the Amazon rainforest. In 19th-century Romania, eating the ashes of those suspected of being vampires was a well-known remedy for vampire attacks. Reports from Amarasti tell of an old peasant woman suspected after her death of becoming a vampire. In order to try and stop the woman's supposed vampiric activity, her sons exhumed her body and found that it had not decayed. The sons took this as proof of their mother's vampirism so they disemboweled her and cut out her heart. The sons then incinerated the heart and mixed the ashes of the heart with water that they fed to the rest of the children in their village in order to protect them from future vampire attacks. In another case, a man from Cusmir was suspected of vampirism so his body was exhumed and his organs removed and cremated. The man's ashes were mixed with water and fed to his relations, all of whom suffered from withered legs, as a way of countering the man's suspected vampirism, which they believed was the reason for their lameness. Having ingested the man's ashes, all his relations are said to have recovered. Similarly, another old man from Cusmir was suspected of being a vampire so he was exhumed, his corpse mutilated, and his liver and heart burned. The resultant ashes were mixed with water and consumed by sick members of the village, all of whom recovered to full health. A similar practice occurred in New England during the 18th and 19th centuries when a number of corpses were exhumed and cremated. The corpses had their organs burned and the resulting ash was combined with medicine and fed to those suffering from consumption.

More recently, an episode of the TLC television reality show *My Strange Addiction* featured a resident of Fayetteville, Tennessee, called *Casie*, who found eating the ashes of her dead husband to be a comfort to her after his death. At first *Casie* carried her husband's ashes everywhere with her but then one day when some ash accidently spilled on to her hand she licked it off and has been addicted to ingesting the ashes ever since. As of 2011, Casie had eaten one pound of her husband's ashes and had about five more to go, describing the taste as a combination of sandpaper, sand, and rotten eggs. Apart from an unpalatable taste, eating cremated remains is dangerous as the ash contains a cocktail of chemicals from the embalming fluid that can cause psychosis if ingested.

See also: Cremation; Endocannibalism

Further Reading

Chagnon, Napoleon A. *Yanomano.* Sixth edition, "The Legacy Edition." Belmont, CA: Wadsworth, Cengage Learning, 2013.

Galvan, Javier A., ed. *They Do What? A Cultural Encyclopedia of Extraordinary and Exotic Customs from around the World.* Santa Barbara, CA: ABC-CLIO, 2014.

Guiley, Rosemary Ellen. *The Encyclopedia of Vampires, Werewolves, and Other Monsters.* New York: Visionary Living, Inc., 2005.

Maddicks, Russell. "Yanomami: The Origin of Eating the Dead." Venezuelan Indians, August 19, 2007. Accessed December 9, 2014, at http://venezuelanindian.blogspot.co.uk/2007/08/yanomami-myth-2-origin-of-eating-dead.html.

Moye, David. "Widow Says Eating Dead Husband's Ashes Helps Her Cope (VIDEO)," *Huffington Post*, August 8, 2011. Accessed December 9, 2014, at http://www.huffingtonpost.com/2011/08/08/eating-husbands-ashes-helps-grieving-wife-mourn-his-death_n_921416.html.

EDIR, ETHIOPIA, AND *ENGOZI*, UGANDA

Edir, also spelled *eddir* or *iddir*, is a traditional Ethiopian burial society that can be based in a neighborhood, at a site of employment, or work along generational or gender lines. Members of the society make voluntary monthly contributions to the society's fund and in return receive payments that help to cover burial costs. It has been estimated that every Ethiopian village has an edir and that virtually every Ethiopian is a member of such a society. Edirs also exist where Ethiopian immigrants have settled—for example, Dallas, Texas, which is home to the Dallas Ethiopian Community Edir.

The ubiquity of edir societies throughout Ethiopia has resulted in some people thinking that the societies are ancient organizations built upon the basis of cooperation that exists among traditional Ethiopian rural communities. Indeed many aspects of traditional Ethiopian death customs require cooperation including preparing and transporting corpses, digging graves, cooking funerary foods, and caring for the bereaved. However it has also been argued that the edir system actually developed at the start of the 20th century in the Ethiopian capital city Addis Abbaba with Lukanda Tra, which dates back to at least 1916, being the oldest edir in Ethiopia. The edir system spread throughout Ethiopia during the Italian invasion of Ethiopia, spreading to other cities and then to the countryside during the late 20th century and early 21st century.

In the past, some Ethiopians have voiced their disapproval that edirs only paid out when someone that had contributed to the society died rather than help them financially when they were ill. In recent years, however, the nature of some edirs has changed somewhat for until recently, most edirs focused exclusively on providing for member's funeral costs. While this is still the case with many edirs, especially those in Ethiopia, some societies now also help to pay for medical treatment and home assistance. This is mainly because a number of edir members have become disturbed at the number of Ethiopians suffering from AIDS and the toll the disease was taking on edir members and their children, many of whom have been left orphaned by the illness. In order to help members stricken with HIV/AIDS, some edirs now also help with the cost of drugs including retroviral drugs for people suffering from HIV/AIDS. Indeed Ethiopian academics and international non-governmental organizations (NGOs) believe the continuance of the edir system is essential in the fight to tackle the AIDS epidemic in Ethiopia because edirs are grassroots organizations to which poor villagers will turn for advice and assistance. Many edirs have also become the center of a network of related associations aiming to raise funds for sick people and helping to facilitate the work of NGOs.

Though some academics assert that the concept of the edir is uniquely Ethiopian, parallel societies exist elsewhere in Africa—for example, the *engozi* organizations of the Bushenyi, Kabale, Kisoro, and Rukungir districts of southwestern Uganda. Engozi groups usually are comprised of between 10 and 50 families with members linked either by belonging to the same clan or through living in the same neighborhood. For the past 100 years, engozi have acted as a traditional health insurance system to which able-bodies adults are obliged to belong or face fines or imprisonment. Engozi are important as they provide care for people that are sick or incapable of supporting themselves, as well as the families of members. Engozi also help the families of pregnant and breastfeeding women and elderly people in need of help, as well as helping to cover the cost of burial ceremonies for members. Engozi members subsidize health care for individuals that do not have sufficient savings to pay for their own medical requirements and also provide transport for patients to and from hospital plus the provision of traditional healers. Members also decide which individuals should look after patient's children or infirm relatives and who should tend a patient's crops.

The engozi system guarantees members sufficient health care, food, and support to maintain their dignity when they are in difficulty. This is extremely important in Bushenyi and Rukungiri districts where malaria and HIV/AIDS are rife. In these areas, public healthcare facilities, however inadequate, do exist but this healthcare provision has led to many engozis being disbanded or being reduced to groups called *twezikye* that help to cover burial costs. However in places where public-health facilities are almost totally absent, such as in Kabale and Kisoro districts, the engozi system continues to thrive.

Also similar to the edir scheme are the village levy schemes found in rural Guinea Bissau that take the form of collective public funds that villagers use to pay for funerals and other public ceremonies as well as the short-lived funeral insurance schemes that flourished briefly in Tanzania. In Democratic Republic of Congo (formerly Zaire), there have been attempts to build community healthcare services from grassroots communal organizations that echo to a degree the health-provider element of the edir system.

See also: Pauper's Funeral

Further Reading

Dallas Ethiopian Community EDIR. "Home." Edirdfw.org. Accessed May 10, 2015, at http://www.edirdfw.org/.

Katabarwa, Moses. "Modern Health Services versus Traditional *Engozi* System in Uganda," *The Lancet,* 354(9175), July 24, 1999, 343. Accessed May 10, 2015, at http://www.thelancet.com/journals/lancet/article/PIIS0140-6736(05)75256-9/fulltext.

Nazret.com. "Ethiopia: 'Edirs' for the Living as Well as the Dead." November 22, 2006. Accessed May 10, 2015, at http://nazret.com/blog/index.php/2006/11/22/ethiopia_edirs_for_the_living_as_well_as.

Pankhurst, Alula. "The Emergence, Evolution and Transformations of Iddir Funeral Associations in Urban Ethiopia," *Journal of Ethiopian Studies, Special Thematic Issue on Contemporary Urban Dynamics,* 41(1/2), June-December 2008, 143–185.

ELEANOR CROSSES, ENGLAND

The Eleanor Crosses are a series of 12 imposing ornately decorated stone mortuary monuments topped by magnificent crucifixes that can be seen in various towns throughout eastern England, including in London, the English capital city.

The Eleanor Crosses were erected on the orders of King Edward I between 1291 and 1294 in memory of the king's beloved wife and mother of his 14 children, Eleanor of Castile. The queen died in the village of Harby in Nottinghamshire and the places where her embalmed corpse rested on its journey southward to Westminster Abbey in London are marked by the crosses known as the Eleanor Crosses. The purpose of the crosses was to remind passersby to pray for Eleanor's soul. The crosses were created by a number of sculptors most of whom were closely allied to the building of royal palaces in Britain. The most famous Eleanor Cross is that which gave Charing Cross in central London its name. Indeed it has been theorized that the name Charing may be a corruption of the French *Chere Reine*, meaning dear or beloved queen.

Edward I was grief stricken when he learned that Eleanor had died on her way to join him in Scotland, having taken ill on the journey and died in Nottinghamshire. On hearing of Eleanor's death, the devasted king rushed back to the south of England to make arrangements for her funeral, which was to take place in Westminster, London. Eleanor's body had to be transported back to London in stages, at each of which Edward arranged for a beautiful memorial cross to be built. Twelve Eleanor Crosses were built in total at Lincoln, Grantham, Stamford, Geddington, Northampton, Stony Stratford, Woburn, Dunstable, St. Albans, Waltham, Cheapside, and Charing. Charing was at this time a village near Westminster and its part in the story of Eleanor is commemorated by the fact that the area is now known as Charing Cross. Today, however, only the Eleanor Crosses at Geddington, Hardingstone, and Waltham Cross still remain for many of the crosses were destroyed by the forces of the English military and political leader Oliver Cromwell in the 17th century. The Eleanor Cross at Geddington is, in the main, an original Eleanor Cross and is maintained by the charity English Heritage. Despite the fact the Eleanor Cross that stands in the forecourt of London's busy railway station Charing Cross is probably the Eleanor Cross that sees the most passersby, it is nonetheless a Victorian reproduction of the Eleanor Cross that stood originally at Westminster.

When Eleanor's body finally arrived in London, the king ordered that two wax candles should burn for all eternity next to her tomb in Westminster Abbey. The king's wish was fulfilled for candles burned next to Eleanor's tomb for 250 years before the tradition ended during the Reformation. Today Eleanor's gilt bronze tomb in Westminster Abbey is seen by thousands of tourists each year though the queen's internal organs (except her heart) are actually buried in Lincoln Cathedral since the queen died at a time when embalming meant that a corpse's viscera were separated from the body. The queen's heart meanwhile was buried at the Dominican priory in Blackfriar's, London, together with the remains of her son, Alphonso, though the statue marking the location of the queen's heart was destroyed during the Dissolution of the Monasteries in the 16th century.

Although the overwhelming reason for the erection of the Eleanor Crosses was Edward I's love for his wife, it has been suggested by architectural historians that the king may also have wished to emulate the French tradition of the *montjoie*, by which is meant a small, free-standing stone memorial that was part of a series of either seven or nine such monuments. French king Philip III erected the montjoie along the route taken by the corpse of King Louis IX on its way to Saint-Denis Abbey, located in the north of the French capital city, Paris. The montjoie were erected between 1271 and 1285 so may well have influenced Edward I. Unlike the Eleanor Crosses, no trace of the French montjoie exist today.

See also: Embalming; Sakalava Royal Death Traditions and *Fitampoha*; Spontaneous Shrines; Tomb of the Unknown Soldier; Tombstone Tourism

Further Reading

Alexander, Marc. *The Sutton Companion to British Folklore, Myths and Legends*. Stroud, UK: Sutton Publishing, 2005.
Eliot, Sara. "The Eleanor Crosses: A Love Story in Stone." TimeTravelBritain.com. Accessed December 14, 2015, at http://www.timetravel-britain.com/articles/history/eleanor.shtml.
Historic England. "Geddington Cross: Eleanor Cross and Conduit House." Accessed December 14, 2015, at https://historicengland.org.uk/listing/the-list/list-entry/1013313.
Hourihane, Colum, ed. *The Grove Encyclopedia of Medieval Art and Architecture, Volume 1: Aachen to Cecco di Pietro*. Oxford, UK: Oxford University Press, 2012.
Johnson, Ben. "The Eleanor Crosses," Historic UK. Accessed December 14, 2015, at http://www.historic-uk.com/HistoryMagazine/DestinationsUK/The-Eleanor-Crosses/.

EMBALMING, UNITED STATES

Embalming is the use of chemicals to preserve human remains and prevent decomposition either for a short time or over longer periods. Embalming is most prevalent in the United States, Canada, the United Kingdom, and Australia, where the embalming process is used to delay the decomposition of a dead body for around one week following a death. Embalming is an expected funeral custom in North America but the practice attracts criticism on a variety of grounds.

The history of embalming dates back to the ancient Egyptians who began to embalm their dead around 3200 BCE and continued to do so for around 4,000 years. The ancient Egyptians performed embalming in order to preserve corpses so that they could be reincarnated. Although the method of embalming performed in ancient Egypt varied depending on the social status of the person whose corpse was to be preserved, in general the embalming technique of ancient Egypt involved eviscerating (i.e., skinning) the corpse and treating the body to a bath in a sodium salt—the internal organs were preserved separately. In ancient Greece, bodies were preserved through the application of spices and perfume—though according to the poet Homer in the *Iliad*, Thetis the sea-nymph preserved the corpse of Patroclus through an injection of nectar and ambrosia, the drink and foods of the gods, up his nostrils. Ancient Scythians also practices embalming. The Scythians would disembowel their kings, fill the empty body cavity with a variety of spices and herbs, and then cover the corpse with wax. Bodies of Agesipolis, the king of Sparta, and Emperor Justin II were embalmed in honey and the body of Alexander the Great was preserved in a mixture of honey and wax so that it could be transported back to Memphis, Egypt, where it was later displayed in a coffin made of glass.

The next significant period in the development of the embalming process came during the Middle Ages through to the U.S. Civil War, an era that saw embalming used as a way to preserve the corpses of important people as well as to prevent decomposition in bodies needed for medical research. The embalming process of this era moved the process away from evisceration and toward the method known as arterial embalming. The development of arterial embalming came about mainly through advances in medical knowledge as the process involves the use of many different types of chemicals—in the 1600s, oil of turpentine and camphorated spirits of wine were used but these were replaced with bichloride of mercury, heavy metal salts, zinc chloride, and compounds of arsenic during the mid-19th century. The increased use of these chemicals meant that the practice of eviscerating the corpse prior to its embalming became fairly rare. Moreover, during the 1700s the development of arterial embalming meant that barber-surgeons were the main practitioners of the technique. During the U.S. Civil War embalming was used to preserve corpses for a short while before they were transported home, with embalming surgeons such as Richard Burr and Thomas Holmes embalming many thousands of dead soldiers by injecting their corpses with solutions applied via gravity fluid injectors. The embalming of U.S. President Abraham Lincoln following his assassination in 1865 further enhanced the popularity of embalming as a method of corpse preservation.

Before the Civil War, embalming was not commonplace as it was the norm for corpses to be contained in coffins. After the war, however, embalming became much more frequent partly through the invention of new machines, the creation of embalmers' associations, and widespread training for would-be embalmers. One of the biggest influences on the increased frequency of embalming was the discovery of formaldehyde during the 1880s. Then, in the 1890s, a 4 percent solution of formaldehyde was invented and remained the most popular embalming fluid for over 100 years replacing highly toxic chemicals such as mercury and arsenic. Another major factor in the development of embalming was the patenting of the trocar for cavity aspiration in 1878. This invention meant that there was no need to eviscerate corpses for embalming and during the 1880s there was much rivalry between embalmers that practiced cavity embalming and those that preformed arterial embalming. Despite the rivalry between practitioners most undertakers used both methods. Another reason that embalming became prevalent in the United States is that the funeral industry became properly organized and training for funeral practitioners became more frequent. For instance, in 1882 the National Funeral Directors Association was founded in the United States with industry publications *The Casket* and *The Sunnyside* having been established a few years earlier as was a textbook on embalming, "The Undertaker's Manual" by Dr. Auguste Renouard, which was published in 1878. Renouard would later go on to open the Rochester School Embalming in 1882.

Then, during the 1880s schools of embalming were established with the first founded in Cincinnati, Ohio, in 1882. In the decades following the Civil War, companies that manufactured funeral products were established too, including the Dodge Chemical Company and the Frigid Fluid Company that produced embalming fluids. Such companies were deeply involved in the nascent American funeral industry. For example, the Dodge family behind the Dodge Chemical Company established and ran the Massachusetts College of Embalming. It was not however until the 1890s that embalming was applied to the pubic in general as opposed to members of the military. When members of the public were embalmed, the corpse was embalmed in the deceased's parlor by an embalmer using a gravity fluid injector and a cooling board. Once it was prepared the corpse would be displayed in the parlor. This tradition gradually died out during the 1950s so that it became usual for an embalmed body to be displayed at a funeral home rather than at the home of the deceased. The exact reason for this is not known but probably owed

Jeremy Bentham's Head

People visiting the South Cloisters at University College London are often surprised to find a wooden cabinet containing the skeletal remains of 19th-century reformer Jeremy Bentham, who declared in his will that his skeleton should be preserved wearing his everyday clothes and sitting on his preferred chair. Moreover, Bentham decreed that his embalmed head be placed atop his skeleton. It is frequently claimed (erroneously) that Bentham's remains are brought to College Council meetings on the minutes of which he is noted as present but not voting. Bentham's head has been stolen by students from rival universities twice and also used as a ball in a soccer match.

something to a decrease in the size of family homes and the increased habitation of tenement buildings.

There is disagreement over why some corpses are embalmed. Many embalmers argue that the process is performed as a method of disinfection that safeguards pubic health. However critics of embalming point out that the process uses many highly toxic chemicals such as formaldehyde that pose a greater hazard to public health than leaving corpses to rot naturally. In an attempt to combat this criticism in recent years some embalmers have tried using other chemicals such as phenoxyethanol and glutaraldehyde, but these chemicals have not proved as effective as formaldehyde. Another reason for embalming seems to be an effort to delay decomposition so that the bereaved can see their deceased loved one for a final time looking attractive. This desired appealing corpse has been dubbed a Beautiful Memory Picture by the funeral industry and is achieved by hydrating body tissues, fixing facial features, applying make-up, and sometimes reconstructing parts of the corpse so that the deceased looks as they did before death. In short, embalming allows a corpse to look as though it were asleep rather than dead. This illusion is fortified by the laying of the corpse on a bed, albeit in a casket, with a mattress and pillow. That embalming allows the deceased to appear to be sleeping rather than dead has fuelled criticism of the practice as critics argue that embalming contributes to the denial of death and over-emphasis on physical good looks that they feel are too widespread in North America.

See also: Mummification; Ossuaries; Plastination; Shrunken Heads; Taxidermy

Further Reading

Bryant, Clifton D., and Dennis L. Peck, eds. *Encyclopedia of Death and the Human Experience 1*. Thousand Oaks, CA: SAGE Publications Inc., 2009.

Clarke, M. J., B. G. F Currie, and R. O. A. M. Lyne, eds. *Epic Interactions: Perspectives on Homer, Virgil, and the Epic Tradition Presented to Jasper Griffin by Former Pupils*. Oxford, UK: Oxford University Press, 2006.

Gow-McDilda, Diane. *The Everything Green Living Book: Easy Ways to Conserve Energy, Protect Your Family's Health, and Help Save the Environment*. Avon, MA: Adams Media, 2007.

Powell, Josephine Price. *Working with the Dead*. Lincoln, NE: iUniverse Inc., 2004.

Quigley, Christine. *The Corpse: A History*. Jefferson, NC: McFarland & Company Inc. Publishers, 1996.

ENDOCANNIBALISM, PAPUA NEW GUINEA AND BRAZIL

Endocannibalism—also referred to as love cannibalism, unification cannibalism, or affectionate cannibalism—is a funeral custom in which the dead are eaten by their close friends and relatives. The relatives and friends of the deceased see this as a way of preserving the essence of the dead by containing their dead flesh within their own living bodies. This is apt for the prefix "endo" means "inside" in Greek.

Some anthropologists consider endocannibalism to be a form of ancestor worship for endocannibals do not simply venerate the dead but actually are partly made up of their ancestors. It is important to note that endocannibalism is a consensual process. The dying know that they will be eaten after death and are pleased that this is the case.

The modern world usually associates cannibalism with fictional killers such as Thomas Harris's anti-hero Hannibal Lecter, or with desperation brought on by extreme circumstance (e.g., the Donner Party or the 1972 Andes flight disaster). Alternatively cannibalism may be associated with acts of savagery such as those perpetrated by Matthew Williams who, in Wales in November 2014, was killed by police having eaten the face and eyeballs of a woman he had met hours earlier or serial killer Jeffrey Dahmer, dubbed the Milwaukee Cannibal. In contrast to random acts of cannibalism, endocannibalism is a very old cultural tradition that practitioners see as both a way of handling grief at the death of a loved one and as a way for a loved one's good characteristics to be passed on and their life force and wisdom to be absorbed by the living. Endocannibalism also reflects fears of the afterlife found in some cultures.

There is evidence of endocannibalism being practiced at various locations around the world throughout history. For example, the ancient Greek historian Herodatus noted that in India the Callatiae tribe ate their dead parents. This is in contrast to modern members of the Aghoris sect living in northern India who eat the bodies of people not known to them.

A form of endocannibalism called Ko Ku and Ko Kan developed in China during the seventh to tenth centuries. This saw children, or more usually sons and daughters-in-law, either extract their own organs, particularly their liver or gall bladder, or slice the flesh off their limbs. The donors would then give the flesh to their ailing elders who in turn cooked the flesh as an ingredient in a supposedly health-giving soup. A case of this medical cannibalism was recorded in China as late as 1987, though by this time the practice was not socially acceptable.

During the 16th century explorer Alvar Nunez Cabeza de Vaca noted endocannibalism among the Karankawas people living on the coast of Texas. However endocannibalism is most often associated with the Fore people of Papua New Guinea and certain tribes living along the Amazon. The Fore practiced cannibalistic funeral rites for many generations and focused particularly on the importance of women and children consuming the flesh of dead males. Those who practiced endocannibalism had to follow certain protocol. For the Fore, endocannibalism represented a way of displaying both grief and affection for the dead for eating the flesh of the dead meant that their very essence continued to exist, a postmortem fate that the Fore considered both comforting and compassionate, since this would allow the dead to live on. To the Fore way of thinking, burying the dead meant that the deceased were consigned to oblivion underground as their body and soul decomposed rather than continuing on within the bodies of the living.

When a member of the Fore tribe died, women would prepare the corpse for consumption. To this end, the corpse was dissected and larger bones cracked open to reveal the marrow. The skull was also cracked open to display the brain. Women and children would eat the majority of the corpse with the brain and spinal cord deemed special. Certain body parts were reserved for women depending on their relationship to the dead. For instance a woman would eat her brother's brain or her brother-in-law's hands with each body part symbolizing a different attribute the consumer would inherit. The Fore reserved reproductive organs for close relatives of the opposite sex. In contrast to women and children who were expected to eat the most flesh, Fore men only had to eat a little flesh. Between them, men, women, and children would consume an entire corpse except for its teeth, bile sack, and other body parts they considered inedible. Remaining body parts (e.g, bone fragments) were burned as the finale to a ritual feast and the resultant calcium-rich dust was sprinkled on food and eaten.

Endocannibalism was banned among the Fore during the 1960s but instances of the custom are still believed to occur. The ban came about after it was discovered that the practice of endocannibalism had given rise to a fatal neurological disease known as *kuru*, meaning shaking or trembling, by the Fore people. Researchers noticed that incidences of kuru, a transmissible spongiform encephalopathy similar to scrapie and Creutzfeldt-Jakob disease (CJD), were highest among women, children, and elderly men—those who were most likely to participate in Fore endocannibalism—and soon realized that the ritual consumption of human flesh as part of the tribe's endocannibal funeral rites were to blame. American neurologist Daniel Carleton Gajdusek won the Nobel Prize for his work on kuru, which included the discovery that kuru had an exceptionally long incubation period of up to 23 years. After the ban on endocannibalism came into force no new cases of kuru were reported. Later research found that kuru was caused by misfolded prions rather than slow viruses. The Fore had become infected because during their funneral rites the tribe cooked the brains of the dead in bamboo containers at temperatures no higher than 95°C. Such temperatures were insufficient to kill the prions leading to tribespeople becoming infected.

Another Papua New Guinean tribe that practices endocannibalism is the Korowai. The Korowai believe that mysterious deaths are caused by witchcraft and when a member of the tribe becomes ill they believe the culprit is a male witch called a *khakhua* who lives clandestinely among the tribe eating away at his victim's innards. The Korowai think that the witch's victim will reveal the name of his or her killer at the point of death and when a person does name the person supposedly responsible for their demise the victim's family kills the witch and eats them in an act of revenge. The Korowai do not consider this to be cannibalism, as they do not view the khakhua as human. However since the khakhua is a member of their own tribe, eating them counts as endocannibalism.

Various tribes living in the Amazon region of Brazil also have a culture of practicing endocannibalism. Until about 1960, the Wari people, of whom there are around 1,500 living in western Brazil close to the country's border with Bolivia, usually ate their dead (a very few corpses were cremated). Indeed all Wari tribal elders living today will either have witnessed or practiced endocannibalism. Unlike other endocannibals, the Wari did not eat select body parts but rather consumed all of the roasted flesh, heart, liver, and bones, and sometimes the ground bones. However the Wari do not eat their close relatives but ask others to eat them on their behalf. This is because the Wari believe that consuming bodily fluids connected people as one individual. Thus to the Wari eating family members would equate to eating themselves, a concept which was anathema to them. To circumvent this problem, the Wari would invite family members from outside the immediate vicinity to gather together and burn the deceased's possessions. As this process usually took some time, the deceased's corpse would often start to rot. The Wari would then cook and eat this decomposing flesh. After the body was eaten, any remaining traces of the corpse were burned along with the tools used to prepare the flesh. This is because in the Wari's belief system the destruction of worldly possessions and the act of endocannibalism let the deceased's soul accept that the physical body has died and proceeded on to the afterlife. According to anthropologists, eating the dead also meant that the Wari could detach themselves from memories of the deceased, altering their perceptions of them and allowing a degree of emotional closure free from grief.

Ritualistic endocannibalism features in a Season 2 episode of the cult American television series *The X-Files*, "Our Town," in which FBI agents Mulder and Scully are called into an Arkansas town after townsfolk start acting bizarrely and the murder rate increases. It soon transpires that a town elder has introduced Papua New Guinean endocannibalism to the town and the townsfolk are suffering from Creutzfeldt–Jakob disease brought on by consuming a town resident suffering from the illness. The episode also features decapitated heads with their lips sewn shut in preparation for shrinking and a tribal mask very similar to that worn during Papua New Guinean malagan ceremonies.

See also: Eating Ashes of the Dead; *Malagan*; Shrunken Heads

Further Reading

Galvan, Javier A., ed. *They Do What? A Cultural Encyclopedia of Extraordinary and Exotic Customs from around the World*. Santa Barbara, CA: ABC-CLIO, 2014.

MacClancy, Jeremy, Jeya Henry, and Helen Macbeth, eds. *Consuming the Inedible: Neglected Dimensions of Food Choice*. New York: Berghahn Books, 2007.

NGC Europe Limited. "Facts About Cannibalism." National Geographic Channel. Accessed December 8, 2014, at http://www.natgeotv.com/se/search-for-the-cannibals-of-the-south-pacific/facts-about-cannibalism.

"Our Town," *The X-Files*. Season 2. First broadcast May, 12 1995. DVD (2001).

Robben, Antonius CGM. ed. *Death, Mourning, and Burial: A Cross-Cultural Reader*. Malden, MA: Blackwell Publishing, 2004.

Ryan, Katie. "The Little Known Ritual of Endocannibalism." Seven Ponds, June 6, 2013. Accessed December 8, 2014, at http://blog.sevenponds.com/cultural-perspectives/the-little-known-ritual-of-endocannibalism.

Smith, Andrew F., ed. *The Oxford Encyclopedia of Food and Drink in America, Volume 1.* Second edition. Oxford, UK: Oxford University Press, 2013.

Sugg, Richard. *Mummies, Cannibals and Vampires: The History of Corpse Medicine from the Renaissance to the Victorians.* Abingdon, UK: Routledge, 2011.

EULOGIES, INTERNATIONAL

A eulogy is a form of public address given during a ceremony to honor the dead. The word eulogy stems from the Latin and Greek word *eulogia* that translates as giving of high praise. As a eulogy often recounts tales of the dead person's life to listening mourners, a eulogy forms a connection between the deceased person and the mourners at the ceremony. A eulogy is often an emotional moment within a ceremony that can kick-start the grieving process for mourners. Eulogies are a nearly universal aspect of funeral services and memorials events as they are a way of marking the demise of a beloved person.

Eulogies are an age-old post-death custom. The ancient Greeks gave eulogies at funerals and public burials while public orations about the dead were also an aspect of the funerals held in ancient Rome. Later in medieval Europe eulogies were delivered alongside sermons at Christian funerals. During the Renaissance and the era known as the Enlightenment there was much discussion as to whether eulogies should be considered a religious rite or secular custom. In Judaism, the eulogy, or *hesped*, is a major element of Jewish funerals. Over the centuries in Western Europe, eulogies have, however, come to be seen largely as a way for extolling the virtues of the dead. Indeed modern eulogies are almost totally divested of any religious overtones even when they are part of a Christian funeral service.

Today, eulogies tend to take the form of personal reminiscences and poems and music enjoyed by the deceased. Above all, however, modern eulogies seek to praise the dead and to function as a final spoken farewell to the dead. As the modern world is on the whole more secular than in times past, modern eulogies do not usually suggest that the deceased seeks a place in heaven; rather, modern eulogies suggest that the dead live on in the hearts and minds of the mourners left behind rather than finding eternal rest in the afterlife. As eulogies no longer tend to be religious in nature it is usual for a family member or friend of the deceased to deliver the oration, as they are best placed to offer a personal insight into the life of the recently dead person. By providing amusing or touching anecdotes about the deceased, the person performing the eulogy not only gives thanks for the deceased person's life but may also be able to raise the spirits of the bereaved and create a sense of togetherness among the mourners, thereby temporary relieving some of their grief. Another common feature of eulogies is that the speech can be used to talk about a cause espoused by the deceased or that has some other connection to the occasion. For example, in 1986 U.S. President Ronald Reagan delivered a eulogy following the *Challenger* space shuttle disaster—in which the shuttle broke up over the Atlantic Ocean shortly after takeoff—that extolled the virtues of the NASA space program for which the crew of *Challenger* had died. Similarly, in 2003 U.S. President George W. Bush gave a comparable eulogy after the *Columbia* space shuttle disaster.

Another function of eulogies is to alter the mood of mourners and get them to adopt an alternative, positive, outlook. In short, eulogies may encourage mourners to look on the bright side of life by looking back on their times spent with the deceased and take solace in having known them. This was the case at the memorial service held in honor of boxing legend Muhammad Ali in June 2016 that featured eulogies from many speakers including actor/comedian Billy Crystal and former U.S. president Bill Clinton.

See also: Christian Death Rituals; Funeral Songs; Jewish Death Customs; President Reagan's Address to the Nation following the *Challenger* Shuttle Disaster, 1986; Tomb of the Unknown Soldier

Further Reading

Brennan, Michael, ed. *The A–Z of Death and Dying: Social, Medical, and Cultural Aspects.* Santa Barbara, CA: ABC-CLIO, 2014.

Bryant, Clifton D., and Dennis L. Peck, eds. *Encyclopedia of Death and the Human Experience* 1. Thousand Oaks, CA: SAGE Publications Inc, 2009.

Garber, Steve. "Explosion of the Space Shuttle *Challenger* Address to the Nation, January 28, 1986, by President Ronald W. Reagan." National Aeronautics and Space Administration: NASA History Office, June 7, 2004. Accessed October 23, 2015, at http://history.nasa.gov/reagan12886.html.

Related Primary Document: President Reagan's Address to the Nation Following the *Challenger* Shuttle Disaster, 1986

The Space Shuttle Challenger *was the second orbiter of NASA's space shuttle program to be put into service.* Challenger's *maiden flight began on April 4, 1983, and the orbiter launched and landed many times before the so-called* Challenger *shuttle disaster. On January 28, 1986, the shuttle broke apart 73 seconds into its 10th mission. This resulted in the death of all seven crewmembers aboard the shuttle, including a schoolteacher (Sharon) Christa McAuliffe, who had beaten 11,000 other applicants to become the first civilian in space.*

The Challenger *disaster led to the NASA shuttle fleet being grounded for more than two years. In response to the disaster, which was seen live on television by millions of people around the world, then-president Ronald Reagan addressed the nation via television and radio with what many commentators consider to be his finest speech. The address stressed the bravery and pioneering sprit of those people that died in the disaster while also acknowledging that they would be remembered by people in the future. The last lines of the address used quotes from a poem called "High Flight," which was written* by 19-year-old American John Gillespie Magee, a wartime Spitfire pilot with the Royal Canadian Air Force, who died in 1941 when his plane collided in mid-air over Lincolnshire, England.

The following is the transcript of President Reagan's Address to the Nation in the wake of the Challenger disaster.

Explosion of the Space Shuttle *Challenger* Address to the Nation, January 28, 1986

by President Ronald W. Reagan

Ladies and gentlemen, I'd planned to speak to you tonight to report on the state of the Union, but the events of earlier today have led me to change those plans. Today is a day for mourning and remembering.

Nancy and I are pained to the core by the tragedy of the shuttle *Challenger*. We know we share this pain with all of the people of our country. This is truly a national loss.

Nineteen years ago, almost to the day, we lost three astronauts in a terrible accident on the ground. But we've never lost an astronaut in flight; we've never had a tragedy like this. And perhaps we've forgotten the courage it took for the crew of the shuttle; but they, the *Challenger* Seven, were aware of the dangers, but overcame them and did their jobs brilliantly. We mourn seven heroes: Michael Smith, Dick Scobee, Judith Resnik, Ronald McNair, Ellison Onizuka, Gregory Jarvis, and Christa McAuliffe. We mourn their loss as a nation together.

For the families of the seven, we cannot bear, as you do, the full impact of this tragedy. But we feel the loss, and we're thinking about you so very much. Your loved ones were daring and brave, and they had that special grace, that special spirit that says, "Give me a challenge and I'll meet it with joy." They had a hunger to explore the universe and discover its truths. They wished to serve, and they did. They served all of us.

We've grown used to wonders in this century. It's hard to dazzle us. But for 25 years the United States space program has been doing just that. We've grown used to the idea of space, and perhaps we forget that we've only just begun. We're still pioneers. They, the members of the *Challenger* crew, were pioneers.

And I want to say something to the schoolchildren of America who were watching the live coverage of the shuttle's takeoff. I know it is hard to understand, but sometimes painful things like this happen. It's all part of the process of exploration and discovery. It's all part of taking a chance and expanding man's horizons. The future doesn't belong to the fainthearted; it belongs to the brave. The *Challenger* crew was pulling us into the future, and we'll continue to follow them.

I've always had great faith in and respect for our space program, and what happened today does nothing to diminish it. We don't hide our space program. We don't keep secrets and cover things up. We do it all up front and in public. That's the way freedom is, and we wouldn't change it for a minute.

We'll continue our quest in space. There will be more shuttle flights and more shuttle crews and, yes, more volunteers, more civilians, more teachers in space. Nothing ends here; our hopes and our journeys continue.

I want to add that I wish I could talk to every man and woman who works for NASA or who worked on this mission and tell them: "Your dedication and professionalism have moved and impressed us for decades. And we know of your anguish. We share it."

There's a coincidence today. On this day 390 years ago, the great explorer Sir Francis Drake died aboard ship off the coast of Panama. In his lifetime the great frontiers were the oceans, and an historian later said, "He lived by the sea, died on it, and was buried in it." Well, today we can say of the *Challenger* crew: Their dedication was, like Drake's, complete.

The crew of the space shuttle *Challenger* honored us by the manner in which they lived their lives. We will never forget them, nor the last time we saw them, this morning, as they prepared for their journey and waved goodbye and "slipped the surly bonds of earth" to "touch the face of God."

[Note: The President spoke at 5 p.m. from the Oval Office at the White House. His address was broadcast live on nationwide radio and television.]

Source: *President Ronald W. Reagan, Explosion of the Space Shuttle Challenger, Address to the Nation, January 28, 1986. NASA History Office, http://history.nasa.gov/reagan12886.html.*

EYAM PLAGUE SUNDAY SERVICE, ENGLAND

Eyam (pronounced Eem) is a picturesque village in Derbyshire, central England, that is synonymous with self-sacrifice, tragedy, disease, and death. Indeed Eyam is known throughout England as the Plague Village. Every year the village holds a remembrance service called the Eyam Plague Sunday Service to recall the self-sacrifice of the villagers. The Sunday Service is normally held on the last Sunday in August at Cucklett Delf (also written as Cucklett Delph), a natural amphitheater set in a small crag located within a secluded valley.

The story behind the Eyam Plague Sunday Service dates back to August 1665 when, according to the most often cited story, the village tailor received a package from London. Inside the box was fabric that the tailor decided was damp and needed to be dried. In order to dry the fabric the tailor spread out the cloth and in so doing released fleas that had been living in the cloth and also carrying germs of the bubonic plague that was raging in London. The bubonic plague had first arrived in England in 1348 and had recurred regularly. During the outbreak known as the Great Plague there were as many as 7,000 plague deaths per week in London.

Six days after receiving the parcel, the tailor died from the disease and people all round the village were falling ill. By the end of April 1666, many villagers had died from the bubonic plague and those that were still healthy were preparing to leave the village. However the village's young rector William Mompesson suggested that since Eyam was the only village in the county to be infected with the plague it was only right that the village cut itself off from the outside world to prevent the disease from spreading and killing many more people. This meant that villagers that had been ready to leave Eyam would have to stay and nobody was allowed in or out of the village. The villagers agreed to the rector's suggestion and said they would stay within the village until the outbreak had concluded. The rector's wife Catherine was reluctant to stay and only agreed once her husband consented to send the couple's children out of the village for the duration of the outbreak. As a precaution, outsiders left supplies for the village at the village boundary and were paid with coins that were cleaned by being dipped in vinegar. Villagers also agreed not to bury any more bodies in the churchyard and also to close the church as they noticed that the plague seemed to be spread by person-to-person contact. The villagers still wanted a weekly church service and so it was decided that regular Sunday services should take place at Cucklett Delf where family groups could sit together but set apart from other families.

Conditions inside the village were said to be terrible with one mother, a Mrs. Hanncocke, having to bury six of her ten children and her husband close to her home between August 3 and 10, 1666. Today, the seven graves dug by Mrs Hanncocke at Riley Farm are listed on local tourists trails as a point of interest known as the Riley Graves. In the midst of such tragedy the villagers remained resolute however and kept their promise not to leave the village. The rector's wife, Catherine Mompesson, who nursed the sick, also died from the plague and for this reason a floral wreath is placed on her grave every time the Eyam Plague Sunday Service is held. Eventually, after 14 months of misery and sacrifice, the plague outbreak ended and life in Eyam slowly returned to normal. Over the course of the 14 months, 260 villagers had died.

Today, the Eyam Plague Sunday Service sees the church bells ring out at noon when the wreath is laid of the grave of Catherine Mompesson. Then the people attending the service make their way in procession to Cucklett Delf where the service begins at 2:30 p.m. A band and a local choir that wears red robes and sings the hymn "Onward, Christian Soldiers," lead the procession. Once at Cucklett Delf the congregation, which is made up of villagers and tourists, sit upon the hillside as the villagers did during the plague outbreak. During the service costumed villagers act out tableaux depicting the time when the plague raged in the village and the "Eyam Plague Hymn," a special hymn sung only at the Eyam Plague Sunday Service, is sung.

See also: "Abide With Me"; Blidworth Cradle Rocking Ceremony (Volume 1); Grasmere Rushbearing (Volume 1); Maidens' Garlands; Passing Bells; Suicide Landmarks; Tombstone Tourism

Further Reading

Alexander, Marc. *The Sutton Companion to British Folklore, Myths & Legends*. Stroud, UK: Sutton Publishing Limited, 2002.

Beautiful Britain. "Eyam Village and the Great Plague." Accessed October 29, 2015, at http://www.beautifulbritain.co.uk/htm/outandabout/eyam.htm.

Derbyshire Guide. "Eyam—The Plague Village." September 28, 2015. Accessed October 29, 2015, at http://www.derbyshireguide.co.uk/travel/eyam.htm.

Paul, David. *Eyam: Plague Village*. Stroud, UK: Amberley Publishing, 2012.

F

FAMADIHANA, MADAGASCAR

Famadihana, or Turning of the Bones, is a funerary festival that occurs amongst the Merina and Betsileo people (part of the predominate Malagasy ethnic group) living in the Hauts Plateaux area of Madagascar. This funerary customs takes place every six to seven years, though the exact time span varies between tombs. However seven years is considered optimal, as this is deemed long enough after death for feelings of grief to have lessened sufficiently for people to be able to contemplate their dead relatives. By law, Famadihana may only occur in the annual dry season that stretches from June to September.

The exact history of Famadihana is unknown but it is thought that the custom may be related to traditions of South East Asia as it is from here that the first colonizers of Madagascar came. However there is no mention of Famadihana having occurred before the 19th century so it seems that the custom is a fairly recent invention.

Malagasy culture is rooted in the need to respect and honor ancestors, as the tribe believes that the spirit world in which the ancestors reside influences the living and controls the physical universe. Thus it follows that the relics of these dead ancestors should be treated with respect. To this end, the bones of the Malagasy dead are taken from their tomb amid much joyous shouting as people recognize the bones of their parents, grandparents, aunts, and uncles.

Famadihana varies between tombs but in general the night before Famadihana begins the names of all the ancestors taking part in the event are read aloud. Then on the first day of Famadihana the skeletal remains are removed from the tomb by being taken from their straw packing and passed over the heads of the line of ancestors waiting to reclaim their ancestors. This element of the celebrations is led by an astrologer accompanied by men bearing photographs of the dead. A Malagasy flag is also on display during the removal of the remains, the presence of which makes the exhumation legal. The flag is attached to the roof of the tomb and then the tomb is opened, allowing the bones to be removed. Once they have been exhumed the bones are squirted with perfume and re-wrapped in a new, hand-woven silk shroud called a *lambamena* in which the names of the ancestor inside the shroud are written in felt-tip pen. When the bones have been re-wrapped, their living relatives, known as *zanadrazana* meaning children of the ancestors, either carry the bones around the tombs several times and then replace the bones safely in the tomb or take them outside. The tomb contains a shelving system so the order in which the re-wrapped bones are replaced is important with freshly entombed bones placed on the lowest shelf and moved up, shelf by shelf, as additional corpses are entombed. When a family retrieves their ancestral bones from the tomb, they may cradle them in their laps or place the remains in a line so that they may have their photograph taken with the bones. Relatives also speak to the skeletal remains as though the ancestor to whom they belong is still alive, telling the bones of family news and recent events. As the ancestors are treated as though they were still living, it is important that the family that has retrieved them from the tomb does not seem upset in their presence and above all the family must not express any grief. The re-wrapped bones are also sprinkled with rum so that families can show their gratitude for all their ancestors do for them. When the relatives take the bones back to their tomb, it is usual for families to leave offerings called *saodrazana*. These offerings usually take the form of of alcohol and a coin, which is known euphemistically as "thanks to the ancestors." Alongside the drink and coin, families often place a photograph of their ancestor in their prime.

Once all the bones and offerings have been placed in the tomb, the tomb is re-sealed and Famadihana is considered almost over. The gathered relatives drift away until only the astrologer and some attendants perform the *fanidi-pasana*, or lock-to-the-tomb ritual, which sees magical charms buried in and around the entrance to the tomb. This procedure is performed to ensure that the ghosts of the ancestors residing within the tomb stay inside the building and do not cause any trouble for the living.

Family members travel from far and wide to attend Famadihana as the festival offers a chance to communicate with dead ancestors that the Malagasy believe are so influential in their lives. Thus, despite being a festival in honor of the dead, Famadihana is a joyous occasion featuring singing by performers called *razana*, dancing, the playing of accordion music, and the drinking of locally made rum. In addition, women that are trying to become pregnant will take a scrap of cloth from an old shroud and place it beneath their mattress in the belief that this will help them conceive.

Though the actual festival of Famadihana lasts for just two days, the actual duration of the event including preparations lasts about a week. The whole family is involved in both the preparations for Famadihana and the festivities so Famadihana involves a significant amount of expense for families. The festival of Famdihana is celebrated by rural families and city dwellers, rich and poor alike. Visitors and tourists are also allowed to take part in the celebrations and outsiders have reported that the festival is extremely moving.

Though Famadihana is Madagscar's most famous celebration, its future is uncertain. Early Christian missionaries to Madagascar disapproved of Famadihana and tried to stop the custom from taking place. However today the Roman Catholic Church, which has the largest following of any religion in Madagascar, no longer disapproves of the tradition. Even so, many Madagascan Evangelical Christians are shunning Famadihana in ever-increasing numbers.

Other peoples of Madagascar also hold their own versions of Famadihana. For instance, the Menabe Sakalava celebrate *fitampoha*, in which the remains of royal ancestors are honored.

See also: Living with the Dead; Ossuaries; Sakalava Royal Death Traditions and *Fitampoha*

Further Reading
Austin, Daniel, and Hilary Bradt. *Madagascar*. Eleventh edition. Chalfont St. Peter, UK: Bradt Travel Guides Ltd., 2014.
BBC. "Madagascar's Dance with the Dead." BBC News, August 16, 2008. Accessed April 15, 2015, at http://news.bbc.co.uk/1/hi/programmes/from_our_own_correspondent/7562898.stm.
Graeber, David. "Dancing with Corpses Reconsidered: An Interpretation of 'Famadihana' (In Arivonimamo, Madagascar)," *American Ethnologist*, 22(2), May 1995, 258–278.
Lonely Planet. "Famadihana: The Festival of Turning the Bones in Madagascar." July 11, 2013. Accessed April 15, 2015, at http://www.lonelyplanet.com/travel-tips-and-articles/77305.
MTV Tour. "Malagasy Origin." MTV Tour, 2013. Accessed April 10, 2015, at http://madagascar-visit-tours.com/orgin_culture.php.
Vlahides, John. "Turning the Dead" Famidahana in Madagascar." Lonely Planet, November 12, 2009. Accessed April 15, 2015, at http://www.lonelyplanet.com/madagascar/travel-tips-and-articles/16951.

FANTASY COFFINS, GHANA

Fantasy coffins are a unique contemporary funerary custom found in the African nation of Ghana, a country well known for both elaborate funeral traditions and processions, and for producing arts and crafts such as basket weaving, pottery, and woodwork. Fantasy coffins are large-scale wooden depictions of objects sculpted from wood, intricately designed and painted with bright colors. (*See* Plate 6.) These wooden sculptures are carved to represent an object symbolizing an aspect of a recently deceased person's life and the person if then laid to rest in their personalized coffin. For example, a farmer might be buried in a coffin depicting one of Ghana's main crops such as an onion or cocoa pod, while a fisherman might be interred in a coffin resembling a fish or a native wooden fishing vessel known as a *pirogue*. Coffins may also be shaped as animals, including chickens, leopards, bulls, lions, fish, or shellfish—all creatures referred to in the proverbs found in the Akan language, the main native language spoken by people living in southern Ghana. For instance, a mother might be buried in a coffin shaped like a hen, the animal that is proverbially representative of a woman who cares for her children, and a politician or community leader might be interred in a coffin shaped like a leopard. However the most popular fantasy coffin is one shaped like a white Mercedes-Benz car, though Cadillacs are also popular. A Mercedes-Benz coffin might be used to bury a successful businessman and symbolizes wealth and good luck. The Ga people living around Ghana's capital city Accra are responsible for crafting nearly all of the country's fantasy coffins.

There is a long tradition of burying the dead along the length of the Ghanaian coast for the Portuguese colonized the country in the 15th century, trading gold and building fortresses along the coast. The Portuguese were Catholics and became the first Ghanaian residents to bury their dead. Over the centuries, Swiss and German missionaries reinforced Christianity in Ghana as well as introducing new woodworking skills. Today, Ghana is a predominantly Christian country and the only fantasy coffins permitted for Christian burial are those shaped as copies of the Bible. Coffins in the shape of the Bible tend to take the form of a large wooden box in the shape of a leather-bound book with writing on the hinged front cover. Other coffins are forbidden from entering Protestant and Catholic churches in Ghana as both churches feel that fantasy coffins are redolent of religious fetishism. However the Christian church does allow the use of fantasy coffins to transport the dead from their home to the graveyard. Both churches are aware of the many traditional Ghanaian customs performed at burial sites but tend to overlook them.

The custom of fantasy coffins did not begin until the 1950s. The tradition started in the remote southern villages inhabited by the Ga people, with some historians citing the village of Teshi as the tradition's geographical origin. Recent history suggests that a carpenter called Ata Owoo, who lived in Teshi, created the first fantasy coffin. Since the end of World War II it has been traditional for the *mantse*, or chief, of Teshi to ride on a type of seat called a palanquin that is carried by the four strongest men of the village. In the late 1940s, Owoo's carpentry shop was the most successful such shop in Teshi and so Owoo was commissioned by the mantse to make him a palanquin in the shape of an eagle. The chief of a neighboring village, who also farmed cocoa, was so impressed by his rival's palanquin that he commissioned his own palanquin in the shape of a cocoa pod. However the chief died before he could ride the cocoa pod palanquin and instead he was buried in it.

The Ga people believe that death is not the end of existence but instead a person continues to exist in the afterlife in the same way they existed in earthly life and maintains the same social status as on earth. Additionally, the Ga believe that when a person dies their soul remains bonded to their body for three days before wandering freely for one year, which is when the *faalo* (final rite) celebration takes place. During faalo the soul crosses the river into the realm of shadows. Fantasy coffins symbolize the deceased's earthly occupation and help them continue their profession in the next world. Dead ancestors are considered to be more powerful than the living, able to influence life on earth. Therefore relatives try to do all they can to help the dead, ensuring they are happy and not holding any ill will toward the living. Indeed the wealthier and more powerful an individual was in life the more their family must do to ease them into the afterlife. In order to do this the family arranges a suitably elaborate funeral.

Many Ghanaian families spend a great deal of money on fantasy coffins. For instance, a coffin shaped like the Bible can cost as much as $400, which represents an average year's salary in Ghana. Therefore it is quite usual for families or even entire communities to unite in paying for a fantasy coffin. Indeed during the part of the funeral service that takes place at the deceased's home the names of those who have contributed to paying for the coffin are read aloud. Such is the community aspect of Ghanaian funerals that burials have become the most important communal activity in Ghana occurring on every Friday and Saturday throughout the year.

In Ghana, the younger someone is when he or she dies the less money is spent on his or her funeral. That said, the amount spent on a young person's funeral is still in excess of the amount spent on his or her health care when the young person was alive. All members of a community are expected to attend a funeral, which can last for several days and involves not just a fantasy coffin, but also musicians, food, and drink—all of which adds to the cost of the funeral. The excessive cost of such funerals has led some religious leaders to call for an end to such elaborate services. However such is the Ghanaian belief that funerals must be elaborate in order to show the esteem in which their loved-ones were held that they are willing to bear the ensuing financial burden, even it means they must sell their property and other assets to cover the cost.

Miniature fantasy coffins are often manufactured as tourist memorabilia while away from Ghana fantasy coffins have been exhibited as art objects and sold to art galleries. Celebrated fantasy coffin makers include Daniel Mensah and brothers Cedi and Eric Adjetey Anang, who run several fantasy coffin carpentry workshops. However perhaps the most famous fantasy coffin maker is Ghanaian sculptor Kane Quayle, known as Seth Kane Kwe in Ghana, who was mentored by Ata Owoo, and who, since the 1970s, has exhibited his work as art in Western galleries. Quayle began making fantasy coffins in order to meet the final request of his dying uncle who had been a fisherman and wanted a coffin in the shape of a canoe. The coffin received a great deal of acclaim and Quayle subsequently opened a workshop given over exclusively to fashioning fantasy coffins and in doing so elevated personalized coffins to the level of art. Quayle's coffins tend to be around five-and-a-half feet long and made either of mahogany or wawa, a wood that weighs less than mahogany and is lighter in color. Quayle's coffins are much admired in his home nation and when used in funerals his coffins are pointed toward the sky, above the heads of mourners, and paraded through the streets until they reach the graveyard.

Over the years, Quayle's coffins have been exhibited in Europe and America, having entered the Western public's consciousness through an exhibition called *Magicians de la Terre* (*Magicians of the Earth*) held in the Pompidou Centre in Paris, the capital of France, in 1989. The exhibition was controversial to a degree for some art critics perceived the show as reinforcing negative concepts surrounding primitive and modern art. In October 1994 Quayle presented 15 coffins as part of an exhibition held at the University of Kansas-Missouri City Gallery of Art called *A Life Well Lived*. Coffins entered into the exhibition included ones fashioned as a KLM aircraft, a Mercedes-Benz car, a lobster, a canoe, and a chicken. Somewhat ironically, when Quayle died in 1992 his coffin was a plain wooden affair decorated with small woodcarvings on each corner depicting a carpenter's tools. Today Quayle's sons and apprentices continue to create coffins in his elaborate style.

See also: Living with the Dead; *Malagan*; *Ngaben*; Ossuaries; Personalized Hearses

Further Reading

Appiah, Kwame Anthony, and Henry Louis Gates Jr., eds. *Encyclopedia of Africa*. Volume 1. Oxford, UK: Oxford University Press, 2010.

Barranger, Nicky. "Ghana's Fantasy Coffin Attraction." BBC News, January 28, 2005. Accessed April 26, 2016, at http://news.bbc.co.uk/2/hi/programmes/from_our_own_correspondent/4196011.stm.

Dumouchelle, Kevin. "Two Journeys: The Deaths and Lives of Ga Fantasy Coffins." Accessed December 6, 2014, at www.columbia.edu. http://www.columbia.edu/~sf2220/TT2007/web-content/Pages/kevin1.html.

Galvan, Javier A., ed. *They Do What? A Cultural Encyclopedia of Extraordinary and Exotic Customs from around the World*. Santa Barbara, CA: ABC-CLIO, 2014.

Murphy, Maureen. "Des *Magiciens de la terre*, à la globalisation du monde de l'art : retour sur une exposition historique [From *Magiciens de la Terre* to the Globalization of the Art World: Going Back to a Historic Exhibition]." Translated by Simon Pleasance. *Critique D'art*. 41. Printemps/Éte 2013. Accessed June 5, 2016, at https://critiquedart.revues.org/8308?lang=en.

National Museum of Funeral History. "Ghana and Fantasy Coffins." Accessed December 6, 2014, at http://www.nmfh.org/exhibits/fantasyCoffins/info.php.

FINGER AMPUTATION, PAPUA NEW GUINEA

Finger amputation is the most ancient form of ritual body modification, having first occurred 20,000 years ago and continued ever since in varying forms. The first evidence of finger amputation occurred in Paleolithic handprints found in Gargas in the south of France. These imprints revealed that it was common practice to remove the fingertips of four fingers per hand probably as part of rituals associated with morning or healing. Finger amputation also occurred in West Africa. For example, if an Ashanti baby died in the first week of life the baby's corpse was beaten by its parents who then cut off a finger and buried the body in the village garbage dump. Meanwhile, sickly Xhosa children would undergo finger amputation to help the child grow up strong and healthy.

Finger amputation was endemic throughout Oceania and the islands of the Pacific Ocean. People who travelled to Papua New Guinea noted that mass finger amputations were conducted on the death of a king with 100 fingers removed to mark the king's burial. Today, the practice of finger amputation is most closely associated with Papua New Guinea's Dani, an ethno-linguistic group who live isolated lives in the country's highlands. For centuries, the Dani have performed finger amputations as a sacrificial funerary custom that usually sees the amputation of females' (often little girls') two smallest finger after the death of male relatives in order to express family grief and placate the ghosts of male relatives killed in battle. Though the government of Papua New Guinea has outlawed this ritual, it is though to continue still and many Dani women bear the scars of the process. Indeed it is common for women to hold their children with hands that consist mainly of thumbs, though it should be noted that even with all their fingers removed at the proximal joints some women remain fairly dexterous.

The Dani's religious system is based around magic and ancestor worship for they believe that the spirit of their ancestors, which dwell in homes and forests, govern every aspect of their lives. Thus the Dani's many customs, ceremonies, and rituals are held to appease the spirits of their ancestors as displeased ancestral spirits can cause negative events such as disease, injury, and poor harvests to happen to individuals and whole communities. Such beliefs make it imperative that ancestors are honored regularly. When a male is killed in warfare, female relatives willingly perform finger amputations without anesthetic as part of the funeral ritual. The male's body is brought back to his village where it is cleansed by being rubbed with oils. The corpse is then placed on a wooden throne and decorated with strings of beads and seashells. Next, the body is paraded via procession to the center of the village amid much singing and dancing. On its arrival the corpse is divested of the beads and shells, which are distributed amongst the warrior's relatives. Once this has occurred the body is cremated on a funeral pyre. During the cremation it is usual for female relatives to cover their faces and bodies with ash and then string is wrapped tightly around the fingers of the females who are to undergo finger amputation. The string acts to cut off feeling to the digits rendering them numb. After about 30 minutes, the fingers are sufficiently insensate for the fingers to be removed. In addition sometimes a sharp blow is delivered to the woman's elbow to deaden the pain (this confuses the ulnar nerve that connects directly with various parts of the fingers). A traditional bamboo or stone blade is used to sever the digits. Once it has been removed the amputated fingers are cremated with ashes placed in a bag and kept in the family home. The females dress the resultant finger stumps with ash and clay wrapped in leaves and hold their hands up vertically with clumps of grass at the elbow to absorb dripping blood.

The Dani believe that amputating the fingers demonstrates the women's dedication to the deceased and serves to gratify the spirits of the dead by allowing the dead to take part of the living with them into the afterlife. In addition to this it has been claimed that finger amputation strengthens bonds between the living as the procedure acts as a symbolic sharing of the misery of death and pain amongst kinsfolk.

See also: Endocannibalism; *Malagan*

Further Reading

Favazza, Armando R. *Bodies under Siege: Self-mutilation, Nonsuicidal Self-injury, and Body Modification in Culture and Psychiatry*. Third edition. Baltimore, MD: Johns Hopkins University Press, 2011.

Galvan, Javier A., ed. *They Do What? A Cultural Encyclopedia of Extraordinary and Exotic Customs from around the World*. Santa Barbara, CA: ABC-CLIO, 2014.

Kirkup, John R. *A History of Limb Amputation*. London: Springer-Verlag London Limited, 2007.

FUNERAL CAKES AND FUNERAL CANDY, INTERNATIONAL

Funerals, like other ceremonial occasions, call for special foods to be served. At funerals, it is sometimes the custom to serve so-called funeral cakes to mourners not only as a form of sustenance but also as a keepsake of the occasion and as a way to remember the deceased. The eating of shared foods also helps to create a sense of communality. Funeral cakes are mostly associated with Protestant traditions.

The tradition of eating funeral cakes can be traced back to northern Europe, particularly areas of rural Sweden, where the custom survives, as well as to medieval Germany where the funeral custom of eating so-called corpse cakes exists as a way of symbolically eating the deceased. According to German (particularly Bavarian) tradition, once a corpse has been washed and placed in a coffin the woman of the house would prepare a type of leavened dough that was left to rise on the corpse's linen-clad torso. This tradition was based on the theory that the dough would in some way absorb the attributes of the deceased and that these personal qualities would, in turn, be transmitted to the mourners that partook of the corpse cakes. A similar custom exists in Hungary and other central European countries where various types of food and drink are typically placed near the corpse for a short time to allow them to take in the merits of the deceased individual before they are eaten. Akin to this is the old Irish custom of leaving a bowl of snuff on the torso of the dead individual, or on the lid of the coffin, with each mourner expected to inhale a pinch of the snuff and, thereby, the virtues of the deceased. A now defunct custom in Britain and Ireland, sin eating, worked along similar lines. A sin-eater was a person of the lowest possible social standing who was paid to attend a wake and eat bread and salt from a dish that had been left on the torso of a dead person. By doing this, the sin-eater was felt to be eating and, therefore, transferring to themselves, the sins of the dead. By absorbing the sins of the deceased, the dead person's soul was considered to be pure enough to enter heaven. Once the sin-eater had finished eating the bread and salt they would typically be kicked and hit by mourners gathered for the funeral. When the sin-eater left the funeral the family members of the deceased would stand beside the coffin and distribute pieces of arvel (or arvil) cake to the mourners by reaching across the coffin to the mourners. This custom is thought to hark back to the Nordic practice of giving bowls of heir ale at funerals. Heir ale was a type of beer used to toast the deceased's eldest male child who would then be granted the deceased's property and authority. Arvel cakes were usually consumed with spiced ale or port before pall-bearers arrived to take the coffin to the burial site. By the end of the 18th century, European funeral food traditions were known in the United States where small cakes (known as funeral biscuits or, by the 20th century, as funeral cookies) would be offered at wakes, funerals, and burials. Funeral biscuits varied widely in appearance but in essence the biscuits performed the same ceremonial function.

Today, most funeral cakes resemble shortbread and are often flavored with spices, especially caraway seeds. Alternatively, a caraway seed cake called seedcake may also be served as funeral cake. Often funeral cake is served with a glass of spiced beer or Madeira, a fortified wine made on the Portuguese archipelago known as the Madeira Islands. According to tradition, the cakes are decorated with symbolic designs that are created by imprinting the uncooked cake mixture with a pattern from a stamp carved from apple wood or beech wood, metal, or stone before baking. The most commonly stamped decorations are roses, hearts, roosters (symbolizing Christ's Resurrection), doves, fish, and Jesus. Alternatively, a pattern taken from a tombstone might be used, as might Masonic emblems, an image of a hearse, or a depiction of three feathers. Funeral cakes are traditionally wrapped in black paper or paper patterned with depictions of skulls. In villages in England it used to be the custom to tie the cakes with black ribbon and distribute them to villagers as a form of invitation to the funeral. It is still the custom in some parts of England and Wales that so-called burying biscuits or funeral cakes be made to mark a funeral. Burying biscuits are small rectangular sponge fingers that some food historians believe were originally made to resemble coffins. According to the custom, as each mourner arrives at the funeral reception he or she is given a biscuit together with a memorial card—a small card printed by the funeral home as a tribute to the deceased. In central England, the tradition is for burying biscuits to be wrapped in white paper that is then sealed with black wax. The biscuits are then sent out to friends and family of the deceased that could not attend the funeral. In Derbyshire, central England, when the keeper of a beehive dies, funeral biscuits that have been soaked in wine are left in front of the beehive so that the bees can toast their keeper. Moreover, in the Derbyshire village of Eyam cake served at the funeral is given to the bees so that the bees can mourn their keeper.

In the United States, the custom of serving funeral cakes is almost extinct. However in Kentucky a pound cake is given to the family of the deceased while Pennsylvania Dutch communities see mourners bring a raisin pie as a gift to the bereaved family with the intention that the pie be served after the funeral. The archives of Dutch communities living in the Hudson Valley in New York State also contain recipes for large *doot coekjes*, meaning death cookies, which were taken to funerals in bushel baskets. Doot coekjes were baked until hard and according to tradition would be softened by mourners dunking them into warm, spiced wine.

In Greece, a cake called a soul cake is served at funerals. In ancient times these cakes were presented to the dead before being left in cracks in the ground surrounding temples as offerings to the gods. Today, however, the cake takes the form of a flat bread covered in honey. Similarly, in nearby Albania funeral cakes made of boiled wheat are transported in procession to the graveside by mourners. Once at the graveside the mourners eat the cakes after the corpse is buried. In other parts of the Balkans these wheat cakes are sometimes decorated with an image of the deceased.

In 19th-century Sweden, it was the custom to give hard, corpse-shaped candies wrapped in black-fringed paper as a funeral favor. The candies were served with wine before funerals and were meant to symbolize corpses wrapped in blacks shrouds with the length of the fringing suggesting the length of life experienced by the deceased. For example, short fringing would suggest the death of a child while long fringing would reflect somebody that died in old age. Sometimes the wrappers were decorated with images associated with death such as crucifixes or tombstones or with prayers or poems. The custom ceased with the advent of World War I and sugar rationing but surviving candies have been used as Christmas tree decorations.

See also: Bees; *Beschuit met Muisjes, Suikerboon,* and *Dragées* (Volume 1); Birthday Cakes (Volume 1); *Dia de los Muertos*: Day of the Dead; Eyam Plague Sunday Service; *Halva; Koliva; Povitica* (Volume 2); Soul Cakes and Soul Bread; Wakes; Wedding Cakes (Volume 2)

Further Reading
Fabricant, Florence. "An Old Custom, Funeral Cakes," *New York Times*, October 12, 1988. Accessed October 30, 2015, at http://www.nytimes.com/1988/10/12/garden/an-old-custom-funeral-cakes.html.
Levins, Hoag. "The Story of Victorian Funeral Cookies: Revisiting a Centuries' Old Tradition." HistoricCamdenCounty.com, September 12, 2011. Accessed October 30, 2015, at http://historiccamdencounty.com/ccnews153.shtml.
Nourishing Death. "Swedish Funeral Candy." February 20, 2015. Accessed October 30, 2015, at https://nourishingdeath.wordpress.com/2015/02/20/swedish-funeral-candy/.
Roud, Steve. *The Penguin Guide to the Superstitions of Britain and Ireland.* London: Penguin Books, 2006.
Simoons, Frederick J. *Plants of Life, Plants of Death.* Madison: The University of Wisconsin Press, 1998.
Simpson, Jacqueline, and Steve Roud. *Oxford Dictionary of English Folklore.* Oxford, UK: Oxford University Press, 2000.
Wright, Elizabeth Mary. *Rustic Speech and Folk-Lore.* London: Oxford University Press, 1913.

FUNERAL PLANTS, EUROPE

Throughout human history flowers have been used to symbolize the fragility of life and represent how the beauty of creation is temporary. Flowers also possess an aesthetic value in the face of death, for their verdant beauty helps balance the emotional response to the ugliness of death and decay by reminding mourners of the freshness of growth. Certain flowers have a specific symbolism and are associated with various superstitions—some flowers even have a dual symbolism. The symbolism and superstitions of flowers vary around the world so a flower that may be associated with happy events in one country may be allied with sadness in another.

Lilies are large ornamental flowers belonging to the genus *Lilium* of the family *Liliaceae*. As lilies are traditionally symbolic of innocence and virginity as well as erotic love they are often to be found in bridal bouquets. However lilies are also used as a symbol of death and rebirth in both art and literature and arum lilies in particular are commonly to be found at funerals, either laid in bunches on top of a coffin or decorating the church where a funeral is to take place. According to English folklore, lilies symbolize the soul of the departed absolved from the sins of the world. While the lily's suggestions of death and sin made them increasingly popular at funerals they fell out of fashion as flowers with which to decorate the home. Indeed so strong is the connection between lilies and funerals that their scent became synonymous with mourning and it became unlucky to have lilies in the home. In some areas of England, they are even thought of as death omens. Contrastingly, however, it was considered fortuitous to grow lilies in the garden as they were said to provide protection from ghosts.

Other European countries also associate lilies with death. For instance, in Hungary lilies are said to yellow when a man is unjustly executed. The association of lilies with death also exists in Asia for in Japan lilies are never grown in gardens or indoors as they are considered the flower of death and ill fortune. In Japan, lilies are also referred to as the equinox flower further highlighting that the flowers are associated with endings and decay. Lily-of-the-valley is also associated with death in some cultures for a common belief across Europe is that the plant came into being when drops of Saint Leonard's blood fell upon the ground when he fought a dragon representative of Satan.

Like lilies, the flowers of the lilac shrub, *Syringa*, are associated with both love and loss. According to English folklore, a person seeing lilacs bloom on any day other than May Day means that the individual will never marry, while a folktale tells of a young woman who, dying on the eve of her wedding, asked that lilacs grow on her grave. Further, it is a well-known old English superstition that bringing lilac flowers indoors, especially into a home, brings death to the house and in the eastern English county of Norfolk it is thought that lilac was used to line coffins and graves. Roses too, so often associated with love, are also to be found at funerals in England for it was traditional for young girls to carry wreaths of white roses when walking behind the coffin of a dead virgin. The wreath would then be hung up above the virgin's seat in church and left to fade in a custom comparable to English maidens' garlands.

Chrysanthemums are also considered funeral flowers in Europe, especially in Italy where they are associated so closely with death that to give a person a bunch of the flowers in akin to saying you wish them dead. Bringing the flowers indoors in Italy is also considered to bring bad luck to a household.

Other plants and herbs are also associated with death and funerals in Europe. For instance, box is included in funerary customs in northern England where sprigs of the plant are placed by the door of a house prior to a funeral and every member of the funeral procession is expected to wear a sprig that they then toss into the grave. This custom also took place in the English county of Lincolnshire where it was known as Burying the Box. Burying box sprigs also occurred in Cambridgeshire and Berkshire too as sprigs of the plant have been excavated from Romano-British graves discovered in these counties.

> ### Alnwick Castle's Poison Garden
>
> Located in the environs of Alnwick Castle (the location of Hogwarts School of Witchcraft and Wizardry in the *Harry Potter* films) in Northumberland, in northern England, is a garden in which every one of the 100 plants is either intoxicating or fatally poisonous—the Poison Garden. The garden, which is open to the public, features plants such as *Nux vomica* (source of strychnine), *ricinus communis* (source of ricin), foxgloves, hemlock, and *Atropa belladonna*. The potentially dangerous nature of the garden's plants means that visitors to the Poison Garden are forbidden to smell, touch, or taste any of the plants.

Evergreen herbs are also associated with funerals in Europe. For instance, rosemary, *Rosmarinus officialis*, is associated with remembrance in England. That rosemary was used at funerals in the time of William Shakespeare is evinced by the fact that Ophelia refers to rosemary's association with remembrance in Act IV of *Hamlet*. Symbolic of remembrance, mourners would place sprigs of the shrub on top of coffins to signify that the deceased would always be remembered. This symbolic association of rosemary with remembrance may stem from the Christian tradition that a rosemary bush would reach the same height as Christ did during his lifetime, but after it had grown to that height the bush would grow no more. English folkloric beliefs suggest rosemary as an amulet against physical assault and being struck by lightening and as a charm to protect against the evil machinations of witches and fairies. Another herb, parsley, is also associated with death in England. It is said that growing parsley in a garden will cause a death in a family before year's end and that it is equally hazardous to transplant it so that it grows elsewhere. It is thought that these superstitions arise from ancient Roman and Greek customs of laying parsley on graves and including it in funeral wreaths. Thyme too, is associated with funerals and death in England where it is considered unlucky and is associated with murder. Members of the British friendship society the Oddfellows carry thyme to funerals of their members and then cast it into the graves. This custom also occurs in Lincolnshire. Thyme is also placed on graves in Wales.

See also: Maidens' Garlands; Planting a Tree or Rose; Remembrance Day and Remembrance Sunday; Wearing Flowers to Honor War Dead; Yew Trees

Further Reading

Alexander, Marc. *The Sutton Companion to British Folklore, Myths & Legends*. Stroud, UK: Sutton Publishing Limited, 2002.
Jones, Alison. *Larousse Dictionary of World Folklore*. Edinburgh, UK: Larousse, 1996.
Watts, D. C. *Dictionary of Plant Lore*. Burlington, MA: Academic Press, 2007.

FUNERAL SONGS, INTERNATIONAL

At some funerals, particularly those of people that were not religious in life, it is usual to play songs rather than hymns. This is particularly the case in the United Kingdom but also happens elsewhere. Funeral directors have suggested that this shift away from the playing of traditional funeral hymns represents a generational change in attitudes to funerals and death in general. Those that advocate the playing of funeral songs rather than traditional hymns point out that it is possible to personalize a funeral by playing the deceased's favorite songs rather than a standard hymn that is sung at many funerals. In this way, funerals songs act as a fitting final farewell to the dead.

In 2014, research by a chain of United Kingdom funeral directors, The Co-operative Funeralcare, studied 30,000 funerals and discovered that the most popular song to be played at funerals was "Always Look on the Bright Side of Life," the irreverent song sung by actor Eric Idle in the 1979 Monty Python film *The Life of Brian*. This was a surprise finding as anecdotal evidence suggested that Frank Sinatra's hit "My Way" was the most preferred funeral song. It is believed that the increased popularity of "Always Look on the Bright Side of Life" was due to the success of the Monty Python musical *Spamalot* in which the song is also performed, the fact that the song was included in the closing ceremony of the 2012 London Olympics, and the fact that those people that enjoyed *The Life of Brian* when the film was released at the cinema are now in their 70s and 80s and made up the majority of funerals overseen by the polled funeral directors.

In the list of popular funeral songs topped by "Always Look on the Bright Side of Life" the hymns "The Lord Is My Shepherd" and "Abide With Me" came in second and third place. Other non-religious songs to appear in the poll's top 10 were "Angels" by Robbie Williams and "Who Wants to Live Forever" by Queen. Also inside the top 20 favorite funeral songs came the television theme tunes for long-running soap opera *Coronation Street*, sitcom *Only Fools and Horses*, and soccer program *Match of the Day*. The poll also found that Elvis Presley was the most oft-requested solo performer.

Such findings seems to tally with the views of some 84 percent of the funeral directors polled who said that hymns and classical music were rapidly falling out of fashion as funeral choices. However "Nimrod" from Elgar's *Enigma Variations*, Pachelbel's *Canon in D*, Vivaldi's *Four Seasons,* and "Ava Maria" by Schubert all appeared in the top 20. Moreover the 20 favorites were rounded out by *Adagio* by Albinoni and Puccini's *Nessum Dorma*, though the popularity of the latter was most probably in part due to the fact that the tune was used, famously, as the theme tune to the BBC's coverage of the 1990 soccer World Cup Finals and has remained popular ever since. Another finding of the poll was that there is a trend to play songs written by the deceased at their funeral.

The poll also found that certain songs are, in general, not allowed to be played at funerals on grounds of good taste. These include the Frankie Goes to Hollywood hit "Relax," "God Save the Queen" by punk band the Sex Pistols, and "Imagine" by John Lennon.

See also: "Abide With Me"; Jazz Funeral; "The Last Post" and "Taps"; Personalized Hearses

Further Reading

BBC. "Monty Python Tune Tops Funeral Songs." BBC News: Entertainment & Arts, November 21, 2014. Accessed August 29, 2015, at http://www.bbc.com/news/entertainment-arts-30143250.

Kyriazis, Stefan. "As Cilla Black Is Laid to Rest, You Won't BELIEVE the UK's Top 10 Funeral Songs," *The Express*. Accessed August 29, 2015, at http://www.express.co.uk/entertainment/music/599645/cilla-black-top-uk-funeral-songs-invlude-monty-python.

Molloy, Antonia. "Monty Python's 'Always Look on the Bright Side of Life' Named Most Popular Funeral Song," *The Independent*, November 21, 2014. Accessed August 29, 2015, at http://www.independent.co.uk/arts-entertainment/music/news/monty-pythons-always-look-on-the-bright-side-of-life-named-most-popular-funeral-song-9875462.html.

G

GOTH SUBCULTURE, INTERNATIONAL

Goth is a subculture that can be found in many countries around the world. People belonging to the Goth subculture differentiate themselves from the normative ideals of the rest of society by wearing certain styles of dress and make-up, listening to particular types of music, and entertaining a Goth aesthetic.

The Goth subculture in its widest sense grew out of the rapidly waning punk rock scene of 1970s England. Early pioneers of Goth music abandoned the guitar-rich sounds of the punk era and instead placed a musical emphasis on strong rhythms, idiosyncratic vocals, and lyrics that were indebted to Gothic literature and British horror films of this time, particularly the stagey, colorful films made by the British Hammer Studios. Especially notable Goth bands of this time include Joy Division, Siouxsie and the Banshees, and UK Decay. However the British Goth band that is most often credited with instituting the genre is Bauhaus, which, in 1979, released the single "Bela Lugosi's Dead." This song is often considered the foundation of the modern Goth movement for not only did it reference Bela Lugosi, who is arguably most famous for portraying Bram Stoker's character Count Dracula in the 1931 film *Dracula*, but the lyrics of the song also revelled in the atmosphere of Gothic literature with references to bats, capes, virgins, velvet, and the undead. Bauhaus play "Bela Lugosi's Dead" during the opening of the 1983 erotic, vampire art film *The Hunger*, starring Catherine Deneuve, Susan Sarandon, and David Bowie. Though a Hollywood film, *The Hunger* is cited by some critics as a cornerstone of a certain type of Goth subgroup as the bisexuality at the film's core appealed to queer audiences. Other important influences on the formation of the Goth subculture during the 1970s and early 1980s included the art movements known as Dadaism and Pre-Raphaelitism, 19th-century Gothic literature that combined horror with romance, politically anarchic sentiments in opposition to the policies of Margaret Thatcher's government, Nazism, Celtic and pagan mythology, and a prevailing air of sexual ambivalence.

Stoker's literary vampire has provided a wealth of inspiring visual prompts for Goth bands, musicians, artists, writers, and dramatists that have all contributed to the fostering of the Goth subculture. Dracula has also provided sartorial cues for members of the Goth subculture as stereotypical Goth clothing includes black capes and long dresses that are often mock-Victorian in styling, accessorised with jewelery that nods toward Victorian mourning jewelry as well as paganism and deathly-white make-up accentuated by darkly rimmed eyes. The stereotypical Goth look that was cultivated by the early Goth bands has fared better than the

Goth music scene itself and even reached levels of haute couture with high-end designers such as Jean Paul Gaultier, John Galliano, and Alexander McQueen all cited as being influenced by the Goth subculture—so-called haute Goth. Indeed fashion by Alexander McQueen was included in the British Library's blockbuster exhibition *Terror and Wonder: The Gothic Imagination* that ran from October 2014 until January 2015. Goth style is not just the preserve of buyers of haute couture however, for watered-down elements of Goth fashion such as the so-called smoky eye make-up look, black nail varnish, and jewel-colored velvets infiltrate winter fashion on a regular basis and are available to buy on the high street.

Even though formative Goth bands began to sell out large stadiums, had top-selling albums, and newer Goth bands such as the Cult and Sisters of Mercy achieved a level of popularity during the 1980s and indeed continue to be popular, on the whole Goth music has faded away. This is in contrast to the Goth subculture in general however as this grows ever more popular with more and more subgroups emerging under its banner. Indeed today the Goth subculture is not easy to define because it spans many countries and has developed to include a diverse range of musical tastes and clothing styles. There are also subgroups within the Goth subculture that wear their own styles of clothing and listen to their own types of music. These subgroups include so-called Mall Goths found in the United States, Australian Gogans, the Cuervos in Spain, and Neogoths in the United Kingdom. Goth subculture tends to be linked to adolescence but there is such variety within the Goth subculture that outlining an average Goth is not possible. It has been theorized that adolescents and teenagers in particular are inclined toward the Goth subculture as they are seeking social acceptance from their peers. However other people may turn to the Goth subculture because they feel alienated from their schoolmates and family or are looking for an outlet to express their feelings. Alternatively, some people that are classed as Goths by others simply enjoy listening to certain styles of music or dressing in a particular way.

In terms of dress, the Goth subculture of today embraces a huge diversity of styles with on the one hand history-inspired looks such as Victoriana and Steampunk (an aesthetic that incorporates science fiction and 19th-century steam-powered technology) and the so-called Lolita look (a Japanese doll-like mock-Victorian look sometimes referred to as GothLoli), but also encompassing fetish-wear, a look influenced by the BDSM (an overlapping term for Bondage and Discipline, Dominance and Submission, Sadism and Masochism) scene and punk that is characterised by women wearing PVC corsets, knee-high boots, straps, and collars. However it should be noted that grouping members of the Goth subculture into such categories is not without controversy, as a substantial overlap may exist between groupings.

Today, the Goth subculture continues to flourish in urban nightspots such as Slimlight in London, the longest-running dark scene club in the world having opened in 1987. The Internet has also opened avenues for member of the various Goth subgroups to communicate, and so-called Goth zines, which were essential in helping Goths communicate in the days before the Internet, are still published. There are several types of Goth zines including glossy magazines like *Permission* and *Propaganda* and small-scale publications such as *Lilith*. Small-scale Goth zines tend to feature hand-drawn illustrations, poetry, and stories by readers plus interviews with musicians and articles on Goth subculture in general. However nowadays the Internet is undoubtedly one of the main ways in which members of the Goth subculture communicate with each other and disseminate Goth culture. In the earliest days of Internet newsgroups such as alt.gothic prevailed but today there is a proliferation of Goth websites and a significant Goth presence on social media. Additional outlets for music such as iTunes and various digital radio stations also mean that lovers of Goth music styles can indulge in their favorite listening material.

In addition to various music outlets, cinema is another channel through which the Goth subculture prevails. Such classic horror narratives as *Dracula* (1897) and *Frankenstein* (1818) have long provided inspiration for filmmakers from the black and white Expressionism of early German cinema to the color-saturated films made by Hammer and the American director Roger Corman, who made a series of horror films based on the writing of Edgar Allan Poe including *House of Usher* (1960) and *The Pit and the Pendulum* (1965). Though these films were popular when they were first release at the cinema, they have found new audiences via DVD distribution and social media sites such as YouTube as well as late-night television screenings. Today, one of the filmmakers most closely associated with Gothic is Tim Burton, who as a child reveled in watching triple bills of these low-budget horror films, especially those featuring actors such as Vincent Price. Burton's films such as *Edward Scissorhands* (1990) and *Sleepy Hollow* (1999) champion the strange and fantastical and have a distinctive look that hinges on artificiality and decorative Gothic excess as well as the deliberate rejection of realism. This is in keeping with Goth sensibilities as is the fact that Burton's films often focus on social outcasts and anxieties about life and death, the real and the unreal, which also chimes with Goth subculture. Mexican filmmaker Guillermo del Toro is also often cited as making films that belong to the Gothic genre. This is especially true of the 2015 film *Crimson Peak*, which was inspired by classic Gothic romances that the film also sought to subvert and combine with scenes of disturbing horror.

One of the highlights of the Goth subculture is the twice-yearly Whitby Goth Weekend (often abbreviated to WGW) during which various subgroups of Goth converge on the small seaside town of Whitby in northern Yorkshire, England. Whitby has long been associated with the Goth subculture because in the novel *Dracula* it is the site of the Count's landing in England and where Lucy Westenra meets the count with fatal consequences. The WGW is a showcase for all types of Goth music, fashion, and lifestyles and generally celebrates everything that is dark and suitably Gothic. (*See* Plate 7.)

A similar event to WGW takes place on the Australian island state of Tasmania, where a 12-day-long festival called Dark Mofo attracts around 270,000 visitors. Dark Mofo is a winter solstice festival that explores cultural attitutdes to death through art, theatre, music, and film. The festival also includes events such as the Funeral Party (a ball held in a funeral parlor) and Hymns to the Dead (a concert featuring black metal and heavy metal bands). Another highpoint of Dark Mofo sees nude attendees dive into the Derwent River at dawn on the morning of the winter solstice. The water temperature at this time of year is about 10°C (50°F) but the swimmers take to the water in order to signify rebirth in the face of the morbidity that is the prevailing mood of Dark Mofo.

In recent years, the media has occasionally portrayed the Goth subculture as being a threatening youth phenomenon populated by malcontents. For example, after the Columbine High School mass shooting several newspapers highlighted what they saw as the dangers of the Goth subculture when they alleged that the perpetrators of the shooting were Goths. The media were quick to suggest that the Goth subculture was the preserve of the weird, freaky, and potentially violent. The singer Marilyn Manson was even forced to cancel concerts in the aftermath of the shooting because of his perceived association with the Goth subculture even though many people who self-identify as Goth do not view Manson as part of Goth subculture. Despite such vilification by the media, however, the Goth subculture continues to attract people for various reasons. Indeed, though Bela Lugosi may be dead, the Goth subculture is very much alive.

See also: *Dia de los Muertos*: Day of the Dead; Doom Metal and Funeral Doom; *Memento Mori* and *Vanitas*; Tear Catchers and Mourning Jewelry

Further Reading

Autstralian Centre for the Moving Image. "The Gothic Imagination of Tim Burton: Education Resources." Melbourne Winter Masterpieces: Tim Burton: The Exhibition. Accessed October 15, 2015, at http://www.acmi.net.au/media/102407/the-gothic-imagination-of-tim-burton.pdf.
Carter, Paul. "Dark Mofo: Australia's Festival of Death and Darkness." BBC News: World: Australia, June 9, 2016. Accessed June 9, 2016, at http://www.bbc.co.uk/news/world-australia-36476354.
The Center for Mental Health in Schools. "About the Goth Youth Subculture." Information Resource. Accessed October 15, 2015, at http://smhp.psych.ucla.edu/pdfdocs/youth/goth.pdf.
Goodlad, Lauren M. E., and Michael Bibby. *Goth: Undead Subculture*. Durham, NC: Duke University Press, 2007.
Townshend, Dale, ed. *Terror and Wonder: The Gothic Imagination*. London: The British Library, 2014.
Wilson, Cintra. "You Just Can't Kill It," *New York Times*, September 17, 2008. Accessed October 15, 2015, at http://www.nytimes.com/2008/09/18/fashion/18GOTH.html?_r=0.

GRAVE RENTAL AND EXHUMATION, EUROPE AND ASIA

The problem of running out of burial space is occurring throughout Europe. For example, a survey conducted in 2013 suggested that almost 50 percent of England's cemeteries would run out of burial room within the next 20 years while in Germany burial spaces are simply reused after a period of time. The issue of running out of grave space is also a problem in Spain and Greece, where families rent a so-called niche, that is, a crypt situated above ground where bodies lie for a number of years. Once corpses have decomposed inside their niche they are transported to communal burial grounds, allowing the niche to be reused. The urban population of Greece has increased rapidly over the past 50 years meaning that in excess of 50 percent of the nation's people live in the two biggest cities—Athens, the Greek capital city, and Thessaloniki. The spread of cities has resulted in cemeteries being encircled by buildings without room to expand. For this reason, Greek graves now tend to be rented on a three-year lease with a set of escalating prices for any additional years of rental. The costs are deliberately prohibitive in order to deter long-term rentals as the quick turnover of grave occupation mean that the grave space can be reused. In November 2015, some Greek cemeteries were seeing an average of 15 exhumations per week as relatives that were unable to pay extra grave-rental costs were forced to have family members exhumed.

In 2006, in an effort to combat the problem of lack of grave space a law was passed permitting crematoria to be built in Greece. The plan was opposed by the Greek Orthodox Church, however, for according to the church a human corpse must be buried so that it may be resurrected during the Second Coming. Leading Greek Orthodox figures claim that cremation renders a corpse a thing of nothingness and today Greece is still without a crematorium. The Greek Orthodox Church is highly influential in Greece with some 98 percent of the country's population identifying as belonging to the church. Some Greek families do, however, have their loved ones cremated by transporting their bodies to crematoria in Bulgaria. Since the Greek Orthodox Church refuses to perform funeral services for people that they know will be cremated, families often pretend to plan a burial just so that a funeral can be held for the departed.

Usually after a Greek exhumation bones are washed and placed in a metal box. The law forbids human remains from being kept outside of the boundaries of a cemetery so bones have to be kept in an ossuary. Here, relatives can visit the bones and occasionally family members may remove the bones from their box so that a priest can bless them. The cost of ossuary rental space in Greece is also increasing, however, meaning that the remains of people whose families cannot afford to pay for ossuary space are thrown into a so-called digestive pit. This is a huge underground mass grave in which the bones of tens of thousands of people are thrown together. Digestive pits are not necessarily the answer to Greece's grave space problem, however, as they too are also filling up rapidly. Indeed the 3rd Cemetery in Athens is full with no room for new bones hence boxes containing jumbles of bones are kept in nearby sheds. Meanwhile, in Israel the creation of multi-story underground burial tunnels has been sanctioned, despite hostility to the idea from some Orthodox Jews.

Outside of Europe, places with limited space are also experiencing the problem of too little grave space. In Hong Kong, China, the last available public burial space was filled during the 1980s. However families able to find and pay for a private grave can purchase a grave for $30,000. Alternatively, Hong Kong families can join a list for a place in a public columbarium where thousands of urns containing cremated ashes are kept, though the wait to place ashes in a public columbarium is, on average, five years long. Another possible alternative to finding grave space in high-tech Hong Kong has seen the government create a social-media network of virtual graves for families that have been forced to cremate their loved ones because of lack of grave space in the city. In this way, families and friends can still pay their respects to the departed even without a physical space at which they can pay their respects. Meanwhile, in Japan large companies such as Panasonic have bought corporate zones within cemeteries for some of their workers. In Kuala Lumpur and other Asian cities, where cremation is the cultural norm, the lack of grave space combined with and the desire of families for a site where they can pay respects to the dead have resulted in giant, mechanized columbaria. These are buildings where thousands of urns full of ashes are kept in a vault from which they can be retrieved through the use of an electronic card key system. The mechanized columbaria are in great demand with one private company, Nirvana, overseeing 12 such sites across Malaysia, Singapore, and Indonesia, and with plans for more. Another option in the face of disappearing grave space is to build cemeteries vertically. An example of a vertical cemetery exists in Brazil, where the Memorial Necrópole Ecumênica in Santos stands some 14 stories high. The building is proving an inspiration to town planners elsewhere with similar building under consideration in the densely populated cities of Bogotá, the capital of Colombia, and Mumbai, India.

The lack of available grave space has also led to an increased interest internationally in so-called green burials and alternative, environmentally friendly methods of corpse disposal such as alkaline hydrolysis. Green burials tend to see corpses contained in biodegradable shrouds or caskets made from materials such as cardboard or banana leaf buried in meadows and woodland areas.

See also: Alkaline Hydrolysis; Cremation; Isola di San Michele: Venice's Cemetery Island; Japanese Funeral Customs; Ossuaries

Further Reading

Brennan, Claire. "Graveyard Overcrowding Stokes Cremation Debate in Greece." *BBC News*, May 3, 2015. Accessed December 15, 2015, at http://www.bbc.co.uk/news/world-europe-32165261.

de Sousa, Ana Naomi. "Death in the City: What Happens When All Our Cemeteries Are Full?" *The Guardian*, January 21, 2015. Accessed December 15, 2015, at http://www.theguardian.com/cities/2015/jan/21/death-in-the-city-what-happens-cemeteries-full-cost-dying.

Hadjimatheou, Chloe. "Why Greeks Are Exhuming Their Parents." *BBC News Magazine*, November 26, 2015. Accessed December 15, 2015, at http://www.bbc.co.uk/news/magazine-34920068.

McManus, John. "The World Is Running Out of Burial Space." *BBC News*, March 12, 2015. Accessed December 14, 2015, at http://www.bbc.co.uk/news/uk-31837964.

Penmellen Boret, Sébastien. *Japanese Tree Burial: Ecology, Kinship and the Culture of Death.* Abingdon, UK: Routledge, 2014.

Suzuki, Hikaru, ed. *Death and Dying in Contemporary Japan.* Abingdon, UK: Routledge, 2013.

THE GREAT PASSING, ROMANIA

The Great Passing, also referred to as the Cult of the Dead, is a three-stage death ritual that occurs in many areas of Romania. Traditionally, the three stages of the passing are the separation of the dead from the living, the preparation of the dead to join the afterlife, and the integration of the deceased into the world of the dead. These stages aim to help the dead leave the realm of the living and the soul to move into the next world. The traditions also reveals the popular Romanian belief that the soul continues to exist after death. As a whole, the tradition of the Great Passing is a mixture of folkloric beliefs and Christianity that suggests ancient traditions continue to play a prominent part in Romanian culture and society.

The death rituals of Romania are thought to date back to the Roman occupation of Romania and are followed particularly closely in the Maramures region of northern Romania, an area steeped in superstition and folkloric traditions that contains eight wooden churches that are listed as UNESCO World Heritage sites as well as the famous Merry Cemetery at Sapanta.

The first stage of the Great Passing sees a priest visit that home of the dying where the priest says prayers and delivers the Eucharist to the dying. The friends and relatives of the dying also visit so that the dying person may apologize for any wrongs he or she has done to them in the past as well as remember fondly happy times. The visit of the relatives, friends, and family are all intended to help the dying achieve separation from the living and help the deceased's soul reach the afterlife. These rituals are followed very closely as Romanians believe that souls of the dead will never be at peace. Once the person has died his or her separation from the living is hastened and the person's soul's path eased by the lighting of a candle. This candle, known as a soul candle, is lit in order to light the soul's path to heaven. Also intended to help the dead move are the placing of money, a stick and bread in the deceased's hands. Before news of the death is announced to the rest of the village the dead person is dressed in his or her best clothing and the deceased's hair is brushed. Also, if the dead is a man his beard is neatened. When these preparations are complete, the women that have gathered at the dead's bedside begin to sob loudly in order to announce that a death has occurred. When they have learned of the death each villager then says, "May the Lord forgive him/her." As a sign of mourning the village men remove their hats and do not shave while women untie their hair and place black handkerchiefs over their heads. A vigil is kept over the corpse for three days and two nights that ensures the soul candle remains lit for the entirety of the vigil. On each evening of the vigil local men keep the corpse company by drinking and socializing around the corpse. Also a glass of water is placed next to the corpse and the level of water within the glass is noted. The next morning the water level is checked to see whether the corpse has drunk from the glass. It is also during the morning that women mourners grieve loudly and the bells of the local church ring out for the first time. The bells also ring out at noon and in the evening. This thrice-daily bell ringing continues over the three days of the corpse vigil. Also during the three days of the vigil preparations are made for the funeral and wake. Enough food is prepared to feed all the mourners (usually all the villagers attend the funeral) and a close relative or friend of the deceased makes arrangements for the funeral such as who will read a psalm at the funeral, what bells will ring to mark the ceremony, who will act as pallbearers, and which mourner will carry a candle, a crucifix, and a religious icon. Usually close relatives of the dead carry these items.

The evening before the funeral, a requiem is held. Then the next day before the funeral begins a procession takes place during which the psalm reader uses a lit candle to trace the shape of the cross on the outside of the deceased's home which the priest enters and gives a reading while the relatives of the dead person kneel around his or her coffin. The priest then proceeds to take the part of the deceased by asking their forgiveness so that he or she can proceed to the next world in peace. A procession of mourners comprising the entire village then travels with the coffin to the graveyard. Oftentimes the procession will stop 12 times en route to the graveyard with the priest reading from the Bible at each pause—sometimes the procession will stop at every intersection of the journey and every time that it passes a crucifix, church, or bridge. These symbolic pauses are called *vamas*. As the coffin is being transported it is usual for some mourners to remain at the dead person's home to sweep the floors and burn the person's bed sheets—a Romanian superstition contends that the direction in which the smoke from this bonfire travels shows where death will strike next.

Once the coffin is lowered into the ground the grave is sealed by the priest who uses a hoe to make the sign of the cross above the grave. After the funeral the mourners gather for a ritual meal called the *praznik* or *pomana* that consists of bread, pasta, potatoes, doughnuts, and *sarmale*, a traditional dish of cabbage stuffed with rice and meat. *Coliva*, a sweet wheat and nut dish known elsewhere as *koliva*, is also eaten, as is a bread called *pomul* that is shaped like a fruit-laden tree and decorated with dried fruits. Pomul not only symbolizes the tree of life but also the passage of the dead into the afterlife and the trees of heaven. If the funeral falls during Advent or Lent then a bean soup will also be eaten and mushrooms will be added to the sarmale. Before anyone starts eating, however, the priest leads the mourners in a prayer for the deceased person. When the meal has finished local teenagers act in a play that depicts the dead person whose funeral they have that morning attended.

The whole funeral procession is re-enacted at intervals after the deceased's burial, usually three and nine days after the funeral and on the six-week, one-year and seven-year anniversaries, and sometimes as part of Sunday church services. This is particularly true if the dead was a member of the Orthodox Church. The purpose of such re-enactments is to ensure that the dead are not forgotten. Additionally 40 days after a burial, incense is wafted over the grave, which is also sprinkled with water or wine.

See also: "Lyke-Wake Dirge"; Passing Bells; Romanian Funeral Customs; Tombstone Tourism

Further Reading

EcoAdventure Ltd. "Funeral Traditions." Tours Romania. Accessed April 13, 2015, at http://www.tours-romania.ro/funeral_traditions.html.

MyCorp. "Traditions and Customs during Life." Echoes of Europe, February 23, 2014. Accessed April 13, 2015, at http://echoesofeurope.ucoz.com/blog/traditions_and_customs_during_life/2014-02-23-80.

H

HALLOWE'EN AND *MARTINSTAG*, INTERNATIONAL

Hallowe'en (also written as Halloween) is the colloquial name for the eve of the festival of All Hallow's Day. Hallowe'en is observed on October 31 in many countries around the world, particularly the United States, Canada, and the United Kingdom. The term "hallow" derives from the Old English word *halig*, meaning holy.

Hallowe'en is named as a Christian feast but actually owes more to the older Celtic tradition of Samhain (pronounced sah-win) that was held to mark the end of summer and beginning of winter on November 1. The eve of Samhain fell on October 31 and ultimately evolved into Hallowe'en. Samhain was characterized as a perilous and magical time when supernatural entities were at their strongest and the pagan gods walked among mortals. Moreover, Samhain was a time when the spirits of ancestors returned to their family homes and acted in a manner that was both playful and destructive. The supernatural element of Samhain was well documented by Irish, Scottish, and Welsh writers and scholars. In order to expel the impish spirits large bonfires were lit and sacrifices were made to pacify malignant supernatural entities. People that were suitably courageous could, however, take advantage of this time of supernatural agency because according to tradition at Samhain the devil could be evoked to assist in divination. Samhain gradually evolved into Hallowe'en as known today when Christian missionaries tried to modify Celtic religious practices.

In the earliest centuries of the first millennium, before Christian missionaries such as Saint Patrick converted the Celts to Christianity, the Celtic people practiced religion through their ecclesiastical order of the Druids, who were simultaneously priests, artists, and scholars. Christians however made efforts to eradicate pagan holidays, including Samhain, and in so doing the Christians affected major changes in Celtic religion. In 601, Pope Gregory I suggested to Christian missionaries that instead of try to eradicate the beliefs, rituals, and customs of the Celts missionaries should appropriate these elements, consecrate them to Christ, and allow worship to continue. This resulted in the spread of Christianity and became the blueprint for the approach of Catholic missionaries. Moreover, through this approach Christian holy days were established to coincide with days considered sacred in indigenous pagan religions and over time Christianity came to influence Samhain with the Christian Feast of All Saints allocated to November 1. The Feast of All Saints was established specifically to honor Christian saints, particularly those saints that did not have their own day of devotion. The Feast of All Saints was supposed to supplant Samhain by capturing the interest and devotion of the Celts, and, ultimately, to replace Samhain forever more. However, although Celtic gods did diminish in status, gradually entering into folklore in diluted form as fairies or leprechauns, the traditional Celtic beliefs connected to Samhain did not die out. Samhain continued to have a hold on people's imagination as the concept of a night on which the dead returned to the living proved too strong either because the idea of ancestors returning was too comforting to the human psyche or because the idea of saints was too abstract for the Celtic mindset. Seeing that it was necessary to dislodge Samhain from the popular imagination, in the ninth century the Church attempted to oust Samhain by instituting another Christian feast day, All Souls' Day, to be held on November 2. This was declared to be a day when the living prayed for the souls of the departed. However yet again old customs proved too strong to eradicate and instead of being eradicated ancient traditions merely transformed and continued in new guises.

All Saints' Day, also known as All Hallows, continued the old Celtic ways with the eve of All Saints' Day the time of the most activity, both human and paranormal. Over time, people continued to observe All Saints' Eve as the time when the dead roamed the earth, but also, over time, these supernatural beings became thought of as evil. People continued to placate these supernatural beings (and those that dressed as them) by leaving out gifts of food and drink. Consequently, All Hallows' Eve became known as Hallow Evening, which in turn became known as Hallowe'en.

However, despite the Christianization of Samhain, even today Hallowe'en is strongly associated with witchcraft, supernatural activity, ghosts, hobgoblins, and the like rather than being seen as the eve of a festival to honor Christian saints. Popular Hallowe'en customs in the United States, Canada, and the United Kingdom include bobbing for apples, which sees people (especially children) pick up apples from a bowl of water using only their teeth. Such customs as this were originally practiced as a form of love divination to see what marriages would occur over the coming year, or as a way of determining a family's future prosperity. Indeed Hallowe'en used to be especially associated with courtship for apart from traditions such as bobbing for apples other things such as the way in which flames crackled in the fire, the way in which stones shifted in the flames, or the way in which nuts cracked were all thought to point toward future marriages.

Another activity synonymous with Hallowe'en is so-called trick or treating, during which children—dressed as characters from supernatural folklore such as cats, witches, ghosts, and vampires or, more recently, horror films and literature—visit houses to demand treats such as sweets. If a householder refuses to provide sweets then the children may well play tricks on them such as throwing eggs or flour at their front door or, more seriously, vandalizing their property or car. One of the most evocative symbols of Hallowe'en is the jack o'lantern. This is a hollowed-out pumpkin (or in Scotland a swede) that is carved to resemble a horrifying face that is lit from within when a candle is placed inside the vegetable. This tradition probably began as way to scare away demons and goblins during Samhain when evil spirits were believed to roam the earth for a night.

Hallowe'en is one of only a few festivals that has increased in popularity over time. Nowadays, around the time of Hallowe'en shops are full of costumes allowing children (and adults if they wish) to disguise themselves as supernatural figures, television schedules are packed with horror films both new and classic, and families stock up on cheap sweets to give to trick or treaters. The increase in Hallowe'en's popularity is in the face of a criticism by both mainstream religious leaders and fundamentalist Christians who argue that the festival could morally endanger people, especially the young. Neo-pagans have added to the ire of Christians that disapprove of Hallowe'en by claiming that as Hallowe'en has its origins in Samhain, Hallowe'en is a festival that was commandeered by Christianity. Such matters are, however, of little interest to those people that each year look forward to dressing-up as vampires, witches, and fairies.

In Austria, Switzerland, Belgium, the Netherlands, Sweden, Hungary, and Germany, people celebrate the old traditional German custom *Martinstag* (also translated as St. Martin's Day or Martinsmas) that has much in common with Hallowe'en. In the German region of Bavaria and in Austria, Martinstag is known as Martini. Martinstag, which occurs on November 11, is the Feast of Saint Martin of Tours, a fourth-century Roman soldier who became a monk and is celebrated in many parts of Europe both Catholic and Protestant. Saint Martin is celebrated for two reasons. Firstly, according to legend, Martin came across a beggar in a blizzard and cut his red cape in half to share with the needy man. Unbeknownst to Martin, the beggar was Christ in disguise and the encounter led to Martin becoming a Christian. Secondly, Martin felt unworthy of being made Bishop of Tours and so hid in a barn full of geese. Disturbed by his entering the stable, however, the geese honked, thereby betraying Martin's location. This is the reason that traditionally a goose (*die Martinsgans*) is eaten on Martinstag. Another traditional Martinstag dish is *Martinsgebäck*, glazed yeast dough that is fashioned into the shape of a man wearing a coat featuring three buttons made of almonds or raisins.

German Catholics observe Martinstag by wearing costumes and holding processions during which children walk holding candles and a man rides a horse while wearing a red cloak as an echo of the tale of Martin and the beggar man. Indeed in areas of Austria, Germany, and Switzerland Martinstag is primarily an occasion for children as they make paper lanterns at school. In some parts of Germany, the Martinstag lantern procession culminates in a special bonfire called a *Martinsfeuer* (Martin bonfire). Then after the bonfire all the children that took part in the procession go from door to door and sing traditional songs such as *"Ich geh' mit meiner Laterne"* ("I Walk With My Lantern") for the occupants of the houses on whose doors they have knocked. In order to show their gratitude for the children's singing, the house-dwellers give children candy in much the same way as occurs in trick or treating.

Another Germanic tradition related to Hallowe'en occurs in the Austrian town of Retz, near the Austrian capital city Vienna, where an annual pumpkin festival or *Kürbisfest*, is held. The area surrounding Retz is known for its pumpkin harvest and

Kürbisfest features carved pumpkins, pumpkin parties, and a Hallowe'en parade called *Halloween-Umzug*.

Meanwhile, on the Isle of Man (a self-governing British Crown dependency located in the Irish Sea between England and Ireland) another custom, *Hop-tu-Naa*, takes place on October 31. Over time, Hop-tu-Naa has come to be seen as a version of Hallowe'en as it involves carving turnips (or swedes) in the manner of jack o' lanterns and processions of singing children visiting houses in the hope of being rewarded with apples, sweets, and coins. Also, as on Hallowe'en, girls would take part in various forms of love divination such as eating a salted fish or *soddag valloo*, a type of cake consisting of flour, salt, and eggs including the shells and soot. It was the belief that eating these items would allow girls to dream of their future husbands. While this form of love divination has largely died out, it is still the custom that children walk in procession along the streets while holding carved turnip lanterns and singing Hop-tu-Naa songs such as "*Ginnie the Witch*."

There is, however, no true connection between Hallowe'en and Hop-tu-Naa despite appearances to the contrary. Instead Hop-tu-Naa is considered Celtic New Year or *Oie Houney* in Manx (the language of the Isle of Man), a date that marks the end of summertime and the start of winter. According to tradition, this was a time when people could rejoice in the safe gathering of the harvest and indicate that their preparations for winter had been completed. The name Hop-tu-Naa is thought by some folklorists to be a corruption of the Manx *Shogh ta'n Oie* ("This is the Night"). Over time, the Celtic New Year moved in line with the secular New Year that occurs on January 1. However the Celtic New Year is still recalled in Scotland where the New Year celebration of Hogmanay, the name of which seems to derive from the same root words and is still celebrated in Scotland as the last day of the year. Another Hallowe'en-esque British custom that is not actually related to the tradition is Punkie Night, which occurs every year on the last Thursday of October in Hinton St. George, in the southwest English county of Somerset. The word punkie is the local name for a hollowed-out mangel-wurzel (large turnip) that is lit from within by a candle in the manner of a jack o'lantern and on Punkie Night all the local children parade through the village streets singing a special Punkie Song and carrying their punkies in order to be given sweets and money by onlookers. According to local legend, the event began when local men went to a nearby village and became so drunk that they could not find their way home. In order to guide their menfolk home, the women of Hinton St. George placed lit candles inside hollowed-out mangel-wurzels to prevent the flames from being blown out by strong winds. Today, the event is very popular with locals and visitors alike, a popularity that has led nearby villages to hold their own Punkie Nights.

See also: All Souls' Day; Burning the Ashen Faggot and The Burning of the Clavie (Volume 2); Changeling Beliefs (Volume 1); *Dia de los Muertos*: Day of the Dead; Japanese Death Customs; *Qingming* Festival; Saining (Volume 1); *Santa Muerte*; Saturday of Souls and *Radonitsa*; Soul Cakes and Soul Bread; *Zaduszki*

Further Reading

The German Way & More. "Halloween and *Martinstag*." Accessed October 31, 2015, at http://www.german-way.com/history-and-culture/holidays-and-celebrations/halloween-and-martinstag/.

Jones, Alison. *Larousse Dictionary of World Folklore*. Edinburgh, UK: Larousse, 1996.

Manx Heritage Centre. "Hop Tu Naa Celebrations at Cregneash." October 26, 2010. Accessed November 1, 2015, at http://www.manx.net/isle-of-man-news/595/hop-tu-naa-celebrations-at-cregneash.

Rogers, Nicholas. *Halloween: From Pagan Ritual to Party Night*. Oxford, UK: Oxford University Press, 2002.

Santino, Jack. "The Fantasy and Folklore of All Hallows," *The American Folklife Center: Halloween*. Accessed October 16, 2015, at http://www.loc.gov/folklife/halloween.html.

Simpson, Jacqueline, and Steve Roud. *Oxford Dictionary of English Folklore*. Oxford, UK: Oxford University Press, 2000.

Vannin, Ellan. "What's the Difference between Hop-tu-Naa and Halloween?" BBC News: Isle of Man, October 24, 2011. Accessed November 1, 2015, at http://www.bbc.co.uk/news/world-europe-isle-of-man-15337057.

HALVA, INTERNATIONAL

Halva (also spelled *halawa*, *halvah*, *halava,* and *halwa*, as well as many other ways) is the name given to a variety of confectionary made in the Middle East, India, and Central Asia, as well as Europe and North America and among immigrant communities in Australia. The name halva derives from the Arabic *hulw*, meaning sweet. As halva is considered a comfort food by many it is often served at funerals or to mark the anniversary of a death. This is especially true in Iran and among Iranian immigrants living in Europe and North America. For many Iranians halva, particularly that made with wheat flour, saffron, and rosewater, is a food symbolic of bereavement and is inextricably linked with times of emotional distress. The association of halva with death may come from the traditional Islamic practice that sees families cook halva made from wheat flour or semolina on the evening of a funeral to distribute among their neighbors and the poor. At Iranian funerals, halva is served alongside mint tea and dates, and rosewater, which is often added as a flavoring to halva, is sprinkled over graves. In Iran, Turkey, and Afghanistan halva is also served on the seventh and fortieth day after a person's death. A type of spiced halva is also served to mourners at funerals in the Republic of Dagestan that is a federal subject of Russia. In Turkey, halva made with *un helvası* flour is made on the day a relative dies. This type of halva is made by browning flour in butter, adding sugar syrup and pine nuts and shaping the dough into balls.

Halva has a long history. In the seventh century, the word halva referred to a paste made from dates kneaded with milk while by the ninth century it had come to resemble the Persian sweetmeat *afroshag*, for it had started to consist of semolina or wheat flour that was fried or toasted and turned into a stiff paste, usually by adding sugar syrup, honey, date syrup, or grape syrup and then combined by stirring over a low heat. Flavorings such as rosewater, chopped nuts, or cooked carrot puree were then added and the finished product was shaped into elaborate shapes or sliced into bars. Over time, halva spread eastward and westward and came to be made using a wide variety of ingredients, preparations, and flavorings. The confection became so popular in India that a caste of confectioners living in the north of the country came to be known as the *halvais*. In India, the sweetmeat was made with semolina that was fried in *ghee* (clarified butter) and flavored with dried fruit, spiced syrup (tasting of saffron and cardamom), and chopped nuts (usually pistachio and almonds but coconut and poppy-seeds in Chennai). Indian halva was also sometimes made with *sathi* (zedoary flour) or purees made from fruits such as melon, banana, papaya, orange, and squash and vegetables such as beetroot, potato, carrot, or yam. In Hindu culture, sesame seeds, from which some forms of halva are made, are associated with immortality for according to Hindu mythology they were blessed by the god of death, Yama. Consequently, sesame seeds are regarded throughout the East as symbolic of eternal life. Moreover, sesame seed oil is considered extremely lucky and so is used in many Hindu rites and prayers. For instance, the Hindu festival held to mark the day that the sun enters the Zodiac sign (*rashi*) of Capricorn (*Makar*) is called *Makar sankrant* (or *Makar Sankranti* or *Makar Sankranthi*) and sesame oil lamps are lit in a temple to Lord Shiva, while devotees perform a ritual honoring their late ancestors (*pitrushraddha*) or *Tarpana*, by making an offering of sesame. The use of sesame oil as an offering to ancestors (*shraddha*) is believed by Hindus to block negative energies from impinging on the rite.

Bangladesh also sees halva made from carrots. Pureed lentils, mung beans, and peanuts are also used to make halva as is egg custard made stiff with the addition of coconut and flavored with nutmeg, cinnamon, cardamom, and saffron and featuring dried fruits, rosewater, and chopped nuts. Halva made from carrot and flours predominate in Nepal, where another type of unsweetened halva is also made in Nepal by mixing barley, salt, water, and ghee.

In the Middle East, it is usual to make halva from semolina to which may be added yoghurt, honey, chopped nuts, dried fruits, rosewater, and spices. In Iraq,

---

Makar Sankranthi: The Hindu Harvest Festival

In India Hindu communities celebrate *Makar Sankranthi* with great enthusiasm. The festival is known by a variety of names across the country, including *Pongal*, *Lohiri*, and *Uttararayan*. The festival is also celebrated in Nepal, Thailand, and Myanmar. Makar Sankranthi marks the day when the sun enters the sign of Makar (Capricorn) from the Tropic of Cancer and it is considered an auspicious time of transition. Makar Sankranthi falls on January 14 annually according to the Hindu solar calendar and is regarded as a special time because, according to the solar calendar, on this date day and night are of equal duration. Moreover from this date days become longer and warmer.

a sweetmeat called *Halawat tamr* is made from chopped walnuts, almonds, and dates that are kneaded together. Similar dishes exist in Iran, Syria, Afghanistan, Pakistan (where halva means "sweet"), and Egypt. The halva sold in Turkey and Greece is made from combining egg with solidified syrup and always includes nuts and sometimes dried or candied fruit. Also made in Europe, as in North America, is sesame halva, which is a by-product of the sesame oil production industry and sees sesame seed ground up and combined with honey or sugar syrup and made to form a solid cake that is often decorated with whole almonds or pistachio nuts.

See also: Eating Ashes of the Dead; Funeral Cakes and Funeral Candy; *Koliva*; Muslim Death Customs; Soul Cakes and Soul Breads; *Tết Nguyên đan*; Wake

Further Reading

Chenciner, Robert. *Daghestan: Tradition and Survival*. Abingdon, UK: RoutledgeCurzon, 1997.
Davidson, Alan. *The Oxford Companion to Food*. Third edition. Oxford, UK: Oxford University Press, 2014.
Edalati, Ali. "Death in Iranian Culture (A Case Study of Abarkouh, Yazd)," *International Review of Social Sciences and Humanities, 2*(2), 2012, 200–202.
Herb Myths and Legends. "Sesame Seed." March 22, 2009. Accessed January 10, 2015, at http://herbmythsandlegends.blogspot.co.uk/2009/03/sesame-seed.html.
Mehran, Azita. "Halva for all Occasions." Turmeric & Saffron, June 16, 2010. Accessed January 10, 2015, at http://turmericsaffron.blogspot.co.uk/2010/06/halva-for-all-occasions.html.
My Persian Kitchen. "Persian Halvah." October 23, 2009. Accessed January 10, 2015, at http://mypersiankitchen.com/persian-halvah/.
Price, Massoume. "A History of Moharram & Other Rituals of Death in Iran." Iran Chamber Society, December 2001. Accessed January 10, 2015, at http://www.iranchamber.com/culture/articles/rituals_of_death.php.
Roufs, Timothy G., and Kathleen Smyth Roufs. *Sweet Treats around the World: An Encyclopedia of Food and Culture*. Santa Barbara, CA: ABC-CLIO, 2014.
Varli Gork, Reyhan. *Death and Funerals in Sunni Communities in Turkey*. Accessed January 10, 2015, at https://www.inter-disciplinary.net/ptb/mso/dd/dd4/gork%20paper.pdf.

HIGH-PLATFORM EXPOSURE OF THE CORPSE, AUSTRALIA

High-platform exposure of the corpse is a traditional method of excarnation or defleshing practiced by Aboriginal Australians who call the practice primary burial. The custom involves the ritualized placing of a corpse in elevated positions such as on a platform lodged in a tree or on a scaffold, where it is covered in leaves and branches but otherwise left exposed to elements including the weather and scavenging creatures. The corpse is left exposed until the flesh disintegrates and leaves the bone, a process that usually takes several months to complete. High-platform exposure is usually reserved for the disposal of high-status adults, especially eminent men. While the practice is not as common as it once was, high-platform exposure of the corpse does take place within several indigenous communities in Australia, being particularly associated with Queensland, Central Australia, the Northern Territory, and the northeast of the country. The practice has also been documented as occurring in New South Wales, Victoria, and southeast Australia. Pentecost Island, one of the 83 islands that make up the South Pacific nation of Vanuatu, sees a similar post-death practice for the corpses of small children and sometimes women are left exposed on cliffs or in caves situated on the side of limestone crags.

Many people around the world practice ground interment thereby providing loved-ones with a peaceful permanent resting place. However many indigenous peoples such as Australian Aborigines incorporate the exposure of corpses to the natural elements into their funerary traditions. Generally speaking, Aborigines feel that after death a body should be placed within the broader natural environment where factors such as the weather and temperature, as well as animals, can help the course of decomposition. Such exposure leads to the bleaching of the corpse's bones, which are subsequently readied for burial.

It is thought that indigenous peoples have lived in Australia for around 60,000 years and Aboriginal populations living in Northern Australia have practiced high-platform exposure of the corpse for millennia. When European colonizers arrived in Australia in the 18th century, settlers noticed that Aborigines lived in sophisticated social patterns and engaged in a rich oral culture. At the heart of this oral tradition lie spiritual values based on belief in Dreamtime, a mythical time of creation also known as The Dreaming or Creation Period. Aborigines see all aspects of life as part of a complex network of inter-relationships that can be traced back to their ancestors' connection to the surrounding environment. For Aboriginal Australians, the spiritual world is inhabited by the ghosts of their ancestors who control the natural world and it is through a great many rituals and customs that the living can placate the dead. Further to this, Aborigines believe that in death the spirit leaves the living world and passes back into Dreamtime, returning to its place of birth in order to be reborn. Post-death rituals help this process of rebirth ensuring a satisfactory return. Therefore it is clear that for Aboriginal Australians all aspects of human existence are interwoven in a mythic structure and connected to the creative force of Dreamtime.

Burial and post-death customs vary across Australia, the world's sixth largest country by land area. Burial and methods of corpse disposal employed by Aboriginal Australians can be divided roughly into seven categories: abandonment of the corpse, burial, carrying of the corpse and bones, cremations, cannibalism, high-platform exposure of the corpse, and secondary disposal. It is usual to see several types of post-death ritual carried out in conjunction depending on the age, sex, and status of the deceased and high-platform exposure nearly always incorporates at least one of these other methods of corpse disposal. However there is great variation in the exact combination of practices that are combined with high-platform exposure of the corpse and these alternate methods of disposal can occur before of after the exposure of the body. Usually, however, it is secondary disposal that is combined with corpse exposure. Secondary disposal sees Aborigines collect all skeletal remains from the high platform and then reposition them after the main funerary rite, either for spiritual or practical reasons, though sometimes a relative of the deceased may carry a bone with them for up to a year before it is reburied. For whichever reason it is performed secondary disposal involves burying the bones at a second site, often in the ground or wrapped in paperbark and placed in a sheltered cave where they can disintegrate over the passage of time. Alternatively, the bones may be placed in a large log that has been hollowed-out by termites. The bones are left inside the log to crumble thereby becoming part of the bush landscape. This is the preferred method of Aborigines living in the Arnhem Land, a region in the Northern Territory. The final resting place chosen depends on soil conditions and local traditions. In East Kimberley, tribes clean the bones and paint them with red ochre before they wrap them in neat bunches tied with human hair prior to their being placed in an ossuary. Other tribes paint the remains with red ochre and then divide them into bundles that are each buried at separate predetermined locations. The specially selected sites often reflect theories about the land as filtered through faith in Dreamtime and are areas with spiritual significance associated with totem beings—the original form of an animal, plant, or other object (e.g., the totem)—as it was in the Dreamtime. A totem being is a generally benevolent mystical figure that shares a bond with a clan or individual. Aboriginal Australians believe in a system of individual totemism for each tribe member is thought to enjoy a mystical kinship with a particular animal (sometimes with an entire species) or with a natural object. This belief system is closely linked to the concept of the bush soul, meaning that the death of one of the pair will result in the demise of the other.

Though high-platform exposure of the corpse still occurs, it is gradually being replaced by Christian-style ground interment. This reflects that Aborigines face many of the same difficulties faced by First Nation groups in North America including augments over land ownership, social upheaval brought about by political marginalization, and a loss of cultural identity caused by forced assimilation. Since legislation was passed in the 1990s recognizing the individual and collective rights of Australia's indigenous people, there has been an increase in the number of Australians who identify themselves as Aborigines. However only a small number of people who identify themselves as Aborigines follow the ancient religious custom of Aboriginal culture, including the high-platform exposure of the corpse.

See also: Alkaline Hydrolysis; Sky Burial; Space Burial; Zoroastrian Funerals

Further Reading

Aboriginalculture.com.au. "Aboriginal Religion." Aboriginal Culture—Religion and Ceremony. Accessed December 16, 2014, at http://www.aboriginalculture.com.au/religion.shtml.

Galvan, Javier A., ed. *They Do What? A Cultural Encyclopedia of Extraordinary and Exotic Customs from around the World.* Santa Barbara, CA: ABC-CLIO, 2014.

Jones, Alison. *Larousse Dictionary of World Folklore*. Edinburgh, UK: Larousse, 1996.
Speiser, Felix. *Ethnology of Vanuatu: An Early Twentieth Century Study*. Bathurst, NSW, Australia: Crawford House Publishing Pty Ltd., 1991.

HINDU DEATH CUSTOMS, HINDUISM

Traditionally, most Hindu people die at home. When death is imminent, the family of the individual is notified and the person is placed in his or her bedroom or in the doorway of their home with the sick and dying person's head facing toward the east. A lantern is lit near the sick person's head and he or she is encouraged to focus on repeating mantras. Meanwhile, the family keeps vigil over the sick person until he or she dies all the while singing hymns, reading holy texts, and praying. If the Hindu person cannot die at home, the family still performs the same rituals, even if they are in a Western hospital. However wherever possible Hindu families will endeavor to take a sick person home to die. If the person is unconscious or dies suddenly, a family member will chant a mantra in their ear, holy ash or sandalwood paste is daubed on their forehead, and milk or holy water is tipped into their mouth, while deceased men will also be shaved. All the while, Vedic scriptures are chanted.

Hindus consider death, like birth, to be a highly polluting experience. For this reason, the icons of deities that are kept in the home are usually removed when a person dies. As death is viewed as extremely polluting, it is very important that the deceased's family performs post-death rituals correctly as only this will allow the spirit of the dead to move on to the afterlife where it will unite with ancestors. As soon as a Hindu person dies he or she is considered to have become a ghost (*preta*) and if funeral rituals are not performed in the right way it is thought that the preta will intrude upon the living by staying with them and causing them mischief and injury. For this reason, Hindu death rituals are intended to change a preta into an ancestral spirit known as a *pitri*. Most Hindus are cremated after death as this method of corpse disposal is considered the most efficient way for a soul to leave the physical body. Cremation is the last of the Hindu *samskaras* (rites of passage) with cremation known as *antyeshti samskara*, or the final reincarnation. The exact rituals of the cremation vary according to local customs but the ritual is normally led by a priest together with the deceased's eldest son. Some of the most common Hindu funeral customs include the placing of a lit lantern near the head of the deceased, the singing of hymns, and the saying of prayers. Other customs include placing rice balls called *pindas* inside the coffin, sprinkling water over the corpse, and placing a necklace of wooden beads called a *mala* around the neck of the corpse. Sometimes a garland of flowers is also tied around the neck while a widow will place her wedding pendant (*tali*) around the neck of her husband to show her enduring connection to him.

In the West, a Hindu coffin will be closed before it travels to a crematorium. However in India Hindus usually wish to have their cremation take place on the funeral *ghats* (platforms) that lie along the shore of the Ganges River. Only men may go to a Hindu cremation. When a Hindu body is cremated close to the Ganges the corpse is laid on a funeral pyre and then the eldest son utters Vedic prayers and sets light to the pyre. Once the pyre is alight, incense and clarified butter (*ghee*) are added to the flames. As the flames burn prayers for the dead are spoken. Once the body has been consumed by the flames, the ashes of the dead are sprinkled on water—either on the Ganges or on the sea close to where the deceased dwelled in life.

After the cremation the deceased's spouse, if any, dons white clothing as a sign that he or she is in mourning. The spouse and the deceased's close family will then mourn for 12 days, a process known as *shraddha*. On the 13th day, the rituals of *Kriya* takes place to signal the end of the reincarnation samskara. During Kriya, pindas and milk are presented in thanksgiving for the life of the deceased. Once Kriya has been completed mourners return to their everyday lives. The Hindu mourning period is brief as Hindus believe that each death brings the soul (*atman*) closer to *moksha*—the ultimate liberation from the continuous cycle of birth and death. On the anniversary of the death, shraddha is held again. During this time of remembrance food including pindas is given to the poor in memory of the ancestral spirits.

Some researchers suggest that the practice of riverside cremation that occurs along the banks of the Ganges is contributing to the pollution of the river with some 32,000 corpses cremated beside the river each year. This frequency of cremation results in around 300 tons of semi-cremated human flesh entering the Ganges annually. However the amount of pollution entering the Ganges through crematory practices is very small compared with the amount of human waste emanating from the living that enters the river for the Ganges acts as a sewer for most of the 450 million people that reside within the river's catchment area. Further it has been asserted that 80 percent of the human waste (mainly fecal matter) that enters the Ganges basin, is untreated.

See also: Hindu Baby Rituals (Volume 1); Hindu Wedding Ceremony (Volume 2); *Kumbh Mela* (Volume 2); Potty Training (Volume 1); Sikh Death Customs; *Thaipusam*: Extreme Ritual Flesh Modification (Volume 2); Vrindavan: The City of Widows; Zoroastrian Funerals

Further Reading

Beliefnet Inc. "Rites of Transition: Hindu Death Rituals." Accessed October 13, 2015, at http://www.beliefnet.com/Faiths/Hinduism/2001/02/Rites-Of-Transition-Hindu-Death-Rituals.aspx.

Firth, Shirley. *Dying, Death and Bereavement in a British Hindu Community*. Leuven, Belgium: Peeters Publishers, 1997.

Fowler, Jeaneane D. *Hinduism: Beliefs and Practices*. Brighton, UK: Sussex Academic Press, 1997.

Hinduism Today. "Death and Dying." January/February/March 2007. Accessed October 13, 2015, at http://www.hinduismtoday.com/modules/smartsection/item.php?itemid=1667.
Melton, J. Gordon, and Martin Baumann, eds. *Religions of the World: A Comprehensive Encyclopedia of Beliefs and Practices. Volume One A–B.* Santa Barbara, CA: ABC-CLIO, 2010.
Murata, Kyoko. "Grieving Tradition in a New Land: Hindu and Death and Dying Rituals in America," in Lucy Bregman, ed., *Religion, Death, and Dying, Volume 3: Bereavement and Death Rituals.* Santa Barbara, CA: Praeger, 2010.
Rowlatt, Justin. "India's Dying Mother." BBC News, May 12, 2016. Accessed June 5, 2016, at http://www.bbc.co.uk/news/resources/idt-aad46fca-734a-45f9-8721-61404cc12a39#four-26696.

ISOLA DI SAN MICHELE: VENICE'S CEMETERY ISLAND, ITALY

Isola di San Michele, or San Michele Island, is a landmass located in the lagoon surrounding Venice, Italy. The island has served as Venice's cemetery (*cimitero*) since the early 19th century.

Prior to the establishing of San Michele as Venice's cemetery, the city's dead were normally buried under paving stones in the city center, a practice that proved a health hazard, especially during times of disease. For this reason, when Austria occupied Venice during the 19th century, Austrian authorities decreed in 1837 that San Michele would be instituted as the only burial ground for most of the city's inhabitants—a Jewish cemetery had already been established on the Venetian sandbar known as the Lido in the 14th century.

San Michele was, originally, two islands that were home to convents, San Michele and San Cristoforo, but these were united during the Napoleonic occupation of Venice allowing the Isola di San Michele to serve as an island dedicated to the dead. The island cemetery is divided into many sections including Orthodox and Protestant cemeteries as well as areas dedicated to memorials to nuns, priests, gondoliers, and foreigners plus the graves of officers and seamen of the British merchant and Royal Navy who perished during World War I. Many of the graves on San Michele attract tourists as they house the remains of famous people. For instance, the Orthodox section contains the tombs of composers Sergei Diaghilev and Igor Stravinsky, both of which are often decorated with offerings left by lovers of ballet and classical music. Modernist American poet Ezra Pound is buried in the Protestant section though his tomb can be quite difficult to see since it is located in the center of a flowerbed.

In 1998, a competition was organized by the City of Venice to try to find a design for an enlarged cemetery island. The competition sought plans that would feature an artificial island that could serve as the base for the island's cemetery services as well as providing additional grave space that could be annexed to San Michele. Today, however, San Michele remains a very small island. This means that in general the dead can stay on the island for only a short time before being exhumed—only a few privileged families are allowed to lease burial space for longer periods. After around 10 to 12 years most people's mortuary remains deposited on San Michele are exhumed before either being cremated or deposited in an ossuary on the Italian mainland. For this reason, discreet noticeboards are posted around the entrance to the cemetery listing the timetable for exhumations.

See also: Grave Rentals and Exhumations; Ossuaries; Tombstone Tourism

Further Reading

Allen Toth, Susan. "Venice's Isle of the Death," *New York Times*, May 16, 1993. Accessed December 14, 2015, at http://www.nytimes.com/1993/05/16/travel/venice-s-isle-of-the-dead.html.

Italy Heaven. "San Michele, Venice's Cemetery Island." Accessed December 14, 2015, at http://www.italyheaven.co.uk/veneto/venice/sanmichele.html.

McManus, John. "The World Is Running Out of Burial Space." BBC News. March 12, 2015. Accessed December 14, 2015, at http://www.bbc.co.uk/news/uk-31837964.

Stoppani, Teresa. *Paradigm Islands: Manhattan and Venice: Discourses on Architecture and the City*. Abingdon, UK: Routledge, 2011.

J

JAPANESE DEATH CUSTOMS, JAPAN

Japanese funeral customs are a mixture of Buddhist rites and Shinto, the native religion of Japan that evolved from a complex set of rituals including funeral rituals and the country's rich cultural history. Buddhist funeral rites were introduced to Japan from abroad and are intended to help the dead make the transition from the world of the living to the realm of the afterlife, or to their reincarnated state if they are not able to escape the cycle of rebirth.

In Japan, the traditions of Shinto and Buddhism amalgamated in 1638 when all Japanese households were made to register as Buddhists. This edict was not to stamp out Shinto but rather to prevent Christianity from gaining a foothold in Japan. However the end result was that while the Japanese built Buddhist shrines called *butsudan* in their homes the families continued to have a Shinto shrine in another room of their house. Today, almost all Japanese families call in a Buddhist priest after a loved one has died and they also take part in Buddhist rituals. However the attitude with which the Japanese view death and death rituals reflects Shinto traditions.

Traditionally, when a Japanese person dies a ritual called *Matsugo-no-mizu* (water of the last moment) takes place during which the lips of the deceased are moistened with water. The corpse is washed with hot water (*yukan*) and cotton gauze is placed in its orifices before being dressed—women wear a kimono and men wear a suit—and having make-up applied to cover the deathly palor. A man will also have his face shaved. The deceased then spends a final night on his or her own futon bed with his or her head pointing toward the north. The body is surrounded with ice and is concealed by a sheet, except for the deceased's face, which is covered with a white cloth. Some Japanese people also put a knife on the corpse's chest so

---

Tama the Cat's Shinto Farewell

In June 2015, around 3,000 Japanese bade farewell to Tama, the cat credited with saving a Japanese railway line from ruin. Tama was given a Shinto-style funeral after she died of heart failure at 16 years of age. Tama was Japan's most famous cat, noted for wearing a stationmaster's cap and whose welcoming presence encouraged people to use the near-abandoned rail line. In recognition for her dedication, Tama was awarded the posthumous status of Shinto goddess, in keeping with Shinto's practice of honoring animal deities, and was also given the title of honorable eternal stationmaster. Tama will also be celebrated at a nearby shrine for cats.

that the deceased is able to protect him- or herself from evil spirits. A small table is also placed next to the futon on which is placed flowers, incense, and candles. Meanwhile, the family shrine is closed and covered with a white paper in a ritual known as *Kamidana-fuji*. This ritual is performed in order to prevent the impure spirits of death from tainting the shrine.

To signal that someone within a household has died, a white paper lantern is placed outside a home. When this is seen, members of the deceased's immediate family, including young children, and friends visit the deceased's home and extend their condolences. The family and friends may also sit with the corpse, touch it, and talk to the deceased as though he or she were alive. This all-night wake is known as *tsuya*.

The following morning the body is part of a slow procession that travels to the place where the various funeral rituals will take place. This can be a temple or, if the deceased was not religious, a secular facility. Many Japanese cities have combined funeral facilities where bodies can rest overnight along with a crematorium. When the procession reaches its destination, the deceased is dressed, laid in a modest coffin, and surrounded with dry ice. Japanese coffins tend to be made from wood and do not feature much in the way of decoration, though they do feature a window above the deceased's face. Traditionally, several items are placed inside the coffin including a white kimono (white is the traditional Buddhist color of mourning), sweets, and six coins with which the deceased can pay to cross the Sanzu River (*Sanzu-no-kawa,* or River of Three Crossings). According to traditional Japanese beliefs, the Sanzu River is located in Mount Osore, in northern Japan and is the river over which the dead must pass on the seventh day after their death as they journey to the afterlife. Once the items are placed within the coffin, it is placed in front of an array of lights, sculptures, and, flowers that symbolize paradise. In addition, a portrait of the dead person is placed with the flowers and lights as is incense, which should be kept burning all the times. If the coffin is taken to a temple then the coffin should be put on the altar with the head of the corpse pointing to the north or west.

Once the coffin is in place, a wake begins close by. Those attending the wake bring gifts of condolence money (*koden*) sealed within special envelopes that are tied with black and white string. The amount of money presented by individual guests varies depending on how well they knew the deceased and is written on the outside of the envelope. Those attending the wake often carry with them a set of tasseled *juzu* prayer beads that are similar to a Catholic rosary. When all the money has been given, the presiding priest kneels before the coffin and chants a *sutra* (i.e., Buddhist scripture). The next part of the Japanese funeral rites varies according to location and the type of Buddhism followed by the family, but it is often the case that the deceased's immediate family steps forward one at a time to offer their respects to the dead. Next, it is traditional for each mourner to take up incense in granular form from a bowl and then hold it to their forehead before dropping the incense onto an incense burner. The mourner then prays and bows to the portrait of the deceased. Each mourner performs this action either in turn or simultaneously at another altar. When all the guests have completed this ritual, they turn and bow to the deceased's immediate family. The guests then depart and on leaving are each presented with a gift that has a value of between 25 percent and 50 percent of the amount of koden given as a sign of their condolences. The deceased's immediate family, meanwhile, retires nearby usually to have an informal dinner accompanied with beer and *sake* (traditional Japanese rice wine) and involving lengthy conversations about the deceased. It is common for men to drink heavily at the wake in lieu of crying at the funeral. The next day the immediate family returns to where the deceased lies in his or her coffin, and the funeral takes place by repeating the entire ritual of the day before. During the repetition of the previous day's ritual the atmosphere is extremely formal. Mourners wear black with men wearing black suits and ties with a white shirt and women wearing either black dresses or a kimono. Though the atmosphere at Japanese funerals is very formal, mourners do not tend to reveal their emotions in public and mourners do not normally cry at funerals. During the funeral the deceased is given a new Buddhist posthumous name, or *kaimyō*. This name is important, as it confers on the deceased a new Buddhist identity thereby helping the deceased to achieve enlightenment. The length of the kaimyō depends on the amount of koden money that the deceased's friend and family give to the temple. Some kaimyō names are free of charge but some names have to be paid for. When the funeral is over, the coffin is opened. This is the emotional climax of the funeral and sees the family and guests take flowers from the arrangement that had stood near the coffin and place them inside the coffin. If Japanese mourners are going to weep in public, this is the moment when the sobbing will occur and only women will cry openly. Sometimes the lid of the coffin is then nailed shut.

Next, the mourners accompany the coffin as it is taken to a crematorium in a decorated funeral vehicle. Once at the crematorium the deceased's immediate family may repeat the incense burning ritual and the closest family member may be asked to operate the furnace. Alternatively, the crematorium staff may conduct this job. While the body burns, a process that takes around two hours, the deceased's closest relatives eat a funeral feast. When they have finished eating, the relatives gather in another room of the crematorium where the furnace's slab, still hot from being among the flames and bearing any residual skeletal remains, is brought forward. Crematorium staff members then give mourners a tour of the bones during which they highlight any visible signs of disease. This tour also sees crematorium staff pick up a special pair of chopsticks of which one is made from bamboo and one is fashioned from willow that is linked together to symbolize that the crematorium is a place that connects life and death. A member of the crematorium staff then uses the special chopsticks to pick up a particular neck bone that seems to contain a seated Buddha figure. All the mourners then also pick up chopsticks and transfers the skeletal remains to a small container with leg bones selected first and head bones chosen last as this ensures that the deceased is not upside-down in death. While selecting the bones it is quite usual for mothers to urge their children to pick up bones from the skull in the belief that this will make the children cleverer. Others mourners may pick up particular bones to battle disease or injuries.

Once all the bones are within the receptacle the vessel is taken to the deceased's home where they are placed on an altar in front of the butsudan with the portrait of the deceased that was employed during the funeral rites placed nearby. The remains stay here for 35 days until they are buried at the family grave (*haka*). All the time that the bones are within the family home incense sticks called *osenko* are burned. The side of family gravestones is often engraved with the name of the person who paid for the memorial as well as the names of persons buried within the grave, though these may also be written on a separate stone located in front of the memorial. When it is time for a new name to be added the name of the deceased is written on a wooden board called a *sotoba* that is kept behind or next to the gravestone. The sotoba is then removed after the funeral or during memorial events. Another quite rare Japanese gravestone tradition occurs on the graves of married couples that are still alive. Both the husband and wife's names appear on the stone with the name of living spouses written in red. When one of the couple dies, the red is removed from that person's name. Another rare gravestone traditions is the inclusion of a box at the side of the grave into which visitors can place their business card to show that they have visited the grave. A modern feature of Japanese graves is to include a small computer touch screen displaying a photograph of the deceased as well as details such as his or her family tree. This custom is reserved for expensive gravestones however.

Buddhism recommends a series of memorial observances be held after death. These ceremonies normally take place at the deceased's family home and normally include a priest chanting a sutra, prayers, and incense burning, just as at the funeral although in a less formal atmosphere. According to Buddhist traditions, these ceremonies should be held every seven days after a death until the 49th day. Today, however, relatives often cannot afford to take time off work or afford to travel to the family home, so it is not unusual for only a couple of memorial ceremonies to be held before the 49th day. The memorial ceremonies are, nonetheless, important, as they are how Japanese ancestor worship begins. After the ceremony on the 49th day, another ceremony should occur on the 100th day after death and then annually until the 33rd, or 50th, anniversary of the death is reached.

In Japan, the yearly memorial ceremony takes the form of Obon (or Bon), a three-day holiday held on different dates according to location that is also known as the Festival of Lanterns. This 500-year-old Buddhist tradition is said to be the occasion on which the spirits of the ancestors return to their family homes. There are many, various Obon traditions throughout Japan. Sometimes lamps are lit at the family butsudan, or small fires are burned in front of houses' front doors in order to guide the spirits back to their homes. Many families also visit their family gravesite where they clean the grave. It is traditional on the last day of Obon to float small lantern-like boats called *Toro Nagashi* that are filled with food and a candle on a river or the sea. The illuminated boats are said to guide ancestral spirits back to the world of the dead. This custom has been banned in most of Japan but this does not seem to have had any effect on the custom's popularity.

See also: Cremation; "Lyke-Wake Dirge"; *Mizuko Kuyo*: Japanese Fetus Memorial Service; *Ngaben*; *Qingming* Festival; Sikh Death Customs; *Tết Nguyên đan*

Further Reading

Howarth, Glennys, and Oliver Leaman, eds. *Encyclopedia of Death and Dying*. Abingdon, UK: Routledge, 2013.
Popovic, Mislav. "Japanese Funeral." TraditionsCustoms.com. Accessed October 13, 2015, at http://traditionscustoms.com/death-rites/japanese-funeral.
Prohl, Inken, and John Nelson, eds. *Handbook of Contemporary Japanese Religions*. Leiden, Netherlands: Brill, 2012.
Reader, Ian. *Religion in Contemporary Japan*. Honolulu, HI: University of Hawai'i Press, 1991.
Suzuki, Hikaru. *The Price of Death: The Funeral Industry in Contemporary Japan*. Stanford, CA: Stanford University Press, 2000.
Van Bremen, Jan, and D. P. Martinez, eds. *Ceremony and Ritual in Japan: Religious Practices in an Industrialized Society*. Abingdon, UK: Routledge, 2002.
Wiren, Alan. "Japanese Funerals: Sunset in the Rising Sun." Japan Tourist Info. Accessed October 13, 2015, at http://www.japanvisitor.com/japanese-culture/japanese-funerals.

JAZZ FUNERAL, UNITED STATES

Jazz funerals are a type funeral synonymous with New Orleans, Louisiana, though in recent years they have also become available elsewhere with jazz funeral companies based in the United Kingdom.

Jazz funerals are festive occasions that celebrate life in the face of death. In the United States, such funerals are usually reserved for prominent males, usually black men who were musicians or New Orleanians who died young. The funerals tend to be arranged by benevolent societies and burial associations that collect dues throughout the year and charge an extra fee for the provision of a brass band at the person's funeral. Jazz funerals are marked by a grand procession of mourners that make their way through the streets of New Orleans on their way to the cemetery. Family and friends of the deceased and funeral directors walk at the front of the procession with the coffin and are referred to as the first line or main line while the musicians and crowds of mourners that follow are referred to as the second line. (*See* Plate 8.) When the funeral procession moves from the funeral service to the burial site the first line and the second line walk in time to the rhythm of a brass band. Once the corpse has been buried the music played by the musicians changes from somber, Christian dirges that necessitate a slow marching pace to upbeat music that is accompanied by dancing and reveling.

The roots of the jazz funeral can be traced back over 400 years to two west African tribes—the Dahomeans of Benin and the Yoruba of Nigeria. These tribes had secret societies that charged a membership fee as a kind of burial insurance to ensure that members received a funeral in the manner that they desired. When the slave trade brought Africans to America, the concept of providing proper burials to fellow slaves remained strong and over time the concept became deeply rooted in African American culture. The custom of playing music during a funeral procession was incorporated into the basic African model of the funeral. Over time brass band music that had evolved from both the military bands of the American Civil War and from French military bands proved popular as funeral processional music. The funeral marches played by the brass bands sounded much like New Orleans dirges as they used the same beat and soon it became customary to play either so-called Negro spiritual songs (e.g., "Nearer My God to Thee") or a slow dirge as a funeral procession traveled to the graveyard. Gradually the tradition evolved of playing hymns over the dirge drumbeat. In addition, once the funeral procession reached the cemetery and the body was "planted" by being buried in the ground, one of the funeral party would declare, "Cut the body loose" and the band would begin to play a livelier hymn such as "When the Saints Go Marching In" or ragtime tunes such as "Just a Little While to Stay Here" or "Oh, Didn't He Ramble." Usually a trumpet would play the first few bars of the upbeat hymn and then drums would play a cadence. Those playing the music, like other general mourners, became known as second line because they traveled behind the corpse and close relatives at the front of the funeral procession.

When slavery was abolished, black funerals continued to include brass band music. By the end of the 19th century and start of the 20th century many benevolent societies such as the Society of the First African Baptist Church, the Odd Fellows, and the Society of Sons and Daughters of Mount Pleasant Baptist Church formed that promised to give members a proper burial as long as they paid a contribution toward the cost of their burial. Up through the 1930s, funerals with music continued to be popular and as at this time ragtime music was in fashion the style of music played at the funerals began to be influenced by prevailing musical tastes and so the jazz funeral was born. Those playing the ragtime music accompanying the funeral processions wore special uniforms as they walked through the streets of New Orleans. Over time, a second line uniform evolved that included an umbrella decorated with feathers, sequins, fringing and flowers, dark suits, white aprons, and handkerchiefs while characteristic dance moves also developed that included gyrating, zigzagging, and bobbing movements, jumping and cake-walking (i.e., a semi-comic dance originating from slaves' mockery of high society dance styles). Sometimes a group circle dance would be included in the procession too during which a solo dancer or duo would be surrounded by other dancers.

During the 1940s and 1950s, however, jazz funerals fell out of fashion, particularly with New Orleans' white population, mainly because the Roman Catholic Church disapproved of the funerals. This scorn led to a deliberate attempt to revive the jazz funeral but as many of the original ragtime musicians had died in the meantime the sound of the revived jazz funeral differed from those of earlier years. One of the most famous jazz funeral bands to evolve during this revival was the Olympia Brass Band, which appeared on film leading a jazz funeral procession in the 1973 James Bond adventure *Live and Let Die* in which a jazz funeral is used as a cover to assassinate a spy. Trumpeter Alvin Alcorn plays the knife-wielding assassin in the film.

Today jazz funerals are held usually for former musicians or young people in which case the playing of dirges is reduced. The uniform worn by jazz funeral musicians has changed over time and nowadays they tend to wear everyday clothes rather than the somber suits of yesteryear. Such changes have not been universally welcomed however with groups such as Black Men of Labor Social Aid & Pleasure Club bemoaning the break with tradition. To this end, the group arranges traditional jazz funerals and sponsors a yearly second line procession for which musicians must dress in the traditional manner and play traditional music and songs.

Over the years, second line musicians have, to a degree, become detached from jazz funerals and developed their own, separate identity. For instance, every September to May at least one second-line parade occurs each Sunday with musicians playing near members' houses and in front of bars. Second lines have also come to be regarded by some as important symbols of New Orleans society and, most especially, as a powerful symbol of black New Orleans. This has led to questions of how to best present the second-line processions both to the tourists that come to New Orleans, especially to see its parades, and to the public in general.

See also: "Abide With Me"; Albanian Funeral Customs; Cajun Weddings (Volume 2); Death Dance; *Edir* and *Engozi*; Funeral Songs; "The Last Post" and "Taps"; "Lyke-Wake Dirge"; Romanian Funeral Customs

Further Reading

New Orleans Tourism Marketing Corporation. "The Jazz Funeral." New Orleans Official Guide. Accessed June 15, 2015, at http://www.neworleansonline.com/neworleans/multicultural/multiculturaltraditions/jazzfuneral.html.

Riley, Herlin, and Johnny Vidacovich. *New Orleans Jazz and Second Line Drumming*. Los Angeles, CA: Alfred Publishing Co., Inc., 2008.

Sakakeeny, Matt. "Jazz Funerals and Second Line Parades." Know LA: Encyclopedia of Louisiana, February 3, 2011. Accessed June 15, 2015, at http://www.knowla.org/entry/860/.

Thursby, Jacqueline S. *Funeral Festivals in America: Rituals for the Living*. Lexington: The University Press of Kentucky, 2006.

JEWISH DEATH CUSTOMS, JUDAISM

Jewish people consider death to be a natural occurrence and feel that as the human body is a sacred vessel belonging to God, corpses should be treated with respect. Jewish people also agree that it is right and proper to mourn someone after he or she has died and keep alive the deceased's memory. It is very difficult to give an all-encompassing overview of every Jewish death custom, as Jews are not one single homogenous group. However in general the process of dying, burial, and mourning within Jewish communities is as follows.

When a Jewish person lies on his or her deathbed, it is usual for the person to say the prayer known as the *Shema* that reiterates the person's showing his or belief in God. Preparations for the burial of the deceased are made as quickly as possible. This reveals that many Jewish post-death customs and rituals are concerned with the treatment of the corpse rather than with the spiritual significance of the soul. Jewish people believe that when a person dies his or her soul or life force leaves the body but that the body retains its sanctity and so must be treated with respect. If a Jewish person dies in his or her own home rather than in a hospital then the first ritual to be performed on the body involves the laying of the corpse on the floor. This ritual is performed to symbolize that in death the body returns to the earth. The family members and friends that are with the person when they die should then rip their clothing in an act known as the act of *keriah*. This age-old tradition is intended to show the grief of mourners and is mentioned in the Hebrew Bible. The gathered people should then perform a prayer called the *Kaddish*, meaning holy. The Kaddish is often referred to as a funeral prayer but is in fact a prayer praising God.

Jewish people show their esteem for the dead through a series of rituals and practices in the lead-up to the funeral and burial. For example, as soon as a Jewish person dies it is considered important that he or she is not left alone. Instead, tradition dictates that a guard, or *shomer*, should be stationed with the corpse from the time of death until the funeral and interment. Often a member of the deceased's family takes on the role of the shomer and though it is traditional for the shomer to read aloud Psalm 23 to the deceased, modern custom dictates that the shomer should recite a poem that the deceased enjoyed or that is appropriate for the occasion. Along with the shomer, it is generally considered appropriate for members of the deceased's family to remain with the body.

Next, a group of volunteers from the local synagogue called a *Chevra Kadisha* (Holy Society) arrives to take care of the body and prepare it for burial. The Chevra Kadisha is not paid for its servies as its members consider preparing the corpse as a good deed (*mitzvah*), for which there is no possible reward. The Chevra Kadisha purifies the corpse by washing it with water in a ritual manner called *taharah* (pure), with male members of a Chevra Kadisha washing dead males and female members of a Chevra Kadisha cleansing females. When the Chevra Kadisha washes a body they do so silently and in sections so that most of the body stays covered when it is not being washed. The washing is performed in this manner so as to preserve the dignity of the corpse. Next, the corpse is dressed is a simple white shroud called a *tachrichin*, the unadorned simplicity of which reflects that everyone is equal in death. Traditionally, deceased Jewish men are also wrapped in a prayer shawl called a *tallit*, the fringing of which is severed to show that the men are now free from the laws of religion, but today this custom also extends to women. Both men and women are also dressed in a gown called a *kittel* that Jewish people wear at Yom Kippur, or the Day of Atonement, that is the holiest day in the Jewish year. When a Jewish person dies in Israel, they are dressed only in these items but if they die in a Western country then they will also be placed in a coffin. This coffin should be fashioned from wood, preferably pine, and should not contain any metal. It is important that materials that will not degrade are not included in the make-up of the coffin because it is of the upmost importance to Jews that the coffin and, subsequently the corpse, will rot quickly and thereby turn to dust as advocated in the book of *Genesis*. The desire for a body to return to dust is the reason that it is not usual for a Jewish person to be embalmed after death. Similarly, Jewish people are not normally cremated as cremation is at odds with the natural process of bodily decay. Moreover, for some Jewish people cremation brings to mind memories of Nazi atrocities involving crematoria during World War II. When a Jewish person is buried it is often the case that a sachet of soil taken from Israel, particularly from the city of Jerusalem, will be included in the coffin with the deceased.

Once the body is washed and placed in the coffin, the coffin is sealed and left to rest until the day of the funeral. A Jewish funeral normally takes place within 24 hours of a death. Just before the funeral all the mourners repeat the act of keriah and recite a blessing to God that reminds the mourners that even at a time of grief they should praise God who created death as part of life. Mourners are divided into categories. Official mourners, the immediate family and spouse of the deceased, participate in the act of keriah and sit in the front row of the funeral. A recent innovation has also allowed life partners, grandparents, and best friends to be included among the official mourners but this is in no way a widespread practice.

According to Jewish tradition, mourning does not actually begin until after the body if buried. Instead, the funeral is focused on honoring the dead and not on comforting those people that are upset during the ceremony. Until after the burial, people that grieve for the deceased are referred to as *aninut* rather than classified as mourners. The aninut are considered to be people that are so upset at the death of the person that they are in shock and cannot be expected to carry out their everyday duties. The aninut are exempt from all normal tasks and only have one duty to perform—to make burial arrangements. It is important for people other than official mourners to attend the funeral too because the Talmud tells that accompanying a person to his or her grave is one of the supreme good deeds (*mitzvot*). Mourners are also expected to give a money donation to a cause that was espoused by the deceased in life—this act is performed instead of giving flowers to the bereaved, who are known as *nihum avelim*.

Jewish funerals tend to be quite simple and short, usually lasting around 20 minutes, as there is no set liturgy that must be followed, no songs are sung, and no flowers are present. There are, however, certain rituals that must be enacted. The funeral, which may or may not be officiated by a rabbi and does not necessarily take place at a synagogue, continues the theme of honoring the deceased. The funeral consists of a poetry and psalm readings and the saying of a eulogy, or *hesped*, that is meant to show the deceased in a positive light but also to be an accurate reflection of his or her life. The ceremony ends with the saying of the *El Mohle Rachamin*. This is a commemorative prayer that implored God to grant peace to the soul of the deceased and connect their soul to the people of Israel.

After the funeral, pallbearers carry the coffin to the burial ground as a mark of respect for the dead. The pallbearers are accompanied by the shomer. The graveside ceremony is completed very quickly as it consists of only a small number of psalm readings and a rendition of the Kaddish. Once the body is buried attention turns to caring for the bereaved. When the bereaved return from the burial they usually go to a family home where mourning practices can be observed—this is known as a mourning house, or *shiva* house. The word shiva means seven in Hebrew and refers to the seven days of morning that mourners are expected to observe—this does not include the Jewish Sabbath as this is not included in shiva. Often a jug of water is left outside the shiva house so that mourners can wash their hands symbolically free from venturing near the dead in the cemetery. The washing of the hands is also a symbolic way of transitioning to the next stage of mourning that involves comforting the bereaved. After mourners have returned from the burial and washed, they then sit down to a ritual meal called *seudat havra'ah,* or the meal of consolation. This meal consists of egg and lentil dishes that are symbolic of the cycle of life and death. Mourners then light a candle that stays alight for the week of designated mourning. During this time mourners must also keep mirrors covered and must not cut their hair or shave. Mourners should also sit only on low stools and wear only slippers as leather shoes denote luxury that is not considered to be in keeping with a time of bereavement. During shiva, mourners should also keep doors unlocked, refrain from having sexual intercourse, and avoid housework, cooking, and studying. Mourners should also say the Kaddish three times each day and receive visitors that wish to comfort them.

Shiva is completed on the morning of the seventh day with the completion signaled by the mourners walking around their block of streets—this symbolizes that the bereaved are ready to return to everyday life. However once shiva is over another period of mourning known as *sheloshim* takes place 30 days after the death. During this period mourners do not go out to pleasurable events such

Jewish Ghosts

There are several types of Jewish ghosts. For example a *dybbuk* is usually the malevolent ghost of a dead person that takes possession of a host body in order to harm the host and to be generally unpleasant. The dybbuk only exits its host once it has completed its mission. A dybbuk may also be a neutral spirit bent on punishing a wrongdoer. Meanwhile, an *ibbur* is the benign spirit of a righteous person that resides inside a host whom it tries to help. Ibburs only incubate within people they feel deserve help to achieve their goals.

as weddings or birthday parties nor do they listen to music. Instead, the bereaved continue to mourn in a low-key manner. In every other way, however, mourners continue with their lives in the manner that they lived before they were bereaved. Sheloshim usually ends with a memorial service for the deceased.

After the periods of mourning have ended, Jewish people are still expected to remember their deceased friends and family. To this end communal memorial services are held at Yom Kippur and on three pilgrimage events—Sukkot, Passover, and Shavuot. At these times, Jewish people light special candles to memorialize the dead. Another period of commemoration occurs on the anniversary of the deceased death—*yahrzeit*. This anniversary is according to the Hebrew calendar rather than the calendars used in the West. On the whole, yahrzeit is not marked by any elaborate rituals though to mark the yahrzeit of a parent children should go to the synagogue to say the Kaddish.

Shortly before the first anniversary of the death, the deceased's family arranges for a tombstone to be placed at the grave. According to tradition, anyone that visits the grave should place a small stone on the tombstone as a mark of respect for the dead.

See also: *Brit Milah* (Volume 1); Jewish Wedding Customs (Volume 2); *Pidyon Haben:* Redemption of the First Born (Volume 1)

Further Reading

Alpert, Rebecca. "Grief and Rituals Surrounding Death: A Jewish Approach," in Lucy Bregman, ed., *Religion, Death, and Dying, Volume 3: Bereavement and Death Rituals*. Santa Barbara, CA: Praeger, 2010.

BBC. "Jewish Funeral Rites." BBC Bitesize: Religious Studies. Accessed October 19, 2015, at http://www.bbc.co.uk/schools/gcsebitesize/rs/death/judeathritesrev2.shtml.

Levine, Emma. "Jewish Views and Custom on Death," in Colin Murray Parkes, Pittu Laungani, and William Young, eds., *Death and Bereavement across Cultures*. Second Edition. Hove, UK: Routledge, 2015.

K

KOLIVA, INTERNATIONAL

Koliva (also spelled *kolyva, kollyva,* or *kollyba*) is a ritual food consisting of boiled or sprouted wheat berry salad that is eaten on special occasions, particularly during events connected to dying in the Eastern Catholic Churches and the Eastern Orthodox Churches. Koliva is eaten in Serbia, Romania, Bulgaria, Ukraine, and Greece, where, particularly, koliva is associated with funerals and death anniversaries. Indeed in the Greek Orthodox Church koliva is a heavily ritualized food that symbolizes death and renewal. In some countries, though not Greece, koliva is eaten on non-religious occasions too. Greek immigrant communities around the world, including those in the United States and Australia, also prepare and eat koliva.

The tradition of preparing koliva dates back to the earliest days of Christianity. In the Eastern Churches, koliva symbolizes Christ's Resurrection for just as wheat must be planted in soil to grow and bear fruit, so Christians must be buried when they die but will grow again, uncorrupted, through the promise of resurrection. Additionally, koliva echoes a quote from the Gospel of Saint John: "Christ said, 'Unless a wheat grain falls into the earth and dies, it remains alone; but if it dies, it bears much fruit'" (John 12:24).

Koliva is prepared in remembrance of the dead, usually to mark Saturday of Souls—a day set aside for the remembrance of the dead within the liturgical year of the Eastern Orthodox Church—and, according to various traditions, on the day of a funeral, the 40th day after death, the third-, sixth-, and ninth-month commemorations, death anniversaries such as five or 10 years after the event. Sometimes no sweetening agent is added to the koliva eaten on the day of a funeral, rendering it suitably bitter to mark a sad occasion. In some instances, only on the 40th-day commemoration is sugar or similar sweet substance added to signify the sweetness of resurrection and the promise that life will, eventually, again be sweet for the friends and relatives of the deceased. The family of the deceased prepares the koliva and brings it to the church for the periodic memorial services known as the *Mnimosinon* during which prayers for the eternal repose of the souls of the dead are said.

In Greece, koliva is served at funerals having been prepared by the family of the deceased and given to mourners. It takes two days to prepare koliva. First, wheat is soaked overnight and then boiled. Next, the wheat is mixed with raisins, parsley, toasted sesame seeds, nuts and sometimes pomegranate seeds. Occasionally, the resulting mixture is sweetened, pressed into a mound, then covered with breadcrumbs, and covered in icing (confectioner's) sugar. It is then decorated with almonds placed in such a way as to form the shape of a crucifix and the initials of the deceased. The koliva is then placed on a silver platter with white paper doilies.

At a Greek funeral, koliva is served to mourners in the courtyard of the graveyard once all of the deceased's immediate family have returned to the family home. The koliva is distributed together with bread and after all the mourners have taken a handful of koliva and a piece of bread, the mourners say a quiet wish for the pardon of the recently deceased. The mourners then travel to the deceased's home to join the family. None of the koliva or bread served at the graveyard may be taken into the bereaved family's house. Once all the mourners have congregated in the house, a tray of koliva is served alongside a slice of bread and a glass of wine. The wine, bread, and koliva are collectively known as *makario*, meaning "that which is blessed." Three days after the funeral, the local priest visits the graveyard along with female mourners and recites a *Trisayio* prayer. After this, koliva decorated with spices, nuts, raisins, and sugar is served.

That koliva is also associated with rebirth is evinced by the sanctification and eating of koliva at the end of the first week of the Great Lent to mark St. Theodore Saturday. This is because in 361 the Roman Emperor Julian, knowing that Christians marked Lent by fasting and praying, ordered that all food on sale at market should be sprinkled with the blood of animals sacrificed to pagan gods, thereby making it impossible for Christians to avoid eating contaminated meat and not be at the mercy of the contagion of pagan idolatry. However according to Christian legend, God sent Saint Theodore to earth to tell Christians not to buy foods from the market but to make koliva by boiling wheat. Thus Christians were not forced into pagan ways. The Eastern Orthodox Church commemorates these events by making koliva on the first Saturday of Great Lent (the last of three Saturday of Souls observed each year) that is then taken to church where a Divine Liturgy and a Memorial Service are held. To commemorate the day, Eastern Orthodox Christians bring koliva and lists of names of deceased friends and family members to church and the names are read aloud by the priest during the memorial service.

In some areas of Greece such as the island of Crete, village women make koliva to feed the souls of the dead on St. Basil's Day, January 1. On this day, the local priest visits every home, sprinkles the houses with water, and blesses them by making a sign of the cross with a sprig of basil.

Koliva Recipe (Serves 40 people)

Ingredients:

    4 cups wheat berries
    salt
    1/2 cup sesame seeds
    1 teaspoon anise seed

1 1/2 cups walnuts, coarsely chopped

1 1/2 cups blanched slivered almonds

1 1/2 cups golden raisins

1 teaspoon ground cinnamon

seeds of 1 pomegranate

3 cups confectioner's sugar, divided

For decoration:

2 cups blanched whole almonds

silver dragees

Rinse the wheat berries and place in a large saucepan. Add two pinches of salt and enough water to cover the wheat berries by 2 inches. Place the pan over a medium gas and bring the wheat berries and salt water to a boil. Cook until the berries are tender and starting to split (usually about 1 ¾ hours)—do not allow the berries to become mushy though. While the berries cook the water level of the pan should be kept high enough to ensure that the berries continue to float and the berries should be stirred from time to time to prevent them from sticking to the bottom of the pan. Once the berries are tender drain them and set aside in a strainer to cool and dry. This will take at least 1 hour. Place the cooled berries in a large mixing bowl. Add the sesame and anise seeds, nuts, raisins, cinnamon, and pomegranate seeds. Then sift in 1 cup of confectioners' sugar and mix everything together. Once mixed transfer to a large serving tray and sift the remaining confectioners' sugar over the top. This will produce a thick sugar coating akin to a frosting. Decorate the top of the koliva with whole almonds and dragées. Just before serving mix everything together.

According to tradition, koliva should be prepared the day before a memorial service. However wheat berries can ferment if left at room temperature overnight and sugar will crystallize if kept in a refrigerator. For this reason it is best to boil and refrigerate the wheat berries beforehand and add the other ingredients and decorations just before serving.

Adapted from "Greek Kolyva (Koliva) (Wheat Berry Memorial Food)" by Olha. *Food.com.* http://www.food.com/recipe/greek-kolyva-koliva-wheat-berry-memorial-food-209462 (accessed February 19, 2016).

See also: *Halva*; Saturday of Souls and *Radonitsa*; Soul Cakes and Soul Breads

Further Reading

Athanasiou, Andrew. "The Significance of Koliva in the Greek Orthodox Church." Greek Boston. Accessed January 11, 2015, at http://www.greekboston.com/religion/koliva/.

Danforth, Loring M. *The Death Rituals of Rural Greece.* Princeton, NJ: Princeton University Press, 1982.

Go Holy Trinity. "Koliva." Accessed January 11, 2015, at http://www.goholytrinity.org/pdf/koliva.pdf.

Greek Orthodox Archdiocese of America. "Feast of the Holy Great Martyr Theodore the Tyron." Accessed January 11, 2015, at http://www.goarch.org/special/theodoretyre/index_html.

Machin, Barrie. "St. George and the Virgin: Cultural Codes, Religion and Attitudes to the Body in a Cretan Mountain Village," *Social Analysis: The International Journal of Social and Cultural Practice, 14,* December 1983, 107–126.

Smith, Andrew F., ed. *The Oxford Companion to American Food and Drink.* Oxford, UK: Oxford University Press, 2007.

Speck, Maria. "A Gift of Grains," *Gastronomica: The Journal of Food and Culture,* 7(4), fall 2007, 84–87.

L

LAKOTA DEATH RITUALS, LAKOTA, NORTH AMERICA

The Lakota people consist of seven Sioux tribes and are the indigenous people of the Great Plains of North America. For the Lakota, death is a communal event and post-death rituals may involve hundreds of people. One of the most important Lakota death traditions is the spirit-keeping ceremony, *wanagi wicagluha*, which translates as to keep one's own. Both the contemporary Lakotan memorial feast and the older ritual of the spirit-keeping ceremony demonstrate the continuity inherent in Lakotan death customs that focus on the need to honor both the recently deceased and long-dead ancestors.

The spirit-keeping ceremony, which has as its foundation the belief that the spirit of a deceased person lingers at that person's place of death, has its basis in Lakota mythology as the Lakota believe Pte San Win, or White Buffalo Calf Woman, instituted the ceremony. The first record of the ceremony having taken place did not, however, occur until the 1860s. The spirit-keeping ceremony sees a person designated the spirit keeper vow to keep alive the spirit of the deceased. To this end, a lock of hair taken from the deceased is wrapped in fabric and kept for 12 months, during which time the hair is handled with great care and consideration. In this way, the deceased is thought to remain near and while in this liminal state the spirit of the deceased is thought to be able to take messages to the spirit of ancestors while also assisting the living. In order to thank the spirit for its help during the yearlong spirit-keeping ceremony, the relatives of the deceased feed the spirit symbolically.

Once the year has passed the family and friends of the deceased gather for the spirit-releasing ceremony. This involves carving a wooden post that is then dressed in the manner of the person whose spirit is being released. Surrounding the carved image are placed the so-called give-away items—cherished or useful items that may or may not have belonged to the deceased—which are laid on the ground in so-called spirit bundles. Prayers are then said and a feast held. In 1883, the spirit-keeping ceremony was made illegal under the Courts of Indian Offenses. Today, however, echoes of the spirit-keeping ceremony survive in modern Lakota death customs. When a Lakota dies, his or her extended family makes arrangements for a wake, a funeral, a feast, and a give-away. The wake usually takes place in a community building or in the home of the deceased, lasts for one to two nights, and involves the saying of condolences and a vigil for which mourners sit around the body in a circle. Mourners may also stand to offer up prayers or songs for the dead. After the wake is the funeral service, which may be a Christian ceremony, a traditional Lakota funeral ritual, or a mixture of the two traditions. In keeping with Lakota tradition, the body of the deceased is typically covered in a star quilt. Star quilts are highly prized by the Lakota because the eight-pointed star that decorates star quilts is a traditional symbol of Anglo-American culture that has been adopted by the Lakota and transformed by the Lakota as a symbol of its tribe, echoing the morning star that is featured traditionally on Lakota ceremonial dress. After the funeral, a feast is held as is a give-away during which the best items are given to people that helped the deceased before he or she died or to individuals that assisted the bereaved.

Sometimes the Lakota hold a memorial ceremony one year after a person's death. This ceremony always includes a certain religious element, a banquet, and a give-away. In this way, the Lakota keep alive the older tradition of the spirit-keeping ceremony. That a memorial ceremony will occur in one year's time is normally announced at the funeral. The person that proposes the memorial ceremony says aloud a pledge to ensure that those living in the deceased's family home should behave in an appropriate manner until the memorial event occurs. Usually the person that makes this pledge will wear black clothes and not attend any other community events over the course of the coming year. Moreover, if the person is a woman then she will typically cut her hair. The memorial ceremony is held 12 months later. During the memorial ceremony food is set aside as an offering and if food is dropped accidently this is taken as a sign that the spirit of the dead person is hungry. If this is deemed to be the case then a plate of food is left outside the eating venue for the spirit to eat. Tobacco may also be left for the spirit to enjoy. The pledge to hold a memorial ceremony is a serious financial undertaking, as the person pledging to sponsor the event must cater for an entire community while also ensuring that enough goods are made or bought by the deceased's family for the give-away. The sponsor will also have to pay for invitations to be made and posted, arranging for news of the memorial service to be broadcast via radio and newspaper announcements, establishing an arbor, and tending the deceased's grave.

One to two days prior to the memorial ceremony preparations for the memorial feast begin with the cooking of beef, buffalo, and soup. During these preparations these everyday foodstuffs cease to be mere food but take on a sacred quality, as they become nourishment for souls. On the morning of the memorial a table is set up on which the food is placed together with flowers and the items for the give-away. The venue is also decorated with star quilts and possibly photographs of the deceased. The way in which the actual memorial ceremony is observed varies for some memorial ceremonies are Christian while others feature traditional Lakota prayers and ceremonies or are a mixture of both Christian and Lakota customs. When it is time for the food to be served, all the guests sit in a circle and are served one at a time until all the food has gone. Ornate cakes are also distributed. It is common for guests to take home food that they could not eat during the ceremony in a *watheca* bucket—watheca meaning food taken home from a feast. The food that is served during the memorial ceremony is not purely for the enjoyment of hungry guests, for the food served is a demonstration of a family's hospitality and is deemed a symbolic offering to guests on behalf of the departed. The foods served include the pre-prepared buffalo, beef, and soup as well as wild turnips (*thipsila*), native fruits, wild chokeberry pudding (*wohapi*), and dried meats. All the food is handled with the utmost care and are first served to tribal elders.

After the feast, the give-away begins. During the give-away some guests are assigned to specific categories of guests (e.g., pallbearers) and then individuals are called forth in turn. When a guest receives a gift the guest shakes the hands of the family members of the deceased. The items given away during this custom include tobacco, which to the Lakota is a symbol of esteem and honor, shirts, shawls, Pendleton blankets, and star quilts. The latter are particularly prized as they take on the role previously filled by buffalo hides as a sign of esteem and prestige. In the recent past it was usual for a family to present only a few star quilts during a give-away but over the course of the last few decades it has become the norm for families to bestow as many as 10 star quilts during a give-away. Critics of this increase in star quilts presentations argue that by giving away so many star quilts families hope to gain in prestige and influence over those to whom they give the quilts.

The give-away ends when the family has give away everything that they intended to give including washing baskets and wooden trunks or even, sometimes, furniture and other sizeable household goods. The items proffered during the give-away are a way of honoring the dead through the act of sharing as it is the family's way of saying that they care more for the deceased individual than they do for their household items and other material goods.

Over time, both the memorial ceremony and the give-away have seen modifications but the rituals remain true to Lakota death-and-mourning customs while continuing to employ traditional motifs and embodying Lakota values, especially the need to ensure that an appropriate relationship exists between the living and the dead.

See also: Christian Death Rituals; Condolences; Delaware Indian Death Rituals; Hopi Naming Rites (Volume 1); Native American Grave Protection and Repatriation Act, 1990; Ray Fadden Letter to President; Wake

Further Reading

Albers, Patricia, and Beatrice Medicine. *The Hidden Half: Studies of Plains Indian Women*. Lanham, MD: University Press of America, 1983.

Cox, Gerry R. "The Native American Way of Death," in Clifton D. Bryant, ed., *Handbook of Death and Dying: Volume One: The Presence of Death*, 631–639. Thousand Oaks, CA: Sage Publications, 2003.

Crawford, Suzanne J., and Dennis F. Kelley, eds. *American Indian Religious Traditions: An Encyclopedia*. Santa Barbara, CA: ABC-CLIO, 2005.

Gagnon, Gregory O. *Culture and Customs of the Sioux Indians.* Santa Barbara, CA: Greenwood, 2011.

Pickering, Kathleen Ann. *Lakota Culture, World Economy.* Lincoln: University of Nebraska Press, 2000.

Related Primary Document: Native American Grave Protection and Repatriation Act, 1990

The Native American Graves Protection and Repatriation Act (NAGPRA), is a United States federal law that came into force on November 16, 1990. The law establishes the ownership of cultural items excavated or discovered on federal or tribal land (not private lands) after this date and also requires each federal agency, museum, or other institution that receives federal funds to organize an inventory of Native American human remains, funerary objects, sacred objects, cultural patrimony objects, and unassociated funerary artifacts discovered at any time including those items found before the date on which the law was enacted. The act also calls for the repatriation of such items if requested by the lineal descendants of the appropriate tribe or to culturally affiliated Indian tribes and Native Hawaiian organizations.

If lineal descendants of a tribe cannot be found, then cultural items may be deemed to belong to either the tribe on whose lands the items were discovered or the tribe that has the closest relationship to the tribe in question. Tribes may need to prove a cultural relationship with the tribe to whom the items originally belonged, something that may be difficult to prove as such links are often not well documented or are intangible.

A program of federal grants exists to help fund the repatriation process for items. Museums that fail to comply with the law may be evaluated by the Secretary of the Interior and be liable for civil penalties. The Native American Graves Protection and Repatriation Act also established ways for dealing with the Native American cultural items discovered unintentionally or excavated on federal or tribal lands. These provisions do not apply to items that are found on private or state lands, unless the land comes under the control of an institution that is awarded federal funding. The Native American Graves Protection and Repatriation Act also makes it a criminal offense to traffic in Native American human remains or Native American cultural items without right of possession. Anyone that contravenes the law risks financial penalties and possible imprisonment. The following document is the text of the act commonly referred to as the Native American Grave Protection and Repatriation Act.

101ST CONGRESS
HOUSE OF REPRESENTATIVES
REPORT, 2d Session, 101-877

PROVIDING FOR THE PROTECTION OF NATIVE AMERICAN GRAVES, AND FOR OTHER PURPOSES

OCTOBER 15, 1990. Committed to the Committee of the Whole House on the State of the Union and ordered to be printed.

SECTION 1. SHORT TITLE.
This Act may be cited as the "Native American Grave Protection and Repatriation Act".

SEC. 2. DEFINITIONS.

For purposes of this Act, the term

(1) "burial site" means any natural or prepared physical location, whether originally below, on, or above the surface of the earth, into which as a part of the death rite or ceremony of a culture, individual human remains are deposited.

(2) "cultural affiliation" means that there is a relationship of shared group identity which can be reasonably traced historically or prehistorically between a present day Indian tribe or Native Hawaiian organization and an identifiable earlier group.

(3) "cultural items" means human remains and (A) "associated funerary objects" which shall mean objects that, as a part of the death rite or ceremony of a culture, are reasonably believed to have been placed with individual human remains either at the time of death or later, and both the human remains and associated funerary objects are presently in the possession or control of a federal agency or museum, except that other items exclusively made for burial purposes or to contain human remains shall be considered as associated funerary objects. (B) "unassociated funerary objects" which shall mean objects that, as a part of the death rite or ceremony of a culture, are reasonably believed to have been placed with individual human remains either at the time of death or later, where the remains are not in the possession or control of the Federal agency or museum and the objects can be identified by a preponderance of the evidence as related to specific individuals or families or to known human remains or, by a preponderance of the evidence, as having been removed from a specific burial site of an individual culturally affiliated with a particular Indian tribe, (C) "sacred objects" which shall mean specific ceremonial objects which are needed by traditional Native American religious leaders for the practice of traditional Native American religions by their present day adherents, and (D) "cultural patrimony" which shall mean an object having ongoing historical, traditional, or cultural importance central to the Native American group or culture itself, rather than property owned by an individual Native American, and which, therefore, cannot be alienated, appropriated, or conveyed by any individual regardless of whether or not the individual is a member of the Indian tribe or Native Hawaiian organization and such object shall have been considered inalienable by such Native American group at the time the object was separated from such group.

(4) "Federal agency" means any department, agency, or instrumentality of the United States and shall include, except as may be inconsistent with the provisions of P.L. 101-185, the Smithsonian Institution.

(5) "Federal lands" means any land other than tribal lands which are controlled or owned by the United States.

(6) "Hui Malama I Na Kupuna O Hawai'i Nei" means the nonprofit, Native Hawaiian organization incorporated under the laws of the State of Hawaii by that name on April 17, 1989, for the purpose of providing guidance and expertise in decisions dealing with Native Hawaiian cultural issues, particularly burial issues.

(7) "Indian tribe" shall have the meaning given such term in section 4 of the Indian Self Determination and Education Assistance Act (25 U.S.C. 450b).

(8) "museum" means any institution or State or local government agency (including any institution of higher learning) that receives Federal funds and has possession of, or control over, Native American cultural items, but does not include any Federal agency.

(9) "Native American" means of, or relating to, a tribe, people, or culture that is indigenous to the United States.

(10) "Native Hawaiian" means any individual who is a descendant of the aboriginal people who, prior to 1778, occupied and exercised sovereignty in the area that now constitutes the State of Hawaii.

(11) "Native Hawaiian organization" means any organization which (A) serves and represents the interests of Native Hawaiians, (B) has a primary and stated purpose the provision of services to Native Hawaiians, and (C) has expertise in Native Hawaiian Affairs, and shall include the Office of Hawaiian Affairs and Hui Malama I Na Kupuna O Hawai'i Nei.

(12) "Office of Hawaiian Affairs" means the Office of Hawaiian Affairs established by the constitution of the State of Hawaii.

(13) "right of possession" means possession obtained with the voluntary consent of an individual or group that had authority of alienation. The original acquisition of a Native American funerary object, sacred object, or object of cultural patrimony from an Indian tribe or Native Hawaiian organization with the voluntary consent of an individual or group with authority to alienate such object is deemed to give right of possession of that object. The original acquisition of Native American human remains which were excavated, exhumed, or otherwise obtained with full knowledge and consent of the next of kin or the official governing body of the appropriate culturally affiliated Indian tribe or Native Hawaiian organization is deemed to give right of possession to those remains. Nothing in this paragraph shall affect the application of relevant State law to the right of ownership of unassociated funerary objects, sacred objects, or objects of cultural patrimony.

(14) "Secretary" means the Secretary of the Interior.

(15) "tribal land" means (A) all lands within the exterior boundaries of any Indian reservation; (B) all dependent Indian communities; (C) lands conveyed to, or subject to an interim conveyance of, Native Corporations pursuant to the Alaska Native Claims Settlement Act; and (D) any lands administered for the benefit of Native Hawaiians pursuant to the Hawaiian Homes Commission Act, 1920, and section 4 of Public Law 86-3.

SEC. 3. OWNERSHIP.

(a) NATIVE AMERICAN HUMAN REMAINS AND OBJECTS. The ownership or control of Native American cultural items which are excavated or discovered on Federal or tribal lands after the date of enactment of this Act shall be (with priority given in the order listed)

(1) in the case of Native American human remains and associated funerary objects, in the lineal descendants of the Native American; or

(2) in any case in which such lineal descendants cannot be ascertained, and in the case of unassociated funerary objects, sacred objects, and objects of cultural patrimony

(A) in the Indian tribe or Native Hawaiian organization on whose tribal land such objects or remains were discovered;

(B) in the Indian tribe or Native Hawaiian organization which has the closest cultural affiliation with such remains or objects and which, upon notice, states a claim for such remains or objects; or

(C) if the cultural affiliation of the objects cannot be reasonably ascertained and if the objects were discovered on Federal land that is recognized by a final judgement of the Indian Claims Commission as the aboriginal land of some Indian tribe

(1) in the Indian tribe that is recognized as aboriginally occupying the area in which the objects were discovered, if upon notice, such tribe states a claim for such remains or objects, or

(2) if it can be shown by a preponderance of the evidence that a different tribe has a stronger cultural relationship with the remains or objects than the tribe or organization specified in paragraph (1), in the Indian tribe that has the strongest demonstrated relationship, if upon notice, such tribe states a claim for such remains or objects.

(b) UNCLAIMED NATIVE AMERICAN HUMAN REMAINS AND OBJECTS. Native American cultural items not claimed under subsection (a) shall be disposed of in accordance with regulations promulgated by the Secretary in consultation with the review committee established under section 8, Native American groups, representatives of museums and the scientific community.

(c) INTENTIONAL EXCAVATION AND REMOVAL OF NATIVE AMERICAN HUMAN REMAINS AND OBJECTS. The intentional removal from or excavation of Native American cultural items from Federal or tribal lands for purposes of discovery, study, or removal of such items is permitted only if

(1) such items are excavated or removed pursuant to a permit issued under section 4 of the Archaeological Resources Protection Act of 1979 (93 Stat. 721; 16 U.S.C. 470aa et seq.) which shall be consistent with this Act;

(2) such items are excavated or removed after consultation with or, in the case of tribal lands, consent of the appropriate (if any) Indian tribe or Native Hawaiian organization;

(3) the ownership and right of control of the disposition of such items shall be as provided in subsections (a) and (b); and

(4) proof of consultation or consent under paragraph (2) is shown.

(d) INADVERTENT DISCOVERY OF NATIVE AMERICAN REMAINS AND OBJECTS. (1) Any person who knows, or has reason to know, that such person has discovered Native American cultural items on Federal or tribal lands after the date of enactment of this Act shall notify, in writing, the Secretary of the Department, or head of any other agency or instrumentality of the United States, having primary management authority with respect to Federal lands and the appropriate Indian tribe or Native Hawaiian organization with respect to tribal lands, if known or readily ascertainable. If the discovery occurred in connection with an activity, including (but not limited to) construction, mining, logging, and agriculture, the person shall cease the activity in the area of the discovery, make a reasonable effort to protect the items discovered before resuming such activity, and provide notice under this subsection. The activity may resume after a reasonable amount of time and following notification under this subsection.

(2) The disposition of and control over any cultural items excavated or removed under this subsection shall be determined as provided for in this section.

(3) If the Secretary of the Interior consents, the responsibilities (in whole or in part) under paragraphs (1) and (2) of the Secretary of any department (other than the Department of the Interior) or the head of any other agency or instrumentality may be delegated to the Secretary with respect to any land managed by such other Secretary or agency head.

(e) RELINQUISHMENT. Nothing in this section shall prevent the governing body of an Indian tribe or Native Hawaiian organization from expressly relinquishing control over any Native American human remains, or title to or control over any funerary object, or sacred object.

SEC. 4. ILLEGAL TRAFFICKING.

(a) ILLEGAL TRAFFICKING. Chapter 53 of title 18, United States Code, is amended by adding at the end thereof the following new section: SEC. 1170. ILLEGAL TRAFFICKING IN NATIVE AMERICAN HUMAN REMAINS AND CULTURAL ITEMS

"(a) Whoever knowingly sells, purchases, uses for profit, or transports for sale or profit, the human remains of a Native American without the right of possession to those remains as provided in the Native American Graves Protection and Repatriation Act shall be fined in accordance with this title, or imprisoned not more than 12 months, or both, and in the case of a second or subsequent violation, be fined in accordance with this title, or imprisoned not more than 5 years, or both.

"(b) Whoever knowingly sells, purchases, uses for profit, or transports for sale or profit any Native American cultural items obtained in violation of the Native American Graves Protection and Repatriation Act shall be fined in accordance with this title, imprisoned not more than one year, or both, and in the case of a second or subsequent violation, be fined in accordance with this title, imprisoned not more than 5 years, or both."

SECTION. 5. INVENTORY FOR HUMAN REMAINS AND ASSOCIATED FUNERARY OBJECTS.
(a) IN GENERAL. Each Federal agency and each museum which has possession or control over holdings or collections of Native American human remains and associated funerary objects shall compile an inventory of such items and, to the extent

possible based on information possessed by such museum or federal agency, identify the geographical and cultural affiliation of such item.

(b) REQUIREMENTS. (1) The inventories and identifications required under subsection (a) shall be

(A) completed in consultation with tribal government and Native Hawaiian organization officials and traditional religious leaders;

(B) completed by not later than the date that is 5 years after the date of enactment of this Act, and

(C) made available both during the time they are being conducted and afterward to a review committee established under section 8.

(2) Upon request by an Indian tribe or Native Hawaiian organization which receives or should have received notice, a museum or federal agency shall supply additional available documentation to supplement the information required by subsection (a) of this section. The term "documentation" means a summary of existing museum or Federal agency records, including inventories or catalogues, relevant studies, or other pertinent data for the limited purpose of determining the geographical origin, cultural affiliation, and basic facts surrounding acquisition and accession of Native American human remains and associated funerary objects subject to this section. Such term does not mean, and this Act shall not be construed to be an authorization for, the initiation of new scientific studies of such remains and associated funerary objects or other means of acquiring or preserving additional scientific information from such remains and objects.

(c) EXTENSION OF TIME FOR INVENTORY. Any museum which has made a good faith effort to carry out an inventory and identification under this section, but which has been unable to complete the process, may appeal to the Secretary for an extension of the time requirements set forth in subsection (b)(1)(B). The Secretary may extend such time requirements for any such museum upon a finding of good faith effort. An indication of good faith shall include the development of a plan to carry out the inventory and identification process.

(d) NOTIFICATION. (1) If the cultural affiliation of any particular Native American human remains or associated funerary objects is determined pursuant to this section, the Federal agency or museum concerned shall, not later than 6 months after the completion of the inventory, notify the affected Indian tribes or Native Hawaiian organizations.

(2) The notice required by paragraph (1) shall include information

(A) which identifies each Native American human remains or associated funerary objects and the circumstances surrounding its acquisition;

(B) which lists the human remains or associated funerary objects that are clearly identifiable as to tribal origin; and

(C) which lists the Native American human remains and associated funerary objects that are not clearly identifiable as being culturally affiliated with that Indian tribe or Native Hawaiian organization, but which, given the totality of circumstances surrounding acquisition of the remains or objects, are determined by a reasonable belief to be remains or objects culturally affiliated with the Indian tribe or Native Hawaiian organization.

(3) A copy of each notice provided under paragraph (1) shall be sent to the Secretary who shall publish each notice in the Federal Register.

SEC. 6. SUMMARY FOR UNASSOCIATED FUNERARY OBJECTS, SACRED OBJECTS, AND CULTURAL PATRIMONY.

(a) IN GENERAL. Each Federal agency or museum which has possession or control over holdings or collections of Native American unassociated funerary objects, sacred objects, or objects of cultural patrimony shall provide a written summary of such objects based upon available information held by such agency or museum. The summary shall describe the scope of the collection, kinds of objects included, reference to geographical location, means and period of acquisition and cultural affiliation, where readily ascertainable.

(b) REQUIREMENTS. (1) The summary required under subsection (a) shall be

(A) in lieu of an object-by-object inventory;

(B) followed by consultation with tribal government and Native Hawaiian organization officials and traditional religious leaders; and

(C) completed by not later than the date that is 3 years after the date of enactment of this Act.

(2) Upon request, Indian tribes and Native Hawaiian organizations shall have access to records, catalogues, relevant studies or other pertinent data for the limited purposes of determining the geographic origin, cultural affiliation, and basic facts surrounding acquisition and accession of Native American objects subject to this section. Such information shall be provided in a reasonable manner to be agreed upon by all parties.

SEC. 7. REPATRIATION.

(a) REPATRIATION OF NATIVE AMERICAN HUMAN REMAINS AND OBJECTS POSSESSED OR CONTROLLED BY FEDERAL AGENCIES AND MUSEUMS. (1) If, pursuant to section 5, the cultural affiliation of Native American human remains and associated funerary objects with a particular Indian tribe or Native Hawaiian organization is established, then the Federal agency or museum, upon the request of a known lineal descendant of the Native American or of the tribe or organization and pursuant to subsections (b) and (e) of this section, shall expeditiously return such remains and associated funerary objects.

(2) If, pursuant to section 6, the cultural affiliation with a particular Indian tribe or Native Hawaiian organization is shown with respect to unassociated funerary objects, sacred objects or objects of cultural patrimony, then the Federal agency or museum, upon the request of the Indian tribe or Native Hawaiian organization and pursuant to subsections (b), (c) and (e) of this section, shall expeditiously return such objects.

(3) The return of cultural items covered by this Act shall be in consultation with the requesting lineal descendant or tribe or organization to determine the place and manner of delivery of such items.

(4) Where cultural affiliation of Native American human remains and funerary objects has not been established in an inventory prepared pursuant to section 5 or where Native American human remains and funerary objects are not included upon any such inventory, then, upon request and pursuant to subsections (b) and (e) and, in the case of unassociated funerary objects, subsection (c), such Native American human remains and funerary objects shall be expeditiously returned where the requesting Indian tribe or Native Hawaiian organization can show cultural affiliation by a preponderance of the evidence based upon geographical, kinship, biological, archaeological, anthropological, linguistic, folkloric, oral traditional, historical, or other relevant information or expert opinion.

(5) Upon request and pursuant to subsections (b), (c) and (e), sacred objects and objects of cultural patrimony shall be expeditiously returned where

(A) the requesting party is the direct lineal descendant of an individual who owned the sacred object;

(B) the requesting Indian tribe or Native Hawaiian organization can show that the object was owned or controlled by the tribe or organization; or

(C) the requesting Indian tribe or Native Hawaiian organization can show that the sacred object was owned or controlled by a member thereof, provided that in the case where a sacred object was owned by a member thereof, there are no identifiable lineal descendants of said member or the lineal descendants, upon notice, have failed to make a claim for the object under this Act.

(b) SCIENTIFIC STUDY. If the lineal descendant, Indian tribe, or Native Hawaiian organization requests the return of culturally affiliated Native American cultural items, the Federal agency or museum shall expeditiously return such items unless such items are indispensable for completion of a specific scientific study, the outcome of which would be of major benefit to the United States. Such items shall be returned by no later than 90 days after the date on which the scientific study is completed.

(c) STANDARD OF REPATRIATION. If a known lineal descendant or an Indian tribe or Native Hawaiian organization requests the return of Native American unassociated funerary objects, sacred objects or objects of cultural patrimony pursuant to this Act and presents evidence which, if standing alone before the introduction of evidence to the contrary, would support a finding that the Federal agency or musuem did not have the right of possession, then such agency or museum shall return such objects unless it can overcome such inference and prove that it has a right of possession to the objects.

(d) SHARING OF INFORMATION BY FEDERAL AGENCIES AND MUSEUMS. Any Federal agency or museum shall share what information it does possess regarding the object in question with the known lineal descendant, Indian tribe, or Native Hawaiian organization to assist in making a claim under this section.

(e) COMPETING CLAIMS. Where there are multiple requests for repatriation of any cultural item and, after complying with the requirements of this Act, the Federal agency or museum cannot clearly determine which requesting party is the most appropriate claimant, the agency or museum may retain such item until the requesting parties agree upon its disposition or the dispute is otherwise resolved pursuant to the provisions of this Act or by a court of competent jurisdiction.

(f) MUSEUM OBLIGATION. Any museum which repatriates any item in good faith pursuant to this Act shall not be liable for claims by an aggrieved party or for claims of breach of fiduciary duty, public trust, or violations of state law that are inconsistent with the provisions of this Act.

SEC. 8. REVIEW COMMITTEE.

(a) ESTABLISHMENT. Within 120 days after the date of enactment of this Act, the Secretary shall establish a committee to monitor and review the implementation of the inventory and identification process and repatriation activities required under sections 5, 6 and 7.

(b) MEMBERSHIP. (1) The Committee established under subsection (a) shall be composed of 7 members,

(A) 3 of whom shall be appointed by the Secretary from nominations submitted by Indian tribes, Native Hawaiian organizations, and traditional Native American religious leaders with at least 2 of such persons being traditional Indian religious leaders;

(B) 3 of whom shall be appointed by the Secretary from nominations submitted by national museum organizations and scientific organizations; and

(C) 1 who shall be appointed by the Secretary from a list of persons developed and consented to by all of the members appointed pursuant to subparagraphs (A) and (B).

(2) The Secretary may not appoint Federal officers or employees to the committee.

(3) In the event vacancies shall occur, such vacancies shall be filled by the Secretary in the same manner as the original appointment within 90 days of the occurrence of such vacancy.

(4) Members of the committee established under subsection (a) shall serve without pay but shall be reimbursed at a rate equal to the daily rate for GS-18 of the General Schedule for each day (including travel time) for which the member is actually engaged in committee business. Each member shall receive travel expenses, including per diem in lieu of subsistence, in accordance with sections 5702 and 5703 of title 5, United States Code.

SEC. 9. PENALTY.

(a) PENALTY. (1) Any museum that fails to comply with the requirements of this Act may be assessed a civil penalty by the secretary of Interior pursuant to procedures established by the Secretary through regulation. No penalty may be assessed under this subsection unless such museum is given notice and opportunity for a hearing with respect to such violation. Each violation shall be a separate offense.

(2) The amount of such penalty shall be determined under regulations promulgated pursuant to this Act, taking into account, in addition to other factors

(A) the archeological, historical or commercial value of the item involved;

(B) the damages suffered, both economic and non-economic, by an aggrieved party;

(C) the number of violations that have occurred.

(3) Any museum aggrieved by an order assessing a civil penalty under this subsection may file a petition of judicial review of such order with the United States District Court for the District of Columbia or for any other district in which the museum is located. Such a petition may only be filed within the 30-day period beginning on the date the order making such assessment was issued. The court shall hear such action on the administrative record and sustain the imposition of the penalty if it is supported by substantial evidence on the record considered as a whole.

(4) If any museum fails to pay an assessment of a civil penalty after a final administrative order has been issued and not appealed or after a final judgement has been rendered, the Attorney General may institute a civil action in a district court of the United States for any district in which such museum is located to collect the penalty and such court shall have jurisdiction to hear and decide such action. In such action, the validity and amount of such penalty shall not be subject to review.

(5) Hearings held during proceedings for the assessment of civil penalties authorized by this subsection shall be conducted in accordance with section 554 of Title 5. Subpoenas may be issued for the attendance and testimony of witnesses and the production of relevant papers, books and documents. Witnesses summoned shall be paid the same fees and mileage that are paid to witnesses in the courts of the United States. In the case of contumacy or refusal to obey a subpoena served upon any person pursuant to this paragraph, the district court of the United States for any district in which such person is located, resides or transacts business, upon application by the United States and after notice to such person shall have jurisdiction to issue an order requiring such person to appear and give testimony or produce documents, or both, and any failure to obey such order of the court may be punished by such court as a contempt thereof.

SEC. 10. GRANTS.

(a) INDIAN TRIBES AND NATIVE HAWAIIAN ORGANIZATIONS. The Secretary is authorized to make grants to Indian tribes and Native Hawaiian organizations for the purpose of assisting such tribes and organizations in the repatriation of Native American cultural items.

(b) MUSEUMS. The Secretary is authorized to make grants to museums for the purpose of assisting the museums in conducting the inventories and identification required under sections 5 and 6.

SEC. 11. SAVINGS PROVISIONS.

Noting in this Act shall be construed to

(1) limit the authority of any Federal agency or museum to

(A) return or repatriate Native American cultural items to Indian tribes, Native Hawaiian organizations, or individuals, and

(B) enter into any other agreement with the consent of the culturally affiliated tribe or organization as to the disposition of control over items covered by this Act;

(2) delay actions on repatriation requests that are pending on the date of enactment of this Act;

(3) deny or otherwise affect access to any court;

(4) limit any procedural or substantive right which may otherwise be secured to individuals or Indian tribes or Native Hawaiian organizations; or

(5) limit the application of any State or Federal law pertaining to theft or stolen property.

SEC. 12. SPECIAL RELATIONSHIP BETWEEN THE FEDERAL GOVERNMENT AND INDIAN TRIBES.

This Act reflects the unique relationship between the Federal government and Indian tribes and Native Hawaiian organizations and should not be construed to establish a precedent with respect to any other individual, organization or foreign government.

SEC. 13. REGULATIONS.

The Secretary shall promulgate regulations to carry out this Act within 12 months of enactment.

SEC. 14. AUTHORIZATION OF APPROPRIATIONS.

There is authorized to be appropriated such sums as may be necessary to carry out this Act.

PURPOSE

The purpose of H.R. 5237 is to protect Native American burial sites and the removal of human remains, funerary objects, sacred objects, and objects of cultural patrimony on Federal, Indian and Native Hawaiian lands. The Act also sets up a process by which Federal agencies and museums receiving federal funds will inventory holdings of such remains and objects and work with appropriate Indian tribes and Native Hawaiian organizations to reach agreement on repatriation or other disposition of these remains and objects.

Source: *Native American Grave Protection and Repatriation Act. Public Law 101-601. U.S. Statutes at Large 104 (1990): 3048.*

"THE LAST POST" AND "TAPS," INTERNATIONAL

"The Last Post" is a haunting tune for bugle or trumpet heard during British and Commonwealth Remembrance Day services such as Remembrance Sunday in the United Kingdom and Anzac Day in Australia and New Zealand, as well as other commemorative events.

"The Last Post" call is thought to have originated in the 17th century as part of a more elaborate routine, known in the British Army as tattoo. In the evening, a duty

> ### The Menin Gate Memorial to the Missing
>
> The Menin Gate Memorial to the Missing is one of four British and Commonwealth memorials to those missing in the battlefield area of the Ypres Salient in Belgium. The memorial bears the names of 54,389 officers and men from the United Kingdom and Commonwealth Forces (except New Zealand and Newfoundland) who fell in the Ypres Salient before August 16, 1917, and have no known grave. Names are engraved on stone panels fixed to the inner walls of the central Hall of Memory, to the sides of the staircases extending between the lower and upper exterior level, and on the interior walls of the loggias on the north and south sides of the building.

officer, accompanied by one or more musicians, had to do the rounds of his unit, checking that the sentry posts were manned and that off-duty soldiers were in their beds or billets. "The First Post" was sounded at 9:30 p.m. when the duty officer started his rounds and, as the party went from post to post, a drum was played. The drumming told off-duty soldiers it was time to rest so any soldiers that had gone into town to relax knew it was time to stop drinking and head back to base. The name tattoo derives from the Dutch for "turn off the taps of beer kegs" and Americans refer to this practice as "taps," though some musical dictionaries state that the word "taps" is more correctly applied to a trumpet call or drum beat played 15 minutes after tattoo. Another bugle call was played when the duty officer's party had completed its rounds. This call was called "The Last Post" and signaled that the night sentries were at their stations and gave one last warning to the other soldiers that they should retire for the night. Since "The Last Post" was played at 10 p.m. to signal the end of the day over the course of time the call, through a process of natural and poetic association, was incorporated into military funerals and memorial events to symbolize that the lives of the soldiers being remembered were also at an end.

Since 1928, "The Last Post" has been played every evening at 8 p.m. at the Menin Gates war memorial in Ypres (also known as Ieper) in western Belgium. The area surrounding Ypres saw several battles during World War I (1914–1918) with the Third Battle of Ypres a notoriously prolonged fight resulting in the deaths of many soldiers on both sides. Just how many British and German soldiers died during this battle, which lasted from July 1917 to November 1917, is a matter still debated today but historians put the figure at between 200,000 and 400,000.

After the end of World War I, many families that had lost family members during the conflict traveled to Ypres to find the graves or memorials to their loved ones. When the Menin Gate memorial was revealed in July 1927, "The Last Post" was played to signal the end of work on the memorial and the start of night. One of those who heard the playing of the call on this occasion was the Chief of Police, M. Vandenbraambussche, who, together with other town dignitaries sponsored the playing of "The Last Post" under the arch of the Menin Gate on a regular basis as a tangible gesture of sympathy on behalf of the residents of Ypres toward those who had lost loved ones in battle around the town. To begin with, "The Last Post" was played for two months after the Menin Gate was unveiled and resumed to mark a visit by British royal the Prince of Wales in August 1928. The ceremony then became a nightly event in 1929. In 1930, the Last Post Committee was formed, later changing its name to the Last Post Association that keeps alive the tradition of playing "The Last Post" as an expression of lasting gratitude to the men who died trying to restore peace and independence to Belgium during the war. The Last Post Association also continues to play "The Last Post" each night to remember the many thousands of French and Belgians who died during the conflict and those who died in the so-called No Man's Land, from both the German and Allied forces. In this respect, "The Last Post" is also a sign of hope as it looks to a unified Europe. On special occasions, six buglers play "The Last Post" simultaneously at the Menin Gate followed by a reading aloud of Laurence Binyon's poem "For the Fallen," the last line of which, "We will remember them," is repeated by those present. The moving Menin Gate ceremony of "The Last Post" attracts many students and tourists that are interested in World War I and sees the local police stop all traffic passing through the Menin Gate as "The Last Post" is sounded.

The haunting quality of "The Last Post" means that it has achieved an almost sacred status. For this reason, the tune is never attacked by satirical comedians and is considered by some to be the most important piece of music Britain has ever produced.

The American equivalent of "The Last Post" is the 24-note bugle call referred to as "Taps", which is played at military funerals, wreath-layings, and memorial events, at the lowering of the United States' flag, and at "lights out" at the end of the military day. Lyrics were put to the "Taps" call as early as 1862 and over the years there have been many different versions of the words. However there are no official lyrics to accompany the call.

The name "Taps" is thought to be derived from a now defunct word, taptoo, which itself evolved from the Dutch *taptoe*. Taptoe, or tap toe, was the order given to turn off a keg's tap, that is, tap to the keg. The revision that gave us "Taps" as known today was made during America's Civil War by Union General Daniel Adams Butterfield who was leading a brigade near Harrison Landing, Virginia. Until this time, the United States' Army's infantry call to signal the end of the day was the French final call, "*L'Extinction des feux*." However Butterfield decided this call was too formal and in July 1862 hummed his own version of the call to an aide, who dutifully wrote down the hummed melody. Butterfield then got brigade bugler, Oliver W. Norton, to play the notes he had hummed and, after listening to the call, amended the duration of some of the notes while retaining his original tune. After this, Butterfield ordered Norton to play this new call to signal each day's lights out. Other brigades heard the call, asked for copies, and adopted the bugle call too. The call was even adopted by buglers in the Confederate army. After the Civil War ended, the call was made the official Army bugle call though it did not receive the name "Taps" until 1874. Taps was probably first played at a military funeral in Virginia soon after Butterfield composed the call, when the head of an artillery battery ordered the call should be played for the burial of a cannoneer. The head of the artillery battery could not risk revealing the battery's position to nearby enemies, so he substituted "Taps" for the triple volley of rifle fire customarily fired over a military grave. Ten months after the call was composed, "Taps" was played at the funeral of Confederate General Stonewall Jackson and by 1891 an official Army infantry regulation required that "Taps" be played at all military funerals.

See also: "Abide With Me"; Chelsea Pensioners; Minute's Silence; Remembrance Day and Remembrance Sunday; Royal Wootton Bassett; Tomb of the Unknown Soldier; Wearing Flowers to Honor War Dead

Further Reading
Australian War Memorial. "The Last Post." Accessed January 9, 2015, at https://www.awm.gov.au/commemoration/customs/last-post/v.
Connell, Royal W., and William P. Mack. *Naval Ceremonies, Customs, and Traditions.* Sixth edition. Annapolis, MD: Naval Institute Press, 2004.
Greatwar.co.uk. "Battles of the Ypres Salient." The Great War 1914–1918. Accessed January 9, 2015, at http://www.greatwar.co.uk/ypres-salient/battles-ypres-salient.htm.
Holt, Major, and Valmai Holt. *Major & Mrs Holt's Battlefield Guide to Ypres Salient and Passchendaele.* Seventh Edition. Barnsley, UK: Pen & Sword Books Limited, 2011.
Last Post Association. "Mission." Accessed January 9, 2015, at http://www.lastpost.be/en/the-last-post/mission.
McNab, Chris. *The Book of the Poppy.* Stroud, UK: The History Press, 2014.
Tuner, Alwyn W. *The Last Post: Music, Remembrance and the Great War.* London: Aurum Press Ltd., 2014.
U.S. Department of Veterans Affairs. "The Story of Taps." Celebrating America's Freedoms. Accessed June 27, 2015, at http://www.va.gov/opa/publications/celebrate/taps.pdf.
Villanueva, Jari A. "24 Notes That Tap Deep Emotions." West-point.org. Accessed June 27, 2015, at http://www.west-point.org/taps/Taps.html.

LIVING WITH THE DEAD, INDONESIA

The Tana Toraja people of South Sulawesi, Indonesia, perform an elaborate funerary custom that is intended to help the spirit of their deceased relatives move on to the afterlife where all souls dwell, which the Tana Torajas call *Puya*. The Tana Torajas do not believe that the spirit of the dead leaves their body the moment they die but instead needs assistance to exit the corpse and move on to the next world. However the rites to help the spirit move to the realm of the afterlife take time to accrue. In the meantime, the relative's corpse is kept in the family home, or *tongkonan*, which are the focus of all Tana Torajan social ceremonies. The tongkonan are very striking architectural features as they have boat-shaped roofs that are traditionally made of bamboo and other natural materials, though today they are often constructed from iron. The layout of a tongkonan is highly symbolic. The house's alignment has cosmological associations and the designs carved on the front of the houses contain messages relating to social structure and the relationship of the living to the spirit world. A tongkonan must face north as this is associated with Puang Matua, who according to Tana Torajan religion is the Creator and built the first tongkonan in heaven. The south of a tongkonan is associated with Puya and with the spirit of ancestors. The west and east of the house equate to the left and right hand sides of the human body, while the east is also associated with the gods and the west corresponds to deified ancestral sprits. Tongkonan may not be traded but instead must pass down through generations.

During this time the family live with the corpse, referring to it as though their relative were ill rather than dead. The family even goes so far as to serve the corpse three meals each day. The custom of living with the dead can continue for months or even years. When the person's funeral finally occurs, the ceremony can last for days and is attended by thousands of people. The duration and attendance level of a Tana Torajan funeral makes them very expensive to hold. The Tana Toraja are enthralled by the idea of dying and spend their entire lives preparing to enter the afterlife. For this reason, funerals are the Tana Toraja's most important rituals. The wealthier and more influential an individual, the more lavish that individual's funeral. The richest families employ funeral planners, dancers, and mourners to organize and attend a funeral.

The Tana Torajans consider death to be a gradual process that can take days, months, or years to complete—completion is marked by the spirit's entry into Puya. In addition, the Tana Toraja people believe that the soul needs the basic supplies that it enjoyed in life.

In order to prepare a corpse for its time residing with its family, it is wrapped in several layers of fabric and placed in a casket and treated as though alive. When sufficient funds have been amassed, the funeral takes place. Funerals usually take place between July and September in order to coincide with the post-harvest period before the sowing of seeds occurs. The funeral is a community event in which everyone, including tourists, may participate. To prepare for the funeral the deceased's family, together with members of the community, build a tower from where they will distribute meat from pigs and water buffalo sacrificed especially for the occasion. The number of water buffalo sacrificed can run into the hundreds but depends on the status of the dead person.

Before the funeral, a private Christian funeral service is held as many Tana Torajans are Christian, having converted to the religion during the Dutch occupation of Indonesia during the early 20th century. The day before the public funeral relatives and friends of the deceased congregate. On the first day of the funeral, a formal procession called *Ma'Passa Tedong* takes place, during which family members and members of the community formally give gifts of pigs, buffalo, drinks, and rice to the close relatives of the deceased. All contributions are recorded so that any debts can be considered recompensed. In the evening, hundreds of people gather to transport the coffin to the funeral ground. This site is called the *rante* and is a large grass-covered field. The rante features several rice barns and shelters for guests as well as other buildings used during funerals. Once the coffins arrive at the rante, cockfighting and bull baiting take place. This is in line with tradition and sees the funeral guests place bets on the outcome of the blood sports. The next day, the family of the deceased decide how many buffalo should be sacrificed in public, their throats slit. The most-prized buffalo sacrificed is that of a spotted or albino buffalo (*tedong bonga*), which are expensive and hard to come by. The buffalo meat is distributed to everyone attending the funeral, including tourists and other strangers, all of whom sing, dance, drink, and make noise. Only after the death of the first buffalo is the deceased considered to be officially dead and his or her spirit able to leave the corpse.

On the day of *Ma'Kaburu'*, or the burial, the coffin is transported by hundreds of attendees, sometimes with thousands of people following behind. The procession walks to nearby cliffs and the coffin is placed in hanging graves in an elevated position on the cliff face or in caves eroded into the cliff face. There are several types of Tana Torajan graves with a single Tana Torajan grave able to house between three and five corpses. Once a grave is full, the family to whom the grave belongs asks a *pande batu* to carve a new grave near the one that is full.

A *liang* is a grave carved into the side of a cliff into which is placed a corpse that has first been wrapped in cloth. This type of grave can be found at Lemo, a UNESCO World Heritage burial site featuring galleries of ancestor statues known as *tau-tau*. Tau-tau are wooden effigies or human-shaped statues that are fashioned to look like the deceased and sit either on balconies carved into the rock or on the cliff tops near the cliff-face graves. The Tana Torajans think that the tau-tau protect villages from evil spirits. Tau-tau are also prevalent at another UNESCO World Heritage site, Londa, a burial cave situated below a cliff face the entrance to which is guarded by a balcony of tau tau.

An *erong* grave is a grave into which a corpse is placed with up to five other dead people and then placed inside a cave. The most modern Tana Torajan grave is a *patane*, with individual families having one patane per family. A patane resembles a house hence the other name given to this type of grave, *banua tang marambu*, meaning house that no longer has smoke. A patane is used by Christian Tana Torajans who consider the grave to be their second home. Coffins are placed inside the house-shaped grave, sometimes with as many as 25 other coffins. Babies are buried in tree graves. If a baby dies before it grows its first tooth then its mother wraps the infant in a blanket or in areca bark. The mother then cuts a hole in a so-called baby tree into which she lays her child. The mother then sews up the hole using palm leaves and over time the tree grows around the baby's body. This leads the Tana Torajans to believe that the dead babies continue to live through the tree.

Another Tana Torajan funeral custom is the *ma' 'nene'*. This ritual occurs every few years in August and sees family members clean both the coffins and corpses of their ancestors as a mark of respect and to show love for their ancestors. The living move the coffins from the cliff face and caves and take them to the site of the ma' 'nene'. Here the corpses are removed from their coffins and given fresh clothes to wear. The corpse is then treated as though it is living and may even be carried around a village. The ma' 'nene' is intended to keep the soul of the ancestor happy so that it will help to protect its family and village community, imbued with good luck and with bountiful harvests. Should a member of the deceased's family become ill or suffer misfortune then they will ask a holy man for guidance. The holy man will consult pieces of bamboo and inform the ill person which ancestor they have angered and how they should appease the ancestor's spirit to try and stop the illness. Occasionally, the holy man will instruct the family member to remove the corpse of the ancestor from their village in order to put an end to the bad luck or illness. However so strong is the Tana Torajan bond between dead and living that if a villager relocates they will exhume their dead relatives and take them along too.

See also: *Ngaben*; Pregnancy and Infant Loss Memorial Day

Further Reading

Bigalke, Terance William. *Tana Toraja: A Social History of An Indonesian People*. Singapore: Singapore University Press, 2005.

Budiman, Michaela. *Contemporary Funeral Rituals of Sa'dan Toraja: From Aluk Todolo to "New" Religions*. Prague, Czech Republic: Charles University, 2013.

Galvan, Javier A., ed. *They Do What? A Cultural Encyclopedia of Extraordinary and Exotic Customs from around the World*. Santa Barbara, CA: ABC-CLIO, 2014.

Holland, Michael. "The Graves of Tana Toraja." *Asia for Visitors*. 2016. Accessed June 6, 2016, at http://asiaforvisitors.com/indonesia/sulawesi/tana-toraja/graves/index.php.

Toraja.net. "Tongkonan: Torajan Kindred Houses." Architecture-Tongkonan. Accessed December 24, 2014, at http://www.toraja.net/culture/arcitecture/.

"LYKE-WAKE DIRGE," ENGLAND

"Lyke-Wake Dirge," sometimes known as the "Cleveland Lyke Wake Dirge," is a traditional northern English song that tells of the soul's hazardous journey from earth to purgatory. The song is recorded as having been sung by Catholics in the county of Yorkshire as early as 1616 when groups of women specially invited for the purpose of singing the song are mentioned. "Lyke-Wake Dirge" was certainly known outside England by the start of the 19th century for Scottish writer Sir Walter Scott included the song in every version of his *Minstrelsy of the Scottish Border* starting with the first edition published in 1802. Later that century, in 1881, the Folk-Lore Society printed the words to "Lyke-Wake Dirge" in their entirety. Nowadays, the song is sung as mourners transport a coffin across the Yorkshire moors from Potto to Ravenscar, a distance of some 42 miles. The coffin is carried across the landscape as it is a local belief that the soul must cross the moors in order to reach heaven.

The word lyke is a very old term for a corpse, specifically an unburied body, and the wake of the song's title refers to a period when mourners keep vigil over the corpse. The concept of a wake evolved out of the ancient superstition that a person's soul can take a little while to leave the physical body after death and the wake was intended to quell evil spirits and ensure that a soul has a clear passage to the afterlife. A more matter-of-fact explanation for keeping watch over the dead in earlier times was to ensure that a corpse was not stolen. This was a particular problem in 19th-century England when body snatchers were known to steal corpses prior to burial for dissection and experiments by anatomists and other scientists as the unburied were fresher, and therefore more valuable, than bodies that had been interred.

A wake was, therefore, a time when the soul of the dead was still nearby and in a precarious state. This is suggested in the lyrics of "Lyke-Wake Dirge", which acts as a protective incantation for the dead, describing the soul's journey to whatever awaits after death. However "Lyke-Wake Dirge" also acts a warning to the living to live a good life. This dual nature is reflected in the fact that each verse of the song ends with the refrain "And Christe receive thy saule" ("And Christ receive thy soul").

"Lyke-Wake Dirge" depicts the soul's journey in three stages. Firstly, the soul must travel across a wild, gorse-covered heath called Whinny-muir (Whinneymoor) and then go on to cross the Brig o' Dread (Bridge of Dread). Finally, the soul must attempt to enter purgatory. The song reveals that only those who in life donated shoes, money, or nourishment to the poor can pass into Purgtory unharmed for if a person gave shoes to the poor while alive they can expect to have clothed feet when crossing the thorny gorse. In contrast, those who did not offer shoes to the poor will have to cross the thorns barefoot, resulting in pain and then unsteady footing when crossing the Bridge of Dread. This, of course, results in the barefoot walker falling from the bridge and falling into hell beneath. "Lyke-Wake Dirge" therefore reflects a common theme in literature written about the afterlife, that there is a narrow bridge connecting this world from the next and that the dead must pass a test to enter the afterlife successfully. This concept of a bridge linking earth to Paradise is akin to beliefs about the afterlife that exist in many religions and mythologies such as those in which the afterlife takes the form of a land reached via a rainbow, boat crossing, or similar.

"Lyke-Wake Dirge" has inspired the Lyke-Wake Walk hiking trail that echoes the route taken by mourners. The route is 40-miles long and on completing the trail walkers are entered into the Lyke Wake Club and issued with a Certificate of Condolence.

See also: "Abide With Me"; Funeral Songs; Jazz Funerals; Wake

Further Reading

Chrystal, Paul, and Mark Sutherland. *North York Moors through Time*. Stroud, UK: Ambleside Publishing, 2013.
Duntemann, Jeff. *Understanding Lyke Wake Dirge*. Accessed October 28, 2014, at http://www.duntemann.com/likewakepage.htm.

Jones, Alison. *Larousse Dictionary of World Folklore*. Edinburgh, UK: Larousse, 1996.

Simpson, Jacqueline, and Steve Roud. *Oxford Dictionary of English Folklore*. Oxford, UK: Oxford University Press, 2000.

Walter Scott Educational Website. "Lyke-Wake Dirge." Minstrelsy Educational. Accessed October 28, 2014, at http://walterscott.eu/education/ballads/supernatural-ballads/a-lyke-wake-dirge/.

M

MAIDENS' GARLANDS, ENGLAND

Maidens' Garlands (also known as Virgins' Garlands, Virgins' Crowns, or crants/crantses from the German *krantz* or Dutch *krans,* meaning crown or chaplet) are English funerary items that take the form of flower garlands usually either carried ahead of a coffin or draped across the coffin of a local person, most especially (though not exclusively) unmarried females, who are known to have lived a chaste, unblemished life and died unmarried. After the funeral the garland is hung up in the church where it remains until it decays. Alternatively, the garland was placed in the grave with the coffin. It is extremely rare to see maidens' garlands atop a coffin in modern-day England, though they can be seen in several churches across the country.

The origins of maidens' garlands are unknown. The earliest garland known to have existed dated from 1680 and could be found at St. Mary's Church in Beverley, a town in the northern county of Yorkshire. By the end of the 19th century, the custom of maidens' garlands was widespread throughout England and was well documented by folklorists who theorized the custom might hark back to Roman times when the iconography of flower garlands was absorbed by the early Christian church to symbolize the Virgin Mary. Meanwhile, historians note that Saints Augustine and Jerome as well as other early writers refer to the custom of placing crowns on the head of dead virgins.

During the 19th century changing social and religious fashions meant that the trend for maidens' garlands gradually declined to the extent that examples of maidens' garlands are most readily seen hanging from the ceiling of churches or as relics in museums. For example, at the parish church of Ashford-in-the-Water, four faded examples are kept, the oldest of which dates from 1747. Indeed only one parish church in England continues the tradition, St. Mary the Virgin in Abbots Ann in the southern county of Hampshire. This church houses 43 garlands, the most recent of which was created in 1973.

Originally, maidens' garlands took the form of a simple circle of flowers placed on the head of a deceased virgin in order to symbolize her chastity, possibly as an echo of the bridal crown she would never wear in life. This is seen in William Shakespeare's play *Hamlet,* in which drowned Ophelia is buried with a garland. Other forms of maidens' garlands also commonly existed, particularly a bell- or crown-shaped wicker construction decorated with flowers, often lilies, which are highly symbolic of both death and purity, and white paper rosettes. It was usual for the deceased's name and age to be written on the garland and for a verse to be inscribed on a white handkerchief, kid gloves, or collar and hung alongside the wicker shape. Sometimes a dying girl would choose her own maidens' garland verse knowing that it would be hung above the pew on which she normally sat when attending church.

Similarly in Greece, the funeral of a spinster is marked by the presence of almonds. Almonds, often associated with weddings, are, in this case, both a reference to the wedding the dead women never experienced in life and a symbol of her union with Christ.

See also: Funeral Plants; *Koliva*; Purity Ball (Volume 2); St. Catherine's Day (Volume 2); *Vinok* (Volume 2); Virginity Testing (Volume 2)

Further Reading

Bunting, Julie. "Take a Look at: Maidens' Garlands and Memorials," *The Peak Advertiser*, June 25, 2001. Accessed May 25, 2016, at http://texts.wishful-thinking.org.uk/TakeaLook/Crantz.html.

Corble, Simon. "Maidens' Garlands or Crantses in the Peak." Peakdistrictonline.co.uk. Accessed October 26, 2014, at http://www.peakdistrictonline.co.uk/maidens-garlands-or-crantses-in-the-peak-c10846.html.

Morris, Rosie. "Background: What Are Maidens' Garlands?" Maidens' Garlands. Accessed October 26, 2014, at http://www.maidensgarlands.com/background.htm.

Simpson, Jacqueline, and Steve Roud. *Oxford Dictionary of English Folklore*. Oxford, UK: Oxford University Press, 2000.

St. Giles, Matlock. "The Crantses." Accessed October 26, 2014, at http://www.stgilesmatlock.co.uk/history/the-crantses.html.

MALAGAN, **PAPUA NEW GUINEA**

The people of northern New Ireland, a province of Papua New Guinea, honor their dead through *malagan* memorial ceremonies that are performed after burial in order to help the souls of the dead to pass into the spirit world and as a means for communities to express their esteem for the dead. These ceremonies are not an occasion for grief but rather to celebrate and honor the dead. The word malagan also refers to the masks, figures, and carvings made for use in these ceremonies that are made from wood, shell, beads, and other natural substances and that are displayed in temporary display houses at the climax of a malagan ceremony. Malagan is the local *tok pisin* (i.e., a language spoken throughout Papua New Guinea) term for both the post-funeral ceremonies and art found in New Ireland and derives from the Tabar language.

Several types of corpse disposal are used in New Ireland—most corpses are buried in the ground, but others are cremated and some are buried at sea. A specific period of mourning follows a funeral no matter which method of corpse disposal has been utilized. In times past, mourners would paint themselves black, not eat certain foods, and refrain for particular activities. Now, however, malagan ceremonies are performed after the period of mourning to mark the completion of all funeral rites.

The art of New Ireland traditionally focuses on post-death ceremonies and feasts that honor the dead. In New Ireland art and life are inextricably linked to malagan ceremonies. The preparations for these malagan ceremonies take place after the funeral but the actual malagan ceremony itself may not take place for between one and five years after an individual dies. During this lengthy post-funeral period malagan performances are organized and feasts are readied. Also sculptors are hired to create the intricate malagan carvings that traditionally incorporate many figures within their design. Such preparations are expensive and so families must spend a great deal of wealth, usually in the form of pigs or shell money, if they are to hold an individual ceremony. Thus it is quite common for families to pool their financial resources together in order to pay for a ceremony for more than one deceased person.

Though various malagan rites are enacted throughout an individual's life in order to mark important rites of passage, the largest and most imposing malagan carvings are exhibited during a final memorial ceremony for the deceased. Throughout life, individuals living on New Ireland seek to acquire rights to specific malagan images, similar to the Western practice of owning copyrights, as well as the rituals associated with the malagan. New Ireland men, in particular, vie to obtain rights to the greatest number of malagan for ownership of the carvings confers status and prestige, thus the more malagan carvings a man possesses the greater the esteem in which he is held. When a person dies on New Ireland a number of malagan are carved for the initial funeral ceremony including raised horizontal malagan carvings in the form of a frieze of birds. However, a greater number of even more spectacular malagan carvings are fashioned for display during the final post-funeral ceremony to memorialize the deceased. This commemorative ceremony, which occurs long after death, features malagan carvings to honor a specific dead individual. These carvings illustrate the dead person's relationship with their ancestors, clan totems, and their living relatives. The malagan carving is also intended to be a representation of an individual's soul or life force, rather than a direct portrait, and effectively functions as a visual résumé of the dead person's lifetime achievements as seen through the deceased's collection of malagan rights. The images of humans and animals depicted in the person's malagan carvings show supernatural beings associated with his or her particular clan and every malagan image denotes a different manifestation of the single supernatural force that sustains that particular clan. There are several types of malagan carvings. Vertical figures are known as *kobokobor*, horizontal figures are called *murumarua*, stacked figures are referred to as *eikuar*, and there are three kinds of helmet masks—*tatanua*, *miteno*, and *wanis*. The tatanua masks are used in the dances that are a traditional part of malagan ceremonies and New Ireland residents believe that the spirits of the ancestors are present in the mask worn by a dancer. (*See* Plate 9.)

During the course of the final malagan ceremony, the carving is treated with the utter care, as it is believed that the soul of the deceased individual to whom the carving is dedicated actually resides within the carving. Once the soul leaves the malagan and, by association, the world of the living, the carvings are no longer needed and by performing a final malagan ceremony the living are liberated from their obligations to the dead. Traditionally, malagan carvings were destroyed at the end of the final ceremony, allowed to rot or sold to outsiders—hence many malagan carvings exist in art collections around the world. However nowadays they are usually kept for future generations.

The most famous malagan carvers are Ben Sisia, Michael Xomerang, and Edward Salle. In the summer of 2009, the Alcheringa Gallery, Victoria, in British Colombia, Canada, presented an exhibition featuring malagan carvings by these artists called *Salle, Sisia, Xomerang: Modern Malagan Masters*. This exhibition looked at the work of these well-established carvers, whose careers spanned nearly 60 years plus the carvings of Sisia's and Salle's sons.

See also: Fantasy Coffins; Finger Amputation; Shrunken Heads

Further Reading

Albert, Steven M. "'Completely by Accident I Discovered Its Meaning': The Iconography of New Ireland Malagan," *The Journal of the Polynesian Society*, 95(2), June 1986, 239–252.
Australian Museum. "Burial—Malagan Ceremony, New Ireland." October 22, 2009. Accessed April 27, 2016, at http://australianmuseum.net.au/burial-malagan-ceremony-new-ireland.
Caglayan, Emily. "New Ireland." Heilbrunn Timeline of Art History. Accessed January 11, 2015, at http://www.metmuseum.org/toah/hd/nwir/hd_nwir.htm.
Craig, Barry, Bernie Kernot, and Christopher Anderson, eds. *Art and Performance in Oceania*. Honolulu, HI: University of Hawai'i Press, 1999.
Gunn, Michael. "Rock Art on Tabar, New Ireland Province, Papua New Guinea," *Anthropos*, 81(4/6), 1986, 455–467.
The Metropolitan Museum of Art. "Funerary Carving (Malagan)." Accessed January 11, 2015, at http://www.metmuseum.org/collection/the-collection-online/search/313662.
Pacific Arts Association. "Alcheringa Gallery Presents Modern Malagan Masters." Accessed January 11, 2015, at http://www.pacificarts.org/node/249.
TraditionsCustoms.com. "Malagan." Accessed January 11, 2015, at http://traditionscustoms.com/death-rites/malagan.

MAUNDY MONEY, UNITED KINGDOM

Each Easter on Maundy Thursday, the day commemorating the day of the Last Supper, the British sovereign presents so-called Maundy Money to local senior citizens during a ceremony called the Royal Maundy Service that is held at a cathedral or abbey in the United Kingdom. The senior citizens are chosen to receive Maundy Money in the form of coins specialy made for the occasion in recognition of the pensioner's charity work. The ceremony is managed by the diocese, or regional Church of England authority, that is hosting that year's Maundy Money ceremony. King Henry IV (1367–1413) began the practice of relating the number of recipients of gifts to the sovereign's age so that in actuality the number of Maundy coins handed out, and the number of people receiving the coins, has been dictated by the sovereign's age—for example, when Queen Elizabeth II was 70 years old, 70 women and 70 men received 70p of Maundy Money coins. The presentation of Maundy Money is the last secular example of a custom that was once widespread through the United Kingdom. This custom recalled Christ's washing the feet of his disciples before the Last Supper for during the Maundy Thursday ceremony a figure of authority washed the feet of the poor and gave them alms in the form of gifts of clothing and food. The Maundy Thursday ceremony of washing the feet of the poor dates back to the fourth century. The commandment "that ye love one another" (John 13:34) that was prescribed by Christ at the Last Supper is still said regularly in Christian churches worldwide. This commandment is also known as a *mandatum* from which the word Maundy derives.

The British royal family has taken part in Maundy Thursday ceremonies since the 13th century, resulting in the ceremony being known as the Royal Maundy Service. The last British sovereign to perform the ceremonial washing of the feet of the poor was King James II (1633–1701). The ritual washing of the poor ceased in the 18th century and money was substituted for the provision of food and clothing in the 19th century. However the giving of Maundy Money began during the reign of King Charles II in 1622. Then the coins presented were one each of a 4p, 3p, 2p, and 1p coin and in 1670 a commemorative set of coins featuring the date was introduced. Prior to the presentation of a set of special coins, ordinary currency was given. Since the 17th century, the giving of Maundy Money has changed little. One change was that traditionally the coins presented are made of sterling silver, though in 1920 this was changed so that the coins were only 50 percent silver. The sterling silver standard recommenced after the Coinage Act of 1946 and in 1971, when the decimalization of the British currency took place, the face values of the coins was increased from old to new pence. While the depiction of Elizabeth II on ordinary British coinage has changed four times during her reign, Maundy Money coins carry the same portrait of the queen as the first coins issued in the year of her coronation in 1953. Apart from changes to the coins presented, one other change in the custom is that the Royal Maundy Service used to take place in London. However not long into her reign Elizabeth II decided that the service should take place at a different venue each year. To this end the Royal Maundy Service has taken place at many locations across the United Kingdom including many services held at Westminster Abbey and other locations in London, the capital of England, and also in Carlisle Cathedral in northern England, Hereford Cathedral in western England, Truro Cathedral, England's most southerly city, and Ely Cathedral in eastern England, plus St. David's Cathedral, Dyfed in Wales. and St. Patrick's Church of Ireland Cathedral, Armagh, Northern Ireland.

Today's recipients of Royal Maundy coins—as many pensioners, male and female, as there are years in the king's or queen's age—are selected on the basis that they have performed Christian service to both their church and their community. During the ceremony the king or queen gives each pernsioner two small leather purses. One, colored red, contains ordinary currency in place of food and clothing.

The other purse handed to the pensioners is colored white and contains silver Maundy Money coins consisting of the same number of pence as the years of the sovereign's age. On April 2, 2015, 89 men and women—the number 89 reflecting the age that Queen Elizabeth II reached on April 21, 2015—received a red purse containing a special commemorative £5 coin to mark the anniversary of the death of Sir Winston Churchill, Britain's leader during World War II, and a 50p coin to commemorate the 75th anniversary of the Battle of Britain, a period of World War II during which the British Royal Air Force fought and defeated the German air force in air combat over Britain.

The Queen's Body Guard of the Yeomen of the Guard (also known as the Indoor Guard and commonly referred to as Beefeaters) perform an important function in the Royal Maundy Service for they ceremonially protect the Royal Body, meaning the sovereign, and also guard the Maundy Money coins. During the Royal Maundy Service the yeomen carry solid-silver, gold-plated dishes, known as The Alms Dishes above their be-hatted heads. The Alms Dishes are heavy and when laden with the Maundy Money coins the dishes become uncomfortably so. Therefore it is necessary for the yeomen to prepare physically for their role by performing many weeks of upper-body training so that they do not embarrassment themselves or the sovereign by dropping one of the priceless Alms Dishes.

Aside from the Yeomen of the Guard, the choir of the Chapel Royal are often present at the Royal Maundy Service, plus six wandsmen that guide recipients of the Maundy Money coins to their allotted place and provide general assistance. Four Maundy Children are also present. Originally known as the Children of the Royal Almonry, the Maundy Children consist of two boys and two girls. The original Maundy Children consisted of four elderly male, charity beneficiaries, who attended at the Royal Maundy Service wearing linen scarves. However the men were paid over £20 per year, which was deemed an abuse of charity, and in 1808 actual children replaced the aged men. However the children appointed to the role of Maundy Children in 1808 did not actually attend upon the king. Rather, their parents received five guineas per year that was to be spent on their children's education up to the age of fifteen years. Today's Maundy Children are selected from religious and state schools and are rewarded with a set of Maundy Money coins for their part in the ceremony. Meanwhile, an official known as the Lord High Almoner wears a linen towel round his waist to symbolize the foundations of the original feet washing ritual performed by Christ. Those who officiate at the Royal Maundy Service wear linen towels over their shoulder and tied at the waist, over their clothing. Officials used to keep their towels but since 1883, the same towels have been used repeatedly, though they are laundered annually.

Recipients of Maundy Money attend a Maundy Lecture in the cathedral in advance of the service. The lecture is given by the Almoner and consists of a history of the service, together with explanations of the ceremony's symbolism and a question-and-answer session with the Lord High Almoner. In particular, those pensioners selected to receive the Maundy Gifts from the sovereign are especially encourage to attend the lecture, though it is open to all.

The cathedral holding the Royal Maundy Service is designated the Royal Chapel for the day of the ceremony. This is signaled by the flying of the Royal Standard flag overhead. The Order of Service for Royal Maundy is straightforward for the ceremony includes a reading of John 13:34 that contains the *mandatum* from which Royal Maundy gets its name. Further to this the ceremony also contains two lessons, the first of which (John 13) also recalls the *mandatum*, while the second contains the part of Matthew 25 that describes the Last Judgment. Once the first lesson has been read, the queen presents half the Maundy Money with the other half handed out after the second reading. Hymns are sung while the presentations take place and are performed by both the Chapel Royal choir and a local choir. The ceremony concludes with George Frideric Handel's coronation anthem "Zadok the Priest," prayers, the singing of the national anthem "God Save the Queen" and The Blessing, which is proclaimed by the member of the clergy that presided over the ceremony.

The Queen interacts informally with those who receive Maundy Money, some of whom give her gifts in return such as homemade marmalade.

See also: Chelsea Pensioners; Croning, Saging, and Elderling Ceremonies; Retirement and Pensions; University of the Third Age

Further Reading

Hall, John. *Queen Elizabeth II and Her Church: Royal Service at Westminster Abbey*. London: Bloomsbury Publishing Plc., 2012.

Office for the Royal Maundy. *Maundy Thursday 28th March 2013*. Accessed June 6, 2016 at http://www.oxford.anglican.org/wp-content/uploads/2013/03/Royal-Maundy-2013.pdf.

Paget, Julian. *Discovering London Ceremonial and Traditions*. Princes Risborough, UK: Shire Publications Ltd., 1989.

Palmer, Richard. "At Her 60th Maundy Service the Queen Is Still Happy to Serve," *Daily Express*, April 3, 2015, p. 3.

Robinson, Brian. *The Royal Maundy*. London: Kaye & Ward, 1977.

The Royal Household. "Royal Maundy Service." *The Official Website of the British Monarchy*. Accessed January 10, 2015, at http://www.royal.gov.uk/RoyalEventsandCeremonies/RoyalMaundyService/Maundyservice.aspx.

The Royal Mint Limited. "Maundy Money." UK Coins. Accessed January 10, 2015, at http://www.royalmint.com/discover/uk-coins/maundy-money.

Westminster-Abbey.org. "Maundy Thursday." Office for The Royal Maundy. April 21, 2011. Accessed January 10, 2015, at http://www.westminster-abbey.org/__data/assets/pdf_file/0011/49358/Royal-Maundy-Service.pdf.

The Yeomen of the Queen's Body Guard of the Yeomen of the Guard. "Maundy Service." Accessed January 10, 2015, at http://yeomenoftheguard.com/maundy_service.htm.

MEMENTO MORI AND *VANITAS*, INTERNATIONAL

Memento Mori (plural also memento mori), which in Latin means remember that you will die, is the term applied to the visual reminders of death that have occur throughout Western art and practical objects since medieval times. The purpose of memento mori is to remind the spectator or user of his or her own mortality rather than to help remember dead ancestors or deceased individuals. Often memento mori depict death as a skeleton carrying a scythe or as skulls, human bones, and skeletons. Alternatively, death may be symbolized by items that represent the passage of time such as hourglasses. Accoutrements of the graveyard are also employed including spades, coffins, and so on. In medieval art these emblems are mainly to be found in works originating from Northern Europe, especially Germany and the Netherlands. This is because after the religious upheaval of the 16th century known as the Protestant Reformation, the break with the Roman Catholic church, artists saw that such universal iconography was a useful way of symbolizing death that people of all religions could comprehend. Famous examples of memento mori from this period includes *The Ambassadors* (1533) by Hans Holbein the Younger, which is noted for the inclusion of the distorted image of a skull in the central foreground that only becomes evident when viewed from the right-hand side.

During the 17th century another type of art redolent of death also became fashionable. This was called *vanitas*, which in Latin means vanity. Vanitas art took the form of still-life paintings that included an even wider range of symbols to represent the temporality and fragility of life such as bubbles, flickering candles, clocks and watches, and skulls. Seventeenth-century artist Pieter Claesz produced many works of vanitas still life paintings featuring motifs such as skulls redolent of human mortality and watches symbolic of the passage of time. Claesz's 1630 still life, *Vanitas*, exemplifies the fact that such paintings are laments dealing with the transience of life for the painting contains a skull, watch, and upturned glass while the artist's use of a monochromatic palette is deliberately melancholic. As well as these symbols of mortality, many other symbols are also included in vanitas art including musical instruments, wine bottles, and books as these sought to remind the viewer of the vanity or worthlessness of enjoying worldly pleasures and goods because everything will end in death. This type of iconography is exemplified by *Still Life with a Volume of Wither's 'Emblemes'* (1696), by Edward Collier.

The term vanitas as employed to describe this type of art derives from the opening lines of the Bible's Book of Ecclesiastes: "Vanity of vanities, saith the Preacher, vanity of vanities, all is vanity." By the 18th century such direct depictions of deathly images fell from fashion and items indirectly linked to death that also harked back to the Classical age became popular including urns, butterflies, weeping willows, cut flowers, and torches. Art historians disagree over whether this change in fashion was due merely to changing tastes or to a more profound reason such as the inability of individuals to deal with the concept of their own mortality. Until the 18th century memento mori appeared frequently on jewelry, thereby creating a strange discord whereby jewelry was worn both to increase the sexual allure of the wearer but also to highlight the concept of human mortality. During the 18th and 19th centuries rings and watchcases decorated with skulls became popular, as did so-called mourning jewelry. The most spectacular memento mori jewelry is probably the Torre Abbey ornament (made circa 1540–1550) housed in the Victoria and Albert Museum in London that takes the form of an enameled, inscribed pendant in the shape of a gold coffin with a detachable lid that conceals a skeleton. The skeleton and coffin were intended to remind the wearer that death, and therefore final judgment, were inescapable, and thus it was essential to lead a virtuous life. Memento mori are also commonly found on memorials to the dead including tombstones in the United Kingdom, Unites States, and elsewhere. On tombstones memento mori normally take the form of winged skulls and skull-and-crossbones. Public memorials also include memento mori. This is exemplified by the *Nightingale Monument* by Louis Francois Roubiliac (1760) that is located in Westminster Abbey, in London, which depicts a skeleton rising up to claim a dying woman (Lady Elizabeth Nightingale) by throwing a lethal dart at her despite the efforts of her husband to shield her from death.

During the 19th century in the United Kingdom and in British colonies such as Australia, the advent of photography led to a new form of memento mori being instituted—memento mori photographic portraiture, also known as death portraiture or death photography. This type of photography featured the dead dressed in everday clothes and posed as though still living, sometimes accompanied by living family members, friends, and pets. The Victorian era was a time when diseases such as diphtheria, rubella, and scarlet fever were often fatal and death portraits allowed the living a final opportunity to obtain a permanent photographic likeness of a deceased loved one, usually a child or mother. Sometimes the dead person would be posed as though asleep or would have eyeballs painted on to their closed eyelids to make it seem as though they were awake. Alternatively the photograph might be altered after printing so that the cheeks of the living were tinted pink while the dead person's appearance went unaltered.

Though memento mori and vanitas became popular in the 16th and 17th centuries, religious eras when most people believed that life was preparation for the afterlife, modern artists have continued to explore both types of art. A recent example of a modern of memento mori is *Self Portrait with Skull* (1997) by English artist Sarah Lucas that takes the form of a self-portrait in which the artist sits behind a skull. Another English artist, Damien Hirst, who like Lucas is often classified as a member of the Young British Artist (YBA) school of art, has also experimented with the motif of the memento mori for his 2007 work *For the Love of God* took the form of a platinum skull set with 8,601 flawless pavé-set diamonds, weighing a massive 1,106.18 carats. The skull was inset with the teeth that belong to the original skull, which according to bio-archaeological analysis and radiocarbon dating, belonged to a 35-year-old man of European/Mediterranean ancestry who lived around 1720–1810. For the work, Hirst combined the iconography of the memento mori with elements taken from Aztec skulls and the Mexican love of decoration and attitude toward death as seen during *Dia de los Muertos* or the Mexican Day of the Dead. *For the Love of God*, which is estimated to have cost around £14 million (approximately $18.7 million) to make, is thought to be the world's most expensive piece of contemporary art and sold in 2007 to an investment group for £50 million, or approximately $100 millon.

> ### Young British Artists
>
> The Young British Artists (YBAs) are a loose group of visual artists who first exhibited together in 1988 as part of the *Freeze* exhibition held in London's Docklands. The YBAs are known for their shock tactics, entrepreneurialism, use of disposable materials, and an open-minded attitude to artistic processes. The YBAs dominated British art during the 1990s with possibly the most famous YBA being Damien Hirst, whose work *The Physical Impossibility of Death in the Mind of Someone Living*, featuring a dead shark preserved in formaldehyde inside a glass cabinet, is often considered the seminal YBA artwork.

Modern fashion has also been influenced by the memento mori as seen in the skull-shaped handbags and skull print scarves popularized by British designer Alexander McQueen, which have greatly influenced mainstream fashion. Indeed McQueen's fashion is famed for reflecting the long history of memento mori, for his designs tended to romanticize death while reminding the wearer of his or her own mortality.

The image of the skull and crossbones has long been used as a symbol to indicate death, danger, and piracy, especially in the form of the Jolly Roger pirate flag. The Jolly Roger usually features crossbones beneath a skull and is thought to have been invented by a Portuguese pirate called Bartolomeu Português who raided Spanish ships sailing the Caribbean in the 1660s. Português was known to make his crewmen take an oath of allegiance on a human skull. The Jolly Roger took its name from the *Joli Rouge*, an all-red flag shown by French pirate ships to warn that an attack was soon to commence. The symbol of skull and crossbones pre-dates piracy at sea by several centuries, however, having been employed as a symbol carved into the entrances to Hispanic graveyards since ancient times. The skull and crossbones were carved into graveyard entrances as they were thought to deter evil spirits and grave robbers.

A similar symbol of death and destruction is the *totenkopf*, the German word for skull, that is also the name given to the symbol of a skull inclined to the right and set against the background of two crossed thighbones. Totenkopf is commonly associated with the German army in the 19th and 20th centuries though it was first employed by the Prussian army's cavalry unit led by Frederick the Great during the 18th century. The totenkopf became an ever-present emblem of the Hussar uniform with the symbol appearing on military tunics and the *kucsma* (fur hats) worn by soldiers. After World War I, the totenkopf fell out of favor but during the 1930s was popularized by the Nazis who made the symbol the emblem of the *Stabswache*, Adolf Hitler's personal bodyguard unit. The symbol was then adopted by various Waffen-SS Panzer divisions and Luftwaffe (German air force) units. Indeed Heinrich Himmler, head of the Gestapo and the Waffen-SS and Nazi Minister of the Interior from 1943 to 1945, chose the totenkopf as the symbol to be used to decorate the silver rings awarded to SS members in recognition for three years' service. Nowadays, these rings are highly sought after by people that, moral questions aside, collect Nazi memorabilia. Furthermore, as a result of the Nazis' use of the totenkopf, the symbol is today frequently associated with rightwing political extremists such as the British neo-Nazi group Combat 18, also known as C18, whose emblem is derived from the totenkopf.

See also: *Ankou*; Death Dance; *Dia de los Muertos*: Day of the Dead; Goth Subculture; Ossuaries; Santa Muerte; Shrunken Heads; Tombstone Tourism

Further Reading

Atkins, Stephen E. *Encyclopedia of Modern Worldwide Extremists and Extremist Groups*. Westport, CT: Greenwood Press, 2004.

BBC. "Hirst's Diamond Skull Raises £50m." BBC News, August 30, 2007. Accessed November 7, 2015, at http://news.bbc.co.uk/1/hi/entertainment/6971116.stm.

Bell, Bethan. "Taken From Life: The Unsettling Art of Death Photography." BBC News: England. June 5, 2016. Accessed June 7, 2016, at http://www.bbc.co.uk/news/uk-england-36389581?ocid=socialflow_facebook&ns_mchannel=social&ns_campaign=bbcnews&ns_source=facebook.

Fare Network. *Monitoring Discriminatory Signs and Symbols in European Football. Version 3*. Accessed November 7, 2015, at http://www.farenet.org/wp-content/uploads/2014/08/Monitoring-discriminatory-signs-and-symbols-in-European-football.pdf.

Howarth, Glennys, and Oliver Leaman, eds. *Encyclopedia of Death and Dying*. Abingdon, UK: Routledge, 2013.

Llewellyn, Nigel. *Art of Death: Visual Culture in the English Death Ritual c.1500–c.1800*. London: Reaktion Books in association with the Victoria and Albert Museum, 1991.

Piercy, Joseph. *Symbols: A Universal Language*. London: Michael O'Mara Books, 2013.

Tate. "Memento Mori." Accessed November 6, 2015, at http://www.tate.org.uk/learn/online-resources/glossary/m/memento-mori.

Townshend, Dale, ed. *Terror and Wonder: The Gothic Imagination*. London: The British Library, 2014.

Vaidyanathan, Rajini. "Six Ways Alexander McQueen Changed Fashion." *BBC News Magazine*, February 12, 2010. Accessed November 6, 2015, at http://news.bbc.co.uk/1/hi/8511404.stm.

Victoria and Albert Museum. "The Museum of Savage Beauty: Memento Mori." Accessed November 7, 2015, at http://www.vam.ac.uk/museumofsavagebeauty/memento-mori/#read_more_1.

Westminster Abbey. "Lady Elizabeth Nightingale." Accessed November 7, 2015, at http://www.westminster-abbey.org/our-history/people/lady-elizabeth-nightingale.

MESSAGE FROM THE QUEEN, UNITED KINGDOM

The British monarch, currently Queen Elizabeth II, sends a message of congratulations when a person celebrates his or her 100th and 105th birthday and every year subsequently, or a couple reach their 60th, 65th, and 70th wedding anniversaries and every year after that. These messages are arranged by the Anniversaries Office at Buckingham Palace, the monarch's official residence in London. Many people consider receiving a congratulatory message from the Queen to be a great honor and a significant part of such special birthday or wedding anniversary celebrations. The queen may send messages of congratulations to people that are current citizens of her realms—including the United Kingdom of Great Britain and Northern Ireland, Australia and New Zealand, Canada, Papua New Guinea, and Jamaica—as well as citizens living in United Kingdom Overseas Territories—including Bermuda, Gibraltar, the Cayman Islands, the British Virgin Islands, and the Falkland Islands. If an individual or couple lives in Australia, Canada, or New Zealand, then applications should be sent to the relevant Governor-General as they are the queen's personal representatives in these countries.

The tradition of the monarch sending a message started in 1917 when King George V, Elizabeth II's grandfather, began to send congratulatory telegrams. Telegrams were discontinued in 1982 and replaced with telemessages. Today messages are sent in greetings cards. A monarch's congratulatory message is sent in the form of a greeting card that contains a personalized message. The card is a special laser-printed card featuring the queen smiling. The message, which is held inside the card by a golden tasseled marker, is signed by the queen.

The card is sent in a special envelope that is mailed through the usual postal service. The message is arranged by the Anniversaries Office, which falls under the auspices of the Private Secretary's Office in the Royal Household, located at Buckingham Palace. The Pension Service tells the Anniversaries Office when an individual that receives a United Kingdom State Pension is about to celebrate a special birthday. People born abroad have to send a copy of their birth certificate with an application form.

For reasons of data protection, however, United Kingdom government records cannot inform the Anniversaries Office of any impending special wedding anniversaries. Therefore relatives and friends must inform the Anniversaries Office if they wish for a couple to receive a message from the monarch ahead of the special date.

Messages from the monarch are provided free of charge. However it is necessary for the Anniversaries Office to see evidence that a couple is entitled to the honor of receiving a message to mark their wedding anniversary. If the wedding that is to be celebrated occurred in England or Wales then the General Register Office for England and Wales can verify the details of the marriage in its records and pass this information directly to the Anniversaries Office at Buckingham Palace. Similarly, if a wedding took place in Scotland, an online application for a monarch's message can be made through the National Records of Scotland that will confirm the details in its records and contact the Anniversaries Office at Buckingham Palace. Meanwhile. if a couple married in Northern Ireland, then a confirmatory letter can be obtained from the General Register Office for Northern Ireland.

In 2014, it was reported that the Department of Work and Pensions, a department of the U.K. government, had to employ additional staff to cope with demand for messages sent by the queen. The so-called centenarian team is dedicated to keeping up to date records on Britain's oldest citizens as the number of people over the age of 100 has increased by 70 percent in the past decade. Estimates published by the Office for National Statistics reveal there are now around 14,000 people age over 100 years living in the U.K. Figures also reveal that in 2014 there were approximately104,000 people alive in Britain that were born during the course of World War I. Indeed the United Kingdom has the seventh largest population of people over 90 years of age coming after Japan and a number of Scandinavian and Mediterranean countries.

See also: Birthday Cards (Volume 1); Chelsea Pensioners; Maundy Money; Retirement and Pensions

Further Reading

BBC. "UK Queen's Birthday Message Gets Personal." BBC News, June 11, 1999. Accessed July 26, 2015, at http://news.bbc.co.uk/1/hi/uk/366998.stm.

Bingham, John. "Queen's 'Birthday Card Team' Expands to Cope with Surge of 100-Year-Olds," *The Telegraph*, September 25, 2014. Accessed July 26, 2015, at http://www.telegraph.co.uk/news/health/elder/11121184/Queens-birthday-card-team-expands-to-cope-with-surge-of-100-year-olds.html.

Hanson, Michael. "If You Want a Telegram from The Queen on Your 100th Birthday, Be Prepared for a Frightful Slog," *The Guardian*, December 11, 2007. Accessed July 26, 2015, at http://www.theguardian.com/commentisfree/2007/dec/11/comment.michelehanson.

The Royal Household. "Queen and Anniversary Messages." The British Monarchy. Accessed July 26, 2015, at http://www.royal.gov.uk/hmthequeen/queenandanniversarymessages/anniversarymessages.aspx.

MINUTE'S SILENCE, INTERNATIONAL

A minute's silence, sometimes called a moment of silence, is a cultural expression of grief that takes the form of a brief period of silent contemplation, prayer, reflection, or meditation. A minute's silence is nearly always a gesture of mourning and respect for individuals that have died recently or to mark a tragic historical event. Over time, a variety of minute's silence has evolved. Some commentators suggest the success of the minute's silence is that during the silence people can think whatever they like, so, for example, a patriot and a highly critical pacifist can mourn together silently while actually holding extremely different views about a situation.

The concept of the minute's silence is widely attributed to Australian journalist Edward George Honey, who in 1919 wrote a letter to the *London Evening News* suggesting five minutes of silence be held to mark the first anniversary of the resolution that ended World War I. It is believed that Honey remembered that when he was a boy, Australians had observed a minute's silence to show respect for victims of a mining accident. Another person credited with inventing the minute's silence to commemorate the end of World War I is South African politician Sir Percy Fitzpatrick who remembered how his fellow South African soldiers stood silent when they received bad news from the front line. The idea of the minute's silence was, however, already practiced in Britain for in 1910 the death of King Edward VII had been marked by a minute's silence, as was the sinking of the *Titanic* in 1912. Whoever invented the idea of a silence to mark the end of World War I, the notion appealed to the British king, George V, who invited Fitzpatrick and others to a rehearsal of the silence performed by the Grenadier Guards at Buckingham Palace. After the rehearsal, it was decided that five minutes of silence was too long and opted for two minutes instead. Ever since, a period of silence has been associated with events held to mark the end of world wars such as Remembrance Day and Remembrance Sunday in the United Kingdom and Commonwealth countries and Veterans Day in the United States.

In the United States, the concept of the minute's silence became commonplace as the country became more secular. During the 1960s, prayer was removed from public schools as a result of the Supreme Court decision of *Engel v. Vitale*, a 1962 a court case that saw the Supreme Court decide it is unconstitutional for state officials to create a school prayer and then encourage the recitation of the prayer in public schools. Once prayer was removed from schools the minute's silence was substituted for the prayers. Despite the fact that in 1985 the Supreme Court ruled in *Wallace v. Jaffree* that the act of holding a minute's silence in classrooms was unconstitutional if there was an obvious religious message behind the silence, the practice of the minute's silence is widely accepted across the United States.

Nowadays the minute's silence is observed regularly from sporting fixtures where fans, players, and officials remain silent for a period to mark deaths ranging from a former player to annual armistice commemorations such as Remembrance Day and Remembrance Sunday. In recent years, however, a great deal of variety in the duration of the silence has developed. Some sad events, such as the death of British royal Diana, Princess of Wales, have been marked by a one-minute silence while others, such as those held to mark death in wartime, tend to be commemorated by a two-minute silence. A three-minute silence was, however, observed across the world after 9/11 as well as after the Boxing Day tsunami of 2004. The same year a five-minute silence was held across Spain after the Madrid train bombings.

Yearly commemorations to mark tragic events also feature minute's silence. For example at the World Trade Center in New York a minute's silence is observed at 8:46 a.m. when the first plane hit the first World Trade Center tower followed by another minute's silence at 9:03 a.m. when the second plane struck the building. These minutes of silence are followed by two more minute's silence at again at 9:59 a.m. and 10:29 a.m.—times that mark the falling of each tower. Though these minute's silence are considered vaguely religious by some commentators, the power of the minute's silence is that the silence crosses all boundaries thereby allowing people to unite in sorrow. The concept of unity in grief transmitted through the power of the minute's silence was evident in November 2015 when, following the terrorist attacks on Paris, France, by the so-called Islamic State, a Europe-wide minute's silence was held. French President Francois Hollande began the silence at noon at the Sorbonne University in Paris. In the French capital people stopped talking and stood silently, while the subway system, buses, and trams came to a halt. Radio programs fell silent and at the scene of each atrocity crowds of people laid flowers in silence. The end of the period of silence was marked by applause and, in at least one case, shortly after the clapping, a person in the crowd at the Sorbonne began to sing the French national anthem, "La Marseillaise." Soon everybody else in the crowd joined the singer with some people even shouting the lyrics of the anthem. The singing made the news across Europe. Elsewhere in Europe the minute's silence was also observed. For instance at St. Pancras station in London, England, from where Eurostar trains depart for Paris, people came to a halt while a silence was also held at Trafalgar Square and busses came to standstill as did people in general. The silence was also observed in other European capital cities, as well as in Antalya, Turkey, where world leaders were attending a G20 summit.

A few days after the Paris attacks, France played England in a friendly soccer match held in London. The match witnessed the laying of wreaths by British royal Prince William and the managers of England's and France's teams as well as the highly unusual instance of the England fans singing "La Marseillaise" as a mark of respect for those killed in Paris. The singing of the anthem was then followed by an impeccably observed minute's silence.

See also: Remembrance Day and Remembrance Sunday; Riderless Horse; Spontaneous Shrines; State Funeral; Wearing Flowers to Honor War Dead; Windmills

Further Reading

Benedictus, Leo. "What Merits a Minute's Silence? It's Time to Speak Up," *The Guardian*, July 3, 2015. Accessed November 19, 2015, at http://www.theguardian.com/uk-news/2015/jul/03/what-merits-minutes-silence-remembrance.

McSmith, Andy. "A Brief History of Silence: When No Noise Is Good Noise," *The Independent*. October 23, 2011. Accessed November 19, 2015, at http://www.independent.co.uk/news/uk/this-britain/a-brief-history-of-silence-when-no-noise-is-good-noise-780200.html.

Morrison, Blake. "A Time to Mourn," *The Guardian*, January 5, 2005. Accessed November 19, 2015, at http://www.theguardian.com/world/2005/jan/05/tsunami2004.features11.

Rowley, Tom. "Paris Attacks: From Gunshots to Silence, a City Mourns," *The Telegraph*, November 16, 2015. Accessed November 19, 2015, at http://www.telegraph.co.uk/news/worldnews/europe/france/11998726/France-attacks-Francois-Hollande-leads-minutes-silence-in-Paris-as-Europe-shows-unity.html.

Webley, Kayla. "A Brief History of the Moment of Silence," *Time*, January 10, 2011. Accessed November 19, 2015, at http://content.time.com/time/nation/article/0,8599,2041686,00.html.

MIRILA, CROATIA

Mirila (singular *mirilo*) are stone funeral monuments to the dead that can be found in rows along the mountain paths, passes, and clearings of Mount Velebit in Croatia. This wild and eerie mountain is a mystical site of folkloric significance and according to an old Croatian folk song, "*Vila Velebita*" ("The Fairy of Velebit"), the mountain is inhabited by fairies.

It has been suggested that mirila were erected when hamlets were formed on the slopes of Mount Velebit from the 17th century to the 20th century. However dates inscribed on the mirila indicate a precise timeline starting in 1717 with most of the stones put in place from 1812 onward and with the most recent being erected in 1971. The custom of erecting mirila was broken during World War I when political and socioeconomic changes meant that old traditions were abandoned. As a practical step, tombstones began to be erected during this period instead of mirila and tombstones became the norm in the area from around 1925. However the outbreak of World War II saw people return to past traditions and mirila were again erected. In the 1950s, mirila fell from favor again but the practice lives on today through place names such as Martinovo mirilo near Mala Paklenica.

Mirila are dedicated to the memory of people that died on the slopes of Mount Velebit, either strangers or inhabitants of the area's scattered villages, and therefore had to be transported to the village church and then on to the local graveyard where they were buried. Those carrying the corpses were allowed to stop once en route to the churchyard and the place where the body rested on the ground was marked by the stone monuments known as mirila. As the stopping en route was the last time that the deceased would encounter the sun, many mirila are orientated toward the sun. Any mirila that are not angled toward the sun are placed in parallel lines, as can be found at Kruscica and Korita. However the magnetic azimuth (i.e., the angle formed between a reference direction—north—and a line from an observer to a point of interest) of the orientation of these rows is 238.5 degrees so that the sun hits the mirila placed in these rows around December 18 and 26, suggesting that they were arranged at these locations in such a way that the mirila would see the final sunsets of the year, as a symbolic last look at the sun. It was to these stone slabs that relatives of the deceased would travel to pay their respects.

Mirila take the form of flat stone tablets that stand upright thereby marking where the head and feet of the corpse rested and, therefore, indicating the height of the corpse. Mirila do not follow a set pattern and necessarily come in various sizes. For instance, the shortest 18th-century mirilo is 143cm long (56 inches) and most likely belonged to a small woman while the shortest 19th-century mirilo is 83cm long (roughly 33 inches) and possibly indicates that some mirila are dedicated to children.

The stones marking the head position were sometime carved with mystical markings such as various types of crucifix, swastikas, pentagrams, and depictions of the sun. These head slabs, called *uzglavnica*, feature various types of inscription. Some show only the initials of the deceased or initials plus a carved crucifix. Others present the person's initials together with their full date of death. Meanwhile a third group of uzglavnica display a complex formula using abbreviations or full phrases to give information and as prayers. For instance, some of the head slabs are inscribed with the following letters: R for (*Roden*, year of birth), U for (*Umra/Umla*, meaning died), DN (for *Dana*, meaning on the day), G (for *Goden*, meaning in the year), and BP (for *Boga/je/i Pomilova*, meaning Lord, have mercy on him/her). It is not possible to identify individuals by their initials alone, but by combining initials with location it is possible to identify the mirila for whole clans at certain places. For instance, the letters "SM" inscribed on mirila in Glavcice identifies the Marasovici clan. A fourth, fuller mirila inscription also exists in which the full first name and family name of the deceased are recorded, sometimes with the name of a family member such as a husband or father.

Similar to mirila are the *mrtva pocivala* (dead resting sites) rocks found in the Karst region of Slovenia that, like mirila, are also ritual resting places on the paths of funeral processions. While both mirila and mrtva pocivala mark the boundary of life and death, mrtva pocivala also mark community boundaries and points where the real and supernatural worlds collide. For these reasons mrtva pocivala are to be found at locations associated with otherworldly beings (e.g., witches) and as they mark the boundary between the living and the dead also highlight places inhabited by intermediary creatures that link the land of the living and the afterlife. Water is often viewed as an entry point into another world and so it is unsurprising that mrtva pocivala can often be found near bodies of water, which also act as community boundaries.

Both mirila and mrtva pocivala fell out of fashion after the introduction of improved transport routes that meant mourners could take alternative routes to cemeteries. Although both mirila and mrtva pocivala are in essence ritual resting places during funeral processions, only mirila is considered a true funeral monument by anthropologists.

See also: Cairn; Mortuary Totem Poles; Ossuaries; Tombstone Tourism

Further Reading

Abraham, Rudolf. "Velebit—A Mountain in Croatia," *Hidden Europe*, No. 22, September 14–19, 2008. Accessed January 1, 2015, at http://www.hiddeneurope.co.uk/assets/files/hidden_europe_22_velebit.pdf.

Pleterski, Andrej, and Goran Pavel Santek, eds. *Mirila*. Zalozba, Slovenia: Institut za arheologijo ZRC SAZU. 2010.

Tourist Board of Starigrad Paklenica County. "Attractions: Mirila." Rivijera. Accessed January 1, 2015, at *Paklenica*. http://www.rivijera-paklenica.hr/en/mirila.

MISSING MAN FORMATION, INTERNATIONAL

The missing man formation, also known as the missing man flyby or missing man flypast, is an aerial salute performed as part of a flyover of aircraft to honor the recently deceased at a funeral or during a memorial ceremony. The missing man formation is usually performed to mark the death of a dignitary or in memory of a recently deceased pilot.

According to military lore, British Royal Air Force (RAF) fighter pilots created the missing man formation during World War I when they flew in formation over the funeral of German flying ace Manfred von Richthofen, nicknamed The Red Baron, who despite being an enemy of the British was nonetheless admired by RAF pilots. However the first written record of the missing man maneuver details the formation being performed by the RAF in 1935. British royal King George V received the missing man aerial salute during his state funeral in 1936. Then, during World War II, the missing man formation developed into a ceremonial tradition as part of RAF commemorative events. The history of the missing man formation in the United States dates back to 1938 during the funeral for Major General Oscar Westover when over 50 aircraft took part in the flyover. The Eighth Air Force, equipped with Flying Fortress heavy bombers, and other combat groups then adopted the maneuver when returning home from a so-called milk runs—a safe, routine flight to signal to people on the ground that losses have been incurred during another mission. Also, in April 1954, U.S. Air Force General Hoyt Vandenberg was laid to rest at Arlington National Cemetery and was honored by a jet flyover in the missing man formation rather than the customary horse-drawn artillery caisson. However the missing man formation was rarely performed in the United States until the maneuver captured the public's imagination during the Vietnam War and conflicts in Laos and Cambodia. The first military acrobatic team to perform the move in the United States was the USAF Thunderbirds that performed the routine for the first time in 1969 to honor prisoners of war held in Vietnam. Today United States aerial demonstration teams regularly perform the maneuver not just at funerals and the like, but also at ceremonial events such as National POW-MIA Recognition Day, Memorial Day, and Veteran's Day.

There are several types of the missing man formation. However the most commonly used variation is based on the "finger-four" aerial combat formation. This formation is so-called because the formation consists of four aircraft, two of which form the lead element with the other pair forming the second element. When this V-shaped formation is viewed from above the formation of the planes looks like the tips of the four fingers of a human right hand. During the finger-four formation the aircraft fly in a V-shaped pattern with the flight leader at the tip of the V and with the wingman to the left. Meanwhile, the leader of the second element and the wingman fly to the right. The finger-four formation then flies over the memorial event venue at a sufficiently low height that it can be seen by those attending the event. Next the second element leader suddenly flies upward and out of the formation while the other aircraft continues in level flight until all four aircraft fly out of sight. A variation on the finger-four formation sees the second element leader left empty to signify loss, or the aircraft may approach from the south at sunset with one aircraft abruptly splitting from the others and symbolically traveling westward toward the lowering sun. Whichever variation is employed, the sudden departure of the aircraft and the flight toward the heavens signifies the death of the person being commemorated by the flyover.

Apart from von Richthofen and King George V, other notable personages to receive the missing man formation salute include U.S. Navy aviator Neil Armstrong, the first man to walk on the Moon, who was honored by U.S. Navy F/A-18 flying in the missing man formation during his memorial service in Cincinnati on August 31, 2012. Similarly, former Australian prime minister Gough Whitlam, who had been a navigator for the Royal Australian Air Force during World War II, was honored by four RAAF F/A-18 Hornets performing the missing man formation during the state memorial service held to mark his death in 2014. Meanwhile, on March 29, 2015, the Republic of Singapore Air Force's Black Knights attempted to perform the missing man formation during the state funeral procession of the nation's founder Lee Kuan Yew. Four Black Knights F-16C aircraft were planned to fly the missing man formation to Lee as his funeral cortege traveled passed Esplanade Bridge. However the flyover salute could not take place because of inclement weather conditions and low visibility.

A similar formation to the missing man formation also occurs in motorsport to honor competitors or officials that have recently died. When a race would usually begin with a rolling start, the missing man formation starts during the pace lap with the driver on pole position dropping back into the second row and the other cars taking position so that there is no car in the lead position. Alternatively, if a race normally begins with a standing start the pole position space can be left empty to signal that a driver is missing. In drag racing, the missing man formation is performed when a driver is killed after qualifying but before the race starts. When this happens the dead driver's lane is kept empty during what would have been the driver's quarterfinal race and the opposing driver, who must necessarily cross the finish line without being disqualified to progress, deliberately drives his or her car slowly along the track in a move known as idling. The deliberate manner in which the deceased driver's lane is kept vacant and the opposing driver's slow pace are both intended to show respect for the dead driver. This occurred after the death of Lee Shepherd in 1985 when Pro Stock drivers remembered Shepherd with a missing man parade at the next national event, in Gainesville, Florida, and in 1996 after the death of Blaine Johnson at the Mac Tools U.S. Nationals in Indianapolis, Indiana. A more recent example of idling in honor of a fallen driver came in 2008 at the NHRA POWERade when Robert Hight performed idling in honor of Scott Kalitta, who was killed during a qualifying pass.

In Formula 1 racing the death of Austrian driver Roland Ratzenberger during qualification for the San Marino Gran Prix in 1994 was marked by Ratzenberger's place on the starting grid being left empty. Similarly, the governing body of Formula 1 motorsport, the FIA, retired the number 17 from the list of car numbers available to Formula 1 drivers as a mark of respect following the death of French driver Jules Bianchi in July 2015. Bianchi died after sustaining severe injuries following a crash at the Japanese Grand Prix in October 2014. Because Formula 1 car numbers are chosen by each driver, the FIA decided that it would be an appropriate gesture to retire Bianchi's number 17. This means that no other driver will be able to compete in a car numbered 17 in the FIA Formula One World Championship.

See also: Changing of the Guard Ceremony; Royal Wootton Bassett; State Funeral; Tomb of the Unknown Soldier; Wearing Flowers to Honor War Dead

Further Reading

Bay Bombers Squadron. "Funeral Overflight & Missing Man Formation for Former United States Military Members." Bay Bombers Squadron Formation Team. Accessed March 31, 2015, at http://baybombersquadron.com/missingman.php.

Burgess, Phil. "A Real Thrill Ride." Dragster Insider. Accessed March 31, 2015, at http://www.nhra.com/blog/dragster-insider/page/114/.

Motorsport.com. "50 Greatest Drivers: No. 12—Lee Shepherd," September 7, 2001. Accessed March 31, 2015, at http://www.motorsport.com/nhra/news/50-greatest-drivers-no-12-lee-shepherd/.

Pearlman, Robert Z. "Neil Armstrong's Family, NASA Remember First Moonwalker." Space.com, August 31, 2012. Accessed March 31, 2015, at http://www.space.com/17415-neil-armstrong-memorial-service-nasa-family.html.

POW-MIA. "The Missing Man Formation." POW MIA Histories. Accessed March 31, 2015, at http://web.archive.org/web/20001121100500/http://www.aiipowmia.com/histories/histformation.html.

Rural Heritage Center. "History of the Missing Man Formation." Accessed March 31, 2015, at http://www.ruralheritagecenter.net/component/content/article/1-latest-news/65-history-of-the-missing-man-formation.

Stephens, Bill. "Hight's Tribute to Kalitta a Moment to Remember." ESPN: NHRA, June 24, 2008. Accessed March 31, 2015, at http://sports.espn.go.com/rpm/racing/nhra/columns/story?columnist=stephens_bill&id=3455766.

The Strait's Times. "RSAF's Black Knights Could Not Perform 'Missing Man' Formation during State Funeral Procession," *The Strait's Times*, March 29, 2015. Accessed March 31, 2015, at http://www.straitstimes.com/news/singapore/more-singapore-stories/story/safs-black-knights-could-not-performed-missing-man-forma.

Sydney Morning Herald. "Live: Gough Whitlam Farewelled at State Memorial Service," *Sydney Morning Herald*, November 5, 2014. Accessed March 31, 2015, at http://www.smh.com.au/federal-politics/political-news/live-gough-whitlam-farewelled-at-state-memorial-service-20141104-3jmf6.html.

MIZUKO KUYO: JAPANESE FETUS MEMORIAL SERVICE, JAPAN

The Japanese ritual of *mizuko kuyo* is a religious ceremony performed in public at Buddhist temples for those who have been affected by miscarriage or stillbirth or have been aborted—no distinctions are made over whether a fetus or baby died or was aborted as Japanese Buddhism does not view abortion as harshly as some other religions, though it should be noted that doubts exist as to whether mizuko kuyo services are authentically Buddhist. The ceremony also commemorates children who died soon after being born. Ceremonies are mainly, though not exclusively, attended by women, but worshippers are drawn from all age groups and every Japanese socio-economic background. The name mizuko kuyo literally translates as "water child memorial service" as *mizuko* means "water child," the Japanese term for a dead fetus or unborn child, while *kuyo* means "offering." Therefore mizuko kuyo refers to an offering for an unborn child—there is no English language equivalent word for a dead fetus or unborn baby that carries the same meaning as the Japanese term. Unborn children and dead fetuses are referred to as water children because it was traditional in Japan to bury the mizuko under their parents' home as it was thought that water would wash them to natural springs hidden under the earth's crust and which are part of the cycle of life. The belief held that the mizuko would therefore travel from the waters of the mother's womb to its original liquid state by becoming part of the waters of the earth. In Japanese Buddhism, water is therefore both representative of death and the knowledge that a child will be reborn. This spiritual aspect is highlighted by the fact that mizuko kuyo is usually held on the three main annual Japanese Buddhist holidays pertaining to ancestor worship—*higan*, held in spring and autumn, and *bon*, the festival of the dead when the spirits of ancestors are invited to return to their homes. However some temples hold the service of mizuko kuyo monthly or even weekly.

The ceremony's history dates back to the 18th century but it has only become widespread throughout Japan since the 1960s. Mizuko kuyo was originally developed as a way of honoring Jizo, or Ojizo-sama, a beloved *bodhisattwa*, or god, in Japan who is believed to be the guardian of children, especially those who die before their parents. According to Japanese mythology, the souls of dead fetuses and children who die before their parents are unable to cross the mythical Sanzu River on their way to the afterlife as they have not lived long enough to accumulate the number of good deeds (*karma*) necessary to do so and because by dying they have made their parents suffer. However Japanese mythology also reveals that Jizo helps the souls of the dead fetuses and children enabling them to traverse the Sanzu River and cross safely into the afterlife. Statues of Jizo have been erected in Japan to commemorate aborted fetuses and victims of child murder and starvation since the 1700s and statues of the god are still placed in Japanese cemeteries usually depicting Jizo wearing babies' clothing such as a red baby's cap and a red bib and surrounded by piles of toys. The clothes and toys are gifts from parents either thanking Jizo for saving their child from ill health, or entreating the god to protect their child in the afterlife.

In 1975, the popularity of the mizuko kuyo service increased hugely after a Japanese television channel broadcasted a film featuring a mizuko kuyo ceremony as part of a show dedicated to peculiar Japanese events. Since the 1980s, the number of mizuko kuyo ceremonies has increased significantly. This is most likely because the number of abortions that take place in Japan has also risen dramatically to the extent that between 1 million and 1.5 million abortions are performed there annually. Abortion is a widely accepted procedure in Japanese society. Indeed after World War II abortion was the most widely used form of birth control and it has been suggested that one of the reasons for the rise in the number of mizuko kuyo services held is to demonstrate that abortion is not a trivial matter despite its frequency.

Today, however, it is not just women who have miscarried or aborted their pregnancies that attend the ceremony but also members of the extended family and friends. The reason for this is three-fold. First, the ceremony provides a sense of shared spiritual consolation. Second, the service exists within the Japanese concept of ancestor worship, and third, people attend the services as they are fearful that the soul of an angry fetus may return seeking vengeance.

The actual ceremony of mizuko kuyo varies widely. Firstly those who wish to take part in the service buy a small stone statue of Jizo depicted as a monk that is then dressed in babies' clothes. Next, the statute is place on the terrace of the temple. Though it may be expected that such terraces would necessarily seem gloomy and depressing, the terraces are actually rather happy places filled with toys and with pretty gardens festooned with childish decorations and filled with playground equipment. The people attending the ceremony usually stand silently in front of their mizuko's statue for a few minutes and pour water over it to symbolize that the statue is a shrine to a water child. Some temples assign a posthumous Buddhist name to a fetus since the fetus was not named in life. A mizuko kuyo ceremony also includes Buddhist prayers and the giving of offerings such as food, flowers, candles, incense and money, as well as toys. In addition to this, it is usual for a woman to pray for her lost child, light a candle in the child's honor, and write a brief message of either apology or remembrance to the fetus or child. The message is then attached to a wooden plaque placed next to the appropriate statue. After a ceremony, some temples hold a tea gathering for people who attended the event to congregate. This is supposed to help form support networks for grieving parents though research has found that these fail to materialize in actuality, mainly because the attendees do not want to talk about the death or aborting of their offspring.

Despite the seeming sincerity of the mizuko kuyo ceremony the rite has garnered controversy. This is because the prevalence of mizuko kuyo in current Japanese society has given rise to temples dedicated to ceremonies such as the one held at Shiun-zan Jizo-ji Temple in Chichibu, a commercial operation that is not actually affiliated with any branch of Buddhism though the building's architecture does reveal Buddhist influences. Many truly Buddhist temples also charge for performing mizuko kuyo services with prices varying widely. Indeed as some temples charge extortionate fees for holding the rite the commercialization of mizuko kuyo ceremonies has caused some anger. This is evinced by the fact that the Japanese media has largely denounced the ceremony as a moneymaking scheme that exploits vulnerable, grief-stricken parents, particularly those who feel guilt over abortions. In addition, feminist groups in Japan have cited the ceremony as a way to continue the subjugation of women that is symptomatic of Japan's patriarchal society. However the number of mizuko kuyo services performed in Japan continues to grow despite these claims, which are well known. Further, researchers whose work focuses on mizuko kuyo point out that no religious practice could become as prevalent in society as has mizuko kuyo unless it fulfilled some profound need in society. Moreover, the practice of mizuko kuyo ceremonies is spreading around the world as Japanese Buddhists emigrate abroad. For instance, the rite was introduced to the United States in 1978 when a Buddhist nun at a Hawaiian temple performed the ritual. Since then a select number of U.S. Buddhist temples have begun to hold the ceremony though the meaning of the service has changed somewhat. In the United States, mizuko kuyo ceremonies act as a way for grieving mothers to mourn their lost children and temples act as the nexus for support groups arising from the ceremonies. In addition to Buddhist temples, some U.S. hospitals have also started to hold the rite in the hope of providing spiritual comfort to grief-stricken families.

See also: Buddhist Attitudes Toward Death; Japanese Death Customs; Living with the Dead; Pregnancy and Infant Loss Memorial Day

Further Reading
Brind'Amour, Katherine, and Garcia, Benjamin. "Mizuko Kuyo." The Embryo Project Encyclopedia. October 30, 2007. Accessed November 16, 2014, at http://embryo.asu.edu/pages/mizuko-kuyo.
Brooks, Anne Page. "Mizuko Kuyo and Japanese Buddhism," *Japanese Journal of Religious Studies*, 8(3-4), September–December 1981. Accessed November 16, 2014, at https://nirc.nanzan-u.ac.jp/nfile/2226.
Galvan, Javier A., ed. *They Do What? A Cultural Encyclopedia of Extraordinary and Exotic Customs from around the World.* Santa Barbara, CA: ABC-CLIO, 2014.
Japanese-buddhism.com. "Jizo Bosatsu." Accessed November 16, 2014, at http://www.japanese-buddhism.com/jizo-bosatsu.html.
Steinfels, Peter. "Beliefs," *New York Times*, August 15, 1992. Accessed November 16, 2014, at http://www.nytimes.com/1992/08/15/us/beliefs-891892.html.

MORTUARY TOTEM POLES, HAIDA AND TLINGIT

Totem poles are tributes crafted by First Nations of the Pacific Northwest to symbolize and honor their lineage, heritage, community, or events. Many peoples around the world erect carved wooden columns for ceremonial or commemorative purposes but the poles raised by the peoples of the Pacific Northwest are notable for their size and the intricacy of their carving. Totem poles are designed to be tall, normally standing between 3 and 18 meters high (though some are over 20 meters tall) so that they can be seen by a community as a whole. Totem poles are usually made from the wood of the red cedar, which is soft and abundant in the Pacific Northwest. There are several different types of totem pole, each built to serve a different purpose.

An especially distinctive type of totem pole is the mortuary totem pole, a type of pole that is particularly associated with the Haida people though the Tlingit also erect such poles. It is not known when such poles began to be erected but there are reports of mortuary carvings from the start of the 1800s. These poles were located in both the Haida Gwaii, an archipelago off the north coast of British Columbia, Canada, that is colloquially referred to as the Queen Charlotte Islands, and extending intermittently some 950 miles along Canada's west coast.

Mortuary totem poles are erected for people of importance or high rank such as a chief and act as both a tomb and a gravestone. This type of pole has a cavity carved into the top into which is placed a burial box, also known as a grave box, containing the remains of the esteemed person. When a Haida person dies, the person's remains are placed in a highly ornate chest that is kept in the community's mortuary house. After a year, the remains are placed inside an undecorated box that is then put in the cavity of the mortuary pole.

To allow enough room for the cavity to be carved into the log used to make the pole, the log is inverted so that the cavity can be carved into the wide end of the pole. This means therefore that the tapering end of the pole is fixed into the ground. The burial box containing the human remains is hidden from sight by a frontal board (i.e., a board made of cedar wood attached to the front of the pole). This board is designed to resemble a large chest and is decorated with carvings or illustrations including the person's ancestral crest. (*See* Plate 10.) Sometimes more wooden planks and rocks are placed on top of the frontal board to prevent the board from moving in high winds. The mortuary poles fashioned by the Tlingit differ in that Tlingit people of high status are usually cremated. Early on in Tlingit history, cremated remains were placed in a box inside a plain totem pole. However more recently it has become traditional for ashes to be placed in a decorated box placed inside a slot at the back of a carved pole.

A second type of mortuary pole reserved for the remains of more than one individual is known as a double post mortuary pole. This is a structure consisting of two poles set slightly apart with a box-type edifice made of wooden planks that connects the two posts. Inside this wooden edifice are placed the burial boxes containing the remains of up to three members of the same family.

Another type of totem pole erected after the death of a notable personage is the memorial pole, also called a commemorative pole. These poles are erected by the successor of the deceased as a sign of honor. These poles tend to be the tallest type of totem pole as they symbolize esteem for the dead. This is particularly true of memorial poles erected by the Tsimshian of the Nass and Skeena Rivers in British Columbia.

See also: Delaware Indian Death Rituals; Fantasy Coffins; Maiden's Garlands; Lakota Death Rituals; *Mirila*; Native American Grave Protection and Repatriation Act, 1990; Ray Fadden Letter to President Harry S. Truman; Personalized Hearses

Further Reading

Huang, Alice. "Totem Poles." Indigenousfoundation.arts.ubc.ac. Accessed May 10, 2015, at http://indigenousfoundations.arts.ubc.ca/home/culture/totem-poles.html.

Kramer, Pat. *Totem Poles*. British Columbia, Canada: Heritage House Publishing Company Ltd., 2008.

Simon Fraser University. "Totem Poles." The Bill Reid Center. Accessed May 10, 2015, at https://www.sfu.ca/brc/art_architecture/totem_poles.html.
Stewart, Hilary. *Looking at Totem Poles*. Vancouver, Canada: Douglas & McIntyre, 1993.

MUMMIFICATION, INTERNATIONAL

Mummification is a method of corpse preservation that can occur accidently by natural means or as a deliberate, artificial way of conserving a body so that the soft tissue is retained. A corpse preserved in this way is called a mummy, a word that probably derives from the Persian word *mummiya* meaning bitumen, which was used to describe the dark color of the mummified bodies. Mummification is synonymous with ancient Egypt but deliberately mummified bodies have been discovered in the Atacama Desert on the border of Chile and Peru, the Canary Islands, China, Italy, Australia, and Japan. Mummified remains of saints and high-ranking members of the Catholic Church can be found in churches around the world, despite the Catholic Church's disapproval of mummification. Indeed there are over 300 mummified, or partially mummified, corpses in churches in Italy including the partially mummified body of St. Victoria in Florence and the corpse of St. Ranieri that is covered in gold and housed in an altar in Pisa. Moreover the preserved corpse of Pope John XXIII (who died in 1963) is on display at the Vatican contained within a glass casket. Many pilgrims to the Vatican consider the Pope's preserved corpse to be a sign of his incorruptibility and, therefore, of his saintliness, but the Pope's corpse is actually the result of various chemical processes and the application of wax to the skin.

Meanwhile, in Papua New Guinea a few tribes continue to mummify their dead by smoke-drying corpses. Naturally preserved mummies have been found preserved in ice in Greenland and the European Alps and in peat bogs in northwestern Europe.

Over the years mummies have been cemented in the popular imagination through works of fiction such as *Jewel of the Seven Stars* by *Dracula* author Bram Stoker (adapted into the film *Blood from the Mummy's Tomb* by English film studio Hammer Horror in 1971) and in films ranging from *The Mummy* (1932) starring Boris Karloff to the various Hammer Horror films featuring mummies made in the 1950s–1970s and *The Mummy* adventure-film franchise of the 1990s. However though these films may be entertaining they tend to forget that behind the desire to deliberately mummify a corpse lay the wish to preserve a body in such a way that it remain as lifelike as possible in order to both provide the soul with a home and also cheat death by denying death the opportunity to putrefy the corpse.

The world's oldest mummies are the remains dating from 6000 BCE that were found in the Atacama Desert on the Chile-Peru border. An ancient people living on the Pacific coast called the Chinchorro created the mummies. The Chinchorro mummies demonstrate a complex mummification technique for the Chinchorro reconstructed their dead by defleshing the corpse and removing the skin, brain, and internal organs. The Chinchorro then dried the bones using hot ashes before reassembling the body using tightly bound twigs for structure. The skin was replaced over the twigs with a thick layer of ash smeared over the body and a painted clay mask placed over the face. (*See* Plate 11.) Each mask was painted similarly so that all the mummies have a uniform appearance. Other Mesoamerican peoples also practiced mummification including the Nazca, Chiribaya, and the Chachapoyas whose mummies have been discovered high above the trees of the Amazon rainforests in a sitting position with their knees pulled up to their chins and mouths open (Edvard Munch's painting *The Scream* was inspired by a Peruvian mummy the artist saw in Paris, France). Incan mummies are often the result of human sacrifice performed on mountaintops where bodies were deliberately left open to the elements resulting in freeze-dried corpses. Hundreds of Incan mummies have been found in the Andes surrounded by ornaments that were offerings to gods accompanying the sacrifices. Incan mummies looked extremely lifelike with their hair, eyebrows, and clothing intact, something that caused Spanish *conquistadors* such disquiet that the Spaniards felt the need to destroy the mummies. Spanish colonialists also destroyed the mummies they found in the Canary Islands where descendants of the North African Berbers, the Guanches, mummified their dead as late as the 1500s. The mummies found in Taklamakan Desert, China, are also thought to be the preserved victims of human sacrifice. These mummies, which are around 3,500 years old, have Caucasian facial features, red hair, and plaid clothing revealing that this area of China acted as a crossroads of early trade routes between Europe and China. The Eurasian Steppes eco-region was also home to the Scythians, a group of Iranian nomads that mummified their dead too. Scythian mummies have been found in the permafrost of the Altai Mountains that lie between Siberia and Outer Mongolia.

However despite the fact that many different peoples practiced mummification the process is undeniably linked with ancient Egypt in the pubic imagination. The Egyptians began to mummify corpses as early as 3400 BCE when they wrapped fabric around corpses. Then in 3000 BCE the Egyptians started to mummify their dead by smoothing plaster over bodies or wrapping corpses in cloth saturated with resin. Then in 2600 BCE the Egyptians realized that extracting the internal organs of bodies delayed decomposition and over subsequent years the Egyptians honed their mummification techniques on both humans and animals to become world leaders in the technique.

In ancient Egypt different versions of mummification existed that varied depending on cost. The most expensive version of mummification involved removing the brain from the corpse by extracting it via the nose while the entrails were removed in order to stop the corpse from decaying. Next, the hollowed-out body was dried using salts and the dried skin was preserved with combinations of oils and resins and natron, a naturally occurring combination of sodium bicarbonate and sodium carbonate. In total, the process took up to 70 days to complete. Extracted internal organs, specifically the liver, intestines, stomach, and lungs were each placed in an individual vessel called a canopic jar. Each jar would have a uniquely shaped lid representing a one of four Egyptian gods known as the Sons of Horus. Each of the Sons of Horus represented a different organ: Qebhsnuf, who had the head of a falcon, cared for the intestines, jackal-headed Duamutef looked after the stomach, Imsety, who had a human head tended the liver, and Hapi, who had the head of a baboon guarded the lungs. Packs of natron were stuffed inside the body cavity to prevent decomposition and then hairstylists and beauticians would get to work to give the corpse a lifelike appearance. Finally, the corpse was swathed in as many as 20 meters of linen that had been pre-soaked in natron. This cloth was either reused household linens or fabric specifically designed for use in the mummification process. The mummy was then placed in an ornate wooden coffin alongside a number of protective amulets, and elaborate funeral ceremonies would take place that were designed to reactivate the soul that was thought to still be residing within the mummy. The words "You will live again for ever. Behold, you are young again for ever" (Fletcher, 2011) were recited and the mummy was interred with plenty of food and drink so that the deceased's soul would be comfortable in the afterlife.

Egyptian mummies were buried in the desert along the banks of the Nile River with the rich interred in specially built tombs while the poor were placed in holes dug in the sand. Once buried in sand the bodies would become desiccated and thus mummified in the heat trapped in the sand. This process meant that the corpses' hair, skin, and nails were all preserved.

Today, very few cultures practice mummification. A few tribes living in the Morobe highlands of Papua New Guinea (e.g., the Anga) do, however, still perform the process as a way of venerating the dead despite the fact that mummification has met with opposition from the Catholic Church and was banned in Papua New Guinea in 1975. Papua New Guinean mummification is performed by highly skilled embalmers who slice into a corpse's knees, feet, and elbows and stab the gut with bamboo sticks to allow body fat to drain out. All the resultant body fluids are then collected and daubed on the hair and skin of the deceased's relatives in a ritual that is thought to confer the strength of the departed on the living. Any liquid leftover is then used to cook food so that the living can ingest the strength of the dead. Next the corpse's eyes, mouth, and anus are sewn closed as this stops the body from taking in air that would make it rot. Soft tissue, such as the tongue, the soles of the feet, and the palms of the hands, are cut from the corpse and given as a memento to the spouse of the deceased. The remainder of the body is smoked over a pit of fire and then coated in a mixture of ochre and clay that dyes the body a reddish color and deters predators from eating the corpse.

Corpses prepared in this manner are then housed within bamboo cages attached to cliffs. The resultant mummies, which number around 200, are something of a tourist attraction but they also have a ceremonial purpose for the mummies are sometimes brought down from the cliff faces to mark special events and then replaced. The mummies are also seen as guardians of their communities with the mummies of fierce warriors placed in positions where they can fend off raiders.

> **Mummy Brown**
>
> Mummy brown, or *caput mortum* (meaning dead head in Latin), was a paint pigment made from white pitch, myrrh, and the ground remains of the linen used to wrap Egyptian mummies, both human and feline. Mummy brown was first made during the 16th century when it was prized for it transparency and ability to convey shadows and flesh tones. The pigment was also a favorite of the group of Victorian artists known as the Pre-Raphaelites. The Victorians were fascinated by mummies and held mummy parties during which mummies were ceremoniously unwrapped accompanied by a brass band as a form of public entertainment.

See also: Eleanor Crosses; Embalming; *Famadihana*; Plastination; Sakalava Royal Death Traditions and *Fitampoha*; Shrunken Heads; Taxidermy

Further Reading

Daily Mail. "The Smoked Corpses of Papua New Guinea: Tribe Pays Respect to the Dead by Curing Them and Hanging Them above Their Village to Look over Them." *Daily Mail*, July 10, 2014. Accessed May 9, 2015, at http://www.dailymail.co.uk/news/article-2687328/The-smoked-corpses-Papua-New-Guinea-Tribe-pays-respect-dead-curing-hanging-village-look-them.html.

Fletcher, Joann. "Mummies around the World." BBC: History, February 17, 2011. Accessed on May 9, 2015, at http://www.bbc.co.uk/history/ancient/egyptians/mummies_01.shtml.

Jeremiah, Ken. *Christian Mummification: An Interpretative History of the Preservation of Saints, Martyrs and Others.* Jefferson, NC: Mcfarland & Company Inc., 2012.

Jeremiah, Ken. *Eternal Remains: World Mummification and the Beliefs That Make It Necessary.* Sarasota, FL: First Edition Design Publishing Inc., 2014.

National Geographic Magazine. "Chile's Chinchorro Mummies," *National Geographic*, March 1995. Accessed May 9, 2015, at http://ngm.nationalgeographic.com/1995/03/chinchorro-mummies/arriaza-text.

Potenza, Theresa. "Vatican's Secret, and Deadly, Project to Mummify Saints." *New York Post*. March 22, 2014. Accessed June 6, 2016, at http://nypost.com/2014/03/22/making-of-a-saint-the-vaticans-quest-to-preserve-its-leaders/.

Science Museum. "Mummification." Accessed May 9, 2015, at http://www.sciencemuseum.org.uk/broughttolife/techniques/mummification.aspx.

MUSLIM DEATH RITUALS, ISLAM

According to Islamic law, a corpse should be buried as soon as possible after the time of death and certainly within 24 hours to 3 days of a person dying. This means that preparations for a Muslim funeral begin immediately after death. Muslims are nearly always buried and cremation is forbidden under Islamic law as Muslims feel that this would prevent a body from being physically resurrected on the Day of Judgment (*yawm ad-din*).

The sanctity of the corpse is very important to Muslims and for this reason Muslims tend to frown upon autopsies as they are considered a desecration of the body. Muslims also shun embalming and post-mortem make-up unless required by local law. Organ donation, however, is, in general, accepted within Islam. The Islamic attitude to embalming means that it is not always possible to repatriate the bodies of Muslims that die in the West but wish to be buried in the country of their ancestors.

When a Muslim person is near death, he or she will try to make sure that his or her dying words are the same as those of the Prophet Muhammad "Allah, help me through the hardship and agony of death" or "To Allah we belong and to Allah we return." When a Muslim person dies the corpse is ritually washed three times (or more but always an odd number of times) by three to four of the deceased's closest family members of the same sex or by the deceased's spouse until it is considered suitably clean. The washing-of-the-corpse tradition is known as *ghusl al-mayyit* and takes place in a secluded room. The corpse must be bathed in the following order: upper right-hand side, upper left-hand side, lower right-hand side, and lower left-hand side thought the private parts of the corpse should remain hidden during the washing. The hair of females should be washed and woven into three plaits. By preparing the body in this way the corpse is considered suitably purified for resurrection. After the ritual washing, the corpse is then shrouded in three sheets of inexpensive white fabric in a ritual known as *takfin*. Deceased women should also be dressed in a long sleeveless dress and a head covering before they are covered in the sheets. To start to shroud the body in the sheets, the corpse should first be laid on top of the fabric (*kafan*). If at all possible, the corpse's left hand should be laid on its chest and the right hand should rest on top of the left hand, as though praying. The sheets should then be gathered over the corpse, first from the right and then from the left, until all three sheets are firmly gathered around the corpse. The sheets should then be tied with ropes with one above the head and two tied around the body. A rope should also be tied below the feet. When the washing and shrouding of the body is complete the corpse is regarded as being ready to say the same phrase as a pilgrim on the *Hajj*: "Here I am Allah."

Once the corpse has been prepared in this manner, it is ready to be transported to the mosque where funeral prayers, known as *Salat al-Janazah*, will be said in the mosque's prayer room or courtyard by all members of the community on the grounds that the death of a Muslim is a death that affects all Muslim not just the deceased's immediate family and friends. During the Salat al-Janazah, everybody praying faces Mecca and all the people praying make three lines with the deceased's closest male relative first in the line followed by other men, then any children, and then females.

Muslims tend not to use coffins but in the West it is not always possible to avoid the use of coffins. Corpses are buried facing Mecca, the Muslim holy site located in Saudi Arabia that is believed to be the birthplace of the Prophet Muhammad. According to Muslim tradition, only men are permitted to be present at a Muslim burial, though some Islamic communities do allow women to be at the graveside during the burial. The grave of a Muslim is dug vertically in the direction of Mecca. Once placed in the grave, the corpse should be placed on its right-hand side also facing Mecca. While putting the corpse into the grave, those lowering the body should say the following words: "In the name of Allah and in the faith of the Messenger of Allah." Then, during the burial the first *surah* or a division of the Islamic holy book the Qur'an is read. During the burial it is acceptable for Muslims to reveal their sorrow over a death so sobbing and such are all considered acceptable modes to manifest grief. Wailing, shrieking, ripping of clothing, and throwing objects are not, however, considered suitable behavior, nor is any sentiment that reveals a lack of faith in Allah.

Once the body is buried, a layer of pebbles or wood is laid on top of the grave so that no direct contact is made between the enshrouded corpse and the ground. Next, each mourner places three handfuls of soil on the grave. When everyone has placed a handful of soil on the grave a stone marker may be put on the grave as a way of identifying the grave. It should be noted, however, that according to tradition, Islam prohibits large grave monument or lavish decorations on graves. It is though important that a grave is visibly distinguishable as a grave however in order to prevent people from stepping on the grave by accident.

After the burial, the deceased's immediate family gathers together and receives other mourners. It is customary on the day of burials for the entire community to provide food for the deceased's family. Indeed the community will normally continue to provide food for three days of mourning. In its entirety, the Muslim mourning period lasts for 40 days, though this depends on how religious a family is. If a family is not that religious then the period of mourning may be much shorter. Muslim widows should, however, observe a much longer mourning period that, in general, lasts for four months and 10 days. While in mourning, widows must not mix with any men that they could potentially consider as future husbands, except for emergency doctors and the like.

See also: Albanian Funeral Customs; *Hajj* (Volume 2); *Halva*; *Hijab* (Volume 2); *Hijra* (Volume 2); Muslim Birth Rites (Volume 1); Muslim Wedding Ceremony (Volume 2); Ossuaries; Vrindavan: The City of Widows

Further Reading

Bergman, Lucy, ed. *Religion, Death, and Dying, Volume 3: Bereavement and Death Rituals*. Santa Barbara, CA: Praeger, 2010.

Everplans. "Muslim Funeral Traditions." Accessed October 13, 2015, at https://www.everplans.com/articles/muslim-funeral-traditions.

Raudvere, Catharina. *Islam: An Introduction*. London: I. B. Tauris & Co Ltd., 2015.

Plate 1 Aymara indigenous people pray on All Souls' Day in El Alto, Bolivia, on November 2, 2013. The day also features the playing of music and the sharing of food and drink in the belief that on this day the souls of the deceased will reunite with their families. (Bert de Ruiter/Alamy Stock Photo)

Plate 2 As the personification of Death, *Ankou* is typically depicted as a skeletal figure. This Ankou is carved on the wall of the parish church in La Roche Maurice in Brittany, France. (Bildagentur-online/Alamy Stock Photo)

Plate 3 A cairn located at the summit of Ceapabhal with a view out over Toe Head, South Harris, Hebrides, Scotland. Cairns are particularly associated with Scotland where they are often to be found marking mountain peaks. (David Forster/Alamy Stock Photo)

Plate 4 Every Good Friday crucifixion reenactments take place in the Philippines. Here Filipino penitent Ruben Enaje, who has portrayed Jesus Christ 27 times, reacts as a nail is removed from his hand on March 29, 2013, at Cutud, Pampanga province. (AP Photo/Aaron Favila)

Plate 5 *Osterbrunnen* are an annual feature of Easter activities in parts of Germany. Osterbrunnen, such as this example located in Bieberach, Bavaria, consist of garlands of colorful hollowed-out eggs. The garlands are placed around public wells one week before Easter Sunday and are removed one week after Easter. (imageBROKER/Alamy Stock Photo)

Plate 6 Ghanaian fantasy coffins take the form of large, colorful, wooden objects carved to symbolize an aspect of a recently deceased person's life. Such is the intricacy of design needed to create fantasy coffins that the coffins are sometimes exhibited as art in Western art galleries. (Spiegl/Ullstein Bild via Getty Images)

Plate 7 A girl attending the biannual Whitby Goth Weekend (WGW) festival in Whitby, North Yorkshire, England, on November 2, 2014. The WGW brings together thousands of goths and fans of alternative lifestyles from across the United Kingdom and elsewhere for a weekend celebrating various aspects of the goth subculture. (Oli Scarff/AFP/Getty Images)

Plate 8 A second line parade consisting of musicians participates in a jazz funeral held in the French Quarter, New Orleans, Louisiana, on November 2, 2007. (Franz Marc Frei/Alamy Stock Photo)

Plate 9 A person takes part in a *malagan tatuana* mask dance on New Ireland Island, Papua New Guinea, in September 2009. Though a type of memorial ceremony, malagan ceremonies are celebratory occasions that honor the dead. (Eric Lafforgue/Alamy Stock Photo)

Plate 10 A Haida mortuary totem pole in Stanley Park, Canada, honoring Chief Skedans. Mortuary totem poles are erected to honor important or high-ranking people and act as both a tomb and a grave marker. (JPL Designs/iStockphoto.com)

Plate 11 A mummified Chinchorro girl in the Chilean town of San Pedro de Atacama. (Eye Ubiquitous/UIG via Getty Images)

Plate 12 A man throws offerings to a bull-shaped sarcophagus during a *ngaben* mass cremation held in Ubud, Bali, Indonesia, in 2014. More than 100 corpses were cremated collectively during the ceremony. The Balinese believe that cremation allows the spirit of the deceased person to be freed in order to reincarnate. (Agung Parameswara/Getty Images)

Plate 13 Human skulls and other skeletal remains decorate a wall in the *Capela dos Ossos* (Chapel of the Bones) ossuary located in Évora, Évora District, Portugal. (imageBROKER/Alamy Stock Photo)

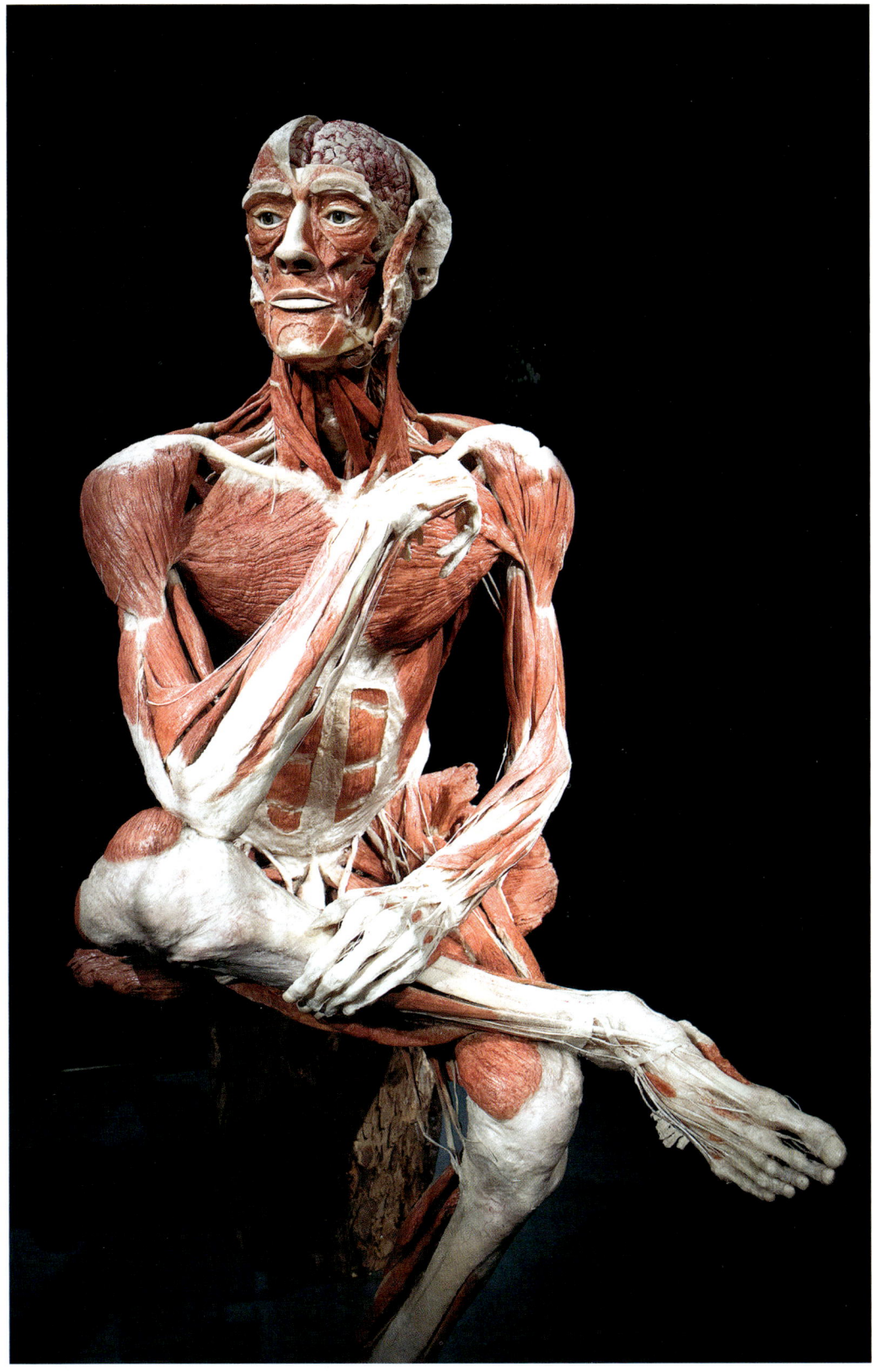

Plate 14 A plastinated human corpse displayed as part of the *Body Worlds* exhibition in Berlin, Germany, in 2015. (Aslu/Ullstein Bild via Getty Images)

Plate 15 A couple prays as they burn paper money at a public cemetery in Shanghai, China, as part of the annual *Qingming* festival, on April 6, 2015. (Johannes Eisele/AFP/Getty Images)

Plate 16 Sunrise over the Tower of London and the art installation called *Blood Swept Lands and Seas of Red*. The artwork consisted of handmade ceramic poppies with each poppy representing a British or Commonwealth military fatality during World War I. (Ray Wise/Getty Images)

Plate 17 A *Santa Muerte* idol dressed as a bride in Santa Maria Cuautepec, Tultitlan, Mexico, on February 7, 2016. (Yuri Cortez/AFP/Getty Images)

Plate 18 Senior athletes compete during the National Senior Games held in Louisville, Kentucky, on June 28, 2007. (Andy Lyons/Getty Images)

Plate 19 The spontaneous shrine established in memory of murdered school girl Alice Gross in Hanwell, West London, England. This photograph was taken on October 5, 2014, a few days after the discovery of the girl's body on September 30. (Danny E. Martindale/Getty Images)

Plate 20 The Tomb of the Unknown Warrior located at the west end of the Nave of Westminster Abbey, London, England. (Justin Kase/Alamy Stock Photo)

Plate 21 Painted wooden crosses, depicting scenes from everyday life and inscribed with poems, mark graves in the Merry Cemetery in Săpânța, Maramures County, Romania. (Caluian/iStockphoto.com)

Plate 22 Widows from Vrindavan listen to speakers during a function intended to honor and assist widows in New Delhi, India, on September 27, 2012. (Raveendran/AFP/Getty Images)

Plate 23 A windmill in Schiedam, the Netherlands, with its sails set in the mourning position to mark the death of Prince Johan Friso. (Robin Van Lonkhuijsen/AFP/Getty Images)

Plate 24 Across Europe yew trees are considered symbolic of death and immortality. In the United Kingdom, the trees are commonly found in churchyards and cemeteries. (David Pearson/Alamy Stock Photo)

Plate 25 A voodoo follower bathes in a sacred pool during the annual voodoo festival held in the village of Souvenance, near Gonaives, Haiti, on March 27, 2016. (Hector Retamal/AFP/Getty Images)

N

NATIONAL MOURNING, INTERNATIONAL

National mourning is a time during which the majority of a country's population observes memorial activities. National mourning is designated as such by the nation's ruling body and can last from one day to several years. National mourning normally occurs to mark the death or funeral of a distinguished individual from that country or elsewhere, to observe the anniversary of a death, or to mark instances of national tragedy. There is no set way in which national mourning is practiced but usually national mourning involves the performance of a number of formalities that manifest sadness. These can include a minute's silence or the lowering of flags on public buildings to half-mast. However academics have noted a difference in how national mourning is observed in the northern and southern hemispheres as national mourning appears to be more reserved in the northern hemisphere than the particularly emotional manifestation of national mourning that occurs in the southern hemisphere.

The pattern of national mourning was established during the reign of British royal Queen Victoria. The rituals of death fascinated the Victorian era and during this time mourning practices became something of a public obsession. It was during the reign of Queen Victoria (r. 1837–1901) that the way of national mourning were founded for in the 1880s it was decided that the period of mourning on the death of a monarch should be 12 weeks and the death of a monarch's child would be marked by 6 weeks of mourning. The scale of national mourning decreased in order of rank so that the death of a monarch's first cousin was marked by just 10 days of mourning. The death of Queen Victoria herself, in 1901, led to a great outpouring of national grief. According to historians, this grief was not so much to signal the death of an esteemed figure but really to symbolize the foreclosure of the nation's future. Though the queen was old the British went into a sort of shock mode as the queen had been such a beloved figurehead that it seemed impossible to her subjects both in Britain and living abroad that she might die. Similarly, there was a large-scale outpouring of public grief in Iran in 1989 when the Ayatollah Khomeini died. Indeed at the Ayatollah's funeral many mourners were killed and thousands hurt in a crush. More recently, people in North Korea were seen to exhibit signs of excessive sadness following the death of Kim Jong-il in 2011 though many Western observers doubted the authenticity of the North Korean people's grief. Previously, the death of North Korean president Kim Il-sung was marked by three years of national mourning from 1994 to 1997.

It is not just royalty and national leaders that are the subject of national mourning instigated by the state. The death of a major religious figure such as the Pope is often marked by national mourning, particularly in countries with large Catholic populations. For example, when John Paul II died in 2005, three days of national mourning were held in Cuba, a communist state that until 1992 was officially atheist. Flags in Cuba were flown at half-mast, the national baseball league play-offs were rescheduled, and bars were shut. Similarly, on November 7, 2012, Bulgaria's Cabinet declared a national day of mourning to be held on November 9 to mark the death of Orthodox Church Patriarch Maxim, who had passed away on November 6 at the age of 98. As a mark of respect for Patriarch Maxim, the Bulgarian government decided that to demonstrate the grief of people belonging to the Eastern Orthodox Church masses would be either postponed or cancelled. Additionally, national flags on all government buildings were flown at half-mast. A requiem liturgy was held on November 8 at the Sveta Nedelya church in the Bulgarian capital Sofia, during which Maxim laid in state. The laying in state was followed by a funeral at the Alexander Nevsky Cathedral on November 9 that saw members of the public pay their last respects to their religious leader.

Occasionally, a country's rulers will also decide to hold a period of national mourning to mark the passing of an exceptional individual that was neither a politician, royal, nor religious leader. This was the case in 1994 when Brazil held three days of national mourning to mark the death of legendary Formula 1 multiple world champion Ayrton Senna, who died when his car hit a barrier during the San Marino Grand Prix. Similarly, to mark the death of Portuguese soccer legend Eusébio in 2014 the Portuguese government announced three days of national mourning.

National mourning is not reserved solely for notable individuals. Sometimes tragic events resulting in the death of many regular individuals from one country also calls for a period of national reflection. In recent times, deaths caused by international terrorism have been marked by days of nationals mourning. For example, in Russia a day of mourning was observed on November 1, 2015, for the 224 people killed when their passenger plane was seemingly blown up over Egypt by a terrorist bomb in October. The group calling itself Islamic State (also known as the Islamic State of Iraq and the Levant, ISIS, Daesh, ISIL) claimed responsibility for the atrocity. To mark the day of mourning, Russians laid flowers and toys as spontaneous shrines at the entrance of Pulkovo Airport in St. Petersburg, where the passengers were headed when they left Egypt. In addition, the Russian national flag was flown at half-mast across the nation, cultural institutions were shut, and television and radio programs were cancelled. In addition, when the so-called Islamic State murdered over 100 people and injured many more in Paris, France, in a series of attacks on November 13, 2015, the French president Francois Hollande declared three days of national mourning across France. Hungary also held a day of national mourning on November 15 to mark the terrorist attacks in Paris. This saw public buildings in Hungary display the national flag at half-mast and flowers and lit candles placed outside the French Institute of Budapest in honor of those who died in the attacks.

See also: Minute's Silence; Remembrance Day and Remembrance Sunday; Riderless Horse; Spontaneous Shrines; State Funeral; Wearing Flowers to Honor War Dead; Windmills

Further Reading

Associated Press. "Thousands of Bulgarians Bid Farewell to Patriarch Maxim, Late Leader of the Orthodox Church." TheRecord.com, November 9, 2012. Accessed November 19, 2015, at http://www.therecord.com/living-story/2617198-thousands-of-bulgarians-bid-farewell-to-patriarch-maxim-late-leader-of-the-orthodox-church/.

BBC. "Reporter's Log: Mourning the Pope." BBC News, April 3, 2005. Accessed November 19, 2015, at http://news.bbc.co.uk/1/hi/world/europe/4400039.stm.

Hungary Today. "Paris Terror Attacks: Hungary Observes Day of National Mourning in Remembrance of Victims," *Hungary Today*, November 16, 2015. Accessed November 19, 2015, at http://hungarytoday.hu/news/paris-terror-attacks-hungary-observes-day-national-mourning-remembrance-victims-70268.

Kasher, Asa, ed. *Dying and Death: Inter-disciplinary Perspectives*. Amsterdam, Netherlands: Rodopi, 2007.

Middleton, John, ed. *World Monarchies and Dynasties*. Volumes 1–3. London: Routledge, 2015.

The Portugal News Online. "Eusébio Dies." The Portugal News Online, May 1, 2014. Accessed November 19, 2015, at http://www.theportugalnews.com/news/eusebio-dies/30329.

Robb, Stephen. "What Is National Mourning For?" *BBC News Magazine*, March 8, 2013. Accessed November 19, 2015, at http://www.bbc.co.uk/news/magazine-21685781.

TASS. "November 1 Declared National Day of Mourning in Russia over Plane Crash in Egypt." TASS: Russian News Agency, October 31, 2015. Accessed November 19, 2015, at http://tass.ru/en/world/833147.

Williams, Richard. "Ayrton Senna: The Day a Million Brazilians Mourned Their Golden Boy," *The Guardian,* April 30, 2014, F1. Accessed November 19, 2015, at http://www.theguardian.com/sport/2014/apr/30/ayrton-senna-death-funeral-formula-one.

NGABEN, INDONESIA

Ngaben (sometimes called *pelebon*), literally meaning "turn to ashes" or cremation ceremony, is an extremely important Balinese Hindu funeral ritual performed to send a soul (*atma*) into the afterlife. The occasion is not a sad one and onlookers do not shed tears. Indeed during the ceremony the living treat the dead as though they are asleep as they believe that the deceased is only temporarily not present and will either be reincarnated or will ultimately find an eternal rest called *moksha*, meaning freedom from the cycle of death and reincarnation. A similar ceremony is practiced by Indian Hindus.

The Balinese believe that gods and deified ancestors dwell in the upper world watching over the inhabitants of the earth and returning acts of homage with kindly acts and general benevolence. The lower realm is inhabited by various evil spirits that move between their world and the middle realm (i.e., the earth). Those who live in the upper world descend to the middle realm to do good, while those in the lower realm rise up to enter the middle realm to wreak havoc and cause harm. If those dwelling in the lower realm rise up in too great a number the cosmos becomes unequal and endangered. The likelihood of the cosmos becoming unbalanced increases when human souls are in a state of flux, crisis, and liminality. This is most apparent when a soul has left its human body in death but has yet to be freed through the act of cremation. Ngaben is intended to help the soul enter the upper realm where it can either wait to be reborn, or it can reach a state of total liberation by leaving behind the cycle of reincarnation altogether. Those attending ngaben fear that the evil inhabitants of the lower realm will try every opportunity to capture a soul waiting to be freed through ngaben and thereby cause disorder in the cosmos. Therefore the Balinese consider it necessary to do all they can to enhance the prospects of the deceased's soul through ngaben.

Ngaben is performed through a series of ceremonies consisting of various rituals, offerings, and symbolism. As ngaben is performed to make the body return to its home and allow the soul to rejoin its ancestors it should be performed as soon as possible after death. However in actuality the ritual is expensive and time consuming to perform and as a result often takes place quite a while after a person has died as communities join together to share the burden of cost by cremating several corpses at once. Indeed lower caste families often bury their dead underground as a temporary measure, while sufficient funds are accrued to pay for the ceremony. Families should not, however, wait longer than a year to carry out the ceremony. However if a family is of a high caste and therefore can afford to bear the expense alone then the ceremony can be held within three days of a death occurring. The appropriate day to hold the ngaben is usually selected after discussions with a Hindu priest or *Brahmin* who will choose the most auspicious day for the event to take place after deciding the auspicious *dewasa* (the day on which a ritual should take place). While they wait for the day of the ngaben to arrive, the family of the deceased make preparations for the ceremony with the help of their community. The family makes a coffin (*bade*) that will be used to transport the corpse to the cremation ground (*kuburan*) along with a replica coffin shaped like a bull (*lembu*) that is made out of bamboo, wood, and paper and which will be burned during the cremation. The replica coffin may also be shaped to resemble a temple (*wadah*).

The night before a cremation, a large wooden drum called a *kul-kul* is struck to tell people that they should assemble at home of the deceased. On the day of the ceremony the community unites with the deceased's family to make final preparations such as washing the corpse. As with all preparations for ngaben, the washing of the corpse is overseen by the Brahmin. Once the corpse has been thoroughly cleaned it is dressed in traditional Balinese attire. Next, all family members amass to pay their respects to the dead and pray that the deceased's soul will know peace. The corpse is then placed in one of the coffins with a white cloth placed at the front and back of the coffin representing a bridge for the soul to reach its place of origin. The corpse is then transported to the cremation ground with relatives and other community members walking in a line behind it. If in transit the procession

> ### The Gamelan
>
> The gamelan is traditional ensemble music found in Java and Bali, which many Indonesians see as an integral element of their national culture. The gamelan consists of percussive instruments, especially metallophones played with mallets and drums called *kendhang* that are played with hands and register the beat. The other instruments included in the gamelan include xylophones, bamboo flutes, the *rehab* (a bowed instrument) and, sometimes, singers known as *sindhen*. The popularity of the gamelan has decreased in the face of an increased interest in modern pop music but the gamelan is still performed on formal occasions and at traditional Indonesian ceremonies.

encounters a junction or crossing then the coffin is rotated three times in order to confuse watching evil spirits and keep them away from the corpse.

The playing of gamelan music, which is intended to summon various gods and ancestors who can then be asked for instructions on how to properly perform ngaben, follows the procession. The gamelan music is also believed to give strength to those carrying the coffin. Holy songs are also sung. Once the coffin reaches the cremation ground the corpse is transferred to the coffin shaped like a bull and a priest recites prayers and mantras over the corpse before it is set alight. The burning of the corpse in the bull-shaped coffin is the climax of the ngaben. (*See* Plate 12.) The fire is important as it frees the soul allowing it to be reborn. During the burning *beleganjur* music, which is traditionally associated with battles including the fight against evil spirits, is played as it is thought this facilitates the soul as it seeks to ascend to the realm of the gods and deified ancestors to await reincarnation. This realm is said to be exactly like Bali except that this realm is totally worry-free.

After the cremation there is yet another stage to fulfill before ngaben is considered complete. After the purification by fire that is ngaben, the final purification rite takes place, usually 12 days after ngaben. This final stage sees the ashes of the body burned during ngaben placed inside the skin of a coconut and scattered in the sea or in rivers that locals consider to be sacred. This allows the water to purify the soul one last time so that it may to return to heaven to begin the process of reincarnation.

In India, a more modest form of ngaben takes place. The Indian version is less complex and does not involve the saying of prayers or mantras. Instead, it requires only a cremation ground and aromatic firewood. Ngaben has a very long history in India. According to Indian Hindu folklore, legendary king Yudhistira cremated warriors killed during battle in Tegal Kurusetra. However a more recent instance of Indian nagben occurred when Indian Prime Minister Indira Gandhi was cremated soon after her assassination. Gandhi's funeral was an elaborate affair attended by foreign government ministers who watched as attendants piled wood on to a funeral pyre until only the head of the corpse was visible. Then her son

Rajiv, who later became Prime Minister of India, poured *ghee* (clarified butter) on to the pyre as this would help the fire take hold. Rajiv then smashed a water-filled clay pot called a *matka* as a symbolic breaking of the final tie of the deceased with earthly life. Rajiv then took a flaming torch and set fire to the end of the pyre where the head lay.

See also: Cremation; Hindu Death Customs; Living with the Dead; Zoroastrian Funerals

Further Reading

BaliGoldenTour.com. "Ngaben Ceremony." Accessed December 19, 2014, at http://www.baligoldentour.com/ngaben.php.

The Economist Newspaper Limited. "The World's Way of Death," *The Economist*, November 12, 1998. Accessed December 20, 2014, at http://www.economist.com/node/176343.

Galvan, Javier A., ed. *They Do What? A Cultural Encyclopedia of Extraordinary and Exotic Customs from around the World*. Santa Barbara, CA: ABC-CLIO, 2014.

Koen, Benjamin, Jacqueline Lloyd, Gregory Barz, and Karen Brummel-Smith, eds. *The Oxford Handbook of Medical Ethnomusicology*. Oxford, UK: Oxford University Press, 2008.

Scattering Ashes. "The Balinese Ceremony of Ngaben: Turn to Ash." April 9, 2014. Accessed December 19, 2014, at http://www.scattering-ashes.co.uk/different-cultures/balinese-ceremony-ngaben/.

NINE-NIGHTS, CARIBBEAN

Nine-Nights, also known as Dead Yard, is a post-death custom that occurs in the Caribbean, most especially in Jamaica, but also in Grenada, Guyana, Trinidad, Haiti and the Dominican Republic. A Nine-Nights takes the form of an extended wake that lasts a maximum of nine nights during which time the friends and relatives of the deceased congregate at the home of the deceased to share condolences and reminisce while singing *sankeys* (hymns focused on the soul's journey to heaven) and African and Christian dirges, sharing food and drinking rum.

The Nine-Nights custom most probably has its roots in the traditions of African slaves that were brought to the Caribbean during the days of the slave trade. African slaves believed that a person's spirit took nine days to travel back to Africa, and this is probably where the tradition started. The gathering of the deceased's family and friends is thought to comfort mourners as well as giving the deceased's spirit a celebratory, yet respectful, farewell. This is important as a long held African belief is that a person's *duppy* (spirit) will refuse to move on and will therefore become a nuisance to the living if it is not treated with respect prior to burial. The Nine-Nights custom is also influenced by the European Christian tradition of the wake and Christian hymn singing.

Nine-Nights, as the name suggests, lasts for nine nights and days with the ninth and therefore, final, night being the eve of the funeral church service. On this ninth night the family of the deceased prepares a great deal of food. According to tradition this ninth night is the night on which the spirit of the deceased passes through the wake collecting food and saying farewells to its loved ones before moving on to its final place of repose. For this reason the ninth night is the most revered part of the Nine-Nights celebration with fond stories about the deceased recounted and with prayers said. It is also traditional for popular games such as dominoes to be played. All the while a table laden with foods and drinks prepared by the deceased's family such as fried fish, goat, pork, chicken, *bammy* (cassava flatbread), and 100-percent proof rum is set up in a tent so that the deceased will not go hungry. A special soup called Mannish Water is also made. This is a soup made from the head, feet, and testicles of a goat that is believed to increase men's sexual prowess. Sexuality is also to the fore during another Nine-Nights customs, in the form of dances such as the so-called *Dinki-Mini*. This is a dance with Congolese origins that features upbeat music peppered with sexually suggestive moves. The dance is not intended to be sexy, but rather a representation of the creation of life at a time when death is at the forefront of people's minds. Moreover, the dance's suggestive moves and rhythmic pounding are intended to show that death is ineffective in the face of life. Similarly, the *Gerreh* dance that is also performed during the Nine-Nights is sexually suggestive in order to request that spirits help defeat death by creating life. Another dance that may be performed during a Nine-Nights is the *Kunima,* though the performing of this dance is usually scorned. The Kumina highlights the spiritual aspects of death but the dance is the focus of much superstition as it is thought by some people to be connected to Haitian Voodoo and incarnations that recall ancestral spirits, which in turn is bound up with superstitions involving zombies. A Kumina is, however, only performed during a wake and is intended to invite the spirits of the family's ancestors to assist the recently departed in their journey to the afterlife.

No living person may eat from the table of food and drink until midnight has struck on the ninth night for it is at the strike of midnight that the deceased is thought to return for his or her share of the food. So that the deceased may move on, a ritual takes place during which a mourner looks at a doorway and claims to see the spirit of the deceased. That person then tells another mourner what they have seen and this prompts the second mouner to tell someone else and so on. The person that started the seeing then greets the duppy and a so-called night song starts up. A night song is a song played especially for the duppy while it is told stories by community leaders. Another Ninth-Night custom sees the deceased's bed and mattress turned upside down against a wall as an encouragement to get the duppy to leave its former home and enter its grave. A community leader may also use a stick of white chalk to draw a crucifix over the exit through which the duppy is thought to have left as this is thought to prevent the duppy from returning once it has departed.

See also: Death Dance; Wake; Zombies and Voodoo Death Traditions

Further Reading

Murrell, Nathaniel Samuel. *Afro-Caribbean Religions: An Introduction to Their Historical, Cultural, and Sacred Traditions.* Philadelphia, PA: Temple University Press, 2010.

Phillips, Nadya-Kaye. "Celebrating Life and Death in Jamaica: The Tradition of Nine-Night," *Mango Salute Magazine*, March 24, 2013. Accessed December 15, 2015, at https://mangosalute.com/magazine/celebrating-life-and-death-in-jamaica-the-tradition-of-nine-night.

Real-Jamaica-Vacations.com. "Jamaican Traditions: Birth and Death Practices." Accessed December 15, 2015, at http://www.real-jamaica-vacations.com/jamaican-traditions.html.

OBITUARY, INTERNATIONAL

An obituary is a type of death notice that occurs in newspapers and other publications, both in print and online. Obituaries are usually written to mark the recent death of a famous person and normally contain details about the deceased individual's life and career. Despite the fact that obituaries are death-related they make very popular reading material with many people heading straight to the obituaries section as soon as they open a newspaper. Indeed some newspapers are particularly noted for their obituary sections—for example, the *Daily Telegraph* in the United Kingdom, which divides its obituaries into various subdivisions such as Military Obituaries, Politics Obituaries, Culture Obituaries, and Sport Obituaries. Moreover, it is also possible to buy books of obituaries that have been written by particular newspapers.

The history of obituaries can be traced back to the newsbooks written in 17th-century England that detailed events such as disasters and deaths and were the forerunner of today's newspapers. The art of obituary writing developed during the 18th century and reached a peak during the 19th century, particularly during the Victorian era. The Victorians tended to be fascinated with death not least because during the mid- to late 19th century most people knew someone that had faced death in war or through illness and because much of Victorian literature included deathbed scenes and a Gothic Revival was ongoing. During the early 20th century obituaries fell out of favor before being revived during the 1980s as a distinct genre of writing.

Today, an obituary is typically written either by someone that knew the deceased or by an employee of the newspaper in which the obituary appears. Often the person that writes a newspaper's obituary section is a specialist that is used to compiling information from various sources very quickly. However obituaries for some very famous people (e.g., members of royal families, leading politicians, or aging film stars) will have been written in advance.

There is a standard format for obituaries that involves logging the date, time, and location of the individual's death, noting in chronological order his or her achievements both career-wise and in his or her personal life, and listing the individual's awards. The biography section of an obituary is often the most interesting part for readers, as it will normally contain information of which the public is unaware such as a famous person's family background, early life, and schooling. This information is usually followed by a more detailed section providing details about any surviving members of the deceased's family such as his or her spouse and children. At the very end of the obituary, the time, date, and place of the deceased's burial or cremation may be published.

One of the most unusual obituaries to have appeared in print came about on August 6, 1975, when the *New York Times* announced the death of Agatha Christie's literary sleuth Hercule Poirot. The newspaper's headline read "Hercule Poirot Is Dead; Famed Belgian Detective; Hercule Poirot, the Detective, Dies" and went on to detail Poirot's life as though he were a real person. Two months later the final mystery to feature Poirot, and in which the detective dies, *Curtain*, was published. Sometimes obituaries are accidently published before a person has actually died. This was the case when the *New York Journal* published an obituary for the American author Mark Twain in advance of his actual demise. The error prompted Twain to remark famously that "the reports of my death are greatly exaggerated."

See also: Eulogies; Fantasy Coffins; Tombstone Tourism

Further Reading

Hercule Poirot Central. "Poirot's Obituary." Accessed October 20, 2015, at http://www.poirot.us/obituary.php.

Howarth, Glennys, and Oliver Leaman, eds. *Encyclopedia of Death and Dying*. Abingdon, UK: Routledge, 2013.

Hume, Janice. *Obituaries in American Culture*. Jackson: University Press of Mississippi, 2000.

The Pennsylvania State University. "Digging Up the Dead: Facts about Obituaries." Penn State University Libraries. Accessed October 20, 2015, at https://www.libraries.psu.edu/psul/researchguides/nml/obituaries/obits.html.

OSSUARIES, EUROPE

Ossuaries, also known as bone houses, are repositories for skeletal human remains found throughout mainland Europe and also in the United Kingdom. The word ossuary is derived from the Latin word *os* (bone; plural *ossa*). An *ossuarium* was the Latin word for a container for bones, typically a box. Related words in other Romance languages derived from these roots include *ossa*, *os*, and *ossos* in Italian, French, and Portuguese respectively. All these words translate as bones, while the word for an ossuary itself also derive from the Latin: *osario* (Italian, Spanish, and Portuguese) and *ossuaire* (French). The word ossuary appeared in English from the 1650s, though at that time the word was used to describe a container for bones such as the James Ossuary, the wooden box initially believed to have belonged to the brother of Jesus but later proved to be a fake. Over time, the word ossuary began to be used to define an architectural edifice rather than a container and now describes a room in which bones are kept. Some ossuaries are minimally decorated while others display ornate design and creativity.

In medieval Europe, ossuaries were a usual method of burial, particularly in densely populated areas where there was little room for ground interment using coffins. The dead would be buried temporarily and then many months later, their corpses would be exhumed and reburied in a separate location in an ossuary. This is the reason that ossuaries do not generally appear in Islamic countries as Islam prohibits the exhumation of skeletal remains under any circumstances. One well-known ossuary located in a Muslim country is that located beneath the floor of the Chapel of Saint Tryphon in Sinai, Egypt. In the Brittany region of France it was usual for corpses to be buried in churchyards for five years before being exhumed with the skull transferred to an individual painted, wooden box displayed in the church or ossuary and the skeleton's other bones placed with undifferentiated bones elsewhere in the ossuary. This treatment of human remains may seem medieval but was customary in parts of Brittany up until the start of World War I in 1914.

Medieval Europeans also believed that those who had lived a good life, particularly saints, would stay incorrupt and their remains would keep well so it seemed logical to keep their remains where they could be seen as a lesson in the benefit of moral correctitude. The bones of many saints were kept by monasteries, churches, and cathedrals as valuable artifacts and often attracted pilgrims and tourists. Some of these saintly remains were incorporated in items of great value such as swords and ornamental crucifixes that were effectively portable ossuaries thought to give their owners great spiritual authority. Some portable ossuaries also served to transport the remains of ancestors as it was felt that carrying the ancestral bones brought ancestral spirits closer to the living.

There is no one set pattern for the architectural design of ossuaries, which can be found across Europe in various sizes. The biggest European ossuaries are to be found in Austria, Italy, Spain, the Czech Republic, and Portugal. The most important Austrian ossuary is located in the village of Hallstatt, in Salzkammergut in Upper Austria and is often referred to as *Beinhaus* (The Bone House). This ossuary is located in the basement of the 12th-century Church of Saint Michael and houses a collection of 700 painted skulls plus 500 unpainted crania together with birth, death, and marriage records. Nearly all the painted skulls bear the emblem of the Maltese Cross and some have snakes depicted crawling from the eye sockets. They also have their name and year of birth and/or death carved on them. These painted skulls are lined up in rows on wooden shelves while the unpainted skulls are piled in corners of the ossuary. Decorating the skulls was the job of the gravedigger and families could request that he paint flowers such as roses on a female's skull and a wreath of oak or ivy on a male's skull. All the skulls are grouped together by family and represent the population of Hallstatt and its neighboring villages through the years—the most recent skull was entered into Hallstatt's ossuary in 1995.

Italy's largest ossuary is also located within a church, the *Santa Maria della Concezione dei Capuccini* or Our Lady of the Conception of Capuchins, in Rome. This ossuary is unusual as all the bones belong to deceased monks—between 1528 and 1870 the resident Capuchin friars used the bones of 4,000 of their departed brothers to fashion an extraordinary sight—a cemetery where everything, including the picture frames and lights are made of human bones (the light fixtures are made from femurs). There is also an arch created from hundreds of human skulls and

> ### Les Catacombes de Paris
>
> *Les Catacombes de Paris* (Catacombs of Paris) are underground ossuaries located in an ancient tunnel network found in Paris. The catacombs contain the bones of around 6 million people. The ossuary was established in the 18th century at a time when such city cemeteries as Saint Innocents were overflowing. Between 1786 and 1788, bones were transferred at night from cemeteries to the tunnels with more bones placed in the catacombs in subsequent years. By the 19th century, the catacombs had become a tourist attraction, opening to the public in 1874. Measuring some 186 miles, the catacombs are sometimes considered the world's biggest grave.

decorated with a fleur-de-lys formed from vertebrae. There are also some mummified skeletal remains clad in monastic robes belonging to Franciscan monks. In fact, nearly every part of the church reveals that an ossuary is located beneath for there is the Crypt of the Bones, Crypt of the Pelvises, and Crypt of the Leg Bones and Thigh Bones. The only part of the church not associated with skeletal remains is the chapel, where mass is said. The ossuary began when in 1631 the Capuchin monks were ordered to relocate from their friary near the Trevi Fountain to Santa Maria della Concezione dei Capuccini, and the pope's brother decreed that the bones of all the deceased friars should be relocated too so that all the monks, living and dead, could be together. This ossuary is said to be the inspiration for Sedlec Ossuary in the Czech Republic that houses between 40,000 and 70,000 sets of skeletal human remains. Many of the bones belong to people who died during the outbreak of the Black Death that occurred in Central Europe in the 14th century while others were killed in wars during the 15th century. In fact, so many people died during this period that bodies buried in the local cemetery were exhumed en masse and their bones placed inside the church, which is also known as the Church of the Bones or the Bone Church. There was such a vast number of bones visible that local artists decided to makes use of them. One of Sedlec Ossuary's most notable works of bone art is the large chandelier of bones that forms the centerpiece of the ossuary. The chandelier contains an example of every human bone including skulls.

The largest ossuary in Portugal is the *Capela dos Ossos* (the Chapel of the Bones). This chapel is part of a 16th-century church in the Alentejo region of southern Portugal. The chapel is notable because its interior walls and pillars are decorated with bones from around 5,000 skeletons taken from at least 10 nearby cemeteries. (*See* Plate 13.) The most talked about part of the ossuary is the macabre sight of two corpses hanging from chains attached to the ceiling. One of the corpses is that of a child and it is believed the skeletons are those of a father and son who were cursed by the man's wife (and therefore the boy's mother) because the man had been unfaithful.

Besides preserving human bones, ossuaries also demonstrate to those who see them that while human life is transitory, death is permanent. For this reason, many ossuaries exhibit inscriptions relating to the transient nature of life. This sentiment is perhaps exemplified by an inscription on a plaque in Santa Maria della Concezione dei Capuccini that reads, in three languages, "What you are now, we once were; what we are now, you shall be."

See also: *Ankou*; Funeral Plants; Jewish Death Customs; *Memento Mori* and *Vanitas*; Tombstone Tourism; Zoroastrian Funerals

Further Reading

Atlas Obscura. "Santa Maria della Concezione Crypts." Accessed January 5, 2015, at http://www.atlasobscura.com/places/santa-maria-della-concezione.

Empire de la Mort. "Ossuaries & Charnels." Accessed January 5, 2015, at http://empiredelamort.com/charnels-and-ossuaries/.

Galvan, Javier A., ed. *They Do What? A Cultural Encyclopedia of Extraordinary and Exotic Customs from around the World.* Santa Barbara, CA: ABC-CLIO, 2014.

Gibson, Marion, Shelley Trower, and Garry Tregidga, eds. *Mysticism, Myth and Celtic Identity.* Abingdon, UK: Routledge, 2013.

Hallstatt. "The Painted Skulls of Hallstatt." *HallstattAustria.net*. Accessed January 5, 2015, at http://www.hallstattaustria.net/the-painted-skulls-of-hallstatt/.

SedlecOssuary.com. "The Church of Bones." Accessed January 5, 2015, at http://www.sedlecossuary.com.

Trinkaus, K.M. "Mortuary Ritual and Mortuary Remains," *Current Anthropology,* 25(5), December 1984, 674–679.

P

PASSING BELLS, ENGLAND AND SCOTLAND

A passing bell is a type of bell ring traditionally sounded to signal a death within a parish. The passing bell would ring when a parishioner was on his or her deathbed and then ring again to mark the parishoner's funeral and the anniversary of the parishoner's death. In this way, a passing bell is a harbinger of death. The bell chime is known as a passing bell because it is sounded to tell listening parishioners that one of their number is passing into the next world. Moreover, the ringing of the passing bell was said to make evil spirits pass over the dying soul at its moment of transition from one world to the next, a time when the soul was especially at risk of falling into the clutches of evil. For this reason, in Scotland a passing bell is referred to as a soul bell. In Scotland, it is customary for a bell chime known as a mort bell to sound when a parishioner was on his or her deathbed while a soul bell would ring out to proclaim that the person had died.

While passing bells are not at all as common a feature of parish life as once they were, passing bells are not extinct as often supposed. Several parishes in England do still ring passing bells. In the town of Richmond in North Yorkshire it is traditional to ring a passing bell to signal the death of a local dignitary. The Richmond passing bell is sounded by a council employee called a town hall keeper who climbs the town hall bell tower and uses a rubber-faced hammer to bang on the tower's large bell. In the past, the passing bell was rung to signal the death of anyone in the parish with the bell sounded nine times for the death of a man and six times for the death of a woman. The passing bell was also rung three times for a child. The Richmond passing bell was last rung in the autumn of 2014. Another English church that still sounds a passing bell is the Parish Church of St. Peter and St. Mary Magdalene in Ely, Cambridgeshire. This church rings a tenor bell to signal the death of a parishioner—the tenor bell is rung slowly in full circle and then set at each handstroke and each backstroke. This bell chime is sounded for five to 10 minutes before the parishioner's funeral.

Another passing bell tradition known as Tolling the Devil's Knell occurs every Christmas Eve at Dewsbury Minster in Dewsbury, Yorkshire. The chime begins with the bell called the Nine Tellers or passing bell that is rung in five sets of five. This chime is the church's version of a passing bell and was traditionally rung to signal the death of a parishioner. Normally, the Dewsbury passing bell chimes four times on the death of a man and three times for a woman but on Christmas Eve the Dewsbury passing bell sounds five times to signal the fact that the birth of Christ marks the death of the devil. The sounding of the passing bell on Christmas Eve is also thought to protect the town from the devil during the coming year. The

Dewsbury passing bell is thought to have originated when a 15th-century local nobleman killed a servant boy by pushing him into a local dam. According to regional folklore, the nobleman provided the local church with a tenor bell as an act of repentance. Ever since, the church has rung out to signal the triumph of good over evil and as a form of mystical protection for the town.

See also: Christian Death Rituals; Maidens' Garlands

Further Reading
Daily Mail, eds. "Question: Do Any Parishes Still Ring a Passing Bell?" *Daily Mail*, December 15, 2014, 46.
Puckle, Bertram S. *Funeral Customs: Their Origin and Development*. Los Angeles, CA: Library of Alexandria, 2009.
Roberts, Kai. *Folklore of Yorkshire*. Stroud, UK: The History Press, 2013.
Simpson, Jacqueline, and Steve Roud. *Oxford Dictionary of English Folklore*. Oxford, UK: Oxford University Press, 2000.

PASSION PLAY, CHRISTIANITY

A Passion play (sometimes called an Easter pageant) is a religious dramatic presentation depicting the Passion of Jesus Christ, by which is meant Jesus's trials, suffering, death, and Resurrection. Passion plays are a traditional Lent custom in several Christian denominations, especially the Catholic tradition. Many scholars accept the crucifixion of Jesus as a real historical event for it is recorded in the writings of Paul, the Gospels, Josephus, and the Roman historian Tacitus. However academics disagree on the historical accuracy of the details, the context, and the meaning of the event.

Most Passion plays open with the events in the Garden of Gethsemane and include the Last Supper, while other Passion plays begin with the events of Palm Sunday (i.e., when Jesus entered Jerusalem to acclaim from spectators). As a drama, Passion plays tell a story of injustice, suspicion, dread, mental and physical suffering, and, ultimately, tortuous death. Passion plays often include explicit, detailed portrayals of Christ's physical suffering during his beatings, whippings, and crucifixion. The reason for this is two-fold. Firstly, since the main aim of Passion plays is to emphasize Christ's humanity by identifying this humanity with his physical suffering, it is necessary to provide audiences with a realistic depiction of the Crucifixion. Secondly, by depicting the final sufferings of Jesus as realistically as possible, Passion plays remind audiences that the execution of Christ was an actual historical event.

The first Passion plays were staged in the 12th century with the earliest-known written Passion play being one found at the Benedictine monastery of Monte Cassino, Italy. Over time, Passion plays also became popular when written in vernacular languages in Germany, France, Flanders, Spain, Italy, and in areas of Celtic Britain. The earliest Passion plays were, however, written in Latin and consisted of excerpts from the Gospels incorporated with poetical accounts of the Passion and other Biblical stories such as the life and contrition of Mary Magdalene, the raising of Lazarus from the dead, the Last Supper, and the lamentations of the Virgin Mary. The use of Latin in these plays led to the development of a separate type of vernacular play, the earliest surviving examples of which are German and date from the 13th century. These plays included dramatic portrayals of the Resurrection and gave rise to a later type of Passion play that was popular in Germany and Czechoslovakia that included the character of Satan and depictions of the fall of Lucifer and the Fall of man. In turn, this type of Passion play developed into cycle plays, that is, plays that tended to focus on religious figures, Biblical writing, and religious sermons. The plays were not generally concerned with the chronology of events and most were by anonymous writers. By the 16th century, Passion plays in general had become degraded through secular influences to the point that the plays had lost much of their religiosity and were viewed by most people as populist, if rather vulgar, entertainment. Indeed such was the debasement of Passion plays at this time that they were banned by ecclesiastical authorities in several countries. Later, after the Protestant Reformation, the plays were also suppressed.

The most famous Passion play to survive into the 20th century is, probably, that staged in Oberammergau, in Upper Bavaria, Germany. This Passion play, which runs from May to September and has been performed since 1634, came into being when villagers promised God that if he saved their village from the plague then they would commemorate his intercession by staging a dramatic depiction of Jesus's suffering, death, and Resurrection once every decade. Ever since, the descendants of these villagers have kept alive their ancestors' vow to stage the play with the only interruptions to the staging of the Oberammergau Passion play occurred in 1870 during the Franco-Prussian War and again during World War II. The Oberammergau Passion play is notable not just because it is a very old tradition but also because the play involves the participation of nearly all the village's inhabitants resulting in a cast of over 2,000 individuals both acting and singing choruses. The Oberammergau Passion play begins with Jesus entering Jerusalem, continues on to the Crucifixion, and ends with the Resurrection. The play is, however, the focus of a certain amount of controversy as some villagers as well as some Jewish organizations claim the play contains anti-Semitic overtones with questionable depictions of Jewish characters that earned praise from Adolf Hitler in 1934. The defeat of Nazi Germany in World War II and the international condemnation of the Holocaust led to many calls to modify the Oberammergau Passion play. However occupying U.S. forces permitted the revival of the Oberammergau Passion play in 1950 as authorities believed that the resumption of the play would lift the moral of locals and create a sense of unity within Germany. Many changes to the Oberammergau Passion play were instituted for the 2000 production that emphasized the culpability of Pontius Pilate with regard to Jesus's execution. Despite such changes, many commentators of varying faiths still consider the Oberammergau Passion play to be anti-Jewish. The next staging of the Oberammergau Passion play is set for 2020.

Elsewhere in Europe the tradition of the Passion play has enjoyed a revival in villages in the mountainous region of the Austrian Tirol as well as villages in northern Spain, in Tegelen in the Netherlands, where a modern play written by the Dutch poet Jacques Scheurs is performed every five years and annually at various locations across the United Kingdom. Outside of Europe, Passion plays are performed regularly in the Philippines, Canada, Australia, Brazil, the United States, and Sri Lanka. However possibly the most famous Passion play is that performed in Iztapalapa, in Mexico City, Mexico, during *Semana Santa*, or Holy Week. In contrast to many Holy Week Passion plays staged in Latin America, the Iztapalapa play dates not from the time of Spanish colonization, but to as recently as 1843. This was when a local cholera epidemic ended and in order to demonstrate their gratitude, residents of Iztapalapa scripted and staged their own version of the Passion of Christ. Since then, the Iztapalapa play has managed to withstand the intense anti-clerical feelings of the Mexican Revolution to become a cherished Catholic tradition that conveys not only devout beliefs but also pride in a cultural identity that is increasingly threatened by modernization, secularization, and encroaching Protestantism.

The Iztapalapa Passion play is performed by a cast of thousands though many of the main parts are played by members of the same local families. Indeed roles in the play are often passed down through generations of the same family in much the same way as family heirlooms—a situation that has led to discontented grumblings from people not in line for an heirloom role. The requirements of the individuals wishing to play the roles of Jesus or Virgin Mary are very strict, for the individuals chosen for these roles must be deemed to be appropriately pure. Therefore according to tradition Jesus and Mary must be played by people that vow not go on dates or to parties and to abstain from alcohol and smoking from the moment that they are chosen to play the roles. In recent years, supplementary restrictions have been added meaning that the actors playing the Virgin Mary and Jesus must also be free from tattoos and piercings. People wishing to play either role must also prove that they have sufficient economic means to buy their own costumes. Despite this list of limitations, competition for the roles of Jesus and the Virgin Mary is intense and the people selected to play the roles do so with great seriousness. Indeed anyone wishing to take on these roles does not do so without serious intentions for the actor that plays Jesus must endure a ritual public whipping as well as carrying a cross weighing in excess of 200 pounds three miles up a steep hill. Once at the top of the hill, the actor must undergo a real crucifixion in which he is attached to the cross for 20 minutes. The actor playing the role of Judas meanwhile, must pretend to display great remorse for betraying Jesus—something that often results in the actor having rotten food sent in his direction as well as being cold-shouldered by his neighbors.

For the past 20 years, the Iztapalapa Passion play has been broadcast via satellite across the Spanish-speaking world and in recent years the play has experienced an increase in popularity. Despite the popularity of the play, however, the Roman Catholic Church's stance toward the play has varied over the years. In the past, religious authorities have protested that the play's script deviates too much from sacred texts as the plays draws not only on the Bible but also on Dante's 14th-century poem *Divine Comedy*. In recent years, however, the church has come to consider the Iztapalapa Passion play as a way of connecting a predominantly indigenous Mexican cast of actors closer to their religion.

See also: Crucifixion Rituals; Easter Eggs; Nativity Play (Volume 1);*Thaipusam*: Extreme Ritual Flesh Modification (Volume 2)

Further Reading

BBC. "The Passion of Christ." BBC: Religion, September 18, 2009. Accessed December 13, 2015, at http://www.bbc.co.uk/religion/religions/christianity/history/passionofchrist_1.shtml.

Hertz, May. "Semana Santa in Mexico." Inside-Mexico.com, March 19, 2015. Accessed December 13, 2015, at http://www.inside-mexico.com/featuresemana/.

Kupfer, Marcia, ed. *The Passion Story: From Visual Representation to Social Drama*. University Park: The Pennsylvania State University, 2008.

Rohter, Larry. "A Mexican Tradition Runs on Pageantry and Faith," *New York Times*, April 11, 2009. Accessed December 13, 2015, at http://www.nytimes.com/2009/04/12/world/americas/12mexico.html?_r=0.

Rudin, A. James. "Oberammergau," in Cunningham, Philip A., ed., *Pondering the Passion: What's at Stake for Christians and Jews?* Lanham, MD: Rowman and Littlefield Publishers, 2004, 809–811.

PAUPER'S FUNERAL, UNITED KINGDOM

A pauper's funeral is the colloquial name given to a funeral funded by the state in the United Kingdom. These funerals are more properly known as national assistance funerals or public health funerals. Under the Public Health (Control of Disease) Act 1984, councils in the United Kingdom have a statutory duty to make arrangements for funerals or cremations of people that die or are found dead in their borough after investigations determine that there is no alternative. In the United Kingdom, if an individual dies without a known next-of-kin councils normally act on written instructions from the coroner's officer. Also it is sometimes the case that the management of residential homes and sheltered accommodation will inform the council when there are no relatives willing or able to make the funeral arrangements for a recently deceased person in their care. Therefore, in short, pauper's funerals are paid for by the local authority when a person dies penniless, without family, or when relatives are unwilling or unable to pay for a funeral service.

The pauper's funeral is a very old type of funeral. In Victorian times, the British working classes had a general but nonetheless deep-seated fear of experiencing a pauper's funeral for during a pauper's funeral a corpse would be stripped naked and then wrapped in very thin material or paper before being placed in a coffin made of flimsy wood and lined with sawdust. The deceased's family would be denied the customary so-called last look at their loved one and also would have no say in where their relative was buried. Pauper's graves were usually dug in land connected to the workhouse or in a neglected part of a cemetery and might be 20 deep with other coffins. To clear space in the grave, the coffins were sprinkled liberally with quicklime and as a further indignity to the deceased, there would be no grave marker though sometimes a number would be assigned to a grave as a means of identifying who inhabited the plot. Such was the dread of the pauper's funeral that during the Depression Era of the 1930s people took out life insurance policies that they could ill afford just so that they would not face the indignity of a pauper's funeral.

Today, when a coroner notifies a council about the death of an individual that has nobody willing to make his or her funeral arrangements, the council will search the deceased's home to try to discover a will or other documents that might reveal the existence of the person's relatives, their religious beliefs, and preferred funeral arrangements. Any family and friends of the deceased that are revealed by the search are then informed of the death and asked if they will make the necessary funeral arrangements. If the family and friends decline to make the arrangements they will have to confirm in writing that they have refused. If no one is willing or able to arrange and pay for the funeral, the council takes responsibility for all funeral arrangements, including the registration of the death, instructing the funeral director to collect the corpse, providing a coffin, and transporting the corpse to the crematorium. Even though family and friends have not arranged the funeral, they will be informed of when the funeral will take place and may attend if they wish.

Usually if there is no reason to think the deceased would have disapproved, the corpse undergoing a pauper's funeral will be cremated. Councils will also try to ascertain the deceased's religious preferences, if any, and arrange a religious officiant to oversee the ceremony. However if a body is buried during a pauper's funeral rather than cremated then the grave may not be marked with a memorial unless somebody has bought the burial plot. After a body is cremated the resultant ashes will usually be scattered in a garden of remembrance. The deceased's personal effects and property will be sold after the pauper's funeral has taken place and any funds accrued will be used to offset some of the funeral costs.

In recent years, both funeral charities and crematorium staff have report a rise in demand for pauper's funerals. These organizations have also noticed that while the pauper's funeral was originally designed for those who died without family and friends, increasingly pauper's funerals are being provided for individuals whose families cannot afford to pay for a ceremony. During the recent economic downturn in the United Kingdom, it has also been asserted that just as the number of pauper's funerals has increased so too has the number of so-called DIY funerals. These funerals are cheaper to hold than traditional funerals as they see a family buy a coffin online and transport the corpse of their loved one to the crematorium in a van or car. Several reasons for the increase in DIY funerals have been proposed all of which are associated with the rising costs of traditional funerals. One suggestion for the rising cost of funerals is that families feel under pressure to put on extravagant ceremonies that they cannot really afford. Meanwhile, funeral directors claim the cost of cremations has risen after the European Union legislated that crematoriums must install expensive new filtration systems that reduce mercury emissions from corpses' fillings that are a significant source of environmental pollution.

In November 2015, it was announced that the cost of pauper's funerals to Welsh councils has increased by almost 30 percent to more than £90,000 (approximately $135,513) over the course of the last five years. Welsh councils spent £92,619 (approximately $139,457) in the year 2013–2014, a figure up from £66,245 (approximately $99,745) in 2009–2010. The councils did, however, manage to recovered some £27,031 (roughly $40,700) and £47,408 (just over $71,382) respectively from the estates of the deceased that underwent pauper's funerals. It was also claimed that the number of pauper's funerals taking place had also risen—from 67 in the year 2009–2010 to 81 in 2013–2014. This was an increase of 17 percent.

See also: Alkaline Hydrolysis; Cremation; State Funeral.

Further Reading

BBC News. "Paupers' Funeral Costs Rise by 30% in Five Years." BBC News: Wales, November 30, 2015. Accessed November 30, 2015, at http://www.bbc.co.uk/news/uk-wales-34963133.

Bracknell Forest Council. "Public Health Funerals—The Council's Role." Accessed July 17, 2015, at http://www.bracknell-forest.gov.uk/funeralnationalassistance.

Gentleman, Amelia. "The Return of the Pauper's Funeral to Austerity Britain," *The Guardian: Poverty*, October 20, 2014. Accessed July 17, 2015, at http://www.theguardian.com/society/2014/oct/20/paupers-funeral-austerity-britain-soaring-costs-bury-loved-ones.

Gilmore, Anne, and Steve Gilmore, eds. *A Safer Death: Multidisciplinary Aspects of Terminal Care*. New York: Plenum Press, 1988.

Strange, Julie-Marie. *Death, Grief and Poverty in Britain, 1870–1914*. Cambridge, UK: Cambridge University Press, 2005.

PERSONALIZED HEARSES, UNITED KINGDOM

A recent funeral trend in the United Kingdom sees people make their final journey in a personalized vehicle. Personalized funeral hearses are setting a fashion for unique funeral transportation. Indeed in a recent poll carried out for Co-Operative Funeralcare, some 23 percent of Britons claimed that they would like to make their final journey in a personalized vehicle. In 2013, 573,452 funerals took place across the United Kingdom, and the poll research revealed that one in fifteen funerals in the United Kingdom—around 38,230 funerals—featured a non-traditional hearse.

The choice of funeral vehicle available to transport the departed has expanded to meet the dying wishes of individuals so that they can express their personalities and the things that they enjoyed in life. For example, dying bikers can opt for a motorbike hearse while a farmer can choose a tractor and a train driver can be transported on a converted steam engine. Other requests for unusual hearses include people asking for their final journey to take place by Rolls Royces, Cadillacs (especially pinks ones), milk floats, and tandem bicycles. Contsruction machinery, camper vans, pickup trucks, lorries, and double-decker buses are also popular vehicles to head funeral processions. In response to such requests, funeral companies such as the Co-operative Funeralcare now frequently invest in unusual hearses such as classic cars and Japanese Buddhist hearses. Research has also found that one in five people would like their last journey to involve a vehicle that reflected their favorite pastime, with horse-drawn hearses and bicycle hearses the preferred options for most people polled. Meanwhile more than one in ten men were keen that their profession be reflected by their final mode of transport. This was particularly the case with van drivers, farmers, milkmen, and men that work in the armed services or emergency services. The Britons polled also revealed people's ultimate dream hearses. These were found to include the Hogwarts Express from the *Harry Potter* books, Dr. Who's TARDIS time machine, the Millennium Falcon from *Star Wars,* and the Trojan Rabbit that appears in *Monty Python and the Holy Grail.* Other preferred dream vehicles included the Batmobile as used by Batman, KITT Car from *Knight Rider*, The A Team's black van, the Ford Gran Torino driven by Starsky and Hutch, and, perhaps least feasibly, the Flintstone's stone car.

Above inflation funeral costs, however, are likely to mean that personalized hearses are too costly for the majority of Britons. Research conducted by the University of Bath shows that the so-called total cost of death is at present £7,600 (approximately $11,442) and is rising by roughly 7 percent per annum. This figure consists of the non-discretionary (i.e., essential) costs of funeral directors and cremation or burial fees plus the cost of including an officiating minister, which total about £3,456 (approximately $5,203). Such costs have risen by 80 percent over the 9 years since the same survey was initially undertaken in 2004. The costs of including a personalized hearse in a funeral procession varies depending on what type of vehicle is chosen, which often have to be hired from third party providers, as well as the distance the vehicle will have to travel as part of the funeral. At the moment it costs between £700 ($1053) and £950 ($1430) to hire a personalized vehicle compare with £350 (just over $526) for a traditional hearse.

See also: Fantasy Coffins; Funeral Songs; Pauper's Funeral

Further Reading

The Co-operative Funeralcare. "Custom Hearses Hit Top Gear." September 25, 2014. Accessed November 30, 2015, at http://www.co-operativefuneralcare.co.uk/news/09-2014/custom-hearses-hit-top-gear/.

Rowe, Tina. "More Brits Opting for Personalised 'Hearse,'" *Western Daily Press*, September 25, 2014. Accessed November 30, 2015, at http://www.westerndailypress.co.uk/Brits-opting-personalised-hearse/story-22978128-detail/story.html.

Smithers, Rebecca. "Personalised Hearses the New Way to Go," *The Guardian*, September 25, 2014. Accessed November 30, 2015, at http://www.theguardian.com/money/2014/sep/25/personalised-hearses-co-op-funeral.

PLASTINATION, GERMANY

The term plastination refers to a method of preserving organic tissues, most particularly corpses, invented by German anatomist Gunther von Hagens while working at the University of Heidelberg's Institute of Anatomy in 1977. The process can be employed as both a method of preserving anatomical samples for scientific research and for showing corpses as public displays that some consider to blur the line between art and science. (*See* Plate 14.) As a method of preserving human corpses for public display, plastination is popular with the paying public in the United States, Europe, and Asia but also highly controversial with exhibitions running into legal and ethical issues in several countries. To date, there are in excess of 400 plastination centers located in 40 nations around the world.

There is some disagreement as to how the name plastination came to be invented for it has been variously suggested that the word derives from the Greek *plassein*, meaning to shape or to form, while it has also been claimed that von Hagens created the word to set his invention apart from the process of plastification that already existed within the sphere of polymer chemistry. Von Hagens applied to patent his process as Polymer Impregnation of Perishable, Biological Specimens in 1977/1978 but decided to change this name to plastination as plastination was shorter, catchier, and more likely to appeal to non-English speakers. In order to have the necessary space and facilities to meet demand for plastination, von Hagens established the Institute for Plastination (IfP) in Heidelberg in 1993.

In the most basic terms, plastination is the process of changing human tissues into malleable plastic through saturation with a polymer substance. In order to preserve a corpse through plastination the following steps are taken. To begin the process a cadaver is first embalmed in a solution of formaldehyde to prevent decomposition. Next, any necessary dissections are made and the body is immersed in a bath of acetone under freezing conditions that elicits all water from the corpse with the water replaced within the body's cells by the acetone. The corpse is then placed in a vat of polymer substances such as epoxy resin, silicone rubber, or polyester. Meanwhile, a vacuum is created that causes the acetone to boil. As the acetone heats it evaporates thereby leaving the cells and drawing into the corpse the liquid polymer with the end result that the body's cells are filled with liquid plastic. The plastic must then be left to cure through the use of heat, gas, or ultraviolet light. Though the process can be applied to an entire corpse, the plastination process works equally well on small pieces of animal tissue. In total, it takes around 1,000 to 1,500 hours to plastinate an entire human corpse.

The plastination process was first developed to help preserve specimens for use in anatomy classes at medical and veterinary schools. Indeed the process is still performed for this purpose with research establishments adopting plastination on the grounds that the process is far more pleasant to undertake than other methods of corpse preservation as it does not result in toxic fumes. Body parts preserved via this process tend to be high quality, durable specimens that do not smell, may be handled safely without gloves as the poisonous fixative has been displaced, and do not need any special storage equipment but rather may be kept like any other inert item. Moreover, plastinated slices of organic tissue may be correlated with computed tomography and magnetic resonance imaging scans allowing for easy reference.

Despite the scientific benefits of preserving tissue in this way, plastination truly entered the public's conscious when von Hagens started to use the process to preserve corpses for public display purposes. The first display of whole human corpses preserved using the plastination technique was exhibited in Tokyo and Osaka in 1995 under the auspices of the Japanese Society for Anatomy. Over the next few years, von Hagens's plastination exhibitions managed to both fascinate and revolt the public leading to von Hagens being considered the world's most well known anatomist. This position was cemented over the next few years as von Hagens developed his *Körperwelten* or Body Worlds exhibitions that feature both entire human and animal corpses posed in lifelike positions and dissected and flayed cadavers all preserved through plastination. To date, in excess of 40 million people have visited the various Body Worlds tours that have taken place in countries including Germany, Austria, England, Ireland, Italy, the Netherlands, Lithuania, Turkey, South Korea, South Africa, Mexico, Singapore, Taiwan, Canada, Guatemala, Puerto Rico, Israel, and many locations across the United States including Los Angeles, Cleveland, Denver, and Chicago. Indeed Body Worlds is the most successful traveling exhibition ever.

Despite the popularity of von Hagens's plastination exhibitions the shows have also proved controversial. Indeed in 2003 officials in the German city of Munich attempted to ban a show on the grounds that it infringed burial laws and went against the principles of human dignity. Many European cities have banned von Hagens's plastination exhibitions yet they remain popular in other areas of the world including the United States. Particularly controversial Body Worlds exhibits have been that of a pregnant woman with her uterus dissected to reveal her fetus and in 2009 von Hagens's *Cycle of Life* exhibition attracted a great deal of criticism for posing two corpses as though they were engaged in sexual intercourse. While von Hagens asserted that the couple whose corpses were posed in this way had asked to be posed in such a manner and that the display was not intended to be sexually stimulating, many German politicians asked for the exhibit to be withdrawn from public display. Others have criticized Body Worlds from a specifically religious, rather than moral, standpoint. For instance, both the Catholic Church and Jewish authorities have aired concerns that plastination does not treat the human corpse with sufficient respect and when von Hagens's laboratory began to sell plastinated slices of human flesh online in 2010, eminent figures in the both Protestant and Catholic in Germany complained that such actions degraded the human body. However supporters of von Hagens's work highlight the fact that the corpses used by von Hagens's Body Worlds exhibitions are willed to the tour by donors through the Institute of Plastination. As of 2012, the Institute of Plastination claims to have more than 13,300 registered donors worldwide consisting of 12,172 living donors and 1,138 deceased donors. Most donors are German, with the second-largest donating nationality being people from North America with 1,385 living donors and 30 deceased donors coming from North America.

Further, in 2011 von Hagens revealed that he wished to be plastinated after his death. Under European Union legislation introduced in April 2006 enforcing a licensing system for transplantable tissues, public exhibition of human tissues such as the Body Worlds displays require written proof of consent before death and a Human Tissue Authority license. In England, in 2008 both the Manchester Museum of Science and Industry and the O2 Arena in London were granted such a license to hold the *Body Worlds 4* exhibition. Meanwhile, in the United States Body Worlds displays have prompted various states to create legislation aimed at governing the exhibition of human corpses and to require tours such as Body Worlds to produce proof that all corpse donations came from willing donors. A donated cadaver was also used in 2002 when von Hagens performed a human dissection in an art gallery in London, England, in front of 500 paying spectators. This was Britain's first public autopsy for 170 years and went ahead despite warnings that the event might be illegal under the Anatomy Act. The autopsy was also screened on the British television station Channel 4, which received complaints as well as praise for deciding to broadcast the autopsy.

During the late 1990s and early years of the 21st century, both the Body Worlds exhibition and the fedora hat-wearing von Hagens became instantly recognizable cultural sensations to the point that some critics consider both to be cultural icons. To this end both the Body Worlds exhibition and von Hagens appear in the 2006 James Bond film *Casino Royale*.

See also: Alkaline Hydrolysis; Embalming; *Memento Mori* and *Vanitas*; Mummification; Shrunken Heads; Taxidermy

Further Reading

BBC. "Controversial Autopsy Goes Ahead." BBC News, November 20, 2002. Accessed April 1, 2015, at http://news.bbc.co.uk/1/hi/health/2493291.stm.

Furness, Peter N. "The Human Tissue Act: Reassurance for Relatives, at a Price," *British Medical Journal*, 333(7567), September 9, 2006, 512. Accessed April 1, 2015, at http://www.ncbi.nlm.nih.gov/pmc/articles/PMC1562465/.

Grindberg, Emanuella. "Donors Sign Up to Have Bodies Dissected, Displayed." CNN: Tech, June 30, 2008. Accessed April 1, 2015, at http://www.cnn.com/2008/TECH/science/06/30/body.worlds/.
Institute for Plastination. "The History of Our Body Donation Program." Body Doation. Accessed April 1, 2015, at http://www.koerperspende.de/en.html.
Institute for Plastination. "The Plastination Process." Gunther von Hagens' Bodyworlds: The Original Exhibition of Real Human Bodies. Accessed April 1, 2015, at http://www.bodyworlds.com/en/plastination/plastination_process.html.
Lantos, John D., ed. *Controversial Bodies: Thoughts on the Public Display of Plastinated Corpses*. Baltimore, MD: The Johns Hopkins University Press, 2011.
Linke, Uli. "Touching the Corpse: The Unmaking of Memory in the Body Museum," *Anthropology Today,* 21(5), October, 13–19, 2005.
Quigley, Christine. *Modern Mummies: The Preservation of the Human Body in the Twentieth Century*. Jefferson, NC: McFarland & Company, Inc., 1998.
Telegraph Media Group Limited. "Gunther von Hagens Exhibition Criticised over Corpse Sex Display," *The Telegraph*, May 7, 2009. Accessed April 1, 2015, at http://www.telegraph.co.uk/news/newstopics/howaboutthat/5289311/Gunther-von-Hagens-exhibition-criticised-over-corpse-sex-display.html.
University of Michigan Plastination Lab. "Plastination of Anatomical Materials." University of Michigan Medical School: Plastination. Accessed April 1, 2015, at http://www.med.umich.edu/anatomy/plastinate/.
Whitaker, Maja I., and D. Gareth Jones. *Speaking for the Dead: The Human Body in Biology and Medicine*. Farnham, UK: Ashgate Publishing Limited, 2009.
White, James. "'I'm Dying, So Put MY Body on Show': 'Dr Death' Gunther von Hagens Plans Grim Farewell in One of His Own Corpse Displays." *Daily Mail*, January 4, 2011. Accessed April 1, 2015, at http://www.dailymail.co.uk/news/article-1343910/Gunther-von-Hagens-Dr-Death-plans-human-corpse-exhibition-grim-farewell.html.

PREGNANCY AND INFANT LOSS REMEMBRANCE DAY, INTERNATIONAL

Pregnancy and Infant Loss Remembrance Day is a day of remembrance for lost pregnancies, the deaths of newborns, and those who died as infants from conditions that include, but are not limited to, miscarriage, stillbirth, birth defects, ectopic pregnancies, molar pregnancies, and sudden infant death syndrome (SIDS). The day is also intended to educate and provide resources for parents that have experienced the death of a baby or suffered miscarriage. The day is symbolized by the wearing of a Pregnancy and Infant Loss Awareness Ribbon colored pale blue and pink, the colors traditionally associated in the West with baby boys and girls, and decorated with the butterfly pattern that is the logo of Pregnancy and Infant Loss Remembrance Day. Some parents also mark the day by releasing bunches of balloons into the sky.

Pregnancy and Infant Loss Remembrance Day is observed in the United States, Canada, the United Kingdom, and in the Australian states of Western Australia and New South Wales. This international day of remembrance is held each year on October 15 through various ceremonies and candle-lit vigils and culminates with the lighting of candles across the world at 7 p.m. in all time zones. When these candles are left lit for at least an hour a continuous band of light is created. This worldwide lighting of candles is known as the International Wave of Light.

The origins of Pregnancy and Infant Loss Remembrance Day can be found in the Pregnancy and Infant Loss Remembrance Movement that started in the United States on October 25, 1988, when Ronald Reagan, the then president, designated October Pregnancy and Infant Loss Awareness Month. The president saw this as a way to increase people's compassion for those who had experienced the death of an unborn or newborn baby, while also hoping to make Americans consider how best they could help bereaved families, on both an individual and community basis.

In 2002, Robyn Bear, Lisa Brown, and Tammy Novak instigated the October 15 Pregnancy and Infant Loss Remembrance Day (PAILRD), petitioning federal government and state governors to observe the day. In the end, 20 states signed up to the proclamation observing the day. To date, every one of the 50 states have yearly proclamations, while Arkansas, Kansas, Kentucky, Louisiana, Missouri, New York, Rhode Island, and South Dakota have adopted permanent proclamations. At present, organizers of Pregnancy and Infant Loss Remembrance Day are attempting to declare October 15 Pregnancy and Infant Loss Remembrance Day permanently in all states of the United States.

Pregnancy experts and grief counselors agree that one of the hardest things for families that have experienced miscarriage and infant death is that the death of a fetus or very young baby is not acknowledged with the same degree of seriousness as the death of older children or other family members. In the case of miscarriage, this may be because many pregnant women do not reveal that they are expecting until the end of their first trimester so a pregnancy may be lost before anyone but the woman is aware that a pregnancy is in progress. In such cases, nobody but the woman is aware of the lost pregnancy potentially making the woman feel isolated and internalizing her anguish. This sense of isolation can be compounded by the fact that many miscarriages occur without medical intervention and with women encouraged to stay at home and look after themselves. Pregnancy and Infant Loss Remembrance Day aims to help women and other people suffering from feelings of bereavement caused by miscarriage and infant death by reminding them that they do not suffer alone.

See also: *Mizuko Kuyo*: Fetus Memorial Ceremony

Further Reading

Fera, Doreen. "About Us." Remembering Our Babies. Accessed January 3, 2015, at http://www.rememberingourbabies.net/store/WsAboutus.asp.

McWhorter Sember, Brette. *The Everything Guide to Pregnancy over 35: From Conquering Your Fears to Assessing Health Risks, All You Need to Have a Happy, Healthy Nine Months*. Avon, MA: Adams Media, 2007.

Reagan, Ronald. "Proclamation 5890—Pregnancy and Infant Loss Awareness Month," 1988. October 26, 1988. Accessed January 3, 2015, at http://www.reagan.utexas.edu/archives/speeches/1988/102588b.htm.

Remembering Our Babies: October 15th. "Welcome." Accessed January 3, 2015, at http://www.october15th.com.

Wearne, Phoebe. "Remembrance Day for Lost Babies." The West Australian, October 16, 2014. Accessed January 3, 2015, at https://au.news.yahoo.com/thewest/a/25269100/remembrance-day-for-lost-babies/.

Q

QINGMING FESTIVAL, CHINA

Qingming, or Tomb-Sweeping Day, also known as Pure Brightness Festival or Clear Bright Festival, is an important annual Chinese festivity to honor dead ancestors. The festival falls on the 15th day after the spring equinox and is traditionally the day of ritual celebration that fell on the first day of the 5th solar term, a time when people enjoy the outdoors and farmers turn their attention to sowing seeds and ploughing.

The ethnically Han Chinese hold Qingming particularly dear. Though the festival has been held continuously in Hong Kong, Taiwan, and Macau, the festival was suppressed under the China's Cultural Revolution (1965–1968) during which many aspects of Chinese history, culture, and religion were curbed by the government and was only reinstated as a national holiday on the Chinese mainland in 2008. Qingming is so intrinsic to Chinese culture that Chinese communities living oversees continue to celebrate the festival. In countries such as the United States, Indonesia, Malaysia, and Singapore that have significant Chinese populations phone calls and letters are sent to China to reconnect with friends and family at this family-orientate time of year. In return, Chinese people may visit the graves of ancestors who died abroad.

Qingming is a very old custom dating back to the Spring and Autumn Period of Chinese history, around 770 BCE–476 BCE, when government officials would honor their dead ancestors to celebrate the start of spring. The festival is thought to have originated as a commemoration to a man called Jie Zitui who cut a piece of flesh from his own leg in order to feed his lord who had been forced to enter into exile during a time of unrest. Nineteen years later, the lord regained his position in society and temporarily forgot about Jie Zitui. When the lord did remember his loyal servant he was embarrassed and felt the need to reward him. However Jie Zitui had encased himself within a mountain together with his mother so in order to find Jie Zitui the lord decreed that the mountain be burned but this killed Jie Zitui and his mother and the lord found them dead. In order to honor Jie Zitui, the lord ordered that the day Jie Zitui died would be known as Hanshi (Cold Food) Festival and that on that day only cold food could be eaten. The next year, when the lord went to the mountain to make a sacrifice to Jie Zitui, he found willow trees had come back to life. For this reason, the lord let it be known that the day after the Hanshi Festival would be called the Qingming Festival. Over the course of history the two festivals have combined as one celebration. A less poetic possible origin for the festival is that Emperor Xuanzong, of the Tang dynasty, in 732 tried to curb his people's continuous and ostentatious honoring of their ancestors by proclaiming celebrations to honor the dead could only occur once per year. Ever since then, those on the Chinese mainland have honored their ancestors each year at Qingming. However people living in Hong Kong celebrate twice per year, once at Qingming and again on the ninth day of the ninth month of the Chinese calendar.

In ancient times, Qingming was the time when families would take long walks to enjoy the outdoors and play *cuju*, a soccer-like game played with a leather ball. Today, there are three main customs associated with Qingming: tomb sweeping, flying kites, and spring outings.

Tomb sweeping is the single-most important custom of the Qingming Festival, leading to the festival's alternative name of Tomb Sweeping Day. Indeed cleaning tombs and proffering offerings in order to honor ancestors are the two most important elements of showing respect to deceased relatives. For Qingming, the living clear weeds from around the tombs and fresh soil is added to show that the living care for the dead. Flowers are brought to the tomb as well as the deceased person's favorite food, wine, and tea are taken to his or her tomb as offerings, along with paper resembling money. Later the food, drink, and paper money are burned in order to ensure the dead do not go hungry or thirsty and are not lacking money. (*See* Plate 15.) Joss sticks (i.e., long, thin incense sticks) are also burned and fireworks are lit to mark the occasion. In urban areas people have begun to attach great significance to willow trees, the branches of which are said to ward off evil spirits. Thus many Chinese urbanites bring branches of willow into their homes at Qingming or attach them to the doors and gateposts. Trees in general are associated with Qingming as it was customary to plant saplings around the time of the festival since young trees planted then had a better chance of survival than trees planted earlier in the year. For this reason, Qingming used to be known as Arbor Day. However since 1979 Arbor Day has been held on March 12 (according to the Gregorian calendar) as a separate holiday. Over the last 20 years or so, many thousands of people born in the Chinese countryside have migrated to urban areas in search of work and so at Qingming many people leave their homes in the towns and cities and travel back to the countryside to visit friends and family. Also, as many people in China are now cremated rather than buried, especially in cities, the Qingming custom of tomb sweeping has been greatly simplified as there are fewer tombs to clean. Therefore the only really tomb-orientated aspect of Qingming in urban areas is the leaving of flowers at ancestral tombs and revolutionary martyrs, plus the saying of prayers. Some people also pay homage to those who killed during the 1989 pro-democracy Tiananmen Square protests and Zhao Ziyang, premier of the People's Republic of China from 1980 to 1987. Further, Qingming is considered the appropriate time for all patriotic Chinese to show respect to dead historical figures, particularly political leaders that shaped China's history. This was demonstrated in 1976 when the death of Premier Zhou Enlai saw thousands of people visit his tomb at Qingming in order to pay their respects. Indeed such was the populace's desire to honor Zhou Enlai that when the time came to remove the offerings left at his tomb, the people strongly opposed the move resulting in protests known as the Tiananmen Square Incident (this is not the same as the Tiananmen Square Massacre of 1989).

In Hong Kong, new traditions have started to become popular. Here, as well as leaving traditional offerings of paper money and joss sticks, the people of Hong Kong now also leave handbags, jewelry, and cigarettes made of paper plus expensive paper decorations fashioned to look like yachts, helicopters, watches, and cars. Also in high-tech Hong Kong, people leave replica iPads, iPhones, laptops, and other electronic devices complete with cables and connectors as offerings so that their ancestors can stay connected and online at Qingming.

Qingming is not, however, just a somber time of honoring ancestors for it is also a time for people to enjoy themselves. In China, March sees nature take on a fresh new look, as trees enter into leaf, flowers start to blossom, and the sun shines more strongly. Thus spring is a good time for people to get out and about to appreciate the beauty of nature. The custom of making spring outings at Qingming can be traced back to the Tang Dynasty (618–907). The outings are seen as joyous occasions that encourage a healthy body and mind. Another outdoor pursuit popular at Qingming is flying kites. Indeed at Qingming kites are not only flown during the day but also in the evening. At Qingming, small lanterns are tied to a string attached to the kite or to the kite's string grasped by the kite's handler. The lanterns look like twinkling stars as they flash through the night sky attached to the kites and create a uniquely beautiful Qingming sight that has caused people to refer to the lanterns as God's Lanterns. It is traditional at Qingming for people flying kites during the day to cut the string while the kite is in the air and to let it fly free. This is said to bring good luck and eliminate diseases.

Another important celebration fundamentally linked to Qingming is *Hanshi*, or Cold Food Festival. This day is celebrated in China as well as Korea and Vietnam. However in China Hanshi takes place just before Qingming and symbolizes the changing of the seasons. The name Cold Food Festival reveals that the celebration has its roots in a time of struggle and it is thought that the festival began in ancient times when the type of wood available to people changed making it necessary to use a new form of starter to light fires. Before the fires could be lit food had to be eaten cold, as there was no way of heating it. This tradition of eating cold food continues today, though now as a form of celebration rather than as a necessity. Hanshi celebrations also see people clean their homes, play tug o' war and watch cockfighting.

Another aspect of Qingming that is only practiced in rural areas of northern China is that of ghost marriages, or *minghun*. A ghost marriage is a ceremonial combination of a funeral and a wedding for the custom sees unmarried dead ancestors given a so-called ghost spouse so that they will be happy in the afterlife. Ceremonial ghost marriages, that some historians think may date back to the 17th century BCE, are increasingly rare in modern China—Mao Tse-tung tried to eradicate the ritual when he assumed power in 1949—but ghost marriages are still practiced in rural parts of Shaanxi, Shanxi, Henan, Hebei, and Guangdong provinces. The practice has its own traditions and customs such as postmortem wedding feasts and dowries and has also led to a corpse matchmaking industry complete with money paid in exchange for helping to find a marital partner for a dead unwed relative. Once a suitable match is found the two corpses are interred together and offerings of foods such as dumplings are placed on the grave. The ritual of ghost marriages has also created an illicit trade in corpses fueled by the fact that the Chinese are newly wealthy but still highly superstitious. This newfound wealth has made it possible for people to afford to purchase desirable postmortem partners with cases of people buying a corpse bride straight from a hospital, financial deals having been made with grieving families. In addition, in February 2012 a woman's corpse was sold by her family to the family of a recently departed young man for 35,000 yuan (roughly $5,327) soon afterward, police caught a grave robber selling the woman's twice-exhumed cadaver to another family for slightly less at 30,000 yuan (about $4,566), as she had been promised in marriage to a dead bachelor in another village. Similarly, in 2009 a grieving father, also in Shaanxi province, paid a team of grave robbers to find a suitable bride for his son, who had died in a car crash. The grave robbers were later arrested for exhuming the remains of a teenage girl who had committed suicide after failing her college entrance exams. In 2013, four men were sentenced to jail terms in Shanxi province for stealing ten female corpses, cleaning the cadavers and counterfeiting their medical records in order to inflate prices, eventually selling the women's corpses on the black market for a total of around $38,000.

Poorer families who cannot afford to pay black-market grave robbers yet still desire ghost marriages may use a non-human proxy such as a silver statuette or human-shaped biscuit with black beans for eyes as the corpse bride. Alternatively a poor family may buy a long-dead, rotten corpse at a discounted price, dress it in ceremonial clothing and reinforce its skeleton with wire.

See also: All Souls' Day; Chinese Death Rituals; Living with the Dead; *Tết Nguyên đan*

Further Reading

China Internet Information Center. "Qingming Festival." Traditional Chinese Festivals. Accessed January 5, 2015, at http://www.china.org.cn/english/features/Festivals/78319.htm.

Galvan, Javier A., ed. *They Do What? A Cultural Encyclopedia of Extraordinary and Exotic Customs from around the World.* Santa Barbara, CA: ABC-CLIO, 2014.

Kaiman, Jonathan. "China Imprisons Four Men for 'Ghost Marriage' Corpse Bride Trafficking," *The Guardian*, March 4, 2013. Accessed January 5, 2015, at http://www.theguardian.com/world/2013/mar/04/china-imprisons-men-ghost-marriage-corpse-bride.

TravelChinaGuide.com. "Qingming Festival (Tomb-sweeping Day)." Accessed January 5, 2015, at http://www.travelchinaguide.com/essential/holidays/qingming.htm.

R

REMEMBRANCE DAY AND REMEMBRANCE SUNDAY, INTERNATIONAL

Remembrance Day is a somber day of commemoration to honor the contribution of British and Commonwealth military personnel and civilian servicemen and women in World War I and World War II as well as later conflicts. Remembrance Day is observed on November 11, a day also known as Armistice Day. Armistice Day is the anniversary marking the end of hostilities of World War I that occurred at 11 a.m. on the 11th day of the 11th month (November) in 1918. Remembrance Day is observed in many countries around the world particularly those that belong to the Commonwealth of Nations or that have been involved in conflicts such as the two World Wars including France, Belgium, and Poland. In the United Kingdom, Remembrance Day is sometimes colloquially known as Poppy Day because people wear red or sometimes white paper poppies in order to remember the people that died in warfare.

In the United Kingdom, a national day of commemoration connected to Remembrance Day is also held. This day is known as Remembrance Sunday and falls on the second Sunday of November, as this is the Sunday that falls nearest to Armistice Day, November 11. At 11 a.m. on Remembrance Sunday a two-minute silence is held to remember service personnel and civilians that died in warfare, not just in World Wars but also in modern conflicts including the Falklands War, the Gulf War, and conflicts in Afghanistan and Iraq. Remembrance Sunday is a major occasion in the United Kingdom and Northern Ireland, Australia, New Zealand, Canada, Singapore, Malaysia, and other Allied countries. Remembrance Sunday events also occur at cemeteries dedicated to Allied war dead in countries that do not belong to the Commonwealth but in which Allied troops fought such as France, and in military camps in countries where personnel are still stationed.

The main commemorative event held on Remembrance Sunday is the National Service of Remembrance that is takes place at the Cenotaph memorial on Whitehall in central London, the capital of England. The National Service of Remembrance commemorates the contribution of British and Commonwealth military and civilian servicemen and women in both World Wars and subsequent conflicts and is attended by many military personnel, veterans of past conflicts, politicians including the British Prime Minister, and members of the British royal family, including the reigning monarch, currently Queen Elizabeth II. The service is also broadcast live on multiple television channels. Although the National Service of

Remembrance is the showpiece event on Remembrance Sunday, many smaller services occur throughout the United Kingdom and the Commonwealth at local war memorials and places of worship. In Australia, the main commemorative event takes place at the Australian War Memorial.

The evening before Remembrance Sunday, the annual Festival of Remembrance takes place at the Royal Albert Hall in London. This event sees military displays by current members of the armed forces, choir singing and prayers and is organized by the charity the Royal British Legion that provides financial and emotional support to current members of the British Armed Forces as well as veterans of the services.

The first two-minute silence was held in Britain on November 11, 1919, when British King George V requested that the public to observe a silence at 11 a.m. in order to remember those people that died in World War I. Up until the end of World War II, Remembrance Sunday was known as Armistice Day but after World War II ended the government of the United Kingdom suggested that the day be renamed Remembrance Day so that the day commemorated both World Wars. This suggestion was agreed upon by Australia and other Allied countries. Today, Remembrance Sunday remembers those people lost in all wars and conflicts while fighting for their countries. As such, Remembrance Sunday is a day of strong national harmony that is almost akin to a nationwide funeral. Indeed there are many parallels between Remembrance Sunday events and Christian funeral customs including the somber demeanor of the participants who tend to wear black or similarly sober colors, the respectful silence that permeates the various ceremonies, and the laying of floral wreaths in tribute to the dead. The sober tone of Remembrance Sunday is very different from the atmosphere of Veterans Day as known in the United States even though Veterans Day began as Armistice Day— the U.S. Congress voted to jettison Armistice Day in 1954. While Veterans Day also occurs on November 11, the tone of the American holiday tends to celebrate war dead as heroes and heroines while Remembrance Sunday has an almost sacred quality that evokes thoughts of pain and suffering and highlights the destructiveness of war.

To mark the centenary of the outbreak of World War I, in 2014 an art instillation called *Blood Swept Lands and Seas of Red* was put in place at the famous London landmark, the Tower of London. The artwork was created by artists Paul Cummins and Tom Piper and saw 888,246 handmade ceramic red poppies progressively fill the Tower's famous moat area between July 17 and November 11, 2014. (*See* Plate 16.) The poppies were planted by a team of 8,000 volunteers and each poppy represented a British or Commonwealth military fatality during World War I with the last poppy placed in the dry moat by a teenage army cadet on Remembrance Sunday 2014. The poppies, colloquially referred to in the United Kingdom as the Tower of London Poppies, proved such a hit with the public that various sections of the artwork toured around the country once the instillation was removed from the Tower of London.

Other countries across the world also hold days to commemorate national war dead. For example, France holds two holidays known as Memorial Days—one on November 11 and another to mark the end of World War II on May 8. In the Netherlands, May 4 is designated Remembrance of the Dead Day that commemorates all members of the Dutch armed forces and civilians that have died in warfare or on peacekeeping missions from World War II to the present. In Belgium, Armistice Day (November 11) is a public holiday and in Germany Liberation Day is held on May 5. This day marks Germany's surrender during World War II and, though it is observed every year unofficially, every fifth year Liberation Day is designated a national holiday. Another national holiday held in Germany is *Volkstrauertag*, meaning People's Day of Mourning. Volkstrauertag is observed two Sundays before the start of Advent as a time to honor the dead, those that have died in war, and to hope for peace. Volkstrauertag was established in the 1920s as a day dedicated to those that died in World War I. The first Volkstrauertag was held in March and was seen as a springtime commemoration of the dead. In these early days of Volkstrauertag, the occasion would be marked by the laying of wreaths at war memorials and at military cemeteries, public calls for the tending of war graves and collections asking for money for war veterans. The day was also synonymous with the symbol of five raised crucifixes that was the insignia of the *Volksbund*, or German people's federation. However the Nazis transformed the day into a celebration to mark their war heroes and to glorify conflict. In this way, Volkstrauertag became intertwined with Nazism. After World War II, an effort was made to break with Nazi ideology and so the date of Volkstrauertag was moved to the second Sunday before the first day of Advent. Each year Volkstrauertag is marked by a commemoration ceremony at the *Bundestag* (the German parliament) where the president gives a speech and members of the parliament sing *"Der gute Kamerad"* ("The Good Comrade"), a song traditionally sung by soldiers. Elsewhere across Germany similar ceremonies are held at memorials erected to the victims of Nazism. As well as various commemorations Volkstrauertag is also a so-called *stiller Tag* or silent day. This means that in some German states law forbids both the playing of music and dancing. Also, in line with all other Sundays in Germany, offices, banks, and schools are kept shut.

See also: "Abide With Me"; Changing of the Guard Ceremony; Christian Death Customs; "The Last Post" and "Taps"; Minute's Silence; National Day of Mourning; Remembrance Sunday Early Day Motion, United Kingdom; Royal Wootton Bassett; Tomb of the Unknown Soldier; Wearing Flowers to Honor War Dead

Further Reading

Army. "Remembrance Day." Accessed October 18, 2015, at http://www.army.gov.au/Our-history/Traditions/Remembrance-Day.

BBC. "Tower of London Poppies: Final Poppy Is Planted." BBC News: London, November 11, 2014. Accessed October 18, 2015, at http://www.bbc.co.uk/news/uk-england-london-30001177.

Diefendorf, Jeffry M., and Janet Ward, eds. *Studies in European Culture and History: Transnationalism and the German City.* New York: Palgrave Macmillan, 2014.

Fanning, Rory. "Why Doesn't the US Observe Armistice Day? We're More Comfortable with War Than Peace," *The Guardian*, November 11, 2014. Accessed October 18, 2015, at http://www.theguardian.com/commentisfree/2014/nov/11/us-observe-armistice-day-more-comfortable-war-than-peace.

Hausen, Karin. "The 'Day of National Mourning' in Germany," in Gerald Sider and Gavin Smith, eds., *Between History and Histories: The Making of Silences and Commemorations.* Toronto, Canada: University of Toronto Press, 1997, 127–148.

Time and Date. "National Day of Mourning in Germany." Accessed October 31, 2015, at http://www.timeanddate.com/holidays/germany/volkstrauertag.

Young, Mitchell, Eric Zuelow, and Andreas Sturm, eds. *Nationalism in a Global Era: The Persistence of Nations.* Abingdon, UK: Routledge, 2007.

Related Primary Document: Remembrance Sunday Early Day Motion, United Kingdom

Remembrance Day is a day on which those military personnel and civilian servicemen and women from British and Commonwealth countries that died in warfare are remembered. Remembrance Day occurs on November 11 annually in many countries around the world, particularly those that have been involved in conflicts such as the two World Wars, including the United Kingdom, France, Belgium, Poland, Australia, New Zealand, Canada, United States, Singapore, and Malaysia. In the United Kingdom the main Remembrance Sunday commemorative event is the National Service of Remembrance at the Cenotaph memorial on Whitehall in London, England. The National Service of Remembrance remembers the contribution of British and Commonwealth military and civilian servicemen and women in both World Wars and subsequent conflicts and is attended by many military personnel, veterans, politicians and royals as well as being broadcast live on television. The event is so significant that the British Parliament passed an Early Day Motion (a debate designed to draw attention to a particular subject) to allow representatives from many countries to lay a wreath at the Cenotaph during the National Service of Remembrance in order to recognize the contribution by members of the armed services from each of the British Overseas Territories during the conflicts of the last 90 years. The countries discussed in the Early Day Motion included the Ascension Island, Anguilla, Bermuda, the British Virgin Islands, the Cayman Islands, Falkland Islands, Gibraltar, Montserrat, Pitcairn Islands, St. Helena, Tristan da Cunha, and Turks and Caicos Islands, as well representatives from the Sovereign Base Areas of Akrotiri and Dhekelia in Cyprus, the British Antarctic Territory, the British Indian Ocean Territory, South Georgia, and the South Sandwich Islands.

The following is an excerpt from the records of the United Kingdom's parliamentary website detailing the proceedings of the Early Day Motion tabled to allow the laying of overseas wreaths at the Cenotaph as well as those Members of Parliament that supported the Motion.

BRITISH OVERSEAS TERRITORIES AND REMEMBRANCE SUNDAY

Main content

- Session: 2008-09
- Date tabled: 28.01.2009
- Primary sponsor: Rosindell, Andrew
- Sponsors:
    - Bottomley, Peter
    - Hoyle, Lindsay
    - MacNeil, Angus
    - Winterton, Ann
    - Winterton, Nicholas

Total number of signatures: **35**

Austin, John	Bottomley, Peter	Brady, Graham	Caton, Martin
Crausby, David	Davies, Philip	Dean, Janet	Dismore, Andrew
Dobbin, Jim	Dodds, Nigel	Donaldson, Jeffrey	Etherington, Bill
Evans, Nigel	Gray, James	Hancock, Mike	Howells, Kim
Hoyle, Lindsay	Hughes, Simon	Jenkins, Brian	Laws, David
Leech, John	MacNeil, Angus	McCrea, Dr William	Moffatt, Laura
Moss, Malcolm	Pope, Greg	Pritchard, Mark	Robinson, Iris
Rosindell, Andrew	Scott, Lee	Vis, Rudi	Williams, Betty
Winterton, Ann	Winterton, Nicholas	Younger-Ross, Richard	

That this House recognises the enormous contribution by members of Her Majesty's Armed Services from each of the British Overseas Territories in wars and conflicts during the past 90 years, fighting for Queen, or King and country; believes that the sacrifices of all these brave men and women should be fully acknowledged in a similar way to members of the Commonwealth of Nations, by granting representatives from Ascension Island, Anguilla, Bermuda, British Virgin Islands, Cayman Islands, Falkland Islands, Gibraltar, Montserrat, Pitcairn Islands, St. Helena, Tristan da Cunha, Turks and Caicos Islands, the Sovereign Base Areas of Akrotiri and Dhekelia, British Antarctic Territory, British Indian Ocean Territory, South Georgia and South Sandwich Islands the right to lay a wreath in their own right at the annual Service of Remembrance at the Cenotaph in Whitehall, each year on Remembrance Sunday; and calls upon the Government to ensure that all the appropriate arrangements for this to happen are correctly in place in time for Remembrance Sunday to be held on 8 November 2009.

Source: *Early day motion 624, House of Commons, United Kingdom Parliament. Available at http://www.parliament.uk/edm/2008-09/624.*

RETIREMENT AND PENSIONS, INTERNATIONAL

Retirement is the act of ceasing to be employed permanently. Many individuals decide to retire when they become eligible to receive a private or state pension, though some people are forced to retire when their physical or mental health deteriorates to the point that they are no longer fit to work or for some other reason. In most countries, the concept of retirement is a relatively new one, being introduced only during the late 19th or early 20th centuries. Prior to the introduction of retirement, low life expectancy and a lack of pension plans meant that most people continued to work until they died.

The first country to introduce retirement was Germany for in 1889 German Chancellor Otto von Bismarck decided that people that were too frail or too old to work should receive help from the state. Initially, Germany set the retirement age at 70 years but then in 1916 this was lowered to 65 years. The United States instituted social insurance in 1935 and, like Germany, set retirement age at 65 years. The German model was not, however, the major influence on the Committee on Economic Security (CES) when it decided to set age of retirement at 65 years. Rather, the CES based its decision on the prevailing retirement ages of the few private pension systems in existence at that time as well as the 30 state old-age pension systems that were then in operation. Moreover, in 1934 the U.S. Congress had set age 65 years as its retirement age for the federal Railroad Retirement System. Currently, 65 years is the retirement age in many countries though increasing life expectancy means that many countries are rethinking the age at which people retire and therefore, begin to receive the state pension. For example, in the United Kingdom the retirement age is set to rise to 66 years in 2016. Many governments feel that they need to raise the retirement age because greater life expectancies result in aging populations and consequently, the need to pay out state pensions to qualifying individuals.

A state pension is a regular payment made by the state to individuals of or above the country's official retirement age. State pensions may also be paid to some widows and disabled people. State pensions are a feature of old age in many countries, particularly in Europe, Australia, and New Zealand and Japan. State pensions are contribution based so in effect the more qualifying years that a person pays into the state via, for example, Nation Insurance in the United Kingdom, the more they should benefit when they retire. Individuals that do not pay into the scheme for as many years as others receive a state pension on a pro rata basis. State pensions differ throughout the world and any changes to pensions tend to be acutely politically sensitive.

Today, the German welfare benefits system has at its heart a comprehensive social insurance system to which most workers contribute. This system covers healthcare provision, unemployment insurance, and pension insurance. Once somebody has paid into all areas of the system—about 15.5 percent of an individual's salary goes toward healthcare, 3 percent toward employment insurance and nursing care insurance, and 18.9 percent toward pension insurance—they are entitled to a number of benefits, including healthcare for senior citizens. Included in this healthcare is the provision of medical prescriptions and spectacles though these are not classed as benefits. In Germany, it is usual for a person to keep paying into the health insurance system even when he or she has started to receive their pension. In general, upon retirement Germans receive half to two-thirds of their net income as a pension with around 85 percent of the German workforce enrolled in the system. The typical retirement age for all Germans born after 1964 is 67 years and women that have taken time off work to have a family see their contributions topped-up by the state. That said, a recent report by the Organisation for Economic Co-operation and Development (OECD) revealed that Germany has the widest pension benefits gap between men and women in both Europe and the United States.

As in Germany, the official pension age in Norway is also 67 years, though in Norway it is possible for someone to draw a full old-age pension from the age of 62 years and still work full-time. Employment among older people is, however, well above the European norm of around 50 percent for in Norway more than 70 percent of people between 55 and 64 years of age are still in employment. This high level of older-age employment may be due to the fact that in Norway there are a number of ways for people to receive partial pensions. Moreover, Norwegians can continue to accumulate pension entitlement until they are 75 years old. 67 years is, however, the age at which most Norwegians retire and also the age at which individuals receiving disability benefits can transfer to pensions schemes. At present, Norway's pension system is transitioning with a new version in operation as a previous scheme is phased out. The earlier scheme is a defined benefit scheme encompassing a flat-rate universal benefit, an earnings-related second tier benefit and a minimum benefit. On average, a Norwegian that has contributed to the system for 40 years at an average wage level can expect to receive a pension of about 67 percent of his or her income after tax. The new Norwegian system consists of a defined pension contribution scheme in addition to a minimum guaranteed pension. The amounts paid out by this scheme are subject to a life expectancy, which some people feel means that old-age benefits for new pensioners will be reduced in proportion to increases in life expectancy.

The pension system in Sweden used to be more generous than that in Norway. Today, however, the average Swedish pension is slightly above 50 percent of wages. Furthermore, this return rate is likely to dip below even that level if life expectancy in Sweden continues to increase and the age of retirement is not deferred. Senior citizens in both Sweden and Norway receive discounted public transport, museum entry, and an income-tested housing allowance. Senior citizens as well as disadvantaged people may also apply for social assistance to cover single large-scale expenses.

The state pension in the United Kingdom has been found to be one of the least generous in Europe for the state pension of £113.10 per week amounts to one-third of the average salary, according to the International Longevity Centre. This figure is much less than the average payment in the rest of Europe, where state retirement payments tend to be worth nearly 50 percent of national average earnings. British pensioners do, however, receive free medical prescriptions, free medical care, and free travel on public transport. One of the ways in which pensioners receive free public travel is by applying for a bus pass. Indeed in the United Kingdom if someone is said to have a bus pass, it is a sure sign that this person is a senior citizen. To this end, having a bus pass is a euphemism for being a pensioner and receiving a bus pass is something of a rite of passage for senior citizens in the United Kingdom.

The British state pension lags behind other European countries in terms of generosity. Indeed British workers that fail to accumulate sufficient private savings can expect to see their incomes decrease further after they retire compared to their European counterparts. For instance, in Greece pensioners receive almost 100 percent of their pay from the state when they retire. The generous Greek state pensions are in line with other European countries where public finances, are like Greece, currently under financial strain. These countries include Spain, Cyprus, Italy, and Portugal. Contrastingly, Austria, Finland, and Belgium also provide generous pensions but maintain relatively healthy public finances. The least generous European pensions in relation to average earnings are to be found in Estonia and Poland. For example, the OECD found that in Estonia pensioners usually receive about a quarter of the income that they earned while in employment.

Outside of Europe, pensions also differ widely. For example, in Australia more than 50 percent of all retired men and 25 percent of retired women cited the state pension as their main source of income. However superannuation payments amounting to 9.5 percent of a salary contributed by employers have been obligatory since 1992. Australian residents over 65 years of age (67 years from 2023) are eligible to receive a state pension if they have lived in Australia for at least 10 years and meet certain income and asset requirements (there are exceptions for people with refugee status). In 2011, this equated to 60 percent of Australians. Additionally, Australians that work past pension age may receive partial benefits or a lump sum. Australian pensioners recieve a maximum payment of AU$776.70 (approximately $550) for singles, or AU$585.50 (approximately $415) for people in couples every two weeks. A supplementary payment of up to AU$63.50 (roughly $45) per fortnight includes a pharmaceutical allowance, plus pensioners can continue to use Australia's publicly funded universal healthcare benefit scheme and also receive a utilities allowance. Each Australian state and territory also provides discounted travel and shopping to people over 60 years of age. Extra services such as a Home Care package or Home and Community Care package are also available though these are means-tested and partially financed by contributions from the individual's pension. Australians over 65 can apply for these packages though Aboriginal Australians and Torres Strait Islanders may apply from the age of 50 years.

In Japan around one in four people are 65 years or older, with the figure expected to rise to one in three by 2025. However, while the Japanese are proud that their life expectancies are among the world's highest, this pride is tempered by worries over how the country will pay for the ageing population's welfare over the coming decades, for there will be fewer people in employment to pay for the welfare services. In Japan, everybody between 20 and 59 years of age has to to contribute to the basic national pension scheme though only people that have contributed for a minimum of 25 years are entitled to receive a pension when they retire at 65 years of age. People that work for a firm full-time (and their spouses) are entered into the employees' pension scheme automatically. This scheme provides supplementary contributions to the basic state pension that are proportional to each worker's salary. The Japanese government believes that about 85 percent of Japan's workforce receives extra help from this scheme. Low-income residents also receive a fuel allowance and people 75 years or older need to pay only 10 percent of their medical costs, though this is means-tested so that those on a higher income pay more. A number of Japanese cities also offer discounted annual travel passes that allow senior citizens unlimited travel for one year.

Other countries, including New Zealand, the Netherlands, Bolivia, Mauritius, and Suriname provide qualifying individuals with another type of pension known as a universal pension, or sometimes referred to as a social pension. Over 100 countries around the world provide some kind of social pension, but the details of such schemes vary greatly. For example, some countries work their universal age pensions geographically. For instance, in Mexico people living in Mexico City, Chiapas state, and in rural areas receive a pension, while in Brazil's *Previdencia Rural,* what is, in effect a social pension is provided to people living in rural parts. A number of other countries are at present experimenting with universal age pensions. These schemes include the Hunger Safety Net Programme in Kenya, the Social Cash Transfer Programme in Zambia, and Uganda's Senior Citizen's Grant. Another type of pension, the universal minimum pension, sees that everyone aged over a specific age gets a pension, though individuals that receive a universal minimum pension may have to undergo means-testing. If people receive other types of pension then they do not usually qualify for a universal minimum pension as well. Countries that provide universal minimum pensions include Barbados, Finland, Swaziland, Latvia, Cyprus, and Bermuda. Meanwhile, in former Soviet states such as Moldova and Kyrgyzstan—where most people are eligible for some type of pension—contributory pensions function as a means of poverty reduction.

See also: Cardboard Box Beds (Volume 1); Childhood Vaccinations (Volume 1); Pauper's Funeral; Social Pension/Superannuation Guide, New Zealand; State Pension Government Guide, United Kingdom

Further Reading
Bracewell, Catherine, Rosaire Gray and Gurcharan S. Ra. *Essential Facts in Geriatric Medicine.* Oxford, UK: Radcliffe Publishing Ltd., 2005.

Clark, Gordon L., Alicia H. Munnell, and J. Michael Orszag, eds. *The Oxford Handbook of Pensions and Retirement Income, Volume 13*. Oxford, UK: Oxford University Press, 2006.

Davidson, Helen, Kate Connolly, Justin McCurry, et al. "Which Are the Best Countries in the World to Grow Old In?" *The Guardian*, March 3, 2015. Accessed November 8, 2015, at http://www.theguardian.com/society/2015/mar/03/which-best-countries-grow-old-in-pensions-benefits-happiness.

Hyde, Dan. "Why Britain's State Pension Is 'One of the Worst in Europe,'" *The Telegraph*, October 27, 2014. Accessed November 8, 2015, at http://www.telegraph.co.uk/finance/personalfinance/pensions/11189414/Why-Britains-state-pension-is-one-of-the-worst-in-Europe.html.

Pension Watch. "What and Where?" About Social Pensions. Accessed November 8, 2015, at http://www.pension-watch.net/about-social-pensions/about-social-pensions/social-pensions-around-the-world/.

Social Security Administration. "Age 65 Retirement: The German Precedent," *Social Security Administration: Frequently Asked Questions*. Accessed November 8, 2015, at https://www.ssa.gov/history/age65.html.

Related Primary Document: Social Pension/Superannuation Guide, New Zealand

In New Zealand, Superannuation (sometimes referred to as an NZ Super) is a fortnightly payment for people aged 65 years and over. To qualify for Superannuation a person should be aged 65 years or over and be a citizen of New Zealand or be a permanent resident who lives in New Zealand at the time of their application for the Superannuation. Alternatively the person should have lived in New Zealand for a minimum of 10 years since they reached 20 years of age with five of those years having been spent in New Zealand since they turned 50 years of age. Years spent living in certain other countries may also count toward a person's New Zealand Superannuation. Any eligible person receives their New Zealand Superannuation regardless of how much money they earned when they were in paid employment, their savings and investments, other assets, or the amount of tax they have paid in the past. Each year New Zealand government establishes the amount paid in New Zealand Superannuation payments with the rates reviewed and adjusted in order to take into account any increases in inflation and the level of average New Zealand wages. Couples comprising of two qualifying individuals receive an after-tax New Zealand Superannuation rate for couples based on 66 percent of the so-called average ordinary time wage after tax. Eligible single people receive an after-tax New Zealand Superannuation rate of around 40 percent of that average wage. When a person qualifies for their New Zealand Superannuation they are automatically sent a SuperGold card too. A SuperGold card is a discount and concessions card that is issued free of charge to all eligible senior citizens, veterans, individuals aged under 65 years but who receive the New Zealand Superannuation, and people who receive some other form of assistance from New Zealand's Ministry of Social Development. The following is an excerpt from the New Zealand government's website detailing eligibility for Superannuation.

New Zealand Superannuation

Who can get it?

You may be able to get New Zealand Superannuation (NZ Super) if you:

- are aged 65 or over
- are a New Zealand citizen or permanent resident
- normally live in New Zealand at the time you apply.

You must also have been resident and present in New Zealand for at least 10 years since you turned 20 years of age (and 5 of those years must be since you turned 50), unless, when you were overseas you were:

- having special medical or surgical treatment or
- doing vocational training or
- working as a missionary/with Volunteer Service Abroad or
- serving in one of the Commonwealth's armed forces or
- working overseas and paid tax in New Zealand on the earnings from that work or
- working on a New Zealand owned or registered ship trading to and from here.

If you spent time overseas, you must usually have been living here before and after you were overseas, unless you spent time in Australia, United Kingdom, Jersey, Guernsey, Canada, Denmark, the Republic of Ireland, Greece, Malta, or the Netherlands. That may also count as time lived here in terms of getting your Super.

How much you can get

How much you get depends on your circumstances, such as:

- whether you're single, married or in a relationship
- your living situation if you're single (eg live alone, live with dependent children, share accommodation with others)
- whether your partner is included in your NZ Super
- any overseas pension/benefit you may get.

NZ Super payments are made directly to your bank account every two weeks on a Tuesday.

Payment rates and dates for NZ Super/Veteran's Pension

Working and getting NZ Super

You can work and still get NZ Super. If you work (or receive other income) while getting NZ Super, this may affect the amount of income tax you have to pay on your combined income.

If you have a spouse/partner who doesn't qualify for their own NZ Super, you can choose to include them in your payments. If you do this, any other income either of you earn could affect how much you get.

We can help you work out whether you're financially better off to include your partner or not.

Including your partner in your NZ Super

If you have a partner we need to ask you about them, as this affects the amount you're paid. This applies even if you're not including them in your payments.

NZ Super is not income tested. We'll only ask about you and your partner's income if:

- you want to include your partner in your payments and they don't qualify for NZ Super in their own right
- you apply for other financial assistance as part of your application for NZ Super.

If you include your partner, any other income either of you earn could affect how much you get.

- If your partner is included in your payments, you can earn up to $100 (before tax) a week between you, before your NZ Super is affected.
- If you earn more than $100 (before tax) a week, your payments are reduced by 70 cents for every dollar of income over $100 (before tax).

SuperGold Card

When you're granted NZ Super or Veteran's Pension, you'll automatically be sent a SuperGold Card.

This gives you access to:

- a wide range of disounts from businesses
- government concessions (such as free off-peak public transport)

Source: *New Zealand Superannuation, Ministry of Social Development, Government of New Zealand. Available at https://www.msd.govt.nz/what-we-can-do/seniorcitizens /entitlements/nz-superannuation/.*

Related Primary Document: State Pension Government Guide, United Kingdom

In the United Kingdom the basic State Pension is a payment made to people considered eligible by the government when they reach State Pension age in order that they do not enter into poverty when they have stopped working in old age. The basic State Pension was introduced in the United Kingdom (which at that time also included all of Ireland) in 1909 following the passing of the Old Age Pensions Act 1908. At this time the payment was referred to as the Old Age Pension and qualifying individuals received 5 shillings per week (the equivalent of 25p which with inflation equates to about £20 or $29), while married couples received 7s.6d per week (37.5p). Today in the United Kingdom in order to receive the State Pension people must have paid National Insurance contributions or been credited with National Insurance contributions. National Insurance contributions are payments made to the government by individuals in order to qualify for certain benefits including the State Pension. In the United Kingdom National

Insurance contributions are paid by people aged over 16 years or who earn above £155 a week (around $224). At present the most a person can receive in State Pension payments is £115.95 per week (roughly $168). Until 2010 men over the age of 65 years and women over 60 years were entitled to claim the State Pension. However beginning April 2010 the age at which women receive their pension has been brought in line with the age for men gradually. In the future the age at which both men and women receive their pension will increase to 68 years. This change will occur no later than 2046 and possibly much sooner.

The following is an extract from the United Kingdom's government website outlining how individuals can qualify to receive the State Pension as well as how they can gain an extra amount of pension by deferring their uptake of the State Pension by at least nine weeks.

2. Eligibility

You'll be able to claim the new State Pension if you're:

- a man born on or after 6 April 1951
- a woman born on or after 6 April 1953

The earliest you can get the new State Pension is when you reach State Pension age.

You'll usually need at least 10 qualifying years on your National Insurance record to get any State Pension. They don't have to be 10 qualifying years in a row.

This means for 10 years at least one or more of the following applied to you:

- you were working and paid National Insurance contributions
- you were getting National Insurance credits, eg for unemployment, sickness or as a parent or carer
- you were paying voluntary National Insurance contributions

If you've lived or worked abroad you may still be able to get some new State Pension.

You may also qualify if you've paid married women's or widow's reduced rate contributions.

Defer your new State Pension

You don't have to claim the new State Pension as soon as you reach State Pension age.

Deferring the new State Pension means that you may get extra State Pension when you do claim it. The extra amount is paid with your State Pension (eg every 4 weeks) and may be taxable.

How much you'll get

You'll need to defer for at least 9 weeks—your State Pension will increase by 1% for every 9 weeks you put off claiming. This works out at just under 5.8% for every full year you put off claiming.

Example

You get less than the full State Pension, eg £120 per week.

That means your State Pension will be £6,240 a year.

By deferring for a year, you'll get an extra £360 (just under 5.8% of £6,240).

After you claim, the extra amount you get because you deferred will usually increase each year.

Source: *The New State Pension, United Kingdom, 2016. Available at https://www.gov.uk/new-state-pension/eligibility.*

RIDERLESS HORSE, INTERNATIONAL

A riderless horse, also called a caparisoned horse or cap horse, is a single horse that accompanies some funeral processions. The horse does not have a rider but is dressed with a pair of boots set reversed in its stirrups. The horse follows the casket as it is borne on the caisson, a two-wheeled cart on which the casket is placed. A riderless horse may also be used to represent fallen military personnel in a military parade. The best-known example of a riderless horse is probably that known as the Lone Charger that takes part in the annual Anzac Day marches held in Australia and New Zealand and Black Jack, which was a famed participant in the funeral of United States President John F. Kennedy. The alternative name for a riderless horse, a caparisoned horse, derives from the decorative cloth, the caparison, which is draped over a horse during a parade.

European folklore tells that a dead horse will find its dead owner in the afterlife. However the tradition of the riderless horse is thought to date back to the time of the founder of the Ottoman Empire, Genghis Khan (1162–1227). At this time, it was customary for a horse to be sacrificed on the death of a soldier so that the horse could serve the deceased soldier in the afterlife. Over time, this tradition was modified and today a so-called cap walker leads the riderless horse that has black boots fixed backward into its stirrups. The backward-facing boots are said to symbolize a leader looking back at his or her troops for the final time.

In the United States, the riderless horse has become part of the military honors shown to Army and Marine Corps officers that have attained the rank of colonel or above. This honor extends to U.S. president, by virtue of the president being the country's commander in chief, and to the Secretary of Defense who oversees the armed forces. The first American to be extended the honor of a riderless horse was 18th-century Secretary of the Treasury Alexander Hamilton while the first U.S. president to be accorded the honor was Abraham Lincoln who was followed by his horse Old Bob. It is also known that George Washington's horse was part of the president's funeral procession carrying Washington's saddle, pistols, and holsters. Zachary Taylor's horse, Old Whitey, also took part in his owner funeral procession. However perhaps the most famous incidence of a presidential riderless horse was

Black Jack, the horse that took part in the funerals of presidents John F. Kennedy, Herbert Hoover, and Lyndon B. Johnson as well as that of General Douglas MacArthur and thousands of funerals at Arlington National Cemetery.

In Australia and New Zealand, ANZAC Day marches and other memorial processions are often led by a riderless horse that has a pair of boots set backward in its stirrups and is dressed with a plain saddle that is stripped bare. The riderless horse is a common feature of ANZAC Day processions as the horse acts as a sign of respect and mourning for fallen military personnel, especially those belonging to Australian Army mounted regiments known as Light Horse units.

See also: "Abide With Me"; Changing of the Guard Ceremony; "The Last Post" and "Taps"; Missing Man Formation; Remembrance Day and Remembrance Sunday; Royal Wootton Bassett; State Funeral; Tomb of the Unknown Soldier; Wearing Flowers to Honor War Dead

Further Reading

Faulkner, Claire A. "Arlington's Ceremonial Horses and Funerals at the White House." White House History, No. 19. Accessed June 29, 2015, at http://www.whitehousehistory.org/history/documents/White-House-History-19-Faulkner-Ceremonial-Horses.pdf.

Inside History Magazine. "The Memorial's Guide to ANZAC Day," *Inside History Magazine*, April 25, 2014. Accessed June 29, 2015, at http://www.insidehistory.com.au/2014/04/the-memorials-guide-to-anzac-day/.

Kovach, Bob. "Riderless Horse Adds Poignancy to Military Burials." CNN, May 23, 2008. Accessed June 29, 2015, at http://edition.cnn.com/2008/LIVING/05/23/arlington.riderless.horse/.

ROMANIAN FUNERAL CUSTOMS, ROMANIA

The funeral customs found in Romania are a mixture of folkloric beliefs and Christianity that reveal ancient traditions that continue to play a prominent part in the country's culture and society. There are a number of Romanian rituals, apart from the Great Passing, that take place when a person has died.

For example one of the most famous Romanian funeral tradition is the singing of melodic, sorrowful burial songs known as *bocete* or *bochirea*. These are sung by women, usually close relatives of the deceased, at the individual's bedside, during the funeral procession, at the graveside, and on dates dedicated to remembering the dead such as the funeral procession re-enactments.

In the Romanian region of Transylvania, additional death traditions exist. For instance, in this part of Romania people believe that for every living human there is a star and a fir tree. Thus a falling star is seen as a harbinger of death and a fir tree, the symbol of life, is placed at the head-end of a grave. The fir is taken from nearby forests by local men and brought to the village of the dead person. At the entrance to the village young village women sing a song about the connection that exists between life and the fir and meet the men. The song sung by the women tells of how the fir is so upset at the death of its sibling—the recently deceased person—that it must dry-up and rot. Another Transylvanian song sung to mark a person's death is the "Great Song" or "Dawn Song." This song, which advises the deceased about how to journey to the world of ancestors, is sung by elderly women at sunrise on the two mornings that fall between the person's day of death and their funeral.

Another common Transylvanian death custom is for people to tell mourners that they wish the sun would rise later in the day so that the deceased's family might have more time to make funeral arrangements. These funeral arrangements include making the coffin and the candle used during the funeral, greeting other mourners, preparing food for the post-funeral meal, and finding bulls that will pull the carriage bearing the coffin. In Transylvania, as in the rest of Romania, a vigil is kept over the corpse though in Transylvania the watching group includes a select group of elderly women. In Transylvania and Moldavia (i.e., the area of eastern Europe that lies partly in Transylvania, Moldova and Ukraine), funerals are announced by alphorn, a musical instrument fashioned as a long wooden horn that is used in mountainous regions of Europe as a means of communication. To signal a death, between two and six alphorn players play alongside the funeral procession. The alphorns are also played in the garden of the dead person at sunrise, midday, and evening during the vigil over the corpse. On the day of the funeral, alphorn-playing not only accompanies the funeral procession but also at the graveside and sounds as the grave is covered with soil. The alphorn also plays occasionally during the wake following the funeral.

In the west of Romania, a number of funeral songs are traditionally sung by elderly women that are not closely related to the dead. The most important of these songs is the "Song of the Dawn," which is sung to announce a death to a village. The selected elderly women sing this song while facing eastward into the dawn and holding lit candles. The "Song of the Dawn" begs the sun to delay its rising so that the dead person may collect everything he or she needs for the journey into the afterlife. Another song sung in this part of Romania is the "Song of the Pine," which is sung on the death of someone young and unwed. In this instance, the pine tree symbolizes the fir that would have been felled in the woods and decorated at the individual's wedding.

See also: The Great Passing; *Hora* and *Horah* (Volume 2); *Koliva*; "Lyke-Wake Dirge"; Tombstone Tourism

Further Reading

Blanco, Maria-Jose, and Ricarda Vidal, eds. *The Power of Death: Contemporary Reflections on Death in Western Society.* Oxford, UK: Berghahn Books, 2015.

EcoAdventure Ltd. "Funeral Traditions." Tours Romania. Accessed April 13, 2015, at http://www.tours-romania.ro/funeral_traditions.html.

Kretsu-Kantsyr, Joanna. "Birth and Death in the Romanian Folk Belief." Accessed April 13, 2015, at http://www.folklore.ee/rl/pubte/ee/usund/ingl/kretsu.html.

MyCorp. "Traditions and Customs during Life." Echoes of Europe, February 23, 2014. Accessed April 13, 2015, at http://echoesofeurope.ucoz.com/blog/traditions_and_customs_during_life/2014-02-23-80.

ROYAL WOOTTON BASSETT, ENGLAND

Royal Wootton Bassett is a town in the southwestern English county of Wiltshire that is synonymous with informal tributes paid during the repatriation of British military dead at the start of the 21st century, particularly personnel transported from Iraq and Afghanistan. Wootton Bassett received the title Royal in 2011 in recognition of the town's dignified efforts to honor the nation's war dead. This was the first time since 1909 that a town had received royal patronage. The conferring of the title was not universally welcomed by the town's inhabitants however as they did not want any particular recognition for their efforts in honoring the dead.

British war dead traveled through Royal Wootton Bassett because the town lies on the route taken by funeral corteges from MoD Lyneham (formerly known as RAF Lyneham) airbase—where British dead used to land and where a formal repatriation ceremony would be held—to John Radcliffe Hospital in Oxford. This hospital is the location of a special armed forces department of pathology that performs autopsies on military dead, especially those that die in Afghanistan. Coffins draped in the Union Flag would be transported in hearses along the town's high street without any publicity. However the presence of the flag-draped coffins caught the attention of the ex-service personnel association the Royal British Legion (RBL), who on discovering the true nature of the corteges decided to honor the repatriated by saluting the hearses as they passed through the town. The first repatriation saw the return of soldiers Aaron Lincoln, 18 years of age, and Danny Wilson, 28. To begin with, only a few members of the RBL would line the streets and bow their heads as the funeral corteges drove past. Over time, however, the number of the town inhabitants as well as many people that traveled to the town

---

MoD Lyneham

MoD Lyneham, previously known as RAF Lyneham, is a U.K. Ministry of Defence (MoD) site situated in Wiltshire in southwestern England. The airfield became well known for being the gateway between the United Kingdom and Afghanistan. As a result of the base's location, MoD Lyneham was where the repatriation of British personnel killed in Iraq and Afghanistan occurred before the bodies were transported through nearby Royal Wootton Bassett. The station closed on December 31, 2012, with most of the site's personnel, flying units, and equipment having been transferred to RAF Brize Norton.

especially to line the high street, grew so that eventually thousands of Royal Wootton Bassett's townsfolk and others would turn out to pay their respects every time a cortege went through the town on its way to Oxford. The procession of the hearses as they traveled along the high street also changed as the townsfolk became more involved in proceedings. For instance, while veteran soldiers, civilian members of the public, and police with dogs would line the street so too would family and friends of the persons being repatriated who would stand nearest to the road, often wearing black. In 2009, a custom began that saw relatives throw flowers at the hearse and applaud the coffin. Relatives would also place flowers on the roof of the hearse. It also became the custom for hearses to pause outside the local church that would then sound its bell in lament. The hearse would then proceed on to, and halt at, the town's war memorial where war veterans would salute the hearse. All the while, the church would continue to chime its bell until the hearse joined the freeway that would take it to Oxford. Once the hearse entered the freeway those lining the high street would drift away slowly.

Royal Wootton Bassett gradually became the focal point for people wanting to recognize the sacrifice of service personnel, and the town went on to garner international attention for its efforts, including a tribute from United States President Barack Obama. Indeed such was the strength of association between Royal Wootton Bassett and military repatriations that in 2010 the now-outlawed radical Islamist group Islam4UK announced its intention to hold an anti-war protest in the town in order to highlight the number of Muslims killed in fighting in Afghanistan. This declaration sparked national outrage throughout the United Kingdom and the proposed protest was abandoned. Royal Wootton Bassett also attracted unwanted attention in 2009 when then-leader of the far right British political party, the British National Party, Nick Griffin, appeared in the town for a repatriation procession for five soldiers murdered by a rogue Afghan policeman. The inhabitants of Royal Wootton Bassett claimed to always strive to keep separate from politics and for this reason were dismayed when the BBC television politics program "Question Time" was filmed in the town in 2009.

The final, 167th repatriation through Royal Wootton Bassett occurred on August 18, 2011, when the body of 24-year-old Lt. Daniel Clack, of First Battalion The Rifles, was repatriated to the United Kingdom. The last repatriation was marked by a special church service for which in excess of 2,000 people lined the town's high street. The service, called the Sunset Service, began with a special chiming of the bell at the Church of Saint Bartholomew. Next the town's mayor addressed those that had lined the streets and declared that the service would be the town's final show of devotion to the repatriated. A war veteran accompanied by his grandson then lowered the town's flag and prayers were said before spontaneous applause broke out. The lowered flag was then draped across the church's altar overnight. At a later date the flag was presented to the people of Oxfordshire during a highly symbolic service.

During the period from April 2007 to August 2011, 345 repatriated British service personnel traveled through Royal Wootton Bassett as they journeyed toward John Radcliffe Hospital from RAF Lyneham. Royal Wootton Bassett no longer receives war dead as repatriated service personnel are now flown to RAF Brize Norton, in Oxfordshire. The town of Royal Wootton Bassett is, however, firmly associated in the British public consciousness with its devotion to honoring the dead while also avoiding jingoistic nationalism or commenting on the politics of war. The town of Carterton, near RAF Brize Norton, continues the tradition of honoring repatriated service personnel that was started at Royal Wootton Bassett. At Carterton, a special area has been created where grief-stricken families and friends can gather with local people to pay their respects to the fallen.

See also: "Abide With Me"; Changing of the Guard Ceremony; Chelsea Pensioners; "The Last Post" and "Taps"; Passing Bells; Remembrance Day and Remembrance Sunday; Riderless Horse; Tomb of the Unknown Soldier; Wearing Flowers to Honor War Dead

Further Reading

BBC. "Wootton Bassett Marks the End of Repatriations." BBC News: Wiltshire, August 31, 2011. Accessed July 19, 2015, at http://www.bbc.co.uk/news/uk-england-wiltshire-14726697.

BBC. "Wootton Bassett to Get 'Royal' Title in War Dead Honour." BBC News: Wiltshire, March 16, 2011. Accessed July 19, 2015, at http://www.bbc.co.uk/news/uk-england-wiltshire-12757984.

Dahl Martinsen, Kaare. *Soldier Repatriation: Popular and Political Responses.* Farnham, UK: Ashgate Publishing Limited, 2013.

Freeden, Michael. *The Political Theory of Political Thinking: The Anatomy of a Practice.* Oxford, UK: Oxford University Press, 2013.

Gillan, Audrey. "How Wootton Bassett Became the Town That Cried," *The Guardian*, February 25, 2010. Accessed July 19, 2015, at http://www.theguardian.com/uk/2010/feb/25/wootton-bassett-audrey-gillan.

Morris, Steven. "Wootton Bassett Timeline: How the Repatriation Ceremony Came About," *The Guardian*, August 31, 2011. Accessed July 19, 2015, at http://www.theguardian.com/uk/2011/aug/31/wootton-bassett-repatriations-timeline.

S

SAKALAVA ROYAL DEATH TRADITIONS AND FITAMPOHA, MADAGASCAR

The Sakalava is a tribe living in the western Madagascar region of Menabe. Central to the Sakalava religion is the *tromba*, or royal ancestors, which are the spirits of dead royalty. Deceased royals are held in great esteem by the Sakalava with royal funerals particularly lavish affairs that often last for several months, or even years. A number of traditions and taboos, known as *fady*, and a specialized vocabulary have evolved around Sakalava rituals surrounding royalty, most especially dead royals. For instance, the Sakalava believe that their royals do not die in the way that non-royals stop living. Rather, the Sakalava employ the verb *mihilana* to describe the way in which a royal has ceased to be alive. Mihilana translates as to turn around, or perform a volte-face, and so suggests that the royal is still alive. One taboo pertaining to Sakalava royal deaths is that a royal corpse must not enter a royal household. Further, if a royal dies inside a royal residence the residence is considered forever polluted and must not be inhabited by other royals. During a funeral for either a royal or non-royal Sakalava tribe member, people may not wash, wear shoes, or comb their hair and they must dress in traditional Sakalava body-wrapping clothing. For a royal funeral to take place, the corpse is transported to a selected location and placed inside a temporary building where it is attended to by a caste of royal slaves called the *Sambarivo*. While the corpse is inside the temporary structure, the Sambarivo collect in special ceramic pots the bodily fluids and such emitted by the corpse as it rots; these fluids are discarded during special nocturnal rituals that take place at consecrated locations.

A particularly noteworthy Sakalava royal death tradition is *fitampoha*, meaning royal relics bath. In fitampoha, the Sakalava celebrate relics, called *dady*, that belong to nine of their dead kings. These relics are very important to the Sakalava as its members believe that their rulers do not stop being royal just because they have died but continue to be noble even in death and in times past these relics were carried into battle to afford supernatural powers to their people. Indeed honoring royalty and ancestors is central to the Sakalava way of life, as is evinced by the way in which the fitampoha celebrations are advertised on Madagascan national television.

Traditionally fitampoha occurred every July. However nowadays fitampoha takes place every 10 years in August on a Friday on which there is a full moon. The ritual sees the living members of the Sakalava royal family wash the relics of their dead ancestors. These relics usually consist of teeth, hair, bones, and fingernails, which are kept in a bag inside an iron trunk housed in a sacred house or royal residence called the *zomba*, in the village of Belo Tsiribihina, which in turn is protected by a fence of sharpened sticks. The zomba is further protected by the so-called guard of the dady, the only person allowed to enter the zomba.

The Menabe royal family and the guard of the dady arrange the cleaning of the relics. Before the ritual washing, 20 oxen are killed in preparation for the feast that is part of the occasion and all the local tribes people contribute to the expense of hosting the event. The washing is performed in the Tsiribihina River, which the Sakalava consider sacred, and starting on the Thursday before fitampoha takes place a form of fitampoha etiquette called *fomba*, meaning customs, comes into force. This etiquette means that from midnight on the Thursday nobody is allowed to wash in the Tsiribihina River nor to wear shoes. Reeds are collected from a certain site along the river amid much singing, dancing, wrestling, and the playing of music on *dabalava* and *hazolahy* drums, the latter being drums played when royalty are present and during ritualistic ceremonies such as coronations and circumcisions. Meanwhile, descendants of the Sakalava royal family wash their ancestors clothing and leave it to dry on the river's reed beds. Also on the eve of fitampoha, tribe members take part in a collective sexual act that the people believe symbolizes the chaos of the world's beginning.

On the Friday the royal relics are cleaned lovingly using dusters, olive oil, honey, and vegetable-based soaps called *fihositry*. Once the relics have been washed they are put on display by hanging them on a line of poles protected by a white awning called the *rivotse*. The Sakalava consider the displayed relics with great pride and affection as the relics shine in the moonlight and reflect the sunset. Once the fitampoha is considered to have ended all the relics are put back in the zomba.

Fitampoha is not just a form of ancestor worship for the ritual also reinforces the idea that the Sakalava royal family possesses supernatural powers. During fitampoha it is also thought that the spirits of ancestors contact the Sakalava people through a possessed woman known as the *bilo*. On a more prosaic level fitampoha is a time when tribal members settle disputes. The royal family also performs a ritual called *lohavony* during which the royal family members pray that their ancestors will bless their tribe.

Burials are not permitted to take place during fitampoha so if someone dies shortly before the ritual washing that person's relatives may not attend the fitampoha ritual.

See also: *Fady*; *Famadihana*; Living with the Dead; *Ngaben*; *Qingming* Festival; Shrunken Heads

Further Reading

Austin, Daniel, and Hilary Bradt. *Madagascar*. Eleventh edition. Chalfont St. Peter, UK: Bradt Travel Guides Ltd., 2014.

Madagascar-Visite.com. "Fitampoha or Relics' Bath." Culture and Tradition of the West. Accessed April 10, 2015, at http://www.madagascar-visite.com/en/culture-ouest.php.

Middleton, Karen, ed. *Ancestors, Power, and History in Madagascar*. Leiden, Netherlands: Brill, 1999.

MTV Tour. "Malagasy Origin." Accessed April 10, 2015, at http://madagascar-visit-tours.com/orgin_culture.php.

Sharp, Lesley A. "Royal Difficulties: A Question of Succession in an Urbanized Sakalava Kingdom," *Journal of Religion in Africa*, (27)3, August 1997, 270–307.

TraditionsCustoms.com. "Fitampoha." Accessed April 10, 2015, at http://traditionscustoms.com/death-rites/fitampoha.

World Culture Encyclopedia. "Sakalava—Religion and Expressive Culture." Countries and Their Cultures. Accessed April 10, 2015, at http://www.everyculture.com/Africa-Middle-East/Sakalava-Religion-and-Expressive-Culture.html.

SALLEKHANĀ, JAINISM

Sallekhanā (also known as Santhara, Samadhi-marana and Sanyasana-marana) is the radical, ascetic practice of facing death voluntarily at the end of one's life that is performed by followers of Jainism, one of India's oldest religions. Sallekhanā is not, however, the same as suicide. Rather, sallekhanā is a special vow that sees individuals perform actions such as abstaining from food and water while meditating on the true meaning of the self until their soul leaves their body. Jains argue that suicide is the killing of oneself by means employed by oneself, whereas sallekhanā sees the person performing sallekhanā enter into a state of spiritual purity and liberation. Moreover, the individual performing sallekhanā does so to be free from the cycle of rebirth and has no desire to die quickly in a state of emotional upset, as do those committing suicide. Additionally, sallekhanā should be adopted only under certain well-defined conditions and should be implemented only with the permission of a person of spiritual authority. As people who commit sallekhanā are thought to have entered a ritualistically purified state, they are often venerated as saint-like beings. Indeed even the ground on which they walk is considered special and stone monuments are erected in their honor. Furthermore, many of these memorials become the focus of pilgrimage. The memorials tend to take the form of images on which inscriptions are carved—the inscriptions provide information and inspiration to those pilgrims that can read while the images serve pilgrims that are illiterate.

Sallekhanā is a very old practice for the king Candragupta Maurya (340–298 BCE) is said to have performed sallekhanā by abdicating his royal position and retiring to the sacred Jain site where he fasted until he died. Moreover, group sallekhanā is said to have occurred in 1331 when a whole Jain congregation performed the practice. Today, it is believed that around 200 Jains perform sallekhanā each year. Most of the people that practice sallekhanā nowadays tend to be Jain priests and nuns though some laypeople also perform the rite.

In order to perform sallekhanā it is necessary for a person to estimate how long they have left to live so that they can adjust their food and water intake as they begin to fast. If for any reason the person performing sallekhanā cannot maintain his or her peace of mind while performing sallekhanā, they should stop fasting and begin to eat and drink again. The word sallekhanā derives from two words *sal* (properly) and *lekhana* (to thin out). Sallekhanā is therefore the tradition of properly thinning out physical passions and the body before death. In general, only individuals suffering from an incurable disease, great physical disability, or who are dying may perform the practice. More precisely, there are four situations under which sallekhanā may be performed: *upasarga*, by which is meant an unavoidable calamity such as being taken prisoner by enemies; *durbhiksa*, meaning great famine; *jara*, a form of old age and senility that makes a Jain unable to keep to the Jainist vows; and *nihpratikara ruja*, incurable disease that makes death imminent.

Sallekhanā is a highly esteemed practice in the Jain community, for according to Jain Agamas (i.e., the canons of Jainism), people that observe sallekhanā subjugate their passions and remove themselves from all worldly, material considerations, which in turn, are considered the root cause of all injury and violence (*himsā*). Moreover, performing sallekhanā is believed to instill in the practitioner a state of complete peace, tranquility, and serenity, which is free of fear.

See also: Assisted Suicide; Buddhist Attitudes Toward Death; *Diwali* and *Kali Pooja* (Volume 2); Hindu Death Customs; Muslim Death Rituals; Sikh Death Customs

Further Reading

Long, Jeffery D. *Jainism: An Introduction*. London: I. B. Tauris & Co., 2009.
Storm, Mary. *Head and Heart: Valour and Self-Sacrifice in the Art of India*. London: Routledge, 2013.
Tukol, Justice T. K. "Sallekhanā." Jain World: Lessons for Seniors 15. Accessed December 10, 2015, at http://www.jainworld.com/education/seniors/senles15.htm.

SAN LA MUERTE, SOUTH AMERICA

San La Muerte (or Saint Death) is a skeletal folk saint that is revered i (where he is sometimes referred to as San Esqueleto, meaning Saint Sk southern Brazil (in the states of Paraná, Santa Catarina, and Rio Gran The folk saint is also venerated in parts of Argentina, especially by peop the province of Corrientes but also in Misiones, Chaco, and Formosa a the area known as the Greater Buenos Aires, where, since the 1960s, of San La Muerte has extended through the process of internal migrati Argentinean national prison system. San La Muerte is typically depicte skeletal figure holding a scythe. Despite the similarities between the Muerte should not be confused with the folk saint Santa Muerte who portrayed as a female skeletal figure and is popular in Mexico and p United States.

Both academics and worshippers alike consider San La Muerte to have originated when an indigenous deity combined in the popular imagination with Catholic iconography. More specifically, it is thought that the Guaraní Indians, an indigenous people of South America living in Paraguay, Argentina, Brazil, Uruguay, and Bolivia, began to combine elements of their previous religion with imported Catholicism after the expulsion of Jesuit missionaries in 1767. A commonly held belief is that after the expulsion of the missionaries the Guaraní Indians took a triptych depicting Jesus, the devil, and death and divided the artwork into thirds so that three different figures of veneration arose: Jesus, Saint Devil (as San Diablo), and San La Muerte. The Catholic Church, however, scorns the veneration of San La Muerte as a tradition that combines paganism with Christianity. Further, the Catholic Church argues that the figure of San La Muerte is contrary to the Christian tenet of Christ overcoming death through his Resurrection. Despite the Catholic Church's attacks on San La Muerte, many devotees of the folk saint are Catholic and regard the figure of San La Muerte as an archangel similar to other supernatural beings belonging to their Catholic faith. Moreover, San La Muerte is also considered by some worshippers to combine the figure of death and the Christian figure of Saint Joseph. Many Christian saints are associated with death: Saint Martha is said to protect the dying from the devil and Christians petition Saint Anne for a peaceful death. It is, however, Saint Joseph that is the Christian (especially Jesuit) patron of good deaths since when Saint Joseph was dying both Jesus and the Virgin Mary attended him. Today, the figure of Saint Joseph has, to a certain degree, become incorporated with that of San La Muerte in those parts of South America where San La Muerte is worshipped with the folk saint invoked by dying people wishing for a good death. For this reason, San La Muerte is sometimes referred to as Señor De La Muerte (Lord of Death) or Señor De La Buena Muerte (Lord of the Good Death).

Devotees of San La Muerte perform prayers and rituals in his honor. Those people who venerate San La Muerte also make offerings to him including human blood, alcohol, and candles. These actions and offerings are made in the hope that San La Muerte will fulfill specific requests, usually helping people with their love lives, restoring people to good health, bringing them luck in gambling, making them wealthy, and protecting them from witchcraft or removing the curse of the evil eye. In addition, San La Muerte is also reputed to help grant requests connected to criminality and violence such as bringing death to enemies of his devotees, arranging for people to be sent to prison, shortening prison sentences, and helping worshippers recover stolen goods. Another type of petition performed to San La Muerte sees prison inmates insert a tiny effigy of the folk saint (made from human, preferably juvenile, bone taken from a baptised individual) under the skin of their arm or leg in the hope that this will help them obtain a good death as well as provide protection against assaults while in prison. In areas of Buenos Aires, the capital of Argentina, in which crime rates are especially high, some devotees of San La Muerte have a tattoo of the folk saint made on their skin rather than introducing a subcutaneous bone effigy. In order to enhance the protective powers of their tattoos, it is common practice for worshippers of San La Muerte to ask a Catholic priest to bless their tattoo of the folk saint.

Icons of San La Muerte are often kept as concealed household objects that are thought to extend the folk saint's protection to everyone living in the home. A number of public altars devoted to San La Muerte can, however, also be found throughout areas in which the folk saint is venerated. Devotees of San La Muerte, who act as the shrines' guardians and caretakers, manage the public shrines, many of which hold public celebrations between August 15 and 20 each year. Furthermore, many devotees of the folk saint consider August 15 to be San La Muerte's saint's day (this is also one of the feast days assigned to Santa Muerte), though since the San La Muerte's saint's day is, obviously, not ascribed as such by the Catholic Church, the date is contested with some devotees of San La Muerte preferring to celebrate the saint on August 13 instead. Whichever date the devotees consider correct, on the feast day of San La Muerte worshippers go to San La Muerte shrines where they make requests for help to the folk saint and vow to make good their previous promises to him. The actual rituals performed at the shrines on San La Muerte's feast day vary but normally involve the use of rosaries, praying, dancing, drinking alcohol, and some sort of procession.

The veneration of San La Muerte is characterized by a strict moral code to which devotees must adhere. Indeed devotion to the folk saint means that people must fulfill numerous duties in order to win his intercession and protection. Those worshippers that make demands of San La Muerte but do not show an appropriate level of gratitude when the folk saint assists them can expect to be punished. San La Muerte is credited with performing many miracles of healings as well as granting protection and favors such as finding jobs for worshippers, improving their finances, and retrieving lost items, but the folk saint is considered to become jealous and vengeful when those he has helped do not demonstrate sufficient thankfulness having received a favor. For example, there are many (apocryphal) reports of politicians being helped by San La Muerte to win elections, but when the winning politicians did not show their gratitude to San La Muerte after their victories they were punished with the death of their children.

A figure similar to San La Muerte is San Pascualito, a folk saint venerated in Guatemala and the Mexican state of Chiapas that is also known as San Pascualito Muerte or El Rey San Pascual. San Pascualito is thought to have originated in 17th-century Guatemala after the folk saint appeared in a vision to a clergyman called Paschal Baylon during an outbreak of the plague. San Pascualito is normally depicted as a skeleton wearing a crown or a cape and is popularly imagined as the King of the Graveyards despite the fact that he is associated with the curing of diseases.

See also: *Ankou*; *Dia de los Muertos*: Day of the Dead; *Memento Mori* and *Vanitas*; Ritual Tattooing (Volume 2); *Santa Muerte*; Warding Off the Evil Eye (Volume 1)

Further Reading

Bigliardi, Stefano. "The Argentinean *San La Muerte* and the Investigations of Walter Alberto Calzato." Foundation for Interreligious and Intercultural Research and Dialogue, Geneva. Accessed December 10, 2015, at http://www.cesnur.org/2015/SanLaMuerte.pdf.

Chesnut, Andrew R. *Devoted to Death: Santa Muerte, the Skeleton Saint*. Oxford, UK: Oxford University Press, 2012.

Deibert, Michael. *In the Shadow of Saint Death: The Gulf Cartel and the Price of America's Drug War in Mexico*. Lanham, MD: First Lyons Paperback, 2015.

Graziano, Frank. *Cultures of Devotion: Folk Saints of Spanish America*. Oxford, UK: Oxford University Press, 2007.

Hecht, Richard D., and Vincent F. Biondo, eds. *Religion and Everyday Life and Culture: Volume 1*. Santa Barbara, CA: Praeger, 2010.

SANTA MUERTE, MEXICO AND UNITED STATES

Santa Muerte—also known as Saint Death, the White Girl (*la Niña Blanca*), Bony Lady (*la Huesuda*), or Skinny Lady (*la Flaquita*) amongst many other soubriquets—is the colloquial name for *Nuestra Senora de la Santa Muerte*, which translates from Spanish as Our Lady of the Holy Death. Santa Muerte is not connected to the Catholic Church and is not a Catholic saint. Instead, Santa Muerte is a Mexican folk saint and the focus of a burgeoning, and controversial, cult religion. Those who worship Santa Muerte are known as *Santa Muertistas*.

Around 8 million devotees from all sections of Mexican society worship Santa Muerte though she is notoriously associated with the Mexican underworld, particularly drug cartels and prostitution. Many Mexicans who follow Santa Muerte are innately fearful of their deity as they know of people whom she has failed and because it is a commonly held Mexican belief that the only way to contact Santa Muerte is by dying or through the death of a loved one. Outside of Mexico, Santa Muertistas are also found in the southwestern United States, particularly in the towns of El Paso, Laredo, and Brownsville, and elsewhere in America, especially Los Angeles, home to the country's largest Mexican immigrant population and where two temples dedicated to Santa Muerte are located. Areas of Central America and Canada also see the worship of Santa Muerte where Mexicans have settled. The worship of Santa Muerte does not have any formal structure nor is there any leader of the cult. Followers cannot join the cult officially as there are no Santa Muerte organizations or associations. However Santa Muerte has appropriated many aspects associated with mainstream religion for there are self-proclaimed Santa Muerte priests, as well as temples and shrines at which rites are held. In addition, believers pray at homemade altars offering candles, fruit, sweets, and tequila to Santa Muerte in the hope that she will grant their wishes. Santa Muertistas also hold an annual celebration on November 1, known as *Dias de la Muerte*, or Day of the Dead. Some Santa Muertistas also hold a feast day for the folk saint on August 15 each year. Devotees of Santa Muerte fuel sales of paraphernalia associated with the folk saint including votive candles, prayer cards, rosaries, and statues in shops and at Mexico City's Sonora Market, the main place of sale for supernatural goods in Mexico.

Santa Muerte is unusual in that unlike most folk saints she is the personification of death itself rather than of a dead individual. As well as being the embodiment of death, Santa Muerte is also the personification of protective healing responsible for the delivery of believers to their destinations in the afterlife. In addition to this, Santa Muerte is also seen as the protector of Mexican homosexual, bisexual, and transgender communities and those considered as outcasts by Mexican society.

Santa Muerte takes the form of an asexual skeleton carrying a scythe, and often other objects, wearing hooded robes or a shroud in the manner of the Grim Reaper. The only outward clue to Santa Muerte's femaleness is the fact that her attire is akin to that worn by the Virgin Mary, a nun, a bride, or a queen for she is often shown wearing a white wedding gown or brightly colored satin robes as well as a crown or floral garland. (*See* Plate 17.) Sometimes Santa Muerte even has a cascade of flowing hair.

The origins of Santa Muerte worship are not known. A few decades ago the folk saint was almost unknown in Catholic Mexico. However Mexico is a country of intense yet unorthodox religiosity and the presence of older, rural cults are pervasive. For instance, Veracruz is associated with *curanderos* (medicine men), folk healers believed to derive curative powers from some supernatural force. The figure of Santa Muerte seems to be linked to vestiges of Aztec beliefs and practices. During the 1970s, shrines dedicated to Santa Muerte began to appear in Tepito, located in the heart of Mexico City's Aztec archeological area. According to local folklore, the saint evolved from the Aztec goddess of death as the patron of women striving to control their wayward husbands. However the recent upsurge in the prevalence of Santa Muerte stems from her association with Mexican criminality, hence the saint is often depicted holding an orb, representing world domination, or a pistol, as well as a scythe, symbolic of death and destruction.

Santa Muerte is a controversial figure. In 2009, Santa Muerte was denounced by the country's administration as both an enemy of the Mexican state and as a "narco-saint," responsible for protecting Mexican drug cartels. This declaration came after the discovery of Santa Muerte shrines and the like at the home of the leader of a major Mexican drug cartel as well as the finding of 11 decapitated bodies, a hallmark of Mexican drug gangs, at a shrine dedicated to the folk saint. As a result of these discoveries, in March 2009 Mexican government authorities bulldozed 40 shrines dedicated to Santa Muerte located on the United States-Mexico border. Later, in 2013, the Vatican condemned Santa Muerte as a sinister, infernal, blasphemous figure and declared that to worship Santa Muerte was to celebrate destruction and hell. Santa Muerte is indeed a problematic figure from a Christian theological perspective, for in Christian teachings the Resurrection saw Christ defeat his last enemy, death. Therefore the worshipping of the personification of death is equivalent to honoring the enemy of Christ, that is, Satan. That there is a satanic element to Santa Muerte worship has been implied by the authorities within the Mexican Church hierarchy who assert that those that follow Santa Muerte participate in satanism unwittingly. Mexican Church officials also claim that criminal Santa Muerte believers have committed crimes in the name of the folk saint. Drug-related assassinations, human sacrifice, and other sensational crimes have been attributed to a minority of believers in both Mexico and the United States who feel that Santa Muerte sanctions their actions. The rise in the number of Santa Muerte followers has also been blamed for an increase in the number of exorcisms performed in Mexico as followers of Santa Muerte turn to the church looking for help to reject their belief in the folk saint.

It is expected that the number of Santa Muerte followers in Mexico and elsewhere will continue to rise, peak, and ultimately wane when the next major folk saint evolves.

See also: *Ankou*; *Dia de los Muertos*: Day of the Dead; *Memento Mori* and *Vanitas*; *San la Muerte*

Further Reading

Brown, Stacy. "Considering *Curanderismo*: The Place of Traditional Hispanic Folk Healing in Modern Medicine." *ETHOS*. Accessed June 7, 2016, at http://www.bc.edu/clubs/mendel/ethos/archives/2008/brown.shtml.

Chesnut, Andrew R. *Devoted to Death: Santa Muerte, the Skeleton Saint*. Oxford, UK: Oxford University Press, 2012.

Chesnut, Andrew R. "Death to Santa Muerte: The Vatican vs. the Skeleton Saint." *Huffington Post*, May 18, 2013. Accessed November 7, 2014, at http://www.huffingtonpost.com/r-andrew-chesnut/death-to-santa-muerte-the-vatican-vs-the-skeleton-saint_b_3291499.html.

Hernandez, Vladimir. "The Country Where Exorcisms Are on the Rise." *BBC News Magazine*, November 26, 2013. Accessed November 7, 2014, at http://www.bbc.co.uk/news/magazine-25032305.

Herrera-Sobek, Maria. *Celebrating Latino Folklore: An Encyclopedia of Cultural Traditions*. Volume 2. Santa Barbara, CA: ABC-CLIO, 2012.

Kail, Tony M. "The Narco Cult of Santa Muerte," *Journal of Counterterrorism & Homeland Security International, 16*(2). Accessed November 7, 2014, at http://www.princetonwebserver.com/SIG/wp-content/uploads/2014/08/The-Narco-Cult-of-Santa-Muerte-Tony-Kail-Symbol-Intelligence-Group.pdf.

News Limited. "The Battle for a Nation's Soul: How the Cult of Santa Muerte Has Infested Mexico's Drug Cartels with Gruesome Consequences." News.com.au, March 28, 2014. Accessed November 7, 2014, at http://www.news.com.au/world/the-battle-for-a-nations-soul-how-the-cult-of-santa-muerte-has-infested-mexicos-drug-cartels-with-gruesome-consequences/story-fndir2ev-1226867231755.

SATURDAY OF SOULS, ORTHODOX CHRISTIANITY, BULGARIA, AND SERBIA, AND *RADONITSA*, RUSSIA

A Saturday of Souls (also known as a Soul Saturday or Memorial Saturday) is a day set aside within the liturgical year of the Orthodox Christian Church, specifically within the liturgical year of the Eastern Orthodox and Greek-Catholic churches, to commemorate the dead. Orthodox Christianity, also referred to as the Eastern

Orthodox Church, consists of many self-governing churches that are united in their faith and by a shared approach to doctrines, rituals, and worship. Orthodox Christianity draws on elements of Greek, Middle Eastern, Russian, and Slav cultures. Eastern Orthodox churches traditionally associate Saturdays with the act of praying for the dead because Jesus lay dead in his tomb on a Saturday before being resurrected on a Sunday. Saturdays of Souls occur in Greece, Bulgaria, and Serbia.

Most of the days on which the dead are commemorated by Orthodox Christianity fall on Saturdays—exceptions include All Saints' Day, which falls on a Sunday, and Joyday, the first Tuesday after Easter. Orthodox Christians remember the dead on the first Saturday of Lent plus the two previous Saturdays, the last three Saturdays to fall within the Advent period, as well as the Saturdays that fall in the two-week-long fasting period before the Dormition of the Mother of God (August 15), Great Saturday that falls before Easter, the Soul Saturday of Saint Demetrius (the Saturday before the feast-day of Saint Demetrius of Thessaloniki that falls on October 26), and All Souls' Day that falls on the eve of Pentecost. The Bulgarian Orthodox Church also sometimes observes a Saturday of Souls on the Saturday prior to the feast of Saint Michael the Archangel (November 8), rather than the Soul Saturday of Saint Demetrius.

On a Saturday of Souls a priest will preside over a service honoring the dead once a regular service has been performed. This service to honor the dead is called *panikhida*. Panikhida is a prayer service led by a priest for the repose of the soul of a deceased Orthodox Christian. Traditionally, panikhida is observed on the third, ninth, and 40th days after the death of an Orthodox Christian and also on each anniversary of the person's death. Panikhida is basically the same as other memorial service offered by Orthodox Churches outside the Russian tradition that are also known as *parastas* and *pannychis*, or as the "Trisagion for the Dead." Panikhida is held exclusively to honor Orthodox Christians.

While commemorating the dead, the priest stands besides a table of lit candles and blesses ceremonial breads and cakes that are then also placed upon the table. One such delicacy is *colybes* (also called *koliva*), which are made from wheat berries or rice, nuts, sugar or honey, and dried fruits. Some researchers believe colybes may be related to the ancient delicacies made from seeds and honey known as *panspermia* that were distributed among worshippers during *Anthesteria*, an ancient Greek festival held to honor the god Dionysius. Wheat is an important element of Saturday of Souls rituals because it has been associated with rebirth and salvation in Greece since ancient times. The friends and family members of people that have died bring the cakes and breads blessed by the priest during a Saturday of Souls service to the church. The delicacies are then eaten after the commemorative service either inside the church, at their home, or beside the grave of the person they wish to remember. When the cakes are eaten at the graveside, a priest will accompany the mourners to the graveyard where he will place a little of the cake beneath a crucifix before pouring some wine onto the grave. Next, a feast is held at the graveside that includes the eating of the blessed cakes.

> ### How the Pussy Willow Got Its Name
>
> According to Polish legend, one spring some kittens fell into a river while chasing butterflies and their mother cat sat by the river's edge weeping for her babies and pleading that they should not drown. The willows growing by the side of the river heard the cat's plaintive cries and swept their long branches into the river. Luckily the kittens grabbed the branches and the willows transferred the kittens safely to the riverbank. Ever since, each spring, willow trees have sprouted furry buds where the little kittens once clung.

The Russian Orthodox Church also celebrates *Radonitsa* (from *radost*, meaning joy), which translates as Day of Rejoicing. Radonitsa is very similar to a Saturday of Souls except it falls on a Tuesday rather than a Saturday. Radonitsa falls on the ninth day after Easter Sunday. The day commemorates all those believers that have died since the Russian Orthodox Church was established and asks that the deceased will be resurrected to gain life eternal. On Radonitsa Russian Orthodox people visit the graves of their dead family members to share their joy in the Easter season. Once at the graves the people clean the graves and decorate them with garlands of flowers and pussy willow and then hold feasts beside the graves, often by holding picnics and drinking vodka—though never clinking glasses together while saying toasts as this is taboo. Russians also leave foods such as eggs, sausages, and candies beside the graves. Members of the Russian Orthodox faith believe that by celebrating by the graveside of their loved one's and leaving them foods they keep alive the spirit of their family members.

See also: All Souls' Day; *Famadihana*; *Halva*; *Koliva*; *Malagan*; Name Days and *Slava* (Volume 1); *Qingming* Festival; Remembrance Day and Remembrance Sunday; Sakalava Royal Death Traditions and *Fitampoha*; Soul Cakes and Soul Breads; *Tết Nguyên đan*

Further Reading

Archangel Gabriel Orthodox Church. "Molieben and Panikhida." Service Schedule. Accessed October 14, 2015, at http://www.stgabrielashland.org/service-schedule/molieben-and-panikhida/.

Cheremeteff Jones, Catherine. *A Year of Russian Feasts*. London: Transworld Publishers, 2003.

Håland, Evy Johanne. *Rituals of Death and Dying in Modern and Ancient Greece: Writing History from a Female Perspective*. Newcastle Upon Tyne, UK: Cambridge Scholars Publishing, 2014.

Orthodox Church in America. "Prayers for the Departed." Accessed October 14, 2015, at http://oca.org/questions/deathfunerals/prayers-for-the-departed.

Roy, Christina. *Traditional Festivals: A Multicultural Encyclopedia, Volume 2*. Santa Barbara, CA: ABC-CLIO, 2005.

SENIOR SPORTING EVENTS, INTERNATIONAL

Senior sporting events are sports tournaments held exclusively for older competitors, usually meaning those competitors aged 50 years and older. (*See* Plate 18.) There are several such sporting events held around the world but perhaps the most well known is the Summer National Senior Games, the largest multi-sport tournament for seniors. The Summer National Senior Games are organized by the National Senior Games Association, which was established in 1985 in St. Louis, Missouri, in order to promote healthy adult lifestyles through sports and education. The National Senior Games Association was originally called the National Senior Olympics Organization (NSOO). In the fall of 1985 the NSOO met with individuals from 33 states in the U.S. that were already organizing sporting events for seniors. At that meeting, the first National Senior Olympic Games, to be held in 1987 in St. Louis, were arranged. The games were a huge success, featuring 2,500 competitors and with the opening ceremony, hosted by comedian-actor Bob Hope, attracting in excess of 100,000 spectators. The second National Games was also held in St. Louis, in 1989, and attracted 3,500 seniors and as well as media coverage. Over time the Summer National Senior Games have continues to grow to the extent that in 2009 the games, held in San Francisco, attracted in excess of 10,000 competitors.

Today, the NSGA is a non-profit organization dedicated to encouraging adults to follow healthy lifestyles through the senior games movement. At present, the Summer National Senior Games take the form of a 19-sport, biennial competition for men and women ages 50 years and older. The large number of events means that the Summer National Senior Games are the largest multi-sport senior sporting event in the world. Sports included in the games include track and field athletics, swimming, cycling, archery, tennis, shuffleboard, and horseshoes. To find competitors for the Summer National Senior Games, NSGA Member Organizations host yearly games as well as qualifying competitions in the year prior to the games.

Other senior sporting events include the World Veterans Games, the World Masters Games (though competitors at this tournaments may be in their twenties depending on the sport), and the United States Senior Games. Individual sports also often have their own senior leagues such as Senior League Softball World Series. The Wimbledon Lawn Tennis Championships also holds senior invitational events each year during the main tennis competitions. Though the senior invitational doubles are not nearly as serious as the main championship matches and are mainly played for fun, many spectators enjoy the opportunity to see previous champions that have retired from regular play. Similarly, the ATP Champions Tour is a series of tennis tournaments that allows former champion tennis players to compete against each other. Former champions—including John McEnroe, Bjorn Borg, Stefan Edberg, and Goran Ivanisevic—have all competed in the series of senior tennis events around the world with the champions taking great pride in displaying their fitness, skill, and competitiveness.

See also: Chelsea Pensioners; Retirement and Pensions; University of the Third Age

Further Reading

ATP Champions Tour. "About." Accessed October 14, 2015, at http://www.atpchampions tour.com/about-atp-champions-tour/about.aspx.

Greenwell, T. Christopher, Leigh Ann Danzey-Bussell, and David Shonk. *Managing Sport Events*. Champaign, IL: Human Kinetics, 2014.

Landry, Fernand, Marc Landry, and Magdeleine Yerlès, eds. *Sport: The Third Millennium*. Proceedings of the International Symposium Quebec City, Canada May 21–25, 1990. Sainte-Foy, Canada: Les Presses de l'Universite Laval, 1991.

National Senior Games Association. "History of the NSGA." Accessed October 14, 2015, at http://www.nsga.com/history.aspx.

Ward, Victoria. "Wimbledon Greats Are Told to Turn Up on Time," *The Telegraph*, July 6, 2015. Accessed October 14, 2015, at http://www.telegraph.co.uk/sport/tennis/wimble don/11719900/Wimbledon-greats-are-told-to-turn-up-on-time.html.

Williams, Victoria. *Weird Sports and Wacky Games around the World: From Buzkashi to Zorbing*. Santa Barbara, CA: ABC-CLIO Books, 2015.

SHRUNKEN HEADS, PERU AND ECUADOR

A shrunken head is a human head that has been severed from its body and specially prepared to act as a trophy or for use in a ritual. The custom of headshrinking is an ancient traditional craft practiced by Jivaroan tribes living in northern Peru and southern Ecuador, including the Achuar, Aguaruna, Huambisa, and, most especially, the Shuar people. Though shrunken heads are an instantly recognizable part of popular culture, it has been claimed that no new shrunken heads have been created for the last 20 years.

Jivaroan tribes call shrunken heads *tsantsa*. After Europeans moved into the upper Amazon region, shrunken heads also proved useful trading items exchanged for weapons and other goods. When Europeans and other Westerners started to travel to South America in the 19th century they discovered the custom of headshrinking, which they found both fascinating and horrifying. This mixture of intrigue and dread meant that the visitors began to collect shrunken heads as souvenirs of their travels that subsequently became museum artifacts. During the 1930s, the selling of human heads was outlawed in most South America countries. At this time a shrunken head would retail for around $25, the equivalent of $330 today. Indeed so fashionable was it to buy shrunken heads that dishonest dealers began to peddle heads made from animals such as sloths, goats, and monkeys masquerading as shrunken human heads. Moreover, it has been claimed that many of the shrunken heads found in museums are in fact fakes, including that found in the American Museum of Natural History. It is difficult to differentiate between human and animal shrunken heads, with the best way of telling the difference being to look at the nasal hairs and the patterns of the ear lobes, which should retain their intricacy when shrunken. In addition, real human shrunken heads should have shiny skin and glossy hair and should display lateral compression of the head among other details.

The removal of a defeated adversary's head was a common way of celebrating victory in many cultures. For instance, the Aztecs, Incas, and Mayans severed the heads of defeated enemies while Native American tribes were known to scalp their foes. However it is imperative that a severed head be preserved if it is to attain the status of a trophy as otherwise it will putrefy and become a source of revulsion. Therefore some form of mummification of the head is necessary. In Indonesia, severed heads were collected by headhunters who used smoke to dry the heads and sometimes removed the skin from the skull and decorated the bone with chalk. Shrunken heads are unique to the Jivaro group of South America, particularly the Shuar, for whom shrunken heads are exceptionally important religious objects. For the Shuar warrior, claiming the head of an enemy meant more than possessing the body part of the enemy as a trophy—it was akin to claiming his soul. Therefore the preparation of the head was an important religious rite.

The Shuar people are famous for their head-shrinking methods. As the only tribe of the area to repel foreign invaders, the Shuar's customs have remained the same for centuries. To create a shrunken head, the Shuar would cut the head from the body of an enemy soon after defeating him, often while the foe was still alive. As the head was to be shrunken it was necessary for the head to be severed from the body lower down than a head would be severed by a guillotine or sword. Instead, the Shuar would cut the head from the body by cutting near the base of the neck, taking with it skin from the chest and back. The warrior then transported the decapitated head back to his home village by threading his headband or a vine through the mouth and then out of the neck, tying together the two ends of the material to make the head easier to carry.

Next, the head would be prepared by carefully separating the skin and hair from the skull so that it could shrink at different rates. The skull and brain were discarded. This separation was achieved by using bamboo knives, shells, or flints—a process that required skill, as it was important that the hair remained intact and the facial features undamaged. Once the skin and hair had been removed the skull, eyelids, and nostrils were sewn shut and the lips clamped shut using a wooden peg. The next stage in the preparation of the shrunken head varied. For instance, after the sewing up of the eyelids and pegging of the mouth to create a balloon effect, the head might be filled with sand and placed over a fire. As the head heated, sand slowly drained out of the neck causing the head to shrink but with facial features retained. When the head was the preferred size, the headshrinker would decorate the face by enhancing the eyes, nose, and lips and cutting the hair so that it fit the proportions of the freshly shrunken head. Alternatively, the head might be boiled in a pot together with plant extracts and bark for two hours or until the head was one-third its original size and the flesh felt rubbery. Once this texture was achieved, the headshrinker turned the flesh inside out, removed the flesh, and then turned the skin back to the right side. A head might also be placed in a pot with tannins and clotting agents. The head was then filled with hot sand causing it to shrink from the inside while at the same time the shrinker applied oils and fats to the outside. Next, the head was smoked over charcoal and plant extracts so that it took on a darker hue. The preparation of the head had tremendous religious and spiritual significance for the head tribes believed the heads held magical powers called *tsarutama*. The Shuar felt it was important that the heads of their enemies were shrunk so that the spirit of their enemies remained locked inside the head, protecting the Shuar from revenge by the spirit of the defeated warrior.

Such processes usually took about a week to complete. Once completed, celebrations were held during which a hole was made through the shrunken head. The head was then threaded to make a necklace worn by the warrior who killed the person to whom the head belonged. The Jivaro believed that the warrior strength (*arutam*) imparted by the wearing of a shrunken head was so powerful that it would constantly benefit both the wearer and the wearer's ancestral spirits. Therefore the Jivaro peoples would hold special ceremonies at which the heads were displayed as a way for the tribes' dead ancestors to see that their descendants continued to fight their enemies. The Jivaro peoples believed that as reward for seeing the display of heads their ancestors would help and protect them. After the ritual was over, the shrunken heads were discarded, given to children to use as a playthings, or used as a decoration. The temporary display of the heads was important so that they could be seen by departed ancestors of the tribe—rather than their continued possession by the living.

See also: *Memento Mori* and *Vanitas*; Mummification; Plastination; Taxidermy

Further Reading

Eveleth, Rose. "How Does One Actually Shrink a Head?" Smithsonian.com, March 20, 2013. Accessed November 8, 2014, at http://www.smithsonianmag.com/smart-news/how-does-one-actually-shrink-a-head-5994665/?no-ist.

Jeremiah, Ken. *Eternal Remains: World Mummification and the Beliefs That Make It Necessary*. Sarasota, FL: First Edition Design Publishing Inc., 2014.

National Geographic Society. "Rare Headshrinking Footage Confirmed?" National Geographic News, November 13, 2009. Accessed November 8, 2014, at http://news.nationalgeographic.com/news/2009/11/091113-shrunken-heads-video-ngc.html.

Peers, Laura. "Shrunken Heads of the Upper Amazon." Pitt Rivers Museum. Accessed November 8, 2014, at http://www.prm.ox.ac.uk/shrunkenheads.html.

SIKH DEATH CUSTOMS, SIKHISM

It is the Sikh tradition to cremate the dead, though if it is not possible to perform a cremation it is also acceptable to the Sikh religion for a person to be buried at sea or in the ground. In India, where Sikhism originated during the 15th century, cremation normally occurs on the day a person dies while elsewhere a cremation may be delayed for up to three days so that relatives of the recently deceased can travel to the funeral venue. When a Sikh person seems close to death, it is traditional for the person who is dying's family to congregate at his or her bedside in order to recite

Sukhmani (the Hymn of Peace) and the dying will attempt to reply to the prayer by saying *Waheguru*, meaning wonderful teacher, which in Sikhism is used to refer to God and to impart spiritual ecstasy. The dying person may also try to drink *amrit*, a blend of water and sugar that has been blessed and stirred with a double-edged sword called a *khanda*.

Once a Sikh person dies, the body is washed with yogurt by the deceased's relatives who recite a holy verse about God called the *Mool Mantar*, as they bathe the corpse and dress it in new clothes in traditional Sikh styles, and, if the corpse is male, a new turban. If the deceased is *Khalsa*—one who has officially joined the collective body of all initiated Sikhs by undergoing a special ceremony—the body will also be prepared in accordance with the symbols of Sikhism known as the five Ks. The five Ks are: *kesh*, uncut hair symbolizing obedience to God that is coiled under a turban; *kangha*, a wooden comb symbolizing order in life that is used to comb ling hair; *kara*, a bracelet the circular shape of which symbolizes that God is unending that is made of steel to represent might; *kachera*, white shorts worn under clothes in order to maintain self-control and chastity; and *kirpan*, a short sword that reminds Sikhs to always fight for truthfulness while defending the defenseless. When the body is appropriately dressed, it is wrapped in a white shroud and a piece of silk called a *rumala* is placed over the shrouded corpse.

Once all the preparations of the body have been performed, the person is placed in a coffin that is then transported to the *gurdwara*, the Sikh place of worship and community, and placed in front of a copy of the Sikh scriptures, Sri Guru Granth Sahib. In India, the coffin is put on a funeral pyre that is then lit by a close relative. As the coffin burns, the *Kirtan Sohila,* or evening prayer, is recited. This prayer reflects the Sikh belief that death is sleep experienced before a person is reborn and receives *moksha*, the ultimate freedom from reincarnation that denotes a person has been released from the cycle of life and death. After the cremation, the Ardas prayer is offered, as is the Anand Sahib prayer that is sung. The word *akal* (undying) may also be chanted throughout a Sikh funeral ceremony in an attempt to release the soul of the departed and allow it to return whence it came. The ceremony concludes with the offering of foods that have been blessed by the guru in a rite known as *karah parshad*. Then the deceased's ashes are collected and disposed of in the nearest river.

Oftentimes the dead person's family will stay home for 10 days after a death occurs all the while reading Sri Guru Granth Sahib. Sometimes a Sikh family will undertake a complete reading of the entire Sri Guru Granth Sahib, known as the *Akhand Path*, that is timed to conclude on the 10th day after a Sikh funeral. This takes place either at the deceased's family home or at the gurdwara with the conclusion of the Akhand Path marking the end of the official period of mourning. The Akhand Path is undertaken to mark both joyous and sad occasions as well as times of adversity. The non-stop reading of Sri Guru Granth Sahib takes around two days to complete and is performed either by family members or professional readers that recite the text while in the presence of the family. Once the reading is complete the *Bhog* ceremony of *Paath* is held to mark the culmination of the Akhand Path and a *Hukam* is chosen. A Hukam is a passage selected at random from Sri Guru Granth Sahib by turning to any page in the text and reciting the hymn on that page. A sacred semolina pudding called *Karah parshad* that is similar to *halva* is then distributed to everybody present.

Sikhs do not mark death with gravestones or other monuments as they see death as the demise of a person's body while his or her real essence survives as the soul.

See also: Cremation; Eating the Ashes of the Dead; Finger Amputation; *Halva*; Hindu Death Customs; *Ngaben*; Vrindavan: The City of Widows; Zoroastrian Funerals

Further Reading
BBC. "Sikh Funeral Rites." BBC: GCSE Bitesize: Religious Studies. Accessed May 7, 2015, at http://www.bbc.co.uk/schools/gcsebitesize/rs/death/sikhdeathritesrev2.shtml.
The Funeral Source. "Religious Traditions: Sikhism Funeral Traditions." Accessed May 7, 2015, at http://thefuneralsource.org/trad0206.html.
Levete, Sarah. *Journey of Life: Death*. New York: The Rosen Publishing Group Inc., 2010.
Sikhs.org. "Ceremonies and Festivals." Accessed May 7, 2015, at http://www.sikhs.org/fest.htm.

SKY BURIALS, AUTONOMOUS TIBET AND CHINA

Sky burial is the English-language term for the custom of *bya gtor* (translated as bird-toss or scattering to birds), a form of excarnation, or the deliberate exposure of a human corpse to the natural environment and scavenging animals, that is the main method of corpse disposal preformed on the Qinghai-Tibetan Plateau of Central Asia. Sky burial involves a human corpse being sliced into pieces with the resulting pieces of flesh then carried away by huge, carrion-eating birds including the bearded vulture and the Himalayan Griffon (also known as the Himalayan vulture) that arrive in the mountainous area in great numbers to consume the remains of the dead. Traditionally two classes of special corpse disposers are employed to slice up bodies—the *topden* and the *ragyapa*, who are considered inferior to the topden—though today it is believed that monks dissect corpses in advance of sky burials. This method of corpse disposal is not performed on children under the age of 18, pregnant women, or those who have died in accidents or from infectious diseases. Tibetans believe that this way of disposing of the dead frees the soul of the deceased allowing it to be reborn. Sky burial is viewed as an act of generosity because not only does it free the dead for rebirth but it also provides nourishment for other living creatures. Although witnessing sky burial is harrowing, the custom is intended to allow the living to make peace with death and to make Tibetans realize the transitory nature of life.

Though other methods of corpse disposal occur on the Qinghai-Tibetan Plateau, including water burial, cremation, and interment, sky burial is the most common as it is a very practical way of dealing with a corpse in a region that is largely covered by permafrost and sees the soil hardened by frost for at least six months of the year thereby making ground burial virtually impossible to accomplish. The Qinghai-Tibetan Plateau, which straddles most of the Tibet Autonomous Region and the Qinghai Region of China, is the largest and highest plateau in the world. The region in bounded by the Himalayas on all sides, lies well above the tree line, and experiences winter temperatures that drop to −40°C (−40°F). In addition, most land is extremely stony with only 10 percent of the area's land available for agriculture. Therefore the geographical and climatic conditions that make life in the region difficult also cause inhabitants problems in death. Though cremation would negate problems of hardened soil, it is not a usual method of corpse disposal on Qinghai-Tibetan Plateau as cremation uses a lot of fuel and as the area is located above the tree line wood is too precious a commodity to use in this way, needed instead as building material. As cremation uses so much precious wood and fuel, it is reserved for religious and political figures, soldiers, teachers, and the wealthy. By contrast, sky burial, which is the preserve of ordinary folk, does not use up resources and so is not expensive to perform. Sky burial also reduces the instances of predation by carnivorous animals as they feed on the dead rather than attacking the living.

The tradition of sky burial is deeply rooted in the Buddhist practices followed in the Qinghai-Tibetan Plateau and in the pre-Buddhist Tibetan religious tradition called Bon. One theory suggests that the Drigung Kagyu order of Tibetan Buddhism established the sky burial tradition but the exact history of the custom is unknown. It is thought that sky burial probably started in Tibet but there is scant archeological proof to substantiate this theory. However the earliest record of the practice dates back to around 640 BCE. Sky burial used to take place across Asia and the Middle East and is still performed by some Aboriginal Australians, Zoroastrians in Persia, and a number of Parsi groups in India. It is not known if the concept of sky burial in Tibet came about through interaction with Zoroastrians and Parsi groups or as a need to find a method of corpse disposal suitable for the terrain found on the Qinghai-Tibetan Plateau. All groups that employ sky burial follow a similar pattern to ready the dead for exposure. The main difference between sky burial and the excarnation practices of other peoples is that other groups collect the bones of the dead and bury them for safekeeping, while in sky burial the bones cannot be collected as they have either been eaten or carried away by scavengers.

Ritual aspects of sky burial prior to the excarnation are familiar to most Buddhist groups, for the ceremonial elements of the process seek to reconcile the dual aim of helping the dead and protecting the living. The funeral element of sky burial encompasses a number of rites and traditions, some of which are performed by laypersons and others by religious figures, though these do vary according to location.

Sky burial would not be successful without the presence of large numbers of vultures and other carnivorous birds on the Qinghai-Tibetan Plateau. Bearded vultures are particularly populous in the area. These birds have a wingspan of seven to nine feet and rarely fly below 6,000 feet but they inhabit large tracts of the region in order to search for food. Bearded vultures are physiologically designed to break down the high fat content found in bone marrow, which makes up 85 percent of their food intake. The vultures of Tibet have learned that sky burial presents a useful food resource and quite aptly vultures engaged in feeding are known as a wake. Inhabitants of the plateau regard vultures as beings similar to angels and called them *Dakinis*, meaning sky dancers. Dakinis are thought to take the souls of the dead into the heavens, which Tibetans take to be a windy place where souls wait to be reincarnated. The donation of human flesh is thought of as virtuous because it saves the lives of the small animals that vultures would otherwise eat. According to Buddhist legend Sakyamuni, one of the Buddhas, demonstrated that feeding vultures human flesh was acceptable when he fed a hawk with his own flesh to stop the predatory bird from eating a pigeon.

The rituals that occur in sky burial can take a number of days to complete with the body left untouched for three days. To start, the sky burial process the corpse is washed, tied in a fetal pose (i.e., the same position as it was born in), and wrapped in a white cloth while chanting monks surround the body. The corpse is then carried to an appropriately sacred place and secured so that it lies away from the ground, usually elevated using stones. At the time of death, a ritual specialist called a *lama* presides over a ceremony that is intended to help the deceased through the time of *bardo*, a liminal state experienced after a person has died but before they are reborn. The lama helps the deceased journey through bardo by engaging in *pawa*, meaning a transfer of consciousness, by making speeches and playing ceremonial musical instruments such as drums, thigh-bone trumpets, and cymbals. Occasionally the lama prepares death horoscopes or name cards for the deceased. These are thought to help the recently dead person on the journey into bardo and they can be displayed in a prominent position after the sky burial in the manner of a tombstone. Once it is thought that the deceased has traversed bardo, ritual dancing and purification rites may take place, before a ceremonial procession sets out for the sky burial location, which is, necessarily, away from the community. During all aspects of sky burial it is rare for a religious figure other than a monk who may be involved with the cutting of the corpse to touch a dead body directly. Instead, religious figures engage with the dead through ceremony and ritual, by leading the procession to the burial location, and overseeing the exposure of the corpse to the elements. After pre-exposure rites have been completed, the person responsible for slicing the corpse releases the corpse from its binding watched eagerly by waiting flocks of flesh-eating birds. The person responsible for slicing the corpse then proceeds to cut the corpse in a ritualized manner using very sharp knives, axes, and hooks. After this dissection, the hungry birds swoop down and devour the flesh and vital organs, leaving just skeletal remains. Once the birds have finished eating the fleshy parts of the corpse, the person that cut the corpse smashes the larger bones to smithereens; these remains are then mixed with *tsampa* (roasted barley flour) to entice the birds to eat them. As the body is broken up, incense is burned to encourage the vultures to swoop down and act as Dakinis. It takes roughly two hours for the birds to devour a human corpse.

To the Western mindset, sky burial may seem a brutal, grisly method of corpse disposal. However sky burial conforms to *gcod* or *cho*, a key concept that occurs in all four branches of Tibetan Buddhism and in Bon. This is because sky burial is viewed as a form of donation intended to demonstrate generosity and compassion—the corpse is donated to the birds as food and thus becomes a life-sustaining resource. The inhabitants of the Qinghai-Tibetan Plateau consider sky burial to be a compassionate process as it helps the deceased navigate the next world. However, as a result of the carrion-eating birds feasting on the dead, it is rare for Tibetans to eat birds. Though sky burial may seem unpalatable to non-Tibetans, the tradition arouses strong curiosity among outsiders. However Tibetans strongly object to visits by strangers and only the funeral party is permitted to be present at the ritual. It is strictly taboo to take a photograph during a sky burial for Tibetans believe that photographing the ritual may negatively affect the soul's ascent to the heavens.

Some archeologists also believe that a form of sky burial excarnation took place in South Ronaldsay in the Orkney Islands, Scotland. This is the location of the Isbister Chambered Cairn, commonly called the Tomb of the Eagles, a graveyard that was used by islanders roughly between 3300 BCE and 2600 BCE. During this time, about 340 people of all ages and both sexes were buried inside the cairn, which contains a rectangular main chamber with stalls and side cells. The number of individuals interred in the cairn is disputed, however, as the people were not buried in the way of interment known today. Rather, only parts of their bodies were stored here, with their skulls housed in the side chambers and their other bones in the two end cells. One theory as to why the remains were disposed of in this way is that the corpses were butchered by hand and then left exposed for animals to scavenge. The cairn is known as Tomb of the Eagles because 70 talons belonging to white-tailed sea eagles were discovered at the site along with the remains of at least 14 sea eagles found inside the tomb that lay alongside the human remains. It has been suggested that the birds excarnated the corpses and were also the totem of the people who built the cairn.

See also: Alkaline Hydrolysis; Buddhist Attitudes Toward Death; Cairn; High-Platform Exposure of the Corpse; Space Burial; Zoroastrian Funerals

Further Reading

Batt, Herbert J., ed. *Tales of Tibet: Sky Burials, Prayer Wheels, and Wind Horses*. Oxford, UK: Rowman & Littlefield Publishers Inc., 2001.

Cuevas, Bryan J. *The Hidden History of the Tibetan Book of the Dead*. Oxford, UK: Oxford University Press Inc., 2003.

Galvan, Javier A., ed. *They Do What? A Cultural Encyclopedia of Extraordinary and Exotic Customs from around the World*. Santa Barbara, CA: ABC-CLIO, 2014.

Gouin, Margaret. *Routledge Critical Studies in Buddhism: Tibetan Rituals of Death: Buddhist Funerary Practices*. London, UK: Routledge, 2010.
Showcaves.com. "Tomb of the Eagles." Accessed December 21, 2014, at http://www.showcaves.com/english/gb/misc/Eagles.html.
TravelChinaGuide.com. "Sky Burial." Accessed December 18, 2014, at http://www.travelchinaguide.com/cityguides/tibet/sky-buria.htm.

SOUL CAKES AND SOUL BREADS, EUROPE

Soul cakes are small, round biscuit-like cakes that are traditionally baked by Christians to mark All Hallows' Eve, All Saints' Day, and All Souls' Day as a way to commemorate the dead, most particularly souls residing in purgatory. There are many different types of soul cakes to be found across Europe, particularly in England, Austria, Germany, Italy, and Portugal. In recent years, there has a resurgence of interest in soul cakes via baking blogs and the availability of old cookbooks online. The cakes are also becoming available outside of their countries of origin by way of being sold in ethnic food shops and bakeries that serve immigrant communities but are also popular with shoppers in general.

There are many theories as to the origins of soul cakes. Some folklorists theorize that the cakes were originally baked on bonfires in pre-Christian times as a type of lottery with the person that picked a burned cake becoming a human sacrifice to ensure a bountiful harvest the following year. Another theory suggests that the cakes were scattered across fields in order to appease evil spirits. Whatever the origins of the cakes, by the eighth century the cakes had been adopted by Christians as a means to aid the souls of the departed. At this time most Christians believed in purgatory as a sort of limbo stage lying between heaven and hell and the eating of soul cakes was seen as a way to assist souls lingering between heaven and hell. Christians consider November 2 to be All Souls' Day—a day on which people remember those who have died and on which the living can commune with the dead and help souls trapped in purgatory. One of the traditions common to All Souls' Day in many different countries is the making of special foods that can be shared by mourners, distributed to the poor, or given to visiting children or left on the graves of loved ones.

In England, an All Souls' Day custom known as souling exists during which children visit houses, sing songs, and collect food, especially soul cakes, as well as money and drink. In England, soul cakes are also known as souling cakes or referred to simply as souls. This custom may have been inspired by the medieval Christian Catholic belief that the dead were allowed to leave purgatory for two to three days in order to call at the homes of relatives with the cakes a gift to the souls. Alternatively, the distribution of soul cakes on All Souls' Day may have derived from the giving out of bread on All Souls' Day during the Middle Ages. Souling has a long history in England but reached a peak of popularity during the 19th century. The tradition, does, nonetheless still take place, particularly in the county of Cheshire where actors known as mummers perform a souling play for All Souls' Eve on November 1. Souling mummer groups such as the Halton Souling are still active today, traveling from pub to pub and between houses to perform their plays, which usually feature a ghastly character known as a souling horse. This is a horse's skull attached to a stick that is then covered in a blanket. A similar character is also found in southern Wales where a skull horse known as Mari Lwyd or Grey Mare is included in mummers' plays and visits people in the hope of receiving cakes and beer. Similarly, in the eastern English county of Kent a custom known as hoodening takes place each year in the villages of Sarre and St. Nicholas-at-Wade a few days before Christmas. Part of the hoodening tradition sees troupes of costumed villagers transport a wooden horse around local pubs to perform plays themed around death and resurrection. Some folklorists believe that hoodening is an Anglo-Saxon practice, with the wooden horse representative of ancestral spirits.

The songs sung during souling vary but nearly always mention the desire for soul cakes. According to tradition, soul cakes are given out to the so-called soulers (i.e., children and the needy), who go from door to door on All Souls' Day saying prayers and singing songs for the dead. Each cake eaten by the soulers represents a soul being freed from purgatory. The practice of doling out soul cakes to children that knock at the door is often viewed as the origin of today's Hallowe'en custom of trick or treating. A similar custom concentrated around the central and northern areas of England is the so-called Caking Night, sometimes called Cakin' Neet. This is a calendar custom that falls either on October 30 or 31 or on November 1 and sees children adopt fancy dress, hats, and masks and then visit each home in the neighborhood all the while chanting a rhyme that goes something like "Cake, cake, cake. Copper, copper, copper. Oil a boil a water. Cake, cake, cake." The children then produce a tin into which homeowners place soul cakes, candies, and money. The visit from the children is supposed to protect homes from evil spirits.

A comparable custom of providing soul cakes to children and the poor on All Souls' Day also exists in the Tyrol region of Austria and Italy. In this area of the world people will go from house to house offering to say prayers for the dead or to sing for their souls in return for a soul cake. In parts of Germany and the Czech Republic, these soul cakes are sometimes dyed black.

Another type of cake given to children that visit houses at the start of November can be found in Portugal, where it is traditional to make a type of sweet bread called *Pão de Deus*, meaning bread of God or heavenly bread, for All Saints' Day and All Souls' Day. Pão de Deus take the form of small, sweet rolls made from butter, eggs, sugar, milk, and lemon zest that are filled with coconut and baked until golden brown. In villages across Portugal on the morning of November 1, children gather together and then visit houses while reciting verses and asking for Pão de Deus. In return for the children's efforts adults place Pão de Deus, pomegranates, and dried fruit into the children's bag. If someone declines to give the children anything then the children exclaim a sort of curse that expresses the hope that the person that did not give them anything will run short of bran to cook. In some rural areas of Portugal, villagers offer children another type of cake called a *Santora* cake. The tradition of Pão de Deus continues strongly in the areas surrounding the Portuguese capital city of Lisbon for the custom reminds city dwellers of the destitution caused by the huge Lisbon earthquake that occurred on November 1, 1755. The earthquake destroyed Lisbon and on the day that the quake struck those that had been made homeless were seen to beg of those whose possessions had survived by imploring for the love of God for some bread to eat. After the earthquake the first few days of November, especially November 1, was considered a day when destitute children could appeal for food. As a sign of love and unity, the wealthier people of Lisbon give food to children in the morning before going with their own families to have lunch and visit the graves of relatives in the afternoon.

In Italy, *Pan dei Morti* (Bread of the Dead) are chewy, moist Italian cookies that are sold by bakeries in the run-up to All Saints' Day and stop being sold after All Souls' Day. Pan dei Morti are flavored with cocoa, cinnamon, nuts, wine, and are smothered in a layer of powdered sugar. Another Italian All Souls' Day delicacy, *Fave dei Morti* (Beans of the Dead) or *Ossi di Morto* (Bones of the Dead) is made from flour, egg, sugar, ground almonds, butter, lemon zest, and cinnamon. The inclusion of the ground nuts gives the biscuits a brittle texture that is supposed to be reminiscent of bones and for this reason when baked as Ossi di Morto the dough is formed into bone-like shapes measuring about two inches long. The dryness of the biscuits means that they are often served with wine.

Sweet doughs and breads are also made to mark All Saints' Day on November 1. For example, there are various All Saints' Day cakes called *Heiligenstriezel* in German, *Strucel Swiateczne* in Polish, and *Mindszenti Kalacska* in Hungarian. On All Souls' Day, the dough used to make these cakes is used to make characters for children—boys receive a cake in the shape of a hare and girls are given cakes shaped like hens. Folklorists have noted that these shapes seem to be redolent of fertility thereby casting the dough figures as an intriguing combination of fertility symbol and soul bread. In Germany on November 1, which is known as *Allerheiligen* (All Saints' Day), it is traditional for Catholics and Protestants to bake *Allerheiligenstriezel* (often called just *striezel*), a type of braided yeast bread. Indeed the word Allerheiligenstriezel means All Saints' Braid in English. The bread generally consists of flour, eggs, yeast, butter, milk, salt, sugar, and almonds with some regional variations adding raisins, rum, or lemon to the dough mixture. The dough is then sometimes decorated with poppy seeds.

In Austria and Bavaria, Allerheiligenstriezel is traditionally given to godchildren by their godparents, a custom that has its origin in ancient funeral cults that saw women sever their braided hair as a sign of mourning. Like Pão de Deus, Allerheiligenstriezel is traditionally given to the needy, especially children living in the German countryside, for the bread was originally seen as a welcome gift to the starving poor who would feel especially hungry during winter. Another Allerheiligenstriezel tradition prevalent in Linz, Austria, is the superstition that how the bread's dough turns out indicates how the forthcoming year will be for the baker. For instance, a well risen, moist bread suggests a good year to come while a bread that comes out of the oven flat and unappetizing implies an unfortunate 12 months ahead. Today, giving Allerheiligenstriezel to godchildren is no longer, perhaps, the ceremonial event it once was but baking the bread is still considered a lovely tradition resulting in a delicious treat to share with family and friends.

See also: All Souls' Day; Changeling Beliefs (Volume 1); *Dia de los Muertos*: Day of the Dead; Funeral Cakes and Funeral Candy; Hallowe'en and *Martinstag*; *Halva*; Japanese Death Customs; *Koliva*; *Memento Mori* and *Vanitas*; *Qingming* Festival; *Santa Muerte*; Saining (Volume 1); Saturday of Souls and *Radonitsa*; *Zaduszki*

Further Reading

BBC. "Local Customs." BBC: Domesday Reloaded. Accessed November 3, 2015, at http://www.bbc.co.uk/history/domesday/dblock/GB-428000-390000/page/7.

Birge Vitz, Evelyn. *A Continual Feast: A Cookbook to Celebrate the Joys of Family and Faith throughout the Christian Year*. San Francisco, CA: Ignatius Press, 1985.

Davidson, Alan. *The Oxford Companion to Food*. Third edition. Oxford, UK: Oxford University Press, 2014.

Dejardin, Juliette. "1 November—PAO POR DEUS: A Portuguese Tradition." Living in Lisbon, October 22, 2009. Accessed November 1, 2015, at http://uk.livinginlisbon.com/en/dossier/pao-por-deus-a-portuguese-tradition/.

Durner, Christina. "Soul Cakes: A Haunted Halloween Tradition and the History of Trick or Treating." Examiner.com, October 16, 2011. Accessed November 1, 2015, at http://www.examiner.com/article/soul-cakes-a-haunted-halloween-tradition-and-the-history-of-trick-or-treating.

The Kitchen Lioness. "All Saints' Braid—Allerheiligenstriezel." November 1, 2014. Accessed November 1, 2015, at http://kitchenlioness.blogspot.co.uk/2014/11/braided-all-saints-yeast-bread.html.

Schler, Jamie. "Pan dei Morti (Bread of the Dead) for All Souls' Day." *Huffington Post*, November 1, 2010. Accessed November 1, 2015, at http://www.huffingtonpost.com/jamie-schler/pan-dei-morti-bread-of-the-dead-all-souls-day_b_776571.html.

Serck, Linda. "Halloween: England's Strange and Ancient Winter Rituals." BBC News: England, October 30, 2014. Accessed November 14, 2015, at http://www.bbc.co.uk/news/uk-england-29742774.

Sheffield Forum. "Does Anyone Remember Caking Night?" Sheffield Forum: For Everything Sheffield. October 30, 2009. Accessed November 3, 2015, at http://www.sheffieldforum.co.uk/showthread.php?t=522410.

Simoons, Frederick J. *Plants of Life, Plants of Death*. Madison: The University of Wisconsin Press, 1998.

Simpson, Jacqueline, and Steve Roud. *Oxford Dictionary of English Folklore*. Oxford, UK: Oxford University Press, 2000.

Smith, Kate. "The Mysteries of the Mummers," *LandLove Magazine*, November/December 2013, 102–105.

Stewart, Nicolette. "Demons and Saints: Unraveling German Holidays." Young Germany, November 1, 2015. Accessed November 1, 2015, at http://blog.young-germany.de/2011/11/demons-and-saints-unraveling-german-holidays/.

SPACE BURIAL, OUTER SPACE

Space burial, sometimes more formally referred to as memorial spaceflights, is a recently invented method of corpse disposal in which a symbolic portion of cremated human remains are loaded on to a small capsule attached to a rocket and then launched into space where they orbit the earth. After a period of time—possibly years—the capsule enters the earth's atmosphere where it burns up. The capsule's disintegration, which often occurs at sunrise or sunset, is visible from earth as a sort of shooting star. The people whose remains enter space are sometimes referred to as participants and come from countries including the United States, Canada, Russia, Japan, China, India, Germany, the United Kingdom, Taiwan, Australia, the Netherlands, France, and South Africa.

Several companies sell space burial packages that offer buyers the chance to send cremated remains into space. For instance, U.S. company Celestis Inc. offers The New Frontier Flight in which remains are packed into capsules containing up to seven grams of ashes. Celestis Inc. hit the headlines in 1997 when its initial memorial spaceflight carried the remains of *Star Trek* creator Gene Roddenberry into space. Celestis Inc. subsequently launched the remains of Roddenberry's wife, Majel Barrett, into space in 2009. Coincidentally, the ashes of James Doohan, who played Scotty in the sci-fi series and died in 2005, were carried into space by the space transportation company SpaceX in 2012, alongside the remains of Gordon Cooper, one of the original seven astronauts involved in Project Mercury, the first manned space program in U.S. history.

The price of space burials varies depending on how much the human remains weigh and how deep into space the remains travel—the further into space the rocket goes the more the service costs. At present, the cheapest Celestis Inc. package starts at $1,295 for launching ashes onto a space flight that then returns to earth, while the most expensive package starts at $12,500 for remains to be launched into deep space. To ensure the ashes travel into space, space burial companies place a small amount of ashes alongside scientific or commercial satellites on board real space missions.

The procedure for launching remains into space is quite simple. A designated amount of ashes is loaded into permanently sealed individual canisters about the size of lipstick tubes and then placed on a spacecraft that is itself attached to a launching device. On the day of the rocket launch, the families and friends of the deceased congregate at the lift-off site and the rocket is then launched into space. Those people gathered below have the opportunity to reminisce at a pre-launch memorial service and the whole event is recorded for posterity on a DVD and on the biography section of the company's website. Another American company, Elysium Space, has created an app allowing the relatives and friends of those launched into space via their own memorial spaceflights the opportunity to track ashes in space before they return to earth in the form of a shooting star.

A variation on space burial is the placing of ashes on the surface of the moon. This was achieved for the first time in January 1998 when the ashes of Dr. Eugene Shoemaker, a leading astronomer and researcher of the moon's craters, traveled to

> ### Pluto Astronomer's Ashes Fly Past Planet
>
> In July 2015, the ashes of astronomer Clyde Tombaugh flew within 7,800 miles of Pluto some 85 years after he discovered the planet. Tombaugh's ashes were aboard NASA's New Horizons spacecraft as it approached the planet nine years after the vessel left Cape Canaveral in 2006. Tombaugh's widow and sons agreed for one ounce of Tombaugh's ashes to be inserted into a two-inch-long aluminum capsule that would then travel aboard the spacecraft. Other items that traveled aboard New Horizon included a 1991 U.S. postage stamp that declared "Pluto Not Yet Explored."

the moon aboard the Lunar Prospector, which was sent to survey the lunar surface for 18 months before hurtling into the moon's surface. Shoemaker's moon burial was arranged by his students as they knew he had always wanted to visit the moon.

A cheaper alternative to space burial is offered by a number of companies based in the United Kingdom and United States that arrange so-called final fireworks, a method of dispersing human ashes by incorporating an eggcup-full of cremated remains into a firework that is then lit. In the United States, prices for ashes fireworks start at around $3,000.

Alternatively ashes can be placed inside a weather balloon or similar balloon able to travel to high altitudes. During this type of ash dispersal the balloon flies up to an altitude of about five miles, at which high altitude the temperature is –40°F (–40°C). As the balloon cools, it crystallizes and disintegrates, allowing the ashes to scatter. This method of ashes dispersal is considered particularly environmentally friendly, as the balloons used in balloon ash scattering are biodegradable.

See also: Cremation

Further Reading

CBS Interactive Inc. "Star Trek's "Scotty" Finally Launched into Space." CBS News, May 22, 2012. Accessed April 1, 2015, at http://www.cbsnews.com/news/star-treks-scotty-finally-launched-into-space/.

Flanagan, Abigail. "We Sent Mum's Ashes Up in a Firework," *The Guardian*, June 7, 2014. Accessed April 2, 2015, at http://www.theguardian.com/lifeandstyle/2014/jun/07/we-sent-mums-ashes-up-in-a-firework.

Garces-Foley, Kathleen, ed. *Death and Religion in a Changing World*. Abingdon, UK: Routledge, 2015.

Hollingham, Richard. "Space Burials: Dying to Go into Orbit." BBC: Future, April 3, 2012. Accessed April 1, 2015, at http://www.bbc.com/future/story/20120402-dying-to-be-in-space.

Marsden, Sara, J. "Overview." US Funerals Online, October 10, 2014. Accessed April 2, 2015, at http://www.us-funerals.com/ash-scattering.html#.VR0YNjqvvR0.

Space Services Inc. "Memorial Spaceflight Services." Celestis. Accessed April 1, 2015, at http://www.celestis.com/services.asp.

SPONTANEOUS SHRINES, INTERNATIONAL

Spontaneous shrines (sometimes referred to as make-shift memorials) are temporary yet heartfelt grassroots memorials to the recently deceased, particularly individuals that have died suddenly or been murdered, and national tragedies. Spontaneous shrines are commonly found at locations of violent death with many such shrines becoming the focal point of mass grief having seemingly sprung up in an impromptu manner. Unlike formal memorial events and monuments, spontaneous shrines are by their very nature unregulated, informal monuments that do not follow traditional ways of mourning. Spontaneous shrines commonly take the form of flowers by the side of a road where somebody has lost his or her life, lit candles, teddy bears for a murdered child, or ribbons. (*See* Plate 19.) Though spontaneous shrines may include sacred objects such as crucifixes, this type of shrine is usually non-religious. Some academics have suggested that the proliferation of spontaneous shrines is a result of people feeling that organized religion and funeral services are impersonal, not easily personalized to suit the deceased individual, and do not fulfill the emotional requirements of mourners.

The term spontaneous shrines was coined by the American folklorist Jack Santino in 1992 to describe the improvised monuments erected to people killed by political assassination in Northern Ireland. It is not known when the first spontaneous shrine was created though an Austrian academic, Konrad Köstlin, suggested that they had been seen in Catholic areas of southeastern Europe since at least the 1960s. From here the practice spread through Hungary to Czechoslovakia (now the Czech Republic and Slovakia), Austria, and France to Germany, Holland, Belgium, and Luxembourg. Spontaneous shrines are now prevalent across mainland Europe, the United Kingdom and Ireland. Spontaneous shrines are not only found in Europe, however, with roadside shrines long reported in the United States and elsewhere, particularly Australia and Mexico. Indeed Mexico has a long-standing folk tradition of roadside crosses called *descansos*, meaning places of rest, which mark the location of an individual's death. The descansos tradition evolved from a combination of Spanish and Mexican customs, folk Catholicism, and indigenous beliefs and has spread from Mexico to the United States.

Some academics theorize that the advent of spontaneous shrines during the 1960s can be linked to increased civil liberties, a more personalized form of mourning and the evolution of the generally held belief that premature, traumatic death is an injustice that needs to be marked. These academics suggest that people's perception that untimely, shocking deaths should be memorialized springs from both the fear that sudden death might befall themselves and the need to perform a mass form of public healing. A more cynical theory is that media interest in spontaneous shrines, particularly television coverage and social media websites, has led mourners to create temporary memorials to the dead partly through a desire to show the importance of each individual's death and partly as a form of performance.

There are several famous examples of spontaneous shrines to individuals. These include the carpet of flowers that was left by mourners outside Kensington Palace in London after the death of Diana, Princess of Wales, in 1997, that was estimated to consist of 15 tons of bouquets or 60 million flowers. While the flowers in memory of Diana have disappeared, an example of a spontaneous shrine to an individual that endures is the running paraphernalia and other items placed at Pre's Rock in Eugene, Oregon, a rock that marks the spot where American long-distance runner Steve Prefontaine died in a car accident in 1973. Today, the rock is something of a tourist attraction to a cult hero that has morphed into a quasi-religious site for runners. An example of spontaneous shrines to many individuals lost through national tragedy includes the so-called wall of the missing detailing the names of people missing after the attacks and other objects that accumulated at Union Square Park in the aftermath of the September 11, 2001, terror attacks on the twin towers of the World Trade Center in New York City. Though the wall of the missing began as a way to try and locate people missing after the terrorist atrocity, the wall and other objects that had gathered at the site gradually began to turn into memorials to the dead with each individual's memorial becoming part of one mass spontaneous shrine.

Because spontaneous shrines are grassroots, public, and informal monuments to the dead they do not tend to receive state funding or care, meaning that spontaneous shrines tend to progressively disintegrate through a combination of weathering and a gradual abandoning of the shrine as time, and mourners, move on from their initial grief. Therefore spontaneous shrines can last anything from several weeks to many months or even years. Sometimes, however, spontaneous shrines can become part of the local geography or give way to more permanent monuments. For instance, though the Union Square Park shrines have long disappeared, New York's 9/11 Memorial now stands as a monument to both the attack on February 26, 1993, when a truck bomb detonated at the World Trade Center, and the attack on September 11, 2001, giving the names of those people killed in the attacks.

See also: *Mizuko Kuyo*: Japanese Fetus Memorial Service; *Santa Muerte*; Suicide Landmarks; Tombstone Tourism; Windmills

Further Reading

Cable News Network, Inc. "London Begins Cleanup of Floral Tributes to Diana." CNN World News. September 11, 1997. Accessed September 9, 2015, at http://edition.cnn.com/WORLD/9709/11/diana.flowers/index.html?_s=PM:WORLD.

Elder, Adam. "Pre's Rock—40 Years On." Competitor.com, June 8, 2015. Accessed September 9, 2015, at http://running.competitor.com/2015/06/features/pres-rock-40-years-later_129573.

Margry, Peter Jan, ed. *Shrines and Pilgrimage in the Modern World: New Itineraries into the Sacred*. Amsterdam, Netherlands: Amsterdam University Press, 2008.

Margry, Peter Jan, and Cristina Sanchez-Carretero, eds. *Grassroots Memorials: The Politics of Memorializing Traumatic Death*. New York: Berghahn Books, 2011.

Senie, Harriet F. "A Difference in Kind: Spontaneous Memorials after 9/11." Sculpture. org. Accessed September 9, 2015, at http://www.sculpture.org/documents/scmag03/jul_aug03/webspecial/senie.shtml.

Tidball, Keith G., and Marianne E. Krasny, eds. *Greening in the Red Zone: Disaster, Resilience and Community Greening*. Dordretch, Netherlands: Springer Science + Business, 2014.

STATE FUNERAL, INTERNATIONAL

A state funeral is a public occasion held to honor the passing of an important public figure regarded as having national significance, often, but not necessarily, a country's head of state. When a state funeral is held for someone that is not the head of state it is because the deceased is considered to be exceptionally distinguished in some way. State funerals normally include a great deal of pageantry and formality as well as exhibiting religious overtones and aspects of military tradition. State funerals tend to be paid for by the nation. Many countries grant a form of public funeral to important public figures when they die though the details of these vary. In some cases a state funeral is conferred by the legislature while in other cases it is the head of state that decides whether a state funeral is appropriate. State funerals are often characterized by the presence of flags draped on the coffin of the deceased and/or flown at half-mast from public buildings, a day of national mourning, and a form of gun salute.

The exact history of state funerals is not known. It is likely, however, that state funerals are a very old tradition. For example, it is known that the Medici dynasty (13th century–17th century), which controlled much of the Florence in what is now Italy during the Renaissance, used *esequie* or funeral rites as propaganda events to bring together its subjects and thereby consolidate its rule. The funeral ceremonies enacted by the Medicis were based in part on the funeral rites of ancient Rome that aimed to mythologize the deceased to which the Medicis added rituals that pointed to the Christian faith in the afterlife. Therefore the ceremonies enacted during the Medici era pointed the way to modern state funerals by using a post-death occasion to foster a sense of togetherness while blending the secular and the spiritual with politics. The use of a state funeral to foster national unity was still evident many years later when in 1805 the British broke with tradition by providing a state funeral for a non-royal, the preeminent naval leader of his era Admiral Lord Nelson, who had died on board HMS *Victory* during the naval battle known as the Battle of Trafalgar. Nelson's funeral is one of the most famous examples of the state funeral and has been likened by historians to a power struggle confined within the structure of a funeral ritual. In awarding Nelson a state funeral tradition was abandoned two-fold for it is traditional to bury someone at sea if they die aboard ship, while Nelson's non-royal status meant that he would not have been considered for a state funeral automatically. Instead of burying Nelson at sea, his body was preserved in a vat of brandy mixed with camphor and myrrh and brought back to England. Nelson's funeral, in January 1806, was an incredibly lavish five-day-long event, which in today's money would have cost around £650,700 (approximately $947,458). A considerable amount of planning went into organizing the event, which saw Nelson laid to rest in a mahogany coffin weighing one ton having lain in state for three days at Greenwich Hospital before his funeral was held at St. Paul's Cathedral.

The most recent state funeral in the United Kingdom was that held for British Prime Minister Sir Winston Churchill in 1965. Churchill's funeral saw silent crowds line the streets of London to watch as his body was transported on a gun carriage to St. Paul's Cathedral where his funeral service took place. Prior to Churchill's funeral, as many as 321,360 people had filed past the catafalque bearing his corpse during a three-day period of lying-in-state. Many people believe erroneously that the British royals known as the Queen Mother as well as Diana, Princess of Wales, were given state funerals. This is not, however, the case as both women were given royal ceremonial funerals, which are almost identical to state funerals but are paid for by the British monarchy rather than the state and do not require a parliamentary vote to take place. More recently, the death of British Prime Minister Margaret Thatcher in 2013 threw into question the issue of who should pay for state funerals. As the prime minister was a highly divisive politician, many British people were deeply unhappy at the thought of paying toward Thatcher's funeral though in the end Thatcher did not have a state funeral but rather was given a ceremonial funeral with military honors—one rung lower than a state funeral. The pomp surrounding Thatcher's funeral was, however, still sufficient to cause a degree of controversy in Britain with protestors jeering, booing, and turning their backs to her coffin as it traveled through London. Potential recipients of state funerals are usually consulted as to whether they would like such a funeral. Thatcher was reported to have declined a state funeral, as did her predecessor Benjamin Disraeli, asked not to lie in state, and also rejected a military fly-past at her funeral on the grounds that a fly-past would cost too much. Despite her wish not to be given a state funeral, some right-wing British newspapers and politicians campaigned for Thatcher to receive a state funeral nonetheless.

Today, state funerals in the United Kingdom tend to follow the following pattern: the deceased is transported from a private place of repose by gun carriage as part of a military procession to Westminster Hall in the Houses of Parliament, where the deceased lies in state. The lying-in-state is usually followed by another procession to either Westminster Abbey or St. Paul's Cathedral where the funeral service takes place. Royal Navy sailors rather than horses draw the gun carriage used in these processions. This is a tradition dating back to the funeral of Queen Victoria that saw the horses drawing her carriage bolt, leaving a group of sailors to drag the carriage to the Royal Chapel at Windsor, which lies several miles outside of London. Another traditional feature of a British state funeral is the gun salute whereby prime ministers receive a 19-gun salute while heads of state such as kings and queens are afforded a full 21-gun salute.

Today, state funerals usually consist of a range of rituals and traditions including the lying-in-state, a funeral procession and service, a burial or other means of corpse disposal, and some sort of reaction on the part of onlookers or the wider community, such as a minute's silence or tolling of church bells. State funerals are often used by the state as vehicles to demonstrate national cultural values that are in effect so-called theaters of power designed to mythologize a significant person on the event of his or her death as well as to signal something about the country that considers the deceased to be important.

The link between state funerals and nationhood meant that in the early days of the United States, state funerals were shunned as the concept owed too much to British rule. William Henry Harrison was the first U.S. president to die while holding the post of president in 1841 and was the first to have a state funeral. However it was the assassination of Abraham Lincoln in 1865 that really instigated the model of the state funeral in America, partly because technological innovations such as the telegraph and railroad made it easier for news to travel fast thereby allowing a sense of national mourning to ensue. Lincoln was not a particularly popular president but his assassination, funeral, and attendant national mourning mythologized his image and rehabilitated his reputation. Some historians assert that by being assassinated Lincoln was cast in the role of martyr with his death seen as an attack on the American people as a whole. Moreover, the magnificence of Lincoln's state funeral fostered a sense of public unity and allowed people to bond together while engaged in the drama of a grand funeral. Historians also claim that Lincoln's funeral points to another factor of state funerals—the need for national catharsis by which is meant a purification and purgation of strong emotions such as pity and fear that results in renewal and restoration. Similarly, historians agree that the state funeral of President John F. Kennedy in 1963 united the nation in grief. On November 24, 1963, two days after the president's assassination, hundreds of thousands of spectators watched Kennedy's horse-drawn caisson, which had also borne the body of Franklin D. Roosevelt, transport the president's body down Pennsylvania Avenue to the U.S. Capitol. The caisson was accompanied by the president's family and flanked by 20 service personnel representing each of the five military services. The president's funeral cortege included heads of state, leading politicians, and royals from around the world. When Kennedy's flag-draped casket arrived at the Capitol, "Hail to the Chief" was played, President Lyndon B. Johnson laid a wreath in front of the bier and the casket was left to lie in state. The following day, Kennedy's funeral took place with leaders and heads of state from 53 countries in attendance. The funeral saw Kennedy's caisson pulled by four horses, with one of the horse being a so-called riderless horse in order to symbolize that the president was a fallen commander-in-chief. The casket was trailed by the president's own American flag and a funeral procession that included the president's brothers, Robert Kennedy and Edward Kennedy, plus dignitaries from across the globe. After the funeral service, the president's casket was transported to Arlington National Cemetery, where a burial service took place that included prayers, a full 21-gun salute, and a silent ceremonial drill performed by Army cadets. The ceremony was concluded by the lighting of an eternal flame that was lit by the president's widow and brothers at the president's grave.

That state funerals can play an important part in facilitating the need for national catharsis was also evident during the state funeral of Mahatma Gandhi, the leader of the independence movement in India, in 1948. According to Hindu traditions, the dead should be cremated and their ashes scattered in bodies of water after 13 days. However the government decided that Gandhi, who had been assassinated, should have a state funeral. Despite the fact that the funeral was arranged very quickly the event was large-scale with Gandhi's ashes shared among Indian villages and towns so that individual communities could mourn the loss of Gandhi.

Sometimes merely witnessing a state funeral is not sufficiently participatory for some onlookers. In such cases people may be moved to join in the state funeral in some way other than merely watching the occasion on live television. While it is often the case that a minute's silence is a feature of a state funeral, a recent development at state funerals has been for people to throw flowers at the funeral procession, and to leave lit candles or photographs at locations associated with the deceased.

See also: Changing of the Guard Ceremony; Embalming; Hindu Death Customs; Minute's Silence; Missing Man Formation; Obituary; Passing Bells; Remembrance Day and Remembrance Sunday; Riderless Horse; Royal Wootton Bassett; Spontaneous Shrines; Tomb of the Unknown Soldier; Tongan Funerals; Windmills

Further Reading

BBC. "1965: Last Farewell to Churchill." BBC: On This Day. Accessed October 25, 2015, at http://news.bbc.co.uk/onthisday/hi/dates/stories/january/30/newsid_2505000/2505981.stm.

Brodzinski, Emma. "Funerals, State," in Clifton D. Bryant and Dennis L. Peck, eds., *Encyclopedia of Death and the Human Experience 1*. Thousand Oaks, CA: SAGE Publications Inc., 2009.

The Economist Newspaper Limited. "What Is a State Funeral?" *The Economist Explains*, April 9, 2013. Accessed October 25, 2015, at http://www.economist.com/blogs/economist-explains/2013/04/economist-explains-what-state-funeral-definition-ceremonial-thatcher.

Garlick, Harry. *The Final Curtain: State Funerals and the Theatre of Power*. Amsterdam, Netherlands: Rodopi, 1999.

Habteslasie, Haben. "Nelson's Funeral Ceremony," *The Guardian*, September 16, 2005. Accessed October 25, 2015, at http://www.theguardian.com/uk/2005/sep/16/military1.

Howarth, Glennys. *Death and Dying: A Sociological Introduction*. Cambridge, UK: Polity Press, 2007.

ITV. "The Difference between a State and Ceremonial Funeral." ITV News, July 29, 2013. Accessed October 25, 2015, at http://www.itv.com/news/central/update/2013-04-17/the-difference-between-a-state-and-a-ceremonial-funeral/.

Percival, Jenny. "Q&A: State Funerals," *The Guardian*, July 14, 2008. Accessed October 25, 2015, at http://www.theguardian.com/politics/2008/jul/14/margaretthatcher.past.
Smith, Stephen. "A Nation Says Goodbye to President Kennedy." CBS News, November 22, 2013. Accessed October 25, 2015, at http://www.cbsnews.com/news/jfk-assassination-a-nation-says-goodbye-to-the-president/.
Taylor, Matthew, and Paul Lewis. "Hundreds of Protesters Turn Backs on Margaret Thatcher's Coffin," *The Guardian*, April 18, 2013. Accessed October 25, 2015, at http://www.theguardian.com/politics/2013/apr/17/protesters-turn-backs-thatcher-coffin.

STATIONS OF THE CROSS, CHRISTIANITY

Stations of the Cross, also known as the *Via Dolorosa*, the Way of Sorrows, or simply as The Way, is the term given to a series of images depicting Jesus on the day of his death as well as the prayers said by Christians when contemplating the images. The Stations of the Cross usually consist of a series of 14 images that are arranged in numbered order around the nave of a church or along a set path. According to tradition, worshippers, either individually or in groups, should travel in sequence from image to image pausing at each station (i.e., image) in turn to say certain prayers and enjoy a period of spiritual reflection. It is very usual, when performing the Stations of the Cross, for Christians to say a stanza of the 13th-century hymn "*Stabat Mater Dolorosa*," which translates as the "Sorrowful Mother Was Standing" and is usually referred to simply as "Stabat Mater," while moving from one station to the next. "Stabat Mater" is considered one of the greatest of all Latin hymns and consists of 20 couplets that describe the sorrows experienced by the Virgin Mary as she stands at the cross on which her son is dying. The hymn originated during the 13th century when the Franciscan devotion to the crucified Jesus was at its peak. For this reason, "Stabat Mater" is often associated with the Stations of the Cross. In 1727, the hymn was recommended as a Sequence for the Mass of the Seven Sorrows of Mary (on September 15) and is still used today.

Occasionally worshippers may exclaim the prayers associated with the Stations of the Cross without being near any image. This occurs, for example, when on Good Friday the Pope leads the Stations of the Cross around the Coliseum in Rome. Though often considered a Roman Catholic ritual, the practice also occurs in numerous Anglican, Lutheran, and Methodist churches. The purpose of the Stations is to assist Christians to make a pilgrimage through prayer by facilitating meditation upon Christ's suffering and death. The ritual of performing the Stations of the Cross is one of most cherished devotions performed by devout Christians, especially among Catholics, Anglicans, and Lutherans who perform the spiritual pilgrimage in a spirit of reparation for the sufferings Jesus sustained during the Passion.

Rituals associated with the Stations of the Cross vary as do the depiction of the stations, which often reflect the artistic sensibility and religious sentiments of the time, place, and culture in which they are created. The stations can consist of small plaques featuring reliefs or paintings, or of simple crucifixes with a number located in the center. In Jerusalem, the Via Dolorosa is an actual walkable route, believed to be the real path taken by Jesus as he carried the cross to his crucifixion. The Stations of the Cross marked along the route are reputed to be the actual places the events took place and are a popular tourist attraction.

The origins of the Stations of the Cross can be traced back to the time of the Roman Emperor Constantine the Great in fourth-century Jerusalem, to where Christian pilgrims would go to visit holy sites associated with the Passion of Christ. By the 12th century, these sites of pilgrimage formed an established route of pilgrimage for European Christians who would walk the Via Dolorosa by observing significant points between the court of Pontius Pilate and Mount Calvary. In the 15th and 16th centuries, outdoor reproductions of the Via Dolorosa were built as shrines throughout Europe, meaning that they themselves became destinations for pilgrims. For example, the Sacri Monti of Piedmont and Lombardy, a UNESCO World Heritage Site, is a series of nine chapels and other architectural features created in the late 16th and 17th centuries that are dedicated to different aspects of Christianity. Sacri Monti offered pilgrims the chance to imagine what it would be like to visit sites where Christ's Passion took place. Sacri Monti stands on high ground away from the local town and is normally reached through the act of pilgrimage, the itinerary of which evokes the Via Dolorosa in Jerusalem along which Christ carried the Cross to Calvary.

By the start of 18th century, Stations of the Cross became common sights inside churches where they were associated with the granting of indulgences—ways of reducing time spent by the souls of the dead in purgatory or hell. Indeed indulgences are still associated with the Stations of the Cross today. The Stations of the Cross that Christians follow nowadays are not necessarily supported by scripture. Indeed only stations 1, 2, 5, 8, 10, 11, 12, 13, and 14 have an obvious basis in scripture with stations 3, 4, 6, 7, and 9 having no scriptural reference. In 1991, Pope John Paul II instituted two new stations that did have a scriptural basis so that all the stations could claim a scriptural foundation. The Pope called the new series of stations the Scriptural Way of the Cross and employed them in the Coliseum Good Friday processions. In 2007, Pope Benedict XVI approved the Scriptural Way of the Cross for use in everyday personal religious meditation and observances.

The traditional Stations of the Cross are as follows:

1. Jesus is condemned to death.
2. Jesus carries his cross.
3. Jesus falls the first time.
4. Jesus meets his mother, the Virgin Mary.
5. Simon of Cyrene helps Jesus carry the cross.
6. Jesus has his face wiped by Veronica.
7. Jesus falls the second time.
8. Jesus meets the women of Jerusalem.
9. Jesus falls the third time.
10. Jesus is stripped of his garments.

11. The Crucifixion—Jesus is nailed to the cross.
12. Jesus dies.
13. Jesus's body is taken down from the cross.
14. Jesus is laid in the tomb.

Sometimes a 15th station is included that features the Resurrection of Jesus.

For believers, the walking of the Stations of the Cross during Lent is a ritual of personal pilgrimage, reflection, and reparation. The devotional act need not take place before an image of Christ for all that is needed is a wooden cross at each station. However images depicting Christ's Passion have come to define the rituals connected with the Stations of the Cross. This is because the visual drama inherent in the stations, whether these depict Christ in a naturalistic or stylized manner, stimulate empathy on the part of the spectator allowing the viewer to participate in the suffering of Christ. Though the Stations of the Cross depict ancient events, modern artists continue to be inspired by the Passion of Christ though modern artists tend to posit the stations as liminal spaces between life and death, ritual and motif.

One of the most famous artistic depictions of Christ's Passion is that by French artist Henri Matisse, whose 1947 Stations of the Cross can be seen in the Chapel of the Rosary in Vence in southeastern France. Matisse's large illustrations of the Stations of the Cross occupy the back wall of the chapel in a grid-like composition on white ceramic tiles. Seven years after Matisse's Stations were unveiled, American artist Barnett Newman produced the first of 14 canvases for his series *The Stations of the Cross: Lema Sabachthani*, which include vertical passages of black and white paint, the monochrome severity of which is simultaneously unsettling and contemplative. Countless artists have treated the subject since many of whom have neutralized the religiosity of the Stations of the Cross so that they can use the stations as a conduit for formal, social, political, and metaphysical inquiries connecting the secular with the divine.

See also: Crucifixion Rituals; Easter Eggs; *Memento Mori* and *Vanitas*; Passion Play

Further Reading

Alston, George Cyprian. "Way of the Cross." *The Catholic Encyclopedia. Vol. 15.* New York: Robert Appleton Company, 1912. Accessed December 14, 2015, at http://www.newadvent.org/cathen/15569a.htm.

Cahill, Timothy D. "Rereading the Stations of the Cross through Art," *The Yale ISM Review,* 1(2), Spring 2015. Accessed December 14, 2015, at http://ismreview.yale.edu/wp-content/uploads/2015/04/v1-2Rereading-the-Stations-of-the-Cross-through-Art.pdf.

Grant, D. L. *The Spiritual Journey of the Stations of the Cross: An Everyday Devotional Journey of Christ.* Bloomington, IN: iUniverse, 2010.

UNESCO World Heritage Centre. "*Sacri Monti* of Piedmont and Lombardy." Accessed December 14, 2015, at http://whc.unesco.org/en/list/1068/.

Winderl, Carl. "Stabat Mater." Accessed December 14, 2015, at http://campus.udayton.edu/mary/resources/poetry/stbmat.html.

SUICIDE LANDMARKS, INTERNATIONAL

Certain landmarks and locations around the world have become associated with suicides and suicide attempts. Experts on suicide refer to such locations as suicide landmarks. Places synonymous with suicide include Beachy Head in England, the Eiffel Tower in France, Aokigahara forest in Japan, the Empire State Building in New York City, the Golden Gate Bridge in San Francisco, the Chesapeake Bay Bridge in Maryland, and the George Washington Bridge that links New York and New Jersey.

According to researchers, some depressed individuals want their act of suicide to be a monumental feat and choose to end their life at famous landmarks because these locations are highly visible and engrained in the public consciousness. Moreover, psychologists point out that some suicidal individuals may feel there is a certain level of romanticism in ending their life at a famous location while other suicidal individuals may feel a certain connectedness with other people that have chosen to die at the same location.

The Golden Gate Bridge has long been associated with suicide and is today considered one of the world's prime suicide locations. This is possibly because the bridge is perceived as an object of beauty and also quite literally as a gateway (to the Pacific). Another reason why the Golden Gate Bridge is popular with suicidal people is that it is very accessible with pedestrian walkways from which it is possible to jump. So strong was the association between the Golden Gate Bridge and suicide that between 1937 and 1979, 58 people drove over the San Francisco-Oakland Bay Bridge that has a comparable height to the Golden Gate Bridge specifically in order to jump from the latter. Also, between these years around 58 people jumped from the Golden Gate Bridge annually. The legendary film director Alfred Hitchcock employed the suicide iconography of the Golden Gate Bridge in his celebrated film *Vertigo* (1958) when one of the lead female characters, Madeleine, seemingly attempts suicide by jumping from Fort Point located beneath the bridge.

Another extremely popular suicide location is Beachy Head, a 535-feet-high chalk cliff in southern England from which people have jumped to their deaths for centuries. According to legend, Saint Wilfrid saw English suicides jumping from the cliff to placate the angry gods for years of crop failure during the seventh century. The first documented death from Beachy Head occurred in 1600. Then, during the 19th century there was an average of three deaths per year. Indeed during the period 1965 to 1989 it is estimated that 236 suicides occurred at the site. Such figures have earned Beachy Head a reputation as the most popular suicide location in Europe, if not the entire world. In fact such is the frequency of suicides at Beachy Head that the Beachy Head Chaplaincy Team has been established. This is a Christian charity set on dissuading would-be suicides from jumping from Beachy Head. Beachy Head Chaplaincy Team is reputed to have prevented over 270 suicides annually since 2009.

In Japan, Aokigahara forest is a sprawling, dense woodland located on the northwest side of Mount Fuji that, over the last 50 years, has gained a reputation as a preferred suicide location. In Japanese folklore the forest is associated with demons and tales abound of poor families abandoning family members to their death in the forest during ancient famines. Stories of people being abandoned to die lingering deaths in the forest mean that Aokigahara is also reputed to be haunted by the ghosts of the forsaken people. Some people attest that Aokigahara's reputation as a suicide hot-spot increased after Seicho Matsumoto published the 1960 novel *Kuroi Kaiju* (*Black Sea of Trees*), which ends with two lovers committing suicide in the forest. Moreover, Wataru Tsurumui's 1993 book, *The Complete Suicide Manual*, actually recommends Aokigahara as an ideal place to commit suicide. Unlike at Beachy Head and various bridges that function as suicide landmarks, most people that kill themselves at Aokigahara commit suicide by hanging. Such is Aokigahara's association with suicide that many Japanese psychics claim that the suicides committed there have seeped into the forest's soil and trees, thereby causing paranormal activity and preventing those that enter the forest bent on suicide but who change their minds from leaving until they have died. When forest workers find the corpse of someone that has committed suicide in the forest they transport the body from the forest to a building that includes a room specifically designed to keep suicide corpses. The forest workers then play *janken*—the Japanese equivalent of paper, rock, scissors—to see which of them will sleep in the room with the body. It is important that one of the forest workers sleep in the room with the corpse as it is believed that if the body is left alone, bad luck will befall the spirit of the suicide victim. Moreover it is said that if the body is left alone then its spirit will scream all through the night and re-animate. The popularity of Aokigahara as a suicide spot seems to stem from the fact that it is symbolically linked with a desire to disappear through legend and the fact that those that commit suicide at the location acquire a sort of camaraderie with other that have also died there.

When a landmark achieves a reputation as a popular suicide destination, governments and police departments usually implement measures to try to curb the number of people that kill themselves there. Such measures are often costly for it is usually the case that crisis phones are installed as well as jump-proof railings. The costliness of implementing suicide prevention measures is evinced by the fact that a proposed net system at the Golden Gate Bridge would cost $45 million. However there is a limit to the effectiveness of suicide prevention schemes, especially when dealing with a natural feature that has become a suicide landmark. For example, at Niagara Falls, the Canadian and American park authorities have sought to reduce the number of suicide attempts by installing signs, video surveillance, and walls. However authorities admit that when an individual is set on committing suicide it is very difficult to prevent him or her, especially when a natural wonder is on a massive scale thereby affording many opportunities to end lives.

It is not, however, only humans that end their lives in large numbers at certain locations for Overtoun Bridge in Scotland has garnered worldwide notoriety as a place where many pet dogs have, for no apparent reason, leapt to their deaths. While animal behaviorists assert that dogs cannot have suicidal thoughts there is no doubt that around 600 dogs have jumped from the 50-feet-high bridge with 50 dogs dying in the past 50 years. For this reason, the bridge has been dubbed the dog suicide bridge. Most of the dogs that have leapt from the bridge have jumped from the same side of the bridge during fine weather and nearly all were breeds with long snouts—Labradors, collies, and retrievers. Theories as to why the dogs have jumped to their death range from the idea that the dogs have been spooked or coerced into the action by some supernatural force—according to Celtic mythology Overtoun is a location where heaven and earth are close together—to the possibility that the pets have responded to the suicidal feelings of their owners. The most mundane suggestion is that the dogs have leapt from the bridge to catch mink, mice, or squirrels living beneath the bridge. Whatever the reason for the dogs' deaths, a sign has been erected warning dog owners to keep their pets on a leash when near the bridge.

See also: Assisted Suicides; Tombstone Tourism

Further Reading

Beachy Head Chaplaincy Team. "Who We Are." Accessed October 14, 2015, at http://www.bhct.org.uk/wp/about/who-we-are/.

DiBlasio, Natalie. "Landmarks Have Fatal Attraction to the Suicidal," *USA Today*, May 24, 2012. Accessed October 14, 2015, at http://usatoday30.usatoday.com/news/nation/story/2012-05-23/suicide-landmarks-niagara/55170340/1.

Gilhooly, Rob. "Inside Japan's 'Suicide Forest,'" *Japan Times*, June 26, 2011. Accessed October 14, 2015, at http://www.japantimes.co.jp/life/2011/06/26/general/inside-japans-suicide-forest/#.Vh6MvDqvvR0.

Hunt, Tom. "Cliffs of Despair," *The Gettysburg Review*, Winter 2000. Accessed October 14, 2015, at http://www.gettysburgreview.com/selections/past_selections/details.dot?inode=40c4ef36-c04d-4585-8434-dc9c82b29469&pageTitle=Tom%20Hunt&crumbTitle=Cliffs%20of%20Despair&author=Tom%20Hunt&story=true.

John. "The Suicide Forest, Aokigahara: Japan's Haunted Forest of Death." Tofugo.com, July 23, 2012. Accessed October 14, 2015, at http://www.tofugu.com/2012/07/23/aokigahara-japans-haunted-forest-of-death/.

Khan, Maria. "Scotland: 600 Dogs Mysteriously Jump Off Haunted Suicide Overtoun Bridge," *International Business Times*, June 25, 2015. Accessed October 14, 2015, at http://www.ibtimes.co.uk/scotland-600-dogs-mysteriously-jump-off-haunted-suicide-overtoun-bridge-1507827.

Lite, Jordan. "Some 'Tourists' Choose City Landmarks for Suicide," *Daily News*, November 1, 2007. Accessed October 14, 2015, at http://www.nydailynews.com/news/tourists-choose-city-landmarks-suicide-article-1.259420.

Maris, Ronald W., Alan L. Berman, and Morton M. Silverman. *Comprehensive Textbook of Suicidology*. New York: The Guilford Press, 2000.

Raven, David. "Mystery as 600 Dogs Jump from 'Haunted Suicide Bridge' Leaving at Least 50 Dead." Mirror.co.uk, June 24, 2015. Accessed October 30, 2015, at http://www.mirror.co.uk/news/uk-news/mystery-600-dogs-jump-haunted-5941044.

TANGIHANGA: MĀORI MOURNING RITUAL, NEW ZEALAND

Tangihanga is a mourning ceremony performed by the Māori indigenous Polynesian people of New Zealand. The ceremony is usually referred to as a *tangi*, a word that means both to weep and to perform a dirge. Māori tradition pays great respect to the dead who are acknowledged at all Māori gatherings, irrespective of the occasion, through calls known as *karanga* and speeches called *whaikōrero* as well as through song. Māoris consider remembering the dead to be an important way to preserve their *whakapapa*, repositories of meaningful stories, as well as to remind people of the importance of life and the people close to them. Another reason that Māoris consider the ceremony to be very important is that tangihanga harks back to a time before *Pākehā*, or New Zealanders of European descent, particularly those with fair coloring. Tangihanga generally takes three days to complete depending on the social status of the deceased and how long it takes for relatives of the deceased to reach the location of the ceremony, which can be on a *marae* (the courtyard of a Māori meeting house that is used on ceremonial occasions) or at a private home. Māoris consider tangihanga to be an essential way to process grief and encourage mourners to show their heartache openly.

For a tangihanga ceremony to take place, a *tūpāpaku* (corpse) is typically prepared by an undertaker and then exhibited in an open coffin. Spoken goodbyes called *poroporoaki* are then said to the corpse as if it were still alive. The Māoris believe that this is because the *wairua*, or spirit, of the dead individual stays within the corpse for some time after death. The coffin, called a *wharemate* (also called a *whare taua* or *whare pōtae*) is then welcomed onto the marae alongside the deceased's bereaved family or *whānau pani*. In recent years the role of the whānau pani has changed. In earlier times families would ritually cut themselves (*haehae*) using shells or stones or even commit suicide (*whakamomori*) to show their grief. The wife of the deceased in particular was expected to perform whakamomori to express her sorrow. Nowadays, the bereaved do not need to cut themselves or commit suicide though they may fast by waiting until sunset to eat—the lowering of the marae's flag signals the end of the fast. Also, a member of the family should always stay with the corpse for the duration of the tangihanga.

The ceremonial rules, or *kawa*, of each marae decree where a coffin should rest before burial. Nowadays, this is usually in a separate house to the side of the *wharenui* (a communal house that is the focus of a marae), under a window on a terrace, or inside the house against the back wall beneath the *pou tuarongo* (the back wall post). Alternatively, the coffin may be placed against the third post or *poupou* on the visitors' side of the house called the *tara whānui*.

During the tangihanga the bereaved family welcomes visitors onto the marae and speeches and songs are performed. Those attending the tangihanga wear wreaths of greenery called *pare kawakawa*. For many people these wreaths are the iconic element of tangihanga but pare kawakawa are made from *kawakawa*, a medicinal plant that is generally used by Māoris on special occasions, including children's *tohi* ceremony, a religious blessing performed in a stream. Also during the tangihanga the family may ask for the body in a ceremony called *tono mate*. The tono mate ceremony sees the bereaved family demand to have the corpse lie in state at their marae or for a memorial service called a *kawe mate* to take place. These ritual arguments over where the corpse is to lie in mourning and where it should be buried are seen as a way to recognize the *mana* (supernatural power) of the dead. Though this form of ceremonial arguing is a recognized tradition, it has been known to prove problematic when the deceased comes from a cross-cultural community.

On the last day of the tangihanga it is usual for a church service to be led by either a member of the clergy or a *tohunga* (an expert practitioner of religion or another subject). The corpse is then taken to an *urupā* (traditional burial ground) where it is interred. Most urupā feature a water container at the entrance. This allows mourners to wash their hands as they leave the urupā thereby removing *tapu*, a sacred yet forbidden force. After this, the ritual of *takahi whare* occurs, where the deceased's home is cleansed of tapu by a minister or tohunga who walks through the house chanting *karakia* (prayers and invocations used to call forth spiritual support and protection).

Until recently, it was traditional for Māoris to exhume bones that they later reburied, a process called *tohunga*. This ritual has, however, been replaced by a ceremony called *hura kōhatu* (the unveiling the gravestone), which takes place about a year after the tangihanga is performed. Also at some point after the tangihanga is performed another memorial ceremony known as carry the dead takes place during which a photograph of the deceased is taken to people that were not able to be at the tangihanga.

Like many areas of Māori life, the traditional tangihanga has changed in the face of modernization and interaction with Pākehā culture. Many Māoris have moved away from their traditional marae to cities, something that has created issues of where to hold tangihanga. This in turn has led to some suburban homes being used as the venue for the tangihanga ceremony. Moreover, as younger generations become removed from their cultural heritage they perform new forms of mourning, meaning that the continuance of tangihanga as a Māori tradition is in doubt to a degree. That said, there is evidence of an increase in the number of tangihanga as some Māoris strive to keep their traditions, including funeral customs, in order to cement Māori traditions as part of modern-day New Zealand society.

See also: "Lyke-Wake Dirge"; Tomb of the Unknown Soldier; Tongan Funerals

Further Reading

Cacciatore, Joanne, and John DeFrain, eds. *The World of Bereavement: Cultural Perspectives on Death in Families*. Cham, Switzerland: Springer International Publishing, 2015.

Gagné, Natacha. *Being Maori in the City: Indigenous Everyday Life in Auckland*. Toronto, Canada: University of Toronto Press, 2013.

Higgins, Rawinia. "Tangihanga—Death Customs—Tangihanga in Modern Times." Te Ara—The Encyclopedia of New Zealand, December 17, 2014. Accessed September 8, 2015, at http://www.teara.govt.nz/en/tangihanga-death-customs/page-5.

Higgins, Rawinia. "Tangihanga—Death Customs—Understanding Tangihanga." Te Ara—The Encyclopedia of New Zealand, December 15, 2014. Accessed September 8, 2015, at http://www.teara.govt.nz/en/tangihanga-death-customs/page-1.

Mitira, Tiaki Hikawera. *Takitimu*. Wellington, New Zealand: Reed Publishing Ltd., 1972.

TAXIDERMY, INTERNATIONAL

Taxidermy is the process of preparing, stuffing, and mounting the pelts of animals so that they look to be still alive. The word taxidermy derives from the Greek words *taxis*, meaning order, and *derma*, meaning skin. Taxidermy is sometimes described as both a thanatological art form and as a type of organic sculpture that uses the bodies of dead animals rather than clay, marble, wood, or other material. Taxidermy may be practiced for a number of reasons, for example, to create hunting trophies or to preserve scientific specimens, as interior design elements or as novelty items.

Taxidermy originated in Europe during the 16th and 17th centuries as a way to preserve animal specimens collected by explorers. These specimens would then go on to become part of a wealthy collector's so-called cabinet of curiosities. In a time before photography, taxidermy presented a rare opportunity for people to see exotic animals, birds, and fish in 3D, something that was both a novelty form of entertainment and an opportunity allowing scientists to study the creatures. One of the main problems with early taxidermy was that the finished, mounted creature needed protecting from ants. This led Jean-Baptiste Bécœur, an ornithologist, bird-skin collector and apothecary, to develop arsenical soap from a mixture of pulverized arsenic, white soap, and calcium oxide in 1743. Bécœur kept the recipe for his arsenic soap secret during his lifetime but after his death in 1777 Bécœur's recipe passed to France's Muséum National d'Histoire Naturelle, and after 1800 the recipe became public knowledge. Moreover other taxidermists and animal collectors had managed to reverse-engineer Bécœur's soap meaning that by the 1830s arsenic soap was widely used by museums and private collectors to safeguard their taxidermy specimens. A little later, from around 1840 to 1914, is the time period sometimes referred to as the golden age of taxidermy. Today, however, the use of arsenic in taxidermy is banned in most countries because arsenic is highly poisonous. Nowadays, Borax, a compound of boron that is also known as sodium borate, and tanning processes tend to be used instead of arsenic. During the 19th century taxidermy was not just a method of preserving animals for scientific study for mounted creatures, especially birds, were a hugely popular home décor feature during the Victorian era, a time that was fascinated with death. Indeed taxidermy was so popular in 19th-century Britain and America that some historians have claimed that a taxidermist could be found living in every town. Moreover, a census taken in London in 1891 shows that there were 369 taxidermists working in that city alone. After World War I, the popularity of taxidermy declined. The main reason for this loss of popularity was the development of new technologies such as photography, which amateurs could indulge in thanks to George Eastman's Brownie camera, the first low-cost camera that was introduced in 1900. Then, in 1907, the Lumière brothers in Paris, France, introduced an early method of color photography called the autochrome process. Such developments in photography meant that where homes were once decorated with taxidermy birds they were now decorated with photographs. Also contributing to the decline of taxidermy was the printing of bird-watching guides as popularized by Chester A. Reed. These birding guides provided amateur and professional ornithologists with definitive reference texts that offered detailed specifics on thousands of birds, meaning that there was little need for birders to keep collections of mounted specimens. Other contributing factors to the unfashionable status of taxidermy were that major American museums such as the Field Museum in Chicago and the American Museum of Natural History in New York had, by the 1940s, completed their extravagant habitat dioramas. Moreover, post–World War II big game hunting became socially unacceptable and as the 20th century continued many governments passed wildlife conservation acts to thwart the illegal ivory and fur markets that were the main reasons for declining numbers of species in Africa.

Taxidermy did not, however, die out. For instance trade magazines such as *Breakthrough Magazine*, which as of 2015 had around 8,000 subscribers, developed while the World Taxidermy Championships were established in 1983.

In the earliest days of taxidermy, practitioners would gut and tan the animals to be mounted before stuffing the creature with straw and sawdust and then stitching the animal closed. As there were no chemicals or techniques used to preserve the mounted animal, the animal would rot eventually. During the 1970s, taxidermists stopped stuffing animals and started to stretch the animal's skin over sculpted models, or mannequins, that were usually made from foam. An alternative to this method sees a taxidermist fashion a mold of a skinned animal and create a solid form using wood or wool that is then wrapped and bound in such as way as to recreate the form of the animal. Sometimes the animal's own skull is used with its muscular facial features reconstructed out of modeling clay. A small animal (e.g., a mouse) takes two to three hours to process whereas a large animal (e.g., a large cat or large rabbit) takes up to three days to complete. To stuff a skinned mouse, which is one of the most basic tasks in taxidermy, the taxidermist will first create a so-called voodoo doll, that is, a version of the animal, made from cotton wool and string, exactly matching the shape and size of the creature being mounted. Eyes are added to the voodoo doll, as these will become visible when they protrude though the animal's eye sockets. Meanwhile the mouse's skin, which has been kept separate, is treated with Borax powder to prevent insect infestations—formaldehyde can also be used to do this but is not as pleasant to work with for the taxidermist. Next, the mouse's legs and innards are discarded with the legs replaced with wires. Alternatively, acetone may be used to clean the mouse's bones if they are going to be used in the finished piece. Once the fur and skin have been treated and dried, often by rubbing cornstarch into the pelt as this removes dirt and moisture, they are placed around the voodoo doll and stitched up. After this, the pelt is brushed with a toothbrush to complete the mount. Another popular animal on which to perform taxidermy is a fish. To taxidermy a fish, a totally different technique is required. As a fish's skin loses its color when it has dried, the taxidermist needs to remove the fish's skin and then recreate it using special pigments. The fish's eyes also have to be removed and the fish's flesh is scraped from its bones. The fish's remains are then treated using Borax or formaldehyde while the skin is either filled with sawdust or stretched over a foam mold.

Taxidermy affects the spectator on two levels. On the one hand, because the stuffed animal exhibits the stillness of death it reminds spectators of the realities of death and their own demise. On the other hand, a stuffed animal that looks alive allows spectators to deny the actuality of death because the animal seems to have transcended death by appearing to live. At the moment, taxidermy is experiencing something of a renaissance. For many modern taxidermists, taxidermy is a trendy art form that exists at the cross-section of art and science. Moreover, knowledge of taxidermy still has a place in science, with taxidermists needed to restore displays in museums and extracting DNA from the mounted bodies of extinct or vanishing species.

See also: Embalming; Goth Subculture; Living with the Dead; Mummification; Plastination; Tear Catchers and Mourning Jewelry

Further Reading

Blitz, Matt. "Why Taxidermy Is Being Revived for the 21st Century." Smithsonian.com, June 19, 2015. Accessed October 27, 2015, at http://www.smithsonianmag.com/arts-culture/why-taxidermy-being-revived-21st-century-180955644/?no-ist.

Bryant, Clifton D., and Donald J. Shoemaker. "Dead Zoo Chic: Some Conceptual Notes on Taxidermy in American Social Life," in Clifton D. Bryant, ed., *Handbook of Death and Dying: Volume II The Response to Death*. Thousand Oaks, CA: Sage Publications, 2003.

Conniff, Richard. *The Species Seekers: Heroes, Fools, and the Mad Pursuit of Life on Earth*. New York: W. W. Norton & Company, 2011.

Poliquin, Rachel. *The Breathless Zoo: Taxidermy and the Cultures of Longing*. University Park: The Pennsylvania State University Press, 2012.

Woollaston, Victoria. "The Science of TAXIDERMY: Expert Reveals the Gruesome Ins and Outs of Mounting and Preserving Dead Creatures." *Daily Mail*, December 31, 2014. Accessed April 2, 2015, at http://www.dailymail.co.uk/sciencetech/article-2847383/The-science-TAXIDERMY-Expert-quite-literally-reveals-ins-outs-mounting-preserving-dead-creatures.html.

TEAR CATCHERS AND MOURNING JEWELRY, INTERNATIONAL

Tear catchers (also known as tear bottles, lachrymatory bottles, lachrymatories, or unguentaria) are, traditionally, small glass or ceramic vessels designed to catch the tears of people experiencing mourning. The collected tears were then either sprinkled over a grave on the anniversary of a burial or kept until the tears held within the vessel evaporated. Tear catchers usually measure between two and four inches with a tear-shaped body and long, narrow neck fitted with a stopper or cap that connects to the vessel. Some tear catchers are fitted with a rubber seal to prevent collected tears from evaporating while others have a cork seal that does allow the tears inside the bottle to vaporize.

The history of tear catchers is very long with a reference to tears being caught in bottles appearing in Psalm 56:8 in the Bible and there is evidence that tear catchers were used in ancient Egypt and ancient Rome. Indeed tear catchers were popular as early as the first century when tear-shaped bottles were left at the base of tombs to honor the dead. At this time, it was also known for professional weepers to be employed by families to augment their own tears for the deceased. Tear catchers were also extremely fashionable during the 19th century, during both the Victorian era in England and during the American Civil War. During the Civil War women would collect the tears that they shed while their husbands were away, with the amount of tears a wife collected seen as an expression of how much she cared for her husband. Civil War tear catchers are highly sought after by collectors of Civil War memorabilia. In Victorian England, it was customary for women to collect their tears in the tear catcher and the vessel's stopper would allow the tears to evaporate gradually. When the tears had eventually vanished, the woman's period of mourning was considered over.

Tear catchers are still made today and used to symbolize emotions associated with mourning and remembrance. Some people buy tear catchers to represent their own mourning though they may also be given to the bereaved as a heartfelt gift. On a happier note in recent times it has been known for tear catchers to be presented as non-funerary gifts at other emotional events such as weddings and births.

Another decorative form of 19th century mourning paraphernalia was mourning jewelry, that is, jewelry specifically designed to be worn to mark a period of mourning after the death of a loved one. As such, mourning jewelry is often described as *memento mori* jewelry. This type of jewelry originated during the 16th century, but is most often associated with the Victorian period when such jewelry was mass produced and adorned with images of skulls and other macabre symbols of death. Mourning jewelry is highly collectable and readily available to buy at affordable prices at auctions and online.

The trend for mourning jewelry is often ascribed to a British ruler, Queen Victoria, who after the death of one of her cousins in the 1850s began to wear jewelry made from Whitby jet, a form of fossilized coal found near Whitby in

> ## Acrostic Jewelry
>
> Acrostic jewelry is a type of jewelry exchanged by lovers and spouses that spell out words in acrostic form—the first letters of the gems used to make the jewelry spell out words. For example, the word "dearest" would be fashioned from a diamond, emerald, amethyst, ruby, emerald, sapphire, and topaz when the stones were viewed from left to right. Other popular words included "adore," "love," and "regard." The trend for acrostic jewelry began in the Georgian period and continued throughout the Victorian era. Today, there is a resurgence of interest in acrostic jewelry at auction with prices ranging from $1,000 to $5,000.

Yorkshire in northern England. Then, after the death of her beloved husband Prince Albert, Queen Victoria decided to wear all black clothing and matching mourning jewelry for many years. The queen also made her courtiers dress in black to show their sadness at Albert's death. Queen Victoria's decision to wear mourning jewelry prompted others to adopt the trend and black jewelry became extremely fashionable. The most popular type of mourning jewelry was that made out of Whitby jet. However Whitby jet was an expensive material. Less expensive mourning jewelry was made from black enamel or glass, a type of hardened rubber called vulcanite or bog oak which was not truly black in color but rather a subdued dark brown that was deemed suitably dark to express the somberness of mourning.

Another type of mourning jewelry was hairwork, which became fashionable around the 1840s. This was jewelry (usually necklaces, rings, and bracelets) made either from human hair, often taken from people that had recently died, though horsehair was also used. In fact, at one point hairwork jewelry was so fashionable in Victorian England that 50 tons of human hair had to be imported into the country so that jewelry manufacturers could keep up with demand. The leading manufacturers of hairwork jewelry were Forrer based in London, and Lemonier and Charleux based in Paris. When making hairwork jewelry, the deceased's initials were often woven into the design of the jewelry so that the mourner associated the item of jewelry with the recently deceased. Another trend in mourning jewelry was lockets, a type of necklace or brooch that contains a photograph or relic of the dead, often a lock of hair or a scrap of clothing of the deceased. Photograph lockets evolved from the practice of painted miniature portraits that had been popular at the end of the 18th century. Other forms of mourning jewelry included cameos carved with an image of the deceased and jewelry featuring silhouettes of the dead. So-called Berlin ironwork jewelry was also commonly used as mourning jewelry. This type of jewelry was made from iron and was very popular during the Gothic Revival experienced in Britain during the 1820s. As the jewelry was made from durable iron and was a very dark grey-black color such jewelry was often worn during times of mourning.

Very similar to mourning jewelry is sentimental jewelry. Indeed sometimes mourning jewelry may be classed as a type of sentimental jewelry. Types of sentimental jewelry include items containing the hair of loved ones, especially fiancés, spouses, and children.

See also: Fantasy Coffins; Goth Subculture; *Malagan*; *Memento Mori* and *Vanitas*; Taxidermy; Wearing Flowers to Honor War Dead; Wedding Dress and Wedding Ring (Volume 2)

Further Reading

Bell, Jeanne C. *Answers to Questions About Old Jewelry 1840–1950*. Eighth edition. Iowa, WI: Krause Publications, 2014.

Lambert, C. S. *A Passion for Sea Glass*. Rockport, ME: Down East, 2008.

Liquid Soul Gifts. "Tear Bottles: A Captivating & Poignant History." TearBottle.com. Accessed April 12, 2015, at http://www.tearbottle.com.

Keister, Douglas. *Stories in Stone: A Field Guide to Cemetery Symbolism and Iconography*. Layton, UT: Gibbs Smith Publisher, 2004.

Market Street Media LLC. "Antique Mourning Jewelry." Collectors Weekly. Accessed April 11, 2015, at http://www.collectorsweekly.com/fine-jewelry/mourning.

Miller, Judith. *Collector's Guides: Costume Jewellery*. London: Dorling Kindersley Limited, 2003.

VictorianGothic.org. "The Enigmatic Lachrymatory, or Tear Bottle," July 23, 2011. Accessed April 11, 2015, at http://www.victoriangothic.org/the-elusive-lachrymatory-or-tear-bottle/.

TẾT NGUYÊN ĐAN, VIETNAM

Tết Nguyên đan (first morning of the first day) is the spring festival that forms an important part of the Vietnamese lunar year and is central to the country's cultural identity. Tết Nguyên đan, which is often shortened to Tết, is a festive, fun occasion that ushers in the New Year. The event also marks the official birthday of every Vietnamese individual. According to the solar calendar, Tết Nguyên đan occurs between January 21 and February 19, on the night of the new moon. The new moon is important because according to the lunar calendar each month starts with a new moon, as does every new year. Therefore by the lunar calendar, Tết falls on the first day of the first month of the year.

Celebrations to honor the start of a new year are found worldwide. Some are religious, others are totally secular, but they all reveal the significance attached to the renewal and continuance of the cycle of life. In short, all new year festivities worldwide can be considered a rite of passage for entire communities. However in Vietnam New Year celebrations are not only a national rite of passage but also a cause for individual birthday celebrations. This is reflected in the customary greetings spoken during Tết Nguyên đan. For example, *Chúc Mừng Năm Mới* and *Cung Chúc Tân Xuân* wish both a healthy, happy year, and by association, happy birthday.

Though Tết is a form of birthday celebration, the number of years a person has lived is considered unimportant compared with the significance of the year in which he or she was born. In Vietnamese cosmology, an animal race was instigated by the Chinese Jade Emperor, a demigod who founded the Chinese civilization and was lord of the cosmos and underworld, with the first animals to finish the race going on to represent a year in the cycle of the zodiac. The Vietnamese substituted the ox of the Chinese zodiac with a water buffalo and the Chinese rabbit with a cat, possibly because cats were regarded as pets in Vietnam. Consequently, every year-animal is thought to mold a person's character and also his or her life pattern. This interconnectedness of humans, the cosmos, the spiritual world, and animals is reflected by the way in which the Vietnamese celebrate Tết and also demonstrates how Vietnamese traditions are indebted to Chinese culture yet have been shaped to conform to the animistic and pastoral lifestyles of southeast Asia.

There are three stages to Tết Nguyên đan. The first is Tết Nien, a seven-day celebration that is held before *Giao Thua* (New Year's Eve), which is the second stage, and *Tan Nien*. Tết Nien sees the Vietnamese unite in rituals that clear the way for the strike of midnight when the old year ends and the new year arrives. In order to see in the new year, all bad luck must be eradicated. As it may take some time to eliminate the bad luck, people leave work early or take the entire day off while school children take a break. Instead of working and studying everyone goes shopping for new clothes, pays off debts, returns loaned goods, and prepares food for the upcoming feast. The traditional food associated with this time is *banh chung* (called *banh tet* in Vietnam's south), a square cake made of glutinous rice, pork, and yellow mung bean paste that is wrapped in bamboo leaves, tied with bamboo strings, and steamed. According to Vietnamese legend, banh chung was invented over 2,000 years ago by a prince of the Hung dynasty who had fallen on hard times. However when his father the king tasted the cake he was so impressed with the cake's simplicity that he named the prince as his heir. Banh chung is only made at Tết symbolic of the Vietnamese people's thankfulness for the abundance of food in the world. All generations of a family participate in making banh chung and there is much excitement in during the wrapping of the cake and steaming process. The cake takes on a green color during cooking and to buy a good-quality cake is extremely cheap, costing around $1. Moon cakes called Bahn *Trung Thu* are also eaten during Tết, sometimes featuring an egg yolk, nuts, or lotus paste in their center. Another traditional sweet eaten at Tết is *miet Tết*, a fruit confectionary made from root ginger, banana, and pumpkin, sometimes with flower blossoms added. On the last day of the old year, Vietnamese families leave miet Tết on the graves of their ancestors as they believe that the sweets will feed the awakened ancestral spirits.

The Vietnamese also leave out sweets for the festival of *Ong Tao*, held seven days before the new moon on the 23rd day of the year's 12th month. During the festival of Ong Tao the household spirits of the hearth or kitchen are said to journey to

> ### The Largest *Tết Nguyên đan* Celebrations in the United States
>
> The city of Garden Grove, California, is the site for the largest *Tết Nguyên đan* celebrations outside of Vietnam. The festivities are overseen by the Union of Vietnamese Student Associations of Southern California, which donates much of the money raised by the event to local cultural organizations. The Californian *Tết Nguyên đan* celebrations last for three days and are very well attended with some 100,000 people believed to have attended the festivities in 2012. Organizers of the event aim to maintain Vietnamese cultural traditions through a combination of live music, dance, food, and other forms of entertainment.

heaven to inform the Jade Emperor of family affairs so that the future of the families can be predicted. Families clean ancestral graves and sweep their homes on the last days of the old year as they fear that sweeping at the start of the new year will brush away Thần Tài, the God of Luck, who brings financial fortunes to families in a new year. The Vietnamese fear that if Thần Tài is expelled they will experience financial hardship. Thus despite being very busy shopping, cooking, and so on to prepare for Tết, the Vietnamese find time to clean their homes before the new year begins. While the women of the household clean the home, the man of each house, usually the father/husband, cleans the ancestral altar to show respect to the dead. The man also sets up *mâm ngũ quả* (the tray of five fruits). This is an essential part of Tết and the five fruits, each a different color, represent the five natural elements: metal, wood, water, fire, and earth. Each element is imbued with meaning or can be wished upon to bring forth wealth, luxury, longevity, health, peace, and the like.

Once the houses are clean they are filled with *cay neu* (decorated Tết trees), flowers, and red ornaments as symbol of Tết in much the same way as Christmas trees and decorations are erected in the West. Vietnamese families, especially those in the north of the country, plant the cay neu, a very tall bamboo tree, in front of their homes in order to keep at bay wayward spirits. The bamboo tree is stripped of all its leaves apart from a tuft at the very top and it is decorated with gongs, bows, bells and arrows plus red paper for good luck that are akin to Western Christmas decorations. In Vietnamese culture, both the cay neu and the color red are said to scare off evil spirits. In other parts of Vietnam families bring peach trees covered in blossom into the home to see off evil or nurture a kumquat tree to encourage flowers, buds, and fruit to grow signifying the continuance of the families' lineage and wealth for the golden fruit of the kumquat and peach, both signify coins. Families also shape the kumquat tree so that it is symmetrical. This symmetry symbolizes the strength of family relationships. Once the trees are erected, red banners are hung up plus good-luck charms, usually cockerels or a trinity of male figures representing wealth, joy, and longevity.

Giao Thea, or New Year's Eve, is a time of merriment and sees people dress in their best clothes. There is dancing, music, gambling on street games such as *bầu cua cá cọp*, poetry, flower arrangements, and a distinctive air of optimism. There are also noisy parades featuring dancers performing in the guise of a *lan*, a creature akin to a cross between a lion and a dragon. The raucous parades aim to drive away evil spirits. Many dinner parties are held too, for the last meal of the year is another important part of family celebrations for families gather together to eat and reminisce about the events of year. Families also watch television programs together including special music shows and art programs, as well as the comedy show "*Gặp nhau cuối năm*," in which famous Vietnamese comedians pretend to be Ong Tao explaining the events of the year to the Jade Emperor in a sarcastic way. It is also usual nowadays to play the ABBA song "Happy New Year."

The stroke of midnight is marked by drumming and the striking of gongs that the Vietnamese see as a way to greet the Ong Tao who they believe return to earth at this moment having met with the Jade Emperor. Midnight also sees every Vietnamese family pray in front of their family altar, which they re-locate to the front of their homes for the occasion. Praying at the ancestral altar is a meaningful custom as the prayers call forth ancestral spirits to unite with the living family so that the dead and the living can welcome the new year together. Most Vietnamese also take this opportunity to make private wishes a year of good health, good fortune, and happiness. To mark the new year, many families also gather in large cities to watch firework displays—firecrackers were banned in 1995 so to enjoy new year fireworks revelers tend to travel to major cities. Another ritual to greet the new year is *Tet Trung Thu* during which children hang rice paper lanterns shaped like stars and fish on long bamboo poles

In Vietnam, the first three days of the new year, Tan Nien, are thought to set the pattern for the rest of the year so people avoid rows, cursing or breaking anything as they believe these could all bring bad luck to a household. On the first day of Tan Nien people invite the most auspicious people they know, usually a husband's best friends, into their home. The first visitor to the home on the morning of Tan Nien is considered very significant—it is preferred that the person be respected, happily married, and wealthy so that the person can bring his or her good fortune to the family whose home the guest is entering. If the family suffers bad luck during the year, they will consider it the fault of their visitor. The first day of Tan Nien also sees the telling of moral stories and the imparting of advice and children are traditionally given *Li Xi*, lucky money presented in red envelopes. Older women choose this day to travel to Ho Chi Min City (formerly Saigon), Vietnam's largest city in order to perform pagoda pilgrimage.

On the second day of Tan Nien the wife's family and friends visit the home along with other guests. Finally, on the third day of Tan Nien, which is also the last day of Tết, families invite teachers, colleagues, and so on into their homes. This event is marked by the consumption of watermelon, the red flesh of the fruit redolent of good luck. This is the day when ancestral spirits are thought to journey back to heaven so families visit the graves of their ancestors that they bedeck with flowers, candles, and miniature paper cars and clothes that are later burned so that they too may ascend to the heavens. Ancestral graves are also purified using incense. Many Buddhists also use this time of reflection to go to temples where they pray and have their fortunes told.

After the third day of Tan Nien Tết festivities wind down. Most of Vietnam, apart from Ho Chi Min City and surrounding areas, sees all cay neu taken down to signify the end of Tết. However in some urban areas of Vietnam Tết may continue until the first full moon of the year as the moon travels across the country.

See also: All Souls' Day; Birthday Cakes (Volume 1); Birthdays (Volume 1); Birthstones (Volume 1); *Qingming* Festival

Further Reading

Dodd, Jan, and Mark Lewis. *The Rough Guide to Vietnam*. Fourth edition. London: Rough Guides Ltd., 2003.
Galvan, Javier A., ed. *They Do What? A Cultural Encyclopedia of Extraordinary and Exotic Customs from around the World*. Santa Barbara, CA: ABC-CLIO, 2014.
Jones, Alison. *Larousse Dictionary of World Folklore*. Edinburgh, UK: Larousse, 1996.
The Ravenous Couple. "Banh Trung Thu Mid Autumn Festival Moon Cakes." September 14, 2010. Accessed June 7, 2016, at http://www.theravenouscouple.com/2010/09/banh-trung-thu-mid-autumn-festival-moon-cakes.html.
Rough Guides Limited. "Vietnam: Festivals and Religious Events." Accessed January 1, 2015, at http://www.roughguides.com/destinations/asia/vietnam/festivals-and-religious-events/.
Vietnam Beauty.com. "The Meaning of 'Cay Neu'." December 10, 2008. Accessed January 1, 2015, at http://www.vietnam-beauty.com/vietnamese-culture/vietnam-culture-value/227-the-meaning-of-cay-neu.html.
Vietnam Online. "Vietnamese New Year (Tet)." Vietnam Travel & Living Guide. Accessed January 1, 2015, at http://www.vietnamonline.com/tet.html.

TOMB OF THE UNKNOWN SOLDIER, INTERNATIONAL

A Tomb of the Unknown Soldier is a monument dedicated to the memory of unknown soldiers killed in warfare that also functions as a commemorative to the memories of all soldiers killed in all wars. Many such tombs exist around the world and are usually high-profile national monuments that act as the centerpiece to nation events of remembrance.

After World War I, a movement arose in the United Kingdom to commemorate the unidentified war dead with a single tomb housing the remains of one anonymous soldier. One of the many tragedies of World War I (1914–1918) was that so many of those who died in battle did not receive a permanent grave, meaning families lacked a focal point for their mourning. Many corpses were buried in makeshift graves with simple markers for headstones that became lost or damaged during battle. Some war dead were also buried in mass graves, their identities lost forever. Other soldiers were simply listed as "missing." Sometimes this was a euphemism for saying that there were no remains, that remains were impossible to identify, or that they were presumed dead as they had been trapped in collapsed underground tunneling operations or had drowned in mud-filled shell-craters. However the term was also used to refer to soldiers whose identity was simply unknown. In total, it is believed that 17 million soldiers and civilians died during the conflict, though even today, these figures are a matter of conjecture.

In 1916, a Church of England clergyman serving on the Western Front, Reverend David Railton, realized that families found the lack of permanent graves profoundly upsetting and, on seeing an inscription on an anonymous grave in Armentieres in France, came up with the concept of the Tomb of the Unknown Soldier. The inscription that so struck Railton read, "An Unknown British Soldier." In 1920, Railton wrote to Herby Ryle, Dean of Westminster Abbey in London, the capital of England, suggesting that a single tomb be created within Westminster Abbey containing an unidentified British soldier. This soldier would then be symbolic of all those missing and killed during the conflict. This suggestion, which echoed an idea proposed by the British newspaper, the *Daily Express* in 1919, was accepted by the British government and plans for the soldier's burial were implemented. However authorities could not decide how to select an individual unknown soldier to bury within the tomb so in the end it was decided that unidentified copses from several battlefields in the Aisne, the Somme, and Arras in France, and Ypres, Belgium, would be placed on gurneys and left at Saint-Pol-sur-Ternoise, near the town of Arras, on November 7, 1920. Then, Brigadier-General L. J. Wyatt and Lieutenant-Colonel E. A. S. Gell from the Directorate of Graves Registration would select the body—this selection was achieved by Wyatt placing his hand on one of the corpses. Neither Wyatt nor Gell had any idea about the soldiers' identities as they were covered by Union Jacks (i.e., British flags). This selection process was followed so that issues of rank, politics, or class could not be said to have been determining factors in choosing the corpse. The officers placed the chosen corpse in an unmarked coffin and reburied the other bodies. The next day, the unknown soldier began his journey to Westminster Abbey, en route being placed inside another coffin this time made from oak taken from the royal palace of Hampton Court and bearing the inscription, "A British Warrior who fell in the Great War 1914–1918 for King and Country." A 16th-century sword donated from King George V's private collection also embellished the second coffin. The coffin arrived in London on November 11, 1920, where it was transported through the capital's streets on a horse-drawn gun carriage until it arrived at the Cenotaph (Greek for empty tomb), the war memorial situated in Whitehall that plays host to the annual Remembrance Service. Londoners looked on in silence out of respect as the coffin went through the streets with many bereaved onlookers wondering if it was the corpse of somebody they knew inside. Eventually, the coffin arrived at Westminster Abbey where it passed through a guard of honor consisting of 100 holders of the Victoria Cross, the highest military decoration awarded to members of the British and Commonwealth armed forces for valor in the face of the enemy. The coffin was then buried at the far west end of the abbey's nave, in soil taken from a battlefield, and is now known as The Tomb of the Unknown Warrior. (*See* Plate 20.) In a unique simultaneous event of remembrance an unidentified French soldier was also buried in La Tombe Du Soldate Inconnu at the Arc de Triomphe in Paris, the capital of France. The first eternal flame to be lit in Europe is to be found at this memorial, placed there in memory of the dead who were never identified. The flame is lit in honor of France's war dead every evening at 6:30 p.m. and war veterans lay wreaths decorated with red, white, and blue, the colors of the French flag, near the base of the flame. The Italian Tomb of the Unknown Soldier also has an eternal flame. This tomb is located at the Monumento Nazionale a Vittorio Emanuele II, also known as Altare della Patria (Altar of the Fatherland) in Rome, Italy's capital city. The tomb was built after World War I and the unknown soldier was buried there in a state funeral on November 4, 1921. Another European Tomb of the Unknown Soldier featuring an eternal flame is The Monument to the Unknown Soldier located in Sofia, the capital of Bulgaria, opened officially on September 22, 1981, to honor the hundreds of thousands of Bulgarian soldiers who have died in wars defending their homeland. The monument also features grass transplanted from Stara Zagora and Shipka Pass, the locations of two important battles of the Russo-Turkish War of Liberation—the Battle of Stara Zagora and the Battle of Shipka Pass—as well as a sculpture of a lion, a national symbol of Bulgaria. After the end of World War I, a group of Bulgarians suggested that a monument should be erected to the dead. However there was strong opposition to this suggestion from Bulgarian intellectuals who thought the concept of a tomb to an unknown soldier implied that the names of the soldiers had been forgotten. This controversy resulted in the monument being designed but not displayed. Even after the monument was unveiled the sculpted lion was singled out for years of abuse because it was depicted sitting and some people saw this pose as a metaphor for military surrender.

While the British unknown soldier was laid to rest with great ceremony, the authorities did not know how the public would take to the memorial. In fact, the British responded positively to the new monument for it has been estimated that in one week 1,250,000 people came to see the tomb. In October 1921, the British unknown soldier was awarded the U.S. Medal of Honor that now hangs on a pillar near his tomb. One month later the British gave a Victoria Cross to the United States' unknown soldier who was buried on top of a hill in the Arlington National Cemetery in March 1921. Nearly one hundred years later the British soldier continues to be honored by governments, royalty and the general public. This was seen on August 4, 2014, when a candle-lit vigil of prayer and reflection was held at Tomb of the Unknown Soldier to commemorate the start of World War I. Later that day, during the Westminster Abbey service to commemorate the start of World War I, an oil lamp was snuffed out at the grave of the unknown soldier at 11 p.m., which was the exact hour that the start of the war was declared.

There are several British royal customs associated with The Tomb of the Unknown Warrior at Westminster Abbey. When Elizabeth Bowes-Lyon married the future King George VI on April 26, 1923, the future queen consort laid her bouquet at the tomb on her way into the Abbey in tribute to her brother Fergus who had died at the Battle of Loos in 1915—before her death, Elizabeth Bowes-Lyon, by then known as the Queen Mother, instructed her daughter Elizabeth II to lay her funeral wreath on the tomb, a wish with which the queen complied the day after her mother's funeral. Ever since, it has been the tradition for royal brides married at Westminster Abbey to have their wedding bouquets laid on the tomb the day after the wedding when all official wedding photographs have been taken. In addition, it is traditional for the red carpets laid during royal weddings not to cover the tomb. Another custom associated with The Tomb of the Unknown Warrior is that heads of state visiting the United Kingdom lay a wreath on the grave in honor of the unknown warrior and all those represented by the grave.

The symbolism of the British Tomb of the Unknown Soldier at Westminster Abbey has been mirrored in other nations for countries in Europe, Africa, Asia, the Middle East, Oceania, Australasia, North America, and South America all have their own memorial to an unknown soldier that is representative of all their people killed in war. In contrast to prevailing feelings in the United Kingdom, Commonwealth countries, and France that made people want to honor the nations' war dead, in 1920s Germany the mood was one of despondency and defeat, which was not helped by economic difficulties and political uncertainty. This mood changed in the 1930s and in 1931 architect Heinrich Tessanow was commissioned by the Prussian government to convert the Neue Wache in the Unter Den Linden boulevard in Berlin into what is known as the "Memorial for the Fallen of the War." The Neue Wache had once been a Prussian guardhouse and it was adapted to resemble a tomb, with a central plinth. Later the Memorial to the Fallen of the War became a centerpiece of Nazi culture and Third Reich grandees were regularly photographed paying their respects at the monument, while rank and file Nazis were pictured saluting the memorial. The Neue Wache was badly damaged in the Battle for Berlin in April–May 1945, and after 1945 formed part of the Russian Zone, that eventually became East Germany. The memorial was guarded by East German soldiers and renamed as the Memorial to the Victims of Fascism and Militarism. When the Berlin Wall came down and Germany was unified the Neue Wache was again rededicated, this time as the Central Memorial of the Federal Republic of Germany for the Victims of War and Tyranny, the focus of which was a sculpture by German artist Käthe Kollwitz. The Tessanow plinth had long since been removed, though its bronze wreath is preserved in the Deutsches Historiches Museum.

In Australia, an unidentified soldier was interred as recently as 1993 at the Australian War Memorial, situated in Australia's capital city, Canberra. The idea of honoring an unknown Australian soldier was first proposed in the 1920s. However, it was not until 1993 that an unknown corpse was at last brought home. In order to mark the 75th anniversary of the end of the World War I, an unidentified Australian soldier's corpse was exhumed from Adelaide Cemetery near Villers-Bretonneaux in France and transported back to Australia. The body lay in state in King's Hall in Old Parliament House and was then buried in the Hall of Memory on November 11, 1993. The coffin was buried with a bayonet and a sprig of wattle and soil from the Pozières battlefield in France was scattered in the tomb. The tomb of the unknown soldier is set into a recess made of granite, suggesting the grave within the ground.

In Canada, an unknown representative soldier was buried in Ottawa in 2000 at the suggestion of the Royal Canadian Legion and other groups. The unknown soldier was selected from among Canada's 6,846 unknown soldiers of World War I and reinterred at the National War Memorial in Ottawa. The chosen unknown soldier was exhumed from a cemetery near Vimy Ridge, the site of part of the Battle of Arras in which four Canadian army divisions fought, and transported to Canada where he lay in state in the Hall of Honour in the Centre Block of Parliament from May 25 to May 28, 2000. In order to show their respect for the soldier, many thousands of Canadians filed past his coffin before his internment on May 28, 2000, a ceremony televised nationwide. Since then, the site has become an important focus of national commemoration, particularly in the national Remembrance Day service held at the National War Memorial on November 11 annually.

In 2004, New Zealand exhumed remains from the Caterpillar Valley Cemetery in the Somme region of France that was the location of fierce fighting during World War I. The body of this unknown soldier was buried at the National War Memorial in Wellington, the capital of New Zealand, in order to symbolize the sacrifice made by all New Zealand servicemen and women. This Unknown Warrior is one of almost 30,000 New Zealanders who died in warfare, and one of almost 9,000 without a known grave. The unknown soldier was repatriated on November 10, 2004, and was honored with campaign medals from both World Wars, the Operational Service Medal and the Royal New Zealand Returned & Services Association's highest award, the Badge in Gold, during a welcoming ceremony. Estimates suggest that around 10,000 people lined up to pay their respects to the unknown warrior during the Lying-in-State vigil that preceded his reburial. On November 11, Armistice Day, after a Memorial Service at the Cathedral of St. Paul, the unknown warrior's corpse was given a full military funeral procession through Wellington to the National War Memorial where it underwent a final interment ceremony. It is thought that 100,000 people watched the procession, which walked to a specially composed slow-time march entitled "Fernleaf Headstones." The burial ceremony included a eulogy, a poetry reading, and the singing of a choral lament of Timothy Hurd's "Memento for an Unknown Warrior." The unknown soldier was laid to rest in his new grave, which featured text of a *karanga* (Māori calls of welcome that can pay tribute to the dead).

A similar London monument to the Tomb of the Unknown Warrior is The Tower Hill Memorial, a Commonwealth War Graves Commission war memorial located on the south side of Trinity Square Gardens. This memorial commemorates those from the civilian Merchant Navy and Fishing Fleets who died during both World Wars and have, in the words of the memorial inscription, "no grave but the sea."

See also: "Abide With Me"; Chelsea Pensioners; Eulogy; "The Last Post" and "Taps"; Minute's Silence; Remembrance Day and Remembrance Sunday; Royal Wootton Bassett; State Funeral; Wearing Flowers to Honor War Dead

Further Reading

Australian War Memorial. "Tomb of the Unknown Australian Soldier." Accessed January 9, 2015, at https://www.awm.gov.au/visit/hall-of-memory/tomb/.

Cacciottolo, Mario. "The Unknown Soldier's Journey from Trench to Tomb." *BBC News Magazine*, November 11, 2010. Accessed January 9, 2015, at http://www.bbc.co.uk/news/magazine-11710660.

Canadian Museum of History. "The Unknown Soldier." Accessed January 9, 2015, at http://www.warmuseum.ca/firstworldwar/history/after-the-war/remembrance/the-unknown-soldier/.

Commonwealth War Graves Commission. "Tower Hill Memorial." Accessed January 9, 2015, at http://www.cwgc.org/find-a-cemetery/cemetery/90002/TOWER%20HILL%20MEMORIAL.

Gillis, John R., ed. *Commemorations: The Politics of National Identity*. Princeton, NJ: Princeton University Press, 1994.

Greatwar.co.uk. "War Graves for WW1 on The Western Front." The Great War 1914–1918. Accessed January 9, 2015, at http://www.greatwar.co.uk/article/ww1-war-graves.htm.

Manatū Taonga, Ministry for Culture & Heritage. "Tomb of the Unknown Warrior." Pukeahu National War Memorial Park, September 29, 2014. Accessed January 9, 2015, at http://www.mch.govt.nz/nz-identity-heritage/national-war-memorial/tomb-unknown-warrior.

McNab, Chris. *The Book of the Poppy*. Stroud, UK: The History Press, 2014.

OpenBuildings. "Monument to the Unknown Soldier, Sofia." Accessed January 9, 2015, at http://openbuildings.com/buildings/monument-to-the-unknown-soldier-sofia-profile-34782.

Sommecourt. "Germany's Unknown Soldier." Military Berlin, October 31, 2011. Accessed January 9, 2015, at https://militaryberlin.wordpress.com/2011/10/31/germanys-unknown-soldier/.

Vivaboo. "Tomb of the Unknown Soldier around the World (History)." Accessed January 9, 2015, at http://www.vivaboo.com/tomb-of-the-unknown-soldier/.

Wittman, Laura. *The Tomb of the Unknown Soldier, Modern Mourning, and the Reinvention of the Mystical Body*. Toronto, Canada: University of Toronto Press Incorporated, 2011.

TOMBSTONE TOURISM, INTERNATIONAL

Some cemeteries attract visitors that are in no way connected to the people buried within the grounds of the graveyard. People that have a greater than average interest in visiting graveyards are sometimes referred to as tombstone tourists or as taphophiles. This word derives from taphophilia, that is, a love of visiting graveyards and interest in all aspects of funerals, graveyard art, and so on. The word taphophile comes from the Greek words for tomb, *taph,* and *philia,* meaning an abnormal love of something. Connected to tombstone tourism is so-called dark tourism that sees people visit sites associated with murders, disasters, wars, assassinations, massacres, and genocide. People that are classed as taphophiles or as dark tourists are sometimes considered to be part of the Goth subculture.

> ### Temple Church's Templar Effigies
>
> The 12th-century Temple Church in central London is home to nine effigies of Knights Templar, medieval soldier-monks. All the knights are depicted lying on their backs, but each is otherwise positioned in a unique manner: some are straight-legged or cross-legged while others have extended legs, some wear tunics over armor while others sport long robes. Additionally, some of the knights clasp swords, while others are shown praying or have their arms by their sides. The oldest effigy dates from 1227. The church is open to the public and became a tourist attraction after being referenced in Dan Brown's novel *The Da Vinci Code*.

Apart from visiting loved ones, people visit graveyards for a number of reasons including an interest in hobbies such as gravestone rubbing, photography, and art, or to discover something about history. Indeed tombstone tourists can be interested in the historical aspects of a graveyard as well as the historical relevance of its inhabitants. For this reason, certain graveyards around the world have become major tourist destinations.

The world's most visited graveyard is the Cimetière du Père Lachaise, often referred to as simply Père-Lachaise, in Paris, the capital of France. Père-Lachaise opened in 1804 and is home to 70,000 elaborate tombs set among 44-hectares of sculpted gardens. Many of the inhabitants of Père-Lachaise are extremely famous, including writers such as Oscar Wilde, Marcel Proust, Gertrude Stein, and Molière; artists including Eugène Delacroix, Camille Pissarro, Georges Seurat, and Gustave Doré; the composers Frédéric Chopin and Georges Bizet; singers including Jim Morrison of the Doors, Yves Montand, and Edith Piaf; and dancer Isadora Duncan. The most visited graves are those belonging to Jim Morrison and Oscar Wilde. Père-Lachaise is also the location to poignant memorials to the many of thousands of French Jews that died when they were deported to Nazi death camps. Another historical aspect of Père-Lachaise is the *Mur des Fédérés* (Wall of the Federalists) that marks the ultimately futile battle between rebels and government forces fought on the night of May 27, 1871. Having fought among the tombstones the insurgents conceded and in the morning, the 147 surviving insurgents were lined up against a wall of the cemetery, shot, and buried in a mass grave.

England's capital city, London, is home to the famous Highgate Cemetery. Highgate Cemetery, which is located in north London and is divided into two parts named the East Cemetery and the West Cemetery, has been designated Grade I on the Historic England Register of Parks and Gardens of Special Historic Interest in England. The cemetery is home to around 170,000 bodies that are interred in 53,000 graves. Notable people buried at Highgate Cemetery include political philosopher Karl Marx, scientist Michael Faraday, authors Douglas Adams and George Eliot, poet Christian Rossetti and actors Corin Redgrave and Sir Ralph Richardson. There is also a so-called Fireman's Corner dedicated to the London Fire Brigade.

Highgate Cemetery is a notable tourist attraction because of the number of people buried within its walls, its status as a sort of nature reserve, and as a prime example of Victorian Gothic architecture that is often used as a film location especially for horror films such as *Taste the Blood of Dracula* (1970), *The Abominable Dr. Phibes* (1971), *Tales from the Crypt* (1972), *From Beyond the Grave* (1974), and *Shaun of the Dead* (2002).

While Highgate Cemetery is famed for its melancholy beauty, another famous graveyard the so-called Merry Cemetery (*Cimitirul Vesel*) in Săpânța, Romania, is known for the cheerfulness and color of its carved wooden tombstones. (*See* Plate 21.) Indeed the Merry Cemetery has been dubbed the world's funniest cemetery. The Merry Cemetery has around 800 colorful grave markers that depict the deceased either as they were in life or at the moment that they died. Each tombstone is accompanied by a simple poem that acts as a final apology for the ordinariness of the dead person's life. According to ethnologists, the cheerfulness of the Merry Cemetery reflects the attitudes held by the early inhabitants of Romania known as the Dacians, who, according to the classical historian Herodotus, were fearless in battle and went happily to their graves because they understood that when they died they would meet their supreme god Zalmoxis. This cheerfulness in the face of death entered into local folklore and ever since the inhabitants of Săpânța have looked on death with ironic amusement. The Merry Cemetery itself was not, however, founded until the 1930s by a local craftsman called Stan Ioan Patras. The grave markers in the Merry Cemetery are carved by hand from planks of local oak that are painted blue and decorated with floral borders. On the grave markers local men use brightly colored paint to depict the dead in wryly mundane images such as women weaving, farmers riding tractors, and teachers sitting at desks. The bright colors fade quickly in the harsh local climate, however, meaning that the grave markers need to be repainted every 15 years.

See also: Changing of the Guard Ceremony; Fantasy Coffins; Goth Subculture; *Mirila*; Mortuary Totem Poles; Ossuaries; Spontaneous Shrines; Suicide Landmarks; Tomb of the Unknown Soldier

Further Reading

Benjamin, Kathy. *Funerals to Die For: The Craziest, Creepiest, and Most Bizarre Funeral Traditions and Practices Ever*. Avon, MA: F+W Media Inc., 2013.

Friends of Highgate Cemetery Trust. "Who's Here?" Highgate Cemetery. Accessed October 19, 2015, at http://highgatecemetery.org/visit/who#architecture.

Green, Peter S. "Sapanta Journal: You'll Die Laughing, if You're Not Already Dead," *New York Times*, May 29, 2002. Accessed October 19, 2015, at http://www.nytimes.com/2002/05/29/world/sapanta-journal-you-ll-die-laughing-if-you-re-not-already-dead.html.

Lonely Planet. "Cimetière du Père Lachaise." Lonely Planet: Paris, 2015. Accessed October 19, 2015, at http://www.lonelyplanet.com/france/paris/sights/cemeteries-memorials-tombs/cimetiere-du-pere-lachaise.

Soper, Steve. "Père-Lachaise." Paris Cemeteries. Accessed October 19, 2015, at http://www.pariscemeteries.com/pere-lachaise.

White, Leanne, and Elspeth Frew, eds. *Dark Tourism and Place Identity: Managing and Interpreting Dark Places*. Abingdon, UK: Routledge, 2013.

TONGAN FUNERALS, TONGA

In the South Pacific nation of Tonga funerals (*putu*) are extremely elaborate events and a source of national pride. Until Christianity became prevalent on the 177-island nation, Tongan funerals were focused on the tradition Tongan afterlife known as *Pulotu*. Christianity, specifically the state church called the Free Wesleyan Church, is now widespread throughout Tonga meaning Tonga is the only nation in the world that has a state religion belonging to the Methodist tradition. However though the spread of Christianity in Tonga means that Pulotu has been replaced with the concept of heaven in much of Tongan philosophy, the idea of Pulotu is still a major element of the songs, poetry, and imagery of modern-day Tongan funerals. Tongans view funerals as an ideal time to reaffirm old traditions and ensure that Tongan heritage is passed on to the next generation of islanders. While Tongans see funerals as an important time to strengthen kinship ties, recently the emphasis has been placed on strengthening bonds within the nuclear family rather than the *kāinga*, or extended network of relatives and kinship groups.

Another major factor of Tongan funerals is subject and social status. Such issues mean little in everyday Tongan life but are considered very important at Tongan funerals. People attending a Tongan funeral are ranked according to their social status and their relationship with the deceased. High-ranking attendees are known as *fahu* with high-ranking relatives referred to as *eiki*. Both groups are accorded certain rights and privileges and asked to perform duties during the funeral ceremony such as preparing the corpse for burial. Moreover, the highest-ranking member of the fahu is required to sit next to the corpse's head. A member of the fahu is also responsible for sprinkling a liquid called *loloku* that is believe to dispel taboos.

Lower-ranking guests are referred to as *liongi* and are given other, more menial, tasks to fulfill during the funeral. For instance, female liongi have to cook food for mourners. Mourners that are neither classed as liongi nor fahu are considered *kāinga* and are required to utter noisy laments for the dead as well as to give the deceased a farewell kiss.

A Tongan funeral begins with a wake called an *'āpō*. This takes place in the dead person's home and is attended by everybody that was in some way linked to the deceased so that they may pay their respects to the dead. During the wake relatives deemed to be liongi stay outside of the building preparing refreshments for the guests while all other relatives of the deceased watch over the corpse and greet mourners. When the mourners have arrived, a ritual gift giving called *koloa* takes place. Koloa translates as wealth or valuables and the gifts given by mourners to the deceased's family during this ritual traditionally include bark cloth and woven mats. These gifts are not kept by the deceased's family however as they are redistributed a few days afterward.

According to Tongan tradition, the funeral should be held within three days of the 'āpō, though in recent years this tradition has relaxed somewhat to allow relatives living overseas time to reach the island for the funeral. In such cases the corpse remains in the hospital mortuary until the funeral occurs. The body may be placed in a coffin or wrapped in a *tapa* or *ngatu,* a fabric made from tree bark that is reserved for special occasions.

Tongan graves, which are normally located within forests of frangipani trees, are considered an art form by some people. The graves take the form of hillocks of white sand that are decorated by women, traditionally with the addition of coral, flowers, black volcanic rocks, and seashells but increasingly with items that reveal the modernization of the country and changing tastes such as syringes and beer bottles that are placed on the sand graves with much care. Sometimes the graves are also painted in the national Tongan colors of white and red.

After the body has been buried, the head of the deceased's household invites all the community to a banquet and announces how long the period of mourning will last. The wearing of special woven mat around the waist called *ta'ovala putu* marks this time of mourning, as does the banning of all games and frivolity in the local area. The tapa will also be beaten during the period of mourning. After the burial, the deceased's family spends weeks sitting next to the grave only leaving at night for fear of ghouls. The frequency of the family visits declines over the course of about a year until finally the grave is left alone. This is because Tongans believe the spirit of the dead can cause illness among the living leading to death. The family does, however, visit to clean the grave on such important occasions as Christmas Day and All Saints' Day.

Tongan funerals were the subject of much international interest in 2012 when the Tongan king, George Tupou V, was laid to rest in the country's capital Nukuk'alofa. The funeral made headlines due to the island nation's unusual mix of traditional Polynesian and Christian funeral rites, specifically Wesleyan Christian hymns, readings from the Bible, prayers, and eulogies. To mark the occasion, buildings in Nukuk'alofa were draped in black and purple fabric, the nation's mourning colors. 150 pallbearers wearing black shirts and long fringed ta'ovala transported the king's flagged-draped coffin to the Royal Tombs on a black and gold colored catafalque, a type of moveable coffin cradle, weighing five tons. The catafalque was so heavy that 1,000 men were needed to move the coffin and every time one man flagged he was replaced with another. Meanwhile, a military band composed of 200 soldiers walked in front of the funeral procession and church bells tolled a military salute lasting 40 minutes. When the coffin reached the wall of the graveyard it was carried over the wall as is traditional in Tonga. Eventually, the king was laid in a grave next to his grandmother. Once the funeral procession came to a halt a fabric screen was erected so that pre-Christian funeral rites could take place in privacy. These rites were performed to ensure that the king could enter Pulotu, a place that according to Tongan lore, only royalty may enter.

See also: Sakalava Royal Death Traditions and *Fitampoha*; State Funeral; *Tangihanga*: Māori Mourning Ritual; Traditional Mourning Colors

Further Reading

Ember, Carol R., and Melvin Ember, eds. *Encyclopedia of Medical Anthropology: Health and Illness in the World's Cultures Volumes 1–2*. New York: Kluwer Academic/Plenum Publishers, 2004.

Reuters. "Tongan King Laid to Rest in Lavish Funeral," *Irish Times*, March 27, 2012. Accessed September 8, 2015, at http://www.irishtimes.com/news/tongan-king-laid-to-rest-in-lavish-funeral-1.706203.

Shears, Richard. "Tears in Paradise: Tonga's Flamboyant King Given Spectacular Farewell as 150 Pallbearers Carry George V's Coffin to Royal Tombs," *Daily Mail*, March 27, 2012. Accessed September 8, 2015, at http://www.dailymail.co.uk/news/article-2120923/Tongas-King-George-Tupou-V-funeral-150-pallbearers-carry-coffin-Royal-Tombs.html.

Stanley, David. *Tonga-Samoa Handbook*. First edition. Emeryville, CA: Moon Publications Inc., 1999.

Völkel, Svenja. *Social Structure, Space and Possession in Tongan Culture and Language*. Amsterdam, Netherlands: John Benjamins Publishing Co., 2010.

TRADITIONAL MOURNING COLORS, INTERNATIONAL

Around the world a number of different colors are associated with mourning. For instance, the color of mourning in both Mexico and Korea is blue; in Thailand, Tonga, and Brazil it is purple; and in Egypt mourning is signified by yellow. By and large, however, the colors most often traditionally associated with mourning are black, white, and red.

Black is considered the color of mourning in many cultures. For this reason in Europe, North America, and Australasia, close family and friends of the deceased will wear black for a period of time. Moreover, black is a common symbol of widowhood. In Iran, it is traditional for widows to wear black for a minimum of 40 days or up to one year while widows in Russia, the Czech Republic, Slovakia, Greece, Italy, Mexico, Portugal, and Spain begin to wear all-black clothing as soon as they are widowed and, traditionally, should continue to do so for the rest of their lives. The custom of wearing plain black clothing as a sign of mourning dates to at least to the time of the Roman Empire, when the *toga pulla* (a toga made from dark gray or brown wool) was worn during periods of mourning and worn to burial services. The custom of wearing black during mourning has been popularly associated with mourning since Victorian times when it was traditional for the bereaved of the United Kingdom to wear black for an extended period of time. This period of mourning generally lasted for two years though widows would be expected to wear black until they died. The custom of wearing black as a sign of mourning traveled far and wide as the British colonized various parts of the world so that it became the norm in countries including the United States for mourners to wear black as a sign of bereavement and respect for the dead.

During the Victorian era, the United Kingdom had established a complex set of rules governing acceptable mourning behavior that was upheld especially by the upper classes. The unofficial rules of mourning meant that when someone died their servants and male acquaintances who had served in the military or some other profession that meant that they wore a uniform, would wear black armbands. Other men were expected to wear mourning suits consisting of black frock coats together with black trousers and waistcoats. Victorian women had to wear heavy, figure-concealing, black clothing, as well as veils of black crêpe fabric—an outfit colloquially referred to as widow's weeds, a term that derived from the Old English word *waed*, meaning garment. Women also wore special mourning bonnets and caps, specifically the so-called widow's peak hood, made from black or dark colored materials, as well as mourning jewelry that was frequently made from the hair of the deceased or from Whitby jet. Widows would wear their widow's weeds for around four years though they could opt to wear the clothing for the rest of their lives. Many writers on the subject have noted that the concept of Victorian widowhood was embodied by Queen Victoria herself, who after the death of her beloved husband Prince Albert, wore only black.

Any Victorian woman that was deemed by her community to have stopped wearing black too soon was considered to show disrespect to the departed and left herself open to charges of sexual impropriety. Additionally, while wearing widow's weeds a woman was not expected to take part in social events, especially happy occasions. For a widow to be seen enjoying herself while wearing her widow's weeds was considered scandalous as is evident from the episode in the novel and film *Gone with the Wind* when beautiful young widow Scarlett O'Hara, dressed in the black of mourning, decides to dance with Rhett Butler under the pretext of raising money for the war effort. Widows and other women were allowed to reintroduce conventional clothing to their wardrobes gradually over a series of specific time periods. These stages, dubbed half mourning, saw women begin to wear muted colors such as lilac, grey, and lavender having worn only black previously. Although mourning customs relaxed somewhat during the succeeding Edwardian era, it was still considered appropriate for men and women to wear dark colored clothing for up to one year after a death in their family. By the late 20th century, this unofficial rule no longer applied, but black continued to be the color most associated with mourning in the United Kingdom and in former British colonies.

Elsewhere, black is also the traditional color of mourning. For instance, in Japan it is customary for women to wear a black mourning outfit called a *mofuku*. The word mofuku can be applied to either Western-style black formal wear or to black kimono worn at funerals. Mofuku kimono are usually made from plain black fabric displaying no adornment save for a design of five white, dyed emblems that identify an individual or family (*kamon*). Japanese mourning clothes used to be white traditionally but once Japan began to be Westernized, black became the standard mourning color. Today, however, most Japanese women wear a black mofuku when in mourning. That said, in some areas of Japan a white mofuku is worn—this is particularly true of Japanese Buddhists who consider white to be the color of mourning. When women opt to wear a black mofuku they usually accessorize the outfit with a black obi belt and black accessories worn over white undergarments, plus black *zori* (sandals) and white *tabi* (split-toe socks). Many Japanese people consider it extremely inappropriate and disrespectful for a black mofuku to be worn on any occasion other than a funeral. At Japanese funerals, men are expected to wear their most formal outfit, which they wear to various ceremonial occasions. Men that are close relatives or friends of the deceased may wear a black, five-crested kimono with a black and white, or gray and white, striped *hakama* (trousers) over white undergarments. These are won with a black crested *haori* (jacket), white or black zori, and white tabi. Similar to the Japanese custom of wearing black or white, in the Philippines mourning customs are influenced by Chinese, Japanese, and Catholic beliefs meaning that mourners tend to wear white or black clothes. Filipinos do not wear red clothing during times of mourning, as according to Filipino tradition, people that wear red within 9 to 40 days of a death will themselves die or suffer ill health.

White, the color of physical purity and spiritual innocence in many cultures, has also long been considered the color of deepest mourning and is still worn in China and India, as well as parts of Japan and Europe. The history of white as a mourning color is very long. For instance, in ancient Egypt the priests of Osiris, the Egyptian god of the dead and ruler of the afterlife, wore white as did the earliest Christians. In medieval times, royalty often wore white during periods of mourning. For example, in 1393, white was worn at the funeral held for Leo V, King of Armenia. In France, queens traditionally wore *deuil blanc*, or white mourning. This was also true of queens closely connected to France such as Mary, Queen of Scots (1542–1587), who as simultaneously the Dowager Queen of France used the symbolism inherent in *deuil blanc* to signal her marital devotion while a widow. This tradition was the inspiration for the so-called White Wardrobe designed by British couturier Normal Hartnell in 1938 for Queen Elizabeth (later known as the Queen Mother), who needed a special wardrobe to wear while making a state visit to France during a period of mourning for her mother. Moreover, the Spanish royal family wore white during mourning until the 16th century, a custom that was revived in 1993 when the Spanish-born Queen Fabiola wore a white dress for the funeral of her husband, King Baudouin I of Belgium, as a symbol of hope. Another instance of European royals wearing white to signal mourning occurred in 2004, when the daughters of Queen Juliana of the Netherlands wore white to the queen's funeral. In 1934, the queen's father, Prince Henry, Duke of Mecklenburg-Schwerin, had been afforded a white funeral featuring white horses and carriages.

It was not just royalty that wore white as a funeral color in Europe, however, for the tradition continued in rural Hungary until very recently. In China, white is considered an unobtrusive color that when worn at funerals makes mourners invisible to the evil spirits that are attendant at such events. Therefore in China, white is worn by mourners as a way of protecting themselves from evil rather than as a way to honor the dead. Although red is often considered lucky in China, the color is also associated with death in China because, like white, red is thought to ward off evil. For this reason, red ink is used to write obituaries. Similarly, to write someone's name in red ink is a signal that you wish to disassociate from the person to the extent that they are cut out of your life. Other Chinese death traditions involving the color red see friends and family of the deceased attach strips of red cloth to their mourning wear, a woman's fiancé will wear a red sash to her funeral, and relatives of the departed may choose to wear a red stripe on the hat that they wear.

Christianity also associates red with death for red is the color of Christian martyrs. For this reason, red may be employed on Holy Thursday (also known as Maundy Thursday) and during Easter, while red, green, and white is the traditional Christmas color palate even in secular households that see Christmas as an annual holiday rather than as a religiously significant period. In the specifically Roman Catholic tradition, red is used to denote all feast days associated with Christian martyrs as well as Palm Sunday, which is obviously connected to the execution of Jesus. Similarly, in parts of Africa red is also the color of death. For this reason, the Red Cross humanitarian organization has had to change the color of its emblem from a red cross on a white background to a green and white insignia in parts of the continent. Meanwhile, several Native American peoples paint red on the faces of their dead. For instance, the Dakota people paint the face of the deceased with red as they consider red to be the color of life. The Comanche also performs this custom. Similarly, the Delaware Indians (also known as the Lenape) also paint red stripes on the faces of their dead. Moreover, deceased Delaware Indians are laid to rest in coffins painted red with the position of the coffins marked by red grave posts.

See also: Buddhist Attitudes Toward Death; Chinese Death Customs; Christian Death Rituals; Coming of Age Day (Volume 2); Delaware Indian Death Rituals; Goth Subculture; Japanese Death Customs; Maundy Money; Obituary; Tear Catchers and Mourning Jewelry; Tongan Funerals; Vrindavan: City of Widows; Warding Off the Evil Eye (Volume 1); Wearing Flowers to Honor War Dead

Further Reading

Bleicher, Steven. *Contemporary Color: Theory and Use.* Second edition. Clifton Park, NY: Delmar CENGAGE Learning, 2012.

Devonshire Jones, Tom, Linda Murray, and Peter Murray. *The Oxford Dictionary of Christian Art and Architecture.* Second edition. Oxford, UK: Oxford University Press, 2013.

Frye, Susan. *Pens and Needles: Women's Textualities in Early Modern England*. Philadelphia: University of Pennsylvania Press, 2010.
Howden, Daniel. "Across Zimbabwe, Red Rags Signify a Nation in Mourning," *The Independent*, June 27, 2008. Accessed December 12, 2015, at http://www.independent.co.uk/news/world/africa/across-zimbabwe-red-rags-signify-a-nation-in-mourning-855428.html.
Mason, Evan. "Mofuku," Immortal Geisha, August 18, 2015. Accessed December 12, 2015, at http://www.immortalgeisha.com/wiki/index.php?title=Mofuku.
Petch, Alison. "Funeral and Mourning Clothing." England: The Other Within. Accessed December 12, 2015, at http://england.prm.ox.ac.uk/englishness-funeral-clothing.html.
Popovic, Mislav. "Native American Death Rites." TraditionsCustoms.com. Accessed December 12, 2015, at http://traditionscustoms.com/death-rites/native-american-death-rites.
Royal Collection Trust. "Queen Elizabeth The Queen Mother's 'White Wardrobe' to Be Shown at Buckingham Palace Next Summer." December 13, 2004. Accessed December 12, 2015, at https://www.royalcollection.org.uk/press-release/queen-elizabeth-the-queen-mothers-white-wardrobe-to-be-shown-at-buckingham-palace-next.
Smith, Bonnie G., ed. *The Oxford Encyclopedia of Women in World History: Volume 4*. Oxford, UK: Oxford University Press, 2008.
Taylor, Lou. *Routledge Revivals: Mourning Dress: A Costume and Social History*. Abingdon, UK: Routledge, 2009.
University College London (UCL). "Red: Symbolic And Cultural Associations." Object Retrieval. Accessed December 12, 2015, at http://www.ucl.ac.uk/museums-static/objectretrieval/node/277.
Wolf, Arthur P. "Chinese Kinship and Mourning Dress," in Maurice Freedman, ed., *Family and Kinship in Chinese Society*. Stanford, CA: Stanford University Press, 1970, 189–208.

U

UNIVERSITY OF THE THIRD AGE, INTERNATIONAL

The University of the Third Age, often referred to as U3A, is an international adult education organization that aims to educate and mentally stimulate people that have retired from work or have entered what the organization deems to be the third age of life—the time after full-time employment and parental responsibilities have ended. The International Association of Universities of the Third Age (IAUTA), established in 1975, is the governing body of University of the Third Age groups worldwide and oversees similar institutions that have different names but hold the same values and objectives.

In 1968, the French government legislated that greater provision should be made to require French universities to engage with local communities. This planted the seed for the University of the Third Age, which was founded in France as the *Universite du Troisieme Age* in 1973 at Toulouse University of Social Science as part of the university's gerontology course. The Universite du Troisieme Age was affiliated with the university's staff and students and set the pattern for the French model of the University of the Third Age. By 1975, the concept of the University of the Third Age had spread from France to Belgium, Switzerland, Poland, Italy, Spain, Canada, and the United States. Then, in 1981, the first British arm of the organization was founded in Cambridge, England. However in the United Kingdom, as elsewhere in Europe with the exception of France, members run the University of the Third Age on a voluntary basis. University of the Third Age groups in France differ somewhat from those in other parts of the world as in France groups tend to be affiliated with local universities and some are awarded charitable status. Also, in the United Kingdom the University of the Third Age does not receive any government funding but rather is totally self-financing. Those University of the Third Age groups that follow the British model are not universities in the usual sense of the word as they do not award degrees, certificates, or other qualifications, and members do not take examinations. Rather, the aim of the British-style University of the Third Age groups is that members simply enjoy the pleasure of learning. At present there are over 800 autonomous University of the Third Age groups throughout the United Kingdom and 250 groups in Australia. Other areas of the world that have University of the Third Age groups based on the British model include New Zealand, Slovenia, the Czech Republic, the Netherlands, Germany, Scandinavia, and South America. In Austria, groups follow neither the French nor British model but rather are associations consisting of older university students. There are also a number of University of the Third Age-type groups to be found in China, though in China the organization is known as Universities for the Ages and is intended to provide academic courses, placement in which is highly sought after. Japan also has many universities for older students, such as Izumi Kenro Daigaku, in Osaka Prefecture, which offers two-year courses and graduate courses.

The classes offered by the University of the Third Age vary from group to group. However groups tend to offer a very wide variety of classes ranging from the academic, such as classical Greek and advanced Latin or the history of philosophy, and modern language courses; to those based around exercise (particularly popular are belly dancing, yoga, and tai chi) and practical skills, including computing and sign language, along with classes that aim to generally improve members' quality of life such as wine appreciation, Reiki healing, stress-reduction, and relaxation. Other classes have a social function that help foster a community feel to the University of the Third Age with regular meetings devoted to the playing of games such as Scrabble, mahjong, and bridge.

Recent research suggests that older people who continue to be intellectually stimulated after retirement by joining establishments such as the University of the Third Age maintain, and may even increase, their cognitive functioning and feel a sense of empowerment that makes them want to contribute to society.

See also: Croning, Saging, and Elderling Ceremonies; Retirement and Pensions; Senior Sporting Events

Further Reading

Boulton-Lewis, Gillian, and Maureen Tam, eds. *Active Ageing, Active Learning: Issues and Challenges. Education in the Asia-Pacific Region: Issues, Concerns and Prospects 15.* Heidelberg, Germany: Springer Science + Business Media, 2012

Laslett, Peter. *A Fresh Map of Life: The Emergence of the Third Age.* London: George Weidenfeld & Nicolson Limited, 1991.

Swindell, Richard, and Jean Thompson. "An International Perspective of the University of the Third Age." Worldu3a.org, September 1995. Accessed April 2, 2015, at http://www.worldu3a.org/resources/u3a-worldwide.htm.

U3A in London. "Home." Accessed April 2, 2015, at http://www.u3alondon.org.uk.

U3A Waltham Forest. "Welcome." Accessed April 2, 2015, at http://u3asites.org.uk/code/u3asite.php?site=427&page=1.

VRINDAVAN: THE CITY OF WIDOWS, INDIA

Vrindavan is a town located in the Mathura district of Uttar Pradesh in northern India. The town is a holy site in Hindu religion, history, and culture and is the location of a great many Hindu temples. However Vrindavan is also known as the "City of Widows" due to the large number of women who move there after the death of their husbands. (*See* Plate 22.) Indeed it has been estimated that between 6,000 and 15,000 of India's 40 million widows live in Vrindavan with many more living in the surrounding countryside. India has one of the highest rates of widowhood in the world with incidents of widowhood rising sharply with age thus 64 percent of women aged 60 years and over are widowed rising to 80 percent of women aged over 70 years. Therefore any older woman in India is most probably a widow. By contrast, only 2.5 percent of Indian men are widowers. This is mainly because it is socially acceptable for men to remarry if their wife dies and because in India mortality rates for males are higher than those for females.

Widowed women gravitate to Vrindavan from across India, especially from Bengal, where it is considered unlucky to even look at a widow. That many widows travel to Vrindavan from Bengal, a journey of approximately 1,000 miles, is particularly noteworthy, for widows from Bengal speak Bengali and so do not necessarily understand Hindi, the language spoken in Vrindavan. However the reason why so many widows journey across India to the town is unknown though it seems that the Indian attitude to widowhood lies at the heart of the matter. Life is very difficult for widows in India, particularly those living in rural areas where old traditions are prevalent. Widowhood is considered a social death by much of Indian society. Indeed when a woman's husband dies the woman loses her feminine pronoun being referred to as "it" rather than "she." Indian nicknames for widows include the term "husband eater" and in the northern state of Punjab widows are called *randi* (prostitute). When their husband dies many Indian widows lose their income and are ostracized by their community. Widows are also often disowned by their husband's family in order to prevent them from inheriting any property or money, mistreated by sons-in-law and daughters-in-law who regard them as a financial burden, and regarded with distrust by married women who fear the widow will try to steal away their husbands.

After the death of their husbands, Indian women are expected to remain in mourning for the rest of their lives, a belief instilled from ancient times for a 2,000-year-old sacred text by Manu states, "A virtuous wife is one who after the death of her husband constantly remains chaste and reaches heaven though she has no son." Widows of all ages are expected to dress in dull clothing rather than colorful saris, and to remove their jewelry and the red dot from between their eyebrows that signifies their sexual energy. In particularly conservative areas, widows are also expected to shave their heads. Such measures are meant to uglify the widow, ensuring that she remain chaste after her husband's death.

One possible reason for some widows journeying to Vrindavan is that the town is synonymous with the story of Lord Krishna and his beloved Radha, which is known to every Hindu. According to the epic narrative *The Mahabharata,* Lord Krishna was born in a forest close to Vrindavan and it was there that the young, mischievous Krishna flirted with female cow herders called *gopis.* Krishna is said to have embarked on a love affair with one of the gopis, the beautiful Radha, to whom Krishna's name is forever bound as RadhaKrisha, the embodiment of the masculine and feminine aspects of God in the Hindu religion. Many of Vrindavan's temples are devoted to Krishna and Radha and the town's association with the couple draws many pilgrims to Vrindavan who walk a ritual circuit of these temples. It has been noted that many of the pilgrims are elderly women dressed in white who come to Vrindavan as genuine pilgrims hoping to devote the remaining years of their lives to the service of Radha and Krishna. However as the widows have no real means of gaining an income, the widows' pilgrimage often ends in a life of destitution. Some widows earn a small wage by looking after a *sadhu*, that is, a man who has renounced worldly pleasures by using meditation to gain enlightenment, while others earn a few coins by singing devotional songs in the temples. However other widows either beg on the streets of Vrindavan or are forced into prostitution. Indeed prostitution is the main way in which widows, especially young widows, survive in Vrindavan, forced into the sex trade and reliant on pimps. Though Indian authorities have established several spiritual communes known as *ashrams* in Vrindavan where widows can live, supposedly unmolested by pimps and townsfolk, many widows have claimed that they are forced to choose between begging in order to be able to pay for rented accommodation or earning the money through working as prostitutes, sometimes for those who are in charge of running the ashrams. As a result of this sexual exploitation, many young widows endure painful abortions, as they cannot afford to care for a child.

Most of the people who abuse the widows of Vrindavan go unpunished for violence against widows is widespread in Indian society despite the fact that laws aimed at protecting women (and therefore widows) do exist in the country. Dr Mohini Giri, a veteran women's rights advocate nominated for the Nobel Peace Prize in 2005, attempted to address this situation when she was chairwoman of the Indian government's National Commission for Women, managing to turn classrooms into courtrooms where rape cases involving widows could be heard—settling 400 cases in one day.

Attempts have been made to end discrimination against widows in India. For instance in October 2013, two widows were permitted to perform religious rituals in a Hindu temple called the Kudroli Shree Gokarnanatheshwara Temple located in Mangalore in the southern Indian state of Karnataka. The women took part in the *Mangalore Dasara*, an annual Hindu festival, having received four months of training from priests. After this training, the women were allowed into the temple's sanctorum, where the Hindu idols of Shiva and Annapoorneshwari were placed. The women then offered *puja* (reverence or worship) to the divinities. According to reports, a multi-faith audience numbering hundreds of people witnessed the ceremony. Having taken part in the ritual, the widows were then to receive further training and be ordained as priestesses, which would enable them to earn a monthly salary. However, perhaps just as importantly, women's rights advocates hoped that the ordination of the widows as priestesses would convey the message that everyone is equal in the sight of God and that no widow should face discrimination on the basis of her marital status. Eminent politician B. Janardhan Poojary, whose initiative it was to ordain the widows of Mangalore, aims to extend the scheme across Karnataka thereby helping to end the prejudice against widows in India.

See also: *Devadasi* System (Volume 1); Hindu Death Customs; *Kumari* and *Deuki* (Volume 1); *Kumbh Mela* (Volume 2); *Mehndi* (Volume 2)

Further Reading
Barrera, Sara, and Corbacho, Eva. "The Ongoing Tragedy of India's Widows." Women under Siege, June 22, 2012. Accessed October 30, 2014, at http://www.womenundersiegeproject.org/blog/entry/the-ongoing-tragedy-of-indias-widows.
Denselow, Anthony. "The Town with 6,000 Widows." *BBC News Magazine*, May 2, 2013. Accessed October 30, 2014, at http://www.bbc.co.uk/news/magazine-21859622.
Ghosh, Palash. "Widows Peak? Women without Husbands Allowed to Perform Religious Rituals at Hindu Temple in Southern India," *International Business Times*, October 7, 2013. Accessed October 30, 2014, at http://www.ibtimes.com/widows-peak-women-without-husbands-allowed-perform-religious-rituals-hindu-temple-southern-india.
Reddy, Adinarayana P. *Problems of Widows in India*. First edition. New Delhi, India: Sarup & Sons, 2004.

W

WAKE, INTERNATIONAL

The word wake can be applied to two post-death customs. Firstly, the term wake refers to the practice of keeping a vigil over a corpse in the run up to the body being buried. This type of wake occurs in many countries including Japan, China, the United Kingdom, Ireland, Australia, New Zealand, and the United States. Wakes are also particularly associated with Roman Catholicism while a similar type of vigil over the dead also occurs in Judaism.

A wake is an interval between the death of an individual and their burial during which the family, friends, and community of the deceased participate in funeral rites that culminates with the interment. There is no set length that a wake should last. Indeed the length of a wake depends on a number of factors including climatic conditions (e.g., hot weather will accelerate decomposition of the corpse thereby shortening the wake), local customs, the need to perform religious rituals and the social status of the deceased. In some places the nature of the death and the need to ensure that the deceased travels to the afterlife will also determine the nature of the wake. Moreover, if a death is considered a so-called bad death—if the individual died suddenly without warning and without being prepared, or if the deceased is an unbaptized child or stillborn baby—then a wake may be curtailed significantly or dispensed with altogether as a way to show that the deceased is looked on unfavorably by those already residing in the afterlife.

The term wake can also be applied as a colloquial word for an informal post-funeral get-together that takes place in the United Kingdom, Ireland, and among British and Irish expat communities abroad. This type of wake normally takes place in the favorite pub or bar of the deceased or at their home and sees the family, friends, and community at large gather to eat and drink to the memory of the deceased, reminisce about events in the deceased's life, and sing songs in their honor. When a wake takes place in a pub it is usual for those organizing the wake, usually the family of the deceased, to arrange a bar tab up to a certain amount of money in advance of guests arriving as the drinking of alcohol is a major feature of this type of wake.

See also: Albanian Funeral Customs; Christian Death Rituals; The Great Passing; Japanese Death Customs; "Lyke-Wake Dirge"; Romanian Funeral Customs; *Tangihanga*: Māori Mourning Ritual; Tongan Funerals

Further Reading

Bregman, Lucy, ed. *Religion, Death, and Dying, Volume 3: Bereavement and Death Rituals*. Santa Barbara, CA: Praeger, 2010.

Howarth, Glennys, and Oliver Leaman, eds. *Encyclopedia of Death and Dying*. Abingdon, UK: Routledge, 2013.

Simpson, Jacqueline, and Steve Roud. *Oxford Dictionary of English Folklore*. Oxford, UK: Oxford University Press, 2000.

WEARING FLOWERS TO HONOR WAR DEAD, INTERNATIONAL

In many countries around the world it is traditional for people to wear flowers to honor the nation's war dead. Perhaps the flower most often associated with honoring war dead is the scarlet common poppy (*popaver rhoeas*), which is a symbol of remembrance in the United Kingdom and Commonwealth countries, France, and the United States. Indeed throughout the United Kingdom and the Commonwealth the red poppy is synonymous with Remembrance Day and Remembrance Sunday. In the United Kingdom it is traditional for people to wear paper versions of red poppies on their coats in the run-up to Remembrance Day and Remembrance Sunday. In the United States, the red poppy has been designated the national flower of remembrance since 1920.

Poppies have long been associated with death. This association dates back to Biblical times for the flower is said to have sprung from the blood of Christ during the Crucifixion. Moreover, the poppy has long been associated with death in European warfare. Indeed this association dates back to the time of the Napoleonic Wars (1803–1815) when poppy seeds that had lain dormant in battlefield soil were disturbed by the surrounding warfare and sprung to life transforming battle-scarred bare earth into fields of blood-red poppies that grew around the corpses of dead soldiers. Around a hundred years later, in 1915 to 1918, the fields of Northern France and Flanders in Belgium were again the site of battle as World War I raged throughout western Europe. Once again, warfare disturbed the soil and this disturbance together with warm weather meant that poppies were the only flowers that would grow on the desolate battlefields. Similarly, a field of poppies was flowering on the battlefields of Turkey's Gallipoli peninsular when the ANZAC and British Forces arrived there at the start of the Gallipoli campaign in April 1915.

That the poppies were blood red seemed to make the symbolism all the more startling. The scarlet flowering poppies captured the imagination of Canadian surgeon John McCrae who used the poppies as a symbol in his poem "In Flanders Fields" that he wrote after his friend died at the battle of Ypres. For McCrae, the poppy represented the immense sacrifice made by his comrades and the poppy soon became a lasting symbol commemorating those that had died in World War I. Over time, the poppy was also used to honor people that died in later conflicts too and the flower was adopted by the charity the Royal British Legion. Indeed each year since 1921 the Royal British Legion employs the symbolism of the poppy during their annual Poppy Appeal, which raises money for people serving in the British Armed Forces.

The history of the Poppy Appeal is surprisingly international. The publication of "In Flanders Fields" inspired an American academic, Moina Michael, to create and sell red silk poppies that were then brought to England by a Frenchwoman, Anna Guérin. The Royal British Legion, which had been established in 1921, ordered nine million of these poppies that were sold on November 11 that same year. The poppies proved hugely popular and sold out almost as soon as they went on sale. The first ever Poppy Appeal raised over £106,000 (approximately $154,267), which was used to help World War I veterans find employment and housing. The next year, Major George Howson set up the Poppy Factory in Richmond-upon-Thames in southwest London to employ disabled ex-servicemen. Today, the Richmond Poppy Factory (together with the Royal British Legion's warehouse in Aylesford in southern England) still makes millions of poppies for the annual Poppy Appeal. The demand for charity poppies in England was such that they tended to sell out before anyone living in Scotland had a chance to buy one. This prompted the wife of Earl Haig to establish the Lady Haig Poppy Factory in Edinburgh, Scotland, in 1926 that produces poppies exclusively for sale in Scotland. Today over 5 million Scottish poppies are handmade by disabled ex-service personnel at Lady Haig's Poppy Factory. The Scottish poppies are distributed by Poppyscotland, the sister charity of the Royal British Legion. However Scottish paper poppies differ from the poppies worn in the rest of the United Kingdom as they have four petals and are leafless. Meanwhile, Moina Michael also played a significant part in the red poppy becoming the flower of remembrance in the United States. In 1920, Michael discovered that the Georgia Department of the American Legion had arranged to meet in August in Atlanta. Knowing where the delegates would convene, Michael searched them out and persuaded the representative of the United States Navy to present her case for a Memorial Poppy to signify the nation's commemoration of its war dead to the convention. The Georgia Convention decided to adopt the Memorial Poppy but omitted the symbol of a torch that had been included in the design of the original Memorial Poppy. The Georgia Convention also decided to support the movement to have the Memorial Poppy adopted by the National American Legion and also agreed to encourage each member of the American Legion in Georgia to wear a red poppy on November 11 each year. Then, in September 1920, the National American Legion agreed to employ the Flanders Fields Memorial Poppy as the United States' national emblem of remembrance.

In the United Kingdom, there are controversies over when to wear a memorial poppy. For instance, there is some disagreement over so-called poppy etiquette. Some people argue that the remembrance poppy must be worn for the period of time from October 31 to November 11, while other people claim that the Poppy Appeal poppy should be worn on the 11 days in the run-up to Remembrance Day. Then again, some people say the poppy should not be worn until after Guy Fawkes Night (also known as Bonfire Night) on November 5. There are also controversies over how to wear the poppy with some people stating the poppy must be worn on the left as this means that the poppy is kept close to the human heart thereby symbolizing that those people who died in warfare and are represented by the poppy also stay close to the heart. Additionally, the left-hand side is also the side on which military medals are worn. Then again, some people say men should wear the poppy on their left and women should wear them on the right. However Queen Elizabeth II wears her poppy on her left. There is also a degree of uncertainty over whether the leaf on the paper poppy worn in the United Kingdom (apart from Scotland) should point to the 11 o'clock position to recall the time of day on which the armistice occurred.

More seriously, while the Royal British Legion's Poppy Appeal is a successful charity initiative that aims to help service personnel and veterans while also educating people about the military, some people in the United Kingdom, and elsewhere, refuse to wear a red poppy as they believe that the flower symbolizes British imperialism and glorifies warfare. There have also been accusations of so-called poppy fascism, the scorning and mockery of people in the United Kingdom that have chosen not to wear a poppy. The term poppy fascism was invented by British television news presenter and journalist Jon Snow, who is vilified each year by certain parts of the British media for his refusal to wear a poppy while reading the news. Similarly, Northern Irish soccer player James McClean, who plays for the English team West Bromwich Albion, receives criticism for refusing to wear a poppy on his team shirt. According to McClean displaying the poppy emblem would be disrespectful to civilians killed during the so-called Bloody Sunday of 1972 during which British soldiers killed a number of unarmed civilians during a protest march.

As some people see the wearing of the red poppy as a symbol of British imperialism efforts have been taken to make the poppy a more inclusive symbol. To this end, in 2014 student Tabinda-Kauser Ishaq made headlines in the United Kingdom for designing a *hijab* decorated with a poppy print in an effort to appeal to British Muslims that wished to mark Remembrance Sunday and commemorate the 400,000 Muslim soldiers and 1.2 million Indian soldiers who fought beside British troops in World War I. However the poppy hijab was accused of perpetuating Islamophobia by suggesting that Muslim women need to in some way prove their loyalty to Britain.

An alternative to the red poppy is the white poppy that some people wear as a symbol of peace. The Co-operative Women's Guild established the white poppy in 1933 as a lasting symbol of peace and to call for the end to all warfare. Though intended as a symbol of peace, the white poppy has proved controversial. The Co-operative Wholesale Society produces the white poppy because the Royal British Legion has refused to be associated with the manufacturing of the white poppies and in the 1930s women that wore the white poppy risked losing their jobs. Moreover, while advocates of the wearing of the white poppy argue that the white poppy was not meant to offend the memory of anyone that died in warfare, many veterans nevertheless feel that the white poppy in some way undermines the contribution of the war dead. Today, the White Poppy Appeal is organized by the Peace Pledge Union.

Other commemorative poppies also exist. For example, the purple poppy was invented in 2006 to remember animals that have died in times of warfare while being used as messengers, scouts, beasts of burden, and rescue animals. All donations from buying a purple poppy go to the charity Animal Aid. Meanwhile, the black poppy is worn by people wishing to make a political statement against what they see as the imperialism of warfare. Those people that choose to wear a black poppy do so because they consider it to be a symbol commemorating people that have died, and continue to die, during imperialist wars and the aftermath of such wars. Advocates of the black poppy argue that wearing a black poppy brings to mind dead soldiers, civilians, and conscientious objectors as well as victims of invasions, occupation, gender-based violence, malnourishment, destitution, and homelessness.

Another flower employed as a way to commemorate war dead is the blue cornflower. *Bluets*, meaning blue cornflowers, was the sobriquet given by older soldiers of World War I to young recruits (those soldiers born in 1895) as they arrived on the battlefield of the Chemin des Dames in northern France wearing brand new blue uniforms. However a more somber reason for the blue cornflower becoming the French flower of remembrance is that the blue cornflower (*bleuet de France*) was adopted by France to memorialize Armistice Day, because, like red poppies, cornflowers managed to flower on the ravaged French battlefields of World War I. For this reason, the French consider the blue cornflower, like the poppy, to be a symbol of survival and resilience.

Meanwhile a plant rather than a flower that is worn to commemorate war dead is the herb rosemary. Rosemary has long been associated with remembrance for, according to Christian legend, the Virgin Mary once rested her blue cloak over a white flowered bush only to find that where the cloak had touched the flowers had turned the bloom blue. From then on the plant was referred to as the Rose of Mary. Moreover, in ancient Greece people wishing to improve their memory took rosemary internally. Today in Australia, small sprigs of rosemary are worn on coat lapels on ANZAC Day by people wishing to commemorate the nation's war dead. Rosemary is especially significant to Australians, as the herb grows wild on the Gallipoli peninsula in Turkey, an area where tens of thousands of ANZAC (Australian and New Zealand Army Corps) troops died for no material gain.

See also: "Abide With Me"; Changing of the Guard Ceremony; Funeral Plants; "The Last Post" and "Taps"; Minute's Silence; National Day of Mourning; Remembrance Day and Remembrance Sunday; Royal Wootton Bassett; Tomb of the Unknown Soldier; Yew Trees

Further Reading

ANZAC Day Commemoration Committee (Qld) Incorporated. "Rosemary Is for Remembrance." Accessed October 18, 2015, at http://www.anzacday.org.au/education/tff/rosemary.html.

BBC. "Gallipoli: Why Do Australians Celebrate a Military Disaster?" BBC iWonder. Accessed October 18, 2015, at http://www.bbc.co.uk/guides/zyj4kqt.
BBC. "Remembrance Poppy: Controversies and How to Wear It." BBC Newsbeat, November 4, 2014. Accessed October 18, 2015, at http://www.bbc.co.uk/newsbeat/article/29848595/remembrance-poppy-controversies-and-how-to-wear-it.
BBC. "Why the Poppy?" BBC: 1918–2008 Ninety Years of Remembrance. Accessed October 18, 2015, at http://www.bbc.co.uk/remembrance/how/poppy.shtml.
Beckett, Ian F. W. *The Great War: 1914–1918*. Second edition. London: Routledge, 2007.
GreatWar.co.uk. "The Story Behind the Remembrance Poppy." The Great War 1914–1918. Accessed October 18, 2015, at http://www.greatwar.co.uk/article/remembrance-poppy.htm.
Jones, Alison. *Larousse Dictionary of World Folklore*. Edinburgh, UK: Larousse, 1996.
The Royal British Legion. "The Story of the Poppy." How We Remember. Accessed October 18, 2015, at http://www.britishlegion.org.uk/remembrance/how-we-remember/the-story-of-the-poppy/.
Saunders, Nicholas J. *The Poppy: A Cultural History From Ancient Egypt to Flanders Fields to Afghanistan*. London: Oneworld Publications, 2013.
Simpson, Jacqueline, and Steve Roud. *Oxford Dictionary of English Folklore*. Oxford, UK: Oxford University Press, 2000.
Sims, Alexandra. "James McClean Explains Why He Chooses Not to Wear Remembrance Day Poppy on West Brom Shirt," *The Independent*, October 31, 2015. Accessed June 12, 2016, at http://www.independent.co.uk/news/people/james-mcclean-explains-why-he-refuses-to-wear-remembrance-day-poppy-on-west-brom-shirt-a6716081.html.
Stop the War Coalition. "Why No Remembrance Day Black Poppies for 16,000 First World War Refusers?" November 9, 2014. Accessed October 18, 2015, at http://www.stopwar.org.uk/index.php/news/why-no-remembrance-day-black-poppies-for-16-000-first-world-war-refusers.
Travel France Online. "Remembrance Day—Bleuet de France." Remembrance Day—Armistice Day—1914–1918, September 13, 2015. Accessed October 18, 2015, at http://www.travelfranceonline.com/remembrance-day-armistice-day-1914-1918/.
Walsh, John. "Is Remembrance Day Being Undermined by 'Poppy Fascism'?" *The Independent*, November 5, 2014. Accessed October 18, 2015, at http://www.independent.co.uk/voices/comment/is-remembrance-day-being-undermined-by-poppy-facism-9842084.html.

WICCAN FUNERALS, WICCA

Many Wiccans regard Wiccan funerals as a rite of passage allowing the spirit of departed believers to travel peacefully from one life to another. As such, Wiccan funerals occur in several Western countries including the United States and the United Kingdom. Apart from a few shared characteristics, there is a great deal of variation between Wiccan funerals. This is partly because there are a great many different ritual Wiccan practices but also because Wiccan funerals are intended to honor the departed Wiccan's wishes for their own individual funeral. Many of the rites practiced at Wiccan funerals are based on the *Book of Shadows*, the book containing Wiccan religious texts as well as instructions for Wiccan rituals. Most

Wiccan covens possess a *Book of Shadows* that contains the various rituals, invocations, and beliefs of their particular group. Traditionally, the High Priestess of each coven writes down by hand all the teachings of the preceding High Priestess, a practice that means that differences exist in the way that Wiccan rituals, including funeral rituals, are performed between covens.

Because Wiccans believe in reincarnation Wiccan funeral ceremonies tend to center around the concept of rebirth. Details may vary but in all cases the Wiccan's body is considered a disposable vessel that will return to the earth once the individual has died. In line with such reincarnation-based beliefs, the majority of Wiccans think that when an individual dies they pass from this life to the Summerlands, by which is meant the place where a person's spirit rests between existences. Wiccans believe that the Summerlands are filled with family and friends that have also passed on from this life and that it is a green and peaceful land that encourages the individual's soul to enter a state of repose before returning to earth where it will complete a new series of tasks. In order to ensure that the spirit of the deceased enters the Summerlands, some Wiccans may hold a special ritual called a Passing Rite or Passing Over that is intended to help a spirit pass into the Summerlands in the appropriate manner.

The Wiccan religion is not totally accepted by all modern societies, something that often results in Wiccans receiving Christian funerals. Although this situation may seem incongruous, many Wiccans understand that non-Wiccan families may need to follow their own death traditions and so will not interfere with their desire to hold a Christian funeral. This is particularly the case since Wiccans see funerals as rituals held more for the living than for the deceased. Moreover, the Wiccan group to which a departed Wiccan belonged may hold a funeral ceremony for their departed member after the Christian funeral.

There are usually several distinct parts to a Wiccan funeral, which often takes place at the graveside and is attended by only the deceased's closest relatives, friends, and coven-mates. The funeral is short in duration and once it has concluded the select group of people that attended the graveside ritual will return to a larger group of attendees that waited at a distance from the grave while the funeral is conducted. The first part of a Wiccan funeral may see the High Priestess and High Priest perform a funeral ritual while their assistants act as ushers. To perform the ritual the area may be cleared and the corpse laid on an altar. The bereaved wait at the boundary of the ritual space while the High Priestess prepares the space while simultaneously performing a ritual chant. Next, the High Priest and High Priestess perform a recitation and then mourners take turns to speak about the dead person. The speeches are intended to help the deceased along his or her journey to the next world but mourners need not speak if they do not wish to do so. Finally, the corpse is shrouded, a candle is lit, and the people acting as ushers direct visitors to food and drink. In the meantime, the High Priestess, High Priest, relatives, and close friends of the deceased take the corpse to the grave. Here, a private funeral is conducted before everyone returns from the graveside to the rest of the mourners to share reminisce about the deceased and offer up prayers. Alternatively, members of the departed Wiccan's coven or Wiccan friends may congregate to hold a private funeral ritual. This type of ritual usually takes place outdoors somewhere the deceased felt most at peace, such as in a forest or by water. This type of ritual sees those Wiccans gathered cast a circle around the corpse as an invisible boundary intended to generate a sacred, secure space in which the ritual may occur. Mourners complete the casting of the circle by calling on the four corners (i.e., the four cardinal points of the compass) and the god and goddess (the identities of the god and goddess are not fixed and vary widely in Wicca). Once the circle is cast, mourners may place lit white candles and flowers along the edge of the circle before stepping inside the space. The candles used are colored white as this is the Wiccan color of death but also denotes rebirth. Each mourner then talks about the deceased and the High Priestess or High Priest may give a final speech including references to the turning of the Wheel of Life and expressing good wishes for the departed's next life. In recent years, the law in many places has prohibited this type of ritual but the ritual may still take place with the individual represented by their ashes, a photograph, or personal possessions rather than their corpse.

Many Wiccan rituals focus on the earth and its elements so for this reason an important part of a Wiccan funeral centers on the act of returning the deceased's body to the earth. Accordingly, it is traditional for a Wiccan corpse to be laid directly in soil without a surrounding casket. In the majority of states across the United States and elsewhere in the world, however, the law does not permit this practice. Instead, in general, Wiccan funerals share elements with green burial customs for today the deceased are often buried wrapped only in cloth or in a wicker casket that allows the corpse to decompose quickly and naturally. Wiccans see the decomposed body as a source of nourishment for other forms of life as well as the soil thereby promoting future growth. Where law does not permit this form of burial, Wiccans are encourage to perform cremation with ashes ultimately buried without a confining coffin as opposed to being buried using embalming fluids and an airtight coffin.

Many Wiccans feel it is important that Wiccan funerals are allowed to take place as a way of allowing people that practice alternative beliefs a final degree of dignity in death as they are permitted to be buried according to their own beliefs rather than in line with the trappings of a religion that they do not follow. Wiccans are often encouraged to make their wishes for their funeral known before they die as this allows them to specify the type of funeral they would like. This is especially important if an individual's relatives are not Wiccans and may not honor their wishes. For this reason, Wiccans may name a fellow coven-mate listed as the executor of their will to ensure that they receive the type of funeral that they desire.

See also: Alkaline Hydrolysis; Croning, Saging, and Elderling Ceremonies; Grave Rental and Exhumation; Hallowe'en and *Martinstag*; Sky Burials

Further Reading

Bett, John. "Wiccan Funeral: Eron the Wizard Laid to Rest in Britain's First Pagan Service for Centuries," *The Mirror*, May 28, 2015. Accessed January 24, 2016, at http://www.mirror.co.uk/news/uk-news/wiccan-funeral-eron-wizard-laid-5778317.

Cantrell, Gary. *Wiccan Beliefs & Practices: With Rituals for Solitaries & Covens*. St Paul, MN: Llewellyn Publications, 2003.

Gardner, Kevin M. *The Wiccan Minister's Manual, A Guide for Priests and Priestesses*. Bloomington, IN: AuthorHouse, 2008.

Universal Life Church Ministries. "Wiccan Funeral Ceremony." Accessed January 24, 2016, at http://www.ulc.org/training-education/guide-to-divinity/religious-ceremonies/28-wiccan-rites/wiccan-funeral-ceremony/.

Related Primary Document: Wiccan Funeral for an Elderly Woman

Wiccan funerals take place in several Western countries including the United States and the United Kingdom. There is no one set Wiccan funeral ritual, as Wiccan funerals are very individualistic but there are, however, several characteristics that are shared by most Wiccan funerals. These common characteristics include rites being based on Wiccan religious texts known as the Book of Shadows and a belief in the concept of rebirth. Most Wiccans believe that the human body is a temporary home for the spirit that will return to the earth after a person's death. In line with these beliefs in reincarnation, most Wiccans believe that when an individual dies they travel from this life to the Summerlands—the place where a person's spirit rests between existences. Not all pagans are Wiccans but all those who follow Wicca as a religion are classed as pagan. As a generic pagan funeral the following ritual includes many of the elements that might be evident at a Wiccan funeral including the presence of an officiating High Priestess and High Priest and a belief in rebirth and reincarnation.

Generic Pagan Funeral for an Elder Woman

She-Wolf

(as written, to be conducted by a group of Priestess, Priest, chief mourner and possibly other coven members as attendants, i.e. ushers.)

The room (perhaps of a funeral home) is decorated with evergreen boughs and roses. This supposes there is a casket, but may be adapted if there is a picture only of the deceased.

Before anyone comes into the room, the priest and priestess may cast a circle, summon the quarters and invoke the Lady and Lord.

As the mourners enter, they will be greeted at the door (and portal to the circle) by the Priest and Priestess. When all are seated, the priestess begins.

PRIESTESS: (adapted from the "Decent of the Goddess," in the Farrars' Witches Bible Complete)

There are three great events in the life of a person: love, death and resurrection to a new life. Of these love is the most important. For by love and in fulfillment of it, we may again be joined with our families and friends, remembering and loving them again. Death cannot take away love or our loved ones.

Without love there is no birth, without birth no death, without death no rebirth. This is the miracle of love.

PRIEST:(name of Chief mourner, here a son), loving son, all here feel your sorrow and with you honor (name of deceased).

Nearest relative or chief mourner tells about the persons life and accomplishments. Others may speak also. When this is finished, the priest continues.

PRIEST:(adapted from memorial service of "Magical rites from the Crystal Well")

For a while we have lost one who is dear to us, but it is only for a time and we should not be sorrowful. There is a reason to be here and a reason to go when we have fulfilled the tasks of a life's work. Dying is only a way of forgetting, of resting, of returning to the eternal source to be renewed and made strong.

PRIESTESS:(adapted from the rite of the Three-Fold-Goddess in the Witches Bible)

Behold a woman who has been three women. First a girl full of dreams and hope. Then a mother who brought forth life and gave love. Finally an elder, rich in knowledge and experience. Her journey is ended and a new one begun. Let us bid her farewell and entreat all her loved ones who have gone before her to greet and guide her on her way.

The priest may then instruct the mourners to bid a personal farewell if they desire, then proceed to the foyer or otherwise outside the room. This is the traditional time to play the departed loved one's favorite song or hymn. Again, some attendant should be at the portal to see all out of the circle. The priest, priestess and perhaps the chief mourner may then thank the Gods, release the quarters and open the circle.

Some refreshment in the outer area might be available to help the people ground a bit. The pall bearers may then return and carry the casket to the conveyance.

At the grave side, salt or ashes, water and wine, and aromatic oil may have been poured to bless the site.

"We wish you all love and happiness. Do not forget us. We will not forget you. We find our peace and hope in the sure and certain knowledge that we shall meet again and at that time we will celebrate in perfect love."

After the casket is lowered, the chief mourner throws earth upon the grave.

This is again a traditional time for all to eat together. This helps in grounding.

Source: *The Pagan Library. Available at http://www.paganlibrary.com/rituals_spells/generic_pagan_funeral.php.*

WINDMILLS, THE NETHERLANDS

Windmills are an iconic symbol of the Netherlands. In fact some Dutch people go so far as to say it was windmills that built the country. Today, the most famous group of mills in the Netherlands is located at Kinderdijk in the north of the country where 19 working windmills have been declared a UNESCO World Heritage site. Kinderdijk's windmills are regarded as the most definite symbol of the contribution of windmills to the nation. Another popular set of windmills can be found at Schiedam. Here some of tallest windmills in the world are located, with the tallest approaching an astonishing 108 feet high. The Netherlands' windmills were built initially in an attempt to keep seawater out of low-lying areas and provide the Dutch people with agricultural land. Windmills would effectively pump water out of lowland areas back into nearby rivers thereby making more space on which to grow crops. Apart from drainage, windmills were also used to grind various types of grain. For instance, the windmills at Schiedam help in the production of Dutch gin while windmills in Zaanse Schans were used in the production of mustard, oil, and paper.

When they are not working, windmills can be used as a communication device for the position of windmill sails are used by the Dutch to give signals pertaining to happy and sad events. The various position of windmills each have a different meaning allowing mill owners to disseminate information, impart news, and also express feelings. Like the burgomaster and schoolmaster, the millers were a central figure in rural Dutch communities as they learned gossip and news via their customers and by means of the position of the windmill's sails could impart this news via the sails. Over time, a code of the windmill sail developed. Windmill sails are visible from all sides, meaning it is easy to see their sails from all positions. In addition, windmills tend to be built on natural or artificial mounds so as the landscape of the Netherlands is particularly flat information indicated by windmill sails was visible for miles around.

When seen from the front, the sails of a windmill always turn counterclockwise so starting with the uppermost sail the sails of a windmill always move from right to left. If a miller wishes to express joy, for example, to announce the birth of a child or a marriage, he makes the uppermost sail stop just before it reaches the highest vertical position and fixes the sail in place. This is known as the "coming" position and is often accompanied by a flag placed in the windmill's cap—the roof of the windmill's tower, which in the Netherlands is often movable. The opposite of the coming position is the "going" position, which is used to signal mourning and sorrow. The going position sees the uppermost sail fixed in place once it has passed through the highest vertical position. This position is representative of death as it shows that the upper sail has traveled past the concluding point of its journey from top to bottom and shows that life is, literally, going downhill. It is usual for this position to be employed when a member of the miller's family has died or some other form of mourning is in progress. When a village funeral procession passes a windmill, the mill will be set in the mourning position and the windmill's cap is turned to face the direction of the graveyard.

The going position is also occasionally used to mark times of national mourning. This was in evidence when windmills across the Netherlands were fixed in the mourning position on the death of Dutch prince Johan Friso in 2013. The prince, who was known as Prince Friso, died at 44 years of age, due to complications following brain damage that was the result of a skiing accident that left the prince in a coma for a year and a half. Upon his death, the Association of Dutch Windmills offered its condolences as the prince had held a ceremonial role within the association. The association also asked all windmill owners across the Netherlands to place their windmill sails in the traditional mourning position. (*See* Plate 23.) To mark the sorrowful occasion, the sails of all the windmills in Zaanse Schaans were pointed to the southwest as this was in the direction of the Dutch city of The Hague, where the prince died. The windmills stayed in this position until after the prince's funeral.

More recently, windmill sails were used to mark the downing of Malaysian Airways Flight MH17. July 23, 2014, was declared a day of national mourning in the Netherlands, the first since the death of Queen Wilhemina in 1962, in honor of those who died on the MH17 flight from Amsterdam to Kuala Lumpur that was shot down over the conflict-hit region of eastern Ukraine killing 283 passengers, including 80 children, plus 15 crew members. One hundred and ninety-three of those killed came from the Netherlands so to express national sorrow all the nation's windmills were placed in the mourning position. As the first coffins returned to the Netherlands, church bells tolled for 10 minutes nationwide, trains came to a stop for one minute at 4 p.m. as the country observed a minute's silence, and no planes took off or landed for 13 minutes at Schiphol Airport in the nation's capital, Amsterdam, from where the Malaysian Airlines flight departed.

Windmills are so central to Dutch culture that in the Netherlands an entire day is dedicated to them every year. The second Saturday of May each year is designated National Mills Day and sees more than 600 mills around the country open their doors to visitors.

Film director Alfred Hitchcock utilized the Dutch windmill code in his 1940 film *Foreign Correspondent*. In a classic scene, the film's hero notices that one windmill in particular is turning the wrong way—against the wind—and deduces that this is a signal that ultimately reveals the actions of a spy ring. A similar tradition to the Dutch windmill code used to be employed in parts of the United Kingdom for a miller would remove the sails of his mill to signal a death in the family. However this tradition no longer takes place in the United Kingdom.

See also: Minute's Silence; National Day of Mourning; Passing Bells; State Funeral

Further Reading

CNBC. "Dutch Mourn First MH17 Bodies Flown to Netherlands." CNBC: War and Military Conflict, July 23, 2013. Accessed January 6, 2015, at http://www.cnbc.com/id/101859164.

Holland Information. "The Dutch Love Affair with Windmills." Accessed January 6, 2015, at http://www.holland-information.com/windmills/.

Let.rug.nl. "Tradition in Windmills." Accessed January 6, 2015, at http://www.let.rug.nl/polders/boekje/tradition.htm.

Righter, Robert W. *Wind Energy in America: A History*. Norman: The University of Oklahoma Press, 1996.

Steinglass, Matt. "Netherlands' Prince Friso Dies after 18 Months in Coma," August 12, 2013. Accessed January 6, 2015, at http://www.ft.com/cms/s/0/876f8a70-0371-11e3-980a-00144feab7de.html#axzz3O2Tww0ll.

Sussex Mills Group. "Post Mills." Accessed January 6, 2015, at http://www.sussexmillsgroup.org.uk/postmill.htm.

UNESCO World Heritage Center. "Mill Network at Kinderdijk-Elshout." World Heritage List. Accessed January 6, 2015, at http://whc.unesco.org/en/list/818/.

Y

YEW TREES, EUROPE

The yew is an evergreen tree belonging to the genus *Taxus* and the family *Taxaceae* in the Northern hemisphere. In Europe, the yew symbolizes both death and immortality for the berries of the tree are poisonous yet the tree is long living and capable of re-rooting from branches so that they produce leaves. In tree lore the yew is, however, thought to bring death to those who pluck it injudiciously. In addition, in Europe, particularly the United Kingdom, the yew is very closely associated with graveyards of which they are a characteristic feature. (*See* Plate 24.) Indeed across Europe the yew tree is viewed as a guardian of the dead and is referred to as the "death tree." For this reason, it is considered unlucky to bring a piece of yew into a home. The association of yews with death means that they were traditionally planted beside the dead to keep witches and demons away from the hallowed ground of the cemetery as it was thought that the trees were able to prevent evil forces from transforming the dead into revenants, that is, a supernatural being that comes back to life either as a ghost inhabiting its own lifeless body or by possessing the body of somebody else. In Medieval England, sprigs of yew were tucked into shrouds, a custom documented in 1651. William Shakespeare also refers to this custom in Act II, Scene 4 of his play *Twelfth Night* when "a shroud of white, stuck all with yew" is mentioned.

The yew tree is also associated with death superstitions in France. For example, in Brittany graveyard yews are said to spread a root into the mouth of every corpse buried in the vicinity, and in Normandy it is traditional to place a branch of yew next to a corpse awaiting burial.

In the 18th century, an England funerary custom saw yew tree leaves placed on top of coffins and graves while the planting of yew trees in British and Irish cemeteries seems to have arrived in Britain and Ireland at the same time as Christianity came to Wales and Ireland. The tradition appears to have started as an imitation of the southern European tradition of planting cypress and laurel trees near the dead. In Britain, during pre-Christian times, yews were revered. Sites of Romano-British burials have been found close to an ancient yew at Claverley in Shropshire, England, and many holy wells are located near yews such as the one at Hope Bagot, beneath Brown Clee in Shropshire. Yews have also entered English culture through place names including Ewhurst in Surrey, Ewshot in Hampshire, and Uley in Gloucestershire. The planting of yew trees in cemeteries spread to England during the 12th century by which time, according to Welsh historian Giraldus Cambrensis, the yews of Ireland were located in old cemeteries and sacred places, planted in ancient times by holy men to provide ornamentation. Also, yews were used by Christians to mark the position of hermits' dwellings. Later generations of British churchgoers found the planting of yew trees in cemeteries perplexing for several reasons. For instance, people wondered if the trees were grown to provide wood to make longbows or to stop cows from eating the grass that covered graves.

It is difficult to assess the age of the yew trees found in graveyards across the United Kingdom but many are thought to be over 1,000 years old and the great age of these yew trees has led some to suggest that many yews trees were planted soon after their churches were built. In 1990, a large yew tree in Selborne in the county of Hampshire collapsed during a spell of strong wind revealing medieval graves beneath its roots. The graves were dated to 1200. However it has also been asserted that Druids planted the largest, and therefore oldest, churchyard yews in Britain around 2,000 to 5,000 years ago for yew trees are sacred to the Druids as Druids make their wands from yew wood. Indeed a yew in the graveyard at Fortingall in Scotland, known as the Fortingall Yew, is believed to be 5,000 years old while a yew tree in Defynnog near Sennybridge, in the Brecon Beacons National Park in Wales is thought to have started life during the Bronze Age. This theory would suggest that churches were erected where yew trees were already planted. However critics say this theory lacks much evidence and is discounted by most historians. The Druids did however bury their dead beneath oak trees, which they considered holy. Indeed the Druids held the oak in such high regard that peeling the bark from an oak tree was punishable, while anybody caught cutting an oak branch would suffer the loss of a limb. Meanwhile, the Druids punished those who cut down an oak by sentencing them to death. Elsewhere in Europe, oak trees were connected with death. For instance, in Croatia witches were buried under oaks, as it was believed their spirits would enter the trees, and in medieval Germany oak tree-burial was practiced. This custom saw corpses buried inside the hollow of an oak tree and it is believed that the concept of wooden coffins may stem from this tree-burial custom.

Another evergreen plant associated with graveyards is ivy. According to Christian lore, a grave on which ivy will not grow is said to house an unhappy soul, while if ivy grows on the grave of a young woman it is thought the woman died for love. Several old English ballads tell of ivy growing on the graves of ill-fated lovers, intertwining its tendrils to show that the lover's everlasting affection continues in the afterlife. Additionally, in England it is generally thought to be unlucky to bring ivy indoors except at Christmas when it is used to decorate homes. Ivy leaves were traditionally used in a form of death divination at Hallowe'en in the English county of Hertfordshire for leaves would be placed in water and if the following morning black, coffin-shaped spots appeared, it was thought a member of the household would die within a year.

See also: *Ankou*; Bees; Birth Plants (Volume 1); Funeral Plants; Hallowe'en and *Martinstag*; Living with the Dead; Mistletoe (Volume 1)

Further Reading

Alexander, Marc. *The Sutton Companion to British Folklore, Myths & Legends.* Stroud, UK: Sutton Publishing Limited, 2002.

Aslet, Clive. "The Ancient, Sacred, Regenerative, Death-Defying Yew Tree," *The Telegraph.* July 9, 2014. Accessed January 1, 2015, at http://www.telegraph.co.uk/news/earth/countryside/10954261/The-ancient-sacred-regenerative-death-defying-yew-tree.html.

Jones, Alison. *Larousse Dictionary of World Folklore.* Edinburgh, UK: Larousse, 1996.

Simpson, Jacqueline, and Steve Roud. *Oxford Dictionary of English Folklore.* Oxford, UK: Oxford University Press, 2000.

Varner, Gary R. *The Mythic Forest, the Green Man and the Spirit of Nature.* New York: Algora Publishing, 2006.

Watts, D. C. *Dictionary of Plant Lore.* Burlington, MA: Academic Press, 2007.

YU LAN JIE: THE HUNGRY GHOST FESTIVAL, CHINA

The Hungry Ghost Festival is an important festival to honor ancestors. The festival is part of the Taoist and Buddhists traditions and occurs in countries such as Malaysia and Singapore but is most closely associated with China. The Hungry Ghost Festival is known by a variety of names including *Yu Lan Jie*, the *Zhongyuan* Festival (Taoist) and *Yulanpen* Festival (Buddhist).

The Hungry Ghost Festival is one of a number of Chinese customs that venerate ancestors, but in Jiangxi Province and Hunan Province the Hungry Ghost Festival is considered more important than the *Qingming* Festival. However unlike during the Qingming Festival when families visit the tombs of their ancestors, during the Hungry Ghost Festival it is the ghosts of the departed that visit the living in search of nourishment. Another difference between the Hungry Ghost Festival and the Qingming Festival is that the Hungry Ghost Festival is held for departed souls that are doomed to hell without any hope of reprieve for their suffering. Moreover, the Chinese believe that during Hungry Ghost Month, most particularly on the night of the full moon, there is a greater connection between the dead and the living than on any other night, so it is important to take precautions to placate the dead as well as to honor ancestors. For this reason, people in China perform ceremonies and customs to protect themselves from the ghosts' mischief and anger. Indeed such is the level of fear of pranks by vengeful ghosts that many Chinese people will not go swimming during Hungry Ghost Month for fear that angry ghosts will hold onto their feet causing them to drown. Indeed the whole of the Hungry Ghost month is considered a generally unlucky time during which new ventures should be put on hold, weddings delayed, and birthdays not celebrated.

According to the indigenous Chinese philosophical tradition known as Taoism, the 14th or 15th day of the 7th month of the lunar year, which usually equates to August or September in the West, sees ghosts return to the world of the living. Although the ancestral ghosts are thought to wander the earth for the whole month, known as Hungry Ghost Month, the Hungry Ghost Festival takes place over just one night. The Chinese believe that during Hungry Ghost Month the gates of hell are opened and every ghost and spirit is permitted to wander the earth in order to find food and drink. The hell of Chinese tradition (*Ti Yu*) is not the frightening place as understood by Christians, but rather it is a realm consisting of different rooms where souls go depending on the sins they committed in life. While in Ti Yu the souls wait to atone for their sins and progress through levels of existence.

It is generally agreed that the Hungry Ghost Festival evolved from various folk traditions including the Buddhist festival, *Ullambana*, or the Festival of Deliverance. Over time, Ullambana merged with the different folk stories of hungry ghosts until one particular folk tale developed. Although Ullambana originated in India, the Chinese gradually adopted it until it came to exemplify Chinese beliefs and mythology and was populated by characters from Chinese tradition. There are several folktales associated with the originating of Ullambana and, subsequently, the Hungry Ghost Festival. One of the most well known tales tells the story of one of the Buddha's followers, Maudgalyayana, who had the psychic ability to see his parents after they died. Unfortunately for Maudgalyayana, he was able to see that his father had entered a heavenly place but his mother, who was covetous and deceitful in life, had entered a lower dominion and turned into a hungry ghost. According to the folk tale, hungry ghosts had huge stomachs but narrow throats that could not tolerate food, meaning that the hungry ghosts were perpetually ravenous. Distressed by what he saw, Maudgalyayana asked the Buddha how he could help his mother and was told a number of things. Firstly Maudgalyayana had to leave food out for the worst type of hungry ghost, the *pretas*, who in life had been the most selfish and greediest of people. Secondly, Maudgalyayana had to say a mantra seven times before snapping his fingers and tip food onto the ground. According to the Buddha, this would allow Maudgalyayana's mother to transform into a dog that he could then look after. Maudgalyayana did not like the idea of his mother transforming into a dog and again asked the Buddha how he could help his parent. This time the Buddha answered that on the 15th day of the lunar month Maudgalyayana should proffer 500 pieces of incense as an offering together with sacrificial food and drink. After this, Maudgalyayana's mother would be resurrected in human form.

Nowadays, the proffering of food, drinks, and offerings are still a major part of the Hungry Ghost Festival as these offerings are said to appease ancestral spirits. The main ritual associated with the Hungry Ghost festival occurs at dusk. The ritual sees people bring photographs and paintings of their ancestors on a table and then burn incense close to the portraits. Additionally, the plates and seats at which the ancestors used to sit are left vacant as this is thought both to commemorate the dead and also to appease the spirits. It is important that plenty of food and drink be available for the ghosts to eat and drink because, having been deprived of nourishment in the netherworld the spirits anticipate the food and drinks left out for them, and sorely disappointed if they are not offered, the ghosts will seek revenge if they are not fed and watered as much as they would like. Indeed Chinese families fear that bad luck will befall them if they do not please the ghosts. In order to please the spirits, offerings of sheep, chickens, pigs, peaches, and rice are also left at Buddhist temples while chants and prayers are said to appease the spirits too. Chinese people consider hungry ghosts to be frightening, polluting creatures able to inflict harm, both spiritual and physical, on the living. Indeed during Hungry Ghost Month many Chinese people fear that the spirits may drag them down to hell, causing them to become ghosts too. For this reason, Chinese people will not walk alone at night during the month when the hungry ghosts are said to roam the streets nor will they wear red clothing or whistle as this is said to attract ghosts to the living.

Another notable tradition associated with the Hungry Ghost Festival is the burning of joss paper money (i.e., pretend paper money made from bamboo paper or rice paper) and also paper money, known as ghost money or hell money, which is a relatively new custom. There are three types of joss money: golden paper (*jin-zhi*) that takes the form of joss paper in the center of which is a piece of gold-colored foil and is burned to honor ancestors and deities, silver paper (*yin-zhi*) that is decorated with silver foil and is less valuable that gold paper, and everyday joss paper that is marked with a red ink stamp in the middle. Silver paper and ordinary joss paper are offered to hungry ghosts because these types of joss paper are low value and so are appropriate to be given to lesser beings. The custom of burning hell money, which resembles high denomination bank notes, occurs particularly on the first day of Ghost Month. The tradition of burning hell money occurs for many reasons. Firstly, burning the notes is meant to allow the ghosts to use the money to pay for a happy afterlife during which they can use the money to buy treats. Burning the money is also said to shorten ancestors' stays in hell. Moreover, the notes can be burned to honor the King of Hell. Also, on the night of the Hungry Ghost Festival families burn incense in front of their house. Indeed families often compete to see which of them can burn the most incense.

As families are either at home or at their favorite temple during the Hungry Ghost Festival the streets are usually left empty to let the spirits roam all the more freely. The empty streets also allow families to burn large amounts of incense in front of their homes without the fear of burning anyone. That said, although the streets are on the whole left empty, a recently developed Hungry Ghost Festival custom are colorful street variety shows, or *ge tai*. The variety shows are performed in order to entertain the hungry ghosts as this ensures that the spirits are kept happy and distracted form making mischief for the living. Meanwhile, another Hungry Ghost festival tradition sees paper boats and red lanterns floated on rivers in order to guide the spirits back to their homes.

According to Chinese beliefs, people should not marry, start new businesses, give birth or move home during Hungry Ghost month and especially not on the night of the Hungry Ghost Festival. This is because the festival is a time when ghosts prevail and so the activities of the living should cease.

See also: All Souls' Day; *Dia de los Muertos*: Day of the Dead; Hallowe'en; Japanese Death Customs; *Qingming* Festival; Saturday of Souls and *Radonitsa*; Tết Nguyên đan; *Zaduszki*

Further Reading

China Highlights. "Hungry Ghost Festival." Accessed October 17, 2015, at http://www.chinahighlights.com/festivals/hungry-ghost-festival.htm.

Koh, Jaime, and Stephanie Ho. *Culture and Customs of Singapore and Malaysia.* Santa Barbara, CA: Greenwood Press, 2009.

Kuah-Pearce, Khun Eng. *State, Society, and Religious Engineering: Towards a Reformist Buddhism in Singapore.* Pasir Panjang, Singapore: Institute of Southeast Asian Studies, 2009.

Montillo, Roseanne. *Halloween and Commemorations of the Dead.* New York: Infobase Publishing, 2009.

Z

ZADUSZKI, POLAND

Zaduszki (also known as *dzień zaduszny*) is a Polish tradition of that sees lit candles (*znicze*) placed on the graves of ancestors by visiting family members. Zaduszki is the equivalent of All Souls' Day and is celebrated on November 2. Indeed the tradition of lighting candles stems from ancient Slavic custom of the *Dziady* (Grandfathers) Feast that was held on All Souls' Day. However, due to a series of misunderstandings, Dziady is now generally held on All Saints' Day rather than All Souls' days. The name Zaduszki derives from *dzień zaduszny*, which can be translated as The Day of the Prayer For Souls. Zaduszki is therefore much more closely allied to All Souls' Day than All Saints' Day. However neither Zaduszki nor the rite of the Dziady Feast were intended to help people connect with the souls of the dead nor to appease the spirit world or gain the favor of the dead. Rather, both Zaduszki and the Dziady Feast are held to pay homage to ancestors. During Zaduszki, Polish people pay tribute to their ancestors and show their appreciation for their forefathers by keeping their memory alive. On Zaduszki people living in Poland thank their deceased relatives for giving them the chance to live.

The main custom associated with Zaduszki sees huge bonfires lit at cemeteries and at crossroads. Most especially fires are lit on the graves of people that have committed suicide, who traditionally, were not buried in Polish cemeteries. The famous Polish poet Adam Mickiewicz (1798–1855) detailed the traditions of Zaduszki in his drama *Dziady*. According to Mickiewicz, working-class people would gather in abandoned houses and chapels located near cemeteries to offer food and drink to the souls of the departed. People would summon the souls of the dead back to life. The gathered people would then discuss the deeds of the deceased and judge them according to the tenets of folk wisdom rather than according to the teachings of the Christian tradition. Moreover, the dead were judged not solely on what they had achieved in life but also on what they had failed to do and what qualities they had lacked. Another Zaduszki tradition sees a special bread baked and broad beans cooked. Also, a version of *koliva* called *kutia*, which is traditionally reserved for funerals in Poland, Ukraine, Russia, and Belarus, is prepared too. These foods would then be offered to the dead along with glasses of vodka. It is also customary for extra places to be set at dinner tables when people have their evening meal. These extra places are reserved for the dead who may wish to join the living as they break bread. Often at the evening meal the bread will be a special type of rye bread that is shaped into long loaves that resemble shrouded corpses. Other foods eaten traditionally on this night include an ancient buckwheat dish called *kasza* that, as it is very old, would have been enjoyed by ancestors. Kasza is passed around the table from diner to diner but servings are always placed on the plates reserved for the dead first before any of the living receive their share. The dead are also given a glass of vodka. After everyone has been served their food and drink, blessings for the dead are said imploring ancestors to enjoy the feast and be welcome.

In many areas of Poland, it is usual to pour a mixture of candle wax mixed with walnut shells on to rivers during Zaduszki. According to tradition, when the wax solidifies on hitting the surface of the water it forms messages that then make their way to the dead. When people return from performing rituals at cemeteries and rivers they return home and indulge in age-old forms of divination. One of these types of divination also involves candle wax for the melted wax—preferably bees' wax, which Polish people consider almost sacred—is poured first into the bowl of a spoon and then into a glass of water. The shape that the solidifying wax takes on is said to foretell the future. Other forms of divination performed during Zaduszki include looking at natural symbols and rune type symbols on objects such as decorated eggs called *pisanki*. Similarly, Polish people also perform a type of divination in a darkened room in which two mirrors are placed facing each other with a candle between them. A person seeking knowledge of the future then stares intently at the candle's flame and the shadows that the candle casts, which, it is believed, will take on the form of things yet to be. People also tend to watch their pets carefully as the animals are regarded as either bringers of good news from the dead or harbingers of doom. It is thought especially bad if a pet sleeps for a long time on Zaduszki. Polish people also take especial notice of their dreams at Zaduszki as the dreams that occur at this special time of year are said to be particularly prophetic.

Outside of the home during Zaduszki the streets are filled with quiet, soberly dressed crowds and cemeteries glow with thousands of candles. One of the main places of Zaduszki observance is the former royal capital city of Poland, Krakow, that is home to many beautiful old cemeteries. One Krakow cemetery in particular, the Gothic styled Rakowicki Cemetery, is particularly notable at Zaduszki when thousands of candles in transparent vases are placed on graves and at the base of memorials, as are fresh flowers. All the while, priests sing psalms and incense is wafted around.

Polish people do not traditionally celebrate Hallowe'en. However in recent years Hallowe'en has become increasingly popular with the holding of Hallowe'en parties and the like. However despite the newfound popularity of Hallowe'en, many Polish people still observe Zaduszki too as they see it as a cherished tradition that is devoid of the commercialism they associate with Hallowe'en.

See also: All Souls' Day; *Andrzejki*: St Andrew's Eve (Volume 2); *Dia de los Muertos*: Day of the Dead; Easter Eggs; Hallowe'en and *Martinstag*; Japanese Death Customs; *Koliva*; *Qingming* Festival; Saturday of Souls and *Radonitsa*; *Tết Nguyên đan*; Tombstone Tourism; *Yu Lan Jie*: The Hungry Ghost Festival

Further Reading

Local-life.com. "All Saints' Day and All Souls." Accessed October 18, 2015, at http://www.local-life.com/krakow/articles/all-saints-day.

Slavorum. "All Souls' Day and All Saints' Day in Polish Tradition." *Exploring Slavic World*, October 2011. Accessed October 18, 2015, at http://www.slavorum.org/forum/discussion/912/all-souls-day-and-all-saints-day-in-polish-tradition.

Szafran, Denice. "All Saints' and All Souls' Day in Poland," *Polish American Journal*, 2014. Accessed October 18, 2015, at http://www.polamjournal.com/Library/Holidays/Zaduszki--All_Soul-s_Day/zaduszki--all_soul_s_day.html.

ZOMBIES AND VOODOO DEATH TRADITIONS, HAITI

A zombie (also spelled zombi) is a revenant spirit or re-animated corpse belonging to Haitian Voodoo (also Vodou) lore. Despite appearing in human form, zombies are no longer connected to life. As such, zombies breach some of the most deeply felt taboos for they are associated with cannibalism and the desecration of graves, and blur the separation of life and death. According to the Voodoo tradition, a zombie is a human whose soul has been corrupted through black magic resulting in it becoming lifeless. Most people are familiar with the idea of zombies through the many horror films featuring the creatures but zombies have a complex folk history and mythological background. Though in the popular Western imagination zombies are mainly associated with horror films, television series, and books, for practitioners of Voodoo zombies seem very real. Indeed many scholars both in the West and in Haiti have tried to prove that zombies do truly exist. Moreover, such is the belief in zombies in Haiti, especially in rural areas of the country, that families may request an autopsy to ensure that the body of a deceased person is actually dead and has not become a zombie.

Scholars believe that the word zombie originates from either the Kongo Bantu language word *nzambi*, meaning soul, or *ndzumbi*, the word for corpse in the Mitsogo language spoken in Gabon. The areas of Africa where these languages were spoken are where European slave traders transported swathes of the population across the Atlantic to work in plantations located in the West Indies. The African slaves brought with them their native religions but under French law the slaves were required to convert to Catholicism—Haiti was at this time ruled by France and known as Saint-Domingue. The end result was that a number of new religions emerged that combined elements of African religions and Catholicism: Voodoo (also spelled Vodou) in Haiti, Obeah in Jamaica, and Santeria in Cuba.

In Haiti and Martinique, the term zombie was originally generally applied to any spirit or ghost. Over time, however, the word became connected to the belief that a *bokor* (sorcerer or witch-doctor) could capture a person's soul and make the victim seem to be dead—either through magic, hypnotic suggestion, or the administering of a secret potion—before reviving the victim as the bokor's personal slave. Thus it seems that even in a deathlike state slaves felt they had no choice but to be trapped in a living death of everlasting drudgery. According to the beliefs held by slaves living in Haiti, dying would allow them to travel to *lan guinée*, by which they meant Guinea, or Africa in general, where they would enjoy liberation in the afterlife. However though many slaves committed suicide those slaves that killed themselves were not permitted to enter *lan guinée*. Instead, slaves that killed themselves were thought condemned to work on plantations forever, as soulless, undead slaves trapped within their own bodies. In this way, therefore, the concept of the zombie was born. By the time French rule of Haiti ended, the zombie had become entrenched in Haitian folklore. The appalling conditions in which Saint-Domingue's slaves existed eventually led to a slave rebellion that saw slaves oust their masters in 1791. Following a revolutionary war of 1804, Saint-Domingue (now renamed Haiti) became the first independent black republic and from then on the country was consistently demonized in the 19th-century European imagination as a place of superstition and death with frequent reports of cannibalism, human sacrifice, and supernatural rituals. Meanwhile, long-held zombie beliefs merged with Voodoo traditions with the result that Haitians believed zombies were actually corpses that had been resurrected by shamans and Voodoo priests.

After the United States occupied Haiti in 1915, rumors about zombies began to spread throughout America. Attempts by United States authorities to eradicate the Voodoo religion only reinforced Haitians' respect for their native beliefs however. It is, perhaps, no co-incidence that the highly influential zombie film *White Zombie* appeared in 1932, two years before the American occupation of Haiti came to an end.

Today, throughout Western popular culture zombies are almost always depicted as being connected to the end of the world via the so-called zombie apocalypse. This is a global pandemic of zombie-ism that will transform the majority of the human population into zombies ravenous for the flesh of non-zombie humans. The zombie apocalypse is the mainstay of the modern zombie movie (*Shaun of the Dead*, 2004; *State of Emergency*, 2011; *Zombieland*, 2009; *World War Z*, 2013; and the like) as well as the hit television show *The Walking Dead* (2010–present).

Today, a majority of Haitians observe Voodoo, which in Haiti, combines many various rites and beliefs originating from African slaves and Catholicism. (*See* Plate 25.) There is no central Voodoo authority, scripture or core doctrine. There are some unifying elements of Voodoo however. For instance, believers worship *Le Grand Maitre*, or Grand Master, who is the equivalent of the Christian God and pray to *loa* (spirits) who are believed to intercede with God on their behalf in the way that Catholics believe saints intervene. Voodoo believers also venerate their ancestors, whom believers feel guide them through their times of difficulty while also believing that everything in the world (e.g., people, animals, and plants) has a spirit.

On the day that a Voodoo follower dies, an *oungan* (Voodoo priest) or *mam'bo* (priestess) is called in to perform a rite called the *dessounen*. This ritual is performed to make sure that the various elements of the deceased are dispatched to their appropriate destinations—the *ti-bon-ange* (the dead individual's characteristics) to the *Grand Met* (akin to heaven), the *gwo-bon-ange* (immortal life force) to the watery realm beneath the earth called *Ginen,* and the body to the earth. During the dessounen, the priest shakes a rattle-like instrument known as an *ason* and speaks into one of the deceased's ears commending the gwo-bon-ange and *met tet* (spirit of the head) to leave the body. As a sign that both entities have left the body of the deceased the priest will become possessed by the *Iwa* spirit that is the deceased's met tet. Once the dessounen has concluded, members of the deceased's community wash the deceased all the while relaying messages from the deceased's family in the belief that the deceased can pass the messages on to ancestors. Additionally, after a Voodoo believer dies a nine-day prayer ritual called a *demier priyem*, which is similar to a wake, takes place. During the wake, the community in which the departed lived is invited to visit the deceased and celebrate their departure from life. To this end, during a Voodoo wake people gather together to eat, drink, chant, and say prayers. The enemies of the deceased are invited to the wake as well in order to heal rifts between individuals. Then, on the ninth day either a ritual known as a *Prise de deuil* is held that is akin to a funeral or the deceased is taken to a cemetery where Catholic burial rites are performed. Once the funeral and burial have taken place the family of the deceased witnesses the ritual breaking and burial of the *pot tet*, a vessel believed to contain a Voodoo practitioner's soul in the form of the gwo-bon-ange and met tet of the departed. One year after the death, the family of the deceased organize a ceremony called the *ouete mo nan ba dlo* that invites the spirit of the deceased back into society of the living as an ancestor. This ceremony is held to allow the living to recognize the knowledge and power of the deceased and to let the living ask the Iwa spirits to help them in their everyday life. Ouete mo nan ba dlo ceremonies are costly, meaning that some families may wish to delay hosting them. After a devastating earthquake struck Haiti in 2010 killing an estimated 200,000 Haitians, Voodoo played an important role in helping the country's population cope with the tragedy. However many Haitian Voodoo believers feared that the sudden number of so many deaths meant the living were unable to hold the appropriate ceremonies to assist the souls of the dead. Deferring such rituals as the *ouete mo nan ba dlo* is, however, considered very risky as failure to hold the ceremony in a timely fashion can result in calamity befalling the family of the deceased and his or her community as a whole. Moreover, not holding the ceremony is thought to result in general bad luck and means that the family of the deceased are unable to connect to their ancestors and, therefore, fail to have access to protective powers and good luck that venerating ancestors provides.

See also: Albanian Funeral Customs; Crucifixion Rituals; *Dia de los Muertos*: Day of the Dead; Eating the Ashes of the Dead; Endocannibalism; Hallowe'en and *Martinstag*; Living with the Dead; Monstrous Punishments for Naughty Children (Volume 1); Wake; *Yu Lan Jie*: The Hungry Ghost Festival; Changeling Beliefs (Volume 1)

Further Reading

Anderson, Jeffrey E., ed. *The Voodoo Encyclopedia: Magic, Ritual, and Religion*. Santa Barbara, CA: ABC-CLIO, 2015.

Bishop, Kyle William. *American Zombie Gothic: The Rise and Fall (and Rise) of the Walking Dead in Popular Culture*. Jefferson, NC: McFarland & Company Inc. Publishers, 2010.

Bradley Hagerty, Barbara. "Voodoo Brings Solace to Grieving Haitians." National Public Radio. January 20, 2010. Accessed December 15, 2015, at http://www.npr.org/templates/story/story.php?storyId=122770590.

Burnett, John. "Quake Takes Its Toll on Haiti's Burial Rites." National Public Radio, February 4, 2010. Accessed December 15, 2015, at http://www.npr.org/templates/story/story.php?storyId=123331644.

Jones, Alison. *Larousse Dictionary of World Folklore*. Edinburgh, UK: Larousse, 1996.

Luckhurst, Roger. "Where Do Zombies Come From?" BBC: Culture. August 31, 2015. Accessed December 15, 2015, at http://www.bbc.com/culture/story/20150828-where-do-zombies-come-from.

Mariani, Mike. "The Tragic, Forgotten History of Zombies," *The Atlantic*, October 28, 2015. Accessed December 15, 2015, at http://www.theatlantic.com/entertainment/archive/2015/10/how-america-erased-the-tragic-history-of-the-zombie/412264/.

Murrell, Nathaniel Samuel. *Afro-Caribbean Religions: An Introduction to Their Historical, Cultural, and Sacred Traditions*. Philadelphia, PA: Temple University Press, 2010.

The Uncanny Valley. "Haiti & the Truth about Zombies." Accessed December 14, 2015, at http://www.umich.edu/~uncanny/zombies.html.

ZOROASTRIAN FUNERALS, INDIA

Zoroastrianism is one of the world's oldest monotheistic religions, established around 3,500 years ago by the Prophet Zarathustra in ancient Iran. For a millennium, Zoroastrianism was one of the most powerful religions on earth. However, today, Zoroastrianism is one of the world's smallest religions with estimates suggesting there are probably less than 190,000 followers worldwide with the majority of followers living in India, Iran, and Pakistan, though small communities of Zoroastrians can be found across the globe, particularly in the United Kingdom, Canada, the United States, and Australia. However in the Western countries where Zoroastrian funerals are either considered impractical or are not permitted by law, Zoroastrians normally choose to be cremated.

Zoroastrians are famous for their funerals for they neither bury nor cremate their dead preferring instead the tradition of corpse exposure sometimes referred to as "laying out the dead." In Mumbai, India, where more than half of India's Zoroastrians reside, the huge "Towers of Silence" set within 57 acres of wooded garden have become a focus of interest because it is one of the few places where this traditional method of corpse disposal can still occur. Similar towers can also be found in Iran, Uzbekistan, and elsewhere.

According to Zoroastrian beliefs, as soon as the last breath has left the body it becomes impure. This is because death is considered to be the work of *Angra Mainyu*, the embodiment of all that is evil, whereas the earth and all that is beautiful is believed to be the pure work of God. It follows therefore that since Zoroastrians believe that earth is sacred the decaying dead should not be buried within it. Zoroastrians also believe water is sacred so polluting corpses should not be thrown into the sea, rivers, lakes, or oceans. Similarly, fire is sacred to the Zoroastrians and so must not be profaned by being used for cremations. Thus the Zoroastrians feel that contaminating the elements of Earth, Air, Fire, and Water with the decaying matter of a corpse is sacrilege. Zoroastrians believe that in order for the living to avoid being contaminated by the evil forces inherent in death, corpses should remain isolated and decaying, untouched and undisturbed by the living. Zoroastrians are taught to avoid the dead as much as possible to prevent the evil at work in the corpse from entering into them through bodily contact. So strongly were these beliefs held that the Prophet Zarathustra asserted that any Zoroastrian that touched a dead body and therefore left him- or herself open to contamination by evil forces should be put to death.

Instead of burying a corpse in the ground or in a body of water, or turning it to ash through cremation, Zoroastrians traditionally lay the corpse out on a purpose built tower called a *dakhma* where the body is left exposed to the sun and can be eaten by birds of prey such as vultures and crows, which Zoroastrians believe were made by God for this purpose. A dakhma is sometimes referred to as a Tower of Silence, the term coined by Robert Murphy, a translator for the British colonial government, in 1832.

Zoroastrian funerals may then fall under the banner of excarnation, or defleshing, the name given to the burial practice of removing the flesh and organs of a corpse so that only the bones remain. There is no set pattern for a dakhma but the building usually takes the form of a massive, squat, round, tower-like walled edifice built on top of a hill and often surrounded by gardens where the exposure of the corpse occurs for the corpse is placed inside the walls of the tower so that it can be excarnated and decomposition can take place.

To gain entry to the dakhma it is necessary to traverse steps that lead up to a door made of iron that is to be found on the eastern side of the high stone walls. This door allows access to a circular platform measuring about 300 feet in diameter. The platform is constructed from stone slabs and slopes toward a central well. The platform is also divided into three concentric circles: one representing good thoughts, one symbolizing words, and one standing for deeds. Children's bodies are placed in the innermost circle with the women's corpses placed in the middle circle. The outer circle is reserved for the bodies of men. All bodies are placed in shallow depressions set into the platform's stone slabs. Dakhmas have many depressions running in rows that allow bodies to be placed alongside each other. Between the concentric rings are raised ledges that act as a path. The dakhma also features rings of narrow drainage channels that connect these depressions so that all fluids travel to the dakhma's central well. The stone slabs are washed by rainwater that also runs along the channels into the central well that travels downward to the base of the dakhma. At the base of the well are layers of sandstone, sand, and charcoal that act as filters through which all the fluids, secretions, and rainwater that collect in the well must pass before draining through grates on side of the well. All fluids then drain into four underground channels, each of which slopes down to underground pits located at four corners of the tower—just outside the walls. The base of the pits is covered in a thick layer of sand, sandstone, and charcoal that is replaced periodically. The fluid filtration system means that water leaving the pits is clean and free from any contamination. In wet climates, gardens surrounding the tower are grown that help absorb the filtered water.

A dakhma may also contain a small building called a *sagri* within which a fire burns continuously. In India, dakhma complexes feature bungalows called *bunglis*. These are temporary homes consisting of bedrooms, bathrooms, kitchen facilities, a dining room, plus a room to house the corpse initially, a ritual bathing room with a stone platform upon which the body is washed, and a large hall for the subsequent funeral service. An India dakhma complex is known as a *doongerwadi* and consists of a tower of silence, surrounding gardens, and the bunglis.

Once the flesh has either been eaten or rotted away from the skeleton, the remaining bones are bleached and dried out by the sun and then collected together and placed in a central well. When this practice is performed in hot, dry countries, the bones naturally turn to dusty powder. In fact so complete is the desiccation of the bones that some dakhmas are said to have accumulated only five feet of bone powder over a period of 40 years.

Zoroastrians believe there are several benefits to this method of corpse disposal, apart from avoiding contamination by evil. For instance, from an ecological viewpoint in dry and rocky regions—where fertile land is scarce soil is left free for agricultural purposes while contamination by soil and water pollution that can result from ground burial is avoided—any run-off water emanating from a dakhma is treated before being used on surrounding land. Zoroastrians also consider placing a body in a dakhma an egalitarian method of corpse disposal as the bodies of rich and poor are disposed of in the same manner lying side-by-side on one common platform. Also, from a practical point of view, ground burial in desert, rocky, or mountainous regions is difficult to perform and often results in shallow graves that leave corpses exposed to the elements. Finally, Zoroastrians also see their method of excarnation as a charitable process as the corpse feeds scavenging birds and animals. In areas with sufficient numbers of scavengers, a body can be completely stripped of flesh within a few hours, if not sooner.

The Zoroastrian funeral practice faces an uncertain future. The scattering of Zoroastrians across the world means that many followers live in countries where dakhmas are illegal or impractical, for instance, because there are no flesh-eating birds. In fact, dakhma funerals are only practiced in India. However the rapid modernization of India means that while dakhmas were originally built away from populated areas, the spread of towns and cities means that construction has brought the general population into close proximity to the dakhmas to the consternation of some. Others in India disapprove of Zoroastrian funerals on religious grounds. For instance, Islam looks upon the eating of the human dead by birds as a mutilation of the corpse, a practice forbidden in Islam. This has resulted in Indian dakhmas being repeatedly attacked by Muslims, much to the dismay and humiliation of the Zoroastrian community. Another issue threatening the future of Zoroastrian funerals is that the numbers of vultures and crows in India is in rapid decline. Further, the actual involvement of birds in the Zoroastrian process of excarnation is endangering birds as the humans they feed upon have increasingly taken medicines and drugs prior to death. This medication, which is poisonous to birds, is still present in the corpses and leads to the death of the birds that are so integral to the Zoroastrian method of corpse disposal. For these reasons, modern Zoroastrians have to consider how best to keep their ancient tradition alive. The Zoroastrian community in Pune, India, has developed an imaginative solution that utilizes spreading urbanization and does not depend on the presence of birds. Here the Zoroastrians have placed solar panels on their dakhma. These panels direct the sun's rays onto the corpses, effectively cremating the corpses using the power of the sun rather than fire. This innovation is akin to an extension of the natural bleaching and drying of the bones that traditionally occurs in a dakhma.

See also: Alkaline Hydrolysis; High-Platform Exposure of the Corpse; Ossuaries; Sky Burials

Further Reading

BBC. "Towers of Silence." Zoroastrian Funerals. October 2, 2009. Accessed January 5, 2015, at http://www.bbc.co.uk/religion/religions/zoroastrian/ritesrituals/funerals.shtml.

Eduljee, K. E. "After Life and Funeral Customs." Zoroastrian Heritage. Accessed January 5, 2015, at http://www.heritageinstitute.com/zoroastrianism/death/page3.htm.

Hinduwebsite.com. "Zoroastrianism—Funeral Ceremonies, Death and Disposal of the Dead." Accessed January 5, 2015, at http://www.hinduwebsite.com/zoroastrianism/funeral.asp.

Nigosia, Solomon Alexander. *The Zoroastrian Faith: Tradition and Modern Research*. Montreal, Canada: McGill-Queen's University Press, 1993.

Stausberg, Michael, ed. *Zoroastrian Rituals in Context*. Leiden, Netherlands: Koninklijke Brill, 2004.

Selected Bibliography for Volume 3

Alexander, Marc. *The Sutton Companion to British Folklore, Myths & Legends*. Stroud, UK: Sutton Publishing Limited, 2002.

Anderson, Jeffrey E., ed. *The Voodoo Encyclopedia: Magic, Ritual, and Religion*. Santa Barbara, CA: ABC-CLIO, 2015.

Austin, Daniel, and Hilary Bradt. *Madagascar*. Eleventh edition. Chalfont St. Peter, UK: Bradt Travel Guides Ltd., 2014.

Bleicher, Steven. *Contemporary Color: Theory and Use*. Second edition. Clifton Park, NY: Delmar CENGAGE Learning, 2012.

Bramshaw, Vikki. *Craft of the Wise: A Practical Guide to Paganism and Witchcraft*. Ropley, UK: O Books, 2009.

Brennan, Michael, ed. *The A–Z of Death and Dying: Social, Medical, and Cultural Aspects*. Santa Barbara, CA: ABC-CLIO, 2014.

Bryant, Clifton D., and Dennis L. Peck., eds. *Encyclopedia of Death and the Human Experience 1*. Thousand Oaks, CA: SAGE Publications Inc., 2009.

Cheremeteff Jones, Catherine. *A Year of Russian Feasts*. London: Transworld Publishers, 2003.

Chesnut, Andrew R. *Devoted to Death: Santa Muerte, the Skeleton Saint*. Oxford, UK: Oxford University Press, 2012.

Clark, Gordon L., Alicia H. Munnell, and J. Michael Orszag, eds. *The Oxford Handbook of Pensions and Retirement Income, Volume 13*. Oxford, UK: Oxford University Press, 2006.

Crawford, Suzanne J., and Dennis F. Kelley, eds. *American Indian Religious Traditions: An Encyclopedia*. Santa Barbara, CA: ABC-CLIO, 2005.

Dahl Martinsen, Kaare. *Soldier Repatriation: Popular and Political Responses*. Farnham, UK: Ashgate Publishing Limited, 2013.

Davidson, Alan. *The Oxford Companion to Food*. Third edition. Oxford, UK: Oxford University Press, 2014.

Devonshire Jones, Tom, Linda Murray, and Peter Murray. *The Oxford Dictionary of Christian Art and Architecture*. Second edition. Oxford, UK: Oxford University Press, 2013.

Dues, Greg. *Catholic Customs & Traditions: A Popular Guide*. Revised edition. New London, CT: Twenty-Third Publications, 2006.

Elsie, Robert. *A Dictionary of Albanian Religion, Mythology and Folk Culture*. London: C. Hurst & Co. Publishers Ltd., 2001.

Galvan, Javier A., ed. *They Do What? A Cultural Encyclopedia of Extraordinary and Exotic Customs from around the World*. Santa Barbara, CA: ABC-CLIO, 2014.

Garces-Foley, Kathleen, ed. *Death and Religion in a Changing World*. Abingdon, UK: Routledge, 2015.

Garlick, Harry. *The Final Curtain: State Funerals and the Theatre of Power*. Amsterdam, Netherlands: Rodopi, 1999.

Gibson, Marion, Shelley Trower, and Garry Tregidga, eds. *Mysticism, Myth and Celtic Identity*. Abingdon, UK: Routledge, 2013.

Goodlad, Lauren M. E., and Michael Bibby. *Goth: Undead Subculture*. Durham, NC: Duke University Press, 2007.

Hecht, Richard D., and Vincent F. Biondo, eds. *Religion and Everyday Life and Culture: Volume 1*. Santa Barbara, CA: Praeger, 2010.

Herrera-Sobek, Maria. *Celebrating Latino Folklore: An Encyclopedia of Cultural Traditions*. Volume 1. Santa Barbara, CA: ABC-CLIO, 2012.

Herrera-Sobek, Maria. *Celebrating Latino Folklore: An Encyclopedia of Cultural Traditions*. Volume 2. Santa Barbara, CA: ABC-CLIO, 2012.

Howarth, Glennys, and Oliver Leaman, eds. *Encyclopedia of Death and Dying*. Abingdon, UK: Routledge, 2013.

Jeremiah, Ken. *Christian Mummification: An Interpretative History of the Preservation of Saints, Martyrs and Others*. Jefferson, NC: Mcfarland & Company Inc., 2012.

Jones, Alison. *Larousse Dictionary of World Folklore*. Edinburgh, UK: Larousse, 1996.

Kasher, Asa, ed. *Dying and Death: Inter-disciplinary Perspectives*. Amsterdam, Netherlands: Rodopi, 2007.

Keister, Douglas. *Stories in Stone: A Field Guide to Cemetery Symbolism and Iconography*. Layton, UT: Gibbs Smith Publisher, 2004.

Koch, John T., ed. *Celtic Culture: A Historical Encyclopedia Volumes 1–5*. Santa Barbara, CA: ABC-CLIO, 2006.

Laslett, Peter. *A Fresh Map of Life: The Emergence of the Third Age*. London: George Weidenfeld & Nicolson Limited, 1991.

Margry, Peter Jan, ed. *Shrines and Pilgrimage in the Modern World: New Itineraries into the Sacred*. Amsterdam, Netherlands: Amsterdam University Press, 2008.

Margry, Peter Jan, and Cristina Sanchez-Carretero, eds. *Grassroots Memorials: The Politics of Memorializing Traumatic Death*. New York: Berghahn Books, 2011.

McManus, Ruth. *Death in a Global Age*. Basingstoke, UK: Palgrave Macmillan, 2013.

McNab, Chris. *The Book of the Poppy*. Stroud, UK: The History Press, 2014.

Miller, Judith. *Collector's Guides: Costume Jewellery*. London: Dorling Kindersley Limited, 2003.

Montillo, Roseanne. *Halloween and Commemorations of the Dead*. New York: Infobase Publishing, 2009.

Morton, Lisa. *Trick or Treat: A History of Halloween*. London: Reaktion Books Ltd., 2012.

Murrell, Nathaniel Samuel. *Afro-Caribbean Religions: An Introduction to Their Historical, Cultural, and Sacred Traditions*. Philadelphia, PA: Temple University Press, 2010.

Poliquin, Rachel. *The Breathless Zoo: Taxidermy and the Cultures of Longing*. University Park: The Pennsylvania State University Press, 2012.

Roberts, Kai. *Folklore of Yorkshire*. Stroud, UK: The History Press, 2013.

Rogers, Nicholas. *Halloween: From Pagan Ritual to Party Night*. Oxford, UK: Oxford University Press, 2002.

Roud, Steve. *The Penguin Guide to the Superstitions of Britain and Ireland*. London: Penguin Books, 2006.

Simpson, Jacqueline, and Steve Roud. *Oxford Dictionary of English Folklore*. Oxford, UK: Oxford University Press, 2000.

Suzuki, Hikaru, ed. *Death and Dying in Contemporary Japan*. Abingdon, UK: Routledge, 2013.

Townshend, Dale, ed. *Terror and Wonder: The Gothic Imagination*. London: The British Library, 2014.

Van Bremen, Jan, and D. P. Martinez, eds. *Ceremony and Ritual in Japan: Religious Practices in an Industrialized Society*. Abingdon, UK: Routledge, 2002.

Venbrux, Eric, Thomas, Quartier, Claudia Venhorst, and Brenda Mathijssen, eds. *Changing European Death Ways*. Volume 1. Zurich, Switzerland: Lit Verlag, 2013.

Watts, D. C. *Dictionary of Plant Lore*. Burlington, MA: Academic Press, 2007.

Werth, James L. Jr., Elena Yakunina, and Jessica M. Richmond, in Clifton D. Bryant and Dennis L. Peck, eds., *Encyclopedia of Death and the Human Experience Volume 1*. Thousand Oaks, CA: SAGE Publications Inc., 2009

White, Leanne, and Elspeth Frew, eds. *Dark Tourism and Place Identity: Managing and Interpreting Dark Places*. Abingdon, UK: Routledge, 2013.

Young, Mitchell, Eric Zuelow, and Andreas Sturm, eds. *Nationalism in a Global Era: The Persistence of Nations*. Abingdon, UK: Routledge, 2007.

Comprehensive Index

The volume in which each entry appears is indicated in **bold**.

Abadinto (baby-naming ceremony), **1**:1
"Abide With Me" (hymn), **3**:1–3, 97
Aboriginal traditions. *See* Australians, Aboriginal
Abortion, **3**:180–182, 310; forced, **1**:256–258
Achambi ceremony, **1**:131
Acrostic jewelry, **3**:287
Adhaan, **1**:234
Adoption, baby showers for, **1**:24
Advent calendars, **1**:349–350
Afghani celebrations and practices: betrothal, **2**:1–3; burqa wearing, **2**:130; forced marriage, **2**:8; *halva*, **3**:113, 115; *Khwahish khwari*, **2**:1; *Labsgriftan*, **2**:1; *Shirin-i-grifgan*, **2**:1–2; *takht e khina*, **2**:2; virginity testing, **2**:357. *See also* Central Asian practices; South Asian celebrations and practices
African American traditions: folk medicine, **1**:30–31; jazz funerals, **3**:127–129; jumping over the broom, **2**:163–165; mistletoe, **1**:219; potty training, **1**:286
African celebrations and practices; arranged marriage, **2**:5, 7; breast ironing, **2**:30–32; cairns, **3**:23; christening gowns, **1**:94; cutting the umbilical cord, **1**:112–113; eating human placenta, **1**:123; female genital cutting, **2**:89–94; food taboos during pregnancy, **1**:146; forehead-cutting initiation rite, **2**:98–101; kangaroo care, **1**:183; lip plugs, **2**:191–195; menstrual customs, **2**:227; mourning color, **3**:305; polygyny, **2**:261; potty training, **1**:286; scarification, **2**:293–296; Tomb of the Unknown Soldier, **3**:295; urethral subincision, **2**:350; virginity testing, **2**:355–358; Wodaabe courtship dance and festival, **2**:383–386; *Yankan Gishiri*, **1**:362–363; *Zur-zur* (*zur zur; zurzur*), **1**:362–363. *See also* North African celebrations and practices; Sub-Saharan Africa; West African celebrations and practices
Afro-Brazilian traditions, **1**:345
Afterbirth. *See* Placenta
Agatharchides of Chidus, **2**:90
Aghoris sect, **3**:77
Aguman Sanduk Festival, **1**:105
Akan tribal groups, **1**:1
Akka goddess customs, **1**:4–7
Alaskan celebrations and practices, **1**:9
Albanian celebrations and practices: *Matura Shtetërore*, **2**:15; Napoleon dance, **2**:234; parental leave, **1**:266. *See also* Albanian funeral customs; Eastern European celebrations and practices
Albanian funeral customs, **3**:3–4; funeral cakes, **3**:93; graveyard traditions, **3**:3–4; "wailing funeral," **3**:3–4; washing the corpse, **3**:3
Alcohol consumption, **2**:16–17, 29, 63, 65, 97, 106, 181–182, 282–283, 316, **3**:313
Algerian celebrations and traditions: hamsa hand symbol, **1**:345. *See also* North African celebrations and practices
Algonquin tribe, **2**:359
Alimony, **2**:1
Alkaline hydrolysis, **3**:5–6, 104

All Hallow's Day, **3**:6, 109–110
All Hallows' Eve, **3**:263
All Saints' Day, **3**:6–8, 59, 263–264. *See also* Feast of All Saints
All Souls' Day, **3**:6–10, 59, 110, 263–265
All Souls' Day cakes, **3**:265
All Souls' Eve, **3**:264
Allerheiligenstriezel, **3**:265–266
Alnwick Castle, **3**:96
Alphorn music, **3**:238
Amajursuk, **1**:79
Ameen ceremony, **1**:47–48
American Indian Religious Freedom Act, **2**:327
American Society for Psychoprophylaxis in Obstetrics (ASOP), **1**:201
Amish practices: baptism, **2**:278; bed-courtship, **2**:23–26; *Rumspringa*, **2**:24, 277–280
Ampe, **1**:149–150
Amphidromia (Running Round) ritual, **1**:23
Amphiphontes, **1**:37
Amrit shanchar, **2**:70
Amulets, protective, **1**:195, 218, 344, 345, **2**:308, **3**:96
Anabaptists, **2**:25
Anal sex, **2**:149
Anatolia, **2**:323–325
Ancestor worship, **3**:20, 77, 91, 126, 181–182, 244
Ancient Babylonia, **3**:7
Ancient Egypt, **1**:22–23, 39, **2**:112, **3**:74; mummification, **3**:185–187
Ancient Greece, **1**:22, 34–35, 37, **2**:285, 375, **3**:7, 96
Ancient Rome, **1**:44, 230, **2**:285, 375, **3**:7, 96, 302
Andrzejki (St. Andrew's Eve), **2**:3–5
Ang pleen **1**:229
Anga people, **3**:187
Anglican Church, **1**:27, 95, 98–99, 142, 231, **2**:185, **3**:275; hymns, **3**:1–3. *See also* Church of England
Animism, **2**:90
Ankou, **3**:10–11
Antambahoaka people, **1**:133, 298–300
Antenatal care. *See* Prenatal care

Antenatal classes, **1**:74
Anthony of Padua (saint), **1**:99
Anti-Social Behaviour, Crime and Policing Act, **2**:8
Anti-Valentine's Day, **2**:315
Anzac Day, **3**:152, 236–237, 317
Aokigahara Forest (Japan), **3**:278–279
Apache ceremonies: baby ceremonies, **1**:7–9; Sunrise Ceremony, **2**:326–331
Apollo (Greek god), **2**:21
Apostle spoons, **1**:313–314
Appalachian traditions: birthday customs, **1**:41; shivaree/chivaree, **2**:257
Apple howling, **2**:44
Aqeeqah (*Aqiqa*) ritual, **1**:235
Aquamation, **3**:5–6
Argentinian celebrations and practices, **3**:247; government-approved baby names, **1**:153; same-sex marriage, **2**:285; *San La Muerte*, **3**:246–249. *See also* South American celebrations and practices
Argile, **1**:71
Arlington National Cemetery, **3**:24–26, 55–56, 178, 237, 273, 294
Armenia: Assyrian populations in, **2**:10; mourning color, **3**:304
Armistice Day, **3**:223
Arranged marriage, **2**:5–7, 10, 37–38, 136, 159, 237, 241, 251–252, 295, 312
Artemis (Greek goddess) **1**:34, 37, 217
Arvel (arvil) cake, **3**:92
Asamoutalik, **1**:79
Asante tribe, **1**:151
Ascension Day, **1**:140
Ashanti people, **3**:90
Ashes fireworks, **3**:268
Asian celebrations and practices: Buddhism, **3**:18; cairns, **3**:23; cremation, **3**:42; eating human placenta, **1**:123; female genital cutting, **2**:89; food taboos during pregnancy, **1**:146; grave rental, **3**:102; kangaroo care, **1**:183; ritual tattooing, **2**:272; teething remedies, **1**:329; Tomb of the Unknown Soldier, **3**:295; virginity testing,

2:355–358. *See also* Central Asian practices; Chinese celebrations and practices; Japanese celebrations and practices; Korean celebrations and practices; South Asian celebrations and practices; South Korean celebrations and practices; Southeast Asian celebrations and practices

Assisted suicide, 3:11–15

Association for Civil Confirmation, 2:300

Association for International Co-operation (*Gesellschaft fur Technische Zusammenarbeit*, GTZ), 2:30

Assyrian betrothal and weddings, 2:9–14

Astrological signs, 1:42, 44–45, 233, 354

Astronomy, Babylonian, 1:45

Atayal people, 2:276

Atiq ceremony, 1:9–11

Attachment parenting, 1:250

Australasian celebrations and practices: birthday bumps, 1:40; christening gowns, 1:94; hair removal, 2:112; mourning color, 3:302; nursery rhymes, 1:250; Tomb of the Unknown Soldier, 3:295; training bras, 2:338–341. *See also* Asian celebrations and practices; Australian celebrations and practices; New Zealand celebrations and practices

Australia, Hmong immigrants in, 2:137

Australian celebrations and practices: "Abide With Me," 3:1–3; alkaline hydrolysis, 3:5–6; Anzac Day, 3:152, 236–237, 317; Australian War Memorial, 3:295–296; bachelor and spinster balls (B and S balls/B&S's), 2:16–19; birthday cakes, 1:35; birthday celebrations, 1:35; breastfeeding, 1:56; Buddhist death practices, 3:21; cardboard box bed scheme, 1:74; childhood vaccinations, 1:85; cremation, 3:42; embalming, 3:73; Gap year, 2:103; Girl Guides, 1:152; Goth subculture, 3:101–102; high-platform exposure of the corpse, 3:115–118; jury duty, 2:168; *koliva*, 3:135; Leaver's Week, 2:283; lotus birthing, 1:201; missing man formation, 3:179; mistletoe, 1:219; mummification, 3:185; parental leave, 1:266, 269–270; Parental Leave Guide, 1:269–270; Passion plays, 3:208; pensions, 3:228, 230; Pregnancy and Infant Loss Remembrance Day, 3:216–218; Remembrance Day, 3:223–224; riderless horse, 3:236–237; Schoolies Week, 2:283–284; space burial, 3:267; spontaneous shrines, 3:269; Steiner schools, 1:318, 320; twenty-first birthday, 2:344; urethral subincision, 2:347–349; wake, 3:313; walkabout, 2:365–367; wedding dresses, 2:374; Zoroastrianism, 3:338. *See also* Australasian celebrations and practices; Australians, Aboriginal

Australian War Memorial, 3:295–296

Australians, Aboriginal, 1:42, 355–356, 2:293, 347–351, 365–367, 3:115–118, 230

Austrian celebrations and practices: All Souls' Day, 3:8; anti-Santa Claus movement 1:297–298; Klawbauf, 1:222–223; *Kürbisfest*, 3:111–112; *Martinstag*, 3:111; ossuaries, 3:201; parental leave, 1:266; Passion plays, 3:208; pensions, 3:230; *Polterabend*, 2:254; *Reifeprüfung*, 2:15; *Schuhplattler* and *Ländler*, 2:297–299; soul cakes, 3:263–265; spontaneous shrines, 3:269; University of the Third Age, 3:307; *Vatertag*, 1:140

Autumn Festival (Diwali), 2:73–75

Aztec practices, 1:283, 2:112, 177, 3:58, 250, 256

Baba Dochia, 1:16

Baba Marta (Grandmother March), 1:13–17

Baba Umer Durga shrine, 1:127

Baba Yaga, 1:223

Babies: *achambi* ceremony for, 1:131; and the Blidworth Cradle Rocking Ceremony, 1:51–52; as mini-gods,

1:253; beds for, 1:72–75; birth year of (Chinese Zodiac), 1:310–311; on cradleboards, 1:109–111; ear-piercing, 1:177, 307; feeding rituals, 1:178–179; first and ritual baths, 1:3, 42, 92, 178; first food, 1:176, 259–260, 275–276; first haircut, 1:177, 227, 232–233; Hindu rituals for, 1:175–177; 100th day celebration, 1:92; keeping from contact with the ground, 1:253–254; learning to walk, 1:93; leaving home for the first time, 1:324; predicting gender of, 1:5–6, 20–21, 187, 348–349; premature, 1:183–184, 194; protection against evil spirits, 1:78–79, 91–92, 114; quilts given to, 1:178; salting, 1:64–65; seventh day celebration, 1:305–307; sleeping with parents, 1:74–75; spitting on, 1:316–317; sprinkling cake on, 1:317; stolen by fairies, 1:77–80; supernatural harm to 1:79; swaddling, 1:195, 320–322; unbaptized, 1:77, 78, 3:313; unregistered, 1:256; vaccinations for, 1:85–87, 320. *See also* Abortion; Baby ceremonies; Baby naming practices; Children; Cutting the umbilical cord; Stillbirth
Babinden, 1:105
Baby ceremonies: Apache, 1:7–9; Atiq, 1:9–11; Hindu, 1:175–177; pagan, 1:24–25; Sikh, 1:311–313
Baby hammocks, 1:300–301
Baby Jumping Festival (*El Salto del Colacho*), 1:126–128
Baby naming practices: Abadinto, 1:1; Akan, 1:1–4; Atiq, 1:9–11; *brit milah*, 1:60–61; Chinese, 1:90; Ghanaian, 1:150; government-approved names, 1:153–157; Hopi, 1:177–180; Korean, 1:188; Latvian, 1:204; Muslim, 1:234–235; Sikh, 1:311–313; Thai, 1:141–142; Wiccan name chant, 1:354; Wik-Mungkan (Wik-Mungknh), 1:355–356. *See also* Naming rituals

Baby racing, 1:21–22
Baby showers, 1:22–24, 175, 90
Baby throwing, in India, 1:127
Babylonian astronomy, 1:45
Baccalauréat (le bac), 2:15–16
Bachelor and spinster balls (B and S balls/B&S's), 2:16–19
Bachelor parties, 2:38, 257
Bachelorette parties, 2:38, 257
Bafia tribe, 2:294
Bahaya people, 1:113
Bajang, 1:79
Bal de noce (wedding dance), 2:47–48
Balangandá (amulet), 1:345
Bali: Barong dance, 1:206; lotus birthing, 1:210; *ngaben* (*pelebon*), 3:193–196; *Nyabutan* ceremony, 1:253; Schoolies Week, 2:284; tooth-filing ceremony, 2:335–337
Bangladesh: cutting the umbilical cord, 1:113; forced marriage, 2:8; *halva*, 3:114. *See also* South Asian celebrations and practices
Bantu people, 2:245
Baoji, 2:50
Baptism and Christening: of adults, 1:28; Amish, 2:278; in Baptist churches, 1:27–29; in the Bulgarian Orthodox Church, 1:65–66; Christian, 1:25–29; *el bolo*, 1:125–126; in Ghana, 1:1–4; gifts for, 1:313–314; by immersion, 1:26–29; of infants, 1:25–26, 28; by pouring, 1:26, 27; Roman Catholic, 1:27; special biscuits for, 1:31–32; by sprinkling, 1:26–27; symbolic, 2:79–80. *See also* Christening gowns
Baptist churches, 1:26, 27–29, 2:60, 185
Bar mitzvah, 1:42, 281–282, 2:19–21
Bara people, 3:51
Barabaig people, 2:295
Barakat Bundle scheme, 1:74
Barbados, 3:231
Bari people, 2:258, 259
Barong dance, 1:206
Baskania, 1:345
Bat mitzvah, 2:19–21

Bathing: of brides, **2**:160, 237, 313; of the groom, **2**:313; for purification, **1**:246–247; in the River Ganges, **1**:233, **2**:173–175; ritual, **1**:49, **2**:134, 160, 226, 227. *See also* Washing
Baule tribe, **2**:294
Bauls (Bengali, India), **2**:225–226
Bavaria, soul cakes, **3**:265
Baznayeh Assyrians, **2**:12
Beachy Head (England), **3**:278
Bealltainn (Beltane), **1**:293, **2**:219
Bean throwing, **1**:308–309
Beards, **2**:21–23
Beauty pageants for children, **1**:80–83
Bed dances, **2**:53–54
Bed-courtship, **2**:23–26
Bedwetting remedies, **1**:29–31
Beer Dance, **2**:54
Bees and death, **3**:12–13
Beinhaus (Bone House), **3**:201
Belarus, parental leave, **1**:266. *See also* Eastern European celebrations and practices
Belgian celebrations and practices: Armistice Day, **3**:225; assisted suicide, **3**:12; *Martinstag*, **3**:111; mourning color, **3**:304; parental leave, **1**:266; pensions, **3**:230; same-sex marriage, **2**:285; spontaneous shrines, **3**:269; *suikerboon*, **1**:32; wedding cakes, **2**:369
Beltane, **1**:293, **2**:219
Bemba people, **2**:52–55
Benedict XV (pope), **3**:8
Benevolent societies, **3**:128
Benin: breast ironing, **2**:30; burial customs, **3**:128; cutting the umbilical cord, **1**:113; female ritual servitude (*trokosi*), **1**:330–333; scarification, **2**:293–294; *Sharo*, **2**:307, 309. *See also* West Africa
Bera út, **1**:214
Berber people, **2**:238
Berlin ironwork jewelry, **3**:287
Bermuda, **2**:371, **3**:231
Beschuit met Muisjes, **1**:31–32
Beshik Toi, in Kyrgyzstan, **1**:194–195
Bétamarribé people, **2**:293–294

Betrothal: Afghani, **2**:1–3; Assyrian, **2**:9–14; in Ethopia, **2**:67; lengthy engagements, **2**:94–95
Betsileo people, **3**:85
Bible, **1**:26, 28, 45–46, 52, 83, 96, 98, 115, 144, 244–245, 281, **2**:22, 91, 93–294, **3**:7
Biddies, **1**:16
Bildungsroman, **1**:135–136
Birth control, **1**:256–258
Birth customs: in the *bashali*, **1**:129–30; in Bulgaria, **1**:63–67; in China, **1**:89–93; confinement after, **1**:226; drink for women after, **1**:208–209; epidural injections, **1**:202; Korean, **1**:186–189; in Kyrgyzstan, **1**:193–194; Lamaze technique, **1**:201–202; in Latvia, **1**:203–204; lotus birthing, **1**:210–213; male re-enactment of birth, **1**:105; mock birthing, **1**:19; Muslim, **1**:234–235; preparation for childbirth, **1**:201–203, **1**:289–290; recovery after childbirth, **1**:290; in Tibet, **1**:323–324; water birth, **1**:346–348. *See also* Churching of Women
Birth trees, **1**:33–34
Birthday candles, **1**:37–38
Birthday celebrations, **1**:42–44; birthday beats, **1**:40; birthday cakes, **1**:34–36, **2**:85; cards, **1**:38–40; first birthday, **1**:92–93, 291; foods for, **1**:34–36; games, **1**:273–274; in Ghana, **1**:149–151; "Happy Birthday" song, **1**:171–173, **1**:263; humiliations for singletons, **2**:26–28; message from the Queen, **3**:171–173; milestones associated with, **1**:43; of notable figures, **1**:43; piñata, **1**:283, 284; *Sockenkrantz*, **2**:318–319; torments, **1**:40–41; twenty-first birthday, **2**:344–345; Vietnam, **3**:288–289
Birthday Parade, **1**:43
Birthday torments, for unmarried persons, **2**:26–28
Birthing blood, **1**:25
Birthing fluids, **1**:69
Birthing pools, **1**:347. *See also* Water births

COMPREHENSIVE INDEX

Birthstones, **1**:44–46
Biscuits, for babies and/or baptism, **1**:31–32
Bismallah ceremony, **1**:47–48
Bizane ts'al (cradleboard ceremony), **1**:7–8
Black Caribs, **1**:106
Black Day, **2**:315–316
Blackening the Bride, **2**:28–30
Blang (Bulang) people, **2**:50
The Blessing (Unification Church weddings), **2**:235
Blessings: for bride and groom, **2**:12, 13, 40; of a child in the womb, **1**:99; given by *devadasis*, **1**:116; of Dinka and Nuer boys, **2**:99; of gifts, **2**:40; in a handfasting ceremony, **2**:121–124; of a marriage, **2**:59–60, **2**:242; pagan baby welcomings, **1**:24–25; with sacred cattail pollen, **2**:157; at Sikh wedding, **2**:313–314; Wiccan, **1**:354; of women after childbirth, **1**:98–100
Blessingway ceremony, **1**:48–51
Blidworth Cradle Rocking Ceremony (England), **1**:51–52
Blind man's buff/bluff, **1**:273
Blood drinking, **2**:205
Blooding, **1**:53–54
Bloodletting ritual, **2**:149
Blue Peter (television program), **1**:54
Blue Peter Badge, **1**:54–55
Body hair removal, **2**:110, 111–113
Body mutilation, **2**:30, **3**:90–91
Bolivian practices, **3**:247; burial of dissected llama fetuses in house foundations, **1**:69; menstrual taboos, **2**:230; pensions, **3**:231. *See also* South American celebrations and practices
Bon Festival, **3**:7
Bonbonniere, **1**:32
Bone houses (ossuaries), **3**:200–203
Bonnet Rippers (Amish Romance Novels), **2**:24
Books, for children, **1**:73, **1**:87–89, **1**:198–201
Borneo: couvade, **1**:104; mother roasting, **1**:228

Bosnia and Herzegovina: *Matura*, **2**:15; parental leave, **1**:266. *See also* Eastern European celebrations and practices; Yugoslav countries
Box, as funeral plant, **3**:95
Boy Scouts Association of the United Kingdom, **1**:302. *See also* Scouts and Scouting
Boy Scouts of America, **1**:303–304. *See also* Scouts and Scouting
Boys: clothing for first communion, **1**:143; feminization of, **2**:149–150; firstborn, **1**:280–283; *pidyon haben* ceremony, **1**:280–283. *See also* Babies; Boys' coming-of-age ceremonies; Children; Circumcision
Boys' coming-of-age ceremonies: Brazil, **2**:41–43; bullet ant initiation, **2**:41–43; China, **2**:51; forehead-cutting initiation rite, **2**:98–101; *Gempuku*, **2**:61; *Gwallye*, **2**:105–106; land diving, **2**:184; Maasai traditions, **2**:205–208; Nkumbi, **2**:245–247; scarification ritual, **2**:294, 295; *Sharo*, **2**:307–309; *shinbyu*, **2**:83, 310–312; *Sünnet*, **2**:323–325; *upanayana*, **1**:337; urethral subincision, **2**:347–351; vision quest, **2**:358–361; *wysoccan* rite of manhood, **2**:359
Bradley method, **1**:202–203
Brazilian practices, **3**:247; All Souls' Day, **3**:9; bullet ant initiation, **2**:41–43; charms against the evil eye, **1**:345; couvade, **1**:104; eating the ashes of the dead, **3**:67–70; endocannibalism, **3**:76–77; fertility symbol, **1**:346; *Festa de debutantes*, **2**:185; jury duty, **2**:165; lip plugs, **2**:192; Matis hunting trials, **2**:215–219; menstrual taboos, **2**:230; mourning color, **3**:302; national mourning, **3**:192; Passion plays, **3**:208; pulling of earlobes on birthdays, **1**:41; same-sex marriage, **2**:285; wedding dresses, **2**:374. *See also* South American celebrations and practices
Brazilian wax, **2**:112–113

Breast ironing, **2**:32–32

Breastfeeding, **1**:55–59, 105, 130, 181, 202, 209, 267, 321; benefits of, **1**:55–56; encouragement of, **1**:73, 75, 306–307; human-animal, **1**:57–58; laws allowing public, **1**:56; long-term, **1**:56–57; and shared nursing, **1**:57; supernatural creatures interfering with, **1**:79; women advised against eating calabash chalk, **1**:71

Breton mythology, **3**:10–11

Bride-price, **2**:1, 11, 100, 117, 195–197, 248, 385

Brides: adorning with henna, **2**:2–3; blackening, **1**:78, **2**:28–20; blessed by *devadasis*, **1**:116; carrying over the threshold, **2**:36; gifts given to, **2**:2, 11, 37–39; gifts of jewelry for, **2**:37, 134, 302–305; giving away, **2**:34; jewelry worn by, **2**:312–313; kidnapping of, **2**:51; removal of body hair, **2**:112; ritual bathing of, **2**:160, 237, 313; throwing the bridal bouquet, **2**:34–35; washing and dressing, **2**:11; wedding superstitions, **2**:33–34

Bris shalom, **1**:62

Brit banot ceremony, **1**:62

Brit milah (*bris milah.bris*), **1**:59–63

Brit shalom, **1**:62

British celebrations and practices: horseshoes, **2**:142; jury duty, **2**:165, 167, 168, 170–171; missing man formation, **3**:177–178; national mourning, **3**:191; official birthday celebrations, **1**:43; Passion plays, **3**:206; Punkie Night, **3**:112; Remembrance Sunday, **3**:152; sin eating, **3**:92. *See also* British wedding traditions; English celebrations and practices; United Kingdom celebrations and practices

British wedding traditions, **2**:32–37; carrying the bride over the threshold, **2**:36; giving away the bride, **2**:34; honeymoon, **2**:36; superstitions, **2**:32–33; throwing rice, **2**:34; throwing the bridal bouquet, **2**:34–35; wedding locations, **2**:32

Brunei, **1**:181

Brunsviger, **1**:35

Bubonic plague, **1**:252, **3**:42, 83–84, 207, 248

Buddhist celebrations and practices **1**:43; attitudes toward death, **3**:18–21; cremation, **3**:42; funeral rites, **3**:123; *Mizuko kuyo*, **3**:180–183; *shinbyu*, **2**:83, 310–312; sky burial, **3**:260; *Ullambana*, **3**:330; *Yulanpen* Festival, **3**:329

Bulgarian celebrations and practices, **1**:63–67; Baba Marta, **1**:13–17; *Babinden*, **1**:17–19, 105; cremation, **3**:103; Enyovden, **2**:177; horo dance, **2**:140; *koliva*, **3**:135; *Ladouvane*, **2**:182–183; *Lazarovden*, **2**:186–188; *Matura*, **2**:15; mock weddings, **1**:19; Monument to the Unknown Soldier, **3**:294; national mourning, **3**:192; pregnancy superstitions, **1**:63; Saturday of Souls, **3**:251–253; spitting on babies, **1**:316; St. Sylvester's Day, **2**:183. *See also* Bulgarian Orthodox Church; Bulgarian weddings; Eastern European celebrations and practices

Bulgarian Orthodox Church, **1**:65–66

Bulgarian weddings, **2**:37–41; arranged marriages, **2**:37–38; engagement, **2**:37–38; *Galena*, **2**:40; parties before, **2**:38; reception, **2**:39

Bullet ant initiation, **2**:41–43

Bull-jumping ceremony, **2**:66

Bullying, **1**:41

Bundling, **2**:24–25

Burakha (marriage service), **2**:12

Burial rituals. *See* Funeral practices

Burial societies, **3**:70

Burkina Faso, **2**:92. *See also* West African celebrations and practices

Burma. *See* Myanmar

Burning the Ashen Faggot, **2**:43–44

Burning the Clavie, **2**:44–45

Burumu (body painting), **2**:154

Burying biscuits, **3**:93

Burying the Box, **3**:95

Cairns, **3**:23–24, 262
Cajun weddings, **2**:47–49; *bal de noce* (wedding dance), **2**:47–48; *charivari*, **2**:48; dancing with broom or mop, **2**:47; food, **2**:48; reception, **2**:48
Caking Night, **3**:264
Calabar stone, **1**:71
Calabash chalk, **1**:71–72
Caldecott Medal, **1**:88
Callatiae tribe, **3**:77
Cambodian practices: Hmong names, **2**:136; mother roasting, **1**:229; treatment of the placenta, **1**:69. *See also* Southeast Asian celebrations and practices
CAME Women and Girl's Development Organisation (Cawogido), **2**:30
Cameos, **3**:287
Cameroon, **2**:30–31, 294
Canada, Assyrian populations in, **2**:10
Canadian celebrations and practices, **1**:9, 10; baby racing, **1**:21; *Baccalauréat (le bac)*, **2**:15–16; bedwetting cures, **1**:30; birthday beats and digs in, **1**:40; birthday bumps, **1**:40; boxes for babies **1**:74; breastfeeding, **1**:56; changeling beliefs, **1**:79; childhood vaccinations, **1**:85; eating calabash chalk, **1**:71; embalming, **3**:73; Gap year, **2**:103; Girl Guides, **1**:152; jury duty, **2**:168; *Mehndi*, **2**:222; mortuary totem poles, **3**:183–185; National War Memorial, **3**:296; noses greased with butter for birthdays, **1**:41; pantomime, **1**:261; parental leave, **1**:266, 267; Passion plays, **3**:208; Pregnancy and Infant Loss Remembrance Day, **3**:216–218; *Pysanka*, **3**:66; Remembrance Day, **3**:223; *Rumspringa*, **2**:277–280; same-sex marriage, **2**:285; Shinerama, **2**:268; sock dances, **2**:319–320; space burial, **3**:267; *Waldkindergärten*, **1**:341; water births, **1**:347; Zoroastrianism, **3**:338. *See also* North American celebrations and practices
Canary Islands, **3**:185, 186
Candlemas, **1**:51, 98, **3**:9

Candles: Advent, **1**:349–350; as baptism gift, **1**:29; birthday, **1**:37–38; on birthday cakes, **1**:34, 37, 38, 42, 171; blessing of, **1**:51, **3**:9; in the Blessingway ceremony, **1**:50, 51; in the Blidworth cradle rocking ceremony, **1**:51; in the *brit banot* ceremony, **1**:62; in the *brit milah* ceremony, **1**:60; candle-leaping, **1**:252; in the Christingle service, **1**:95–97; on Christmas trees, **1**:38; in the Churching of Women service, **1**:99; around a corpse, **1**:37; in the *Klausjagen* procession, **1**:296; in midwife folklore, **1**:64; penis-shaped, **1**:278–279; for Pregnancy and Infant Loss Remembrance Day, **3**:217; for *Quccija*, **1**:291; used for sacred severance, **1**:113; for the saining rite, **1**:294; in the *Sebou* ceremony, **1**:306–307; for Slava, **1**:242, 243; soul candle, **3**:105; in the Wiccaning ceremony, **1**:354; for *Zaduszki (dzień zaduszny)*, **3**:333. *See also* Candlemas
Canopic jars, **3**:186
Caparisoned horse (Cap horse), **3**:236
Cardboard box beds, **1**:72–75
Caribbean: *La Quinceañera*, **2**:177–180; Nine-Nights, **3**:196–198
Carnet de Santé Maternité, **1**:238
Carrera Día del Padre, **1**:139
Castration ceremony, **2**:132
Catholic Church: on assisted suicide, **3**:14; on cremation, **3**:42; Greek, **3**:251; missionaries in North America, **1**:283–284; objection to plastination, **3**:214–215; opinion of jazz funerals, **3**:128; opinion of mummification, **3**:185; opposition to alkaline hydrolysis, **3**:6; opposition to *Famadihana*, **3**:86. *See also* Folk Catholicism
Catholic Church celebrations and practices, **1**:37, 45, 98–99; All Souls' Day, **3**:6–10; color symbolism, **3**:305; combining with indigenous beliefs, **3**:246–247; crucifixion rituals, **3**:47–50; *Dia de los Muertos*, **3**:60; first communion, **1**:142–144;

funerals, **3**:36–37; *La Quinceañera*, **2**:177–180, 187; Martinstag, **3**:111; May crowning ritual, **1**:217–218; Name days, **1**:241; Passion plays, **3**:206–209; prayers at Filipino debut, **2**:96; Saint Nicholas, **1**:294–298; wedding anniversaries, **2**:368; wedding ceremony, **2**:58–59. *See also* Christian Church celebrations and practices; Eastern Orthodox Church celebrations and practices; Greek Orthodox Church celebrations and practices

Celestis Inc., **3**:267

Celtic Reconstructionist Paganism, **1**:293

Celtic traditions, **3**:109–110; handfasting, **2**:32; New Year, **3**:112; Passion plays, **3**:206

Cemeteries: Arlington National, **3**:24–26, 55–56, 178, 237, 273, 294; blessing of, **3**:8; bonfires in, **3**:333; burial ceremonies in, **3**:20, 337; Caterpillar Valley, **3**:296; Chinese, **3**:33–34; Cimetière du Père Lachaise, **3**:298; in France, **3**:296; in Greece, **3**:103; taking Easter eggs to, **3**:66; in England, **3**:102; Highgate Cemetery, **3**:298–299; Isola di San Michele (San Michele Island), **3**:121–122; in Japan, **3**:104, 181; Merry Cemetery, **3**:299; in Poland, **3**:333–334; procession to, **3**:3, 54, 127–128; vertical, **3**:104; visits on All Souls' Day, **3**:9; Yew trees in, **3**:327–328. *See also* Ossuaries; Remembrance Sunday; Tombstone Tourism

Central Africa. *See* Cameroon; Central African Republic; Chad; Democratic Republic of Congo

Central African Republic, **2**:192. *See also* African celebrations and practices; Sub-Saharan African celebrations and practices

Central American practices: belief in the evil eye, **1**:343; the umbilical cord, **1**:113; kangaroo care, **1**:183; water births, **1**:346. *See also* Guatemalan practices; Mexican celebrations and practices

Central Asian practices: arranged marriage, **2**:5; forced marriage, **2**:8; *halva*, **3**:113. *See also* Afghani celebrations and practices; Asian celebrations and practices; Kyrgyzstan; Mongolia; Uzbekistan

Central Europe, *Pysanka*, **3**:66

Ceremony of the Christmas Cheese, **3**:28–29

Cerne Abbas Giant, **1**:75–77

Chachapoya people, **3**:186

Chad, **2**:30, 192–193. *See also* African celebrations and practices; Sub-Saharan African celebrations and practices

Chambri tribe, **2**:295–296

Changeling beliefs, **1**:77–80

Changing of the Guard Ceremony, **3**:24–26

Charades, **1**:274

Charing Cross, **3**:72–73

Charitable giving, **2**:267–268

Charivari, **2**:48

Chelsea pensioners, **3**:26–29

Cheppewa tribe, **1**:119

Chesapeake Bay Bridge (Maryland), **3**:278

Chevra Kadisha, (Holy Society), **3**:130

Child beauty pageants, **1**:80–83

Child, Early and Forced Marriage (CEFM), **2**:9, 136. *See also* Forced marriage

Childermas (Feast of the Holy Innocents), **1**:83–84, 245

Childhood vaccinations, **1**:85–87

Child-rearing, slow parenting, **1**:314–315

Children: All Souls' Day traditions involving, **3**:8; and the blooding ritual, **1**:53; books for, **1**:73, 87–89, 198–201; and breastfeeding, **1**:55–59; celebration of one-year milestone, **1**:141; development of, **1**:106; exploitation of, **1**:80, 82; exposure to heavy metals, **1**:71; in Finland, **1**:72; First Steps celebration, **1**:66–67; goddess protector of, **1**:5; Jesus's regard for, **1**:28; Muslim, **1**:47; names of, **1**:42; napping in cold temperatures, **1**:249–250; sexualization of, **1**:82–83; washing of, **1**:18. *See also* Babies; Boys; Girls

Children's Act (Nepal), **1**:192
Children's Day (Japan), **1**:184–186
Children's Day Olympics, **1**:184
Children's Laureate, **1**:87–89
Children's Peace Monument, **1**:185
Chile, **3**:185. *See also* South American celebrations and practices
Chinchorro mummies, **3**:185–186
Chinese celebrations and practices: baby racing, **1**:21, 22; birthday celebrations, **1**:36; Buddhist practices, **3**:18, 20; government-approved baby names, **1**:153, 155; hair removal, **2**:112; Hungry Ghost Festival, **3**:7; Long-Horn Miao minority group, **2**:138; *Moon-Yuet*, **1**:226–228; New Year messages, **1**:39; one-child policy, **1**:256–258; origin of the piñata, **1**:283; potty training, **1**:286, 287; *Qingming* Festival, **3**:219–222; same-sex marriage, **2**:285; Shanghai Marriage Market, **2**:305–307; *Shengziao*, **1**:310–311; Singles' Day, **2**:315–316; Sisters' Meal Festival, **2**:317–218; treatment of the placenta, **1**:68; Universities for the Ages, **3**:307–308; *Yu Lan Jie*, **3**:329–332; *Zui yuezi*, **1**:361–362. *See also* Asian celebrations and practices; Chinese coming-of-age ceremonies; Chinese pregnancy and birth rituals
Chinese coming-of-age ceremonies, **2**:49–52; *baoji*, **2**:50; Dong ceremony, **2**:51; Guan Li, **2**:49–50; Ji Li, **2**:49–50; Puni ceremony, **2**:50–51; Yi ceremony, **2**:51
Chinese funeral customs, **3**:29–34, 305; cemeteries, **3**:33–34; funeral strippers, **3**:30; grave rental, **3**:103–104; mourning color, **3**:304, 305; mummification, **3**:185, 186; sky burials, **3**:259–263; space burial, **3**:267; wakes, **3**:32–33, 313
Chinese lunar calendar, **1**:20
Chinese philosophy, **1**:310–311
Chinese pregnancy and birth rituals, **1**:20–21, **1**:89–93; 100th day celebration, **1**:92; baby hammocks (*yao lan*), **1**:300; baby naming, **1**:91; birth announcements, **1**:91; childbirth conventions, **1**:90–91; eating human placenta, **1**:123; bath, **1**:92; first birthday, **1**:92–93; learning to walk, **1**:93; pregnancy taboos, **1**:89–90, 145–146; *Zuo yuezi*, **1**:92. *See also* Chinese celebrations and practices
Chinese wedding customs: arranged marriage, **2**:5, 7; kidnapping of the bride, **2**:51; Visiting-girls courtship tradition, **2**:360–364; walking marriages, **2**:391–393; wedding cakes, **2**:371–372; wedding dresses, **2**:374
Chinese Zodiac signs, **1**:310–311, **2**:30
Chiribaya people, **3**:186
Chisungu, **2**:52–55
Chivaree/Chivari, **2**:257
Chokha thavani viddhi (purification ritual), **2**:55–56
Chola temples, **1**:117
Chopi people, **2**:254
Christening. *See* Baptism and Christening
Christening gowns, **1**:26, 93–95
Christian celebrations and practices, **1**:83–84; baptism and christening, **1**:25–29; birthstones, **1**:44; christening gown, **1**:93–95; color symbolism, **3**:305; Churching of Women, **1**:98–100; confirmation, **1**:42; Easter eggs, **3**:65–67; female genital cutting, **2**:90; first communion, **1**:142–144; hymns, **3**:1–3; menstruation as unclean, **2**:228; Mothering Sunday, **1**:230–232; Passion plays, **3**:206–209; Protestant, **1**:27; purity ball, **2**:264–268; saining, **1**:294; Saint Nicholas, **1**:294–298; Stations of the Cross, **3**:275–277. *See also* Catholic Church celebrations and practices; Christian churches; Christian funeral practices; Christian weddings; Eastern Orthodox Church celebrations and practices; Greek Orthodox Church celebrations and practices; Lutheran Church; Orthodox Church celebrations and practices; Pentecostal Church;

Protestant Church celebrations and practices; Russian Orthodox Church celebrations and practices

Christian churches: Coptic, **2**:302; Episcopal, **2**:60; evangelical, **2**:265; Free Wesleyan, **3**:300–301; in Ghana, **3**:87–88; Methodist, **1**:27, **2**:60, **3**:275, 300; Moravian, **1**:95; Mormon, **1**:303, **2**:161–162; objection to Dipo rite by, **2**:73; opposition to *Famadihana*, **3**:86; Pentecostal, **1**:26–27; Presbyterian, **1**:27, **2**:60; saints associated with death, **3**:247; view of beards by, **2**:22. *See also* Anglican Church; Church of England

Christian funeral practices, **3**:35–37; for Wiccans, **3**:319

Christian missionaries, **2**:343

Christian weddings, **2**:58–61; Catholic ceremony, **2**:59–60; marriage banns, **2**:210–215; Protestant ceremony, **2**:60–61; wedding music, **2**:379–381; wedding rings, **2**:375–376

Christingle, **1**:95–98

Christmas Cheese, Ceremony of, **3**:28–29

Christmas celebrations: Americanization of, **1**:297; Christmas carols, **1**:245; Christmas Eve traditions, **2**:44; Christmas stockings, **1**:294; Christmas trees, **1**:38; commercialization of, **1**:297; and the Nativity play, **1**:244–246; piñatas, **1**:284

Chrysanthemums, as funeral plants, **3**:95

Chudakarm/Chudakarna, **1**:232

Chupa (huppah), **2**:160–161

Church of Body Modification, **2**:272

Church of England, **1**:26–27, 76, 231, **2**:60, **3**:164, 293; on assisted suicide, **3**:13; marriage banns, **2**:210–211. *See also* Anglican Church

Church of Jesus Christ of Latter-day Saints (Mormons), **1**:303, **2**:261–262

Churching of Women, **1**:98–103

Cimetière du Père Lachaise, **3**:298

Circumcision, **1**:59–63, 298–300, **2**:149, 245–247; criticism of, **1**:61–62; of girls, **2**:206; Maasai, **2**:206; Muslim, **1**:234, 235–237; *Sünnet*, **2**:323–325; Xhosa, **2**:387–389. *See also* Female genital cutting; Male genital cutting

City of Widows, **3**:309–311

Civic confirmation, **2**:300–302

Claddagh ring, **2**:376

Clava Cairns, **3**:23

Clean-birth kits, **1**:74

Clear Bright Festival, **3**:219

Cleveland Lyke-Wake Dirge, **3**:158

Clitoral excision, **2**:91. *See also* Female genital cutting

Clypping the Church, **1**:230

Cold Food Festival, **3**:219, 221

Columbaria, **3**:104

Comanche tribe, **3**:305

Coming-of-age ceremonies: Brazil, **2**:41–43; China, **2**:49–52; Coming of Age Day (*Seijin no Hi*), **2**:61–64; *Gwallye*, **2**:105–106; Mosuo ceremony, **2**:391; secular confirmation, **2**:300–302. *See also* Boys' coming-of-age ceremonies; Chinese coming-of-age ceremonies; Girls' coming-of-age ceremonies

Commedia dell'arte, **1**:261–262

Condemned prisoner's last meal, **3**:37–40

Condolences, **3**:40–41

Confirmation: Christian, **1**:42; secular, **2**:300–302

Convention on the Elimination of All Forms of Discrimination Against Women, **2**:8, 358

Convention on the Rights of the Child, **2**:8, 31

Coptic Christianity, **2**:302

Cornflowers, for remembrance, **3**:317

Corpus Christi Festival, **1**:126–127

Cot death, **1**:321

Côte d'Ivoire, **2**:30, 294. *See also* West African celebrations and practices

Courtship whistling, **2**:64–66

Couvade, **1**:104–107

Covering the belly button, **1**:108–109

Cow jumping, **2**:66–68

Cradleboard, **1**:109–111, 119

Cradleboard ceremony, **1**:7–8

Cradlesongs, **1**:213–215

Crants/Crantses, **3**:161

Cremation, 3:41–44, 68–69; in Asia, 3:104; in Greece, 3:103; Hindu, 3:118–119; in Indonesia, 3:193–195; in Japan, 3:124–125; liquid, 3:5–6; in Papua New Guinea, 3:162; in the Sikh tradition, 3:257–258; and space burial, 3:267–268; by Zoroastrians, 3:338
Creutzfeldt-Jakob disease (CJD), 3:77
Croatian celebrations and practices: danse macabre, 3:52; *Lindo*, 2:190–191; *Matura*, 2:15; *Mirila*, 3:175–177; parental leave, 1:266; *Sokacko Kolo*, 2:194; Summer Festival, 2:194. *See also* Eastern European celebrations and practices; Yugoslav countries
Croning ceremonies, 3:44–46
Cross-dressing, 1:19, 263
Crucifixion rituals, 3:47–50
Crying-baby sumo competition, 1:111–112
Cuba: *La Quinceañera*, 2:185–188; national mourning, 3:192
Cult of Dionysus, 1:279
Cult of the Dead, 3:105
Cumberland Sound Inuit, 1:10
Cutting the umbilical cord traditions, 1:112–114, 130, 210–213
Cyprus, 2:234, 3:230, 231
Cyriac's Mead, 1:77
Czech Republic: Andrzejki, 2:3; anti-Santa Claus movement 1:297–298; Cert, 1:222–223; *Majáles*, 2:208–209; *Matura*, 2:15; May Day, 2:220–221; mourning color, 3:302; *Oblévačka*, 2:79; ossuaries, 3:201–202; parental leave 1:266; soul cakes, 3:264; spontaneous shrines, 3:269; University of the Third Age, 3:307. *See also* Eastern European celebrations and practices

Dahomean tribe, 3:128
Dakota people, 3:305
Dala (Dalecarlian) horse, 1:115–116
Dalit caste, 1:118
Dallas Ethiopian Community Edir, 3:70
Dancing: *Abang*, 2:88; in the cow-jumping ceremony, 2:67; Death Dance, 3:51–52; Dinki-Mini, 3:197; *Ekombi* (wedding dance), 2:88; fertility dance, 1:255–256; at Filipino debut, 2:96; *hora (horah)*, 1:19, 2:20, 40, 139–140; in Indonesia 1:204–207; *Kunima*, 3:197; at *La Quinceañera*, 2:179; in *Lazarovden*, 2:187; *Lindo*, 2:190–191; around the Maypole, 2:219–220; Morris dancers, 2:220; peccary dance, 2:217–218; puberty dance, 2:72; *Schuhplattler* and *Ländler*, 2:297–299; *Sokacko Kolo*, 2:194; at wedding celebrations, 2:13, 35, 47–48. *See also* Death Dance; Money Dance
Dandelions, and bedwetting, 1:31
Dani people, 3:90–91
Danish celebrations and practices: birthday customs, 1:35, 2:26–28; cutting the groom's socks, 2:320; danse macabre, 3:52; Girl Guides, 1:152; government-approved baby names, 1:153; *kagemand* and *kagekone*, 1:35; *kanelmø* (cinnamon maid), 2:26; *kanelsvend* (cinnamon man), 2:26; Nordic napping, 1:249; *pebermø* (pepper maid), 2:26; *pebersvend* (pepper man), 2:26; *Polterabend*, 2:254; same-sex marriage, 2:285; secular confirmation, 2:300; *slå kitten af tønden*, 1:285. *See also* Scandinavian celebrations and practices
Danse macabre, 3:52
Daruma Doll, 1:185
Dastaar Bandi (Dastar Bandi), 2:69
Daughters of Eve, 2:93
Dawn Songs, 2:154
Day of Delivery Assistance, 1:17
Day of Flowers, 2:184
Day of the Commemoration of All the Faithful Departed, 3:6–7. *See also* All Souls' Day
Days of the week, 1:220–221
Death: Buddhist attitudes toward, 3:18; Christian saints associated with, 3:247; personification of, 3:10–11; symbolic depictions of, 3:168–170. *See also* Death rituals; Funeral practices

Death Dance, **3**:51–52
Death divination, **3**:328
Death rituals: Albanian, **3**:3–4; Buddhist, **3**:18–21; Catholic, **3**:6–10; Chinese, **3**:29–34; Delaware Indian, **3**:53–56, 305; The Great Passing, **3**:105–107; Muslim, **3**:188–190. *See also* Death rituals; Funeral practices; Lakota death rituals
Death with Dignity Act (Oregon), **3**:13–14
Debut (Philippines), **2**:95–97, **2**:345
Debutante balls, **2**:96
Dekate (Tehtn Day), **1**:23
Delaware Indian death rituals, **3**:54–56, 305
Democratic Republic of Congo: funeral insurance schemes, **3**:71; *Nkumbi*, **2**:245–247; tooth sharpening, **2**:143. *See also* African celebrations and practices
Den to (baby-naming ceremony), **1**:1–4
Denmark. *See* Danish celebrations and practices
Denville Hall and Brinsworth House, **3**:56–57
Depilation, **2**:111–113
Descansos, **3**:269
Desert Flower (Dirie), **2**:93
Deuki, **1**:192–193
Devadasi system, **1**:116–119
Devi (Hindu goddess) **1**:189
Devipujak purification trial, **2**:55–56
Dewaqthad idha, **2**:10
Dezalik (fertility goddess) **1**:129–130
Dia de los Muertos, **3**:52, 58–61, 169
Diana, Princess of Wales, **1**:199, **3**:40–41, 174, 270
Dias de la Muerte, **3**:249
Dignitas, **3**:13
Diné. *See* Navajo ceremonies
Dinka tribe, **2**:98, 142–143, 294
Dipo Womanhood Ceremony, **2**:71–73
Dirie, Waris, **2**:93
Divination: with candle wax, **3**:334; folk, **1**:348–349. *See also* Death divination; Love divination
Divorce, **1**:48, 58, **2**:1, 160, 189, 221, 241, 262, 370, 392; handparting, **2**:127–128

Diwali, **2**:73–74; celebrated by Barack Obama, **2**:76–77
DIY funerals, **3**:210–211
Djibouti, **2**:89, 91, 93. *See also* Sub-Saharan African celebrations and practices
Dogon tribe, **2**:143
Doll Festival (*Hina Matsuri*), **1**:184, 185
Domestic violence, **2**:247–248
Dominican Republic, Nine-Nights, **3**:196–198
Dong people, **2**:51
Donkey party, **1**:274
Doom Metal, **3**:62–63
Doot coekjes, **3**:93
Dowry and dowries, **2**:1, 40, 117, 136, 159–160, 240–242, 303, 312, 373, 375
Dragées, **1**:32
Dream catchers, **1**:119–122
Dreamtime, **2**:347–348, 365, **3**:116–117
Druid practices, **1**:219, **2**:32, **3**:109, 328
Dumagat tribe, **2**:338
Dunmow Flitch Trials, **2**:78–79
Dunstan (saint), **2**:141
Dwynwen (saint), **2**:322
Dyngus Day, (*Śmigus-Dyngus*), **2**:79–81
Dzień zaduszny (*Zaduszki*), **3**:333–335
Dzinto (baby-naming ceremony), **1**:1

Ear piercing, **1**:177, 307, **2**:83–84
Earth's Prayer (Navajo), **1**:49
Easter egg trees, **3**:67
Easter eggs, **3**:65–67, 334
Easter Island, **2**:272
Easter Monday, **2**:79
Easter pageants, **3**:206
Easter traditions: Bulgarian, **2**:40; crucifixion reenactment, Philippines, **3**:47–50; Greek Orthodox, **1**:17
Eastern Catholic Church, **3**:135
Eastern European celebrations and practices: arranged marriage, **2**:5; looking for fern blossoms, **2**:199–201; *Povitica*, **2**:263–264; *Pysanka*, **3**:66–67, 334; *Śmigus-Dyngus* (Dyngus Day), **2**:79–81. *See also* Albanian celebrations and practices; Belarus; Bosnia and Herzegovina; Bulgarian celebrations and practices;

Croatian celebrations and practices; Czech Republic; Hungary; Kosovo; Latvian celebrations and practices; Lithuanian celebrations and practices; Macedonia; Moldova; Montenegro; Polish celebrations and practices; Romanian celebrations and practices; Russian celebrations and practices; Serbian celebrations and practices; Slovakian celebrations and practices; Slovenian celebrations and practices; Ukrainian celebrations and practices; Yugoslav countries

Eastern Orthodox Church celebrations and practices, **1**:26, 27, 65–66, **3**:7, 135–136, 192, 251, 252; Easter eggs, **3**:65–66; Saturday of Souls, **3**:251–252. *See also* Greek Orthodox Church celebrations and practices; Orthodox Church celebrations and practices; Russian Orthodox Church celebrations and practices

Eating Sisters' Rice Festival, **2**:317–318

Eating the ashes of the dead, **3**:67–70

Ecuadorean practices: cutting the umbilical cord, **1**:113; shrunken heads, **3**:255–257. *See also* South American celebrations and practices

Edir (*eddir, iddir*), **3**:70–72

Education: admission to university, **2**:57–58; in Amish communities, **2**:24, 277–278; *Baccalauréat* and *Matura*, **2**:15–16; choosing Options, **2**:56–58; Gap year, **2**:103–104; Hindu *upanayana* ceremony, **1**:337; *Majáles* festival, **2**:208–209; Steiner schools, **1**:318–320; University of the Third Age (U3A), **3**:307–308

Efe tribe, **2**:143, 245

Efik tribe (Nigeria), **2**:86

Eggs, **1**:144–145, 149. *See also* Easter eggs

Egyptian celebrations and practices: burying the placenta, **1**:235; female genital cutting, **2**:89–90, 93; mourning color, **3**:302, 304; *Sebou*, **1**:305–307; *shabka*, **2**:302–303; water births, **1**:346. *See also* Ancient Egypt; Middle Eastern celebrations and practices; North African celebrations and practices

Eid Al-Adha, **2**:115–116

Eileithyia (goddess of childbirth), **1**:23

Ein Risz in der Maurer (*A Break in the Wall*), **2**:25

El bolo, **1**:125–126

El Salto del Colacho (The Devil's Jump), **1**:126–128

Elderling ceremonies, **3**:44–46

Eleanor Crosses, **3**:72–73

Elimination communication, **1**:286

Elizabeth II (queen of England), **3**:171–172, 295

Embalming, **3**:73–76

Empire State Building (New York City), **3**:278

Endocannibalism, **3**:67, 76–77

Enfant changé, **1**:77

Engagement. *See* Betrothal

English celebrations and practices: *Ankou*, **3**:10–11; bedwetting cures, **1**:29–30; belief in the evil eye, **1**:343; Blidworth Cradle Rocking Ceremony, **1**:51–52; Burning the Ashen Faggot, **2**:43–44; burying biscuits, **3**:93; Cerne Abbas Giant, **1**:75–77; Chelsea pensioners, **3**:26–29; Childermas, **1**:84; choosing Options, **2**:56–58; danse macabre, **3**:52; Denville Hall and Brinsworth House, **3**:56–57; Dunmow Flitch Trials, **2**:78–79; Eleanor crosses, **3**:72–73; Eyam Plague Sunday Service, **3**:83–84; funeral plants, **3**:95; Goth subculture, **3**:99–101; Grasmere Rushbearing ceremony, **1**:164–166; grave rental, **3**:102; Highgate Cemetery, **3**:298–299; Kissing Friday, **2**:80; Ladybird Books, **1**:198–201; Little Edith's Treat, **1**:207–208; "Lyke-wake Dirge," **3**:158–160; Maidens' Garlands, **3**:161–162; marriage banns, **2**:210; Maypoles, **2**:220; minute's silence, **3**:174–175; "Monday's Child," **1**:220–221;

Mothering Sunday, **1**:230–232; passing bells, **3**:205–206; Royal Wootton Bassett, **3**:239–241; same-sex marriage, **2**:285; Scroggling the Holly, **1**:304–305; soul cakes, **3**:263; souling, **3**:9; Tomb of the Unknown Warrior, **3**:293–295; war memorials, **3**:293–296; wassailing (apple howling), **2**:44; wedding cakes, **2**:369; wedding traditions, **2**:32; witch balls, **1**:356; yew trees, **3**:327–328. *See also* British celebrations and practices; British wedding traditions; United Kingdom celebrations and practices

Engozi, **3**:71

Entering the *Bashali* (Pakistan), **1**: 128–132

Enyovden, **2**:182

Epilation, **2**:111–113

Epiphany, **2**:44

Episcopal Church, **2**:60. *See also* Anglican Church; Church of England

Episiotomy, **1**:187

Eritrea, **2**:89, 92, 93. *See also* Sub-Saharan African celebrations and practices

Estonia, **3**:230

Ethiopia: betrothal, **2**:67; cow jumping, **2**:66–68; *edir*, **3**:70–71; lip plugs, **2**:193–194. *See also* African celebrations and practices

Etoro tribe, **2**:149

Etruscan culture, **1**:345

Eucharist: for the dying, **3**:105; at funeral services, **3**:37; in a wedding ceremony, **2**:59, 61. *See also* Holy Communion

Eukonkanto (wife-carrying), **2**:35

Eulogies, **3**:80–83

European celebrations and practices: *Baccalauréat (le bac)*, **2**:15–16; belief in the evil eye, **1**:343; biscuits for baptisms, **1**:31–33; cairns, **3**:23; christening gowns, **1**:94; Easter eggs, **3**:65–66; eating human placenta, **1**:123; funeral plants, **3**:94–96; government-approved baby names, **1**:154; grave rental, **3**:102; interrailing, **2**:147–148; kangaroo care, **1**:183; *Matura (Mature, Matur, Maturita, Maturità, Maturität, Mamypa)*, **2**:15–16; Maypole, **2**:219–222; mourning color, **3**:302, 304–305; Nordic napping, **1**:249–250; ossuaries, **3**:200–203; pensions, **3**:228; secular confirmation, **2**:300–302; soul cakes and soul breads, **3**:263–266; spontaneous shrines, **3**:269; Steiner schools, **1**:318; *tand-fé*, **1**:326; Tomb of the Unknown Soldier, **3**:295; training bras, **2**:338–341; water births, **1**:347; yew trees, **3**:327–329. *See also individual European countries by name*

Euthanasia, **3**:11–12

Evans, Thom, **2**:23

Evergreen herbs, as funeral plants, **3**:96

Evil eye and evil spirits (devils): amulets/ charms against, **1**:14, 344–345, **2**:324; protection against, **1**:306, 316, 318, 324, 356–357; **2**:191, 294, **3**:33, 305; warding off, **1**:235, 305, 306–309, 318, 342–346, 356, **2**:12, 39, 237, 243, 254; release of, 349

Excarnation, **3**:259–262, 339–340

Exhumation, **3**:102–105, 121, 202

Exogamy, **2**:343

Extreme ritual flesh modification, **2**:333–335

Eyam Plague Sunday Service, **3**:83–84

Face in birthday cake, **2**:85

Fady, **1**:33

Fairies: on Mount Velebit, **3**:176; protection from, **1**:78; stealing human babies, **1**:77–80

Fairy bread, **1**:35

Fairy Day, **1**:304

Fairy Investigation Society (FIS), **1**:78

Fairytales, **1**:134–138, 262; alluding to menstruation, **2**:230–231. *See also Weihnachtsmärchen*

Famadihana, **3**:85–87

Family and Medical Leave Act (U.S.), **1**:265
Family Federation for Peace and Unification, **2**:235
Family planning. *See* Birth control
Fantasy coffins, **3**:87–90
Fassi people, **2**:373
Fat Buddha (Hotei), **1**:214
Fat Tuesday, **3**:66
Father Christmas, **1**:296–297, 304–305. *See also* Saint Nicholas; Santa Claus
Father's Day, **1**:138–140
Fathers: bonding with children, **1**:75; preparation for childbirth, **1**:104; traditions involving, **1**:350–351
Fattening room seclusion, **2**:86–89, 153–155
Fave dei Morti, **3**:265
Feast of All Saints, **3**:109. *See also* All Saints' Day
Feast of Corpus Christi, **1**:126–127
Feast of Saint Joseph, **1**:139
Feast of the Banners, **1**:184
Feast of the Holy Innocents, **1**:83–84, 245
Feast of the Presentation, **1**:98
Feast of the Willow Branches, **2**:188
Fellatio, **2**:149–152
Female circumcision. *See* Female genital cutting (FGC)
Female genital cutting (FGC), **2**:8–9, 86–87, 89–94
Female Genital Mutilation. *See* Female genital cutting (FGC)
Female impersonators, **1**:263
Feminism and feminists, **1**:5, 23, **2**:189–190, 196
Fertility: celebration of, **1**:13; deities associated with, **1**:5–6, 34–35, **2**:225; government control over, **1**:256–258; promotion of, **1**:18, **2**:237; rituals, **1**:19, 256–257; symbols of, **1**:14, 75–76, **1**:218–219, 346, **2**:200
Festival of Lights. *See* Diwali
Festival of Lily-of-the-Valley, **2**:321
Festival of Remembrance (British Legion), **3**:2. *See also* Remembrance Day
Fetish-wear, **3**:100
FGM National Clinical Group, **2**:93

Fidanzamenti, **2**:94–95
Fidanzati in casa, **2**:94–95
Figa (amulet), **1**:345
Fiji: birth trees, **1**:33; ritual tattooing, **2**:272–273; Schoolies Week, **2**:284; urethral subincision, **2**:349
Filahta, **1**:345
Filipino debut (Filipino Cotillion), **2**:95–97, **2**:345
Final fireworks, **3**:268
Finger amputation, **3**:90–91
Finnish celebrations and practices: birthday celebrations, **1**:35; cardboard box beds, **1**:72–75; changeling beliefs, **1**:79; Girl Guides, **1**:152; leap year proposals, **2**:189; Nordic napping, **1**:249; parental leave, **1**:266; pensions, **3**:230; *Polterabend*, **2**:256–257; Prometheus Camps, **2**:301; same-sex marriage, **2**:285; universal minimum pension, **3**:231; wife-carrying (*eukonkanto*), **2**:35. *See also* Saami people; Scandinavian celebrations and practices
Fire-Hair Shaving ceremony, **1**:140–142
First communion, **1**:142–144. *See also* Holy Communion
First Nation people, **3**:117, 183–185
First Steps celebration, **1**:66–67
Firstborn males, **1**:280–283
Fistulas, **1**:362
Fitampoha, **3**:86, 243–245
Flanders Fields Memorial Poppy, **3**:315
Flanders Passion plays, **3**:206
Flower garlands, **3**:161
Folk art, Dala horses, **1**:115–116
Folk Catholicism, **3**:49, 269
Folk divination, **1**:348–349
Folk medicine, **1**:124, 130–131
Folk narratives. *See* Fairytales; Folktales
Folk saints, **3**:246–250
Folklore: monsters, **1**:221–226; Ozark and Appalachian, **1**:356–357; pagan, **1**:126; Roma, **2**:44; Saint Nicholas, **1**:294
Folktales, and nursery rhymes, **1**:252
Food and Agriculture Organization of the United Nations (FAO), **1**:146

Food taboos in pregnancy, **1**:86, 89–90, 144–147, 187
Forced marriage, **2**:7–9, 136
Forced Marriage Unit (FMU), **2**:8
Fore people, **3**:77–78
Forehead-cutting initiation, **2**:98–101
Founder's Day (Chelsea pensioners), **3**:28
France: government-approved baby names, **1**:153, 155; Hmong immigrants in, **2**:137
French celebrations and practices: *Ankou*, **3**:10–11; *Baccalauréat (le bac)*, **2**:15–16; baptism customs, **1**:32; birth commemorations, **1**:32; *Carnet de Santé Maternité*, **1**:238; Cimetière du Père Lachaise, **3**:298; danse macabre, **3**:52; jury duty, **2**:165; *La Soupe*, **2**:181–182; La Tombe Du Soldate Inconnu, **3**:294, 295; *Le Bal des Débutantes*, **2**:97; Memorial Days, **3**:225; minute's silence, **3**:174–175; mistletoe, **1**:219; mourning color, **3**:304; national mourning, **3**:192; nursery rhymes, **1**:251; parental leave, **1**:266; Passion plays, **3**:206; St. Catherine's Day, **2**:320–322; same-sex marriage, **2**:285; space burial, **3**:267; spontaneous shrines, **3**:269; sugared almonds, **1**:32; swaddling, **1**:321; tooth mouse, **1**:326; *Universite du Troisieme Age*, **3**:307; water births, **1**:347; wedding customs, **1**:32; yew trees, **3**:327
Frau Perchta, **1**:223
Free Wesleyan Church, **3**:300–301
French Guiana, **2**:185. *See also* South American celebrations and practices
Fulani (Fulbe, Fula) tribe, **2**:307, **2**:383–386
Full moon, **1**:37
Fundoshi, **2**:110
Funeral cakes, **3**:92–93
Funeral candy, **3**:93–94
Funeral Doom, **3**:62–63
Funeral monuments, *Mirila*, **3**:175–177
Funeral music and songs, **3**:97–98, 127–129
Funeral plants, **3**:94–96, 328

Funeral practices: Aboriginal, **3**:116–117; candles around the corpse, **1**:37; Christian, **3**:155; DIY funerals, **3**:210–211; *Famadihana*, **3**:85–87; fantasy coffins, **3**:87–90; green burials, **3**:104, 320; high-platform exposure of the corpse, **3**:115–118; Netherlands, **3**:323; pauper's funeral, **3**:209–211; personalized hearses, **3**:211–213; ritual feasts, **3**:53–55; Romanian, **3**:237–239; snuff, **3**:92; state funerals, **3**:271–275; Tongan, **3**:300–302; Voodoo, **3**:336–337; Wiccan, **3**:318–322; involving yew trees, **3**:327–328; Zoroastran, **3**:338–341. *See also* Death rituals; Japanese funeral customs; Jewish funeral customs
Funeral processions, **3**:273; riderless horse, **3**:236–237; Royal Wootton Bassett, **3**:239–241
Funerary sculpture, **3**:163–164

Ga people, **1**:149, **3**:87–88
Ga'anda people, **2**:100, 294–295
Gaelic festivals, **2**:219
Galena, **2**:40
Gambia, **2**:92. *See also* Sub-Saharan African celebrations and practices; West African celebrations and practices
Gamelan music, **1**:204–206, **3**:195
Gap year, **2**:103–104
Garifuna people, **1**:106–107
Gautama Buddha, **1**:210
GAVI (Global Alliance for Vaccines and Immunisation), **1**:86 –87
Gay marriage. *See* Same-sex marriage
GCSE subjects (General Certificate of Secondary Education), **2**:56–58
Geishas, **2**:292–293
Gempuku, **2**:61
Gender issues: gender equality, **1**:33–34; gender segregation, **2**:279; *hijra* population, **2**:131–133; short-term gender transformation, **1**:106
General Certificate of Secondary Education (GCSE), choosing options, **2**:56–58
Geophagia, **1**:71

George Washington Bridge (New York/New Jersey), **3**:278

German celebrations and practices: Advent calendars, **1**:349–350; All Souls' Day, **3**:8–9, 265; assisted suicide, **3**:13; *bar mitzvah*, **2**:21; birthday customs, **2**:26–28; breastfeeding, **1**:56; candle superstitions, **1**:37; changeling beliefs, **1**:77; danse macabre, **3**:52; Easter egg trees (*Osterbrunnen*), **3**:67; eating human placenta, **1**:124; Frau Perchta, **1**:223; glass blowing, **1**:357; government-approved baby names, **1**:153, 154, 155; grave reuse, **3**:103; jury duty, **2**:165; *Kinderfest*, **1**:36–37, 42, 273; *klinken putzen*, **2**:27; Krampus, **1**:221–223; Liberation Day, **3**:225; love divination, **2**:3; *Martinstag*, **3**:111; May Day, **2**:221; Memorial to the Fallen of the War, **3**:295; Memorial to the Victims of Fascism and Militarism, **3**:295; mistletoe, **1**:219; *Mutterpass*, **1**:237–238; nursery rhymes, **1**:251; parental leave, **1**:66; Passion plays, **3**:206–208; plastination, **3**:213–216; *Polterabend*, **2**:254–258; Round Birthdays, **1**:43; Saint Nicholas, **1**:297; *Schuhplattler* and *Ländler*, **2**:297–299; secular confirmation, **2**:300–301; silver spoon, **1**:313; sock garlands, **2**:318–319; soul cakes, **3**:263–264; space burial, **3**:267; spontaneous shrines, **3**:269; Steiner schools, **1**:318; swaddling, **1**:321; University of the Third Age, **3**:307; Vatertag, **1**:139–140; *Volkstrauertag* (People's Day of Mourning), **3**:225; *Waldkindergärten*, **1**:341–342; *Weihnachtsmärchen*, **1**:349–350; witch balls, **1**:356

German Federation of Nature and Forest Kindergartens (BVNW), **1**:341

Germany: Hmong immigrants in, **2**:137; retirement and pensions, **3**:228–229

Gesellschaft fur Technische Zusammenarbeit (GTZ), **2**:30

Ghanaian practices: baby-naming ceremony **1**:1–4; birthday traditions, **1**:149–151; Dipo Womanhood Ceremony, **2**:71–73; fantasy coffins, **3**:87–90; female ritual servitude (*trokosi*), **1**:330–333. *See also* West African celebrations and practices

Ghost marriages, **3**:221–222

Ghosts: Chinese, **3**:329–332; Jewish, **3**:132

Girl Guides movement, **1**:151–153, 303. *See also* Scouts and Scouting

Girl Scouts of the United States of America, **1**:152. *See also* Scouts and Scouting

Girl Summit, **2**:8

Girls: circumcision of, **2**:206 (*see also* Female genital cutting); clothing for first communion, **1**:143; given in marriage to a deity, **1**:116–119; offered to Hindu temple, **1**:192–193; and ritual servitude, **1**:330–333; serving as incarnation of goddess Devi, **1**:189–190. *See also* Babies; Children; Girls' coming-of-age ceremonies

Girls' coming-of-age ceremonies, **2**:269; *ameen* ceremony, **1**:47–48; *Brit banot* ceremony, **1**:62; Chinese, **2**:51; Dipo Womanhood Ceremony, **2**:71–73; Filipino debut, **2**:95–97; *gryerye*, **2**:106; Iria ceremony, **2**:153–155; *Isanaklesh Gotal*, **2**:155–159; *La Quinceañera*, **2**:177–180; *Lazarovden*, **2**:186–188; Maasai traditions, **2**:205, **2**:206; *Mehndi*, **2**:223; menstrual customs, **2**:226–227; *Mogi*, **2**:61–62; *nahtwin*, **2**:83; *Pika* and *Nora*, **2**:253–254; scarification ritual, **2**:294–295; Sunrise Ceremony, **2**:326–331; Tamil celebration, **2**:226; training bras, **2**:338–341; vision quest, **2**:359; Zambia, **2**:52–55. *See also* Coming-of-age ceremonies

Goddesses: Aztec, **3**:58; of childbearing and children, **1**:5–6, 23, 90; Devi (Hindu), **1**:189–190; earth, **1**:69, 194, 203, **2**:71; Earth Mother, **1**:8, **2**:155; of fertility, **1**:117, 129–130, **2**:225; of fertility, childbirth and

water, **1**:4–7; of love, **1**:6, **2**:182; of luck/fate, **1**:203–204; of menstruation, **1**:6; of pregnancy, **1**:4–7
Godparents, **1**:26, 66, 125, 204, **2**:178
Gokarna Aunsi, **1**:139
The Golden Bough, **1**:218
Golden Gate Bridge (San Francisco), **3**:278–279
Golden Week (Japan), **1**:184
Gongua ba Buniwae (the Care), **1**:106
Good Friday, **3**:275. *See also* Holy Week
Goth subculture, **3**:99–102, 297; bands, **3**:99–100; cinema, **3**:101; fashion, **3**:100; magazines, **3**:100–101
Government-approved baby names, **1**:153–157
Grasmere Rushbearing, **1**:164–166
Grave rental, **3**:102–105, 121
The Great Passing, **3**:105–107
Greek celebrations and practices: almonds at spinsters' funerals, **3**:162; Childermas, **1**:84; cremation, **3**:103; *filahta*, **1**:345; grave rental, **3**:102; *koliva*, **3**:135–136; leap year marriage, **2**:189; love divination, **2**:3; March celebration, **1**:16–17; money dance, **2**:234; mourning color, **3**:302; parental leave, **1**:266; pensions, **3**:230; soul cake, **3**:93. *See also* Ancient Greece; Greek Orthodox Church celebrations and practices
Greek Orthodox Church celebrations and practices: charms against the evil eye, **1**:345; Churching of Women script, **1**:100–103; Easter, **1**:17; *koliva*, **3**:135; Name days, **1**:241; opposition to cremation, **3**:42, 103. *See also* Eastern Orthodox Church celebrations and practices
Greek-Catholic churches, **3**:251
Green burial customs, **3**:104, 320
Green Day, **2**:316
Greenland, **1**:9, 10, **2**:285
Grenada, Nine-Nights, **3**:196–198
Gretna Green, **2**:104–105, 210
Groaning Cake (Kimbly), **1**:166–169
Groaning Cheese, **1**:166–167

Grooms: blackening, **2**:28; carrying the bride over the threshold, **2**:36; creeling, **2**:29; gifts given to, **2**:13, 37–38; Jewish ceremony for, **2**:159–160; ritual bathing of, **2**:11, 213
Groom's cakes, **2**:48
Grýla, **1**:223
Guanches, **3**:186
Guanyin (Buddhist deity), **1**:90
Guaraní Indians, **3**:247
Guatemalan practices: covering the belly button, **1**:108; *Tuj* or *Temascal*, **1**:333–335; worry dolls, **1**:357–358. *See also* Central American practices
Guinea, **2**:30. *See also* West African celebrations and practices
Guinea Bissau, **3**:71. *See also* Sub-Saharan African celebrations and practices; West African celebrations and practices
Gulab Jamun, **1**:36
Guyana, Nine-Nights, **3**:196–198
Gwallye, **2**:105–106
Gyerye ceremony, **2**:106
Gypsies. *See* Roma celebrations and practices

Hadaka Matsuri (naked festival), **2**:109–110
Haida Gwaii, **3**:184
Haida tribe, **3**:183–185
Hair cutting: ceremonial **1**:9, 195; on *Hajj*, **2**:116
Hair removal, **2**:111–113
Hair shaving, **1**:338, **2**:207, 116
Hair-pinning ceremony (Ji Li), **2**:49–50
Hairwork, **3**:287
Haiti: Nine-Nights, **3**:196–198; zombies and voodoo death traditions, **3**:335–338
Hajj (pilgrimage), **2**:113–116
Hallowe'en (Halloween), **3**:109–111, 328, 334
Halva (halawa, halvah, halava, halwa), **3**:113–115
Hamar people, **2**:66
Hammaspeikko (Tooth Troll), **1**:325
hampas-palayak, **1**:285

366 COMPREHENSIVE INDEX

Hamsa hand symbol, **1**:344–345
Handfasting, **2**:32, 117–119; ceremony, **2**:119–126
Handkerchief test, **2**:357
Handparting, **2**:127–128
Hanselling, **1**:351
Hanshi Festival, **3**:219, 221
Hanuman (monkey god), **1**:117
"Happy Birthday" Song, **1**:171–173, 263
Hatsu Miyamairi, **1**:174
Haulage of the Midwife (*Vlechugane*), **1**:19
Hausa people, **1**:362–363
Hawai'i, **1**:67–68, **2**:272
Haworth Traders Christmas Committee, **1**:304
Head shaving ritual, **2**:116, 207
Healthcare, for pregnant women, **1**:72, 73, 237–238. *See also* Indigenous medicine
Hearses, personalized, **3**:211–213
Henna, **1**:51, **2**:2–3, 222–224, 237–238, 242, 312
Herbal remedies, **1**:30, 90, 181, 229, 307
Herodotus, **2**:90
Herrick, Robert, **2**:44
Hesono-o, **1**:173–175
Hesperides (Herrick), **2**:44
Highgate Cemetery, **3**:298–299
High-platform exposure of the corpse, **3**:115–118
Hijab, **2**:128–130; poppy-print, **3**:316
Hijra population, **2**:131–133
Himalayas, **3**:23. *See also* Tibetan practices
Hindu celebrations and practices: arranged marriage, **2**:6; baby rituals, **1**:175–177; birthstones, **1**:44–45; British weddings, **2**:32; cremation, **3**:42; *devadasi*, **1**:116–119; Diwali, **2**:73–75, 77; extreme ritual flesh modification, **2**:333–335; forced marriage, **2**:8; *halva*, **3**:114; and the *hijra* population, **2**:131–133; Karva Chauth (Karwa Chauth), **2**:224; *Kumbh Mela*, **2**:173–175; lotus birthing, **1**:210–211; *Makar Sankranthi*, **3**:114; Mangalore Dasara, **3**:311; *Manjal Neerattu Vizha* (Turmeric Bathing Ceremony), **2**:226; menstruation as unclean, **2**:228; Mundan ceremony, **1**:232–234; *ngaben* (*pelebon*), **3**:193–196; *Pasni*, **1**:275–276; polygyny, **2**:261; tooth-filing ceremony, **2**:335–338; *Upanayana* (Sacred thread ritual), **1**:337–339; Vrindavan, **3**:309–311; wedding ceremonies, **2**:133–136
Hindu death customs, **3**:118–120; mourning, **3**:119; post-death rituals, **3**:118; riverside cremation, **3**:119
Hitler Youth, **2**:298
HIV/AIDS, **2**:31, 92, 132, 248, 269–270, 343–344, **3**:71
Hmong people, **2**:317–318; names, **2**:136–139; treatment of the placenta, **1**:67
Hogmanay, **1**:293
Hogueras festival, **1**:128
Holi (springtime festival), **2**:75–76
Holiva, **3**:333
Holland. *See* Netherlands
Holly Queen and Princesses, **1**:304–305
Holy Communion, **1**:32; first, **1**:142–144; in a wedding ceremony, **2**:59, 61. *See also* Eucharist
Holy Mosque (Mecca), **2**:116
Holy Week, **3**:47–50. *See also* Good Friday; Palm Sunday
Homosexual communities, **2**:8, **3**:250. *See also* LGBT issues
Homosexuality, ritualized, **2**:148
Hong Kong: grave rental, **3**:104; jury duty, **2**:167; *Qingming* Festival, **3**:219–221. *See also* Asian celebrations and practices
Hopi traditions: *Katsina* (*katchina*, *kachina*) dolls, **1**:179, 358–359; naming rites, **1**:177–180
Hop-tu-Naa, **3**:112
Hora (*horah*) dance, **1**:19, **2**:20, 40, 139–140
Horseshoes, as good luck charm, **2**:141–142
Hotei, **1**:214
Hounen Matsuri, **1**:277
Huitzilopochtli (Aztec god of war) **1**:283
Human rights, **2**:30
Humanist confirmation, **2**:300–302

Hungarian celebrations and practices: All Souls' Day, **3**:8, 265; birthday customs, **1**:41; eating human placenta, **1**:123; funeral plants, **3**:95; Krampusz, **1**:222–223; *Martinstag*, **3**:111; *Matura*, **2**:15; mourning color, **3**:305; national mourning, **3**:192; parental leave, **1**:266; spontaneous shrines, **3**:269; *Vizbevető*, **2**:79; wedding cakes, **2**:371. *See also* Eastern European celebrations and practices

Hunger Safety Net Programme, **3**:231

Hungry Ghost Festival, **3**:7, 329–332

Hyakunichimairi (*Hyaku niche mairi*), **1**:259

Iban people of Borneo, **2**:144

Ibani tribe, **1**:68, 69

Ibo tribe, **2**:142

Icelandic celebrations and practices: *Eddas*, **1**:326; government-approved baby names, **1**:153, 154–155, 157–164; *Grýla*, **1**:223; lullabies, **1**:214; parental leave, **1**:265; same-sex marriage, **2**:285; secular confirmation, **2**:300; wedding cake, **2**:370

Ifaluk Island, **1**:287

Igbo tribe, **1**:68, **2**:234

Imbolc, **2**:219

Imilchil Moussem (Berber Marriage Festival), **2**:238–240

Incan practices, **3**:186, 256

Incubus, **1**:79

Indian celebrations and practices: arranged marriage, **2**:5–7; baby hammocks, **1**:301; baby-throwing, **1**:127; belief in the evil eye, **1**:343; birthday traditions, **1**:36, 40, 41; boxes for babies, **1**:74; Buddhist practices, **3**:18, 20; cremation, **3**:41; *devadasi* system, **1**:116–119; Devipujak purification trial, **2**:55–56; Diwali, **2**:73–75; endocannibalism, **3**:77; food taboos during pregnancy, **1**:146; forced marriage, **2**:8; hair removal, **2**:112; *halva*, **3**:113–114; *hijra* population, **2**:131–133; Kali Pooja, **2**:74–75; Karva Chauth, **2**:224; *Mehndi*, **2**:222, 223; menstrual taboos, **2**:228–229; mourning color, **3**:304; navjote ceremonies, **1**:247–248; *ngaben*, **3**:195–196; polyandry, **2**:258, 260; potty training, **1**:286; *sati* (*suttee*), **3**:43; Sikh death customs, **3**:257; Sikh wedding ceremonies, **2**:312–315; space burial, **3**:267; state funerals, **3**:273; teething remedies, **1**:329; virginity testing, **2**:356; Vrindavan (City of Widows), **3**:309–311; Zoroastran funerals, **3**:338–341. *See also* South Asian celebrations and practices

Indian Arts and Crafts Act (1990), **1**:120

Indigenous medicine, **1**:181

Indonesian celebrations and practices: birth trees, **1**:33; birthday celebrations, **1**:36; cutting the umbilical cord, **1**:113; eating human placenta, **1**:123; food taboos during pregnancy, **1**:145; headhunters, **3**:256; *Jamu* medicine and massage, **1**:181–182; *Legong*, **1**:204–207; living with the dead, **3**:155–158; Muslim dress for women, **2**:130; *ngaben* (*pelebon*), **3**:193–195; *Nyabutan* ceremony, **1**:253–254; tooth sharpening, **2**:143; tooth-filing ceremony, **2**:335–338; wedding cakes, **2**:372. *See also* Southeast Asian celebrations and practices

Indra Jatta Festival, **1**:190–191

Infant mortality: in China, **1**:226; in Egypt, **1**:306; in Finland, **1**:72; in Ghana, **1**:2; in Kyrgyzstan, **1**:195; in Texas, **1**:75; in Tibet, **1**:323

Infibulation, **2**:91. *See also* Female genital cutting

Initiation ceremonies: bullet ant initiation, **2**:41–43; cow jumping, **2**:66–68; forehead-cutting, **2**:98–101; for *hijra*, **2**:132; ritual, **1**:53; by semen transferal, **2**:148–152. *See also* Boys' coming-of-age ceremonies; Chinese coming-of-age ceremonies; Coming-of-age ceremonies; Girls' coming-of-age ceremonies

Institute for Plastination (IfP), **3**:213
International Association of Universities of the Third Age (IAUTA), **3**:307
International Child Protection Day, **1**:22
International Cremation Federation (ICF), **3**:41
International Day of Zero Tolerance for Female Genital Mutilation, **2**:93
International Needs Ghana (ING), **1**:332
International Wave of Light, **3**:217
Interrailing, **2**:147–148
Inuit people, **1**:9–11, **1**:79
Iran: Assyrian betrothal and weddings, **2**:9–14; *halva*, **3**:113, 115; mourning color, **3**:302; national mourning, **3**:191; Zoroastrianism, **3**:338. *See also* Middle Eastern celebrations and practices; Persia
Iraq: Assyrian betrothal and weddings, **2**:9–14; *Halawat tamr*, **3**:114–115. *See also* Middle Eastern celebrations and practices
Iria ceremony, **2**:153–155
Irish celebrations and practices: Beltane, **2**:219; birthday customs, **1**:40; changeling beliefs, **1**:77; funeral snuff, **3**:92; Girl Guides, **1**:152; Lisdoonvarna Matchmaking Festival, **2**:16–17; RAG Week, **2**:267–268; Saint Brigid and the Biddies, **1**:16; same-sex marriage, **2**:285; spontaneous shrines, **3**:269; sprinkling cake, **1**:317–318; wakes, **3**:313; yew trees, **3**:327
Isanaklesh (Mescalero Apache Earth Mother Goddess), **1**:8, **2**:155
Isanaklesh Gotal (The Feast), **2**:155–159
Isbister Chambered Cairn, **3**:262
ISIL (Islamic State), **3**:192
Isla de las Munecas, **3**:61
Islamic celebrations and practices: *Adhaan*, **1**:234; *ameen* ceremony, **1**:47–48; *aqeeqah* (*aqiqa*) ritual, **1**:235; baby naming, **1**:234–235; beards, **2**:22; betrothal and marriage, **2**:1; birth rites, **1**:234–235; *bismallah* ceremony, **1**:47–48; British weddings, **2**:32; burying the placenta, **1**:235; circumcision, **1**:234, 235–237; death rituals, **3**:188–190; female genital cutting, **2**:90; forced marriage, **2**:7–8; hair removal, **2**:112; *Hajj*, **2**:113–116; head shaving, **1**:234; *Hijab*, **2**:128–130; and the *hijra* population, **2**:131–133; *Id-el-kabir*, **2**:307; menstruation customs, **2**:228; opposition to cremation, **3**:44; polygyny, **2**:261; prayer for babies, **1**:194; ritual ear-piercing, **2**:83–84; *shabka*, **2**:302–305; *tahneek* ritual **1**:234; *taweez*, **1**:234; *Umrah*, **2**:113; wedding ceremonies, **2**:40, 222, 241–242
Islamic State (ISIL), **3**:192
Islamophobia, **3**:316
Island of the Dolls, **3**:61
Isle of Man: Beltane, **2**:219; Hop-tu-Naa, **3**:112
Isola di San Michele (San Michele Island), **3**:121–122
Israel: birthday child on a chair, **1**:40; food taboos during pregnancy, **1**:145. *See also* Middle Eastern celebrations and practices
Italy: birthday customs, **1**:41; birthstones, **1**:44; danse macabre, **3**:52; Father's Day, **1**:139; *Fave dei Morti*, **3**:265; *Fidanzamenti* and *Fidanzati in casa*, **2**:94–95; Isola di San Michele (San Michele Island), **3**:121–122; La Befana, **1**:223; *mano fico*, **1**:346; Marantega (tooth witch), **1**:326; *Matura*, **2**:15; mourning color, **3**:302; mummification, **3**:185; Nativity play, **1**:245; ossuaries, **3**:201; *Pan dei Morti*, **3**:265; parental leave, **1**:266; Passion plays, **3**:206; pensions, **3**:230; soul cakes, **3**:263–264; Tomb of the Unknown Soldier, **3**:294
Ivana Kupala, **2**:353
Ivy, **3**:328
Iztapalapa Passion play, **3**:208–209

Jack o'lanterns, **3**:110, 112
Jailbreak, **2**:267
Jainism, **3**:245–246; Diwali, **2**:73–74, 76–77

Jamaica: Nine-Nights, **3**:196–198; pantomime, **1**:261; treatment of the placenta, **1**:69

Jamu medicine and massage, **1**:181–182

Jāṇi Day, **2**:200

Japanese celebrations and practices: baby naming ceremony, **1**:259; baby racing, **1**:22; Bon Festival, **3**:7; Buddhist practices, **3**:18, 20; crying-baby sumo competition, **1**:111–112; cutting the umbilical cord, **1**:113; government-approved baby names, **1**:153, 155; *Hadaka Matsuri* (naked festival), **2**:109–110; *Hatsu Miyamairi*, **1**:174; *Hesono-o* (wrapping umbilical cord as keepsake), **1**:173–175; *Hyakunichimairi* (*Hyaku niche mairi*), **1**:259; *Kanchu Misogi*, **2**:110–111; *Koshikijima no Toshidon*, **1**:225; log riding, **2**:197–199; lullabies, **1**:214; mistletoe, **1**:219; *Namahage*, **1**:223–224; *Okuizome*, **1**:259–260; *Omiai*, **2**:251–252; *Omiya-mairi*, **1**:174; *Onbashira* festival, **2**:197–199; *Oshichiya Meimeishiki*, **1**:259; *Ososo Matsuri* (Vagina Festival), **1**:279; parental leave, **1**:266, 267; pensions, **3**:228, 230–231; phalllus festivals, **1**:277–280; ritual tattooing, **2**:276; *San-san-kudo* (*san san kudo*; *sansan-kudo*), **2**:291–293; *Seijin no Hi* (Coming of Age Day), **2**:61–64; *Setsubun*, **1**:307–309; shrine outing, **1**:259; teething remedies, **1**:329; universities for older students, **3**:308; Valentine's Day, **2**:316; *Waldkindergärten*, **1**:341; wedding cakes, **2**:372; wedding dresses, **2**:374; *Yamadashi*, **2**:198. *See also* Asian celebrations and practices; Japanese funeral customs

Japanese funeral customs, **3**:123–127; arrangement of the corpse, **3**:123–124; cremation **3**:125; fetus memorial service, **3**:180–183; funeral plants, **3**:95; grave rental, **3**:104; memorial observances, **3**:126; mourning clothes, **3**:303–304; mourning colors, **3**:303–304; mummification, **3**:185; Obon, **3**:126–127; procession to location of the funeral, **3**:124; space burial, **3**:267; *Toro Nagashi*, **3**:127; wake, **3**:124–125, 313

Japanese matchmaking, **2**:251–252

Jazz funeral, **3**:127–129

Jerusalem and the Via Dolorosa, **3**:275–276

Jewelry: as gifts for brides, **2**:37, 134, 302–305; mourning, **3**:286–288; ritual wedding and betrothal gifts, **2**:1–2; worn by brides, **2**:312–313

Jewish celebrations and practices: *bar mitzvah*, **2**:19–21; *bat mitzvah*, **2**:19–21; beards, **2**:22; birth trees, **1**:33; birthstones, **1**:44, **1**:46; *brit banot*, **1**:62; *brit milah*, **1**:59–63; *brit shalom* (*bris shalom*), **1**:62; British weddings, **2**:32; female genital cutting, **2**:90; forced marriage, **2**:8; *hora* dance, **2**:138–140; menstrual customs, **2**:226–228; *Pidyon haben* (Redemption of the first-born), **1**:280–283; *Pidyon habit* ceremony (Redemption of the firstborn daughter), **1**:282; wedding customs, **2**:159–162, 222. *See also* Jewish funeral customs

Jewish funeral customs, **3**:129–133; burial, **3**:130–131; dying, **3**:130; mourning, **3**:131; objection to plastination, **3**:214; opposition to cremation, **3**:44; Shiva, **3**:132

Jewish ghosts, **3**:132

Jia Liang (Sisters' Meal Festival), **2**:317–318

Jicarilla Apache tribe, **2**:330

Jivaroan tribes, **3**:255, 256–357

John XXIII (pope), **3**:185

John Paul II (pope), **3**:192, 276

Jolly Roger, **3**:170

Joninės, **2**:200

Jordan, **2**:262. *See also* Middle Eastern celebrations and practices

Jugendweihe, **2**:300–301

Juks-akka (childbirth goddess), **1**:5

Jumping over the broom, **2**:163–165

Jury duty, **2**:165–171

Kachina. See *Katsina*
Kagekone, **1**:35
Kagemand, **1**:35
Kaiapo (Kayapo) tribe, **2**:190
Kalash (Kalasha or Nuristani) people, **1**:128, **2**:225
Kalash religion, **1**:128–129
Kali (Hindu goddess), **2**:74
Kali Pooja, **2**:74–75
Kami-dana (god-shelf), **1**:214
Kanamara Matsuri (Festival of the Steel Phallus), **1**:278–279
Kanchu Misogi, **2**:110–111
Kanelmø (cinnamon maid), **2**:26
Kanelsvend (cinnamon man), **2**:26
Kangaroo care, **1**:183–184
Karan people, **2**:275–276
Kare-Kare community, **1**:362
Kashiwa mochi, **1**:185
Katarzynki (St. Catherine's Day), **2**:3–4, 320–322
Katarzynki gingerbread, **2**:4
Katsina (*katchina, kachina*) dolls, **1**:179, 358–359
Kayan people, **2**:243, 244
Keesta, **2**:330
Kenya, **1**:316, **2**:93, **3**:231. See also African celebrations and practices
Keraki tribe, **2**:149
Ketubah, **2**:160
Khandoba (god of farming and herding), **1**:117
Kheyapta-d khitna, **2**:11
Khitan, **1**:235. See also Circumcision
Khoya, **1**:36
Khwahish khwari, **2**:1
Khwan ceremony, **1**:140–142
Kickapoo Indian tribe, **2**:64–66
Kikuyu people, **2**:262
Kimbly, **1**:166
Kimono rental, **2**:62
Kinaalda, **2**:330
Kinderfest, **1**:37, 42, 273
Kingdom of Swaziland, **2**:269–272
Kiriwina Islands, **2**:341–344
Kiss Day, **2**:316
Kissing Friday, **2**:80
Kite flying, **3**:221

Kiv people, **2**:142
Klama puberty dance, **2**:72–73
Klausjagen, **1**:296
Klinken putzen, **2**:27
Kodomo Noi Hi (Japan), **1**:184–186
Kola Peninsula, **1**:4
Koliva (*kolyva, kollyva, kollyba*), **3**:135–138
Konaki sumo (Crying Sumo), **1**:111–112
Korean celebrations and practices: baby naming, **1**:188; childbirth customs, **1**:186–189; mourning color, **3**:302; placenta in folk medicine, **1**:124; pregnancy customs, **1**:186–187. See also Asian celebrations and practices; South Korean celebrations and practices
Koroonduk, **1**:195
Korowai tribe, **3**:78
Koshikijima no Toshidon, **1**:225
Kosovo, **2**:15. See also Eastern European celebrations and practices; Yugoslav countries
Kotobuki Bako, **1**:173–174
Krada, **1**:150
Krahonowska-Malkowska, Olga, **1**:152
Krampus **1**:221–223, 298
Krampusnacht, **1**:222
Krobo people, **2**:71–73
Krustaba, **1**:204
Kulemba, **2**:100
Kumari and *Deuki*, **1**:189–193
Kumbh Mela, **2**:173–175
Kunstmärchen, **1**:135
Kuru, **3**:77
Kusti ritual, **1**:246–248
Kutema nyora, **2**:253
Kyrgyzstan, **1**:193–196, **3**:231. See also Central Asian practices

L'Ankou, **3**:10–11
La Befana, **1**:21:23
La Calavera Catrina, **3**:58
La Cincuentañera, **2**:180
La Craie, **1**:71
La cuarentena, **1**:197–198
La Fête du Muguet, **2**:321
La fiesta de quince años see *La Quinceañera*
La Quinceañera, **2**:96, 177–180

La Soupe, **2**:180–181
Labsgriftan, **2**:1
Lachrymatory bottles, **3**:286
Ladouvane, **2**:182–183
Ladybird Books, **1**:198–201
Laetare Sunday, **1**:230
Laima (Latvian goddess of luck/fate), **1**:203–204
Lakota death rituals, **3**:139–152; giveaway, **3**:141; memorial ceremony, **3**:140–141; Native American Grave Protection and Repatriation Act, **3**:142–152; spirit-keeping ceremony, **3**:139; spirit-releasing ceremony, **3**:139–140
Lakota tribe, **1**:120, **2**:358–359
Lamaze technique, **1**:201–202
Land diving competitions (*Gol, Nanggol, Nagol, N'gol*), **2**:183–186
Ländler, **2**:298–299
Langsuir, **1**:79
Lanie wosku (pouring wax), **2**:4
Lanimer Day, Scotland, **1**:353
Lany poniedzalek (Wet Monday), **2**:79
Laos: Hmong names, **2**:136; mother roasting, **1**:228–229; tooth dyeing, **2**:144. *See also* Southeast Asian celebrations and practices
Las Posadas, **1**:284
Last meal of condemned prisoner, **3**:37–40
"The Last Post," **3**:152–155
Latin American celebrations and practices: anti-Santa Claus movement, **1**:297–298; christening gowns, **1**:94; covering the belly button, **1**:108–109; danse macabre, **3**:52; *Dia de los Muertos*, **3**:52, 58–61; *La cuarentena*, **1**:197–198; *La Quinceañera*, **2**:177–180; *Las Posadas*, **1**:284; Name Days, **1**:241. *See also* Central American celebrations and practices; Mexico
Latvian celebrations and practices: birth traditions, **1**:203–204; birthday customs, **1**:40; childhood vaccinations in, **1**:85; Ligo, or Jāņi Day, **2**:200; parental leave, **1**:266; universal minimum pension, **3**:231. *See also* Eastern European celebrations and practices
Laughing Buddha (Hotei), **1**:214
Lazarovden, **2**:186–188
Le Bal des Débutantes, **2**:97
Leap Year Proposal, **2**:189–190
Leaver's Week, **2**:283
Legong, **1**:204–207
Les Relevailles, **1**:98
LGBT issues, **2**:8, 280, **3**:250
Liechtenstein, *Matura*, **2**:15
Ligo, **2**:200
Lilacs, **3**:95
Lilies, **3**:94–95
Lily-of-the-Valley, **3**:95
Lindo, **2**:190–191
Linga (Philippine deity), **1**:256
Lip plugs, **2**:191–195
Liquid cremation, **3**:5–6
Lisdoonvarna Matchmaking Festival, **2**:16–17
Lithuanian celebrations and practices: baby racing, **1**:21–22; birthday customs, **1**:40; government-approved baby names, **1**:153, 155; Joninės, **2**:200; parental leave, **1**:266. *See also* Eastern European celebrations and practices
Little Edith's Treat, **1**:207–208
Living with the Dead, **3**:155–158
Llama fetuses, dissected, **1**:69
Lobola, **2**:195–197
Lockets, **3**:287
Log riding, **2**:197–199
Lohusa Şerbeti, **1**:208–210
Lolita look, **3**:100
Lone Charger, **3**:236
Long-Horn Miao minority group, **2**:138
Longoria, Eva, **2**:112
Looking for fern blossoms, **2**:199–201
Lotus birthing, **1**:210–213
Love divination, **1**:167, **2**:3–5, 44, 177–178, 353, **3**:110, 112
Lovespoons, **2**:201–203
Lucia celebrations, **2**:256–257
Lughnasadh, **2**:219
Luk Thep dolls, **1**:358
Lullabies, **1**:213–215

Lutheran Church, **1**:27, 349, **2**:60, 185, 300, **3**:275. *See also* Christian celebrations and practices
Luxembourg: parental leave, **1**:266; same-sex marriage, **2**:285; spontaneous shrines, **3**:269
"Lyke-wake Dirge," **3**:158–160

Maasai traditions, **1**:316; blood drinking, **2**:205; Maasai warrior initiation, **2**:205–208
Mabele, **1**:71
Macau, *Qingming* Festival, **3**:219
Macedonia, **2**:15, 140. *See also* Eastern European celebrations and practices; Yugoslav countries
Madagascar, **1**:133; death dance, **3**:51; *Famadihana*, **3**:85–87; Sakalava royal death traditions and *Fitampoha*, **3**:243–245; Sambatra mass circumcision festival **1**:298–300
Madder-akka (Mother Goddess), **1**:5
Madrasah school, **1**:47
Madrinas, **2**:178. *See also* Godparents
Magnetoscope, **1**:348
Mahandeo (Kalash deity), **1**:129
Maidens' Garlands, **3**:161–162
Majáles festival, **2**:208–209
Makar Sankranthi, **3**:114
Make-shift memorials. *See* Spontaneous shrines
Makonde people, **2**:143
Malagan ceremonies, **3**:162–164
Malagasy ethnic group, **3**:85
Malawi, **2**:192, **3**:51. *See also* African celebrations and practices
Malaysian celebrations and practices: belief in demons, **1**:79; birth trees, **1**:33; breastfeeding, **1**:56; ear-piercing ceremonies in, **2**:83–84; food taboos during pregnancy, **1**:145; government-approved baby names, **1**:153; indigenous medicine in, **1**:181; *moon-yuet*, **1**:227; mother roasting, **1**:228; Muslim dress for women, **2**:130; Remembrance Day, **3**:223; *sarung buaian*, **1**:300–301; tooth sharpening, **2**:143; treatment of the placenta in, **1**:67. *See also* Southeast Asian celebrations and practices
Male genital cutting, **2**:347–351. *See also* Circumcision
Mali, tooth sharpening, **2**:143. *See also* West Africa
Malta, *Quccija* (*il-Quccija*), **1**:291–292
Mangalore Dasara, **3**:311
Mani-Mala: A Treatise on Gems, **1**:44
Manjal Neerattu Vizha (Turmeric Bathing Ceremony), **2**:226
Mano cornuta, **1**:344
Mano fico, **1**:346
Māori people, **1**:69–70, **2**:230, 273–274, 345; mourning ritual, **3**:281–283. *See also* New Zealand celebrations and practices
Mara (Latvian earth goddess), **1**:203
Marantega, **1**:326
Marawtungwni ceremony, **1**:180
March celebrations, **1**:16
Märchen. *See* Fairytales
Mardi Gras, **3**:66
Marriage Act (Britain), **2**:32, 211–215
Marriage banns, **2**:210–215
Marriages: arranged, **2**:5–9, 10, 37–38, 94, 100, 136, 159, 237, 241, 251–252, 295, 312; exogamous, **2**:343; forced, **2**:5–9, 136; Ghost, **3**:221–222; handfasting, **2**:117–118; leap year, **2**:189–190; mixed (Catholic and non-Catholic), **2**:58–59; multi-racial, **2**:378–379; polyandrous, **2**:258–261; polygamous, **2**:240, 247; polygynous, **2**:261–263; same-sex, **2**:117, 119, 247–249, 256, 285–291; as union of families, **2**:10; *urfi* (unregistered), **2**:304. *See also* Wedding traditions and customs
Martenitsi, **1**:13–16
Martini, **3**:111
Martinique, zombies, **3**:335
Martinsmas, **3**:111
Martinstag, **3**:111
Martisor (Romania), **1**:16
Massacre of the Innocents, **1**:83–84, 245
Massage, *jamu*, **1**:181

Matchmakers: and arranged marriages, **2**:5; Irish, **2**:17; Japanese, **2**:251–252, 291; Jewish, **2**:159; *nayan*, **2**:6–7, 159; in the Shanghai Marriage Market, **2**:305–306
Maternity boxes, **1**:72–75
Maternity Grants Act (Finland), **1**:72
Maternity leave, **1**:266–268. *See also* Parental leave
Matetha-d dhamanta, **2**:10
Matis hunting trials, **2**:215–219
Matronales Feriae, **1**:230
Matronalia, **1**:230
Matura (Mature, Matur, Maturita, Maturità, Maturität, Mamypa), **2**:15–16
Matura Shtetërore, **2**:15
Maundy Money, **3**:164–167
Mauritius, **3**:231
May Day celebrations, **1**:76, 217–218, **2**:209; Maypoles, **2**:219–222
May Queen, **2**:220
Mayan traditions, **2**:177, **3**:256; hair removal, **2**:112; midwives, **1**:112; therapeutic steam bath (*Tuj or temascal*), **1**:333–335; worry dolls, **1**:357–358
Maypoles, **2**:219–222
Mbuti (Efe) tribe, **2**:143, 245
Mecca, pilgrimage to, **2**:113–116
Medical students, white coat ceremony, **2**:381–382
Mehinako tribe, couvade, **1**:104
Mehndi, **2**:222–224, 312. *See also* Henna
Melanesia, **1**:104, **2**:272
Memento Mori, **3**:167–171; jewelry, **3**:286
Memorial feasts, **3**:4–5, 7
Memorial to the Fallen of the War (Germany), **3**:295
Memorial to the Victims of Fascism and Militarism (Germany), **3**:295
Menabe Sakalava, **3**:86
Mende people, **1**:113
Menin Gate Memorial to the Missing, **3**:153–154
Mennonites, **2**:254
Menstrual customs, **2**:224–228; African, **2**:227; of the Bauls, **2**:225–226; Hindu, **2**:226; Jewish, **2**:226–227; in Pakistan **2**:225; in Polynesia, **2**:224–225

Menstrual taboos, **2**:228–233
Menstruation, **1**:14, **2**:52–54; access to sanitary products, **2**:231–232; celebration of, **2**:225–226; goddess of, **1**:6; seclusion during, **1**:129, **2**:225–226, 229–230; as unclean, **2**:228. *See also* Menstrual customs; Menstrual taboos
Mentawai tribe, **2**:142, 143
Mere-Ama (water goddess), **1**:6–7
Merina people, **3**:85
Merry Cemetery, **3**:105, 299
Mescalero Apache, *Isanaklesh Gotal* (The Feast), **2**:155–159
Mesmerism, **1**:348
Mesoamerican practices, **3**:185–186
Message from the Queen, **3**:171–173
Methodist Church, **1**:27, **2**:60, **3**:275, 300
Metrosexual look, **2**:22–23
Mexican celebrations and practices: birthday customs, **2**:85; courtship whistling, **2**:64–66; cutting the umbilical cord, **1**:112; *Dia de los Muertos*, **3**:52; Father's Day, **1**:139; food taboos during pregnancy, **1**:145–146; money dance, **2**:234–235; mourning color, **3**:302; Passion plays, **3**:208–209; pensions, **3**:231; *piñata*, **1**:283–286; placenta as folk medicine, **1**:124; same-sex marriage, **2**:285; Santa Muerte, **3**:246, 249–250; spontaneous shrines, **3**:269. *See also* Central American celebrations and practices; Latin American celebrations and practices
Miao people, **2**:317–318. *See also* Hmong people
Mice, as bedwetting cure, **1**:29
Micronesia, **2**:272
Mictlan (Aztec god), **3**:58
Mictlancihuatl (Aztec goddess), **3**:58
Middle Eastern celebrations and practices: female genital cutting, **2**:89–94; forced marriage, **2**:8; hair removal, **2**:112; *halva*, **3**:113–115; *Mehndi*, **2**:222, 223; Muslim modes of dress for women, **2**:128–130; Tomb of the Unknown Soldier, **3**:295; virginity testing, **2**:355–358. *See also* Egyptian

celebrations and practices; Iran; Iraq; Israel; Jordan; Palestine; Qatar; Saudi Arabia; Syria; Turkish celebrations and practices

Midsummer celebrations, **2**:182, 221

Midwives, **1**:5, 131; Aboriginal, **1**:355; Bulgarian, **1**:17–19, 63–64; celebration of, **1**:17–19; Guatemalan, **1**:334; kidnapped by fairies, **1**:77; in Kyrgyzstan, **1**:194; Mayan, **1**:112; Mexican, **1**:112; Southeast Asian, **1**:229; treatment of umbilical cord by, **1**:112, 114; Zulu, **1**:112

Mieszko I (Poland), **2**:80

Milk names (*ru ming*), **1**:91

Minghun (ghost marriages), **3**:221–222

Ministry for the Promotion of Women and Family (Cameroon), **2**:31

Minute's silence, **3**:173–175, 224

Mirila, **3**:175–177

Miscarriage, **3**:180, 216

Missing man formation, **3**:177–180; in motorsports, **3**:179–180

Missouri, shivaree/chivaree, **2**:257

Mistletoe, **1**:218–220

Mithras cult, **1**:42

Mizuko kuyo, **3**:180–183

Moccasin ceremony, **1**:8

MoD Lyneham, **3**:239

Mogi, **2**:61–62

Mohel, **1**:60

Moldova, **1**:16, 266, **3**:231. *See also* Eastern European celebrations and practices

Moment of silence. *See* Minute's silence

"Monday's Child," **1**:220–221

Money dance, **2**:233–235

Mongolia, **1**:266, **3**:24. *See also* Central Asian practices

Monstrous punishments for naughty children, **1**:221–226

Montenegro, **2**:15. *See also* Eastern European celebrations and practices; Yugoslav countries

Montjoie, **3**:73

Moon burial, **3**:267–268

Moonie weddings, **2**:235–237

Moon-Yuet (Full Moon), **1**:226–228

Moravian Church, **1**:95

Mormons (Church of Jesus Christ of Latter-day Saints), **1**:303, **2**:161–162

Morning sickness remedy, **1**:71

Moro reflex, **1**:321

Moroccan celebrations and practices, **2**:237–240; eating human placenta, **1**:123; government-approved baby names, **1**:153, 155; wedding dresses, **2**:373. *See also* North African celebrations and practices

Mortuary totem poles, **3**:183–185

Moses (biblical), **1**:62

Mosquito netting, **1**:74

Mosuo people, **2**:391–393

Mother Goose songs and rhymes, **1**:250

Mother Nature, **1**:13

Mother roasting, **1**:228–230

Mother's Day, **1**:138

Mothering Sunday, **1**:230–232

Mothers. *See* Women

Mounukyia, **1**:37

Mourning jewelry, **3**:286–288

Mourning rituals, Māori, **3**:281–283

Mozambique, *Pika* and *Nora*, **2**:253

Mrtva pocivala, **3**:177

Mummification, **3**:185–188; of heads, **3**:256

Mummy brown, **3**:188

Mundan ceremony, **1**:232–234

Mundana, **1**:232

Mursi tribe, **2**:193–194

Music: Alphorn, **3**:238; Dawn Songs, **2**:154; doom metal and funeral doom, **3**:62–63; for funerals, **3**:1–3, 97; in the *Isanaklesh Gotal* ritual, **2**:156–158; Punk Rock, **3**:99; for weddings, **2**:379–381

Muslim celebrations and practices. *See* Islamic celebrations and practices.

Mutterpass, **1**:237–238

My Home Library scheme, **1**:88

Myanmar (Burma): Buddhist death practices, **3**:20; ear-piercing ceremonies, **2**:83; Hmong names, **2**:136; mother roasting, **1**:228; neck elongation, **2**:243–244; ritual tattooing, **2**:275. *See also* Southeast Asian celebrations and practices

Naam karan naming ceremony 1:311–313
Nachisungu, 2:52–53
Naga sadhus, 2:174
Nagashi-bina, 1:185
Nahtwin, 2:83
Nakisumo (Sumo of Tears), 1:111
Namahage, 1:223
Namahage Sedo Festival, 1:224
Name days, 1:241
Naming rituals: adult names, 2:106; "ox names," 2:100. *See also* Baby naming practices
Nana Kloweki (earth goddess), 2:71
Naozot ceremony, 1:246
Napoleon dance, 2:234
National Matchmaking Association (Japan), 2:251
National Mills Day (Netherlands), 3:324
National mourning, 3:191–183, 324
National Organization for Marriage (NOM), 2:287
National Senior Olympics Games, 3:254
National Service of Remembrance, 3:223–224
National Tooth Fairy Day, 1:325
National War Memorial (Canada), 3:296
National War Memorial (New Zealand), 3:296
Native American celebrations and practices: cradleboard, 1:109–111; Death Dance, 3:51; Dream catchers, 1:119–122; eating human placenta, 1:123; hair removal by, 2:112; herbal remedies, 1:30; Hopi naming rites, 1:177–180; menstrual customs, 2:225; mourning color, 3:305; preserving the umbilical cord, 1:174; same-sex marriage, 2:285–286; scalping, 3:256; vision quest, 2:358–361. *See also* Apache ceremonies; Hopi traditions; Navajo traditions
Native American Grave Protection and Repatriation Act, 3:142–152
Native Americans: Cheppewa tribe, 1:119; Delaware Indians, 3:53–56, 305; Ojibwa people, 1:119–120
Native Hawaiian Religion, 1:68
Nativity play, 1:244–246

Navajo traditions: Blessingway, 1:48–51; *kinaalda*, 2:330
Navjote ceremony, 1:246–249
Nazar boncugu, 1:344
Nazca people, 3:186
Nazism, 2:380, 3:171
Ndau people, 2:253–254
Ndebele tribe, 2:244–245
Ndwandewe clan, 2:269
Neck elongation, 2:243–245
Neo-pagan practices, 3:111; croning ceremonies, 3:44–46; handfasting, 2:117–119; jumping over the broom, 2:163–165. *See also* Pagan celebrations and practices; Wiccan funerals
Nepal: cremation, 3:41; Father's Day, 1:139; *halva*, 3:114; killing of royal family, 1:191; *Kumari* and *Deuki*, 1:189–193; menstrual customs and taboos, 2:225, 229–230; Pasni weaning ceremony, 1:275–277; treatment of the placenta in 1:67; vision quest, 2:360. *See also* South Asian celebrations and practices
Netherlands celebrations and practices: anti-Santa Claus movement, 1:297–298; assisted suicide, 3:12; Assyrian populations in, 2:10; *beschuit met muisjes*, 1:31–32; cremation, 3:42; Gap year, 2:103; lovespoons, 2:202; *Martinstag*, 3:111; mourning color, 3:304; National Mills Day, 3:324; national mourning, 3:324; parental leave, 1:266; Passion plays, 3:208; pensions, 3:231; Remembrance of the Dead Day, 3:225; Saint Nicholas, 1:295–296; same-sex marriage, 2:285; silver spoon, 1:313; space burial, 3:267; spontaneous shrines, 3:269; *suikerboon*, 1:32; University of the Third Age, 3:307; windmills, 3:323–325
Netsilingmiut people, 1:79
Network of Aunties Association, 2:31
New Brunswick, 1:41
New Ireland, 3:162–163
New Order Amish, 2:25
New Year cards, 1:39

New Year traditions, **2**:44–45
New Zealand celebrations and practices: "Abide With Me," **3**:1–3; Anzac Day, **3**:152, 236–237, 317; birth trees, **1**:33, 35; Gap year, **2**:103; Girl Guides, **1**:152; government-approved baby names, **1**:153, 155; jury duty, **2**:168; menstrual taboos, **2**:230; National War Memorial, **3**:296; parental leave, **1**:266, 267; pensions, **3**:228, 231–234; Remembrance Day, **3**:223; riderless horse, **3**:236–237; ritual tattooing, **2**:272, 273–274; same-sex marriage, **2**:285; Steiner schools, **1**:318, 320; *Tangihanga*, **3**:281–283; treatment of the placenta, **1**:69–70; twenty-first birthday, **2**:344–345; University of the Third Age, **3**:307; wake, **3**:313; wedding dresses, **2**:374. *See also* Māori people
Newbery Medal, **1**:88
Newfoundland, **1**:41
Ngaben, **3**:193–196
Ngilai, **1**:79
Niagara Falls, **3**:279
Nicholas (saint). *See* Saint Nicholas
Niger: arranged marriage, **2**:7; Wodaabe courtship dance and festival, **2**:383–386. *See also* African celebrations and practices; West African celebrations and practices
Nigerian celebrations and practices: breast ironing, **2**:30; burial customs, **3**:128; cutting the umbilical cord, **1**:113; eating calabash chalk, **1**:71; fattening room seclusion, **2**:86–89; female genital cutting, **2**:93; migration to Nigeria, **1**:1; money dance, **2**:234; *Sallah*, **2**:30; scarification, **2**:294–295; *Sharo*, **2**:307–309; treatment of the placenta in, **1**:68–69; *Yankan gishiri*, **1**:362; *Zur-zur*, **1**:362. *See also* African celebrations and practices; West African celebrations and practices
Nikolaustag, **1**:222
Nine-Nights, **3**:196–198

Nirwaan (*nirvana*) ceremony, **2**:132
Nkumbi, **2**:245–247
Nomkhubulwane fertility festival, **2**:356
Nora, **2**:253
Nordic napping, **1**:249–250
Norse myths, **1**:135
North African celebrations and practices: Mehndi, **2**:222, 223; *shabka*, **2**:302. *See also* Algerian celebrations and practices; Egyptian celebrations and practices; Moroccan celebrations and practices; Sudan
North America, First Nation groups in, **3**:117
North American celebrations and practices: "Abide With Me," **3**:1–3; Groaning Cheese and Groaning Cake, **1**:166–169; hair removal, **2**:112; *halva*, **3**:113; horseshoes, **2**:142; lotus birthing, **1**:210; mourning color, **3**:302; nursery rhymes, **1**:250; Santa Claus, **1**:296; teething remedies, **1**:328–329; Tomb of the Unknown Soldier, **3**:295. *See also* Canadian celebrations and practices; United States celebrations and practices
Northern Ireland: choosing Options, **2**:56–58; political assassinations, **3**:269; Remembrance Day, **3**:223; wedding traditions, **2**:32
Norwegian celebrations and practices: Girl Guides, **1**:152; jury duty, **2**:165; parental leave, **1**:265; retirement and pensions, **3**:229; *Russefeiring*, **2**:281–283; same-sex marriage, **2**:285; secular confirmation, **2**:300; wedding customs, **2**:370, **2**:373; wedding spoons, **2**:202. *See also* Saami people; Scandinavian celebrations and practices
Nose buttering, **1**:41
Nova Scotia, **1**:41
Nuba tribe, **2**:295
Nuer tribe, **2**:98
Nuliayuq (Inuit spirit of the sea), **1**:11
Nursery rhymes, **1**:250–253
Nurses, pinning ceremony, **2**:382–383
Nwaotam (placenta-related festival), **1**:69

Nyabutan ceremony, **1**:253–254
Nyakyusa tribe, **3**:51
Nyumba Ntobhu, **2**:247–249
Nzu, **1**:71

Oak trees, **3**:328
Obama, Barack, **2**:76–77
Obando fertility dance, **1**:255–256
Oberammergau Passion Play, **3**:207–208
Oberon's Palace (Herrick), **1**:325
Obituaries, **3**:199–200
Oblievačka (Oblévačka), **2**:79
Obon (Bon), **3**:126–127
Oceania, Tomb of the Unknown Soldier, **3**:295
Odd Fellows (Oddfellows) society, **3**:96, 128
Oie Houney, **3**:112
Ojibwa people, **1**:119–120
Okuizome, **1**:259–260
Old Order Amish, **2**:25
Ombliguera, **1**:108
Omiai, **2**:251–252
Omiya-mairi, **1**:174
Onabasulu tribe, **2**:149
Onbashira festival, **2**:197–199
One-child policy, **1**:256–258
Onge people, **1**:57–58
Operation Mercy India (OM), **1**:118
Origami cranes, **1**:185
Orkney Islands, **1**:293, **2**:28, **3**:261
Orthodox Catholic Church, **3**:66
Orthodox Church celebrations and practices: funeral practices, **3**:107; Name days, **1**:241; Saturday of Souls, **3**:251–253. *See also* Eastern Orthodox Church celebrations and practices; Greek Orthodox Church celebrations and practices; Russian Orthodox Church celebrations and practices
Oshichiya Meimeishiki, **1**:259
Ososo Matsuri (Vagina Festival), **1**:279
Ossuaries, **3**:103, 200–203
Oto, **1**:149
Our Lady of Salambao, **1**:256–257
Overtoun Bridge (Scotland), **3**:279–280
Ovoo (cairn), **3**:24

Pachamama (earth goddess), **1**:69
Pacific Northwest, lip plugs, **2**:191
Padaung people, **2**:243
Padmasambhava, **1**:210
Padrinos, **1**:125, **2**:178. *See also* Godparents
Pagan celebrations and practices: baby welcoming, **1**:24–25; croning ceremonies, **3**:44–46; elderling ceremonies, **3**:44–46; jumping over the broom, **2**:163–165; Saging ceremonies, **3**:46; saining, **1**:293–294. *See also* Neo-pagan practices; Wiccan funerals
Pakistan: burqa wearing, **2**:130; entering the *Bashali*, **1**:128–132; forced marriage, **2**:8; *halva*, **3**:115; *Mehndi*, **2**:222, 223; menstrual customs, **2**:225; Zoroastrianism, **3**:338. *See also* South Asian celebrations and practices
Palaa ritual, **2**:314
Palestine, **1**:235, **2**:302. *See also* Middle Eastern celebrations and practices
Palm Sunday, **2**:188
Pan American Health Organization (PAHO), **1**:86
Pan dei Morti, **3**:265
Pancake Day, **3**:66
Pang-sai, **1**:323–324
Panikhida, **3**:252
Pan-Indian Movement **1**:120
Pantomime, **1**:261–265
Panuda, **1**:65
Pão de Deus, **3**:264–365
Paoli Amish, **2**:25
Papua New Guinea: couvade, **1**:104, 106; cutting the umbilical cord, **1**:113; endocannibalism, **3**:76–77; finger amputation, **3**:90–91; initiation by semen transferal, **2**:148–152; *Malagan* ceremonies, **3**:162–164; mummification, **3**:185, 187; ritual tattooing, **2**:275; ritualized sex, **2**:341–344; scarification, **2**:293–296; urethral subincision, **2**:349–350
Paraguay, **3**:247
Parental leave, **1**:265–267
Paris, *Le Bal des Débutantes*, **2**:97

Parsley, **3**:96
Party games, **1**:273–275
Paschal (saint), **1**:256
Paschal eggs. *See* Easter eggs
Pasni weaning ceremony, **1**:275–277
Passing bells, **3**:205–206
Passion plays, **3**:206–209
Paternal/Paternity leave, **1**:267, 270–272. *See also* Parental leave
Pauper's funeral, **3**:209–211
Peace Memorial Park, **1**:185
Peace Pledge Union, **3**:316
Pebermø (pepper maid), **2**:26
Pebersvend (pepper man), **2**:26
Pelebon, **3**:193–196
Penda idols, **1**:13–14
Penile subincision, **2**:347–351
Penis. *See* Phallus
The Penis Festival, **1**:277–278
Pennsylvania Dutch practices, **3**:93; bed-courtship, **2**:24–25
Pensions and Retirement, **3**:228–236
Pentecostal church, **1**:26, 27
Persia, **1**:42. *See also* Iran
Personalized hearses, **3**:211–213
Peruvian practices: menstrual taboos, **2**:230; mummification, **3**:185; shrunken heads, **3**:255–257. *See also* South American celebrations and practices
Peterson, Frederick, **2**:64
Phallus: broomstick as, **2**:163–164; Cerne Abbas Giant, **1**:75–76; used in chisungu ceremony, **2**:53; Maypole as, **2**:221
Phallus festivals, **1**:277–280; Clean (or Dirty) Monday (Tyrnavos, Greece), **1**:279–280; *Kanamara Matsuri* (Festival of the Steel Phallus), **1**:278–279; The Penis Festival (Tagata Jinja), **1**:277–278
Philippine celebrations and practices: Aguman Sanduk Festival, **1**:105; breastfeeding, **1**:56; crucifixion rituals, **3**:47–50; Filipino debut/Cotillion, **2**:95–97; *hampas-palayak* or *pukpok palayok*, **1**:285; money dance, **2**:234; mother roasting, **1**:228; Obando fertility dance, **1**:256–257; Passion plays, **3**:208; piñatas, **1**:285; tooth-filing, **2**:338; twenty-first birthday, **2**:345. *See also* Southeast Asian celebrations and practices
Physician Assisted Suicide (PAS), **3**:11
Pidyon haben (Redemption of the firstborn), **1**:280–283
Pidyon habit ceremony (Redemption of the firstborn daughter), **1**:282
Pika, **2**:253
Pilgrimage, **2**:173–175
Piñata, **1**:274, 283–286
Pinning ceremony, **2**:382–383
Pin-the-tail-on-the-donkey, **1**:274
Pirts (*Pirtiņa*), **1**:204
Pisanki, **3**:66–67, 334
Pius X (pope), **1**:143
Pius XII (pope), **1**:201
Pizho idols, **1**:13–14
Placenta: burying of, **1**:25, 67–70, 235; eating, **1**:123–125; in folk medicine, **1**:124
Placentophagy, **1**:123–125
Plastination, **3**:213–216
Pogacha, **1**:65
Poison garden, **3**:96
Polish celebrations and practices: All Souls' Day, **3**:8, 265; *Andrzejki* (St. Andrew's Eve), **2**:3–5; birthstones, **1**:44; Easter eggs (*pysanka*), **3**:66; first communion, **1**:144; government-approved baby names, **1**:153, 155; Hallowe'en, **3**:334; *Katarzynki* gingerbread, **2**:4; *Lanie wosku* (pouring wax), **2**:4; *Matura*, **2**:15–16; Nordic napping, **1**:250; *Pani Mloda* (money dance), **2**:233; pensions, **3**:230; *Polterabend*, **2**:254; *Śmigus-Dyngus* (Dyngus Day), **2**:79–81; spring celebration in, **1**:16; *Talerzyki*, **2**:4; *Zaduszki* (*dzień zaduszny*), **3**:333–335. *See also* Eastern European celebrations and practices
Polterabend, **2**:254–258
Polter-Lucia celebration, **2**:257

Polyandry, **2**:258–261
Polygyny, **2**:259, 261–263
Polygyny-fertility hypothesis, **2**:262
Polynesia: menstrual customs, **2**:224–225; ritual tattooing, **2**:272–273; urethral subincision, **2**:347, 349
Poppies: black, against imperialism of warfare, **3**:317; purple, for animals killed in warfare, **3**:317; red, as symbol of remembrance, **3**:314–318; white, as symbol of peace, **3**:316
Poppy Appeal, **3**:314–316
Poppy Day, **3**:223
Poppy etiquette, **3**:315–316
Portugal: Father's Day, **1**:139; Girl Guides, **1**:152; government-approved baby names, **1**:153; money dance, **2**:234; mourning color, **3**:302; ossuaries, **3**:201–202; *Pão de Deus*, **3**:264–365; pensions, **3**:230; same-sex marriage, **2**:285; *Santora* cake, **3**:264; soul cakes, **3**:263
Post-traumatic stress disorder, **2**:31
Poto, **1**:71
Potty training, **1**:286–288
Povitica, **2**:263–264
Prayers: for baby's gender, **1**:187; at baptisms, **1**:29; in *bismallah* ceremony, **1**:47; in Blessingway ceremony, **1**:49; for the dead, **3**:7; in *Dia de los Muertos* celebrations, **3**:59; for the dying, **3**:105; at Filipino debut, **2**:96; at funeral services, **3**:273; Hindu, **1**:175–177, 275–276; Hindu death rituals, **3**:118; Islamic, **1**:194, **3**:189; Jewish, **3**:130, 132; at a Jewish wedding, **2**:161; during labor and childbirth, **1**:211; for a new baby, **1**:234, 312; for the new mother and baby, **1**:209; at *pidyon haben* ceremony, **1**:282; by pregnant women, **1**:312; in *Quinceañera* mass, **2**:186; to San La Muerte, **3**:247; at Setsubun, **1**:308; Sikh, **2**:70; at Sikh wedding, **2**:313–314; on the Stations of the Cross, **3**:275–277; to the sun, **1**:179; in *upanayana* ritual, **1**:338; at weddings, **2**:13, 59–60; in Zoroastrianism, **1**:246–248
Pre's Rock, **3**:270
Pregnancy and Infant Loss Remembrance Day, **3**:216–218
Pregnancy yoga, **1**:289–290
Pregnant women: Blessingway ceremony for, **1**:50–51; classes for, **1**:74; eating calabash chalk, **1**:71; food for, **1**:166–169; food taboos, **1**:71, 89–90; 144–147; in Malaysia, **1**:79; targeted by trows, **1**:78. *See also* Women
Prehistoric Burial Cairns of Balnuaran of Clava, **3**:23
Prenatal care, **1**:72, 73, 237–238
Pre-Raphaelite Brotherhood (PRB), **1**:136, 137
Presbyterian church, **1**:27, **2**:60
Prince Edward Island, **1**:41
Prinsessornas Kokbok, **1**:35
Prinsesstårta, **1**:35
Prophet's Mosque (Medina), **2**:116
Prostitution, **1**:116–118, 193, 278, **2**:392–393, **3**:249, 310
Protestant Church celebrations and practices, **3**:35–36; funeral cakes, **3**:92; objection to plastination, **3**:214; wedding ceremonies, **2**:60–61. *See also* Christian celebrations and practices; Christian churches
Psychoprophylaxis, **1**:201
Public flogging, **2**:307–309
Puerto Rico, **1**:40–1
pukpok palayok, **1**:285
Pumi (Primi) people, **2**:50–51
Punk rock, **3**:99
Punkie Night, **3**:112
Pure Brightness Festival, **3**:219
Puritans, **2**:25
Purity ball, **2**:264–266
Pussy willows, **3**:253; spanking with, **2**:80, 81
Putting on Moccasins, **1**:8
Pygmy people, **2**:245
Pysanka, **3**:66–67, 334

Qatar, **2**:304. *See also* Middle Eastern celebrations and practices
Qinghai-Tibetan Plateau, **3**:259–260
Qingming Festival, **3**:219–222, 329
Qiqiqtamiut Inuit, **1**:10
Quarter Days, **1**:293
Quccija (il-Quccija), **1**:291–292
Quebec, **1**:40. *See also* Canada
Queen Charlotte Islands, **3**:184
Quinceañera, **2**:96, 185–188
Qur'an, **2**:128–129, 242, 261

Radonitsa, **3**:253
RAF Lyneham, **3**:239
RAG Week (Raising and Giving Week), **2**:267–268
Reagan, Ronald, eulogy on the *Challenger*, **3**:81–83
Reed Dancing Chastity Ceremony, **2**:269–272
Reifeprüfung, **2**:15
Religious holidays, birthdays of religious figures, **1**:43
Religious milestones, **1**:42. *See also* Baptism and Christening; Confirmation; First Communion; Holy Communion
Remembrance Day, **3**:152, 174, 223–226, 296, 314–315
Remembrance Sunday, **3**:2, 152, 174, 223–227, 314, 316; Early Day Motion, **3**:226–227
Renaming procedures, **1**:11
Reproduction, government control over, **1**:256–258
Requiem mass, **3**:8
Reschtach, **2**:28–30
Reseau National des Associations de Tantines (RENATA), **2**:31
Resomation, **3**:5–6
Retirement and Pensions, **3**:228–236, 308
Retirement homes: Denville Hall and Brinsworth House, **3**:56–57; Royal Hospital Chelsea, **3**:26–29
Riderless horse, **3**:236–237
Rite for the Blessing of a Child in the Womb, **1**:99
Rites of passage. *See* Boys' coming-of-age ceremonies; Chinese coming-of-age ceremonies; Coming-of-age ceremonies; Girls' coming-of-age ceremonies
Ritual body mutilation, finger amputation, **3**:90–91
Ritual sacrifice, **1**:235, **2**:72, 99, 115
Ritual servitude, female, **1**:116–118, 331. *See also Devadasi* system; *Kumari* and *Deuki*
Ritual tattooing, **2**:272–277
Ritualized homosexuality (RHS), **2**:148
Ritzenthaler, Robert, **2**:64
River Ganges, **1**:233
Roma celebrations and practices: arranged marriages, **2**:37–38; forced marriage, **2**:8; jumping over the broom, **2**:163–165; virginity testing, **2**:357
Roma folklore, **2**:44
Roman Catholic Church. *See* Catholic Church; Catholic Church celebrations and practices
Romanian celebrations and practices: eating the ashes of the dead, **3**:69; funeral traditions, **3**:237–239; The Great Passing, **3**:105–107; *koliva*, **3**:135; love divination, **2**:3; *martisor* (March celebration), **1**:16; Merry Cemetery, **3**:299; parental leave, **1**:266; *Pysanka*, **3**:66; spitting on babies, **1**:316. *See also* Eastern European celebrations and practices
Rosemary, **3**:96, 317
Round Birthdays, **1**:43
Roy, Sandip, **2**:76–77
Royal Air Force (RAF), **3**:178
Royal British Legion, **3**:314–316
Royal Hospital Chelsea, **3**:26–29
Royal Maundy Service, **3**:164–167
Royal Wootton Bassett, England, **3**:239–241
Rumspringa, **2**:24, 277–280
Running Round (*Amphidromia*) ritual, **1**:23
Rushbearing ceremonies, **1**:164–166
Russefeiring, **2**:281–283
Russia, Assyrian populations in, **2**:10
Russian celebrations and practices: Baba Yaga, **1**:223; birthstones, **1**:44, 46; love divination, **2**:3; mourning color, **3**:302; national mourning, **3**:192; *Polterabend*, **2**:254; *Pysanka*, **3**:66; Saint Nicholas, **1**:294; space burial,

3:267; water births, 1:347. *See also* Eastern European celebrations and practices; Eastern Orthodox Church celebrations and practices; Russian Orthodox Church celebrations and practices; Soviet Union

Russian Orthodox Church: name days, 1:241; opposition to cremation, 3:44; *Radonitsa*, 3:253; wedding dresses, 2:374

Saami people (Sami, Samer, or Lapps), 1:4–7
Sacred ceremonies, 1:37
Sacred severance, 1:113
Sadhus, 2:174
Saging ceremonies, 3:46
Saining, 1:293–294
Saint Aidan, 1:165
Saint Apollonia, 1:326
Saint Brigid, 2:189
Saint Catherine of Alexandria, 2:320–321
Saint Claire, 1:256
Saint Francis of Assisi, 1:245
Saint Jerome, 1:45
Saint John the Baptist, 1:26, 2:200
Saint Martin of Tours, 3:111
Saint Nicholas, 1:294–298. *See also* Father Christmas; Santa Claus
Saint Odilo of Cluny, 3:7
Saint Oswald, 1:165
Saint Oswald's Day, 1:165
Saint Oswald's Hand, 1:165
Saint Patrick, 2:189
Saint Walpurga's feast day, 1:217
Saint Wilfrid, 3:278
Saints: feast days of, 1:241; folk, 3:246–250
Sakalava royal death traditions, 3:243–245
Sake, 1:224, 2:63, 291–292
Sallekhanā, 3:245–246
Salting the baby, 1:64–65
Sambatra mass circumcision festival, 1:298–300
Sambia tribe, 2:148, 149–152
Samburu tribe, 2:350
Same-sex marriage, 2:285–291
Samhain, 2:219, 3:109–111
Samoan practices: hair removal, 2:112; ritual tattooing, 2:272–273
San La Muerte (Saint Death), 3:246–249
San Pascualito, 3:248
San Pedro Cutud Lenten Rites, 3:48–49
San-san-kudo (*san san kudo*; *sansan-kudo*), 2:291–293
Santa Claus, 1:296. *See also* Father Christmas; Saint Nicholas
Santa Muerte, 3:246, 249–250
Sar-akka (childbirth goddess), 1:5–6
Sarung buaian, 1:300–301
Sateré-Mawé tribe, 2:41–43
Sati (*suttee*), 3:43
Saturday of Souls, 3:135, 251–253
Saudi Arabia,1:56. *See also* Middle Eastern celebrations and practices
Scalping, 3:256
Scandinavian celebrations and practices: cairns, 3:24; changeling beliefs, 1:77; kangaroo care, 1:183; nursery rhymes, 1:250, 251; parental leave, 1:265; protection from fairies, 1:78; secular confirmation, 2:300; trolls, 1:78; University of the Third Age, 3:307; wedding cakes, 2:370. *See also* Danish celebrations and practices; Finnish celebrations and practices; Norwegian celebrations and practices; Saami people; Swedish celebrations and practices
Scarification, 2:98–101, 253, 293–296
Schmidt Sting Pain Index, 2:41–42
Schoolies Week, 2:283–284
Schuhplattler, 2:297–299
Schwuhplattler Group, 2:299
Scottish celebrations and practices: belief in the evil eye, 1:343; Beltane, 2:219; blackening the bride, 2:28–30; Burning the Clavie, 2:44–45; cairns, 3:23; changeling beliefs, 1:78; christening gown, 1:95; Gretna Green, 2:104–105, 210; handfasting, 2:117–118; hanselling, 1:351; Lady Haig Poppy Factory, 3:315; Lanimer Day, 1:353; Nordic napping, 1:250; passing bells, 3:205–206; saining, 1:293–294; same-sex marriage, 2:285; silver spoon, 1:351; wedding traditions, 2:32; wetting the baby's head, 1:351; Whuppity Scoorie, 1:351–353; yew trees, 3:328

Scouts and Scouting, **1**:152–153, 302–304
Scriptural Way of the Cross, **3**:276
Scroggleve, **1**:304
Scroggling the Holly, **1**:304–305
Sebou, **1**:305–307
Secular coming of age, **2**:300–302
Secular confirmation, **2**:300–302
Sedreh-pushi (*Sedreh-pooshi*), **1**:246
Seelënnacht, **3**:9
Seijin no Hi (Coming of Age Day), **2**:61–64
Seijin-shiki, **2**:61
Semen practices, **2**:148
Senegal, **2**:93. *See also* West Africa
Senior Sporting Events, **3**:254–255
Senofo tribe, **2**:294
Sentimental jewelry, **3**:288
September 11 attacks, **3**:2, 174, 270
September Romance, **2**:239
Serbian celebrations and practices: *koliva*, **3**:135; Saturday of Souls, **3**:251–253. *See also* Eastern European celebrations and practices; Yugoslav countries
Serbian Orthodox traditions, Slava, **1**:242
Servia, *Matura*, **2**:15
Setsubun (Children's bean-throwing festival), **1**:307–309
Sex taboos, **2**:53
Sexual intercourse: after childbirth, **1**: 104–106, 197, 361; on the Cerne Abbas Giant, **1**:76; with a *deuki*, **1**:192; with a *devadasi*, **1**:117–18; with an incubus, **1**:79, 222; in marriage, **1**:175; while menstruating, **2**:228; in Moonie weddings, **2**:236; during pregnancy, **1**:90; ritualized, **2**:341–344; with a succubus, **1**:79; with a *trokosi*, **1**:331–332
Sexually transmitted disease (STD), **1**:118, 278, 363, **2**:248, 349. *See also* HIV/AIDS
Shabka, **2**:302–305
Shalaluo (skirt-changing ceremony), **2**:51
Shanghai Marriage Market, **2**:305–307
Shared nursing, **1**:57. *See also* Breastfeeding
Sharo, **2**:307–309
Shashu, **1**:69

Shengxiao (Chinese Zodiac), **1**:310–311
Shinbyu (*shin-byu; shinpyu*), **2**:83, 310–311
Shinerama, **2**:268
Shinto traditions: deities, **1**:214; funeral rites, **3**:123; *Kanchu Misogi*, **2**:110–111; *Onbashira* festival, **2**:197–199; *Ososo Matsuri*, **1**:279; thanksgiving ritual, **1**:174
Shipibo tribe, **2**:261
Shirin-i-grifgan, **2**:1–2
Shiva, **3**:132
Shivaree/chivaree, **2**:257
Shona people, **2**:195
Shortbread, pinned to christening gowns, **1**:94
Shoutao, **1**:36
Shrines, spontaneous, **3**:269–271
Shrove Tuesday, **3**:66
Shrovetide, **1**:293
Shrunken heads, **3**:255–257
Siad, Fatima, **2**:93
Siberia, **1**:310. *See also* Russian celebrations and practices
Sicily, *Fidanzamenti* and *Fidanzati in casa*, **2**:94–95
Sierra Leone, **1**:113, 145. *See also* West African celebrations and practices
Sikh celebrations and practices: *Amrit shanchar*, **2**:70; baby rites and *naam karan* naming ceremony, **1**:311–313; beards, **2**:22; British weddings, **2**:32; cremation, **3**:42; *Dastaar Bandi* (*Dastar Bandi*), **2**:69; death customs, **3**:257–259; Diwali, **2**:73–74, 77; Five Ks, **2**:69–70, **3**:258; forced marriage, **2**:8; wedding ceremonies, **2**:312–315; women wearing turbans, **2**:69
Silver Spoon, **1**:313–314, 351
Simnel cake, **1**:231
Simplicity parenting, **1**:314–315
Sin eating, **3**:92
Singapore; indigenous medicine, **1**:181; jury duty, **2**:167; missing man formation, **3**:179; Remembrance Day, **3**:223. *See also* Southeast Asian celebrations and practices
Singings, **2**:278

Singles' Day, **2**:315–316
Sinterklaas, **1**:296
Sisters' Meal Festival, **2**:317–318
Skirt-changing ceremony (*shalaluo*), **2**:51
Sky burials, **3**:259–263
Slå kitten af tønden, **1**:285
Slava, **1**:242
Slava cake, **1**:242
Slovakian calendar, **1**:241
Slovakian celebrations and practices: love divination, **2**:3; *Matura*, **2**:15; mourning color, **3**:302; *Oblievačka*, **2**:79; spontaneous shrines, **3**:269. *See also* Eastern European celebrations and practices
Slovenian celebrations and practices: childhood vaccinations, **1**:85–86; danse macabre, **3**:52; *Matura*, **2**:15; *mrtva pocivala*, **3**:177; parental leave, **1**:266; Parkelj, **1**:222–223; same-sex marriage, **2**:285; University of the Third Age, **3**:307. *See also* Eastern European celebrations and practices; Yugoslav countries
Slow parenting movement, **1**:314–315
Śmigus-Dyngus (Dyngus Day), **2**:79–81
Soccer games, **3**:2
Social Cash Transfer Programme, **3**:231
Sock dances, **2**:319–320
Sock garlands, **2**:318–319
Sockenkrantz, **2**:318–319
Sokacs, **2**:191
Solomon Islands, **1**:33, **2**:296
Somalia, **2**:89, 91. *See also* Sub-Saharan African celebrations and practices
Song, in the *Isanaklesh Gotal* ritual, **2**:156–158
Sor Sai Karchey, **1**:229
Soul bells, **3**:205
Soul cakes and soul breads, **3**:263–266
Souling, **3**:263–264
Soulmas Day, **3**:6
South African celebrations and practices: boxes for babies, **1**:74; breast ironing, **2**:30; breastfeeding, **1**:56; cutting the umbilical cord, **1**:112; Girl Guides, **1**:152; jury duty, **2**:167; neck elongation, **2**:244–245; same-sex marriage, **2**:285; space burial, **3**:267; virginity testing, **2**:356; Xhosa circumcision, **2**:387–389
South American celebrations and practices: All Souls' Day, **3**:9; belief in the evil eye, **1**:343; eating human placenta, **1**:123; hair removal, **2**:112; kangaroo care, **1**:183; lip plugs, **2**:191–195; polygyny, **2**:261; potty training, **1**:286; *San La Muerte*, **3**:246–249; Tomb of the Unknown Soldier, **3**:295; University of the Third Age, **3**:307; urethral subincision, **2**:350. *See also* Argentinian celebrations and practices; Bolivian practices; Brazilian practices; Ecuadorean practices; French Guiana; Peruvian practices; Uruguay; Venezuela
South Asian celebrations and practices: belief in the evil eye, **1**:343–344; forced marriage, **2**:8. *See also* Afghani celebrations and practices; Asian celebrations and practices; Bangladesh; Indian celebrations and practices; Nepal; Pakistan; Sri Lanka
South Korean celebrations and practices: Black Day, **2**:315–316; *Gwallye*, **2**:105–106; Moonie weddings, **2**:235; *Waldkindergärten*, **1**:341; wedding cakes, **2**:372. *See also* Asian celebrations and practices; Korean celebrations and practices
South Pacific, **1**:46
Southeast Asian celebrations and practices, **3**:85; *Mehndi*, **2**:224; mother roasting, **1**:228–230; potty training, **1**:286. *See also* Asian celebrations and practices; Cambodian practices; Indonesian celebrations and practices; Laos; Malaysian celebrations and practices; Myanmar; Philippine celebrations and practices; Singapore; Thailand; Vietnam
Southern Africa, *Lobola*, **2**:195–197
Soviet Union, **1**:201. *See also* Russian celebrations and practices

Space burial, **3**:267–268
Spanish celebrations and practices: *Dia de los Muertos*, **3**:52; *El Salto del Colacho*, **1**:126–128; Father's Day, **1**:139; government-approved baby names, **1**:153; grave rental, **3**:102; mourning color, **3**:302, 304; ossuaries, **3**:201; Passion plays, **3**:206, 208; parental leave, **1**:66; pensions, **3**:230; Perez Mouse (Ratón Perez), **1**:326; same-sex marriage, **2**:285
Spitting on babies, **1**:316–317
Spontaneous shrines, **3**:269–271
Spring celebrations, **1**:16, 307–309; *Tết Nguyên đan*, **3**:288–292
Spring cleaning rituals, **1**:13
Sprinkling cake, **1**:317–318
Sprinklings (second baby showers), **1**:23
Sri Guru Granth Sahib, **1**:311–312, **2**:313–314, **3**:258–259
Sri Lanka: Buddhist practices, **3**:18, 20; Passion plays, **3**:208; polyandry, **2**:258, 259; virginity testing, **2**:357. *See also* South Asian celebrations and practices
Sri Santeswar temple, **1**:127
St. Andrew's Eve (*Andrzejki*), **2**:3–5
St. Basil's Day, **3**:136
St. Brigid's Day, **1**:16
St. Catherine's Day (*Katarzynki*), **2**:3–4, 320–322
St. Dwynwen's Day, **2**:322–323
St. John's Day, **2**:200
St. Lazarus's Day, **2**:186
St. Martin's Day, **3**:111
St. Mary of the Purification church, **1**:51–52
St. Mary's church in Hanwell, **1**:96
St. Nicholas Day, **1**:222
St. Sylvester's Day, **2**:183
St. Theodore Saturday **3**:136
St. Theodore's Day (*Todorovden*), **2**:40
State funerals, **3**:271–275
Stations of the Cross, **3**:275–277
Statutory Maternity Pay (SMP), **1**:267
Steam baths, **1**:228–229, **1**:333
Steampunk, **3**:100
Steiner schools, **1**:318–320
Steiner Waldorf Schools Fellowship (SWSF), **1**:318
Sterilization, forced, **1**:256, 257
Stillbirth, **3**:180, 216, 313
Stiller Tag (Silent Day), **3**:225
Student Zone, **2**:209
Sub-Saharan African celebrations and practices: fattening room seclusion, **2**:89; *Yankan Gishiri*, **1**:362–363; *Zurzur* (*zur zur*; *zurzur*), **1**:362–363. *See also* Central African Republic; Chad; Djibouti; Eritrea; Gambia; Guinea-Bissau; Somalia; Sudan; Zimbabwe
Succubus, **1**:79
Sudan: burying the placenta, **1**:235; female genital cutting, **2**:89, 91; lip plugs, **2**:191; scarification, **2**:294–295. *See also* North African celebrations and practices; Sub-Saharan African celebrations and practices
Sudden infant death syndrome (SIDS), **3**:216
Sudreh, **1**:246, 248
Suicide landmarks, **3**:278–280
Suikerboon, **1**:32
Sukusendal, **1**:78
Sumatra, **2**:142
Summer National Senior Games, **3**:254
Summer solstice, **2**:199–201
Sun God offerings, **1**:254
Sünnet, **2**:323–325
Sunrise Ceremony, **2**:326–331
Sunset Service, **3**:240
Suriname, **3**:231
Surrogacy, baby showers for, **1**:24
Swaddling, **1**:320–322
Swaziland, **2**:269–272, 356, **3**:231
Sweden, Assyrian populations in, **2**:10
Swedish celebrations and practices, **1**:4; birthday cakes, **1**:35; Dala horse, **1**:115–116; funeral cakes, **3**:92; funeral candies, **3**:93; government-approved baby names, **1**:153, **1**:155; lullabies, **1**:215; *Martinstag*, **3**:111; Maypoles, **2**:221; Nordic napping, **1**:249; parental leave, **1**:265; pensions, **3**:229; royal family, **1**:35; same-sex marriage, **2**:285; wedding cakes, **2**:370–371. *See also* Scandinavian celebrations and practices

Swiss celebrations and practices: assisted suicide, 3:12–13; birth trees, 1:33; danse macabre, 3:52; *Klausjagen*, 1:296; *Martinstag*, 3:111; *Matura*, 2:15; parental leave, 1:266; *Polterabend*, 2:254
Sympathetic pregnancy, 1:104
Syrian celebrations and practices: Assyrian betrothal and weddings, 2:9–14; Childermas, 1:84; forced marriage, 2:8; *halva*, 3:115. See also Middle Eastern celebrations and practices

Taapu, 1:109
Tahara, 1:235. See also Circumcision
Tahneek ritual, 1:234
Taishen (God of the Pregnant Womb), 1:90
Taiwan: baby racing, 1:21; breastfeeding, 1:56; pregnancy and birth rituals, 1:89–93; *Qingming* Festival, 3:219; ritual tattooing, 2:276; space burial, 3:267. See also Asian celebrations and practices
Takht e khina, 2:2
Talerzyki, 2:4
Talmud, 2:21
Tama the Cat, 3:123
Tana Toraja people, 3:155–157
Tangihanga, 3:281–283
Tango no Sekkui (Feast of the Banners), 1:184
Tantrics, 2:55–56
Tanzania, 1:46, 3:71; death dance, 3:51; female genital cutting, 2:93; food taboos during pregnancy, 1:145; lip plugs, 2:193; *Nyumba Ntobhu*, 2:247–249; scarification, 2:295; spitting on babies, 1:316; tooth sharpening, 2:143. See also Maasai traditions
Taoism, 3:329; *Zhongyuan* Festival, 3:329
"Taps," 3:152–155
Tattoing, ritual, 2:272–277
Tawaf, 2:114–115
Tawba people, 2:100
Taweez, 1:234
Taxidermy, 3:283–285
Tear bottles, 3:286
Tear catchers, 3:286

Teething remedies, 1:327–330
Teknonymy, 2:138
Templar effigies (Temple Church), 3:298
Temple Church (London), 3:298
Tét Nguyên đan, 3:288–292
Thailand: Buddhist practices, 3:18, 20; Fire-hair shaving and Khwan ceremonies, 1:140–142; Hmong names, 2:136; *Luk Thep* dolls, 1:358; mother roasting, 1:228; mourning color, 3:302; neck elongation, 2:243–244; treatment of the placenta in, 1:69, 124. See also Southeast Asian celebrations and practices
Thaipusam, 2:333–335
Thanksgiving of Women after Childbirth, 1:98, 100
Theravada Buddhism, 2:310–312, 3:18. See also Buddhism
Threading, 2:112
Thula Baba Box, 1:74
Thyme, 3:96
Tiananmen Square protests, 3:220
Tibetan Buddhism, 3:18. See also Buddhism
Tibetan practices: Buddhist death practices, 3:19–20; polyandry, 2:258, 259; sky burials, 3:259–263. See also Tibetan pregnancy and birth customs
Tibetan pregnancy and birth customs, 1:323–324; one month leaving home, 1:324; *pang-sai*, 1:323–324; *tshe dbang* ceremony, 1:323
Tikinagan, 1:109
Tipos'asna, 1:178
Tiv people, 2:295
Tlingit tribe, 3:183–185
Tobasichine (Child of Water), 1:8
Toda people, 2:258
Todorovden (St. Theodore's Day), 2:40
Togo: breast ironing, 2:30; female ritual servitude (*trokosi*), 1:330–333. See also West African celebrations and practices
Toilet training. See Potty training
Tolling the Devil's Knell, 3:205
Tomb of the Eagles, 3:262
Tomb of the Unknown Soldier (Tomb of the Unknowns), 3:24–26, 292–297
Tomb Sweeping Day, 3:219–220

Tombstone tourism, **3**:297–300
Tongan practices: funerals, **3**:300–302; mourning color, **3**:302; ritual tattooing, **2**:272
Tooth dyeing, **2**:143–144
Tooth fairy and tooth mouse, **1**:324–327
Tooth sharpening, **2**:142–143
Tooth Troll (*Hammaspeikko*), **1**:325
Tooth-filing ceremony, **2**:254, 335–338
Torah, **1**:59–62, 281–282, **2**:19–20
Totem poles, mortuary, **3**:183–185
Totems, **3**:117
Totenkopf, **3**:170–171
Tourta, **1**:65
Tower Hill Memorial, **3**:296
Traditional Chinese Medicine (TCM), **1**:89, 145–146
Traditional mourning colors, **3**:302–306
Training bras (trainer bras, bralettes), **2**:338–341
Trick or treating, **3**:110
Trinidad, Nine-Nights, **3**:196–198
Trobriand Islands, **2**:112, 341–344
Trokosi (female ritual servitude), **1**:330–333
Trolls, **1**:78, 223, 293, 325
Trooping the Colour, **1**:43
Trough dance, **2**:319
Trows, **1**:78, 293. *See also* Trolls
Ts'aal, **1**:109
Tsach, **1**:109
Tshe dbang (long life) ceremony, **1**:323
Tsimshian tribe, **3**:184
Tsue shen, **1**:90
Tuareg people **2**:7
Tuatha de Danann (People of the Goddess Danu), **1**:77
Tuj (*temascal*), **1**:333–335
Tumpeng, **1**:36
Turkish celebrations and practices: Assyrian betrothal and weddings, **2**:9–14; evil eye beads, **1**:344; hair removal, **2**:112; *halva*, **3**:113; *Lohusa Şerbeti*, **1**:208–210; Saint Nicholas, **1**:294; spitting on babies, **1**:316; *Sünnet*, **2**:323–325; treatment of the placenta, **1**:70. *See also* Middle Eastern celebrations and practices
Turkmenistan, money dance, **2**:234

Turning of the Bones, **3**:85–87
Tuvalu, ritual tattooing, **2**:272
Twelfth Night, **2**:44
Twenty-first birthday celebrations, **2**:344–345
Two-finger test (TFT), **2**:356

Uganda: *engozi*, **3**:71; female genital cutting, **2**:93; Senior Citizen Grant, **3**:231
Ukrainian celebrations and practices: *koliva*, **3**:135; love divination, **2**:3; money dance, **2**:234; parental leave, **1**:266; *Pysanka*, **3**:66–67, 334; *Śmigus-Dyngus* (Dyngus Day), **2**:79–81; treatment of the placenta, **1**:70; Ukrainian wreath, **2**:353–355; *vinok*, **2**:353–355; wedding cakes, **2**:370. *See also* Eastern European celebrations and practices
Ukrainian diaspora, **2**:15
Ukrainian Orthodox Church, **1**:241
Uks-akka (childbirth goddess), **1**:5–6
Ukuingishya abanacisungu, **2**:53
Ullambana, **3**:330
Umbilical cord: burial of, **1**:69–70; traditions for cutting, **1**:112–114, 130, 210–213; wrapping as keepsake, **1**:173–175
Umbilical non-severance, **1**:210
Umcwasho, **2**:269
Umhlanga, **2**:269
Umkhosi woMhlanga, **2**:269
Umrah, **2**:113
Unguentaria, **3**:286
Unification Church, **2**:235, 374
United Kingdom celebrations and practices: "Abide With Me," **3**:1–3; alkaline hydrolysis, **3**:5–6; bees and death, **3**:12–13; Beltane, **2**:219; birthday traditions, **1**:40; blooding, **1**:53–54; Blue Peter Badge, **1**:54–55; breast ironing, **2**:30; breastfeeding, **1**:56; candles on birthday cakes, **1**:38; cardboard box bed scheme, **1**:74; child beauty pageants, **1**:80; Children's Laureate, **1**:87–89; choosing

Options, **2**:56–58; christening customs, **1**:32; Christingle, **1**:95–96; cremation, **3**:42, 44; cutting the umbilical cord, **1**:113; eating calabash chalk, **1**:71; embalming, **3**:73; Father Christmas, **1**:296–297; female genital cutting, **2**:90; forced marriage, **2**:8; funeral songs, **3**:97; Gap year, **2**:103; Girl Guides, **1**:152–153; Groaning Cheese and Groaning Cake, **1**:166–169; jazz funerals, **3**:127–129; jumping over the broom, **2**:163–165; jury duty, **2**:165, 167, 168, 170–171; kangaroo care, **1**:183; lotus birthing, **1**:210; marriage banns, **2**:210–215; Maternity Leave Guide, **1**:267–268; Maundy Money, **3**:164–167; *Mehndi*, **2**:222; menstrual taboos, **2**:231; message from the Queen, **3**:171–173; Mothering Sunday, **1**:230–232; mourning customs, **3**:303; Muslim weddings, **2**:241; Name Day celebrations, **1**:241; nativity plays, **1**:245; Nordic napping, **1**:250; nursery rhymes, **1**:250; pantomime, **1**:251–265; parental leave, **1**:266; Passion plays, **3**:208; Paternity Leave Guide, **1**:270–272; pauper's funeral, **3**:209–211; pensions, **3**:228–230, 234–236; personalized hearses, **3**:211–213; Pregnancy and Infant Loss Remembrance Day, **3**:216–218; Protestant wedding ceremonies, **2**:60; RAG Week, **2**:267–268; Remembrance Day, **3**:223–226; Remembrance Sunday, **3**:152; same-sex marriage, **2**:285, 288–291; Scouting movement, **1**:152–153, 302–304; silver spoon, **1**:313–314; souling, **3**:263–264; space burial, **3**:267; spontaneous shrines, **3**:269; state funerals, **3**:272–273; Steiner schools, **1**:318, 320; teething superstitions and remedies, **1**:327–328; tooth fairy, **1**:325; twenty-first birthday, **2**:344; University of the Third Age, **3**:307; wakes, **3**:313; *Waldkindergärten*, **1**:341; water births, **1**:347; wearing of poppies, **3**:314–316; wedding anniversaries, **2**:368; wedding customs, **1**:32, **2**:32–37; wedding dresses, **2**:374; wedding ring test, **1**:348–349; Wiccan funerals, **3**:318; witch balls, **1**:357; Zoroastrianism, **3**:338. *See also* British celebrations and practices; English celebrations and practices; Irish celebrations and practices; Scottish celebrations and practices; Welsh celebrations and practices

United Nations, on breast ironing, **2**:30

United Nations Children's Fund (UNICEF), **1**:85, 86, 183, 192, **2**:8

United Nations' Convention on the Elimination of All Forms of Discrimination Against Women, **2**:8

United Nations' Convention on the Rights of the Child, **2**:8

United Nations' Development Fund for Women (UNIFEM), **1**:332

United States: Assyrian populations in, **2**:10; Hmong immigrants in, **2**:137; Polish communities in, **2**:80–81

United States celebrations and practices: alkaline hydrolysis, **3**:5–6; assisted suicide, **3**:12–14; baby racing, **1**:21, 22; *Baccalauréat (le bac)*, **2**:15–16; bedwetting cures, **1**:29–30; birthday customs, **1**:40; breastfeeding, **1**:56; Buddhist death practices, **3**:21; cairns, **3**:23; cardboard box bed scheme, **1**:74; Changing of the Guard ceremony, **3**:24–26; child beauty pageants, **1**:80; childhood vaccinations, **1**:85; christening gowns, **1**:94; condemned prisoner's last meal, **3**:37–40; cutting the umbilical cord, **1**:113; *Dia de los Muertos*, **3**:58–61; eating calabash chalk, **1**:71; eating human placenta, **1**:123; embalming, **3**:73–76; Father's Day, **1**:138–139; Girl Guides, **1**:152; government-approved baby names, **1**:153, 155;

Hindu celebrations, **2**:75; jazz funerals, **3**:127–129; jumping over the broom, **2**:163–165; jury duty, **2**:168, 169–170; kangaroo care, **1**:183; *koliva*, **3**:135; *La Quinceañera*, **2**:177–180; marriage banns, **2**:210; *Mehndi*, **2**:222; Memorial Poppy, **3**:315; menstrual taboos, **2**:231; minute's silence, **3**:174; missing man formation, **3**:178–180; money dance, **2**:234; pantomime, **1**:261; parental leave, **1**:265; Passion plays, **3**:208; Pregnancy and Infant Loss Remembrance Day, **3**:216–218; Protestant wedding ceremonies, **2**:60; purity ball, **2**:264–268; riderless horse, **3**:236–237; ritual tattooing, **2**:272; *Rumspringa*, **2**:277–280; same-sex marriage, **2**:285; Santa Muerte, **3**:246, 249–250; shivaree/chivaree, **2**:257; *Śmigus-Dyngus* (Dyngus Day), **2**:79–81; space burial, **3**:267; spontaneous shrines, **3**:269; state funerals, **3**:273–274; Steiner schools, **1**:320; Sunrise Ceremony, **2**:326–331; swaddling, **1**:321; *Tết Nguyên đan*, **3**:290; tooth fairy, **1**:325–326; training bras, **2**:338–341; Veterans Day, **3**:224; wakes, **3**:313; *Waldkindergärten*, **1**:341; water births, **1**:347; wedding cakes, **2**:371; wedding dresses, **2**:374–375; Wiccan practices, **1**:354, **3**:318; witch balls, **1**:356; Zoroastrianism, **3**:338. *See also* Amish practices; Cajun weddings; North American celebrations and practices

United States Centers for Disease Control and Prevention (CDC), **1**:86

United States Senior Games, **3**:254

Universal minimum pensions, **3**:231

University of the Third Age (U3A), **3**:307–308

Upanayana (Sacred thread ritual), **1**:337–339

Urethral subincision, **2**:347–351

Uruguay, **2**:285, **3**:247. *See also* South American celebrations and practices

Utah, *Holi* celebration in, **2**:75

Uzglavnica, **3**:176

Vaccinations, **1**:85–87, 320

Vado Mori, **3**:52

Vagina festival, **1**:279

Vaginal cutting, **1**:362–363

Valentine's Day, **2**:315–316, 323

Valentines cards, **1**:39

Vanitas, **3**:167–171

Vanuatu: exposure of the corpse, **3**:116; initiation by semen transferal, **2**:148–152; land diving competitions (*Gol, Nanggol, Nagol, N'gol*), **2**:183–186

Vatertag, **1**:139–140

Venezuela: eating the ashes of the dead, **3**:67–70; polyandry, **2**:258, 259. *See also* South American celebrations and practices

Vesak (Wesak), **1**:43

Veterans Day, **3**:224

Via Dolorosa, **3**:275–277

Victorian Era practices: baby showers, **1**:23; birthday parties, **1**:273; christening gowns, **1**:94; Christmas celebrations, **1**:297, 304–305; *dragées*, **1**:32; fairytales, **1**:135; Kissing Friday, **2**:80; lovespoons, **2**:202; mourning customs, **3**:302–303; national mourning, **3**:191; obituaries, **3**:199; pauper's funeral, **3**:209–210; wedding ring test, **1**:348; wedding superstitions originating in, **2**:33; writing of condolences, **3**:40–41

Victoriana, **3**:100

Vietnamese celebrations and practices: *Giao Thea*, **3**:290–291; Hmong names, **2**:136; mother roasting, **1**:228; New Year celebration, **3**:288; placenta in folk medicine, **1**:124; Tan Nien, **3**:291–292; *Tết Nguyên đan*, **3**:288–292; tooth sharpening, **2**:143. *See also* Southeast Asian celebrations and practices

Vigils, **3**:105–106

Vinok (Ukrainian wreath), **2**:353–355
Virgin Mary, **1**:45, 51, 64, 98–99, 203, 217–218, 242, 244, 251, 314, 326, 344, **2**:43, 178, **3**:9, 161, 207, 208
Virgin of Guadalupe, **2**:186
Virginity testing, **2**:72, 355–358; handkerchief test, **2**:357; two-finger test (TFT), **2**:356
Virgins' Crowns, **3**:161
Virgins' Garlands, **3**:161
Vision quest (vision fast), **2**:358–361
Visiting-girls courtship tradition, **2**:360–364
Vizbevető, **2**:79
Vlechugane (Haulage of the Midwife), **1**:19
Volkstrauertag (People's Day of Mourning), **3**:225
Voodoo death traditions, **3**:335–338
Vrindavan, **3**:309–311
Vrubnitsa, **2**:184

Wagner, Richard, **2**:380
"Wailing funeral," **3**:3–4
Wakes, **3**:31–32, 36, 54, 92, 106, 124–125, 139, 158–159, 196–197, 238, 261, 300, 313–314, 337
Walbiri people, **2**:249
Waldkindergärten, **1**:341–342
Waldorf schools, **1**:8, 318
Walkabout, **2**:365–367
Walking marriages, **2**:391–393
Walpurgisnacht (Walpurgis Night), **1**:217
Wandervogel, **2**:298
War dead, wearing flowers to honor, **3**:314–318
Wari people, **3**:78–79
Washing: of bride and groom, **2**:28; of the corpse, **3**:189, 258; of relics, **3**:243–244; ritual, **2**:72. *See also* Bathing
Wassailing, **2**:44
Water birth, **1**:346–348
Water children, **3**:181
Water: used for Amrit Sanchar, **2**:70; used for baptism, **1**:26–29; symbolism of, **3**:181
Waxing, **2**:112
Weaning, **1**:275–277

Wearing flowers to honor war dead, **3**:314–318
Weather balloons, ashes inside, **3**:268
Wechselbalg, **1**:77
Wedding anniversaries, **1**:32, **2**:367–369
Wedding cakes, **1**:317, **2**:35–36, 48, 369–373
Wedding dresses (wedding gowns), **2**:373–375
Wedding march and Bridal Chorus, **2**:379–381
Wedding receptions, **2**:35; Bulgarian, **2**:39; Jewish, **2**:162
Wedding ring test, **1**:348–349
Wedding rings, **2**:12, 39, 60, 94, 123–124, 375–376
Wedding traditions and customs: Afghani, **2**:1–3; Assyrian, **2**:9–14; besom weddings, **2**:163; blackening, **2**:28; bride-price, **2**:195–197; British, **2**:32–37; Bulgarian, **2**:37–41, 182–183; Cajun, **2**:47–49; chimneysweeps, **2**:33; Chinese, **2**:51; Christian, **2**:58–61; cutting the groom's socks, **2**:320; food, **2**:2, 263–264; French, **2**:180–181; German, **2**:254–258; Hindu, **2**:133–136, 222; horseshoes, **2**:142; Japanese, **2**:291–293; Jewish, **2**:159–162, 222; Latino, **2**:234–235; *Mehndi*, **2**:222; mock weddings, **1**:18–19; Moonie weddings, **2**:235–237; Moroccan, **2**:237–240; Muslim, **2**:40, 222, 241–242; music, **2**:379–381; piñatas, **1**:284; popular locations, **2**:104–105; Saami, **1**:6–7; Sikh, **2**:312–315; Sisters' Meal Festival, **2**:317–318; solo weddings, **2**:316; superstitions, **2**:374; Trobriand Islands, **2**:342–344. *See also* Marriages; Wedding cakes; Wedding receptions; Wedding rings
Wee Bell Ceremony, **1**:352
Weihnachtsmärchen, **1**:261, 349–350
Welsh celebrations and practices: birth trees, **1**:34; burying biscuits, **3**:93; choosing Options, **2**:56–58; forced

marriage, **2**:8; funeral plants, **3**:96; handfasting, **2**:117–118; lovespoons, **2**:201–203; pauper's funerals, **3**:211; same-sex marriage, **2**:285; souling, **3**:264; St. Dwynwen's Day, **2**:322–323; wedding traditions, **2**:32; yew trees, **3**:327
West African practices, **1**:1, 71. *See also* Africa; Benin, Burkina Faso; Côte d'Ivoire; Gambia; Ghana; Guinea; Guinea Bissau; Mali; Niger; Nigeria; Senegal; Sierra Leone; Togo
Western Europe, **2**:112. *See also* European celebrations and practices; *individual Western European countries by name*
Wet Monday (*lany poniedzalek*), **2**:79
Wetting the baby's head, **1**:350–351
Whistling, as courtship communication, **2**:64–66
Whitby Goth Weekend (WGW), **3**:101
Whitby jet, **3**:286–287
White coat ceremony, **2**:381–382
White Day, **2**:315–316
White Poppy Appeal, **3**:316
Whuppity Scoorie, **1**:351–353
Wiccan celebrations and practices: British weddings, **2**:32; croning ceremonies, **3**:44–46; handfasting, **2**:117–118; handparting, **2**:127–128; Wiccaning, **1**:353–355. *See also* Wiccan funerals
Wiccan funerals, **3**:318–322; *Book of Shadows*, **3**:318–319; for an elderly woman, **3**:321–322; graveside, **3**:319–320
Wife carrying, competitive, **2**:35
Wigs made from ancestors' hair, **2**:138
Wik-Mungkan (Wik-Mungknh) naming ceremony, **1**:355–356
Windmills, **3**:323–325
Witch balls, **1**:344, 356–357
Witchcraft, **1**:5, 293, **2**:12
Wodaabe courtship dance and festival, **2**:383–386
Wogeo tribe, **2**:349–350
Women: blessing after childbirth, **1**:98–100; bodily functions of, **1**:6; breast ironing as crime against, **2**:30; celebration of mothers, **1**:306; as Chelsea pensioners, **3**:28; forehead scars, **2**:99, 100; hair removal, **2**:111–113; head covering, **2**:128–130; henna night for, **2**:2; Muslim dress practices, **2**:128–130; ordination of, **3**:311; postpartum confinement, **1**:65, 188, 229, 334, 361–362; postpartum recovery, **1**:197–198, 228–230; pre-delivery confinement, **1**:166; rights of, **2**:261, **3**:310; rituals after childbirth, **1**:130–131, 165; seclusion of during menstruation and pregnancy, **1**:129, **2**:225–226, 229–230; at the *shirin-i-griftan*, **2**:2; subjugation of, **2**:262; violence against, **2**:66, 247–248; wearing Sikh turbans, **2**:69; widows, **3**:309–311. *See also* Breastfeeding; Menstrual customs; Menstrual taboos; Menstruation; Pregnant women
Women and Law in Southern Africa (WLSA), **2**:271
Women's rights, **2**:261, **3**:310
World Association of Girl Guides and Girl Scouts (WAGGGS), **1**:151, 302
World Food Programme, **1**:146
World Health Organization (WHO), **1**:55–56, 85, 86, 183, 275, **2**:91, 355, 357
World Masters Games, **3**:254
World Organization of the Scout Movement (WOSM), **1**:302. *See also* Scouts and Scouting
World Veterans Games, **3**:254
Worry dolls, **1**:357–358
Wrapping umbilical cord as keepsake (*Hesono-o*), **1**:173–175
Wuwsimtungwni ceremony, **1**:180
Wysoccan rite of manhood, **2**:359

Xhosa people, **3**:90; circumcision, **2**:387–389

Yam festival, **2**:341–342
Yamadashi, **2**:198
Yang phai, **1**:229
Yankan Gishiri, **1**:362–363
Yanomamö people, **2**:258

Yanomani people, **3**:67–69
Yellamma (fertility), **1**:117
Yemen, **2**:90
Yentas, **2**:159
Yew trees, **3**:327–329
Yoga, pregnancy, **1**:289–290
Yoruba tribe, **1**:68–69, 113, **2**:234, **3**:128
Yorubaland, ritual servitude in, **1**:331
Young British Artists (YBAs), **3**:169–170
Yu char kuei, **1**:93
Yu Lan Jie, **3**:329–332
Yugoslav countries, **2**:234. *See also* Bosnia and Herzegovina; Croatian celebrations and practices; Eastern European celebrations and practices; Kosovo; Macedonia; Montenegro; Serbian celebrations and practices; Slovenia
Yulanpen Festival, **3**:329
Yule logs, **2**:45
Yuletide traditions, **1**:293. *See also* Christmas celebrations

Zaduszki (*dzień zaduszny*), **3**:333–335
Zaire. *See* Democratic Republic of Congo
Zambian celebrations and practices: *Chisungu*, **2**:52–55; cutting the umbilical cord, **1**:112–113; *Nachisungu*, **2**:52–53; Social Cash Transfer Programme, **3**:231; *ukuingishya abanacisungu*, **2**:53
Zen Buddhism, **3**:18. *See also* Buddhism
Zenkoku Nakodo Rengokai, **2**:251–252
Zhongyuan Festival, **3**:329
Zhuazhou, **1**:93
Zimbabwe: *Pika* and *Nora*, **2**:253. *See also* Sub-Saharan African celebrations and practices
Zionism, **1**:62
Zo'e people, **2**:192
Zodiac constellations and signs, **1**:42, 44–45, 354; Chinese, **1**:233, 310–311, **2**:30
Zombie apocalypse, **3**:336
Zombies, **3**:335–338
Zoroastran practices: funerals, **3**:338–341; initiation, **1**:246–249
Zou hun, **2**:391–393
Zulu clans: midwives, **1**:112; Reed Dancing Chastity Ceremony, **2**:269–271; virginity testing, **2**:356–357
Zuo yuezi (sitting the month) **1**:92, 226, 361–362
Zur-zur (*zur zur; zurzur*), **1**:362–363

About the Author

Victoria Williams, PhD, is an independent writer and researcher living in London. She is author of ABC-CLIO's *Weird Sports and Wacky Games around the World: From Buzkashi to Zorbing* and has written on a variety of subjects, including Hollywood film (for ABC-CLIO's *Movies in American History: An Encyclopedia*), human sacrifice, and Mesoamerican mythology (for ABC-CLIO's *Conflict in the Early Americas*), British folk customs (for ABC-CLIO's *They Do What? A Cultural Encyclopedia of Extraordinary and Exotic Customs from around the World*), and other topics. Williams wrote her doctoral thesis (King's College, London) on European fairy tales in 19th-century British art and literature and on film, with special reference to the Brothers Grimm.